I

The Basics

1

Feature Writing in the Mid-1990s

A profile of the hottest new Washington political leader in *The New Yorker*? A compelling article about babies with cancer in *Family Circle*? A highly descriptive piece about the latest Italian fashion trends for *Vogue*? A human interest article about grandchildren in *Modern Maturity*? A travel feature focusing on finding bargain airfares in the *Los Angeles Times* Sunday edition? Or maybe a how-to home electronics article in *Popular Mechanics*? Too much for you right now?

How about a short review of a new Oliver Stone movie in your local daily newspaper's Weekend section? A humorous column for your campus newspaper? Perhaps a holiday story about foreign students at your school experiencing their first Thanksgiving or Fourth of July? Maybe a personality sketch of a nearby high school athlete who recently set a school record? More reachable goals for you? Perhaps. Perhaps not yet. Feature writing includes all of these possibilities, even those for the top national and international publications, and they are attainable with a lot of hard work and development of your talents.

You may wish to become a feature writer. You may have an interest in the subject and thought you would pick up this book to see what feature writing is about. Did someone out there once tell you that you could write, saying that you might have what it takes to become a journalist? If you want to be a successful *professional* feature writer, then you have to be willing to sweat. You have to like people and be willing to spend time with them, too. You have to be willing to live with frustration. You have to make personal and professional sacrifices. You have to be willing to work long hours. You have to be willing to take little or no remuneration in the beginning. You have to have a strong desire to publish your writing. If you think you lack the motivation or potential to overcome these obstacles, forget it. Pick another subject to read about. If you are starting a class, find the drop–add line. Think about another career interest or specialization.

If you are still reading after those admonitions, welcome to the world of feature writing for magazines, newspapers, and newsletters. You might just have what it takes to be a staff or free-lance feature writer, so read on!

It is important to emphasize the difficulty of being a successful professional writer these days. Yet for those who do have the drive and talent to succeed, there can be significant personal and professional rewards. Your first byline can be highly satisfying. So can the second, or third, or four hundredth. The euphoria you feel from this accomplishment at any level, from student newspaper to major international magazine, is equaled by little else in professional writing. And beginners do have a chance at making it. With the right idea at the right time, you can become a published feature writer early in your career.

Myrick E. Land (1993), professor of journalism at the University of Nevada at Reno, wrote that success in writing requires intelligence, imagination, talent, and persistence. This book gives you the basic tools for writing feature stories for newspapers, magazines, and newsletters.

What really motivates you to be a writer? If you can answer that question by the time you finish this book, you might have the foundation for becoming a professional feature writer.

WRITING NONFICTION

You write because you want to pass along facts and other information to your readers. You write to share what you have learned. Readers learn from you. They are entertained. They are thrilled. They are saddened. People react to what you have to say in print. At the same time, you have a tremendous responsibility to be accurate, concise, timely, and responsible.

You also have to know how to express yourself. This basic communication skill is your starting point in feature writing for the news media. You have to have the interest and you have to have writing ability. At some point in your life, you began to think of yourself as a writing-oriented person. And you wound up with this book, opened to the first few pages of the first chapter, perhaps wondering if you could write features for a living.

But knowing you have basic writing interest and ability is not enough, according to the late Scott Meredith (1987), who managed a New York literary agency. He wrote: "To have basic writing ability and no technical knowledge, and to try to earn a living as a writer, is equivalent to finding yourself suddenly endowed with a large amount of steel, lumber, and bricks and, without any knowledge of architecture or building, setting out to earn your living building and selling houses" (p. 3).

DEFINING FEATURE WRITING

If you take the term literally, a feature is a special part of something. Feature articles are often special portions of the periodicals that publish them. They do take many different approaches and forms, of course. Most persons familiar with *nonfiction* writing for the news media think of the conventional *straight news* or *hard news* topics and approaches—police and courts, sports, local government, or business—written to give the *who, what, when, where, why,* and *how.* These stories emphasize the important persons, the activities, current events, local and regional orientation, explanation of importance, and nature of the event.

Feature stories go beyond this level to be special. Feature writers often employ some "license" or flexibility and emphasize the unconventional or the different. Feature writers look for the story about someone who is not necessarily a newsmaker. Instead, the story is about something or someone offbeat and entertaining. Feature stories are emotional, and they involve readers. They demand reader reaction because these articles can be serious or light, timely or timeless, funny or sad, joyful or joyless. These articles tell us much about the human condition. All you have to do is pick up a recent copy of your local newspaper or favorite magazine to see the variety of subjects and approaches that are a part of feature article writing.

One professional writer defines feature writing as *creative, subjective* article writing that is designed to *inform* and *entertain* readers. Daniel Williamson's (1975) interpretation emphasized the four words that have been italicized. These points help to show features are different from "straight" news or information writing.

First, features certainly contain more *creative energy* than routine nonfiction. Writers and editors take a bit more freedom in their writing style or approaches, selection of sources, and packaging of articles. Second, these articles are *often less objective* than conventional news writing, offering a particular point of view or the author's personal impressions, perceptions, and opinions (in addition to those of sources). Third, the articles remain *informative* even if they are more creative and personalized by the writer. The level of reader utility of a story often determines its success with readers. Fourth, the article must *entertain* the reader while accomplishing all three other goals. The article makes readers satisfied they chose to spend 5 minutes or even an hour reading the article instead of doing some other activity. Williamson (1975) noted one other characteristic: A feature is *less perishable* than conventional nonfiction or news writing. Stories often are held for appropriate seasons or for slow news periods at newspapers. And simply because of their less frequent publication schedules, magazines often hold stories for considerable lengths of time prior to publication.

Other professionals compare feature writing to writing fiction such as short stories. The major difference, of course, is that feature writers deal with reality. Benton Rain Patterson (1986), who has written for newspapers and magazines across the United States, says:

> A feature writer deliberately puts people (characters) into what he writes. He describes them and shows them (description) doing and saying (action, expressed through narrative and quotes) whatever it is that makes the characters worth writing—and reading— about. When he puts those elements into his

---

JAMES J. KILPATRICK ON THE ART OF WRITING

[T]he crafts of writing and carpentry are deceptively simple. The carpenter has to begin with a plan; the writer must begin with a thought. There must be at least the germ of an idea. Before the first board is nailed to the second board, or the first word connected to the second word, there has to be some clear notion of where we expect to be when we have finished nailing or writing.
—Red Smith lecture in Journalism, University of Notre Dame, 1985 (Kilpatrick, 1985, p. 2).

---

piece, a writer is *ipso facto* featurizing his subject, handling his material and writing his piece as a feature. (p. 21)

Patterson's three basic rules for features are straightforward:

1. Put people into the story.
2. Tell a story.
3. Let the reader see and hear for himself or herself.

Just about all feature stories have these elements in common and often in large quantity. Good features use people in the story, quoted often about what they do that is so interesting. Feature stories are *not* written like meeting minutes. Features are *not* dreary matter-of-fact research reports. They are *not* lifeless summaries of big events. They *are* often factual short stories written in *active voice*. They have a plot. There is a story line. There are characters. There is a beginning, a middle, and an end. Many writers will say that feature articles fall somewhere between news writing and short story writing.

You will see the major types of magazine, newspaper, and newsletter feature articles as you read further. You can focus on such story forms as color stories that emphasize descriptive writing, human interest stories, personality sketches and profiles, seasonal feature stories, reviews and critical feature writing, aftermath and follow-up feature stories, the feature series, travel article writing, personal experience stories, how-to-do-it articles, humor writing, and technical and specialized features.

There is discussion of the tools you need as a feature writer. You will learn how to find a good feature idea and how to mold it into a story, how to research story ideas, how to write and edit feature articles, and how to successfully free-lance feature articles for publication. You will also learn professional and ethical standards of professional feature writers.

You will see these types of stories applied in their major forms: weekly and daily newspapers and general and specialized magazines. The writing strategies and information-gathering approaches for feature writing are discussed in broad terms, but often with particular application to the print media.

NONFICTION PUBLISHING IN THE MID-1990s

Like many other businesses in the United States, the newspaper, magazine, and newsletter industries suffered through their worst economic recession since World War II at the beginning of this decade. The recession affected growth, caused failures, and left the three industries in a state of uncertainty. But by the mid-1990s, this was changing.

There were 1,570 morning and evening daily newspapers with an average circulation of 38,270 copies in the United States in 1993 (Newspaper Association of America staff, 1993). There were 7,406 weekly newspapers with an average circulation of 7,487 copies in 1993, including paid and free circulation newspapers, according to the National Newspaper Association (Okola, personal communication, 1993). The largest daily newspapers circulate over 1 million copies daily. These are the *Wall Street Journal* and *USA Today*, both national and, lately, internationally oriented publications with circulations over 1.6 million each. *The New York Times* and *Los Angeles Times* are both very large, each with circulations over 1 million copies per weekday (Fitzgerald, 1993).

There are plenty of small newspapers, also. These are often the best markets for beginning feature writers because they have small staffs, limited resources, and welcome contributions from student and free-lance writers. Weekly newspapers publish from once every 2 weeks to as many as three times a week. Their circulation sizes vary considerably, too. Most weeklies are very small—in the 1,000 to 4,000 copies per issue category—but there are several dozen weeklies with circulations over 100,000 copies per issue (Okola, personal communication, 1993).

But newspapers are experiencing relatively hard times. Fewer people are reading them, preferring to find information from television or other sources. Some experts, such as one Atlanta marketing consultant, have already labeled newspapers as "irrelevant," in fact (Glaberson, 1993, p. D7). But others will not go so far in making that judgment. Other authorities think it is an overstatement to call newspapers irrelevant, but the point is well taken: No one seems to know what the future of the newspaper will be for the next generations of writers and editors. We are unsure of the content and the form in the generations ahead. But for now there is some optimism, especially if newspapers can adapt. Some major news/information and telecommunications companies that publish newspapers and other news products are developing such bold changes as electronic versions of their products. This, of course, is not a new idea, because such services have been available for a decade or more, but these companies are exploring new ways to use computers, telecommunications, and other common consumer technology to deliver news to customers. For the mid-1990s, this not only means personal computers, but such innovations as pocket-sized wireless computer receivers or such things as personalized newspapers printed within the home of subscribers (Markoff, 1993). The implications for all writers, not just feature writers, seem to be massive.

Such changes may be necessary for newspapers and other periodicals to survive in the electronic age. One news media observer has written that all is not bad. "Newspaper readership remains extraordinarily high despite years of declines," writes *New York Times* media columnist William Glaberson (1993, p. D7). "Every day, 115 million people read a newspaper in America. On Sunday, 125 million read a newspaper."

There are many more magazines than daily and weekly newspapers. There are about 11,100 U.S. periodicals, according to compilations of the Magazine Publishers of America. In terms of editorial pages circulated in 1992, the largest single category is culture and humanities magazines (14.8% of all 200 million pages in that year). Sports, hobbies, and recreation constituted the second-largest proportion (8.8%). Food and nutrition pages (8.6%), national affairs (8.4%), and health (7.8%) round out the top five categories (Magazine Publishers of America staff, 1993).

The largest magazines in the country as of late 1992 reach older, or retirement age, citizens. *Modern Maturity* and the *NRTA/AARP Bulletin*, the two largest periodicals according to independently audited paid circulation figures, each distribute about 22.8 million copies per issue. *Reader's Digest* and *TV Guide* both publish over 16.3 million and 14.5 million copies per issue, respectively, and *National Geographic* publishes almost 10 million copies a month. The top 50 magazines in the United States circulate over 200 million copies per edition, or an average of about 4 million per periodical, and the top 100 magazines circulate more than 250 million copies, or roughly 2.5 million copies per edition per magazine (*Folio:* staff, 1993; Magazine Publishers of America staff, 1993). Of the top 100 magazines, about half experienced circulation gains and half experienced losses when comparing 1991 and 1990 figures. Whereas other magazines geared toward older Americans are largest in circulation, including largest in subscription sales, *TV Guide* is the largest newsstand sales magazine. Of its 15 million circulation (fourth overall), over 6 million copies (43%) are sold in newsstands, grocery stores, and other locations each week. A few major magazines have experienced "dramatic" single-copy sales increases in recent years, analysts at *Folio:*, the monthly for magazine management, report. But most magazines have experienced "flat" growth at the newsstand in the past several years (*Folio:* staff, 1993; Magazine Publishers of America staff, 1993).

The biggest magazines continue to be very big. But there are thousands of smaller monthly, bimonthly, and quarterly publications. And some of the smaller national or regional magazines, such as *Velonews* (competitive bicyclers, circulation about 38,000) or *Videomaker* (video camera users, 44,000), are comparatively small but are growing very fast. They are smaller because they reach more specialized audiences, but they often offer marvelous opportunities for serious feature writers.

"What we are going through right now is a massive and very rapid change. By the year 2000, we will see totally different economic formulas being used in our industry," says John Klingel, vice president for development for Time

Publishing Ventures (*Folio:* staff, 1992, p. 140). "In the decades ahead of us, the size and diversity of the company are going to become much more critical factors."

Magazine industry and financial consultant Wilma Jordan feels periodical publishing can remain viable because of its willingness to change. "I think that publishing is truly an organic business; it's always going to change because it has to adapt to a new environment each year. I would assert that if we look back over the years, it's changed every decade—and the challenges have been different every time" (*Folio:* staff, 1992, p. 140).

Jerry Reitman, an executive vice president for the advertising firm Leo Burnett Co., in Chicago, is also optimistic. "I still think what makes magazines stand out . . . is that they play a special role in people's lives. No electronic media will change that, because of a magazine's physical and intellectual nature, compared to the various forms of video communications" (*Folio:* staff, 1992, p. 141).

A smart feature writer seeking free-lance markets will not overlook newsletter journalism. There are small organization-based newsletters and large public subscription-based newsletters, and lots in between. In this decade, careers are developing in this new and growing field. Newsletters are not all small "mom and pop"-type editorial operations. Commercial business-to-business newsletters have become a major industry with thousands of editions each business day, week, month, or quarter. It may be impossible to estimate the number of newsletters regularly published in the United States. With so many new publications beginning each month and others closing down because funding becomes difficult to find or interests change, the numbers are difficult to estimate. Many newsletters are organizational and not widely circulated. Others are distributed to the public or to private groups free or for sale, but their circulation numbers or simple existence are not regulated or monitored by any national organizations. It is safe to say, however, there are thousands of such periodicals, and the figure is growing with the recent development of inexpensive production and printing technology. Some are large and some are small.

These thousands of newsletters are published by people who need to communicate something. Gale's directory of newsletters, *Newsletters in Print*, lists over 11,000 newsletters in the United States and Canada (Krol, 1992), but this total does not include many of the smaller circulation newsletters for internal corporate, institutional, organizational, or other proprietary purposes. Other estimates, such as that of the Oxbridge directory, go as high as 21,000 newsletters in the U.S., but even those do not include private publications and others not sold to the public (Greenberg, 1992).

For writers, the newspapers, magazines, and newsletters of the mid-1990s depend more and more on technology. Because of computers, fax machines, and other modern hardware, you are able to gather information in ways impossible for a generation before you. You are able to work on machines that make preparation of manuscripts much easier than ever before.

Publications are much more sophisticated in production techniques in this decade. This means feature writers, on deadline, can produce stories faster and closer to printing deadlines than ever before and supplement the usual news coverage of an event, whether it be for a daily newspaper, a daily fax newsletter, or a weekly news magazine.

Trends in group ownership of newspapers and magazines have changed the nature of the business over the past two decades. The largest newspaper groups, such as Gannett and Knight-Ridder, have purchased major dailies. Other companies have gathered up available small dailies and weeklies. Magazines have experienced the same phenomenon, with many ownership changes in the past decade. Companies have bought up independently owned magazines to form new or larger groups.

The effect has been less independent management of publications. At times, staff positions have been eliminated to create more profitable operating costs. It has meant a harder time to make a living for feature writers in some markets and some specializations. It has also meant greater resources and new ideas. It has meant some publications near failure got a second chance, and this has helped writers.

Newspapers are in the midst of significant change in the middle of this decade. They are using feature material in larger quantities. Because of this, they seek better quality from writers to keep the demand for their editions high. Reacting to television and other electronic media vying for the growing entertainment and leisure time of Americans, newspapers are offering material once found only in magazines, such as longer in-depth profiles and analyses. Stanford University Professor William Rivers has labeled this phenomenon the "magazining of newspapers" (1992, p. 13). Recently, some newspaper feature sections have shown interest in shorter, tightly written pieces with the same "television story" flair of USA Today.

Some experts feel these changes have not been enough for newspapers in a visual era. The first Photo Systems Manager for the Pasadena Star-News, Mark Loundy, believes newspapers must change or they will continue to suffer from declining audiences. "Color, graphics, contests, and zoned editions may have slowed the readership decline, but decline it continues to do. After more than 15 years of reading, discussing, following, and participating in the bleeding edge of this issue, I've come up with the Information Appliance (IA), my concept of what newspapers must become," Loundy (1992) explained. His "IA" is small, works like a radio receiver, and will receive news from as wide a range of sources as the user desires (subscribes), replacing paper-based publications.

There is a variety of scenarios such as Loundy's in the literature these days. Although it is not certain what will happen in the next few years, such ideas show how dramatically the final format of your writing will change during your professional career.

Television, film, and other influences changed newspapers and magazines in the 1960s and 1970s. Newspapers began to develop regional, or zoned, editions and to look at other dissemination techniques. General interest consumer magazines closed when operations became more costly than circulation and advertising revenues could cover. In an effort to segment the general audience, more specialized magazines evolved in the 1960s and 1970s to replace general interest publications. Suddenly, readers interested in health and medicine did not have to depend on news magazines or the coffee-table magazines of another era. They, instead, subscribe to *Total Health, Prevention, Vim & Vigor,* or other similar magazines.

City and regional magazines became the rage of the 1960s and underwent a major shake-up in the late 1980s. These periodicals have matured as a distinct category of magazines over the past quarter century, perhaps having passed their zenith at the beginning of this decade, according to one industry expert (Couzens, 1988). Yet, large metropolitan areas such as Chicago, Boston, Washington, Los Angeles, and Atlanta, or smaller urban areas such as Hartford, Sacramento, and Cincinnati continue to support them. However, they failed in Houston and Austin, for example, and have been severely remodeled in other cities, such as Miami. Entertainment and personality–celebrity publications such as *People* and *US The Entertainment Magazine* were created during the 1970s and 1980s and have grown in popularity.

Magazines, like newspapers, have changed as well in the past three decades. There have been very difficult times, forcing basic survival decisions by editors and publishers in some cases, for magazines in the early 1990s, and the problems are not always caused by choice of content. Magazines such as *Psychology Today, Savvy Woman, Fame, Taxi,* and *Smart* were forced to close during the harsh realities of advertising slumps caused by economic recession at the beginning of this decade. It has been a case of "too many titles chasing too few ad pages," according to magazine industry consultant George Simpson (Wolk, 1991).

Some magazines have survived on sound fiscal management and other rare publications have existed on subscriber and newsstand sales alone. The bimonthly *Ms.* magazine, for example, did not suffer as much as other publications during the same recession period because it does not accept advertising. It has never depended on advertising since it debuted in 1972.

But circulation revenue has been falling for some traditional women's magazines. The mass market women's magazines known as the "Seven Sisters" (*Better Homes & Gardens, Family Circle, Good Housekeeping, Ladies' Home Journal, McCall's, Redbook,* and *Woman's Day*) have even suffered from an eroding reader base. Many readers simply switched to more specialized publications. In 1979, those magazines had a combined circulation of about 45 million copies a month. In 1991, it was only about 37 million, or a decrease of almost 18% (*Folio:* staff, 1993). Advertising suffered as well, in a severe recession that affected the entire publishing industry. These magazines have been through retooling and are offering changes in covers, interior design and organization, revised traditional content, and other completely new features to attract new readers (Carmody, 1990c).

Whereas some magazines, such as the "Seven Sisters," continue to aim at women readers, some other magazines, in their efforts to survive in a growing competitive media market, are focusing more of their attention on men in this decade. Magazine industry circulation statistics show strong showings by some male-oriented publications in sales growth in recent years. Magazines geared to male readers such as *Men's Health, Sport Truck, Texas Fish & Game, Mountain Bike Action, North American Hunter, Stock Car Racing, Low Rider*, and *Game & Fish* are each in the top 20 in growth (*Folio:* staff, 1993).

New York Times reporter Deirdre Carmody, who covers the magazine industry, observed this trend and wrote, "Ever on the lookout for what is truly hot, the magazine industry has come up with a sizzler. It has discovered men" (Carmody, 1990a, p. 1D). Carmody says that a sudden spurt in new men's magazines is indicative of the trend. Some of the new publications, such as *Men, Men's Health, Men's Journal*, and a revamped *Details*, join the well-established *Esquire* and *GQ* in trying to find their niche. *Men's Life* was tried in 1990 and lasted through only one issue. "Publishers and editors say they are aiming at a liberated man of the 90s who has thrown off the shackles and stereotypes," Carmody wrote. Readership research studies, she explains, show as many men read magazines as women, with local and regional publications being their favorites. Evidence exists that some of these, such as outdoor periodicals, may be slipping. Some industry analysts feel more general interest publications aimed at men will succeed in the mid-1990s. But, Carmody concedes, "Editing a men's magazine these days—to say nothing of starting one—is like shooting at a moving target, as men's roles continue to evolve" (Carmody, 1992b, p. 1E).

Bridal and wedding magazines seem to be another mid-1990s magazine growth area, *The Times'* Carmody believes (1992a). She cites changing values as a reason. In 1982, there were about 1 million marriages a year. In 1992, there were about 2.3 million. And these involved adults waiting until their mid-20s and later, waiting longer during the engagement period, and often with more money to spend. It means a strong market for magazines that write about everything from engagements to honeymoons and setting up households. In fact, the well-established *Bride's* recently renamed itself to become *Brides and Your New Home*. "There is a huge appetite out there for pages and pages of pictures . . . and answers to endless questions," Carmody writes (1992b, p. 1F).

Another category of magazines showing encouraging growth are magazines geared toward children. *Folio: First Day*, an industry publication, said 1993 was the "year of the children" because of the proliferation of new publications. Staffs of established ones, such as *Sesame Street Magazine, Disney Adventures*, and *Sports Illustrated for Kids*, have witnessed the addition of *Nickelodeon Magazine, Outside Kids, Family Adventures*, and *Family Life*. These publications target kids aged 3 to 14, or even more specific bracketed markets than those ages. Articles focus on indoor and outdoor activities, travel, food, the environment, basic science, television programs, clothing, toys such as video games, and activities designed to enhance quality time with parents (Colford, 1993). Corporate endeavors such as these show the continuing evolution of the magazine writing market. Writers, as well as editors and publishers, have to keep track of the evolving industry.

On the other hand, one category that is not doing well is teen magazines. Publications such as *Super Teen*, *Teen Machine*, and *Teen Beat* have lost from 40% to 60% of their total circulation in recent years, involving major losses in both subscription and single-copy sales (*Folio:* staff, 1993).

NATURE OF NEWSPAPER FEATURE WRITING

What makes a newspaper feature different from a magazine or newsletter feature? There are a number of answers to that question that go beyond simple frequency or timing of publication. First, let's discuss newspapers and how they use features in this section. Then the following two sections of this chapter discuss how magazines and newsletters use feature material.

Newspaper features are used throughout the newspaper, but some sections use features more often and very differently from others. The front section, generally containing the spot news of the day from state, national, and international sources, will use features for balance. Features in these sections offer insight into the day's newsmakers and major events. Features are used as *sidebars* to supplement straight news reporting. For example, a story about a truck–van traffic accident that killed nine people might be boosted by a feature sidebar focusing on the one surviving child. The announcement of a nomination of a U.S. Supreme Court justice will often be supplemented by a feature profile of the career of the person seeking the position.

The local section of most daily newspapers will often run features on unusual individuals or events of community interest. Certainly local sidebar features are also used. However, newspapers that have segmented their local news coverage into neighborhood sections will frequently fill these sections with features about people, school, religion, home repair, pets, arts and crafts, parks and recreation, and small businesses.

In lifestyle and living sections, editors will devote most of the day's space to a wide variety of feature material. These stories focus on home how-to-do-it subjects, consumer and shopping ideas, profiles, health and medicine suggestions, child-care news, gardening, cooking and food ideas, and much more.

In some newspapers, entertainment news is part of lifestyle coverage, but this category of news creates a different set of feature needs for newspapers. Writers specializing in entertainment provide features on individuals, reviews of performances, and insight into creative activities.

Sports sections provide feature content to break the routine of daily results stories. Features also supplement spot sports coverage. Regular readers look for features such as profiles on coaches and players, descriptions of facilities, and in-depth analysis of outstanding strategies and performances. Sports features are less focused on professionals and outstanding amateurs than they were a decade ago. Editors have found that readers want to read features about participation sports, such as jogging and swimming, in addition to the National Football League or Major League Baseball. Editors have also learned that readers would like increased feature coverage of "minor" sports, such as soccer, giving writers more opportunities and broader scope for features than in past decades.

Business sections have experienced growth in many daily newspapers in recent years. Even newspapers that do not have separate business sections, such as special tabloids on Mondays, still devote considerable space to business news and features. For writers interested in business, this is an upbeat and opportune time. These section editors demand regular features describing new companies, new products, consumerism, successful executives, and trends in the marketplace.

Feature material occasionally is found on the opinion or editorial pages also. It is often in the form of a column, but the same general principles of feature writing have been used to write the feature column. These creative columnists use satire for humor, or write a profile of an individual, or give how-to-do-it advice on a subject.

Even newspapers have outlets for magazine-style writing. The Sunday magazine supplements of major newspapers depend a great deal on solid feature essay writing of traditional magazine length each week to build regular readership. Feature subjects are wide ranging in nature. From humor columns to portraits of individuals to accounts of historical events to chronologies of conflicts, these articles are the foundations of Sunday magazines. Sunday magazines also include shorter departmentalized features, such as listings of events, reviews of new restaurants, and summaries of new products on the market.

Newspaper features are usually much shorter in length than magazine features, but this tendency does not hold as firmly as it once did. It is not unusual to find a 5,000-word feature story in a newspaper, even in an era influenced by the brevity and graphics of *USA Today*. And, of course, magazines often run short feature items, also. But the majority of newspaper features are short and to the point—500 to 1,000 words. Space does not often provide the chance for depth and development of "characters" in the article. Frequency of publication does, however, provide the opportunity for newspaper features to be more timely than magazines.

Newspapers depend less on outside material than do magazines, as detailed in later chapters. Because most newspapers have staffs of writers and reporters available, most sections do not buy much free-lance material. Sunday travel sections or pages, however, are an exception because very few newspapers employ full-time travel writers other than a travel editor.

Certainly, newspaper feature articles are produced in a shorter deadline framework. There are not too many newspaper feature writers who have not had to research, write, and turn in a complete feature within a few hours. Although this also occurs in magazine feature writing, it is not as likely to happen with monthly or weekly deadlines.

NATURE OF MAGAZINE FEATURE WRITING

Magazine features are quite different from newspaper features in a number of ways. First, these articles are often written free-lance by nonstaff members of a magazine. Many writers are attracted to the freedom of free-lance writing and are able to make good supplemental income as free-lance writers. However, it is worth repeating: It is quite difficult to make a substantial career and a living from free-lance writing. A good number of individuals do well selling their work to magazines while working another career, both in and out of the news media. You will learn more about free-lance writing in the final two chapters of this book.

There are many opportunities for magazine-oriented, nonfiction writers. You can select the subject, the market, and the magazine you wish to write for. You can specialize if you desire to do so, or you can be a generalist who writes on whatever subject is appealing for whatever reasons. You can certainly set your own work schedule for writing and researching articles. A staff writer for a newspaper or a magazine staffer cannot enjoy this luxury most of the time. You can set up an office at home or elsewhere, but you are responsible for whatever costs you incur. The expenses for such things as equipment, furniture, and supplies have to come out of your writer's fees. And, it follows, you are able to live wherever you want as an independent writer.

The magazine industry is still changing. This means the beginning of opportunities for feature article writers, but also the end of other opportunities. For example, one of the real growth areas in the magazine industry over the past two decades has been computer consumer publications. The new wave of 1990s computer user magazines is exemplified by CMP Publications' *Windows Magazine* and Ziff-Davis Company's *PC Sources*, both started in 1989. Numerous new publications such as these have been introduced each year since the first PCs were introduced to the mass market in the late 1970s.

On the other hand, "shelter" and home decorating magazines— those devoted to home, interior design, and lifestyles—were hard hit by the early 1990s economic recession and competition has been intense for readers and advertisers. In 1993, for example, the venerable *HG*, or *House & Garden* as it was known for most of its years, which had been published since 1901, was closed by Condé Nast Publications. *Metropolitan Home,* which began in the early 1970s as *Apartment Life*, was sold to the French publishing firm Hachette and scaled back to six issues a year (Kantrowitz, 1993; Winship, 1993). The 1990s, some experts believe, are the decade of success for service-oriented publications that focus on decorating, remodeling, and other home topics. The shelter and home decorating magazine market is intensely competitive, even if it further segments into smaller and more specialized publications within the genre (Carmody, 1990b; Kantrowitz, 1993).

You have a reasonable chance as an unknown writer to be published by a successful major magazine. However, you do have to work hard on good ideas at the right time. Magazine feature writing is a field with tremendous opportunity. With hundreds of major magazines and thousands more specialized business publications, you can do much as a magazine feature writer—if you have the drive.

Magazines, like newspapers, have their own styles or personalities. Part of this is the look, or graphics of the magazine, but the other major part is the *writing* style. Magazine writing generally is in essay form with longer, more fully developed paragraphs. Usages are more formalized, also. This subject gets more attention in later chapters.

And they change from time to time. Sometimes, when a new editor takes control, changes occur. At other times, magazine editors retool their products to enhance them. *The New Yorker*, for example, is one of the industry's best regarded periodicals even though it is not one of the largest. But it recently underwent major changes under a new editor. Some industry analysts say the new version under editor Tina Brown is not as "highbrow" as it once was thought to be (Wilson, 1992). Television programs are reviewed. Language usages are more contemporary. Long articles, some over 20,000 words and some as long as 70,000 words, still grace its pages. Lengthy discussions of New York politics remain. So do the long "letters" about American events and trends. And the magazine still depends on fiction, such as short stories and poetry, to entertain and attract readers.

Despite occasional changes in established publications or the debut of completely new ones, you will also find that magazine writing itself tends to be somewhat constant. After all, good writing is good writing. Magazine articles, generally, do tend to be more descriptive and detailed than newspaper writing, but this is partly due to the additional space given to major features in magazines. And, as noted earlier, these articles are a bit more subjective, as writers offer their perspectives on the subject.

Just remember that, regardless of the writing approach and topic, you will find the magazine industry to be quite different from what it once was. Individuals beginning careers as magazine writers in the postwar 1940s and 1950s found general interest magazines flourishing. Due to the influences of television and other mass media influences on society, leisure time demands are quite different two generations later. To meet this challenge, magazines began to specialize. Your writing challenge will be to handle specialized subjects with the authority of an expert. This, you will find, is still another reason magazine feature writing differs so much from newspaper feature writing.

FEATURE WRITING FOR NEWSLETTERS

Newsletter publishing is growing fast, according to Frederick Goss (1988), a newsletter industry leader. The industry is quite fluid, he says, and ripe with opportunities. Some newsletters have grown larger than some newspapers and magazines in terms of circulation and staff size. Most are quite small, though. One relatively new newsletter for example, the *Tightwad Gazette*, circulates about 50,000 copies each month to individuals interested in ways for their families to live frugally. The Maine-based newsletter has found a major market by "promoting thrift as a viable alternative lifestyle" (Krol, 1992, p. 253). Newsletters such as the *Tightwad Gazette* have existed for as long as newspapers and magazines, but they are enjoying a growing role in mass communication in the 1990s. The *Tightwad Gazette* provides feature articles about product purchasing, recipes, recycling and new uses of old products, insurance, thrift store bargains, and balancing food budgets with nutrition. Newsletters like this one mean new and growing markets for feature writers. Many newsletters are produced by comparatively small staffs and need both talented staff writers and free-lance writers.

Just about everyone reads a newsletter of some sort on a regular basis. Some might even come to you, your business, or your family residence unsolicited. Newsletters are necessary because they, like newspapers and magazines, contain news and information (Greenberg, 1992). Newsletters are highly specialized, reflecting the interests of members of groups, clubs and organizations, institutions, and other entities that need to communicate information. Newsletters give members of organizations information and a sense of belonging. Newsletters sell. They inform. They motivate. "Successful newsletters convey specialized information to narrow markets," wrote Goss (1988, p. 1). "The public's demand for specialized information has made the growth of newsletters in the information industry phenomenal."

They come and go. A lot of new newsletters begin each year, but an equal number fail because of overoptimism, poor financing, weak reporting, writing, and editing, or all of these factors. Nevertheless, newsletters in the mid-1990s are, with their wide range of specialized subjects, perhaps the single best potential market for beginning feature writers. Not only are newsletters available in traditional 8½" by 11" format, but also by electronic media such as online (computer to computer) transfer, fax machine, computer diskettes, and compact disc/read-only memory (CD-ROM).

"Newsletter jobs are not necessarily easier to find than jobs with other news media organizations. (Some newsletter publishers say they never hire people straight out of journalism school)," writes *Criminal Justice Newsletter* editor Craig Fischer (1990). "Nevertheless, J-school grads should be aware that newsletters can offer excellent opportunities to practice *bona-fide* journalism, using the same skills as those applied at a newspaper, magazine or wire service job" (Fischer, 1990, p. 2).

Many newsletters are just a few pages and are the effort of just one or two persons. In terms of format and content, most are published on 8½" by 11" pages and contain some sort of nameplate, general news and information, feature articles, graphics (both art and photographs), and editorials, and some even contain advertising. They are often photocopied in black and white and stapled before being mailed to readers. They may only be published on a quarterly or monthly basis. These small publications serve an important mass communication need in the contemporary world.

THE AMERICAN SOCIETY OF MAGAZINE EDITORS HONORS AMERICA'S LEADING MAGAZINES

Each spring, the American Society of Magazine Editors presents its National Magazine Awards for excellence in magazine publishing. To be honored signifies that a publication has reached the top of its class.

In 1994, the major awards went to *Harper's* and *Health* magazines. Other winners included *Fortune, Wired, Philadelphia, Print, BusinessWeek, Outside, The New Yorker, Allure,* and *Martha Stewart Living*.
• *Harper's* won three awards in the feature writing, fiction writing, and essays and criticism categories.
• *Health* won two awards for best single-topic issue—a practical guide to aging—and for general excellence in its 400,000 to 1 million circulation category.
• The public interest award was won by Philadelphia magazine for Stephen Friend's article on the antibiotic Floxin.
• The prize for general excellence among large magazines (over 1 million circulation) was won by *BusinessWeek* (United Press International staff, 1994).

Other newsletters are more substantial. They may have dozens of pages, glossy paper, two-color or even four-color commercial printing, and be distributed two or more times per month, perhaps even weekly. In addition to a publisher and editor, there may be news and feature writers on staff. These newsletters are much more commercial and professional in their orientation, circulate more copies, and must make a profit for the publisher. In between, there is a wide range of forms and styles of newsletters.

But what exactly is a newsletter? Gale's *Newsletters in Print* editor John Krol (1992) says newsletters have a number of special characteristics, including publications that are serial in nature, are readily available to the public, have national or broad regional interest (but often also have local or community focus), treat specialized interests and topics for readers, and use a variety of formal and informal presentations for readers.

"Although Webster's provides a concise definition of the term 'newsletter,' in practical application the word is used to describe publications of all kinds, ranging from journals that report on science to occasional bulletins that carry commercial product notices. Conversely, publications that are arguably newsletters in format and content call themselves 'magazines,' 'newspapers,' or 'journals,'" writes Krol (1992, p. xiii).

The Newsletter Publishers Foundation, based in Arlington, Virginia, differentiates between "house organ" publications and subscription-based newsletters. "The type of newsletter which employs legitimate journalists covers a beat for interested subscribers. The source of support—subscription fees—distinguishes it from 'house organs' and other types of publications that are essentially public-relations initiatives," the NPF argues in its *Newsletter Career Guide* (Newsletter Publishers Foundation staff, 1992, p. 3).

Newsletters begin where an informational gap exists. Someone identifies it and the new publication is launched. The beat can be relatively broad in the beginning but will eventually develop into related or spin-off publications that give more information about subdivisions of the topic. One successful newsletter, *Communications Daily*, focuses on electronic communications. It has generated several related publications such as *Video Week, Audio Week,* and *Public Broadcasting Report* (Newsletter Publishers Foundation staff, 1992).

Writers contributing to newsletters provide an important informational service, especially in a fast-paced information-oriented world. "Because they can be produced so quickly, they are often the first purveyors of important news, such as announcements of medical breakthroughs, results of statistical studies, identification of trends in society, or new shortcuts for professionals," Krol (1992, p. xi) explains.

Newsletter writers are most often free-lance contributors or staff writers doubling as editors. Most newsletter publishers cannot afford a large full-time staff. Instead, publishers and editors purchase articles or take contributed articles for free from interested people. These outlets, even the ones that cannot pay contributors, can be important starting points for feature writers. Newsletters that succeed are a mix of mostly traditional hard news peppered with features, profiles, humor, and the human element with liberal use of direct quotations (Goss, 1988).

"Journalism graduates who investigate the newsletter job market not only increase their odds of finding professional employment, but also may find their jobs more interesting, challenging, and lucrative," advises Newsletter Publishers Foundation President Shirley B. Alexander (personal communication, 1992). "Newsletter journalists drive hard, but they travel in the express lane for important news assignments other beginners may take years to earn."

A clear advantage is that writers are often working with small organizations and with editors directly. Access is often faster and easier. Opportunities may be greater because they are less competitive than on newspapers and magazines. However, there is a trade-off. Although there may be less competition, newsletters are highly specialized and require feature writers who have an ability to work within the specialization and communicate at the level of the often sophisticated audience.

Internal newsletters for companies and other types of organizations contain articles that inform and build loyalty to the organization. They can unify through the features on employees or members. The news and information keep members up to date. *External newsletters* are often used for sales and publicity purposes. News and feature articles serve customers and potential customers, or members, and tell them about developments such as new products or services. In essence, the types and purposes of feature articles in newsletters may differ somewhat from newspaper and magazine features, but the writing forms and styles will probably not be too different.

Commercial newsletters—those published with subscriber fees only—are, in a sense, the purest form of journalism. There are no advertising and no organizational interests to represent or promote. These newsletters are expensive, but valuable, to their subscribers. Anyone willing to spend from $200 to $4,000 a year for a newsletter has a demand for rare information that cannot be obtained elsewhere and this individual wants it without the sanitized editing that may occur at other publications.

NEWSPAPER FEATURE WRITERS

Newspaper feature writers come in two varieties. The most common is the staff writer, an individual who works full time or steady part time for a single publication. Free-lance newspaper feature writers often work for local newspapers, but most newspapers do not use their work as often as they use staff-written feature material.

Most newspaper staff members work regular schedules. Most work 40 hours, but some who work on a salary find their schedule and demands of the job require more than the conventional week. The work of newspaper feature writers is not limited to a 9-to-5, Monday through Friday schedule. Nor is the work limited to "scheduled" times. Most top newspaper feature writers, even on a regular work schedule, find they never really stop working even when off duty. If you want to succeed, you must take advantage of the opportunity whenever a good article prospect presents itself.

Whether you work general assignment or a beat, the intense nature of newspaper feature writing dictates that you be prepared at all times. With daily, two or three times a week, or even weekly deadlines, a large amount of feature production is expected. You must have an endless stream of strong ideas to develop into stories. You cannot "switch off" your alertness as a feature writer.

There are challenges and rewards working in this environment. The challenge of the newspaper feature writer is to know a great deal about a wide range of subjects in a given community. As a specialist on a beat at a newspaper, your challenge is to know a great deal about a restricted range of subjects, but you carry the burden of responsibility for your entire publication.

As a newspaper staff writer, you will take advantage of public familiarity with your newspaper. Few communities now have more than one newspaper. If you work for that newspaper or your community weekly, readers and sources will recognize it immediately. This means you will have stories come to you, and you might find a higher level of cooperation from sources.

You will eventually also enjoy the advantage of being known by your readers. Your name will become known to the community you serve as a feature writer. If you are good, this can become a major asset in your work as a feature writer. If you are not professional in your work, it becomes the opposite—a liability.

MAGAZINE FEATURE WRITERS

Magazine feature writers are most often free-lance writers. Most magazines maintain very small full-time writing staffs, and most staff members are responsible for postwriting activities such as editing, layout, and other production tasks rather than original writing and reporting. Therefore, magazines depend a great deal on free-lance writers to submit their work, or they solicit work by known free-lance writers.

The traditional staff feature writer position at a magazine will vary, depending on the type of magazine. At a news magazine, for example, the differences between writers and reporters remain great. The functions of writer and information gatherer differ widely for large news organizations such as *Time* or *Newsweek*. Although more and more reporter-originated material is being published, reporters in bureaus around the world still produce information, much of it in memo form, for writers in the main offices in New York to organize and perfect through rewriting.

At other types of magazines, the work of reporter and writer is less specialized. Most staffers, especially those at specialized consumer magazines, write and report. At some smaller magazines, writers may also double as editors to help handle material that comes from experts and free-lance writers.

The routine at magazines, although deadlines are less frequent, is still similar to those at a newspaper for editors and staff writers. The pressure as deadline approaches is intense. Expectations are high. Performance can be no less than top level. Hours are often not within the standard 9-to-5, Monday through Friday week that beginners might expect from the corporate publishing world.

Because some magazines in the mid-1990s are organizing into groups under single ownership and often single publishers and editors, this could mean a growing emphasis on staff writers and shrinking emphasis on free-lancers. In fact, some publications have completely eliminated the need for free-lancers by hiring full-time staffs of writers, correspondents, editors, and others, with bureaus around the world or across the country. McGraw-Hill's *BusinessWeek* illustrates this point.

In fact, Time Inc.'s Sandra Kresch (1986) says this trend toward concentration of ownership will continue as competition within the industry increases and costs of launching a large magazine escalate. She also sees more specialized publications focusing on individual topics for consumers. "If consumers are looking for more specificity in the information available to them, in the next fifty years the industry may change significantly, resulting in an environment where a few, large, general interest magazines are supplemented by thousands of small ones focused on the needs of well-defined market segments" (p. 18).

If you do not become a magazine staff writer, your life as a free-lance writer for a magazine will be quite different. You are your own boss until you commit to work for a publication on an assignment. Your work will require that you interact with many editors throughout a year, and you will likely be an employee of several bosses at one time.

Small magazines offer the best chance for regular work for beginning feature writers. It is also a different working environment. Writers will be less specialized within the scope of the magazine and will be asked to produce a greater variety of writing, reporting, and editing/production work. Staffs may be closer at smaller publications because of the need to interact more often. Writers and editors work together more frequently and will often exchange duties. Writers become editors; editors become writers; publishers become editors and writers. A beginner can learn a variety of feature writing tasks and skills.

NEWSLETTER FEATURE WRITERS

Individuals writing feature articles for newsletters work under a wide range of circumstances, but the model is much more like that of magazines than newspapers. Newsletters rarely have full-time staff writers and depend a great deal on free-lancers or part-time contributors. Larger, well-established news-letters may have small staffs, but these writers probably also have other responsibilities such as editing or other work for the organization the news-letter serves.

Most newsletters, even expensive ones with significant national or interna-tional circulation, have small full-time staffs and seek much of their material from outside contributors. Organizations that publish newsletters—compa-nies, associations, country clubs, schools, government departments and agen-cies, neighborhood groups, and even extended families—may have a single editor who depends on a stable of contributors who have information of interest to readers. This approach to publishing newsletters opens opportuni-ties for beginning and experienced free-lance writers, of course.

Full-time journalists working for newsletters are reporters and feature writers just like those at newspapers and magazines. Their audiences may be much more sophisticated and specialized, but they use the same tools and techniques. Newsletter journalists may also be more expert on subjects they cover. "For some, the difference is that newsletters provide more detail, more background, more analysis, and more follow-up to a story than required by the average newspaper or magazine reader," says the Newsletter Publishers Foundation in its *Newsletter Career Guide* (Newsletter Publishers Foundation staff, 1992, p. 4). "Some newsletters include the entire texts of government reports . . . and other documents. . . . Newsletter subscribers are experts and they demand expert reporting."

On the other hand, newsletter feature writers can be, and often are, mem-bers of special groups publishing the newsletters, or they are individuals with a particular specialization or interest. Assignments are obtained by contacting editors and either asking for assignments or proposing article ideas. Much of the time, there will be less competition and easier access to editors of these publications. This means it may be easiest for beginners to try writing features for newsletters, rather than newspapers and magazines.

It is also important to note that because of the more independent nature of newsletter reporting and feature writing, there is more flexibility for individual lifestyles. Many writers work out of offices in their homes, using personal computers, modems, fax machines, and overnight mail services. Pay may be per story or per issue, but the additional freedom is worth it for many individuals.

Advancement is also rapid for some persons. A writer one day may find himself or herself as an assistant editor, associate editor, or editor in chief the next. Or with experience, you may start your own publication and serve as a writer and editor. It is clear, regardless of the level of work, that opportunities are present in this news medium as never before.

CONTEMPORARY MARKETS FOR FEATURE WRITERS

The numerous markets for feature article writers offer many opportunities for good free-lancers. Magazines are increasing in number and so are the markets for your work. Though there are fewer dailies than in years past, newspapers emphasize feature material even more to compete as an information and entertainment source with other soft news sources such as television, radio, and magazines.

Although you might not think much about it, smaller newspapers are the best chance for a beginning writer to find markets for feature articles. Small dailies that do not have large staffs will more often be responsive to queries or completed manuscripts for timely features. Weekly newspapers, with even smaller staffs, often seek assistance when it does not come to the editor. It is likely that your own journalism school or campus placement service receives telephone calls from time to time from weekly editors seeking part-time or free-lance help in covering their neighborhood or community.

Magazines follow the same model of opportunity for writers. Although most magazines seek good writers outside their staffs, many small and specialized publications need quality free-lance assistance year-round. This demands that you know about what you write for a specialized magazine, and you can still become a valuable part of a publication if you do.

A beginning feature writer need only look at the latest edition of the *Editor & Publisher International Yearbook*, issued each April, to find out which newspapers are published in the region or area. Similarly, the annual edition of *Writer's Market*, published each fall, gives a complete look at the magazine markets that buy free-lance feature work.

And, of course, it goes without lengthy explanation that you can simply pull out the local telephone directory yellow pages, especially if you reside in a metropolitan area, to see which publishers maintain offices in your community.

Various specialized subjects have increased visibility in the past decade. The growing number of separate and larger business sections in newspapers and business magazines means new and more writing opportunities as well. As the Business Press Educational Foundation says, business stories focus on supercomputers, genetic engineering, manufacturing in space, and other unlikely business topics because these activities are financed by businesses and are the work of privately funded laboratories of corporations, not the federal, state, or local governments. "The results [of these stories in the business press], moreover, promise to have major impact on existing industries and, perhaps, bring entire new industries into existence. It explains why these developments are getting even more diligent attention from the business/industry press than from the mass media" (p. 1), the foundation has stated. You will find there are more than 3,000 business publications in the United States alone, presenting a growing market for writers.

There are other examples. You could make many points about the growth in sports publications, computer publications, and even a rebirth of some general interest publications, such as *Life*, in the past decade. These changes, of course, mean better opportunities for feature writers at present and in the future. And for the beginning feature writer, these publications are probably more accessible than established consumer magazines or daily newspapers.

NEW WAYS TO USE FEATURE WRITING

There are many excellent approaches to feature writing that you will discover. Certain specific features and subjects that are getting inadequate attention or no attention might draw greater readership. Some publications are re-examining how they define and present news in light of dramatically changing markets and readers. Modern readership research has given editors and publishers new insights into more effective ways to serve readers.

Features are one of them. Magazines have always had high, if not dominant, feature content, but they are learning new ways to use and present features. Newspapers are becoming more magazine-like in their use of features in the mid-1990s. For example, in 1993 the *Philadelphia Daily News* began publishing a special section of features each week for high school students, named "Fresh Ink." The articles focus on the lifestyles and interests of younger readers by presenting such serious subjects as drug abuse and health matters to such lighter material as fashion and hair care features. The *Myrtle Beach Sun News* developed a new feature section, called "kicks!", which presents readers—especially tourists visiting this resort area—with a weekly focus on such fun as local amusements, attractions, events, and contests. And to attract more women readers, the *Charlotte Observer* ("Connect") and *Lexington Herald-Leader* ("YOU") recently developed sections appealing to women with regular features about jobs and careers, families, health, and children. Other newspapers seem to be making major policy decisions about coverage that decrease focus on government news and increase attention given to family or "kinship" news. Typical of this approach are increased features about relationships, marriage, children, friends, support groups, community and church groups, and the places where people spend much of their lives, such as home, the office, church, neighborhoods, and schools.

Naples Daily News executive editor Colleen Conant (1993) says features are one way to bring Southwest Florida readers to her newspaper. Her newspaper has recently incorporated new emphases on teens, food, books, shopping, education, outdoors activities, and business. Another important feature, she says was named "faces of hope" in the newspaper's People section. These articles, she says, were "a series of 50 features on people in our community who had overcome obstacles. They were nominated by readers. These stories were about people you'd not normally come across in the course of a day. The stories have been very successful in building readership through *access* to the newspaper."

Like Conant suggests, editors believe they have to study their communities and both respond to and anticipate what they are becoming. "Newspapers are looking at the changing demographics of America and their communities, and are creating new editorial pages or sections to reflect fresh ideas," writes Knight-Ridder Newspapers Consulting Editor Michael P. Smith (1993, p. 8).

It is also important to note the significant role alternative publications are playing in the mid-1990s. Many of these "magazine-type newspapers" are filling informational roles for younger markets. Popular in major urban areas, alternative publications highlight lifestyles news and features with a strong emphasis on entertainment, leisure activities, self-improvement, and "anti-establishment" views of politics and government activity in the community. Growing circulation figures point to the success of these publications among younger audiences. In California, for example, there are at least 18 alternative publications that fill their pages with longer, feature-style articles. Most publications are weekly or even less frequent. The *San Francisco Bay Guardian*, published for the San Francisco–Oakland area, circulates about 135,000 copies each issue. The news and feature-based content of alternative publications is often magazine length and magazine quality, some observers feel (Duscha, 1993), and offers writing assignment opportunities for both free-lance and staff feature writers.

A CAREER AS A FEATURE WRITER FOR YOU?

Wendy Grossman (personal communication, 1993), a metropolitan London-based free-lance writer who specializes in science writing about subjects such as computers and the paranormal world, was raised in New York City. She did not think she would necessarily wind up a writer regularly contributing to such publications as *Personal Computer World, PC Magazine* (UK edition), and *Skeptic*, but was not sure what she would do with her life. Sound familiar? She explains she evolved into a free-lance science writer and founder-editor of *Skeptic* magazine in one of Europe's largest cities through a chance series of decisions.

> I went to a private school in New York City and then to Cornell University, where I was an English major simply because that gave me the most freedom to take anything I wanted. I had a fair bit of science: a year each of high school chemistry and physics; two years of high school biology; lots of math through calculus. I also studied both French and Spanish. At Cornell, I did another year of biology and two years more of math (I was originally going to be a math major, but quit when I found I was losing interest), plus a year of German, a lot of theatre arts, and so on.

After finishing college, she did not go into a typical 9-to-5 corporate office routine. In fact, she did just the opposite. She became a musician.

> I was a folk singer for 6 years and traveled a lot. While this sort of background won't get you any kind of a "good job," in some ways it's ideal for a journalist. Unless you know absolutely definitely and for sure what you're going to write about, having a varied background keeps your options open. It means when you're inevitably asked to write about something you know nothing about, you actually do have a place to start.

What background will best prepare you for work as a writer, especially a feature writer? Jack Hunter (1983), who is a free-lance writer and writing coach of Jacksonville's *Florida Times-Union* and the nearby *St. Augustine Record*, says careers based on good writing are a combination of good journalism, good business, and art. And, at the same time, he says such background is good for you. This motivation to excel, combined with the satisfaction excellence can generate, may help you decide if you are destined for a career in feature writing.

Free-lance writers Clay Schoenfeld and Karen Diegmueller (1982) composed a self-analysis of writing potential. Answer these questions as honestly as possible for another indicator of whether you have what it takes to write features:

1. *Do you have talent?* This means an urge to write that creates a capacity to produce good writing.
2. *Do you really want to write?* Can you accept failure as a writer? Success requires a devotion to long hours of hard labor.
3. *Will you work hard yet imaginatively at writing for your readers?* This means concentration on hitting the reader target every time. Do you know your readers?
4. *Can you take advice?* Rejection and evaluation of work should help you improve what you do.

5. *Will you rest on initial laurels?* A one-shot writer will not get far. You cannot expect a publication or sale because the last article was published or bought.
6. *Will you always write your very best?* Writing your best for all publications is required.
7. *Do you start with a knack for narrating interesting experiences, telling colorful stories, or stating clear-cut opinions?* You should say yes. You must be able to document these stories and accurately. Readers must react positively.
8. *Do you start with keen powers of observation, analysis, and reporting?* You must learn how to enliven your facts and get reader identification with what you are writing (Schoenfeld & Diegmueller, 1982, pp. 13–14).

Barrie J. Atkin, former director of Corporate Planning for Rodale Press and former magazine marketing consultant, says magazines attract people who are like the publications they produce. "[Magazine publishing] attracts dynamic, lively people—idea-oriented people who want to present fresh concepts, new insights and exciting information to the public" (1986, p. 29), Atkin says. So why do magazine publishing people select their careers? Atkin lists many reasons: "the excitement of working on an ever-changing product; the pleasure of being around talented and articulate people; the psychological satisfaction of being associated with an idea leader" (pp. 29–30).

Whatever the qualifications necessary and the motivations for the choice, you are now more conscious of your own starting point for a career in professional feature writing. Some of you will start closer to the goal than others. Some will have to work harder. Some will have to invest more to succeed.

THE REST OF THE BOOK

As you move on, you will find many useful ideas in the following chapters. Here's a brief look at what's in store:

Chapter 2 focuses on finding a good story idea. Chapter 3 offers approaches to tools you need for research, such as reference materials, libraries, and interviewing, for idea development into a story. Chapter 4 equips you with proper writing and editing skills when you are ready to write the story.

The next 11 chapters take close-up looks at specialized feature writing approaches. Chapter 5 starts the odyssey with descriptive writing and color stories. Chapter 6 emphasizes people and the human interest story. Chapter 7 looks further at people by describing personality sketches and profiles. Chapter 8 tells the secrets for success in seasonal feature writing. Chapter 9, venturing into subjective writing in any depth for the first time in the book, should strengthen your understanding of reviewing, critical writing, and entertainment-oriented feature writing.

Chapter 10 looks at specialized types of features used to enhance news coverage: aftermath stories, follow-up stories, and series approaches to subjects. You will get a thorough understanding of travel writing from chapter 11. Chapter 12 focuses on personal experience stories from the perspective of the writer and the source through the writer. Chapter 13 outlines the steps to successful service features such as how-to-do-it articles and listings. Humor is the central focus of chapter 14 and a review of technical and specialized writing is found in chapter 15.

To conclude, chapters 16, 17, and 18 focus on the collegiate and professional writing environments. Chapter 16 focuses on campus publications feature writing, with emphasis on newspapers, magazines, and organizational newsletters. Chapter 17 provides an introduction to free-lance writing and then looks at article preparation and marketing techniques. Chapter 18 focuses on financial, legal, ethical, and organizational considerations involving free-lance writing.

The book is peppered with examples integrated into the text at appropriate places to illustrate good writing and information gathering. Newspaper, magazine, and newsletter feature writers are utilized to show the similarities and distinctions of the two approaches of professional feature writing.

Welcome!

PROFESSIONAL'S POINT OF VIEW

Lucille S. deView
Orange County Register

The feature writer is like the dancer grounded in ballet who can switch to tap, jazz, or modern dance—and enjoy performing all of them.

The grounding comes from solid reporting skills honed through writing obituaries, doing the police beat, covering sports, any and all tasks that bear down hard on the who, what, where, when, and why.

The joy comes from leaping beyond these vaunted five w's, to write with style and grace. The skilled feature writer borrows techniques from literary masters to infuse stories with a lyrical quality.

Within a short span of time, the feature writer may twirl from a scientific breakthrough to the newest discovery in fashions; from explaining the stock market to a how-to piece on cultivating roses.

The rewards are great, especially for the writer open to new ideas but blessed with common sense. Some suggestions:

• *Do not mistake celebrity or education for the only sources of intelligent discussion, wit, or sagacity.* People whose occupations are humble and names unknown may provide the deepest insights and most compelling quotes. Factory workers go to the symphony; a housemaid becomes an opera star; stevedores publish poetry; homemakers become bank presidents, and more.

• *Be unbiased in your writing.* Sexism and racism often take subtle forms and ethnic stereotypes persist unless we are careful to avoid them. Because a majority of women are in the workplace, a writer's vocabulary must keep pace. Use the word *executives*, not *businessmen; firefighters* instead of *firemen.* And do not write *woman doctor;* just say *doctor.*

• *Don't make racial exceptions.* If you say *the articulate black professor,* you imply most are inarticulate. Don't indicate race unless it is relevant to the story. Why mention *the Hispanic bookkeeper* when you would not say *the German bookkeeper?*

• *Use the word* disabled, *not* handicapped. People *use* wheelchairs; they are not *confined* to wheelchairs. Use appropriate terminology for specific disabilities. Is the person *hearing impaired* or *deaf?* For guidelines, write the Media Project, Research and Training Center on Independent Living, BCR/3111 Haworth, University of Kansas, Lawrence, KS 66045.

• *In general, don't call older people senior citizens.* They prefer being called older persons. When so many are active and healthy, it is not appropriate to say a person is *80 (or 90, or more) and still going strong.*

• *Don't portray younger people as always troubled.* See the individual, not the group.

• *Practice problem-solving journalism.* Explaining the dimensions of a dilemma is helpful to your readers; finding an answer is curative. Seek the solution, test it, and pass it along if it has merit.

• *Do interviews in person, not on the telephone.* Not seeing the person's raised eyebrows or scowl is a risk—and a lost opportunity for colorful writing.

• *Make each assignment a learning experience.* See it as an opportunity to enrich your writing and your life (de View, personal communication, 1993).

Lucille S. de View, the writing coach for the *Orange County Register* in Santa Ana, CA, writes a weekly syndicated column on aging. She was assistant to the editor and writing coach for *Florida Today* in Melbourne, FL, before moving to California. She was also a columnist for the Gannett Co. newspapers and continues to be a free-lance poet and short story writer. She has also conducted a writing program for the *Christian Science Monitor* and she was a staff writer in the feature department of the *Detroit News.*

2

Finding a Good Feature Article Idea

Do you notice things around you? When you drive to work or to school, do you make the little extra effort to notice people or places or what is happening on that routine trip? Do you take time to look around when you go someplace new? What do you see? Is it interesting to you? Wouldn't it be interesting to others?

Have you met anyone new today? What does the person do for a living? Has your regular network of friends and acquaintances brought anything different or unique into your life in the past week? What did you do out of the ordinary this week? Was it fun? Significant? Did you learn anything from the experience? Would anyone else be interested?

Chances are high that any of these questions, if answered in the affirmative, might lead to a very good feature story. Finding story ideas can be that easy. Some subjects practically announce their potential as a story to an alert writer. Others need the experienced eye and ear of a feature writer to work them into readable and salable articles.

Paying attention to what is going on around her is one of the major ways in which Liz Balmaseda, columnist and feature writer for *The Miami Herald*, comes up with ideas for her award-winning columns and feature articles for the local section of her newspaper. Balmaseda, who won the 1993 Pulitzer Prize for commentary, says the entire city is what gives her ideas. "I look around and see what's going on," Balmaseda (personal communication, 1993) says. "I talk to a lot of people and ask them to tell me what's going on where they work and where they live."

Balmaseda says she also depends on people to call her with column and feature article ideas. As a highly visible columnist for one of the nation's major daily newspapers, she gets large numbers of telephone calls and letters. "People will call me and give me ideas," she says. "And I also talk to people in the newsroom. Reporters around the newsroom are crucial teammates for me. With their help, I look for wrongs—people who have been wronged."

Writers Vincent Coppola and James McPherson and the editors of *Atlanta* magazine also look carefully at what is going on in their city. Not too long ago, they noticed their city's population characteristics were changing. Their keen observations about the changing nature of the minority population of the South's largest metropolitan area and the upcoming 25th anniversary of the death of Martin Luther King, Jr., led to a 1993 theme issue on race relations in Atlanta. A three-article package of primary features included a look back at the day King—an Atlanta resident—died and his subsequent funeral, which put the city in the national spotlight, speculation on what might have happened had King lived, and the new minorities of Atlanta. The issue was an anniversary look at the death of one of Atlanta's most famous residents. In addition to the two major articles about King, a third highly creative story looked at the new immigrants who have created a new minority population in the metropolitan area. Coppola, a senior editor for *Atlanta*, who wrote the article, focused on the growing Asian and Latin American population, individuals from Laos, Vietnam, and Mexico who now embrace Georgia as their homeland. The article is not packed with census data as you might expect. Instead, the article paints the picture with stories of individuals representative of this new population. Here's how Coppola (1993) begins his article, illustrated by photographer David Zeiger's stirring black and white portraits of the people Coppola writes about:

The images are hauntingly familiar.

Where have we seen them before? The guy in the Dodgers shirt. Does he whisper to us of the Boys of Summer? The little girl in the velveteen dress, spit curl so carefully placed, fingers in faint rebellion against Mama's picture-perfect pose. A Baptist preacher calling out to his God. A bride of rose petal beauty searching her new husband's face—as he looks away. Chopsticks and beer spread out on the floor. Luminous children in Sunday-white dresses holding colored balloons.

Images from our scrapbooks, our albums, our lives. Unerringly American. Grandchild with grandma who's trying to pray . . . .

. . . The Vietnamese wedding was an arranged marriage; the rose petal bride, it is rumored, has since run away. She's American now.

Immigrant lives. Hundreds of thousands being lived in the corners and shadows of Atlanta's endless sprawl . . . . (pp. 46, 48)

You have to be willing to get out of your ordinary habits and routines to find good feature stories. You have to notice details of things around you. If you drive the same road to work or school every day, try to vary the route. Look at the scenery with an eye for story possibilities. For example, if you drive past the same house every day, look in the driveway. The old cars that the owner of the house is working on might be more than what they seem to be. Is there a chance this person restores valuable older cars? Isn't this a story prospect? Why not stop and ask a few questions?

University of Wisconsin at Oshkosh journalism professor Margaret Davidson believes being a keen observer is what makes the biggest difference between a good writer and an average one, especially in terms of finding news and story ideas. "A good writer is a good observer—of people, surroundings, ideas and trends, and the general flotsam and jetsam of the world around," Davidson (1990, p. 7) says. "Some people seem to go through life with blinders on. They are so wrapped up in their own comings and goings they are unaware of the ebb and flow around them. But others observe the world in sharp detail with the vision to see everything in perspective, appreciating its true value." Davidson also says this is especially true of college students. "For some of the students . . . the world seems to be a colorful and fascinating place with an endless supply of worthwhile news stories. But for many others it appears to be a very sterile, boring existence where little that is exciting ever happens."

If you go somewhere new, think even before you leave home about what possibilities for stories and articles exist. If you like the destination, why? Would others like it also? If that new boutique has unusual or new designs, tell others about it—in a feature story.

Meeting someone new and different can be exciting, also. However, don't think about the new acquaintance from a personal perspective. Think about him or her from a writer's professional point of view. Is this person worthy of a feature story? What makes him or her interesting to readers? What has this person done that others would like to know? Perhaps the person is in town for just a few days and really lives in a foreign country—perhaps a relatively unknown small country like Belize in Central America. Wouldn't this be a chance to write about the person, the country, and all the unusual aspects of life in a country that many Americans do not know much about?

Finding story and article ideas is related to natural curiosity. Often, the best ideas occur when writers think like 3- or 4-year-olds, always asking "Why?" and "How?" And you have to think about what you do each day—you did something unusual, even something as simple as deciding where to go for spring break or over a long weekend. You could write a story listing your own favorite places. Or compile a list from the information provided by tourism and visitors bureaus. Those might just make a good story.

A stronger story requires you to select the right angle with the right point of view. Like what? *The Boston Globe* publishes its summer vacation guide in the spring to allow readers to use it to plan their own vacations. Instead of taking the conventional approaches such as those described above, the *Globe* staff, including staff writer Richard P. Carpenter (1993), conducted a Summer Guide reader survey of how New Englanders view New England's six states as a recreation and vacation destination. There was a wide range of interesting findings, including a few surprises. Although the desire to go to Cape Cod may be no shocker, some locations offered new and creative vacation suggestions in Carpenter's well-illustrated article. Accompanying his article was a colorful chart listing questions from the questionnaire and the top five or six answers in an easy-to-understand format not burdened with any statistics. Here's Carpenter's personalized lead to set up a place-by-place review of the six most overlooked "jewels" of New England for readers:

Ah, New England. In the summer, you sing to me of cool Maine forests, rugged New Hampshire hills, sandy Cape Cod beaches and calming Connecticut landscapes. Your trendy tourist towns entice me and your crusty characters delight me. Your attractions are everywhere ... but not all get the attention they deserve.

In our survey, we asked our readers what they considered the region's most underappreciated attractions. Now, they were good choices, ranging from scenic islands to cozy inns to challenging trails. But it seemed to me the list was incomplete. New England has many more seldom-mined jewels, including those found in our cities. Such attractions may lack the panache of a week surrounded by Vermont's greenery, for example, but they offer their own rich rewards. Here are some examples .... (p. B29)

This *Sunday Globe* travel feature package went far beyond the ordinary story because it was a unique approach to a routine assignment. In addition to running the results of the survey, Carpenter supplemented his cover article with some of his own ideas. Inside, the section included articles on the most popular lake in the region, Cape Cod, a state-by-state listings tour, special articles focusing on New Haven and Hartford, the best beaches, and visitable islands. In other words, some article ideas like these will be quite successful if you let your imagination and your creativity take off when story situations present themselves. A widely read story might result from it! This chapter gives you some basic advice and professional tips to help you generate story ideas for features for newspapers, magazines, and newsletters. In fact, as you will see, the process is much the same for all three types of publications.

IDENTIFYING FEATURE ARTICLE MATERIAL

What makes a great feature article idea? One that gets published. Just about everything around you is *possible* feature material. Use your senses. Look around. Absorb. Notice. Listen. Look. Your job is to take these undeveloped ideas and turn them into something interesting for readers.

People make some of the best story ideas. Often a powerful story about a successful person's problems helps readers to see the "real" side of that individual. We learn from how he or she has battled adversity and won, or made the comeback to succeed a second time, lost a loved one, or survived a brush with death. These stories often make wonderful feature articles. One such example is the story about the up-and-down career of television journalist Linda Ellerbee. She made it to the top of her craft but had her share of problems along the way. She fought them and began producing award-winning work again. This is how free-lance writer Claudia Dreifus (1993) opened her *TV Guide* cover article about Ellerbee, using the free-flowing descriptive style common with novelists in re-creating an opening scene with dialogue:

Not long after newscaster Linda Ellerbee finished chemotherapy for breast cancer, she quit smoking, threw away the wig that had been covering her stumpy hair, and guested on CBS This Morning to promote a video she'd narrated about cancer recovery.

"You're looking great, Linda," offered a friendly Deborah Norville backstage, who was coincidentally appearing on the same program. "You know, I've found that when bad things happen, you just put one foot in front of the other. Next thing you know, you're at the corner."

"Right, that's what I did," Ellerbee said, grinning.

When it comes to survival, Linda Ellerbee knows all the steps. At 48, she's been married four times; raised two kids as a single mom; recovered from alcoholism at the Betty Ford clinic; endured the comings and goings at CBS, CNN, NBC, and ABC. And now, a victory over the disease that strikes one in nine American women—breast cancer . . . . (p. 8)

Writer and professor Daniel Williamson says finding a feature story idea should be easy, especially if it is a story as appealing as Dreifus' piece about Ellerbee. Those stories seem to jump out and practically scream, "Write me!" Williamson (1975) argues, "A great advantage in being a reporter is that you have a 'license' to find out about all those things you've always been curious about" (p. 70).

The key, then, is curiosity. Once you notice things, once you meet someone, once you discover something interesting to you, let your journalistic curiosity take over. Satisfy your inquisitiveness by finding out about the subject. How? If you always wanted to learn about sailing, go to interview a local sailor or take lessons at a nearby lake. Or go to a nearby sailing club meeting.

Finding the right story idea is also dependent on the publication for which you will write the story. You need to know what sort of material the publication publishes. This is more easily done if you work for the publication, but it can be relatively easy to find out if you take time to research the publication and its market.

You also need to know the basic characteristics of feature ideas. What are they? Traditionally, good feature ideas have eight basic elements, according to authors Clay Schoenfeld and Karen Diegmueller (1982). Those elements are:

1. *Appeal to people.* The story has to meet a need of the reader.
2. *Facts.* A feature that works will contain certain information, or facts, about that subject that will be beneficial to readers in some way.
3. *Personalities.* Facts are enhanced with personality. A story that can offer some unusual person or personality with facts and appeal will be much stronger.
4. *Angle.* The right "slant" or theme makes the subject tie together better.
5. *Action.* Can you make the story come alive? It will if you have some activity in the story. It is relatively simple—people should do something in your story.

6. *Uniqueness and universality.* The topic should be different and should have broad appeal at the same time.
7. *Significance.* Timeliness, proximity, prominence, and relevance create significance in a story.
8. *Energy increment.* The story should stir your readers just as the idea stirred you to write the story. You should show your enthusiasm and sincerity.

Finally, let's think about the necessity that all feature ideas remain fresh. Just like bread, a feature idea has a certain shelf life and it is up to you as a writer to make certain the idea is developed and published in story form while it is still fresh. The best idea won't work with editors or with readers if it is stale.

TAKING THE RIGHT STEPS TO IDEA SUCCESS

Nonfiction and fiction writing have a lot of similarities, and many of them are discussed throughout this book. One is the formation of ideas. Successful mystery novelist Elizabeth Peters (1992) says *ideas* are quite different from the *plots* she uses in her books. She writes:

> It [the idea] begins with a "one-liner"—a single sentence or visual image, characterized by brevity and vividness. Since an idea is not an avocado, you can't simply go out and get one. In fact, the technique of finding a usable idea is more akin to birdwatching than to chasing butterflies: There are ideas all over the place, the trick is to recognize one of the elusive creatures when it flits past. I'm not being whimsical. It is certainly possible to search actively for an idea, but unless you know one when you see one, there is no point in looking. (p. 88)

Free-lance writer Lorene Hanley Duquin (1987) has a four-step plan of attack for shaping story ideas before actually writing the article. She says these four steps require "simple brainstorming" by asking yourself the questions and writing down the answers. "It's that information that I mold and shape into a proposal that captures an editor's interest and imagination" (p. 38). Her four steps are:

1. *Capture the idea.* Build an idea file, because writers cannot always use ideas when they come along. You can do this with notebooks, file cards, file folders, shoe boxes, and even your word processor. At times, ideas have to wait until a market prospect presents itself, too.

2. *Develop the idea.* Do some preliminary research to develop that idea into a proposal. Not all ideas are easy to develop, of course, so be prepared to do some work. Think about the idea. Is it too broad or too narrow? Does it have wide enough appeal to your potential readers?

3. *Tailor the idea.* Shaping the idea to the readers you wish to reach is very important to a successful feature story. Ask yourself questions: What readers will be interested in your article? What has already been done on the subject? What publication will want to publish the article?

4. *Test the idea.* Duquin says you should be able to answer these questions: Do you really want to write the article? Are you capable of doing the article? How much will the article cost you (in money and time)? What else can you do with the material if an editor does not want it? Are there markets for reprints? Can you do spin-off articles?

For another approach to turning an idea into a workable story, Wisconsin writer Marshall Cook (1986) suggests seven steps:

1. *Feed the mind.* Try new experiences. Relive old ones through journals and diaries. Read extensively. Talk to people. Do stimulating things.

2. *Nurture the idea.* Ideas come with a flash of lightning or with the graduate speed of a sunrise. Be ready for an idea to come to you and give it your attention by examining it from all angles.

3. *Ignore the idea.* After pampering the idea, forget about it for a while. This incubation period helps divert you from pressure of creation on demand. Decide to come back to the idea at an appointed date and time a few days later.

4. *Welcome the idea back.* When you return to the idea at the appointed hour, be fresh and alert. Be at your most productive period of the day. Write in your regular, yet special, writing place. Be comfortable.

5. *Create!* Concentrate on your idea, organize, and get going. Let the ideas flow and worry about style and clarity later. Get something on paper now.

6. *Sustain the flow.* Regular writing momentum makes a big difference. Successfully developing your idea into an article will depend on continuation of the work.

7. *Revise.* This involves polishing the original draft into a final product.

LOOKING AT THE WORLD AROUND YOU

You can do stories on an endless list of topics. Start by thinking about your own personal experiences and lifestyle. Stop reading for a moment. Take a piece of paper from your notebook and make a list of possible story ideas. It can be very general. You can refine it later. Compile your list before you read the next paragraph.

Done? Compare your list to the idea categories that follow. If you are a typical college student, it might include such things (in no particular order) as: cars, music, movies, dancing, clothing styles, housing, food, relationships and dating, classes, grades, fitness and exercise, travel, credit cards and bank accounts, friends, roommates, church, clubs and social groups, part-time jobs, parents/grandparents, and even your hometown. Your list probably includes some things like these and perhaps more. Your list might be more specific. Not bad for a just few minutes of brainstorming.

Every one of those categories can be divided into story prospects. You just need to get more specific, that is, give each one a little more focus. You might not realize it, but you are an *expert* on subjects already and can write about them. If you are interested in fitness and exercise, for instance, do you like to jog? Take an aerobics class? If you do, you know much more about jogging or aerobics than those who don't jog or do aerobics. You've experienced shopping for running and exercise clothes, conditioning, selection of the right foods, and the choice of best places to run, best clubs, and trainers.

Personal expertise can be personal experiences also. These can develop into wonderful feature articles for the right publications. How about those categories we called parents/grandparents and hometown? Some writers can turn an ordinary aspect of their lives, such as their family or the home in which they grew up into a marvelous experience for readers. Suddenly an ordinary part of your life, if reinvestigated, becomes a feature idea, a story prospect, and ultimately an article for a magazine. An example of this personal experience approach that developed into a magazine feature article comes from novelist Janette Turner Hospital, author of *The Last Magician*. Hospital (1993) wrote a moving, highly descriptive memoir of her childhood home for a recent issue of Hearst Corporation's *Victoria* magazine. Here's how Hospital opened her article, which was illustrated with black and white photographs from her family album:

> It was never just a house, it was where the world began, right there at 30 Station Street, Ringwood, in the city of Melbourne, Australia. There were wide verandahs on three sides, gables, stained glass borders on the living room windows, figured glass on the front door, a riotous garden with the scent of camellia, gardenia, and wisteria careless in the air.

> It was a Federation house (built, that is, around 1901, the year of Australia's graduation from the status of British colony to its federation as an independent nation), the kind of house much sought after and fetching prices unimaginable to my grandparents who scraped together a down payment in 1918, just as World War I was ending . . . . (p. 40)

Hospital described the house and her memories of the secret trails, her favorite places, and the people who lived there. She weaved these stories into a surprise ending, which described the fate of the house. On a trip back to Australia in 1985, 20 years after her family sold the home to a neighboring church, she learned what had happened to this place of her beginning, her "first dreams." It had been leveled and the lot paved for parking. Like Hospital, you can develop such experiences into stories to tell. You have to take advantage of your experiences—good or bad—and use them as a base to start your work.

Your story ideas can come from a lot of different places. Now, think of your experiences beyond the most immediate personal levels of your life. Professional and personal contacts can be useful, too. Do you belong to a club or business group? Or does someone in your family? Sometimes these organizations provide numerous professional and personal contacts that can be used as sources for story ideas or for stories themselves. For example, that neighborhood fitness and exercise club you belong to can become a source spot for stories. You can write how-to-do-it stories, for example, from what you learn about the aerobics classes and other features of fitness, good eating habits, exercise clothing, membership plans and costs, and so forth about the clubs in your community.

Certain groups will often host programs with instructional and educational value. Speeches and discussions can produce dozens of potential stories, ranging from child care to income tax preparation. All you need to do is look through the listings in your local newspaper or the newsletters of organizations in your community for upcoming events that could lead to interesting stories. Think about the *subject*, not the event itself. The speech or panel discussion might not become an article through the event itself. A speech or panel discussion about sexual harassment in the workplace could lead to a feature article about the unique problems some women face in their offices in your community, and the speaker could become a major source for your story about how women should handle such problems and their courses of legal and internal policy action.

Conventions are still another area that might suggest stories for feature writers. National and regional meetings always attract the most active and authoritative persons who are interested in discussing recent developments in their respective specializations. If you are in a metropolitan area or resort region where conventions are frequently held, this source can be very valuable. To keep up with the schedule of conventions, simply make regular contact with your local convention and visitors office or major convention hotels.

Another set of sources will be at local libraries. Every community has a public library. A few minutes spent in browsing through periodicals or new books at the library will inform you about the latest treatments of subjects that may interest readers. Larger libraries, such as those at universities and colleges, often offer exhibitions and programs with speakers, even authors, and other experts who provide material for potential stories. Some larger, more active commercial bookstores have similar programs.

If your community has a museum, the exhibits and specialists assembled may be useful for story ideas. Both permanent and temporary exhibits will offer possibilities for stories, of course, even if the stories are limited to just the fact that these events are occurring. Often, though, you can go beyond the exhibit itself to generate stories about the artist or event being highlighted. Numerous local, regional, and national markets exist for these features.

In most areas, local history makes good story material. This can be a subject area to cultivate for stories, especially if you can find a local historian who is also a good storyteller. Many of your readers will be interested in their community's history, especially if you can *explain* how and why events, buildings or other landmarks, and people wound up as they did. Former *Miami News* executive editor Howard Kleinberg, now a busy syndicated Cox Newspapers international political affairs columnist, still finds time to develop ideas, research them, and then write a weekly local history column for *The Miami Herald*. He began the column in 1981 and has even written two South Florida history books based on his research for the widely read column.

Because house and home are important to just about everyone, writing about these topics is a natural. Numerous "shelter" magazines, such as *Better Homes & Gardens* and *Architectural Digest*, exist on the subject. Many major newspapers publish home and garden sections on Sundays or in certain seasons of the year.

Just roaming around can generate ideas for stories, too, if you know a good idea when you see it. When was the last time you drove through a neighborhood of your community that you haven't seen for a few months? Or maybe there are parts of your community that you have *never* visited. The curiosity and inquisitiveness a good feature writer needs should eventually motivate you to take a look at different places and people. In other words, explore and look around you.

COLLEGES AS A SOURCE FOR STORY IDEAS

Where do we get a good feature idea? Everywhere. Well, it seems like it. For starters, people at local colleges or universities can be very good sources. Campuses offer both *diversity* and *expertise*. Combine that with relatively easy *access* and a campus is hard to beat for generating article ideas. If you are a student, think about the story prospects in your own classes. What interesting research is underway in the sciences at your campus? What work is being done by your own professors? Have you ever thought to ask? Many are working on serious and important projects that are often worthy of a feature or news story. This is particularly true if your campus has a medical school or other health education programs in which human health and human life may be affected by the work that is being done. Even if you are no longer a student, you will find these schools can be rich with story possibilities. You just have to know where to go to start.

Many universities and colleges have public affairs or public relations individuals who can suggest contacts for you on particular subjects. With a telephone call, these persons can suggest story ideas to you based on their knowledge of the current research and service projects on their campus. Some schools publish experts directories that are excellent sources for reporters and writers. Organized by topic, these directories quickly tell you what experts exist in your own backyard. These are free on request and often require only a telephone call to acquire.

Marshall Swanson (1979), a free-lance writer based in Columbia, South Carolina, uses the University of South Carolina campus as a base for many of his feature articles. He suggests these five steps in tracking story ideas:

1. *Get to know how things run on campus.* Use the public relations people. Get maps and student, staff, and faculty telephone directories of large campuses.

2. *Subscribe to the student newspaper on campus.* Often these publications will tell you a great deal about campus goings-on. You can extend this suggestion by reading the campus magazines and faculty-staff publications, also.

3. *Get to know the director of the student center.* There are many campus events that are coordinated through this office.

4. *Establish contact with various deans and chairpersons of departments.* Do this in person if possible.

5. *Stop off for a visit at the campus research office.* Many universities have offices for funded research programs, a campus clearinghouse for funded research. There is often a list produced of this work, or of grants received, that might propose interesting ideas before anyone else gets them.

Swanson also suggests people on campuses are good prospects for profiles. Both faculty and students can become story ideas if you ask around to find out who is doing what. Columnist Dennis Hensley (1979) also suggests this, saying, "Colleges are the homes of the greatest minds we have in this country and the free-lance writer who doesn't tap this source of free information is literally missing the buck—the royalty buck, that is" (p. 34).

Off campus, of course, there are numerous places to find story ideas.

LISTENING TO IDEAS FROM READERS

Many times, readers will suggest story ideas. You know you have become established as a writer when readers contact you to pass along their ideas for stories. Although some ideas will not be worthy of a story, or are just not practical given your resources, others will be workable and you should follow up on the suggestions.

One important thing: *Never* ignore tips from readers. Whereas one tip just will not work, the next one might be ideal. You cannot afford to forget about these suggestions. If you cannot follow up on a tip right away, pass it along to someone who can or, if time permits, write it down for later use. But you must take the time to check out each and every tip.

Most reader ideas come in the form of casual conversations. Someone will find out you are a feature writer and want to pass along the idea, or someone will call. There will be times when someone tries to be a public relations person for a friend or relative and write some sort of announcement or article to start you on your way.

If you get a call, or a letter, or someone pulls you aside in an office, listen to the idea even if you are busy and cannot do anything about it right away. Write that idea down for action later. Writer Marshall Cook (1986) says, "You [should] scramble for paper and pencil to capture this . . . . You know better than to wait. Write it down now or risk remembering later only that you had a great idea but not what that great idea was" (p. 26).

Tips and other ideas for stories from readers will need to be checked out. Occasionally, someone will present an idea to you that seems good, but it might be false, exaggerated, or otherwise problematic. You have to take the time, at the outset, to confirm and verify information before you dig in to begin work.

The value of tips cannot be overlooked. Some feature writers make their living off them. Gary King, a free-lance magazine article writer and book author who specializes in serial crime, finds tips to be his bread and butter. He combines tips with other sources, such as the news media and online computer databases. King (personal communication, 1993) explains:

> At first I got all of my leads for article ideas by following the news—all of it: TV, radio, newspapers, magazines. If I found a particular case that interested me, I would follow up by contacting (either in person, by phone, or by mail) the primary persons involved. After a while, however, people began contacting me, particularly those in the law enforcement community whose trust and respect I managed to garner. During the past 2 to 3 years, I learned about the power of the computer, and now make scanning the news wires part of my daily routine. Nothing, however, can fully take the place of the in-person interview.

GETTING IDEAS FROM OTHER WRITERS

There's absolutely nothing wrong with looking at what other writers and publications are using as sources for ideas. An idea that you see in a West Coast magazine or newsletter might not work in an East Coast market, but then again, it might. You might be able to adapt it for your own purposes. Start by reading all of your local newspapers, magazines, and newsletters. If you live in a metropolitan area, this might be a chore, but you have to know what is happening locally. This keeps you informed about potential for publishing when you have an idea, but it also gives you ideas that you can market elsewhere.

Certainly, you should try to read as many out-of-town newspapers, magazines, and newsletters as you can. This is especially true to help you learn markets where you might sell your work, but also to give you new ideas. If your budget is tight and you cannot always buy subscriptions to newspapers, magazines, and newsletters, then head to your local college or public library, where you will find many major publications that arrive regularly.

Serious staff and free-lance feature writers make this a part of their daily work habits. "I find that a writer should read everything in order to get article leads. The *Wall Street Journal* is quite valuable to me for that reason. I often spend several hours a week at the library going through newspapers," says free-lance feature writer Susanna K. Hutcheson (personal communication, 1993). "Often, just a small item can be a major story or, at the least, a human interest piece that can be resold a number of times."

USING SPECIALIZED PUBLICATIONS, PROGRAMS

Specialized publications and programs take this concept one step further. Specialized magazines and journals are excellent sources for feature article ideas. If you write about a particular subject, whether it be gardening, cardiac care, office equipment, or restaurant food, you need to be in touch with the industries about which you write. The best way to do this is to read about the concerns, news and developments, problems, opinions, services, lifestyles, and major issues in these publications designed to be read by the professionals, the artists, and other experts.

These publications can help you understand the language, contemporary issues, and general concerns of these specialists, as well. *Foodservice Product News* is an industry monthly produced by Young/Conway Publications Inc., in New Jersey, and *Food Service Director* is published by Bill Communications in New York. Both are aimed at individuals working in the business of school, factory, and business food-service facilities such as factory or school cafeterias. Readers are most often managers and directors of these locations who are interested in information about new products, services, promotions by suppliers, special success stories, and even the law. If part of your work as a student writer for your campus newspaper included covering the university or college dining service, publications such as these (and several others like them) would seem to be required reading. In them you could discover what was available, what was happening at other schools, and whether your own campus measures up. You would also learn a lot about the language of the industry (e.g., "steam tables," "nutrient standard menus," or "ecumenical dining rooms").

A recent sampling might include writer Michelle Breyer's article for *Food Service Director*, which featured a description of the new mini food court designed to serve individuals working in the Texas Capitol Building in Austin. Breyer's (1993) full-page article, which described the food served, prices, the decor, facilities, the menu, and the customer reaction, began this way:

> Some Texas lawmakers called it the Black Hole. To most, it was formally known as the Linoleum Club.

For more than 40 years, this cramped snack bar with a row of vending machines tucked beneath a dingy stairwell in the Capitol building basement in Austin was their cafeteria.

Many Capitol staffers, dissatisfied with the facilities, limited offerings and less than desirable ambiance, were forced to take their meals at cafeterias in other state buildings or at restaurants in downtown Austin.

The Linoleum Club served its last meal in November 1991 to make way for an ongoing Capitol restoration project.

In early April, the new Capitol Dining Room opened its doors for business. Today, a sign greets customers with traditional Texas hospitality: "Welcome Y'all."

Although the greeting was downhome, the dining room is plush and modern. The facility is located on the first floor of the new $62 million underground Capitol Extension . . . . (p. 46)

These sorts of specialized magazines are generally available to members of organizations or employees of companies clearly involved in the industry, but nonmembers can often obtain subscriptions or single copies. Or, of course, these can usually be obtained by borrowing them or requesting the discards from members or subscribers you know. But if you are serious about developing story ideas in a specialized area, you have to have access to these publications while they are current.

Research journals are also good regular reading for story ideas. One of the most widely read is the *Journal of the American Medical Association*, which regularly publishes new medical research findings. The journal is a mainstay for health and medicine writers but provides ideas for many general assignment reporters and free-lance writers as well.

Most journals are published quarterly, but some are monthly and even more frequent. You simply need to familiarize yourself with the existence of these publications by heading to a library or by asking sources you respect for the names of publications they regularly read.

Bulletins and newsletters from organizations are equally valuable. Although these publications often do not offer the depth that a magazine or journal might offer, they still present issues that should suggest stories for you. Regular reading of these topics will make a difference in how you cover your subject.

With the uniqueness of some cable television networks of the mid-1990s, some specialized television programs may be a useful source for story ideas also. With cable television systems growing to over 100 channels in some communities and 24-hour on-air television and radio broadcasting in many other markets, programs of a narrow and specialized nature are getting opportunities to be aired. Talk radio, popular on AM stations in many metropolitan markets, can generate odd and unusual ideas simply by your listening to callers respond to the topic of the day. Shows devoted to local issues or specific concerns, such as business or the economy, are available and often become good sources for development of stories.

Furthermore, public access channels on cable systems provide relatively obscure groups with special interests the time to broadcast. The convenience, for example, of tuning to your local school board meeting or local county government meeting on a cable channel saves time and still allows you to pick up concerns of the community.

WORKING WITH EDITORS' IDEAS

Editors know their markets well. Regardless of whether they are newspaper, magazine, or newsletter editors, these persons are in contact with their readers and other writers, and they probably have had access to research about their publication's readership and reader demographics. You need to know as much as you can about a given publication if you want to free-lance for it, and, of course, you need to know who your readers are and what they want to read if you are a staff member.

You will have countless opportunities to work with your editor on story ideas. Beginning general assignment staff writers at newspapers will often start this way and gradually begin to initiate stories on their own as they gain confidence on the job. Magazine and newsletter staffers can expect much the same, but because magazines and newsletters may often depend more on free-lance material, editors will usually only request articles or pass along ideas for articles to experienced writers they already know and trust.

Editors work from idea lists, just as you should do. When something interests an editor, he or she usually puts it in some sort of holding spot until planning for a new edition or issue is underway. These idea lists, when stories are assigned or when they are finished, are often called *budgets*. Like your own ideas, editors' article ideas come from an equally wide range of possible sources. Editors read extensively. They talk to people. Tips come in.

Your part of the system is to complete the legwork. You research and write. But you should not limit yourself to this role when working with an editor on a story idea. You bring into the situation different perspectives, experiences, and orientations. There will be occasions when you have begun to research an assignment and decide the original article idea was not exactly right, so you refocus the story after discussing this with the editor who assigned the article. You should always share these concerns with your editors and offer to modify their suggestions if you have an angle that will make a good idea a better one, and your editor should be willing to listen. Don't change the story without talking to the editor. The editor needs to know what you are doing because your article is just one part of a larger plan for the department, section, or even the entire magazine.

On occasion, you will find a group brainstorming session can generate workable story ideas. You can do this with your supervising editors, with other writers, and even your friends or roommates. Simple conversation around the office or the apartment or dorm floor during a break or after work might do the trick. For free-lancers not working in a regular news media environment, writers' clubs and other similar professional organizations can offer the same support.

INFORMATION AND COMMUNICATION CENTERS

You can generate ideas by exploring the communication networks of your community. Many institutions and organizations today provide local telephone numbers or toll-free long-distance telephone numbers to information lines. These lines are regularly updated reports designed either for the public in general or the news media. When you know you have a subject to write about, and you know some of the source organizations and institutions you will use, you should find out if these services exist.

Community bulletin boards exist just about every place where people regularly congregate. Shopping centers, for example, often have community bulletin boards for wide varieties of goods, services, and other items. You will often find these at larger grocery stores, too. Churches, senior citizen centers, park centers, and other community "living rooms" will be good places to find story ideas.

For example, go to the recreation center of a park near you. Dance classes, exercise programs, arts and crafts groups, and other organized activities will be promoted in a variety of ways, and you probably see the article possibilities already. At universities, colleges, and even high schools, campus student centers will have a lot going on. Message centers will often tell you about lectures, meetings, organizations, programs, and so on. These information centers are not limited to buildings. Electronic bulletin boards often find their way into your home on cable television channels. Community access channels often run listings of activities that can lead to stories.

Personal computers are now a part of the article idea search process, also. A computer BBS—short for bulletin board service—can list useful information for you if you know the telephone number, access information, and operating hours. Some organizations will use these services to distribute information about their activities. The key is to regularly and routinely check these sources of information. Consistent use of the sources will eventually pay off with a unique and salable story idea.

IDEA FILES, CALENDARS, AND DATEBOOKS

A well-organized writer will keep an idea file, a calendar, or datebook to plan ahead. Without it, your life as a writer will be filled with scheduling chaos. Idea files can be as simple as scraps of paper with ideas scribbled on them and thrown into a box or file folder, or they can be more sophisticated and better organized. You can use computer database programs or even work with a word processor to keep a list. Some writers will use a card file system for managing their ideas for articles. Others prefer to use calendars or datebooks.

Calendars and datebooks of the mid-1990s can be quite sophisticated. Perhaps some of the best are called personal information managers. You may already have one. For serious writers, it may be easier to work with two of these: Keep one for personal matters and the other for your writing and professional activities. These can be bound and professionally organized in a notebook format. Also, they can be purchased in fairly expensive computer software packages that allow you to put all your appointments, addresses, notes, "to-do" lists, and other events into an electronic format. The address section is ideal for compiling a source list in an electronic address book (and you can print them out for your binder that comes with it). Or, calendars and datebooks can be quite simple, such as the pocket-size calendars that are often given away each semester at school bookstores. In short, you have many ways to keep track of upcoming events and activities that might lead to article prospects. Office supply houses, bookstores, and even variety stores sell these tools for your work.

Regardless of what form they take and where you get them, calendars and datebooks are among the basics of the well-organized writer. You might consider a hybrid form of a calendar-idea list. Some writers like to use file folders, one for each month of the year. Others will keep desk books and clip ideas onto each appropriate day or week. Some professional writers, using their publication's office or their home work space, will use a large wall calendar for a big picture of upcoming article prospects and deadlines. Find a system that works for you. Try different approaches until you find something that fits your personal style. You will find that if you are organized, you will be more efficient and productive in your work.

Don't forget the seasonal nature of feature writing. Although this is discussed further in a later chapter, it is important enough to mention here. For example, *Writer's Digest* contributing editor Frank Dickson (1980) wrote two articles for his magazine more than a decade ago that proposed rather timeless story ideas based on the fall and winter seasons. His point, in addition to listing more than 70 ideas in the articles, was that you must plan ahead as much as 6 months for some stories if you want to sell your work.

FINDING FEATURE IDEAS ON A BEAT

Staff writers for newspapers, magazines, and newsletters often find themselves on a beat assignment. Although there is considerable freedom in being a general assignment staff member who takes just about any story assignment that comes along, the opportunity to specialize on a beat appeals to many writers.

Whereas a newspaper reporter's beat can be defined as just about any subject—such as health and medicine, transportation, the public zoo, education and the schools, or parks and recreation—magazine and newsletter writers' beats are often even more specific and specialized because of the narrow scope of the publication.

For some newspaper, magazine, or newsletter beat writers, feature stories can be the exception rather than the rule. Many times, beat reporters are bound by the demands of spot news reporting and find little time for features. However, a good feature article can serve several purposes for beat writers. First, they give a needed *diversion* from the daily deadline writing. Second, they can *build bridges* with sources, because these stories, if accurate and fair, seldom ruffle feathers. Third, they offer readers a *new perspective* on a familiar subject.

Let's think about the police beat as an example. A writer covering the police department on a regular basis will have plenty of breaking spot stories for his or her editors without writing feature articles. Yet, some of the most interesting stories will take readers behind the scenes, profile officers with special achievements, highlight special crime prevention programs, or offer depth and insight to an unusual event, such as a shocking crime that has recently occurred, or a crime trend affecting a segment of the community, such as senior citizens. Looking at a different beat, a writer covering education can produce many feature articles about schools, students, programs, teachers, administrators, parental activities, organizations, and the successes and failures of the school system.

Daniel Williamson (1975) says beat reporters generate most newspaper features. He says, "Regardless of the reporting specialty you may inherit, feature stories will present an ever-present opportunity to win news sources, educate and inform your readers, and impress your editors with steady, high production" (p. 75).

YOUR BEST SOURCES FOR STORY IDEAS

Personal experiences
Personal and professional contacts
College and university campuses
Meetings and conventions
House and home
Libraries, museums
Historians
Other publications (newspapers, magazines, and newsletters)
Television programs
Readers and sources
Editors and fellow writers
Telephone information lines
Community bulletin boards and communication centers
Calendars and datebooks

Magazines, on the other hand, also depend on beat writers, but these people are not always on staff. As we have already noted, many magazines depend on free-lance writers to be their specialists for articles. Or, if you become a specialist on a magazine *staff*, remember that either way, it is likely that you will be a specialist for a publication quite narrow in its scope. There are few general interest magazines that remain successful in the mid-1990s. Unless you work for one of them, it is likely you will be covering a specialized area for readers who have a high level of interest in the subject and, it is also quite likely, a high level of knowledge as well.

This simply means the demands on you to find feature articles that are educational and informative will be tougher. Let's consider another example. If you are a writer for a food and home entertaining magazine such as Knapp Communications' *Bon Appetit*, feature articles about such subjects as British cooking must have something *new* to offer before America's cooks will bother to read your work. The Los Angeles-based magazine recently succeeded with an entire issue devoted to the subject. Articles told readers about the top restaurants, more traditional dishes, desserts, and British breads. Being a beat feature writer has its advantages. You can carve out a niche and learn much about the topic. You become authoritative, and this, of course, makes your work even more sought after.

CHOOSING THE RIGHT ANGLE

All feature articles have a particular approach. It really doesn't matter whether your article is written for a magazine, newspaper, or newsletter. It has to have some sort of angle, some major thrust within the subject you have selected. It should also limit itself to one angle or it will have too much direction to it.

After you have determined the subject for the article, make a list of all the possible angles of the subject. By exploring your list of options, you will begin to get the overall picture and available approaches. Then organize the list. Reorder it. Which one is best? Rank the items on the list according to which you feel are the most appealing and unique to readers. This should help you eliminate some of the less desired approaches. With a practical point of view, determine what angles are within your resources. How much time is needed? Are sources available? Is travel involved? Can you afford the approach within your operating budget? What topics interest you the most? Make second, third, and fourth choices for the story's focus in case your favorite choice does not work out. Always have a backup angle to the idea.

As an example of giving some focus to a general idea, let's suppose you want to write an article for your local city/regional magazine about bicycling. The process of finding the best angle is similar to a narrowing-down process. What do you want to write about bicycling? Because it is a city/regional magazine, do you write about urban or suburban bicycling? Touring the countryside? Competitive racing? Bicycling clubs? Buying a bicycle? Other equipment? Clothing? Training? You make these types of decisions many times in conjunction with an editor. As a free-lancer, you are on your own. It is a good idea to have this angle set before you pitch the story in a query letter or article proposal.

For this assignment, you decide you want to write about riding bicycles from a consumer or participation angle. Can you narrow this down further? Probably. You think this through and decide one approach might be the public bicycle routes or riding paths built in your metropolitan area in the past few years. However, you still have to go further to determine your final focus. Will you do a user "review" of these trails? Will you simply do a descriptive piece with maps that tells readers where they can be found? You decide on the descriptive review and set out to ride every mile of the trails, taking notes along the way about rest stops, traffic, smoothness of the trail, bicycle shops along the way for emergencies, staging or parking areas, and even how busy the trails get after work and on weekends. Then you stop some fellow riders and interview them. Other sources, such as officers of local bicycle clubs and local government officials who oversee the trails, become part of the story also. The purpose of this example is to illustrate that you must keep things specific and focused in your article. Without focus, your article will drift without any real beginning, middle, or end, and worse, it will not seem to have any point to it.

Professor Benton Rain Patterson (1986) calls an article angle "a frame that contains all the pertinent material. Material not pertinent to the angle is left out of the piece. The angle is also like a clothesline from which the piece's bits of information are hung" (p. 59). He adds that a feature article's angle helps structure information around a central idea that gives the reader's mind a clear place to rest.

TRYING OUT IDEAS BEFORE WRITING

To be fair to yourself and to your potential readers, you must try out an idea before you devote time and resources to it. As noted earlier, free-lance writer Lorene Hanley Duquin (1987) offers a strategy for polishing your story ideas before you sit down to write. She says the approach requires asking yourself questions and writing down the answers. Here is a much closer look at the questions posed earlier:

1. *Do you really want to write the article?* You have to consider the motivation level. If it is interesting to you and a worthy subject, you should do it. If you cannot seem to get excited about it, how can you expect your article to show that excitement? How can you expect your readers to be stimulated by what you have written?

2. *Are you capable of doing the article?* Some topics are simply beyond a writer's abilities to complete. Because of technical complexity, or the time

involved, or the expenses, it might not be workable. Some great article ideas are just out of reach for average writers. Sometimes, a subject requires the sensitivity or personal experience that you might not have. A mature writer will recognize this and hold the idea until later or give it up completely.

3. *How much will the article cost you?* Both staff writers and free-lancers have to consider the resources needed to do a story. Staff writers might have a news media organization behind them, but its budget has limitations and priorities that may prevent traveling, calling, or otherwise gathering the information needed. This is a serious problem for free-lancers when you are not sure if a publication will pay your expenses. Can you afford to take the chance? Some ideas will be worth the risk; others will not be. Finally, there is the consideration of time. If you have the resource backing you need, does this idea merit the time it will require to do it right? Some long magazine pieces require a month or two of full-time research and writing. Other features can be done in a few hours.

4. *What else can you do with the material?* What happens to your idea and its development if a particular targeted publication does not want it? Do you have other publication options? Can this idea become part of another writing project? If you are a staff member, does your publication permit you to market your work to other outlets?

5. *Are there markets for reprints?* For free-lance writers, this is a concern that may not be so important to staff writers. If you write your article from this idea, can you find second and third outlets for the story in the form of reprints? Some magazines regularly reprint major feature articles. Staff writers might not concern themselves with this, because they have less control over distribution of their work. However, some newspaper and magazine groups often exchange the best of their editions through news services and syndicates.

6. *Can you do spin-off articles?* For the free-lance writer, this is a critical point. To make your work pay off at a level that can sustain you, ideas must generate more than one possible story. Can you take the idea and move into several markets with it? For a staff writer on a regular income, this is a little less important. Yet, from a similar perspective, even a staff writer might consider if the idea will have potential for a series approach or other stories for later issues or editions.

DEVELOPING AN IDEA INTO AN ARTICLE

Two steps in developing your idea into a finished manuscript are:

1. *Giving the idea an angle.* Narrow it down. Cut out unnecessary approaches.
2. *Testing the idea for its soundness.* Does it seem logical? Does it make sense on its face? Would you want to read this article if someone else had written it?

Once you are satisfied that these steps are taken, then the prewriting and editing process continues with your first efforts to gather and organize materials for your article. These additional three steps are:

1. *List the research sources you will need.* This subject is covered in depth in the next chapter, but in developing an article idea before the writing stage, you now should consider what research will be necessary. Where do you go?

2. *Make a rough outline of the idea as you turn it into an article.* Although outlining is discussed in more depth in chapter 4, you should have some idea of the thrust or angle of the story by now and can begin to list major sections of the article on paper. This will help you understand what needs to be done next.

3. *List possible interviews/sources you will need.* What persons will be a part of the article? What areas of expertise will they represent? How will you find them? Are they accessible?

PROFESSIONAL'S POINT OF VIEW

Pat Clinton
Chicago magazine

To come up with good ideas, start by coming up with bad ones. Don't try to censor yourself. Write them all down: bad ones, incredibly bad ones, baldly stolen ones, embarrassing ones. Don't stop the flow by trying to judge them— first go for volume.

Build new ideas by doing variations on old ones. Extrapolate. Look for common threads, related topics, parallels in different fields. One writer I know calls it the "Beverly Hillbillies"/"Green Acres" strategy. If you read a story about country folk who come to the city, you look for one about city folk who go to the country.

That's what you do with your bad ideas. Say you've read a news story about a particularly bloody divorce, but it's been covered so much you don't think anyone would buy a story on it. What are the variations? You could try to find another bloody divorce. A divorce lawyer. A lot of divorce lawyers. Expert witnesses in divorce cases. New ideas about financial support. Child-support cheating. People who track down child-support cheats. Children who live in poverty while their half-siblings are affluent. Alimony for men. For a specific man. Don't stop.

Detectives who do divorce work. Your city's most notorious local detective who does divorce work. Detectives who get in trouble with the law over their divorce work. The multiple ex-spouses of some locally famous divorced person. Ways people have of not getting divorced. People who remarry. Other kinds of partnerships that dissolve: law firms that split, for instance. How about a bitter lawsuit over dissolving a family-held corporation? Or a bloody bankruptcy. Bankruptcy lawyers? And on and on and on.

Most of the ideas will be terrible; many of them will need to be filled out by calls to sources of one sort or another—experts, associations, participants, and so on. (These sources in turn will be sources of still more ideas.) But at least you're thinking along new lines.

Don't stop. Make a list of every category, every story genre you can think of. Subdivide them: Don't just put down "profile," put down "*New Yorker* profile, *Vanity Fair* profile, celebrity profile, obit, oral history"—draw as many distinctions as you can. Make lists of kinds of people—old, young, living, dead, black, white, starting out, retired, entertainer, sports figure, politician, teacher, lawyer. Combine your categories and see what you get: retired black entertainers, female lawyers starting out in their careers, very young athletes. Think of some specific story ideas that arise from these kinds of people. Do variations on them. Make some calls. Don't stop.

Look at the ideas on your list. Think of them in terms of real pieces of stories. Mentally sketch a lead, a scene, a headline, a potential interview. Think about what you've sketched: Does it suggest other story ideas? Are you slowing down? Think of some deliberately bad ideas—clichéd, overdone, boring, stupid. Write them down. Work with them.

By now you should have a fair-sized list. Read it over. Some of the ideas you'll like. Why? What is it that draws you to a story? Personalities? Conflict? Complex processes that need to be explained? New solutions to old problems? Look for themes in what you like and try to turn them into still more ideas. Try to anticipate sources for the kinds of stories you seem to like. (One writer I work with discovered that the state licensing office's disciplinary file was filled with stories he liked. He reads it every week now, and he's probably the only journalist in town who does.)

Make up your own rules. Remember, if you write down enough ideas, eventually you'll come up with some good ones. Don't stop (Clinton, personal communication, 1988).

Pat Clinton is a senior editor for *Chicago* magazine. He says "in our scheme of things, [senior editor] means I edit and develop stories and badger and cajole writers." Prior to joining *Chicago*, he was managing editor of *Chicago Reader*. He also was on the staff of *Building Design & Construction*. He studied medieval English literature at the doctoral level at Northwestern University.

3

Researching Feature Article Ideas

News research is undergoing a metamorphosis. Like Franz Kafka's famed short story in which a man becomes an insect, news research is nothing like it used to be. These days, the serious researcher is becoming a computer whiz, weaving his or her way in and out of electronic libraries in a wide range of forms. Mix this with the already looming size and vastness of traditional library collections, and the research process has taken on new meaning when applied to article writing.

Have you found a good idea that you want to develop into a feature article? Do you need to find some basic information about it? Perhaps dig deeper for all there is on a current subject? That's what you will learn how to do in this chapter. Focus is on both using traditional library resources and employing newer computer-based resources. Brief attention will also be given to interviewing and observation as significant information gathering tools.

Research is diligent investigation and inquiry into a subject. It is such an important step, all writers take time to do it. Not only would it be rare to write an article without *any* research, it borders on foolish. It is a common pitfall for beginners who think they know enough to write an opinion feature or some other type of article with little or no background work. Effective research requires a plan. Free-lance writer Gary Stern (1993) advises getting organized before beginning any research. "Before you launch your research, plan your strategy," he advises (p. 36). "Do your homework." Yet, because professional writers must do research for their articles, they often take it for granted, but they take the time and expense to do the research and are always glad they did.

Free-lance feature writer Andy Rathbone is a believer. He subscribes to the "research first" approach in his work. Rathbone, author of books, magazine articles, and newspaper stories about such wide-ranging topics as computers, food preparation, dining in restaurants, humor, travel, and electronics, says research is one of the first steps in his work. Not only will he spend time on it, he is not afraid to spend considerable money when it is necessary. "When writing computer books, I've spent $300 at the bookstores to grab all the competing books. It's important to know what's been discussed by the competition," Rathbone (personal communication, 1993) says. "It's easier to see what approaches work well—and what approaches fail—by seeing it appear on the printed page." Rathbone often writes specialty material for beginners who are being introduced to a new subject or product:

> I drop by several online services. CompuServe's "New User" forum, for instance, is a gold mine for finding out the questions that confused computer users are asking. Prodigy's "Beginner" forum works the same way. It's important to see what's been written previously about a subject. Before, it meant a trip to the library. Today, I search computerized databases on ZiffNet's Computer Database Plus and Knowledge Index. By scanning for some key words, I can trace a subject's history, and perhaps find other angles.

Feature writer Steve Perlstein agrees with this approach to research. He finds the writing and reporting-researching processes to be inseparable. Perlstein, who has written as a staff member at major daily newspapers as well as for United Press International, has written two books and numerous national magazine articles. To add to what Rathbone says, Perlstein (personal communication, 1993) comments:

> For me, writing and reporting mesh; one begets the other, and one cannot exist without the other. I've always considered myself a natural writer who had to learn reporting. Some are the other way around. When I pull in an assignment, I first write a list of all the possible sources I can think of from all sides of the issue. Unless I can come up with a compelling reason otherwise, I wind up calling everyone on this list. And usually, each of these people gives me one or two others to call (I always ask), or a book or article I should read for my research.

> I regularly use databases from the library and online services to flesh out my background knowledge before I call anybody—I've found most sources are exponentially more forthcoming when you indicate you have at least a rudimentary knowledge of what you are asking them. They also are more likely to think you'll know if they are lying, so they don't try it as often.

News research—and reporting—are in a new world of computers and database research, as Perlstein's discussion suggests. If computer-based research is all new to you, you might wonder, "Where can I start? What sources can I call on? Where do I go?" Start with, and master, printed sources. There are still the basic categories of interview-based resources. But these days, you will soon need to add computer-based sources to the list. We devote our attention to all three of these areas—published sources, people sources, and computer databases—in this chapter because you may need to employ all of them in working on a feature article. It may be easiest to start with printed materials in a place with which you are familiar, such as your campus or local public library. Then you can ease into the more challenging specialized, online, or other electronic reference materials when you are ready to do so.

Expect to do some serious work and spend some time on it, no matter what research resources you use. Authors Clay Schoenfeld and Karen Diegmueller (1982), who have written both books and articles, say you should expect to spend *10 hours* of research for every 1 hour you spend at your computer when working on a feature article.

Free-lance feature writer Karla Harby (personal communication, 1993), who has written for such publications as *Psychology Today*, *The Mother Earth News*, and the *New York Times*, firmly believes research has to come first. "I believe in doing background reading before doing any interviews. Science journalists [her specialty] are people who are intensely curious about anything and everything related to science, so much of your working framework is obtained just by living, reading, and listening. If you do your homework first, you'll know exactly whom you need to talk to, and why."

Generally, there are two categories of written sources for research: (a) those open and available to you, and (b) those that are not generally available to the public. Although we spend most of our time discussing public sources, we also give you some ideas about how to contend with limitations of restricted information that you might need for a story.

MEDIA LIBRARIES

Most established news organizations will have good to excellent libraries to use. As companies have seen these grow into potential revenue centers (e.g., some now sell access to their information to the general public), budgets have grown and so have usable resources. A larger newspaper, magazine, or newsletter will have a staff of professional news librarians and sophisticated computer systems to assist you in your work. In fact, some companies insist on librarians conducting computer searches because that will control costs. However, smaller newspapers, magazines, and newsletters, as well as bureaus of larger news organizations, usually are not as well equipped. As a writer for a smaller publication, you may have to pay for search expenses yourself. This forces you to be more resourceful in finding information on your own.

If you are fortunate enough to have a news library (once known as a *morgue*) at your office, information is usually filed two ways—by newsmaker's name and by subject matter—and there are usually two categories: article clippings and still photographs.

All news libraries seem to have a standard set of atlases, abstracts, directories, handbooks, encyclopedias, almanacs, and other general reference books. Libraries should update their holdings as often as new editions are published. Later in this chapter, there are some suggested titles to consider acquiring in starting your own desktop reference library. Many writers feel you can never have too many reference books within arm's reach of your favorite writing spot.

The standard tools for finding information at full-service libraries are card and online catalogs, as well as book and automated indexes. Specialized news libraries are not often that well organized. When it doubt, get someone to help you.

PUBLIC AND OTHER PRIVATE LIBRARIES

Both public and private libraries will be your next options in conducting research for your article. If you cannot find what you seek at your own organization's news library, then go to your local public library. In many communities, there will also be university and college libraries, but these are sometimes restricted. Many state university and college libraries are open to the general public, but some private schools limit access to faculty, students, staff, and alumni. If you need to use a private library, contact the director of the library for permission to use it.

Public libraries, such as those supported by city or county funds, often contain excellent sources, particularly for local and regional subjects. If you reside in a metropolitan area, then the wealth of library resources should be great. The only restrictions for public libraries will be hours of operation and demand on resources. Some special collections will be accessible only by advance arrangement, but the reference materials you need most likely will be available for your use.

Besides your office library, public libraries, and academic facilities, there are three types of special libraries to remember. First, you can often use area historical society libraries. Many communities have these, and in state capitals there may be several that are usually open to the public. Second, there are museum libraries. Presidential libraries and topical museums are an example of this type of facility. Third, there are company and corporate libraries. Large corporations, such as those on the Fortune 500 list, maintain these for employees but facilities may be available for your use if you request permission. If you are not permitted on site, it is possible that through the public relations or public affairs department of the company you may reach the company's specialists to get assistance.

Most libraries have open stacks. That is, the shelves are open for you to browse and to find your own materials. However, some libraries do not open their stacks because of theft, misshelving, and other loss of valuable materials. Closed stacks are a hardship for you because you must list the books you want and request a clerk to get them for you. Needless to say, this takes time. You might want to talk to the director of the library for permission to use the stacks if your research project is complex and you can establish that you will use the privilege with responsibility.

Your ability to take advantage of whatever library you use will depend on you and one other person: an experienced professional reference librarian who specializes in the subject you are writing about. Subject specialists are on staff to assist you, so call on them as you need assistance.

Another service to remember is the networking that libraries use to multiply their resources. Many libraries link together in national, state, or regional networks to loan and exchange materials needed by borrowers. These interlibrary loan services may be fee-based and may take time to use, but they can save you a lot of travel expense to find materials not locally available.

Finally, check the facility's hours of operation before you leave home. Hours can change and a telephone call may save you valuable time.

USEFUL REFERENCE BOOKS

Do you need to know a quick fact for a travel feature, such as the average daily temperature in Toronto and Mexico City in summer? Go to a reference book. (The answers may surprise you: an average high of 79° and a low of 59° in Toronto and only 74° and 54° in Mexico City in July, according to *The 1993 Information Please Almanac*; Johnson, 1993.) Even a rather common reference book such as this one, available for a few dollars at just about any neighborhood drug store or bookstore, can be a boon when you are researching a quick fact for an article.

If you take a step further, you will find your local library's reference section to be one of the most useful sections of any library for any writer. You'll find many types and sources of books and periodicals. A few of the major reference books that will be helpful to writers are discussed later in this chapter.

For starters, *directories* are specialized books that list wide-ranging content, such as membership lists and statistics. One example of particular interest to you as a writer is *city directories*. These can be extremely helpful for finding names, addresses, telephone numbers, and building occupants. Writers for newspapers and news magazines find them particularly helpful in locating sources. There are directories for several thousand cities in the United States that are published annually by private companies such as Detroit's R. L. Polk. These books (each is different, depending on the company that produced it) contain traditional white pages (alphabetic listings by last name), but also color pages that list (a) address listings in alphanumeric order, (b) telephone listings in numeric order (often called reverse phone listing), and (c) directories of major buildings and occupants. Some even include directories of government officials, addresses, and telephone numbers.

There are also *almanacs*. As mentioned previously, some of these basic references are inexpensive and easy to buy. These books are published independently by companies or often cosponsored by news organizations such as Associated Press or *Time*. They are published annually and list facts and figures on many contemporary items. There are other types of almanacs, too. Some almanacs are more specialized and focus on subjects such as politics, business, agriculture, or an entire state. The *Wisconsin Blue Book* is just one example.

Atlases and *gazetteers* are useful because they include a great deal more information than just maps and geographic data. For starters, though, you can learn a great deal by simply studying a map of an area. These books often contain statistics and other listings of value to writers. When geography is the subject you need to study, atlases and gazetteers will likely contain the answers. You can use them to verify locations, distances, spellings, population, trade, industry, available natural resources, economic development politics, and distribution systems.

Encyclopedias and *yearbooks* should not be overlooked either, because these books can often give you an authoritative introduction to a subject. Encyclopedias are often thought of as general sets of books that are updated every 1 to 3 years and have a universal application. However, these books are often much more useful as specialized volumes devoted to limited information on subjects such as world history, physical science, and music. Yearbooks are usually supplements that update existing editions of books or series of books such as encyclopedias. One example of a very useful specialized encyclopedia for finding expert sources at the national level is the *Encyclopedia of Associations*. Simply look up the specialty and find the organization or organizations representing that interest. Call the organization's media relations office and you will probably be given names and telephone numbers of individuals who are willing to be interviewed.

Abstracts are valuable because these books take sets of statistics and other data and condense the data into useful form for the user. Abstracts can also list bibliographic information and offer annotations or summaries of books, articles, theses, or dissertations (such as *Dissertation Abstracts* or *Psychological Abstracts*).

Chronologies are reference books that list events in chronological order over a period of time. Many of these are limited to certain periods of time, such as a decade or century, or are limited to the duration of a historic event, such as the 1992 presidential campaign, the 1990–1991 Persian Gulf War, or the Great Depression.

Dictionaries are critical to research and writing. Many general dictionaries are available, of course, some within very low price ranges. Yet there are many more expensive dictionaries within particular disciplines, such as law, medicine, or the physical sciences, that can help you when working with technical subjects that require explanation for your readers. If you want to specialize in a subject as a feature writer, consider obtaining a dictionary for that specialty if one exists, even if it is a considerable investment. It may help you through interviews and, even more importantly, prevent errors. For legal sources, a good source is *Black's Law Dictionary*.

Biographical dictionaries are extremely helpful in researching well-known persons. There are different types of biographical dictionaries, many focused on specific disciplines, so you need to know where to go to find information about the person you are researching. Good examples are *Current Biography*, *Contemporary Authors*, or *Who's Who*. There are biographical master indexes to these reference books that are kept in most major libraries. Many of these books are updated regularly.

Books of quotations are another category of reference books that are a valued source to writers. When you need an authoritative quote or a familiar quote to make your point, these books are the source to use. The leading example is *Bartlett's Familiar Quotations*.

USEFUL GOVERNMENT PUBLICATIONS

Tens of thousands of federal, state, and local government publications are created each year and these can help you during research for an article. As has often been said about Washington, most of the time the information you need is there, but you just have to know how and where to find it. This applies to government publications. All branches of government produce publications. These are mostly public documents, although some are classified and unavailable to the public.

To help find the information you want, there are indexes—especially at the federal level. General indexes, such as the *Monthly Catalog of U.S. Government Publications*, can help. This contains a subject index of new materials that are issued.

Congressional sources provide us with hearings documents on specialized topics such as pending legislation or ongoing concern about medical care, agriculture, and even the routine daily activities of Congress. These documents are available at local libraries that are designated U.S. Government document depository libraries or from the bookstores of the U.S. Government Printing Office. USGPO materials are sold, of course, but often at prices lower than what a commercial publisher might charge.

Executive branch sources cover subjects as broad as the various departments that help the White House carry out the laws of the land. The *Federal Register* and *Code of Federal Regulations* are both good sources for orders, proclamations, and regulations that are announced by the White House. A writer interested in the words of the president may check the *Weekly Compilation of Presidential Documents*.

Want to know how U.S. population trends are changing or how many appliances are in a state or county? Use current census data provided by the federal government's Bureau of the Census in the Department of Commerce. There are both lengthy census reports and shorter, more accessible abstracts of census data. The most popular one is the *Statistical Abstract of the United States*, which is published annually. However, there are several other statistical abstract publications produced either annually or at other regular intervals, such as the *City and County Data Book*, produced every 5 years.

For the judicial branch, the *Index to Legal Periodicals* is a good starting point. For court decisions, the West Publishing Company of St. Paul publishes reports from many federal courts, all state appellate courts, and some state courts in its National Reporter System. This material is also available online at most law school libraries. The published version is often found in county and city libraries, law school libraries, and in some law offices.

In law enforcement, you can find reports by the Federal Bureau of Investigation (such as the *Uniform Crime Report*, issued annually). For other regulations, reports and books are frequently issued by agencies such as the Food and Drug Administration and the Federal Communications Commission.

At the state level, there are many useful publications and documents. Look for handbooks, directories, guidebooks, and other volumes produced by official and private sources. One good example of an official reference book is the *Blue Book* produced by the state of Wisconsin each year.

Other general reference books include works produced state by state. These books can be excellent regional sources and are published by both public and private sources. These books, such as the *Texas Almanac* and *Florida Almanac*, are published annually or biannually. There are also general indexes of state publications. One such book is the *Monthly Checklist of State Publications*, which is produced by the Library of Congress. Some states, such as Virginia and Kentucky, produce their own similar lists. For most state documents, start with the secretary of state's office. This person is the state's official record keeper.

Local government publications vary in quantity and quality. Most metropolitan areas will produce a substantial number of publications and local reference materials. Small cities and towns will not always have the resources to do so. Generally, they can neither afford, nor have the space, to archive much information, except that required by law. If you cannot find what you want at a city hall, go to the county or parish as your main regional source. Some private sources can be helpful. For example, the International City Management Association produces the *Municipal Year Book*.

GOING ONLINE: USING COMPUTERS FOR RESEARCH

For those who have toiled long hours in libraries searching for literature about a subject, the computer is the best thing that has come along since movable type. Computer-based databases have been available for public use for more than a decade now and promise to be the way to do your research work in the future. Of course, this assumes you can use a computer. There are other problems, too, such as cost and time-sharing access restrictions.

One of the fastest growing ways to use databases is through a personal computer from the office or home. In the early days of computer database searching, the effort had to be made from a library or other special facility. With the use of a modem, just about any computer and, therefore, any location, can use a computer database. With news breaking at any time, the instant long-distance reach provided by online computer-based research is increasingly important for feature writers. Online means your computer is linked to a second computer by a telephone line. The information that you transfer is known as *datum* (singular) or *data* (plural). The link is completed by use of *modems* in each computer. Modem is an acronym for modulation–demodulation, the process that data go through to be transferred over a telephone line. Technically what occurs is that the data in the computer of an online information provider are converted into analog wave form by the modem to be transferred to your computer's modem, where the analog wave version of the data is transferred back into data (Davis, Byrkett, Schreiner, & Wood, 1990).

Confusing? Well, take consolation in the fact that most computer programs that operate modems are very simple and require little programming effort (the most difficult things might be setting up and acquiring accounts and passwords). Almost all computer databases are "read-only" files that allow you to look at information but not modify it in any way. You are allowed to copy the information to your own computer and use it later, of course, subject to any copyright restrictions that apply. Almost all services also require a search fee based on time or some other unit charge. These are national commercial services and you pay for the time you are "logged on." These fees are not inexpensive. Some are free, whereas others run as little as $8 to $10 per month with unlimited use and some run as high as $200 or more per hour for more exclusive systems at corporate, prime usage time rates. Most searches cost just a few dollars, however, and may be well worth the investment in terms of time and other expenses saved. Popular news media database providers are CompuServe, Prodigy, America Online, Nexis/Lexis, Dialog/Knowledge Index, Dow Jones News/Retrieval, DataTimes, and Burrelle's Broadcast Database. At Cable News Network, the favorite databases of librarians and reporters seem to be Nexis, Dialog, DataTimes, and Vu/Text. Dialog lists, for instance, are quite large. It has over 320 databases through its "boutique" system, for example, and the number grows larger each month.

"The most popular newspaper databases are Vu/Text and Nexis," according to journalist Brock Meeks (1991, p. 9). "Between these two databases, one can find the full text of hundreds of newspapers, large and small. It's the small, regional newspapers that often contain the real gems."

However, don't despair. Most colleges and universities have libraries with access to these and other databases at a completely subsidized, or at least a reduced rate, for students. You should ask about this by checking with your professors or reference librarians.

Another growing tool to access databases is called *CD-ROM*, which is an acronym for *compact disc, read-only memory* systems. These are not online services, but CD-ROM databases often contain the same information. These permit use for unlimited periods at no additional cost. Libraries often make a one-time purchase of a database, such as a newspaper or magazine, over a period of time such as a year, and make the data available to users at no cost. This is a popular tool at many university and college libraries. CD-ROM systems are available for home PCs also but are an expensive investment compared to modems. Usually, these are best for high-volume users.

Most current databases used for literature searches are electronic versions of indexes that have traditionally been published in hardbound form. The convenience is obvious, if you are willing to pay for the time to do a broad search. Most of the searches that your library can do for you are through a central computer located somewhere else. Your library simply links its computer to the larger, mainframe computer and requests a particular database for you. The database you request will, of course, depend on the subject of your article. As noted earlier, you can conduct many searches yourself, though, if you want to learn and want to acquire the additions to your home computer.

The most challenging aspect of computer database use is search strategy. The secret to inexpensive searching is to narrow down the *key words* that the computer uses to make its search. A key word or series of key words will define what the computer searches for in the database. Because most databases are bibliographic—that is, they contain authors, titles, and subjects—you have to have an idea who the authors are or what correct words might appear in titles. A search of "animals," for example, would work if you wanted to find articles on domestic house cats, but it would generate a lot of information not central to your interests. It would be even better to request "pets" or "cats" or a specific breed such as "Maine coon cats" if you need to be that narrowly focused.

Some databases, such as the contents of many daily newspapers and major national or specialized magazines, are full-text. These databases, when accessed, permit users to look at entire articles as they were published. Naturally, these can be extremely valuable for feature writers searching for previously published, but recent, information.

Many larger libraries are beginning to computerize their card catalogs for easy searching, also. The scope of these databases may be limited to the last 5 or 10 years, primarily because of the high cost of entering older acquisitions. Yet these databases are helpful in finding the most recent editions of books, or, at least, the most recent acquisitions by libraries. These searches work on the same principle as the database searches: You search for the author, the title, or a subject as key words. Terminals set up in the card catalog room or elsewhere make the work convenient. This would permit searching the catalog of your local or university library through your personal computer from your office or home. Think of the time savings from this convenience alone. You can often obtain the access codes and telephone number from the library. To encourage use of their resources, some libraries provide access to online systems to qualified individuals such as legal local residents, registered students, or alumni. Some public colleges and universities that have placed their catalogs online will give connection numbers to the public if their computer systems have the capacity for public inquiries in addition to school users.

Many newspapers, magazines, and newsletters are also getting into the act. Through computers you can access the articles of most major daily newspapers published since the early to mid-1980s. In mid-1993, at least 160 newspapers in the United States had their contents online for public access (Paul, 1993). There are literally thousands of other databases available to check—some larger magazines and magazine groups are following suit. Time Inc. magazines, including *Time, Money, Sports Illustrated,* and *Fortune,* have been online for several years. In the near future, it will be easy to find an article through a service such as Knight-Ridder Inc.'s Dialog, which allows access to many of the corporation's newspapers (e.g., *Philadelphia Inquirer, Detroit Free-Press, Miami Herald*), as well as other major dailies such as *The Washington Post.*

RESOURCES FOR PEOPLE RESEARCH

Edmund J. Pankau, a Houston private investigator, does a lot of research about people to make a living. Reporters and feature writers, to be more specific, of course, are often a lot like detectives. Both journalists and detectives need information about people for their work. For writers, it is often background information for a profile or other feature. Pankau (1993) has suggested nine useful commercial sources of information, some easily available to the public in instant online computer form or by telephone or mail request. The services provide easy access to information about individuals. Here is Pankau's annotated list:

1. *American Data Research Inc.*—motor vehicle information for the insurance industry and other users.
2. *Disclosure Database*—information about publicly held American companies.
3. *Dow Jones News/Retrieval*—emphasis is on financial resources about businesses from such sources as the *Wall Street Journal.*
4. *Electronic White Pages*—online directory assistance for 120 million names in the United States.
5. *Marquis Who's Who*—biographies of over 100,000 business executives.
6. *Metronet*—national directory of names, addresses, and neighbors.
7. *MVR Services*—provides vehicle registration and driving record searches for all 50 states.
8. *Phonefile*—a part of the electronic information service, CompuServe, that searches a national telephone directory.
9. *Standard & Poors Register (Biographical)*—listings of over 70,000 high-level American business executives in biographical form.

A computer database of periodicals called Info Trac is now available in many libraries. Like some other databases discussed earlier, it is available on CD-ROM and is regularly updated. It includes newspapers and magazines and is comprehensive in scope. The service includes recent reviews and uses the U.S. Library of Congress subject headings. The service is provided by Information Access Company and encompasses its *Magazine Index.*

INTERVIEWING: A KEY FORM OF ARTICLE RESEARCH

Certainly an important step in preparing an article is *interviewing.* After you have done your "homework" on the subject and learned what you can about it, you still have to consider the special demands of interviews. Each interview, if done well, should have its own preparation effort, customized for the source.

Columnist Art Spikol (1987a) tells *Writer's Digest* readers the two words all writers need to remember about interviewing are "be prepared." He argues, "there's no excuse for sounding ill-prepared" (p. 10). The journalist who turned the celebrity interview into an art form for *Playboy* magazine, interviewer Lawrence Grobel, agrees that interviewing is the most crucial step in the entire process. "You should know as much about your subjects as they remember about themselves," he believes (Wood, 1991, p. 29).

There might be a need for numerous interviews for most feature articles. Some writers interview dozens of individuals for an article. There is a mix of types of sources, too, of course. Some are experts or authorities. Some are eyewitnesses. Some are consumers or users. Some are simply typical "people on the street." You will use and choose sources on the basis of need for your article and you may need all of these sources for an article.

California State University-Sacramento Professor Shirley Biagi (1986) says there are four basic questions a writer needs to answer when conducting research for an interview:

1. What information do you want to know?
2. Why do you want to know that information?
3. How will you use the information?
4. How much time do you have to do your research?

Without the right preparation or focus, an interview may waste both your time and your source's time. Biagi (1986) writes, "Well-documented research gives you the background you need to ask good questions, to match your interviewee's answers with what your research tells you. To be a truly good researcher, you can't be satisfied with just *an* answer. You must always look until you find the *best answer*" (p. 44). When you get the best answer, you can then set up the interview. Most of the time, your research will tell you what direction to take.

You should write down or type out your questions in advance, each one based on the research you have done. These question lists can serve as a crutch during the interview. They show the sources that you took the time to prepare for the time you have with them. You must remain flexible during the interview to get into other subjects and concerns beyond what your research told you. There are times when your well-researched questions will wind up only as a jumping-off point for an interview.

In most cases, the article you are writing will require that you do some detective work to get the information you need to do the article right. A few subjects will give you the luxury to get by without significant research. Your best bet, regardless, is to know where to go to get the answers when you need to get them *before* you go into an interview.

CONDUCTING INTERVIEWS

Too many good books are written solely about journalistic interviewing to attempt to tell you everything in part of a single chapter. This discussion focuses on interviewing as part of the overall research and reporting process

BASIC SOURCES FOR FEATURE WRITERS

1 *Editorial Research Reports*, Congressional Quarterly, Inc., Washington, DC, weekly.
2. *Europa Year Book*, 2 volumes, Europa Publications, London, annual.
3. *Facts on File*, Facts on File, New York, annual cumulation and regular updates.
4. *Editorials on File*, Facts on File, New York, annual cumulation and regular updates.
5. *Followup File*, P.O. Box 330, Hastings-on-Hudson, N.Y., 10706, paid subscription service, weekly newsletter with up-to-date story suggestion lists.
6. *McGraw-Hill Concise Encyclopedia of Science & Technology*, 2nd ed., Sybil P. Parker, ed., 15 volumes, McGraw-Hill, New York, 1989.
7. *New York Times Cumulative Subject & Personal Name Index*, Edward A. Reno, series ed., Microfilming Corp., of America, Glen Rock, NJ, annual. Covers 1913–present.
8. *Guide to Reference Books*, 10th ed., Eugene P. Sheehy, American Library Association, Chicago, 1986.
9. *Wall Street Journal Index*, Dow Jones, New York, annual. Covers 1958–present.
10. *World of Learning*, 2 volumes, Europa Publications, Ltd., London, annual. Issued since 1947.
11. *Access, The Supplementary Index to Periodicals*, John Gordon Burke Publishers, Inc., Evanston, IL, annual. Covers 1979–present.
12. *NewsBank Index*, NewsBank, Inc., New Canaan, CT, updated monthly. Covers 1982–present.
13. *The Magazine Index: Hot Topics*, Information Access Co., Belmont, CA, updated monthly.
14. *Associated Press Stylebook and Libel Manual*, Norm Goldstein, ed., Associated Press, New York, 1992.

and offers advice on how you can use interviews to gather information needed for a feature article. After you have done your preinterview homework, the time arrives to go to the telephone or to your source in person. Assuming you have found the right sources for your story, the next step is to set up the meeting to talk.

Your interpersonal communication skills are put to test during an interview. You should try to relax the person you are talking to and make the experience seem less like an interview and more like a conversation between two people who just met. How is this done? If you can, start by chatting about something neutral. Take a moment to get to know the person. Tell the person about yourself. Let them get to know you and become more comfortable with you. You have to judge how much casual conversation is enough. It is obvious that a busy banker is less interested in casual conversation than a relaxed grandfatherly craftsman might be. Remember, you will have different experiences, depending on whether the interview is conducted in person or on the telephone. Although the telephone saves time, you lose the familiarity and depth of detail of being there with the source.

Treat your source as you would like to be treated if you were the source. Dress professionally. Be polite and considerate. *Identify* yourself. This is especially important if you are conducting an interview by telephone. Explain your purpose and estimate how much time you need. If you plan to use a tape recorder for accuracy and completeness, ask if it matters to the source before you use it. Some state laws require it, especially if it involves a telephone conversation. Remind the source that you are also going to be taking notes during the interview.

Because getting information is your goal, always be certain of the information you are getting during your interview, regardless of whether it is in person or on the telephone. Verify spellings and the meaning of technical terms. Ask a second time if necessary. Follow up the responses with questions designed to clarify, such as "Why?" Don't be afraid to show you don't know something.

These context and verification elements of the interview are quite important, says magazine editorial consultant and former *BusinessWeek* Senior Editor John Campbell. Campbell (1993) believes context should be made clear when questioning a source. This can be done as part of the questioning, such as prefacing a question with a brief factual statement. Verification is equally significant, Campbell says, because "you must understand not just what the interviewee said, but what he really meant to say" (p. 31).

Interviewing in-person in the "street" for an article has its own problems. Many people resist strangers, especially ones with notebooks. Kevin McManus (1992), a reporter for *The Washington Post*, recommends avoiding the outdoors (people prefer indoor situations), taking time to warm up people, using a tape recorder, putting in the time (avoiding quick hit efforts), finding an escort (someone from the neighborhood, the business, or school), using a sign (in large group situations, use posterboard to make a sign to tell people you want to talk), and developing a thick skin (don't let refusals from strangers to do spot interviews to bother you).

Because many interviews in the course of the research process are vital to the article you do, it is often wise to take a tape recorder with you. In fact, some professional writers use *two* recorders to guard against failure of one of the machines. But, as already noted, be sure your source knows you are taping the interview. At the same time you record, you should continue to take notes as you would normally because your notes will help you in finding quotes on the tape later during the writing process. Susanna K. Hutcheson (personal communication, 1993), a free-lance magazine writer, says she depends on her tape recorder for accuracy. "My interviews are taped, as is my practice, because it keeps me from misquoting a subject and could help me if I ever had to go to court."

John Campbell (1993), who has served as editorial director for the Hearst Business Publishing Group, says interviews are best if you give a little to get a little information. He believes the interview should be kept conversational and not overly rigid and organized. Let the interview flow naturally, he advocates. Talk to your sources; don't just question them. This helps to establish rapport, allows a chance to test your ideas more effectively, and gives some feedback to the sources to ensure their involvement in future requests. This is what he calls an informal "payback" for their involvement this time around by letting the sources know how they have helped you.

Shirley Biagi (1986) agrees with the conversational approach. She recommends that during the interview you should relax and let your source do the talking. Simply bite your tongue if you are inclined to talk too much or interrupt before someone finishes answering your question. Biagi also says you should display empathy and concentrate on what your source is saying. She also says it makes a difference if you note gestures and expressions by your source, as well as physical characteristics. It is helpful, of course, during in-person interviews to look around the room when you get the chance—to learn more about the person. Biagi also cautions beginning writers to watch for sudden shifts in direction of the interview. And, she says, be prepared to get away from the questions you developed if something more interesting arises.

Experienced professionals also recommend that you remain firm and in control while using the conversational approach. Be honest and do not pretend to be something you are not. Being prepared through preinterview research is one way to accomplish that. Keep your composure. Relax. This is a natural outgrowth of knowing your material going into the interview. Mixing easy and tough questions will vary the pace and intensity of the interview, also, giving respites to both you and your source, but be sensitive. If you can prepare question lists in advance, keep this in mind as you order the questions (Bottomly, 1991; Ritz, 1993).

Clearly, the telephone is the most convenient method of interviewing. It is indispensable when working on a feature article. Although an in-person interview can yield much richer information and depth of detail, often time or expense will not permit it. A good feature writer needs to refine his or her telephone interviewing skills. Minneapolis free-lance writer Steve Perlstein (personal communication, 1993) offers a tip from his decade of experience as a journalist:

> I can't stress how important it is to sound *relaxed* on the phone. Remember, interview subjects either like you or are intimidated by you because you are writing about them—you are in control. Even when someone is hostile, that's because they feel they don't have the upper hand and they need to get it. Always have your questions written down, so in case someone is short with you, you always have something else to move on to without foundering. That contributes to your air of knowledge, your control of the interview. Without that, you'll almost never get the information you need.

Pauline Bartel (1992), who has written free-lance articles for numerous national magazines such as the *Saturday Evening Post* and *Mademoiselle*, says

---

A WRITER'S LIST OF BEST PERIODICAL INDEXES

Free-lance writer and librarian Lois Horowitz (1986) compiled this list of indexes for *Writer's Digest* that is particularly useful for writers:

Abstracts of Popular Culture
Access
Applied Science & Technology Index
Art Index
Biological and Agricultural Index
Business Periodicals Index
Catholic Periodical and Literature Index
Chicorel's Index to Abstracting and Indexing Services in the Humanities and Social Sciences
Consumer Index to Product Evaluations and Information Services
Education Index
Film Literature Index
Humanities Index
Index to Free Periodicals
Index to How-to-Do-It Information
Index to Jewish Periodicals
Index to New England Periodicals
Index to Periodicals By and About Blacks
Magazine Index
Music Index
New Periodicals Index
Physical Education/Sports Index
Physical Education Index
Poole's Index to Periodicals
Popular Music Index
Popular Periodicals Index
Psychological Abstracts
Reader's Guide to Periodical Literature
Runner's Index
Social Sciences Index
Sociological Abstracts
Subject Index to Children's Magazines
Ulrich's International Periodicals Directory

---

organization is the key to efficient use of time for interviews. There is a risk that a disorganized interviewer can spend too much time on interviews and postinterview review of notes and tapes. To save time, she recommends setting up advance appointments, using the telephone as much as possible, tape recording often, and clustering interviews around the same topic.

Some of the most readable and interesting feature articles are often based on very difficult interviews to set up and carry out. Free-lance writer Toni Wood (1993), who has written as a staff writer for the *Kansas City Star* and for national magazines, strongly recommends putting in the effort to get tough interviews. "Compelling nonfiction is often based on intimate losses, victories or mistakes. But learning to draw those stories from people is an art. It requires that you ask tough, personal questions with compassion, patience, persuasion and tenacity" (p. 28). Here is Wood's useful list of 10 recommendations for successfully completing a tough interview:

1. Watch your body language and tone of voice.
2. Start the conversation in neutral territory.
3. Tape recording can be frightening.
4. React to what you hear.
5. Slow down as you move to the sensitive territory.
6. Don't rush to fill gaps in conversation.
7. Pose the most challenging questions with simplicity and be direct.
8. Take time in developing the relationship with the source.
9. There may be source resistance, so be ready and make space for it.
10. Try to keep professional distance and don't melt down emotionally.

Remember the value of follow-up questions as well. Often a source will give a partial answer to your question or may offer a response that is not completely understandable. Be prepared to ask follow-up questions such as "Can you explain that better?" or "Give me an example of what you mean" or "I'm not sure I understand. Can you expand a little on what you just said?"

And a final tip: When you are winding up the interview, make certain you know how to find your source later if you need to conduct a second, or follow-up, interview. Get a telephone number. It may not always be in the same place as the first interview. Remember to double check critical information before you leave or hang up the telephone.

Remember, this is how just one interview goes. Just about all but the most basic feature articles require that you repeat this process in preparing an assignment. Seldom can you get a complete picture of a situation by depending on only one interview. Unfortunately, this is the error of many beginning writers. There is always more than one point of view and one side to a feature story. It is your job to find the others.

RESEARCH USING OBSERVATION

There are times when a portion of an article can be researched simply by going to a location and looking around. You might be writing a piece on flood damage, and a tour of a flooded area can tell you much more than reading books or talking to people who had previously experienced floods. Your own firsthand observation can add much depth of detail and description to your article.

Most of the time, you will be combining observation with interviewing and other research skills. You do not need to be a detective, but you cannot be oblivious to what is going on, either. If you find yourself dependent on others for detail and description, you must contend with possible distortions of fact. Thus, the more you see for yourself, the richer your article will be. Most people are simply not accustomed to noting detail as detectives do, and you have to train yourself through practice to do it well.

Given that there are certain risks in using observation, Stanford University Professor William Rivers (1975) recommends these guidelines to avoid the potential pitfalls:

1. *Remember the process of distortion.* People tend to change what they see to make it consistent with their own previous experiences. And there is also distortion of perspective. Point of view can give you a different look at matters from someone else's point of view.

2. *Recall emotional states.* Your emotional response to a situation can affect what you see and later recall.

3. *Concentrate on important details.* It is possible to observe too much.

4. *Seek other evidence.* Consider the perspectives of others.

5. *Observe unobtrusively.* If people know you are intentionally watching, it may affect their normal behavior. This does not preclude observation that is known to the source, but do not interfere with what you are observing.

6. *Become a participant if you can, but only if you want this special point of view.* You are certain to distort behavior of those around you if your purpose is known, but often the experience is still worth it for your article.

7. *Watch for nonverbal communication such as body language.* What a person says is not all that the person communicates.

Author Jacqueline Briskin (1979) recommends one rather unusual technique that may lend a guiding hand to your observational talents. She suggests that when you are out looking around—touring a museum, for example, to research a story— sometimes your camera can help you with your notetaking. The pictures don't have to be publishable, and the approach makes good sense. The detail contained in a picture might just jog your memory or provide the image for a description needed in your article. In fact, Briskin calls her 35mm camera (or any inexpensive pocket-size *instant* camera, for that matter) her most important research tool. Just consider how a camera might help you capture the color and pageantry of a festival or block party. You might just decide this tool will help you also, especially if you do not plan to write your article right away. In this case a picture might really be worth a thousand words—in your notebook.

GETTING PERSONALLY INVOLVED IN THE STORY

The participant form of journalistic observation is unique because you get involved in the story *personally.* As a participant, you may actually become part of the story. This can have certain advantages, such as in travel writing

GETTING A TOUGH INTERVIEW: TWO REPORTERS TELL HOW THEY INTERVIEWED CUBA'S CASTRO

It might not seem like a difficult task for the casual observer, but for any reporter from the United States to interview Cuban President Fidel Castro is a nearly impossible assignment to complete. He is generally inaccessible to the news media. Security is extraordinarily tight, especially when Castro is on the road. But persistence, imagination, and luck led to a timely, and exclusive, feature article by two *Miami Herald* reporters who got 10 minutes with Castro for a story that revealed how the long-time world leader had aged and become out of touch with the changing Communist world. Reporter Chris Marquis described how he and colleague Mirta Ojito were able to talk with Castro, who was at a meeting with the leaders of the Spanish-speaking nations in Mexico City:

"I had placed several formal requests for an interview with Fidel, but as soon as he arrived in Mexico, I feared all bets were off. He moved amid tight security and was plainly taking no chances. A hotel waiter told us Fidel brought his own food, vegetables, and ice with him.

"The trick, Mirta and I decided, would be getting into the luxury hotel where all the presidents were staying. But the El Camino Hotel was awash in guards and even had sharpshooters on rooftops, and there was no U.S. delegation to help. So we tried the next-best thing: We called the Panamanians to ask for an interview.

"OK, they told us, come in. Once there, we chatted up a Chilean security guard. Gee, we said, it would be nice to talk to the president of Chile. Come on, he said, whisking us through metal detectors and past the German shepherds, to the inner garden, where presidents and their aides were meeting in poolfront suites.

"The Chilean walked off to look for the Chilean press aide, leaving us standing by the pool. Mirta spotted a knot of Cubans standing near a cabana. We started taking baby steps that way, and soon, we were within 20 feet of Room 1114. A maid emerged, carrying an olive drab uniform: Fidel's.

"Mirta and I tried to look nonchalant, which was hard as it became increasingly obvious that we represented a major breach of security. Before we knew it, the King of Spain strode by, close enough to touch. Mirta and I were struck dumb. We didn't want to call attention to ourselves, and weren't sure about the protocol: 'Hey King?'

"Gabriel Garcia Marquez, the famous [Nobel Prize-winning] novelist, zipped past. Alberto Fujimori [president] of Peru was next. We were gambling, risking good interviews for a chance with Fidel.

"Then he appeared, on the other side of a hedge—tall, green-garbed, looking famous. He was headed straight toward us. 'Commandante,' I exclaimed. 'Where are you from?' he asked. '*The Miami Herald*,' we told him.

"Fidel wanted to talk, so we caught our breath and fired away. His gray and white beard made him look old. He had sleep in his eyes. Still, he seemed thoughtful, taking time to ponder the questions we frantically poured forth. As he talked, he seemed smaller, became personable, grabbed our arms to emphasize his words. The anti-Yankee rhetoric and bombast was gone. Like everyone else, he said, he was worried about Cuba. Was this Fidel?

"After about 10 minutes, the bodyguard shoved us aside and Fidel ducked into his room. Mirta and I triumphantly walked out the hotel's front door" (Seibel, 1991).

Reprinted with the permission of *The Miami Herald.*

when you relate your personal travel experiences to readers. Other approaches are more third-person oriented and do not thrust you as a writer into the middle of the story.

You can accomplish some research for stories by experiencing an activity yourself. Usually this is research that you simply could not find from other sources. Some serious subjects require it, especially if the article subject involves illegal or, at least, questionable, activities. Because sources, when confronted with tough questions about illegal or morally and ethically questionable activities, will almost always deny involvement, you get firsthand knowledge by becoming a participant and witness. However, in addition to being potentially dangerous, these stories present ethical problems because there can be no disclosure that you are a writer. Many professionals discourage this because they believe it is a form of deception. But in some cases it may be necessary. Other professionals feel it is a necessary and legitimate form of information gathering. Ultimately, you and your editors must judge that.

On less serious feature stories, some excellent feature articles can result from do-it-yourself experiences. One student, when assigned to write a feature story based on participant observation, took a flying lesson and learned the basics of piloting a private plane. Another student took the assignment a step further and actually jumped out of a plane! She was taking parachuting lessons, of course, with a licensed instructor. Both experiences resulted in fine first-person feature stories that dependence on another person's descriptions would not produce.

Other stories may be supplemented by participating in one or more activities. A feature article about hospital volunteers might be strengthened if the writer took the time to go through a training program and actually volunteer for a few hours. But the story would not necessarily stand on observation alone. To make the article more complete, you would also interview veteran volunteers, managers of the program, hospital officials, doctors and nurses, patients, and even a beginning volunteer or two. All this would be beyond the library research you started with when the article idea first was chosen.

BEST SOURCES FOR RESEARCHING FEATURE ARTICLES

1. Recognized authorities and experts such as professors and researchers
2. Reference books and periodicals
    Dictionaries
    Encyclopedias
    Biographical dictionaries
    Atlases, wall maps, and gazetteers
    Yearbooks
    Almanacs
    Books of quotations
    Abstracts
    Chronologies
    Indexes
3. Databases
    Online services
    CD-ROM (compact disc, read-only memory) systems
    Other information retrieval systems
4. Libraries
    Your own organization's library
    Public and private libraries
    Library telephone reference services
5. Others with access to experts
    Corporate and commercial public relations practitioners
6. Your trained observations of others
7. Your participant observation experiences

CURRENT ISSUES FACING RESEARCHERS

You should take a brief look at some of the current issues affecting your research for feature articles. Certainly, there are ethical and legal considerations involving research. In conducting research, you may not have *access* to restricted public and private information. The reasons are many, but these restrictions come in both the public sector and the private sector. Public limitations come in the form of closed records. They can be closed for security reasons, personnel reasons, and other stipulated reasons in local ordinances as well as state and federal laws. Private limitations are imposed by those owning the information you wish to use. You may risk legal penalties if you use information that you have obtained without permission. There is public debate from time to time about what information should and should not be classified by the government, for example. Ethically you must consider, even when you have legally obtained information, whether or not that information is best used or best not used.

On another level, computerization of government records has created still another research problem. Many persons who once could inspect public records freely using the actual documents can no longer do so as easily, because the records are stored in electronic databases that often require clerical assistance to access. Storage and access to information in many public and private libraries face the same problem as more and more libraries computerize their holdings to save precious storage space.

Remember that whatever barriers you encounter and regardless of how you hurdle them, you must remain accurate in your research in any article you write. Authors Patricia Kubis and Robert Howland (1985) advise you in this way: "If you are inaccurate in your research, and your article or book is published, you will have every specialist writing to your publisher and pointing out all your discrepancies. If you write articles, inaccuracy will not have a favorable effect on your career—because truthfulness is a major part of being a journalist. . . . [B]eing inaccurate destroys your credibility as an authority figure" (p. 145).

PROFESSIONAL'S POINT OF VIEW

Jacqui Banaszynski
St. Paul Pioneer Press

Reporting—especially the daily newspaper variety—is fabulous improvisational theater.

Each day we start with a blank paper and set out to tell the history of the world. Much of that history is fairly predictable and, thus, familiar: politics, taxes, worn-out debates about abortion and gun control, sporting events won and lost.

But often history-in-the-making catches us by surprise. Only a few of us who covered the meltdown of Three Mile Island had ever studied the innards of a nuclear power plant. Fewer still had firsthand knowledge of volcanoes when we were sent to Washington for the eruption of Mount St. Helens. AIDS remains such a mystery that we struggle to find the questions—to say nothing of the answers.

Yet we are expected to write about these subjects with accuracy and authority. Often, we are expected to do that on deadline.

So we improvise. We learn to be quick with our pens, quicker with our questions, instant with our analysis. In a few days or a few hours, we cull the pertinent wisdom from experts who have spent lifetimes studying a topic. Unless we settle into a specialized beat and nurture our own expertise, we bounce from story to story armed with little but instinct and moxie.

In-depth research is a luxury in the business. Doing your homework—most would call it backgrounding—is a necessity. However rushed the assignment, there are a few basics that will save you embarrassment and mistakes:

• Start in the newsroom library, or morgue, then expand your search to the public library. Read everything available in the popular press about your subject. Tap into your newspaper's electronic library and cull some national stories for context. But beware: You are seeking information, not attitude.

Don't let background reading shape your point of view. Don't enter an interview looking for a few quotes to drop into an already-written story.

• Gather quick tips from other people. Corner an editor or veteran reporter for summaries about your subject. Ask colleagues, friends, and relatives what they want to know about the subject. Supplement your curiosity with theirs. When I did a profile of North Pole explorer Ann Bancroft, my newsroom curiosity survey revealed a question I would have overlooked: How did she go to the bathroom when it was 70-below? That question led to a wonderful anecdote that gave the story some humor, humanity, and dimension.

• If you have time, conduct a few preinterview interviews. Written research will give you background, but it won't give you quotes or character. Glean impressions of your subject firsthand—from boosters, from detractors, and from knowledgeable, but detached, observers. Check their comments against those of your subject.

Since being awarded a Pulitzer Prize, I have been on the receiving end of reporters' notebooks—a vantage point that has underscored some basic journalistic tenets that we too often take for granted.

When reporters interview me, I expect them to already have our Pulitzer series "AIDS in the Heartland" and a few other accessible clippings from local newspapers that would include my basic biography. The diligent ones also will have talked to one or more people about me—perhaps an editor or a colleague or one of my story subjects. If they haven't done that legwork, I find myself feeling impatient and a bit insulted. I am not willing to give my time and candor to someone who hasn't shown me the courtesy to do their homework. I imagine my interview subjects feel the same way (Banaszynski, personal communication, 1993).

Jacqui Banaszynski, Special Projects Editor and a reporter for the *St. Paul Pioneer Press,* was awarded the 1988 Pulitzer Prize in feature writing for "AIDS in the Heartland," a moving series on a gay farmer and political activist who died of AIDS. The series also received the national Society of Professional Journalists Distinguished Service Award and the Sweepstakes Award from the Minnesota chapter of SPJ. Banaszynski was also a finalist in the 1986 Pulitzer Prize competition for international reporting for her "Trail of Tears," a personal story of famine in Africa. She has been a reporter and feature writer at the *Pioneer Press* since 1984, covering what she calls "the bummer beat"—stories about victims and human grief. Banaszynski interned at *The Wall Street Journal* and *The Indianapolis Star.* She also worked for the *Minneapolis Star and Tribune, The (Eugene, OR) Register-Guard, The Duluth News-Tribune,* and *The Janesville (WI) Gazette.*

4

The Writing and Editing Process

The late E. B. White (Strunk & White, 1979) said writing rules are "somewhat a matter of individual preference, and even the established rules of grammar are open to challenge" (p. xv). These are the tools of the trade, the rules of the game. Good writing has a certain foundation upon which it is built and a certain polish or finish on which it is sold to the buyer.

Yet, as White (Strunk & White, 1979) observed in the writer's little bible, *The Elements of Style*, his Cornell professor, William Strunk, once said, "The best writers sometimes disregard the rules of rhetoric. When they do so, however, the reader will usually find in the sentence some compensating merit, attained at the cost of the violation. Unless he is certain of doing as well, he will probably do best to follow the rules" (p. xvi).

Good writing is difficult to achieve, but with the right desire and right tools, you can do it. Good ideas put on paper (or a computer screen) still need good massaging—good polish, that is—to make them presentable to readers. This chapter gives you the basics of good article-writing style and organization. It also offers time-tested suggestions for editing your own manuscript to get it ready for an editor or publisher. You will investigate the art and craft of article writing. After reading it, you will know the ways and means of getting an article onto paper. You will learn how experts manage their writing and how varied the approaches might be to achieve the same goal of publication. You have to, ultimately, sell your idea and yourself.

Some news media critics feel that writing has deteriorated in recent years. New York University Professor Neil Postman (1985) blames it on television and a video-oriented society. He laments about "the most significant American cultural fact of the second half of the twentieth century: the decline of the Age of Typography and the ascendancy of the Age of Television. This change-over has dramatically and irreversibly shifted the content and meaning of public discourse, since two media so vastly different cannot accommodate the same ideas" (p. 8).

Columbia University cultural historian Jacques Barzun (1992) agrees, especially about the decline of writing skills within the news media. "The unhappy truth is that the prose of the press, and of broadcast news as well, has fallen below the level of competence that was once obtained and that can reasonably be expected. It is not uniformly bad, but the faults are frequent and of many kinds . . . blurred meanings; pretentiousness; and irrelevant fiction-style" (p. 3).

THE ELEMENTS OF GOOD WRITING

Much work goes into good writing. William Zinsser (1980), who has written for newspapers and magazines and authored numerous books, considers good writing a disciplined, rigorous effort that comes from practice. It takes rewriting, what he calls "the essence of writing" (p. 4). It takes the same regular, daily schedule that a craftsman might use in making furniture or artwork. Zinsser also explains that writing is a solitary effort of people who do not mind being alone. Yet he also believes writing can be easy and fun.

Lawyers, for example, often write with clutter and complexity in their search for precision. Good writers keep it simple while retaining meaning. Zinsser (1980) calls clutter the "disease of American writing" (p. 7). He is right. This is especially true for writers for mass publications such as newspapers, magazines, and newsletters. Because there is no particular reason for newspaper and magazine feature articles to be complex or difficult, you should keep it simple. This means you have to translate complicated material, such as medical or other scientific terms, for your readers. "We are a society strangling in unnecessary words, circular constructions, pompous frills and meaningless jargon," Zinsser believes (p. 7).

Columbia's Barzun (1992) is deeply concerned about false meaning in news media writing. He points to vogue words and malapropism. *Vogue words* reduce precision in meaning by giving slangy new meanings to words, keeping better fitting words out of use. *Malapropism* is the misuse of often similar but incorrect words. These sorts of writing mistakes, he argues, come from laziness and from ignorance of the language.

There are ways to be successful and avoid such pitfalls in writing. Freelance feature writer Steve Perlstein (personal communication, 1993) believes in simplicity for success:

> Writing style is surely important, but so is keeping your prose simple and straightforward. The great writers never waste words, and their stories are never one word longer than they need to be. Superfluous words—whether they are to pad the word count or to make the piece sound more important—are invariably cut in the editing process anyway. If you write too many words about the same thing over and over again, or just more words than you need, your work winds up looking overblown and tedious, or just plain too long. See what I mean?

A good newspaper, magazine, or newsletter writer will keep thoughts easy to understand. This is done several ways. First, it is done through your word selection. Use the right words, but don't use too many of the right words. Be concise. Be precise in meaning. Another way to keep your thoughts easy to understand is to use basic subject–verb–object sentence structure. Even if you can find a way to write a sentence with the verb before the subject, it is likely to be hard to understand and you have wasted your reader's time. If you do that often enough, you lose the reader permanently. A third way to help the reader understand what you are writing is to use correct grammar. Usages do help the communication process. People are accustomed to seeing certain forms of grammar, such as subjects and verbs that are in agreement and consistent use of tense. Still another way to write in simple English is to keep an eye on sentence length. The longer the sentence, the harder it is to follow. You do not want your reader going through your article and wondering to himself or herself, "What did that mean? Am I crazy? Why can't I figure out what this means?"

Style is another consideration when you think about good writing. Every writer has a style. Every publication has a style manual. Both points are discussed here. Writing style is much like one's personal appearance. Your appearance reflects your own way of dressing, your mannerisms, and your physical uniqueness. Writing does much the same thing, but it reveals a bit about our minds, our thinking, our logic, and our expression of those processes.

Most experienced writers and writing teachers will tell you that to teach writing, you have to start with basics, no matter whether it is sixth-grade theme writing or freshman composition at a Big Ten university. As Zinsser (1980) has said, "You have to strip down your writing before you can build it back up" (p. 19).

Free-lance nonfiction writer Gary C. King (personal communication, 1993) believes in sticking to the fundamentals when he writes his specialty, crime features. King, who has written three books and numerous articles about major crimes, emphasizes that writing success is found in the basics.

> In writing for the crime magazines, the writer must use good, standard English. Don't use shortcuts, but don't be stiff and too formal, either. Avoid long "travel-ogue" descriptions of the locale where the crime took place (a mistake that many first-timers make) in the introduction, and get right to the story, usually the discovery of a body. Try to tell the story in chronological order, and emphasize the detective work that leads to the solution of the case. In other words, milk the investigative process for everything you can. Don't pinpoint the guilty person too early in the story, and use active writing constructions wherever possible. There's no reason that nonfiction writing has to be dull. Novices should decide which publication(s) they want to write for, read several copies of the publication, and by all means send off for the magazine's writers' guidelines.

After mastering cumbersome language, complex sentence structure, and the like, you can begin to build your own style. The late novelist Paul Darcy Boles (1985) called style a "way of saying" and a "way of seeing." He said it is somewhat born into the owner, but it is also borrowed. Many writers become the product of other writers they admire. The process of stealing technique is

---

WORD USAGE AND CHANGES IN MEANING

Columbia University Professor Ernest Brennecke (Wardlow, 1985, p. 24) created the following eight sentences and eight different meanings by changing the location of one word. Read the sentences or say them out loud. Notice how the meaning of each sentence changes as the location of the word *only* changes. Here's a lesson—one you should not forget—about saying precisely what you mean in a sentence.

Only I hit him in the eye yesterday.
I *only* hit him in the eye yesterday.
I hit *only* him in the eye yesterday.
I hit him *only* in the eye yesterday.
I hit him in *only* the eye yesterday.
I hit him in the *only* eye yesterday.
I hit him in the eye *only* yesterday.
I hit him in the eye yesterday *only*.

---

a rather accepted one in the business of writing—we become a mixture of the styles of writers we read and enjoy the most while we are learning to write.

Really, you don't have to work too hard to develop a style. It is not so much a conscious matter of writing as it is an unconscious matter of writing. It evolves and comes through in your writing whether you want it or not. Everyone has a writing style. On the other hand, the business of a style manual is another issue altogether. You will find most, if not all, publications have their own style manuals or have adapted the manuals of other organizations. Magazines such as *U.S. News and World Report* have their own manual. Newspapers such as *The New York Times* and *Chicago Tribune* have their own. Wire services such as the Associated Press and United Press International have widely used manuals for writers and editors. You will find some of these stylebooks are for sale to the public as well. These books are reference books containing the rules of usage for local and not-so-local matters that commonly are used. The range covers basics such as numbers and names, and more complicated matters such as religious titles, foreign geographic names, and even medical terms. So, even if you are an independent writer, you need to know the major style usages of a publication when you prepare a manuscript for its editor.

Another element of good writing focuses on the audience, or, in the language of communication theorists, the receiver of your message. In communication, there has to be an area of common, or shared, experience. In writing for a newspaper, magazine, or newsletter, the area of shared experience is reduced because a writer must have a shared experience with thousands of individuals. "The chances soar that a message will go awry when you start factoring more receivers into the equation," says Jack Hart (1990b, p. 3), an editor and writing coach for *The Oregonian* in Portland. You need to consider: Who is going to read your article? Do you know? Have you thought about it?

How can you find out? There is a high degree of seriousness in those questions. If you don't know the answers, can you honestly write well for that audience? No.

For some publications, it is easy to know who reads each edition. For others, it is difficult to tell without research. A specialized publication, such as an industry magazine or a legal newspaper, will have a well-defined audience. But the general circulation daily or weekly newspaper and some consumer magazines must be researched before you know anything certain about the audience.

You want to be careful to write at the level of the audience. If you write too far below it, you will turn off readers. If you write too far above it, you will lose readers as well. In fact, if you miss estimating the audience too much, you won't even get past first base with your editor and will never reach any readers.

Certainly you have to have a sense of timing with readers and audiences, too. The right mood, writing style, and sensitivity make an article work. Make the wrong choices and the article will work against you. Thus, you have to know when to use humor, when to be serious, when to be gentle, and when to be emotional. Knowing your audience will help you chart the course through these dangerous waters.

Some general points about writing mechanics have already been made. You have read about the value of grammar in this chapter already. In reality, not enough can be said to beginning feature writers about spelling, about syntax, and about punctuation. In fact, former *Hartford Courant* editor and publisher Bob Eddy (1979) calls spelling the curse of the working journalist. For writers, each of these skills *is* important. If you cannot handle basic skills such as spelling, you will eventually lose your job. Often writing students dismiss spelling or punctuation as unimportant at the moment because, they say, "It is the idea that matters. I'll learn the rules of spelling later." If a carpenter were to say that about building a house, it would come crashing down. The same goes for your writing. It will cause your plan to fail unless you use the right tools and materials: language, words, spelling, punctuation. Correct use of words can be helped by regular use of a dictionary, a thesaurus, and other word reference books available at most bookstores. Your shelves should be stocked with at least one dictionary, a thesaurus, and a handful of stylebooks— at least one, but several if you work for a number of publications or use different writing styles. Several good reference books were suggested in the previous chapter.

Unity is like an anchor for good writing, Zinsser says. Some might call this concept a matter of consistency in your writing. Whatever you wind up calling it, remember it is a critical element of good writing.

Tense, pronoun point of view, and mood are all indicators of unity in your writing. It is best to maintain a level of consistency in each. Don't mix tenses. Past and present tenses in the same sentence will only confuse your reader. Articles that jump around from first to second to third person are equally disconcerting for readers. Mixture of mood can cause perhaps the most serious

---

FINDING YOUR WAY TO A SATISFACTORY STYLE

William Strunk, Jr. and E. B. White (1979), in their classic *The Elements of Style*, offer "cautionary hints" to help you find a style that works. Consider these items:

1. Place yourself in the background.
2. Write in a way that comes naturally.
3. Work from a suitable design.
4. Write with nouns and verbs.
5. Revise and rewrite.
6. Do not overwrite.
7. Do not overstate.
8. Avoid the use of qualifiers.
9. Do not affect a breezy manner.
10. Use orthodox spelling.
11. Do not explain too much.
12. Do not construct awkward adverbs.
13. Make sure the reader knows who is speaking.
14. Avoid fancy words.
15. Do not use dialect unless your ear is good.
16. Be clear.
17. Do not inject opinion.
18. Use figures of speech sparingly.
19. Do not take shortcuts at the cost of clarity.
20. Avoid foreign languages.
21. Prefer the standard to the offbeat.

---

confusion for a reader who does not know whether to laugh, cry, be sad or happy, or how to otherwise respond to your message.

Tone is also important in feature writing. Writers establish the mood or texture of their features with use of language. This is the tone of the article. Diction, or word choice, contributes to this characteristic of your writing. "When we select one word over another of equal denotative value, we likely make the selection based on the connotative meaning of the word. And by using that connotation, we effectively establish a mood or texture—the *tone*—of the story. In fact, tone is one of the most important elements of writing—and perhaps the most frequently overlooked," writes Roane State (TN) Community College professor David Brill (1992, p. 32).

Each of these points about good writing requires your attention and time. If you learn to manage them, you should find great improvement in your ability to communicate to the world.

GIVING AN IDEA FOCUS AND DEPTH

A large portion of chapter 2 was devoted to finding a good article idea. Although some attention was given to developing the idea and giving it focus and depth, let's return to this in the context of writing. Focus comes throughout the article, but it begins with the lead. A well-chosen lead, or introduction, tells the reader what you mean to achieve in the article. It is up to you to guide the reader through the article, much like a road map, with the theme or idea you have introduced in the beginning paragraphs of your article.

For a writer, focus is the key. If you can remember this, you will do better as a writer. Your articles will be stronger. The focus of the article must carry through the rest of the article after you have constructed the lead. It carries through the body of the article as well. Then it dominates the ending, also.

Think of the focus as the article's "angle" that you read about earlier. To write a feature article only about "appliance repairs" leaves so much to write that a series of books could be produced, but to write about a shop that repairs household appliances is another matter. And to center the attention on the 85-year-old owner who does all the work himself redirects the article still again.

You must be disciplined not to fall to the temptation to drift in your writing. Examine each paragraph as a unit. Is it necessary? Does it help get to the point? Then examine each sentence within each paragraph. Does each sentence help maintain the point of the paragraph? Then, finally, examine each word within each sentence. Are all words needed? Do they help the purpose of the individual sentence?

GETTING AN IDEA DOWN ON PAPER

How do you get the ideas in your mind on paper? Surely, as there are many outlets for your work, there are many approaches to the physical act of writing. Some veteran writers like to labor over a manual typewriter as they have done for years. Others use electric typewriters. And others have entered the computer age with a technological leap to powerful personal computers and multifeatured word processors.

There are writers who will want to work in the early morning because they are morning people. These people rise and jump at the chance to get their creative juices flowing while they are fresh. Others, it seems, cannot get going until finishing several cups of coffee, a newspaper, the mail, and other activities. These afternoon writers seem most comfortable at that time of day. And, as you have guessed, some writers thrive at night. When all is quiet and the day is almost done, these writers are busy at creating and work through much of the night, only to rest in the morning.

There are writers who will use a dictation machine or tape recorder to write, turning over the mundane duties of typing and preparing a manuscript to an assistant. These "idea" writers don't want to be bothered with the clerical duties of typing or setting up a printer. Yet, some writers feel much closer to their work when they can do just that—control the typewriter and other effects of the writer's private work environment. Some still prefer to handwrite their manuscripts and don't deal with any machines at all, not even tape recorders.

You can find writers who want to work in absolute silence to enhance their concentration. Some like to work in a social environment where other people are present, such as an office. The interaction seems to stimulate and inspire rather than interrupt and retard. Still others like to have a stereo playing loudly, or softly, or the television tuned to a program for background noise.

Some writers will produce a manuscript in one long and exhausting effort. Others will produce it in bits and pieces. Some writers will write a manuscript as it is presented, from beginning to end. You will find others who will write the middle first, the end, and then the beginning. Some authors' styles will be to research first, then write. Some professionals will simultaneously research and write. There also are writers who revise as they write, a sentence at a time. You also can find writers who write many pages and then revise. Some people like to write in an office at home. Some lease office space to get away from distractions at home. And others, who have full-time jobs doing something else, like to write in their regular work environment.

Writer's Digest Senior Editor Thomas Clark says a critical step in getting started as a writer is setting up. "One of the most important commitments you can make to your writing is to *set aside an area where you write*," Clark says (1990, p. 24). "What is essential to your mindset is that your office have an air of exclusivity about it . . . . You're telling yourself that writing is important" (p. 26).

Beyond this first step, Clark strongly recommends these other nine tips to establish yourself in the professional writer frame of mind:

- Involve yourself with writing, such as by attending writing classes or conferences.
- Equip yourself with writing tools.
- Read books about writing and other writers.
- Put words on paper.
- Write every day.
- Decide what type of writer you seek to be.
- Think small to build confidence.
- Send out your work after completing it.
- Expect some rejection and analyze the reasons for rejections.

These work styles are as unique as any other personal habits. You have to find what is right for you. Try a variety of combinations to determine what is the most productive and efficient environment for your writing. Then, as Zinsser has said, stick to it. The habit of writing counts. It isn't so important what constitutes the habit, as you see in the next sections.

ORGANIZING ALL THAT INFORMATION

To be organized in your writing means you are more efficient and, likely, more effective and productive. Organizing gives focus by giving each story a

A PEEK AT *WHERE* ONE WRITER WRITES

Each writer needs his or her own "nest" for productive writing. It can be a corner in the bedroom, an office in the basement, or any other secluded location. British free-lance newspaper and magazine writer Wendy Grossman (personal communication, 1993) specializes in computers and paranormal science writing. A member of the Association of British Science Writers and former editor of *Skeptic* magazine, she began free-lance writing in 1990 from her home outside London in Richmond, Surrey. She was asked to describe her individual writing work habits She provided the following:

Other people think I'm disciplined, but I think I'm as disorganized as hell. I have an office in the largest room in my flat, which has a full-sized desk, and a board over a couple of filing cabinets. At the moment it also has three computers and a laser printer. If you're going to review hardware, you need space to put all the boxes in. But really, I can write anywhere, and often do: on planes, in coffee shops, outdoors, in the living room, in bed. For me, a notebook computer is vital—spend 14 hours a day sitting in the same office, and you go mad. I have the office set up with a TV, speakers for the stereo system, and a radio, plus two telephones—I make outgoing calls on the fax line so people can call in on the number I give out. I grew up working in front of the TV, and I find it helps to have some evidence that the outside world is continuing to revolve.

dominant element (Sweeney, 1993). Organizing does not come easy to some people. Some writers are naturally disorganized people, so they have to work harder to get to their writing goals. University of Pittsburgh magazine editor David Fryxell (1990) believes that: "By getting organized—wresting order out of the chaos of your writing process—you will be liberated to be all that you can be as an author. Once you know where a story is going and how you'll get there, it's a lot easier to pay attention to the scenery en route. In other words, by getting organized, you'll write not only faster, but also *better*" (p. 42).

There are several concerns when organizing the information you have collected for your article. Remember that the organizational approaches will vary depending on the style of writing and the medium, but there are several standard ways of organizing yourself before you even start writing. You will find discussions of common newspaper and magazine organizational strategies in the sections that follow.

Different organizational approaches represent the personality of the writer as much as do the space where you work, your typewriter (or computer), and work habits. Probably the most common way to get the mass of information you have collected is to use an *outline* to get started. Writers who use outlines have different styles of outlining as well. Some write formal sentence outlines and others use simple topical outlines. Others will sketch an outline of an article on their computer screen or on paper in their typewriter and begin to fill in the gaps as they sift through the notes of interviews that have been completed. A good procedure for beginners might be the following steps:

1. Think of the main points of the article and make these topics the Roman numerals of your outline. These are also your article's main sections.

2. Next, divide each of the main sections into subsections. What are the major characteristics, or concerns, of each Roman numeral section? There might be just one characteristic or several dozen. *List each* so you will not forget to include these as you begin to write portions of the manuscript. You should letter each of these A, B, and so on.

3. If the article is going to be lengthy, you might want to go beyond the alphabetic listings. If you do extend the outline, these will be details of each subsection and they can be numbered 1, 2, and so forth.

4. On longer articles, or articles with sidebars and boxed inserts such as many magazines use, you should use separate outlines for the sidebars. Often, after writing the main article, you will spot a portion of the main article outline that will lend itself to a "take out" or sidebar.

These steps will help you to write and organize, especially longer manuscripts. Shorter articles (under 1,000 words) common in newspapers might not need this sort of rigorous organizational plan, but even shorter pieces will benefit if you find yourself confused about what you have before the writing stage.

The newest and more complete mid-1990s full-feature word processors offer outlining tools in addition to all of their other features. This does not mean, of course, that your computer will do the outlining for you. However, the word processor software does contain features that permit creation of collapsible outlines based on text that you have entered. This is a way of viewing the words you have written that may help you to create, organize, and move text more easily. "Big three" word processing software such as Microsoft Word, WordPerfect, and AmiPro offer such features and more. But these can be costly for beginners on a budget and you may wish to use a less expensive package with fewer features.

Another one of the conveniences of personal computers and word processors is the ease of moving things around. If you use a computer to write, take advantage of the flexibility and ease of organizing and reorganizing your facts even at the outline stage.

Whereas paper outlines and computers are one approach, there are others. Some experienced writers prefer the standard file cards in 3" x 5" or 5" x 7" sizes. This approach works well for shuffling and reordering the information once it is listed on cards. The approach, again, is pretty straightforward:

1. List each important point on an individual card.
2. Place cards with related information in the same pile as you begin to sort through the deck.
3. Order the piles according to the sequence you want the information to flow in the article.

4. Then sort each individual pile to logically support the general point that the pile of cards represents.

Still another approach is to use a notebook. Divide it into sections and place relevant information about each section into the binder. Then you can move material as necessary, page by page, or section by section, until you get it into a sequence that you want to use to write. Another technique some writers use helps them to get "the big picture" of the organizational plan of their article. This approach requires these steps:

1. Write a very rough draft of as much of your manuscript as you can.
2. Take scissors and cut it up, a paragraph at a time.
3. Tape the pieces or tack them to a wall or bulletin board.
4. Study the pieces on the wall. Move the pieces as needed to improve the flow and direction of your article.

You have other basic decisions to make when contemplating the organizational plan of your article. Consider these as you move into the next sections that discuss the particulars of newspaper and magazine organization and structure. The American Press Institute (Wardlow, 1985) says these are the three basic questions in organizing your information:

1. What type of lead?
2. What manner of telling?
3. Third person, or first?

BASIC STRUCTURE OF FEATURE ARTICLES

Newspaper features employ a variety of leads and organizational plans. You want your article to start well and retain readership for the rest of the article. This part of the chapter discusses approaches to leads, tools to hold the parts together, general organizational techniques used in features, developing and using writing style rules, and point of view.

Developing the Right Lead

Writing authorities Patricia Kubis and Robert Howland (1985) have stated that the lead, or opening paragraph, of a magazine article should achieve three goals:

1. Tell the reader what the article is about.
2. Provide the tone and mood of the article.
3. Catch the reader's attention and entice the reader to go further into the article.

Certainly the lead works with the title of the article and the layout of the first two pages to grab the reader. But the best package of color graphics won't keep a reader unless the author has done a big part in hooking the reader with a strong lead. The lead is crucially important. It can help determine the mood of the article. It should persuade the reader to stay with the article. Here are some of the basic newspaper (as well as magazine and newsletter) leads commonly used for features:

1. *Summary lead.* This lead gives the traditional five w's and h (who, what, when, where, why, and how) in as few words as possible. Some summary leads focus on one or two of these elements of the story and save the others, that are judged less important, for later in the story.

2. *Salient feature lead.* This lead focuses on one major characteristic of the story. Instead of several points in a color story about a festival, the salient feature lead emphasizes one point about food, music, or weather, for example.

3. *Anecdotal lead.* This lead is also called a case approach lead and *Wall Street Journal* feature lead. The reason is simple: Stories with this lead use a specific representative example or story to illustrate a point about a situation that is discussed in general after the lead of the story. Thus, instead of writing about the woes of unemployed oil workers in Texas, this approach would describe one person or family in the lead.

4. *Quotation lead.* Some writers like to open a feature with a quotation. The quotation can be from a person being profiled or an expression of sentiment common at a meeting or concert, but it must catch the gist of the article and be the exact words of a source important to the story.

5. *Delayed-suspended interest lead.* This lead deliberately holds the big news of the story from the reader to tease the reader further into the story. It is a lead that works well when there is some question of the outcome of a situation, such as an article about a lost memento that is found or an article describing the sudden joy of a big contest prize winner.

6. *Question lead.* This sort of lead asks a question of the reader, usually in direct address. The key here, of course, is to be sure to answer the question in the story, preferably in the top half of the story while the question is still in the reader's mind.

There are still other frequently used approaches to leads. Many writers like to use straight narrative or highly descriptive writing. Some like to employ comparison and contrast for effect. Some use startling statements for impact. You will spot some leads that play on words, using puns as attention grabbers. Also, you might find others with use of direct address as a tool to get to readers who might otherwise find their interest drifting off (Cook, 1991; Garrison, 1990).

Leads should entice readers into the article. University of Oregon adjunct professor and free-lance writer Sally-Jo Bowman (1990) puts the work of a good article lead in this interesting manner: "Writing nonfiction articles is like feeding a baby. You warm the little fellow up with a couple of bites of chocolate cake, and when he opens his mushy mouth for more, you cram in some broccoli" (p. 38).

Whatever the lead approach, it should be a stirring paragraph. Pulitzer Prize-winning reporter Edna Buchanan says this about her lead-writing philosophy: "My idea of a successful lead is one that might cause a reader, who is having breakfast with his wife, to spit out his coffee, clutch his chest and say, 'My God, Martha! Did you read this?'" (Knight-Ridder, 1986).

American essayist and novelist Edmund White (1993) wrote a major feature article for *Vogue*, profiling German-Swiss artist Rebecca Horn. He used a little contrast and a lot of description to hook the reader into his article about her new exhibition. Here's how White's article began:

> Everything in the work of Rebecca Horn is intimate, yet nothing is personal. A sculptor who makes fantastic machines, a filmmaker who realizes her wildest dreams, a writer who concocts wry texts to accompany her museum and gallery installations, this German-Swiss artist (with a pure profile worthy of a cameo) never stops telling her secrets—only they're coded, as in dreams. Those secrets are now on display in New York City during a major retrospective at the Guggenheim Museum through September 8; the show fills half the museum.

> Horn's sculpture runs an extraordinarily broad gamut. A blue electric charge sizzles and glows between fourteen pairs of brass rods suspended from the ceiling; paint splatters down on high-heeled shoes fixed on rods to the gallery wall; gray feathers, stuck to a wheel, turn in a circle, spreading open, then suddenly snapping shut, shuddering off balance. Waves gently undulate over the surface of a black pool; piles of black and yellow pigment slowly build up on the floor; liquid drops into open cones; an electric-powered rod revolves like a geometer's compass . . . . (p. 184)

National Geographic senior writer Joel L. Swerdlow (1993) used a direct quotation to open his lead article about New York City's Central Park, evolving into a lead using dialogue and first-person voice like a scriptwriter might use it for a television or film scene:

> "Will you wander through Central Park with me?" I ask a friend. He is a tough guy with whom I have shared many adventures. "No thanks," he says, smiling nervously. "I want to live."

> Despite its reputation as a crime scene, Central Park attracts 15 million visitors each year. To find what draws them in, I enter the 843-acre park at its southeast corner, where fancy hotels and Fifth Avenue shops make Central Park most glamorous. My plan is to meander north to where it borders on rough, poverty-ridden neighborhoods . . . .(p. 6)

In terms of structure, magazine leads are not bound by the same rules of newspaper lead writing in that most newspaper editors prefer short leads that are supported by subsequent paragraphs. Magazine leads are more flexible and are quite long as often as they are short. Their purposes remain the same, however.

Pulling the Various Pieces Together

Another important part of the article is a single sentence or paragraph that gets to the real point of the article. You can create a very strong lead, but few leads truly give focus to a feature article. A lot of writers give different names to that function, but it is a paragraph or sentence that tells readers what is really going on. The article may get off to a great start, but that super lead might not get to the essence of the article. You do that—get to the point of the article—with what is called a *billboard paragraph*, a *nut graf*, or a *summary paragraph*. These statements offer your theme or thesis. This part of the article can be the lead, but it is rare in feature writing. Instead, it usually comes right after the lead is established, or played out. The focus statement is short and to the point."[W]riters lead in with several paragraphs—frequently anecdotal—then pop in the billboard to sum up the main point, the angle of the story," writes John Wilson (1990, p. 31), a free-lance editor with the *Los Angeles Times*. "It's not unusual to follow a billboard with a supporting or amplifying graph, or a quotation for impact and validity."

Miami Herald reporter Pamela Ferdinand (1993) uses a nut graf in the following lead to her story about pain sufferers who legitimately need marijuana for treatment. See how the italicized nut graf works:

> Chris Woiderski, a Tampa psychology student paralyzed from the chest down, used to take 490 prescribed pills a month to stop his muscle spasms and kill pain. He says he lived in a pharmacological stupor.
>
> Irvin Rosenfeld, a Lauderhill stockbroker whose body is riddled with hundreds of bone tumors, underwent eight operations but could not prevent constant pulled muscles and hemorrhages. Heaven would be lying on a rack to stretch his tight muscles, he says.
>
> Bound by their pain, both men sought relief in marijuana and found it. The difference is, one of them is breaking the law.
>
> *Woiderski, and others like him, say they have no choice but to defy a law they deem both irrational and cruel. Using their own lives as examples of marijuana's medical value and pinning fresh hopes on a new political climate, they are part of a movement putting medical marijuana back on the nation's agenda.*
>
> *More people in Florida than anywhere else in the United States use marijuana legally for medical reasons. And more Floridians were approved for and awaiting their legal marijuana supplies when the Bush administration banned new users in 1991.*
>
> "Every time I buy it in the street, I don't know what it's going to be mixed with," says Ronald Shaw, a Cocoa engineer who suffers post-polio muscle spasms.

Shaw was approved for the 14-year-old program, but never received any legal marijuana. "The government is making me a criminal. I don't want to be a criminal."

Times are changing, though, and many illegal medical marijuana users believe they may not be considered criminals for long. They're counting on Surgeon General-designate Joycelyn Elders, whose office at the Arkansas Department of Health has been flooded with pro-marijuana letters.

She supports its medical use, although aides say she may be reluctant to speak out immediately. More pressing are other, less controversial health issues, they say. "Her belief is that if there is some medical benefit to the patient and the doctor feels it's in the best interest of his patient, the doctor should have (marijuana) as a tool," said Carol Roddy, Elder's executive assistant. "It's just not her battle."

Medical marijuana users are also heartened by high-profile backers. The American Medical Student Association, which represents 48,000 pre-med students and residents, endorsed marijuana's medical use at its Miami conference last month. Marijuana relieves symptoms of AIDS, cancer, glaucoma and neurological disorders, the association contends.

Recommendations issued in January by Gov. Lawton Chiles' Red Ribbon Panel on AIDS also encouraged its medical use. People with AIDS—there are more than 26,440 in Florida—say marijuana reduces nausea, a side effect of chemotherapy, and stimulates appetite. In other words, marijuana gives AIDS patients a classic case of the "munchies" (p. 1F).

Transitions are also critical for success in writing, especially in longer pieces. Transitions, as *Mademoiselle* editor Michelle Stacey notes later in this chapter, are often misused and underrated. Transitions link major portions of an article together in an effective way. These can be road maps for longer articles, of course. They tell readers where they have been and where they are going. This might not always be obvious to your readers. Transitions can be a sentence or two, or just a phrase or few words, often containing the common elements of the two parts being linked (Garrison, 1990).

Organizing the Article

Story organizational forms are also broad in scope to give you flexibility in fitting the organizational plan to the story. There will be variations in approaches, often based on length and not whether the article is written for any particular print medium.

There are some differences involving lengthier magazine articles, of course. The body, or middle, of a magazine article is the meat of the sandwich. Once the article gets started with a well-conceived lead, the momentum must continue with the body of the article. Linking together the pieces with transitional sentences and paragraphs, this is where you must bring in the material that you promised your reader in the lead.

Regardless of what organizational plan you use for your topic, your conclusion serves a completely different purpose. This is where you clean up, wrap up, and tie everything together. In magazine feature writing more than most newspaper or newsletter writing, the conclusion plays a vital role. It is a chance to summarize the major points again for the reader and to reveal the delayed or surprise "finish." Conclusions can be several pages or several sentences. Regardless of the length, the conclusion should not leave the reader hanging in midair by what you have chosen to say. Reach some form of resolution. Close it out. But be careful of writing too much, as some beginning writers will do. Remember that you do get a second chance at the conclusion, if you need it, when you rewrite.

These are the main time-tested story structural approaches of features:

1. *Inverted pyramid.* This approach might work for some features, but it is best used in straight news writing. This approach is less appropriate for feature material because it is structured by most important to least important priorities. It usually requires a summary lead.

2. *Chronological order.* This follows sequencing of events. When a feature recounts events or describes a procedure, this approach might be best.

3. *Essay.* A rather standard approach to all writing, this is found in columns, analyses, reviews, and other personal opinion or subjective writing. The essay format is standardized with an introduction, a middle, and a conclusion.

There will be many occasions when a combination of these three plans will work best for your article. Certainly there will be some subjects that will best be handled by one approach or another, but be prepared to mix the best of each of these when the subject calls for it.

Writing with Stylebooks

Although leads and organizational plans are at the top of the list for beginners to learn about feature writing, there are other concerns. First, remember that most news organizations maintain their own stylebooks, and usages in writing will vary from newspaper to newspaper. Certainly the differences will be distinct when compared to magazine usages. Two of the most popular stylebooks are those published by the Associated Press and United Press International. Whatever book is used by the newspaper, magazine, or newsletter you write for, get a copy of it and use it as you write. You will notice the professional touch it gives your work.

Using the Right Point of View

Another consideration is point of view in your writing. Feature stories for newspapers are most often written in third person, but in some situations, such as personal experience articles, columns, and travel articles, the writing is often in first person. Remember that when you choose to write in first person, you become a significant part of the story. Do you want to be the focus of the article? If so, chose the first person "I." If not, write in third person or even second person.

A LOOK AT A PULITZER PRIZE-WINNING ARTICLE

Miami Herald columnist and feature writer Liz Balmaseda won the 1993 Pulitzer Prize for commentary for her columns and feature articles for the newspaper's local section each Wednesday and Saturday. Her articles show a variety of approaches focused on people. Her features, written as fixed-length columns, always seem filled with lots of direct quotations from the people about whom she writes. Balmaseda wrote human interest feature articles for *The Herald* from 1987 to 1991 after 6 years of news reporting and production for *The Herald* city desk, *Newsweek*, and NBC network news. She began her award-winning column in late 1991.

Balmaseda (personal communication, 1993) said one of her 10 articles in her Pulitzer-winning package almost did not get written. She was in Haiti on assignment and went with her photgrapher to a particularly poor part of the island near Port-au-Prince. She explained what led to the story:

I went to this village while the photographer took some photos and did not plan to write anything. We went behind this old slaughterhouse and saw a strip of little houses. We went to one to meet a family there. I saw that it was a wonderful look at daily life in a poor, poor place. When we went into the house, I did not plan to write anything, but suddenly, on this hot day, it started raining very hard. We were trapped because my photographer could not take his equipment outside. So, I sat there and thought to myself, "this is a blessing." I had been staying in a nice hotel on another part of the island and was suddenly dropped into a life and culture I'd never come into contact with before. It was the real Haitian life and its rhythms.

The man's wife came home soaking wet. The kids from the village were dancing in the rain, but the man protected his kids by keeping them inside. The dynamic of the scene was really incredible. In that moment, I learned what kept life going on that island. In the rain, I saw hope. There was hope in the kids dancing, in the kids catching rain drops with their tongues, in the refreshment they felt from the rain on such a hot and humid day. In it, they saw hope.

I went back to the hotel and thought, "I can't write this. There's no news peg. No press conference. No quotes. No real news." But I thought, what the heck? What's the worst they [her editors back in Miami] can do? So I wrote the story. Of all the stories I did, they [her editors] liked this story best and put it on the front page. They loved it. And that was one of the stories that won the Pulitzer. Something inside me said to take the risk and write that story. I did it. If you have the instinctive reaction—if something moves you—then do it. Follow that feeling.

Her story of the man and his family demonstrates a sensitive first-person approach to writing about the political and economic oppression, as well as the indomitable spirit, of the people of Haiti. "It is my favorite of all of them," Balmaseda (personal communication, 1993) says. This is her story of one family in Haiti:

PORT-AU-PRINCE, Haiti—Those are the neighbor's children dancing in the rain, thrusting their faces skyward, trying to catch the raindrops in their mouths, singing a song that gets lost in the deluge.

Those are not the children of Morales Leger. His children are inside, dry, pleased nevertheless to witness the downpour on such a suffocating day.

From his house across the alley, he and I watch the neighbor's girls in their euphoric convulsions, drenched, entranced.

Morales, a man of 64, has put out large tin pots to catch the clean rainwater, a blessing on this humid Feast of the Ascension.

He pulls his young son close to him, kissing his cheek, explaining that "he easily gets the flu."

The sudden storm caught me as we talked in his home. Entirely by chance, I found myself dropped in the middle of daily life in a squalid shanty strip where a desperate existence churns on endlessly, even on feast days.

The rain hammered on the tin roof, veiling doorways and windows in misty curtains. A shower of relief.

To arrive at his house, I crossed the ancient slaughterhouse, walked along the muck-filled canal where pigs slept. The stench of human and animal and vegetable waste clung to my face like a mask. I took quick, shallow breaths through my mouth.

A young woman bathed in the pig water, scrubbing her arms with a pink bar of soap, as if the rosy suds could extinguish the film of God-knows-what-is-dumped-in-there.

I had passed more than a dozen wooden doorways framing swollen, naked children. Inside, their mothers and sisters and maybe cousins lounged in a darker dimension. Because this was a holiday, no one was working. Normally, this place is alive from 4:30 a.m. with wailing animals and haggling merchants who later sell the fresh, warm meat at the market.

Then, I slipped into the home of Morales Leger.

Within dim, green walls there are two beds over which gauze mosquito nets dangle. There is a pink, child-size potty chair where his youngest girl, Philocles, 2, fidgets, naked.

We talk about his life. He has not worked steadily in years. He was a sergeant in the military for 26 years, though he says he is not a political man. He left the service 17 years ago and has worked odd jobs since.

He married a woman much younger, Margareth Coustan, 29. He delivered their four children in his home, on their matrimonial bed. He writes their names in my notebook in a spidery hand: Gina, 8, Philomene, 5, Philippe, 3, Philocles, 2.

He lifts the youngest from her chamber pot, slides a piece of cardboard over its seat, and kisses the girl gently.

"My consolation," he whispers, kissing her again.

Then it begins to rain.

I ask him about Haiti, about politics and refugee boats, and the *regime du jour*. But he shakes his head.

"It is a divine presence that guides us. That is all," he says, offering me a seat in his home.

The rain is powerful and relentless. In a while, his wife arrives, soaked and shivering. She sets down a flat basket of bruised chayotes and mangoes on the kitchen floor.

From what I can understand, she brings back what the market ladies don't sell.

A 25-year-old neighbor named Jonny explains that friends sometimes help her buy food.

"She has many mouths to feed," he says. "She has plenty babies."

And another is on the way. Margareth is five months pregnant.

Why so many babies? I ask.

Morales answers for her.

"They are my security," he says, clutching his chest. "They are my future."

The gray canal outside his window has become a swift river rushing away from the shanty strip, rushing toward the bay, washing the putrid smells, washing the mud off the pigs, cleansing the woman who bathes in the pig water.

After the rain, everything along the alley glistens, and in the distance a rainbow has appeared.

A couple of days later, I watch a storm approach from my hotel balcony high above the capital. The city seems to dissolve gradually into silver sheets of water that sweep inland from the bay, across the slums and markets.

I think of the slaughterhouse and the resilient souls who dwell on its fringe. Probably, they're happily getting wet.

I know I learned something that afternoon at the house of Morales Leger. I learned that neither poverty nor politics can break the Haitian spirit.

I learned that sometimes it can rain on the most putrid of days.

I learned that in this place where hope is too often elusive, the children of Morales Leger, his hope and consolation, are truly his wealth (Balmaseda, 1992, p. 1A). Reprinted with the permission of *The Miami Herald.*

USING DIRECT QUOTATIONS

Good feature articles come alive with liberal use of direct quotations from a variety of people and, occasionally, even documents. People make features work and their words, through your use of direct quotations, give *life* to your story. There are some rules about quotations in magazine and newspaper features that you should remember. First of all, in much of your article writing, you will find that quotations help to back up generalizations made about a person, place, or thing. Quotations give the article an element of reality beyond the perspective of the writer. For features, it means you can let someone else speak in the article, using their *exact* words.

Liz Balmaseda, Pulitzer Prize-winning feature writer at *The Miami Herald,* says she depends a great deal on direct quotations for her articles and columns about people. Balmaseda (personal communication, 1993) says:

> I don't always have a lot to say about a subject. I ask a question and let people say it for me. Sometimes people say it better. Many times, people who never get into the paper say things very beautifully and I feel compelled to use what they say. Quotes give you something to hang the story on. But you also have to recognize that some people don't have something to say and you have to be selective.

Paraphrasing can work as effectively as direct quotations. Sometimes, paraphrases work better. There will be occasions when you can state something more efficiently and more meaningfully. This avoids the sense of overquoting and overstating. Full-time free-lance writer Hank Nuwer (1992), author of a book on pledging and hazing, believes paraphrases are the desired alternative to bad and inappropriate quotations, also.

Writer's Digest columnist Art Spikol (1993) feels direct quotations can add much to nonfiction, if they are used effectively. "Quotation marks have a power far beyond the space they occupy in print," he argues. "Use a quotation mark, and the reader infers: *Here's something somebody actually said. Here's a living, breathing individual about to speak to me. Here's something the writer thought was important enough to set off with those funny little apostrophes*" (p. 55).

In addition to quoting one individual at a time, many experienced feature writers use quotations to re-create dialogue to provide the reader with the effect of being there—getting to watch history occur, for example, through the words of the persons who were present. It seems to make the passage move more quickly, too. Here are some helpful guidelines in using quotations in your writing:

1. *Make certain it is clear in the flow of your article just who is speaking.* This is especially true if you change the person being quoted.

2. *Vary your verbs of attribution.* At times, you should rely on the standard verb *said*, but there are other more precise verbs. Most feature writing uses the past tense verb, *said*, instead of the present tense verb, *says*. Remember that verbs and verb tenses have specific meaning when used, so take care in selecting just the right word.

3. *Vary placement of attribution verbs.* It will be necessary to place them at the beginning of a sentence on some occasions; avoid using the verbs only at the end of sentences. Thus, use past tense as your standard tense for attribution.

4. *Be careful in using long quotations.* If you must use a lengthy quote from a person or text from a document, make certain you have introduced it to the reader to explain what you are doing and why.

5. *Dialogue quotations add a great deal.* Use them, but be clear who is saying what. And break up long passages of dialogue, if they are necessary, with some description of action by the speakers.

6. *Quote exact words and* do not *change the words in the quotation.* Even incorrect grammar will give the reader insight into the personality of the individual speaking.

You must also be very careful to be *accurate* with direct quotations. Quotations cannot be made up. Most professional journalists do not subscribe to the approach that modifying direct quotations is acceptable. This debate continues, because some journalists and writers feel it is not troubling to "clean up" direct quotations to make them more understandable without changing the sense or meaning, whereas others believe writers should not "play with" reality.

There are some legal limits, too. A writer for *The New Yorker* magazine had a suit filed in federal court against her because a doctor believed he had been libeled by misused and even fabricated quotations in the article based on personal interviews by the writer. Although the case was dismissed on two occasions, it was returned to court a third time and the writer was found by a jury to have been wrong in her use of quotations. But when the jury could not decide a judgment award for the plantiff—the foreman said it was hopelessly deadlocked on that issue—the judge eventually declared a mistrial. Regardless of the judgment, these matters of honesty and accuracy are serious for feature writers. The safest way to avoid such legal problems is to be accurate and correct and not to fabricate or alter what was said in any deliberate manner (Salant, 1993).

REWRITING, REWRITING, AND MORE REWRITING

Some writing experts call *rewriting* an art form. Writers Patricia Kubis and Robert Howland (1985) have said, "If you are a real writer, you *know* that *rewriting is the name of the game"* (p. 205). Unless you are a particularly gifted writer, you will seldom find that a first draft is sufficient for publication. Most writers will find that to finish a manuscript is an achievement of note, but the real work comes in revision.

The best policy is to finish the first draft, then let it sit a while—overnight or longer, if possible. Then read it from top to bottom with a fresh mind and clear head. You can be more critical and make some true improvements in the work. Each time you do this, the manuscript will get better as words are changed or cut, sentences are revised, and passages reorganized.

Your goal is to revise until what you have to say flows smoothly. Revise the work until it seems to glide as you read it. Although beginning writers might need more rewrites, you will find that as you become more experienced, you will write, revise, and polish to finish an article in three distinct stages.

Rewriting will help you make your thoughts clearer and, at the same time, more efficient. You can use this stage to add information, or delete it, or clarify it. Rewriting is a necessary step. Even after that initial surge of creativity in writing the first draft, you will see rewriting makes a significant difference in the quality of your work. Thus you must make the time to rewrite. It is really a part of the writing process. Build it into the article production cycle you use. And remember one key question: If what you have written is not clear to you, how can it be clear to someone else? Rewriting is the answer.

BORROWING FROM FICTION WRITERS

Some of the best nonfiction writers in the United States also write in a fiction style or use the tools of short story writers and novelists. They may not always realize it, but they use the same techniques. Use of dialogue, discussed earlier in this chapter, is but one frequently found example.

Countless successful American novelists began as nonfiction writers, of course: Mark Twain, Walt Whitman, Ernest Hemingway, Tom Wolfe, and Gay Talese. Numerous modern journalists have crossed into fiction and crossed back. There is as much in common as there isn't with the two approaches. Four elements in particular—levels of abstraction, storytelling, use of tension, and development of characters—work effectively in many forms of feature writing.

Abstraction

Summaries, separate from the specific, seem to be the opposite of what most feature writers use in their writing. Feature writers seldom delve into the theoretical world, right? Without getting overly philosophical, they do. Because an abstract is the essence of something, such as a series of events or a single event, writers often write in the abstract. You do. There are often times when you are general, others when you are specific. *The Oregonian* writing coach Jack Hart (1991e) makes this proper observation: "The best literary writers recognize the importance of varying abstraction levels, depending on the purposes they have in mind. But lots of journalists pay little attention to the degree of abstraction in their writing. Out of habit, they stay at the same middling abstraction levels all the time. That cruise-control approach robs their writing of both meaning and impact" (p. 1). Hart likes to use a ladder metaphor in referring to levels of abstraction in writing. Think of the bottom of the ladder as the most concrete, or single item, and the top of the ladder as the most general, or everything. And in between, you find varying degrees gradually going from the specific to general as you refer to the item in your article.

Storytelling

Humans have always been storytellers. And when typesetting came along, the stories began to be preserved. Journalism, in its most primitive form, began to evolve. Feature writers are storytellers. There are both long and short stories to tell. We tend to tell the short ones. However, think of telling stories as something more than just anything you might write. Stories in the strictest form involve more than what most news and feature writers offer. Some experts say that journalists simply tell the *end* of a good story. Because storytelling involves an entire plot, a good feature writer using storytelling techniques will include the beginning, middle, and then the ending. And the story is often told in this manner, also. Storytelling, in the most traditional manner, is done firsthand. It uses common literary devices such as shifting points of view, irony, dialogue, and surprise endings. In the 1990s, it may seem to be a lost art. It was common earlier in this century and remains popular with some magazine and nonfiction book writers (DeSilva, 1990; Hart, 1991d).

Tension

Another tool used by successful feature writers who borrow from fiction writers is tension, the stretching and straining of human emotions to their limits. Pulitzer Prize-winning feature writer Madeleine Blais (1984) says she likes to build her feature articles around tension involving the central sources, or the characters, in her articles. Without it, she says, her articles would not be worth writing. "Tension offers an element of surprise. It allows the reader to imagine many possible endings to the course of the piece. If there isn't some kind of tension, there's no story." One effective method for creating high levels of tension is foreshadowing, or hinting at things to come through some description in the article. This works since it hooks readers into finding out what will happen later in the narrative (Hart, 1992).

Characters

In the preceding paragraph, *sources* were also described as characters. It is often helpful for feature writers to think of their sources as characters in the

A PEEK AT *HOW* ONE WRITER WRITES

Veteran free-lance writer Bill Steele (personal communication, 1993) has written and edited for newspapers and magazines. He has worked with both large and small publications. His own writing habits are well established and he shares them:

I usually begin at the beginning, (i.e., by writing my lead). That's the newspaper background showing. However clever or cutesy it may be (I try to avoid cutesy but some publications want it), it has to tell the reader what the article is about; if you don't know that yet you need to do more research, or at least more thinking.

The lead pretty much determines what I have to talk about first, and that helps set up the structure of the article—what some people would call the outline. I seldom do an outline *per se*, although I may scribble a few sentences that show what comes first, what comes second, and so on. Often the sentences are transitions that show how I'm going to get from one area to the next. I think of the structure from the point of view of a teacher: What does the reader need to know before I introduce this piece of information?

Sometimes I get stuck and have no idea what comes next. In that case, I may pick up some other part of the article and write that—say, some biographical information on the person I interviewed. Thanks to the computer, I can have that floating around until I figure out where it goes, then just paste it in. Sometimes when I'm stuck I just go out for a walk; I'll start out thinking about other things, but after about a mile, the article ideas will come back in and I'll see a way to solve the problem. Then again, often the answers will come to me when I'm in bed trying to go to sleep, which is a nuisance because I have to get up again and write it all down.

I do see writing as a problem-solving process, a sort of engineering job if you will: How do I put this structure together with the materials I've got?

These days I write perforce in front of the computer. That's not much of a change, since I used to write in front of the typewriter. I was never much for writing in longhand; I can go faster on a keyboard, and the only way to keep up with my thoughts in longhand is to write illegibly. The workspace now is sort of L-shaped, with the computer screen in front of me and the disk drives and printer off to the right. I have a swing-arm lamp that illuminates the space on the desk to the right of the keyboard and the keyboard itself without throwing much light on the screenscreen. Notes and stuff I have to look at go on the desk under the lamp—and eventually get piled up to where I spend a lot of time leafing through for the thing I need. The dictionary, thesaurus, White, and a few other basic references sit on the desk just behind that space, and works in progress get stuffed into stacked trays to the left.

I get some of my work done in my head while walking or lying in bed. The majority of the work, really, gets done inside my head; the computer is just the place I put it after it's done. I remember a panel of the comic strip "Shoe" in which someone says, "Why are you staring out the window when you should be working? Start pounding the keyboard." To which Shoe replied, "*Typists* pound keyboards. *Writers* stare out windows."

overall story they are telling. Naturally, in nonfiction feature writing, the realities of the situation limit what the characters do and do not do. Feature writers develop sources/characters in their articles through description and use of direct quotations. There is little else. Although all sources cannot be developed into characters, it helps in some articles. Sources are distinct. If feature writers could use some of the descriptive techniques that novelists use in describing their characters, readers would benefit from deeper knowledge of the people in the stories. We should take opportunities, when they come along, to describe people through their words and our observations of their behavior, of course, but we also should describe them in terms of their appearance, their possessions, their values, their beliefs, and even how they move, express themselves with their hands, and how they talk (Hart, 1991a, 1991b).

WRITING ABOUT COMPLEX SUBJECTS

Writers who diversify their topics will find they occasionally will write about complicated and difficult subjects. Even those who write about one particular subject will find this challenge to their writing from time to time. You have to explain relationships, make comparisons, evaluate importance, or differentiate among a dozen elements in an article. If you can write in a clear manner about complicated matters, your reader wins. The American Press Institute's Associate Director, Elwood Wardlow (1985), proposes three ways to explain a difficult subject and to develop a sense of comparatives and relationships. Here they are:

1. *Knowledge and awareness.* You have to be a generalist in many ways, learning as much as you can about a wide range of subjects.

2. *Practice.* The more you repeat something, the better you get at it. Try some exercises to develop your ability to describe people, places, or things. Take notes while watching events such as public hearings or meetings on television. If you can synthesize and reduce the information to an understandable form without holes, you are on your way to success.

3. *Relating the unknown to the known.* If your reader has never been to a faraway place, can you describe it in terms of local nature? As Wardlow says, this is particularly true in science and technical writing. Although Wardlow notes this type of writing is common in the news magazines, it is not limited to those publications. All good writers, he says, should strive to do whatever is necessary to make this talent a strong point in their writing.

COMPUTERS, WORD PROCESSORS, AND PRINTERS

Most writers who use electronic systems to write prefer personal computers. Some personal computers are, however, dedicated to only one task and have permanent software for word processing. The machines can do only this task.

You must find what is best for you. If you feel you might use your computer for purposes other than writing (such as data processing or communications with other computers by telephone line), then you probably should invest in a personal computer and purchase software for particular tasks as they are needed. On the other hand, if you feel you want to keep things simple, then a dedicated system for word processing might be best for you.

The text of this book was written at times on an IBM-compatible desktop PC and at other times on an IBM-compatible notebook PC, both with Microsoft Word for Windows Version 2.0, a word processing program. It is one of dozens of full-feature word processing software packages on the market. Most writers have specific needs for word processing (e.g., their writing) and you should make certain your software can handle your writing demands.

When looking at word processors, you will find the price often indicates the number of available features. For example, the more expensive programs (about $200, but up to $500) will often offer features not found in less expensive programs. You should search for software that offers all basic word processing functions. *PC Sources* magazine writer C. David Stone (1993) listed the most important considerations of modern word processing software:

1. Ease of installation or setup on your computer.
2. Ease of use.
3. Data exchange with other applications such as spreadsheets, databases, or desktop publishing.
4. Text formatting features.
5. Editing features.
6. Customizing options.
7. Management of document files.
8. Supporting features.
9. Quick-access help available on screen.
10. Quality of printed documentation.

Another feature of some computers, mentioned in the previous chapter, is the ability to communicate with other computers or to be compatible with other computers. In the end, you must make these choices about your own writing hardware (and software) needs. They must fit what you do most. The decisions are not unlike those involved in buying a car. Some authors require only the basic pencil and paper or manual typewriter. Other writers must not only have a PC, but the fastest PC with all of the assorted peripherals. Sounds like hunting for a car, doesn't it?

READABILITY OF WRITING

Regardless of what you use to write your manuscript, good writing must be readable, just as it must be understandable. *Readability* is simply a term that describes how easy something is to read. Writing experts have been studying readability for about 50 years and have devised various rules and formulas for readability. As American Press Institute's Wardlow (1985, p. 15) has observed, these tools for measuring readership have different ways of getting to the same points about readable articles:

1. Short is better than long.
2. Simple forms are best.
3. Personal is better than impersonal.

Well-known readability formulas include those created by Rudolph Flesch (1946, 1949) in the 1940s and Robert Gunning (1968) in the 1960s. Flesch found that there is an ideal number of words per sentence (17 to 19), an ideal number of syllables (150 per 100 words), an ideal percentage of personal interest words (such as pronouns: 6 per 100 words), and an ideal percentage of sentences that have human interest (such as direct address, questions, quotations: 12%). However, *The Oregonian* writing coach Jack Hart (1990e) cautions: "[W]e all need to understand that while readable writing may be simple, it isn't necessarily simplistic" (p. 1).

The late 1980s brought personal computing into writing education. As a result, there are now numerous programs available in secondary and higher education that address writing and readability. Students of writing, as well as writing teachers, now can use computer programs to calculate these readability assessments on the spot. Some grammar and writing "checkers" are now a part of more sophisticated word processing packages, going well beyond the usual spelling and thesaurus features. Other forms of analysis of writing are also possible, through computers, to determine mechanical and structural writing errors that would reduce readability. Many of these programs are available at low cost through software clearinghouses or local personal computer stores.

POLISHING AND EDITING MANUSCRIPTS

You can also think of rewriting as a self-editing process, but you will learn that the process is somewhat different. Rewriting means writing it over and over until it is right. Self-editing is making changes on the existing manuscript without rewriting major portions. The focus here is on *self-editing*.

There are two ways of looking at manuscript editing. First, you must consider what has to be done on your own part to improve your manuscript. This is an important stage and it is the most significant portion of this discussion. The other, the handling that another person will give your manuscript, also remains vital to the writing process, yet it is out of your control for the most part.

But what can you do to improve your article? What is within your control? One editor has an answer. Phil Currie (Wardlow, 1985, p. 45), a Gannett Company news executive, offers this checklist of the most significant problem areas to look for:

1. Dull, wooden phrasing.
2. Poor grammar, spelling, and punctuation.
3. Story organization.
4. Errors of fact or interpretation.
5. Holes in stories, completeness.
6. Clutter.
7. Redundancy.

There are other concerns in tuning a manuscript. You must, as noted before, match a publication's stylebook. You must answer the unanswered questions. You have to check for attribution strengths and weaknesses. Finally, as any copy desk chief will tell you, tightening is always a concern about a manuscript: Watch for wordiness.

PROFESSIONAL'S POINT OF VIEW

Michelle Stacey
Mademoiselle

First drafts are for putting it all on paper, for getting over the staring-at-a-blank-page stage, for thinking up a wonderful lead that you'll probably hate in the morning. They are not for publication. There's always that dangerous, heady moment when you've finally finished a draft of the piece, when the whole thing sits there in a neat (or not-so-neat) package. You're in the throes of first love. "This is so great," you think. "I may not even need to revise this!"

Don't you believe it.

That's the moment to dive back in, pencil in hand, and revise, rewrite, reorganize, rethink. But once you've gone through another draft or two and you really know it's close this time—how do you make it into a piece your editor will love, too?

When it comes to final polishing of a story, I like to think in terms of *danger points*. There are three danger points in every piece you write, and there are points every editor looks at and usually ends up having to revise. Save your editor the trouble on these and your stock will rise immediately.

1. *The lead.* Yes, you have already tinkered with this. You may have gone through two or three different ones. But there's a trick I've had to do as an editor so many times that it's become a basic rule: Look at the second or third

paragraph. Chances are your real lead is right there. I can't count the number of times I've had to chop off the first one or two paragraphs of a story—paragraphs that, when you were writing them, made you feel comfortable, buttressed, and safe, but that turn out to be completely unnecessary. Beat your editor to the chopping block.

2. *Transitions.* The most misused and underrated parts of a story, these turning points can be the weak links in the strongest of chains. There is a popular misconception that transitions consist of latching on to a stray word or concept in the last sentence of a section and using that poor stray as a rope to swing, Tarzan-like, to an entirely new section. "Speaking of cows," you write, "Mrs. O'Leary . . . ." This is the sort of lazy writing that has made many a weary editor write "weak trans." in the margin of a piece. Good transitions always have some connection to the main thrust of a piece; they are your opportunity to ask yourself: "Why am I writing this next section? How does this fit in with my overall thesis?" Once you've answered those questions, you can convey the answers to the reader. Transitions remind the reader of where you've been and where you're going; they shouldn't exist in a void. Don't be afraid that you're explaining too much. "Another aspect of municipal disasters that historians tend to ignore is the element of plain bad luck," you write. "Take, for instance, the case of Mrs. O'Leary's cow . . . ."

3. *Favorite parts.* Those luscious turns of phrase that make your heart beat a little faster every time you read them, those especially creative sentences where you've really found a new way to say something . . . be suspicious of these. They're probably the worst writing in your story. I know it seems unlikely—and painful—but trust me on this one. Those lovely phrases are more likely to be overwritten, hard to understand, high-falutin', and low in content. The best writing does not go out of its way to be cute or beautiful; it is good because it is clear, informative, and says what needs to be said in the most succinct and effective manner. That is elegant writing—it doesn't draw attention to itself. Go back to every favorite part you have and don't give it any breaks: Is it doing its job in the piece, or is it just serving your ego? Be ruthless.

Now you've got a piece to warm an editor's heart. Is that the last work you'll ever have to do on that story? Don't bet on it—at least if you're writing for a magazine. The nature of magazine writing, with its finely tuned attention to voice and a very specific audience, almost always requires that an author make further revisions. But if you can make your editor say, "This piece is close, really close!" when she reads your story, you've made her day. Trust me on this one (Stacey, personal communication, 1988).

Michelle Stacey is the managing editor of *Mademoiselle* magazine.

II

The Basics

5

Descriptive and Color Writing

Like hundreds of other news organizations, *The Miami Herald* dispatched a reporter to Los Angeles in the spring of 1993. There was great concern across America about what was happening during the federal civil rights violations trial of police officers involved in the videotaped roadside beating of motorist Rodney King. Many people feared the worst—a repeat of the disturbances of a year earlier. There was tension in the air as the trial was about to go to the jury for a verdict. *The Herald* sent senior writer and roving national correspondent Martin Merzer, a veteran of many of the nation's major stories over the past several decades, to the city a little less than 2 weeks before the verdict was announced. Other reporters followed. Merzer's assignment was to set the scene and establish his newspaper's coverage. "It was my job to set the framework for our coverage over the next 2 weeks," Merzer (personal communication, 1993) recalls. "This was my first story of many I wrote there. I was trying to give a feel for the community. I combined my reporting with some facts I got off the wires. Later in the week, when I had had some time, I went into the community to interview residents and did a lot more face-to-face. I listened to voices and let them talk about how they felt." The coverage in Los Angeles was an example of what Merzer labels as *parachute work*, in which reporters are quickly sent to cover a breaking story. For the Thursday morning front-page story for his newspaper, he tried to describe the mood of Southern California about 10 days before the verdict would be rendered. This is Merzer's first story filed from Los Angeles:

> LOS ANGELES—Helicopters will pluck jurors from the courthouse rooftop. Virtually every police officer will be on duty, most in riot gear. The National Guard is armed and ready; the populace is armed and tense.
>
> Long lines form at gun stores. Rumor hot lines ring incessantly. A city still wounded by last year's firestorm of madness cowers in fear and uncertainty.
>
> After six weeks of testimony, final arguments begin today in the potentially explosive second chapter of the Rodney King beating trial. The federal civil rights case against four white officers accused of beating the black motorist could go to the jury Friday.

U.S. District Judge John Davies, who is overseeing the trial, said Wednesday he feared the jury might be unable to reach a verdict, a result that could be as inflammatory as another acquittal.

No one can guess the outcome of the case or predict the nature and scope of the reaction, though most people expect trouble. Authorities—criticized for their slow response last year—are mapping extensive battle plans.

"We want people to be able to come out, turn, blink and see an L.A.P.D. officer," said Los Angeles Police Chief Willie Williams, who has replaced the controversial Daryl Gates.

In addition to service revolvers and nightsticks, officers will be armed with tear-gas sprays and rubber bullets, part of $1 million in riot gear recently purchased by the city.

Patrols will be beefed up as soon as the jury gets the case, and 6,500 of the city's 7,900 officers will be on the streets when the verdict is announced, Williams said.

The National Guard has moved armored personnel carriers into area armories and has 1,500 troops on standby, this time with ammunition and equipment at the ready. All major law enforcement agencies are conducting high-profile riot training maneuvers. Attorney General Janet Reno is monitoring events.

"We will not be sitting in command posts waiting for something to happen," said Williams, who is black. "Our plans include saturation of the entire city of Los Angeles with additional officers."

Some fear that a swift, formidable show of force will incite the very violence it is intended to discourage. But others welcome the hard line taken by police.

"They can't abandon the streets," said Lamar Jackson, a television and movie producer who lives near Los Angeles and returned to his jittery hometown Wednesday after a brief visit to South Florida. "That's the mistake they made the last time. They have to show they mean business."

Jackson was traveling against the current. Southern California travel agents report a surge of last-minute reservations. Destination: any place out of town.

Authorities, hoping for the best, insist much has changed since last year, when the officers accused of pounding King 56 times in 81 seconds were cleared of most charges despite the amateur videotape seen around the world.

Those acquittals fueled a three-day orgy of violence that left 53 people dead, 2,383 injured and $1 billion in property damage. The nation's worst riot in a century triggered unrest in other American cities, many of them now watching this second phase with rising unease.

Said Williams: "I get calls every day from agencies around this country that say, 'We'd like to know when the verdict is about to come in.'"

The first jury was nearly all white, and the trial was conducted in suburban Simi Valley. This time, the jury that includes two blacks and one Hispanic will be deliberating in downtown Los Angeles.

Unlike last time, King testified during this trial and courtroom observers rated him an effective witness.

But the passions reawakened by this second trial, the still-fresh memories of Los Angeles ablaze, the sheer uncertainty all combine to generate apocalyptic visions of disorder.

One poll found that nearly seven of 10 residents believe an acquittal will fuel new riots. Many also fear that a conviction will trigger celebrations that will turn violent.

Unsubstantiated rumors waft through the region: Police privately expect 10,500 deaths. Large stockpiles of weapons, many stolen during last year's riot, are in the hands of troublemakers. Gangs from the inner city and from out of state are targeting suburban communities.

One of the area's three rumor control hotlines logged 450 calls Monday, its first day of existence.

Police cannot confirm any of the rumors, but they sense that trouble is brewing and they are unsettled by the pace of weapons sales.

Nearly 114,000 guns were purchased in Los Angeles County last year alone, and gun store managers said sales have doubled since the trial reached its final stages last week. Customers have waited in line as long as 2½ hours, despite extended store hours.

Many of those weapons are in the hands of suburban homeowners and inner-city merchants, including Asian-Americans whose stores sustained nearly half the total property damage last year.

In an environment that could hardly be more combustible, the judge is expected to hold any verdict for no more than three hours so authorities can position their forces. The defendants face 10 years and $250,000 in fines if convicted.

And despite all the plans, police stop short of promising they will be able to short-circuit trouble everywhere, but they promised to do their best.

"I know it's very difficult for the chief of police to say to a community that has already experienced what we experienced last April to take it easy," Williams said. "But we're here. We're not going to fail you this time." (Merzer, 1993a, p. 1A) Reprinted with permission of *The Miami Herald*.

Merzer, an award-winning reporter, was experienced in working in such tension-filled environments. After all, he had lived in Israel and covered the Middle East for *The Herald* during 1983–1985. The New York native and Hunter College graduate had worked for the Associated Press in New York and Miami. After Merzer had been in Los Angeles for several days and had time to get a feel for the communities involved, he prepared a longer Sunday feature. He interviewed residents: blacks, whites, Asians, Hispanics, all living in the area near or in South Central L.A., where the worst problems occurred a year earlier. The story, a series of mood-revealing miniprofiles, was published on the front page also. This goes into more depth about how all the tension was affecting the behavior and the emotions of the residents of Southern California who were forced to conduct their daily lives during that tense spring week:

LOS ANGELES—They speak of fear and resentment and widening polarization, of broken dreams and shattered faith in humanity, of something pulverized near the heart of what America should be.

The white suburban accountant in tasseled leather shoes buying a Chinese assault rifle: "The bottom line is, man, I'm scared." The black woman from South Central Los Angeles: "So now they're resorting to the same thing they say we've become—violent."

The Korean merchant regretting her resettlement in America: "I still have a hurting." The black lawyer striving to serve peace on Easter Sunday: "Let's talk about cooling the 'hood."

The voices of Los Angeles.

A jury began deliberations Saturday night in the civil rights trial of four white police officers accused of beating black motorist Rodney King. Apprehension gripped the city, and police flooded the streets with officers.

Religious and civic leaders pleaded for calm and tolerance, for faith and empathy. No place needs that more than Los Angeles this weekend.

Here are some voices from the City of Angels, a city on the edge:

Nick Galuzevski, 39, stood in line for a half-hour last week just to enter B&B Gun Sales in North Hollywood.

Thirty-two people gathered outside, waiting for the fortress-like store to open. They were men, women, white, Hispanic, Asian, a few blacks. They drove up in Toyota compacts, Ford pickups and Lexus sedans.

A sign said: "Open Easter Sun 11-5." The owner called that a public service and in some ways it was.

Los Angeles-area residents are shopping for shotguns and pistols this weekend like South Floridians shopped for plywood and bottled water last Aug. 23. Grimly, with trepidation.

California requires a 15-day waiting period before newly purchased weapons can be picked up. Nevertheless, stores are jammed. Some customers are first-time buyers, gambling that a verdict will be delayed; others pick up weapons ordered two weeks ago; others grab boxes of ammunition.

Galuzevski, an accountant, has an 11-year-old daughter, Natalya. He was picking up a Mak-90 Chinese semi-automatic rifle and 300 rounds of ammunition:

"It's like a giant feeding frenzy. If you don't buy it, someone else will buy it in five minutes. It's a real mania now. We're all caught up in the riot thing and the crime thing.

"It's like a civil war. To have such widespread lawlessness, like what I read about happening in Miami the other day with that poor German woman. I never conceived of anything like that.

"We're all basically fed up. We all have kids. We worry about the future. There's got to be an end to all this madness.

"And beyond today, I'm really concerned about what the world will be like 10 or 15 years from now for my daughter and her family.

"Now, because of all this, I'm less likely to give strangers the benefit of the doubt. It used to be when I met someone I would give them an 'A' to begin with and then as they progressed through the class, the more mistakes they made, I would whittle them down. Now, I start them out with a 'Z.'

"I'm not going to say I'm going out looking for trouble, but if trouble comes my way, I'll deal with it. If someone starts shooting at me, I'll probably start shooting back.

"I mean, the law is great and it's well-intentioned, but I'd rather be alive and get in trouble with 'the man' than be dead and be a good citizen.

"I'm scared. The bottom line is, man, I'm scared. I don't want to have to shoot someone. I don't want to be shot at."

A MATTER OF SURVIVAL
Blacks now fearful, too

Etha Robinson, 51, lives in predominantly black South Central Los Angeles, the area most ravaged by last April's riots.

Born in Mississippi, a former teacher, she now runs a small business baking and selling "Teacakes." The lemon-flavored cookies are based on a family recipe. It originated in slavery 200 years ago.

Robinson has a friendly, open face, but underneath the surface simmers a deep anger. Whites and Asians are buying guns because they fear blacks and, in some cases, Hispanics.

After all the progress, after all that has happened, people like Robinson are again judged first and foremost by the color of their skin. And many are frightened by the firepower and the emotions arrayed against them:

"Why would I have to fear a white person if I'm not infringing on their civil liberties? Just because I'm black? That's how our laws were set up. They've always considered me to be a threat.

"They're just becoming more desperate. So now they're resorting to the same thing they say we've become—violent. I guess the slave cannot be too far from the master.

"I'm a little afraid, but let me tell you something. I'm no more afraid of the people with the guns than I am afraid of the people who have written laws and created situations with the pencil.

"I think the pencil is the most dangerous weapon to our community. It has killed and mutilated more people than any firearm.

"I'm a Southerner, I'm a woman and I'm black. And that gives me the whole spectrum of vantage points as far as segregation goes.

"We spent years of effort and suffered indignation just to be able to drink out of a fountain that said 'White' or go up to a rest room that said 'White.' But now we should develop our own thing.

"Did anything ever come out of a situation that was not violent, especially in America? It's just a matter of who will survive and who won't."

DESPAIR IN KOREATOWN
Baker recalls looters

Joy Ahn, 50, moved her family to America from South Korea in 1976. Four years ago, she bought the Koryo Bakery in Koreatown, a mixed Asian-Hispanic neighborhood about a mile north of South Central.

Korean merchants were particularly hard hit during last year's riots. Ahn's bakery was spared, but only because her adult son enlisted friends who protected the place at gunpoint.

At the time, she said, "America is a terrible place." In the last year, she has seen little to change her mind. Police have promised to protect the sprawling neighborhood this time, but she doesn't see how that is possible:

"Last year, we called the police station, everybody called the police station for protection. They tell me, 'We can't do nothing right now. You guys protect yourself.'

"Three hundred looters came up to my shopping center. They looted all the TVs, the furniture. Every store they set on fire.

"I still have a hurting. I still can't change my mind. I still see the looters here.

"Shooting. Fires. Pain. My family's eyes were red. So much smoke. All the electric wires burning. So scary, just like war.

"Most of my neighbors, the Spanish, they were looting the stores. We were surprised. My neighbors were looting the stores with their kids. It's a very bad education for their kids, looting stores.

"It is a shame to steal somebody else's merchandise. These people, they think it is fun. It is not fun. They ruined somebody else's life.

"This time? It's getting worse. All the weapons. Before the riots, we didn't have a gun. Now, we have four guns. All the Korean people have guns.

"My hope is for my next generation, that this country can be clear of all these problems for the next generation, but I don't know.

"When we came here, we enjoyed life here. We tried to build up life here and tried to have the highest education.

"But now I know. I made a big mistake to bring my kids over here."

IN SEARCH OF PEACE
Lawyer: an opportunity

Julius Butler, 53, is a public interest lawyer now serving the most fundamental public interest he can imagine—peace. He directs Operation Cool Response, a new group of community leaders and former gang members who will try to extinguish any hot spots that erupt.

His people will cruise certain neighborhoods in South Central, ready to reason with those who seem headed toward violence. Like other black leaders, he is not sure what to expect.

Very little reconstruction has begun in the area; very little has been done to address the underlying causes of the blight and hopelessness.

The feedback Butler has received suggests the streets may remain calm, but he has also seen the posters: No Justice, No Peace.

Whatever happens, he is angered that others assume that blacks will take to the street again, assume that they know no other way:

"Contrary to what everyone else seems to believe, we see this as an opportunity to build more linkage in the community.

"We're trying to convince people to look at the process this time rather than the verdict. I think the judge has pretty well managed this trial, which is a difficult trial to manage.

"But people with racist agendas are fanning the flames and we're very concerned that these people who are arming themselves will end up hurting themselves or each other.

"Look, this is all coming down on Easter Sunday. Let's use that as an opportunity for religious leaders to influence their congregations, for people all over the country to think about what's going on.

"I'm saying, 'Let's take what happened last April 29 as a wake-up call and let's take this April as an opportunity for change.'

"I'm saying, 'Let's talk about cooling the 'hood.'" (Merzer, 1993b, p. 1A) Reprinted with permission of *The Miami Herald*.

Writing with a feel for the sensitivities of strangers as Merzer does in these articles, achieved by using his honed observation, interviewing, and information collating skills—his senses, in other words—does not come automatically to the news feature writer. It takes considerable effort and experience to write well and to convey color and atmosphere in a story, any story. You have to get out and look around. Pay attention to detail. People have to be persuaded to talk, to open up. Merzer accomplishes his goals in his stories. He wanted to show South Floridians, veterans of their own civil disturbances, how tense, how nervous, and how fearful residents of Los Angeles were during the week the trial went to the jury for a decision.

Some stories need to set a scene or establish a mood as their most important objective for readers. If this is your assignment, your goal in short is to make the reader "see," "feel," and "touch" the subject of your writing. Can you sense the fear and apprehension of Southern Californians from the descriptions and quotations contained in Merzer's articles? You want to create mental images of the person, the place, the scenery. You want to present the opportunity for readers to use their mental senses—that is, to imagine the smell, sound, feel, the emotion, the physical appearance, and even the taste of the subject.

This is what descriptive and color writing are all about. You will find these types of articles published often in newspapers, magazines, and newsletters. This approach to writing can be applied to just about every feature subject you care to mention, yet the approach is best suited for specific subjects and types of articles. This chapter discusses these approaches and outlines the best ways to use the technique in writing features.

You will soon learn that this type of writing requires great concentration and highly tuned observational skills on your part. An alert writer will notice the colors, odors, noise, and other elements of a setting and put the reader in the middle of the action by describing these in depth. You accomplish this by using precise adjectives and adverbs, as well as exact nouns and verbs to convey the right image.

Writers achieve descriptive effects in their articles in a variety of ways with a wide range of writing tools. Some like to focus on their observations and use adjectives, and lots of them, throughout their writing. Others work hard to find the right nouns (for example, *dirge* instead of *song*). This requires a superior command of the English language. Using a broad vocabulary will not be enough. This type of writing also requires timing—you must be able to determine when to go heavily into description and when to back away from the temptation. Some like to let the story be told by the well-chosen words of others in direct quotations.

The primary rule is simple. When you think description will help a story, make certain what you are writing about is *distinctive*. The description and color should have a *purpose*. If you can find unique characteristics instead of the ordinary, then the additional color, or atmosphere, you add to a story through detailed descriptive writing will usually work. Certainly, as noted in the last chapter, the way you write also makes a difference. Choosing words and putting them together will also affect the impact description will have on your readers. Organization, or order, of the information will have a similar impact.

Jack Hart, an editor and writing coach at *The Oregonian* in Portland, feels description and color add spice to writing:

> Ordinarily, descriptive color or interesting details brighten news writing, helping draw readers into stories by sparking vivid images in their minds. When used skillfully, such details help motivate readers to make the paper part of their daily routine. But color, like everything else in a story, should serve some larger purpose. Well-chosen details may help to create a mood important to the story. They may serve as evidence for a generalization. Maybe they reveal something about the personality of a key character. Or they introduce an object that will be important to an action line. (Hart, 1990a, p. 3)

CREATING IMAGES IN THE MIND

As Hart (1990a) notes, detail and color must do *something* for a feature article when a writer uses them. Ultimately, they should advance the story or contribute to the main theme, he says. A good feature article will be enhanced with strong artwork, such as photographs or drawings, when the artwork and story come together as a unit on the page. Yet, you often have to write as if there is no art with the story; you must write to allow your readers to create *images* in their minds from reading your article. It does not take much to illustrate this point. Pick up most magazines and you will find at least one article rich in description and detail that gives a certain color or atmosphere to the article. Rowland Stiteler (1993), senior editor and writer for *Orlando* magazine, set this scene and mood in the opening paragraph of his cover article about how moving a television program such as "Ed McMahon's Star Search '93" is becoming big business for Central Florida's economy:

> The tourists walking the faux Hollywood streets of the Disney-MGM Studios Theme Park one morning just before Christmas must have thought they had arrived in show biz Nirvana. There was Ed McMahon, sitting in a director's chair in a small roped-off area on the side of the street, camera fixed upon him as he did a live satellite interview for a Hartford, Conn., television station to promote the upcoming Disney Christmas Parade, of which he would be grand marshal. He would also put in a pitch for his decade-old television show, "Ed McMahon's Star Search '93," which moved from Hollywood to Orlando last year and is taped at Disney-MGM.
>
> McMahon, being one of those rare celebrities who is as salt-of-the-earth convivial for an audience of one as he is for an audience of 20 million, spent time just before the broadcast session kibitzing with the tourists. He asked them where they lived and offered to autograph the programs and odd pieces of paper they pulled from their pockets and purses when they found that he had no intention of ignoring them . . . .(p. 52)

Although Stiteler's lead sets a scene and mood in an effective manner, it does not have quite the detailed descriptive power of James Watson's series of short portraits of several "secret gardens" he wrote for *Gold Coast*, a regional magazine based in Southeast Florida with a considerable home decorating and gardening focus. Watson's article is intentionally overdescriptive to get across the quiet and soothing feel of these unusual places. Here is a brief passage from one of the descriptions, and it is typical of Watson's (1993) writing throughout the article that forces the reader to walk with him through the gardens:

> Like a house, this landscape has a floor plan. Brick and coral rock-paved corridors wind lazily beneath a canopy of palms, evergreens and flowering trees, linking several themed gardens: Chinese; rose; a colonial garden; white-flowered vines and shrubs in a moonlight garden; a jungle garden; and one illustrating the use of tropical fruit trees in the everyday landscape.
>
> Pushing away palm fronds that overhang the path, new vistas unfold. A subtle blend of texture and color, fragrance and sound, conspire to wake each of our senses. Outside the library building adjoining the garden, gardenias and roses perfume the air while bunches of rosemary, oregano, basil and parsley spill onto the weather-worn pavers. In the Chinese garden, a wall embellished with a patina of algae contrasts with the lacquered red doors through which one passes. And deeper within, ferns, palms, papyrus and vines intertwine to cloak a quiet pool with the mystery of an Amazonian adventure . . . .(p. 40)

Clearly one goal is to provide *information* to readers through the description and color in your articles. In this way, color and description do something significant for the article. They are not padding or simply there to impress editors. A contribution of value to the entire piece occurs in the lead to Stiteler's article because it sets a scene. The middle passages quoted from Watson's carefully worded images are critical to telling readers about the attention to detail the gardeners have given to their work. However, the two writers get to their goals in different ways. One is comparatively general and less specific, yet still presents a picture in the mind to set up a later narration and the overall theme. The second example is extraordinarily precise.

Writers must also, as Stanford University's William Rivers (1992) says, make the effort of reading a rewarding experience. Some element of satisfaction should result for readers. "Success [of your article] pivots almost entirely on whether readers finish a descriptive [article or passage] with the feeling that they have been through a satisfying reading experience. The most evocative descriptives—those fashioned by writers who have developed and refined a talent for using visual words—are also *viewing* experiences," Rivers (1992, pp. 242–243) says.

Although they were written over three decades ago, these two short passages from Tom Wolfe's (1963) article in *Esquire* about stock car driver Junior Johnson illustrate that point as they set the scene for the profile:

Ten o'clock Sunday morning in the hills of North Carolina. Cars, miles of cars, in every direction, millions of cars, pastel cars, aqua green, aqua blue, aqua beige, aqua buff, aqua dawn, aqua dusk, aqua Malacca, Malacca lacquer, Cloud lavender, Assassin pink, Rake-a-Cheek raspberry, Nude Strand coral, Honest Thrill orange, and Baby Fawn Lust cream-colored cars are all going to the stock car races, and that old mothering North Carolina sun keeps exploding off the windshields.

Seventeen thousand people, me included, all of us driving out Route 421, out to the stock car races at the North Wilkesboro Speedway, 17,000 going out to a five-eighths-mile stock car track with a Coca-Cola sign out front. This is not to say there is no preaching and shouting in the South this morning. There is preaching and shouting. Any of us can turn on the old automobile transistor radio and get all we want . . . .(Wolfe, 1966, pp. 105–106)

Not much later in the same article, a different but equally powerful image-provoking passage by Wolfe appears:

And suddenly my car is stopped still on Sunday morning in the middle of the biggest traffic jam in the history of the world. It goes for ten miles in every direction from the North Wilkesboro Speedway. And right there it dawns on me that as far as this situation is concerned, anyway, all the conventional notions about the South are confined to . . . the Sunday radio. The South has preaching and shouting, the South has grits, the South has country songs, old mimosa traditions, clay dust, Old Bigots, New Liberals—and all of it, all of that old mental cholesterol, is confined to the Sunday radio. What I was in the middle of—well, it wasn't anything one hears about in panels about the South today. Miles and miles of eye-busting pastel cars on the expressway, which roar right up into the hills, going to the stock car races. Fifteen years of stock car racing, and baseball—and the state of North Carolina alone used to have forty-four professional baseball teams—baseball is all over within the South. We are all in the middle of a wild new thing, the Southern car world, and heading down the road on my way to see a breed such as sports never saw before, Southern stock car drivers, all lined up in these two-ton mothers that go over 175 m.p.h. . . .(1966, p. 106)

Even if you know little about the subject, Wolfe's methodical descriptive writing makes it seem as if you are there. After reading this, ask yourself why this article creates such vivid images in your mind. Is it the unusual colors (adjectives) he describes? Is it the emphasis on an action event (driving to the races) you are able to experience? Is it the writer's enthusiasm and excitement (emotions) for the subject? Or could it be the reconstruction of dialogue (direct quotes)? In fact, it is probably a little of each of these factors that contributes to Wolfe's success. Wolfe often utilizes what he calls the *four techniques of realism* in his writing. In a style that has been labeled *new journalism* by the writers and scholars studying it, these "new journalists" of the 1960s and 1970s often employed these basic steps that Wolfe described:

1. *Scene-by-scene construction of events.* Scene-by-scene construction is the most basic of organizational schemes and is different from narrative writing. It is a form of storytelling illustrated by Wolfe's description of the drive on a Sunday morning to the stock car races.

2. *Full record of dialogue in the scenes.* Magazine writers, with the luxury of more space, often can take advantage of this by using longer passages of exact dialogue from sources or between sources and the writer. In this way, however, sources nearly become characters as this type of writing edges toward the fiction form called a short story.

3. *Third-person point of view.* Although this is the norm in most feature writing, this type of writing exhibited by Wolfe shows less involvement by the writer than a first-person point of view would offer.

4. *Detailing of descriptive incidentals.* Wolfe calls this sort of writing technique a "social autopsy," the attention the writer pays to minute details of the source's life in characterizing the person.

Whenever you try to create images in your reader's mind, remember you cannot drift from reality. In writing nonfiction, there must still be some information value to the article. You should always ask yourself, "What is the news hook or news peg of the story?" Its focus and current value must be clear to you and to your reader.

DESCRIPTIVE WRITING AND INTERVIEWING

There will be times when you will be assigned to conduct an interview as a basis for an article and find that the piece needs enrichment through description. This makes your challenge as a writer even tougher, because you must not only concentrate on the interview itself by listening to your source's answers, but you must also be concerned with using your observational skills to note details before, during, and after the interview. For example, you should be concerned with your source's *body language*, or your source's physical responses to your questions, in addition to what the source says. Watch for facial expressions, shifts in seating position, gestures, and other mannerisms. Listen carefully for intonations and other characteristics of speaking.

You can employ techniques of detailed and descriptive writing to set a single impression of an interview for your reader. Often, as you have probably noted, this is not necessarily objective. For magazine writers in particular, this is possible. Many newspapers will permit such "writer's license" in certain types of features such as columns, analyses and interpretive articles, and Sunday magazine features. Remember, however, you still remain objective in your writing by being fair and careful about what you observe. When done well, this becomes an asset for the writer and for the article itself. The most common interview-based feature article that employs descriptive writing in large quantities is the profile.

When writer David Kaplan was dispatched by *Newsweek* to California's Skywalker Ranch, the Marin County home of filmmaker George Lucas, Kaplan interviewed the now-legendary leader in the film industry. Kaplan's article was part of a series of articles for a cover package focusing on the spurt in growth in the interactive technology of computers, television, telephone, and other systems. Kaplan's article presents the perspectives of Lucas, who had earned a reputation as a technological visionary with nearly two decades of high-tech and special-effects Hollywood films in the *Star Wars* trilogy and the *Terminator* series. In an article designed to convey the thoughts of an industry leader, Lucas' views combined with a bit of intricate description to show the contrast of the high-tech thinking Lucas with his rather low-tech home and office. This is how Kaplan (1993) began the article:

> For filmmaker George Lucas, it's just another noontime in the undulating hills of his high-tech paradise north of San Francisco. The chef at Skywalker Ranch has prepared a simple tray of sautéed trout with balsamic vinegar reduction, soft polenta with Parmesan and organic greens grown out by the Chardonnay vineyards. Many employees lunch on the sun porch. Lucas is upstairs in the modern Victorian mansion that serves as headquarters for Lucasfilm, Ltd. His oak office is spare: no PCs, no pixels, no toys that byte—just a spectacular westward view of his 2,541-acre Marin compound.

> With all that is percolating inside his head these days, it's no wonder that the 49-year-old Lucas needs a little serenity . . . .(p. 45)

Regardless of the sort of interview-oriented story you are writing, use of description must be built on careful word selection. Remember that you will be serving as the eyes, ears, and other sense organs for your readers. During your interview, take advantage of interruptions to notice things about the room you are in. What is on the desk? How is the room decorated? What objects are on the walls? How is the person you are interviewing dressed? How is his or her hair cut? What sort of food is being served? What color are the eyes? Look for characteristics no matter how minute they seem. Look for subtle things such as brand names and positioning of furniture. What do they tell you about your source?

Also remember that you are not the brains of your readers. Leave the conclusions about what you have observed to your readers. You are better off not making judgments about what you describe. Personal conclusions and interpretations are most often not used in newspaper features and many times not desired in magazine article writing unless you are a qualified expert on a subject and can make such comments with authority.

Syndicated *New York Times* columnist and feature writer Anna Quindlen (1984) says, when covering an event for an atmosphere piece, she writes down everything she sees. "I take down quotes, names of signs and all those things. Just in case it might fit in. And I don't want to trust my memory. Sometimes you remember something red and it's really pink or blue."

USING THE RIGHT SUPPORTING CAST

As a writer, words are your supporting cast. Like a play or a film, you need the right ones for the right script. You have two basic strategies to writing when it comes to word selection and usage: writing with general, ambiguous words and writing with specific, clear words. Consider, for a moment, the value of the right nouns and verbs and their grammatical assistants, adjectives and adverbs. What exactly are their roles in your script?

Adjectives and adverbs convey distinct impressions. *Adjectives* express qualities of the nouns they modify. Adjectives can be descriptive, proper (similar to proper nouns), and restrictive. These words tell us more about the noun.

Adverbs do much the same thing, except they can also modify adjectives in addition to expressing time, place, manner, degree, or cause. Adverbs limit, or further define and describe, the verbs with which they are used. In descriptive or color writing, these are perhaps the most important category of words feature writers can use. "Strong modifiers also evoke strong images," Jack Hart (1990d), writing coach for *The Oregonian* in Portland, reminds us. "Writers who consistently pick winners look for specific adjectives and adverbs" (p. 1).

Writers most often use *verbs* to connote movement, action, or an assertion. Verbs are necessary in sentences, performing the expression of action, existence, and occurrence. Writers who do not vary verb usage, or stick to the same dull verbs all the time, will take much of the life out of their writing. "Our audience naturally focuses on action," Hart (1990c) also notes. "Journalists sell information about action. And when they lose sight of that simple truth, they lose readers" (p. 1).

Nouns, of course, describe something substantive such as things, concepts, people, places, and objects. There are *common* nouns, such as generic words (automobile). But writers also use *proper* nouns (Lexus or Ford). Abstract nouns describe ideas and qualities (love or loving) and concrete nouns are more definitive objects (bird or sidewalk). Collective nouns describe groups (faculty) while mass nouns describe things not usually counted (sand).

The goal is to emphasize prevailing characteristics of the subject about which you are writing. And, at the same time, you want to convey excitement or other emotions.

WRITING DESCRIPTIVE LEADS

Descriptive features that convey the color of an event have the important duty of helping to balance the content of a newspaper, magazine, or newsletter. Of the three major types of magazine leads—descriptive, expository, and narrative—only the descriptive lead draws the reader into the article by painting pictures for the reader at the outset. The idea of giving features special descriptive content and attention to detail and color is, of course, not a new one. Nor is giving the lead of a story a particularly heavy dose of description to interest readers in the subject a new device of writers.

In fact, University of Wisconsin Professor Willard Bleyer (1913), in his textbook about journalistic writing that was published over 80 years ago, said description in the lead of an article is crucial to the success of feature stories. "A vivid bit of description is sometimes used to advantage at the beginning," he wrote (p. 229). "If, instead of merely describing and explaining a mechanical process, the writer portrays men actually performing the work involved in the process, he adds greatly to the interest of the article. The effectiveness of an explanation of a new surgical operation can be increased to a marked degree by picturing a surgeon as he performs the operation" (p. 229).

Miami Herald assistant travel editor and former lifestyles feature writer Jane Wooldridge (1993) wrote an appealing lead to her story about her first visit to Vietnam. Her first sentences describe her emotions when her flight touched down in that place she says she felt she knew, not because she had been there, but because she grew up in the era during the U.S. involvement in war there. She describes what she saw in fine detail, while surprising us—she was surprised as well—with some rather unique firsthand observations. This personal approach remains highly descriptive and captures a bit of drama and her excitement at the moment of arrival:

> The U.S.-crafted Boeing 737—not the usual rickety Russian junk heap, thank God—settles in, then descends over mud flats pocked by bomb craters and patchwork fields of tender green. The conical hats of women bent over the rice paddies come into view; an ethereal yellow light washes the few buildings.
>
> Hello, Vietnam.
>
> Like most Americans of my generation, I grew up with one foot in a place I had never seen—Vietnam—and, at least then, never wanted to visit. The *Life* magazine photos of the war, the nightly news footage, the antiwar demonstrations were as much part of my teenage years as my first kiss and playing hooky from Sunday School.
>
> But that was all long ago—before Apocalypse Now and Deer Hunter and Indochine, before I had a career and a mortgage.
>
> When I flew to Vietnam in March, I knew the country had changed; I'd read articles on increasing tourism, the search for MIA remains and the possible lifting of the U.S. economic embargo.
>
> Still, I didn't expect this: attractive women in smartly tailored pant suits zipping along the streets of Hanoi on Honda motorbikes; chic restaurants and an anything-goes attitude in Saigon; magnificent ceramic-encrusted tombs from the Imperial dynasties; a hundred religious devotees cloaked in crimson and white kneeling on the exquisitely patterned floor of a strange, vast temple; the dazzling smile and warmth of the Vietnamese toward even—some will say especially—Americans. (p. 1F)

Your goal is to capture the drama, the excitement and overall emotion of an event and to share the experience of the moment with your readers. Even with good artwork accompanying the article, a strong descriptive lead such as Wooldridge's example will grab the interested reader and not let go. The two elements, artwork and a strong lead, should work together to create the right feel for the article's treatment of the subject. Professor Myrick Land (1993) says there are numerous options for leads that can employ description and detail. Land lists the anecdote, the narrative series of examples, the first person, the straightforward statement, the surprising statement, the surprising quote, the question, the "you" or direct address, the quotation, the single example, the opinion statement, and the general descriptive leads. Regardless of the type of lead, he says, it should "emerge naturally from the research on your article. An effective lead can be written only if you have shown imagination in selecting a subject, have focused sharply on one aspect of that topic, have been thorough in gathering background information, and have conducted enough well-planned interviews" (p. 85).

Readers thrive on details, especially when the writer is focusing on something unfamiliar to most readers. An article that starts with richness in detail and imagery will win readers from the first sentence to the last. If you don't buy this, just take a look at a piece of fiction on the current best-seller list or read a short story by a well-known writer. Good nonfiction writers use this technique as well.

ADDING COLOR TO WRITING

Color stories are important feature forms. These stories are often used to provide readers with the most descriptive aspects of a news event or other activity. Newspapers use color stories as sidebars to help explain a major news story by providing atmosphere or mood—happy or sad, warm or cold, exciting or dull—for those who could not be there.

Frequently, color stories in newspapers are used with the major news of the day—tragedies such as airline crashes or car accidents or joyful moments such as a papal visit or the opening of a new public facility. Color stories are used to relate the mood of crowds at events such as football games, festivals, parties, celebrations, parades, concerts, funerals, and memorial services. For example, at a major college football game or the opening day of baseball season, a color story angle might be the activities and reactions of a group of fans who followed the home team on the road several hundred miles to see the big game. It might focus on the team on the sidelines or in the dugout during the game. It might focus on celebrities in the press box or in elsewhere in the stadium. It might reflect the party-like atmosphere before the game in the parking lot at the tailgate or tent parties of alumni, season-ticket holders, and other fans. It can focus on the reaction of a single person who might be pivotal to the major story of that day.

Rarely does a color story focus on the results of the game or even the principal action of the game. That is likely the purpose of another story by the same reporter or, as preferred by most editors, by a second or even a third reporter. In short, the idea behind this sort of writing is to permit the reader who did not attend to share the event with the writer and others who were there. Color stories take advantage of certain types of sources of information. You will find color stories almost always include people, your perceptions as an observer, your observations, and a common thread.

These are often reaction stories, but the reaction is often that of the writer. Professor Louis Alexander (1975) says these types of stories are usually written with a point of view or a focus that directs the article. What are you trying to say about the subject? What story line, or other literary device, are you using? How can you arrange the information to give the event some of the atmosphere it needs? Alexander adds that when you successfully answer these questions, you have done your job well. He says, "Overall, because you have all the colors in it [the article] you give the reader a much stronger, more meaningful, more colorful picture—the blacks and the whites, the grays, the blues and peppermint stripes and everything else. You accomplish this by planning your story to make one major point or leave one message and by selecting a story line on which to hang or arrange your materials" (1975, pp. 58–59).

When violence became severe in several local South Florida high schools, in the nearby neighborhoods, and even church parking lots, some parents and clergymen began to work to stop it. Teenage students, some just innocent bystanders, were dying. Weapons were commonplace. The parents and their clergymen felt the school system and local police were not doing enough. John Barry's (1993) Sunday feature appeared on *The Miami Herald*'s Living section front page. The section, which focuses on family and other lifestyle concerns, needed an article which took the *micro* view, looking at how one couple handled the problem. He began with a close-up look at the couple trying to do something, regardless of how small or insignificant it seemed. This is how Barry's story began:

> Tall, stately Elonia Reynolds, who reveals her grief in her solemn gaze, had to brace herself to go back to Norland High, the school her murdered daughter LaToy loved dearly. But after another child was shot to death she decided to take a stand.
>
> So in January, the morning after the second shooting, Elonia, LaToy's two sisters and a small group of parents took up positions at the school's entrance, holding signs demanding an end to teenage violence.
>
> But the Hondas and Chevys stopped just long enough to unload kids. Only hours after a boy was riddled with bullets on campus, no one stopped to talk, no one came by to ask, "What can we do?"
>
> So far, taking a stand in Norland is a lonely job.
>
> The Norland neighborhood in North Dade, in the shadow of the aqua and orange Joe Robbie Stadium, is most of the time a sleepy collection of homes.

It is a neighborhood of bone-tiredness and grit, where parents make themselves upwardly mobile the hard way, by working two jobs, day shifts, night shifts—the unvarnished side of the American Dream.

You could say the shootings of two teenagers had nothing to do with the school or the neighborhood, that either could have happened anywhere.

Or you could say the shootings had everything to do with the school and the neighborhood, and whether they will endure or fail.

Another good neighborhood in the heart of Dade finds itself on the edge: facing surrender to decline, or a daunting long-term battle against it.

And you could say this is a test—one that could happen, or is happening, in your own neighborhood—of whether people today have the guts to fight for their children's futures and for their own safety.

That's what the parents and clergy who want the Norland neighborhood back say.

That's what Elonia Reynolds says.

Elonia and her husband David, who themselves split day and night shifts as nurses, are selling and moving to Broward. Memories of their 8-month-old tragedy are too painful. Each young kid marching by to class reminds them of LaToy.

But they don't blame the neighborhood or the school for the shooting. They blame the pathological few who would hold the community hostage.

They are the few who leave their shell casings in the church parking lots, who rip off purses from car seats when mothers drop their kids off for day care, who make it necessary. (p. 1J)

The story, like Barry's riveting account of the efforts of the Reynoldses, must be continuously interesting, William Rivers (1992) emphasizes. "One sentence should grow out of another; one paragraph should grow out of another. The middle and end should be as interesting as the beginning. Although a color story has no standard structure, the 'hard news' should usually be somewhere near the beginning," he advises (p. 249).

New York Times' syndicated columnist Anna Quindlen has a tested and proven successful strategy she uses in writing features. The approach works to portray events such as the Feast of St. Anthony on Sullivan Street in Manhattan, which she covered as a feature writer. When she wrote features for the newspaper's "About New York" column, she loved to cover such "quintessential New York events." Quindlen (1984) explains: "In something like this, where I'm basically going to take the reader and put him on this street, on this day, on this beat, my problem more than anything else is figuring out how to organize and then pick and choose the telling details that are really going to make him feel like he was here with me." She likens covering such an event to painting a picture—she is an artist with words:

If you try to hold up a mirror to an event, if you paint it in broad strokes, you're going to miss on colors, you're going to miss on sights, you're going to miss on all kinds of things. I think if you're going to hold up a mirror and do the painting, the best thing to do is pointillism—a whole bunch of little points. . . . [W]hen the reader steps back and looks at it, when they're done, they're not going to see the little points, they're going to see a whole big picture. (Quindlen, 1984)

Color writing is a very personal style of writing, Quindlen explains. Each person will gain a different perspective on the same event and will probably write a different story. "Everybody faced with the same event will give you a different viewpoint, a different answer, a different set of people." And, she adds, you have to have confidence in yourself as a writer to write about your own perceptions and reactions to a given situation. "It's the self-confidence that comes from self-confidence in your personality and not so much your skills. I'm just different. I have different perceptions."

CREATING MOODS

Good color writing will set a tone for the reader. You can manipulate moods by your choice of words, organizational approach to the information you have and, of course, the subject about which you are writing. Louis Alexander (1975) says that if you can do well writing color, that is, creating a mood for the reader, the rewards are high for both the reader and writer: "When you get your story across, when you convey the color and drama that make other people feel it, you the feature writer gain genuine satisfaction" (p. 59).

As you move into other specific types of feature articles in the next chapters, you will begin to get ideas for application of the techniques of descriptive and color writing in these varieties of articles. For example, you will see wide possibilities for descriptive writing on seasonal topics and on travel subjects. As you will see, some of these types of stories are easy to write and others do not lend themselves to descriptive writing approaches very readily. Writing with heavy emphasis on detail is a valuable tool for feature writers.

Miami Herald reporter Richard Wallace (1993) was assigned to cover the annual Coconut Grove Bed Race, a large Miami event that raises money for charity. Thousands of people were at the races, some participating but many just people-watching. It is a day-long series of races with oddly decorated beds and even more oddly dressed and costumed participants. Notice how Wallace weaves people, through numerous direct quotation reaction comments from those present and involved, into a description of the event in his story for the city desk:

A wacky concept. Firm-bodied competitors. Some racy action. Throw in a sunny day in May, and the result is another vast crowd for that double entendre on wheels, the Coconut Grove Bed Race.

Dozens of crews of competitors sprinted along South Bayshore Drive in the Grove, pushing lightweight beds on wheels for fun and glory.

And tens of thousands of spectators took it all in—for a variety of reasons.

"I've got a friend running in the race," said Jose Torres, 22, as he stood next to a temporary guard rail watching beds whiz past. "He's with Baptist Hospital."

Torres turned out to be rooting for a winner. Baptist was the first-place finisher in one of the race's four sections, the Bed Pan Division, which featured hospitals and other health-care facilities.

But for Dave Mustaine, 23, the event might as well have been named the Coconut Grove Bud Race.

"I came here for the exercise—12-ounce curls," said Mustaine, bending his arm to heft a can of Budweiser to his lips.

Alex Mutis, 23, and Angie Morales, 22, found the day at the races simply a pleasurable way to while away a Sunday.

Morales liked some of the colorful designs of the beds and costumes worn by some of the competitors.

"Have you seen the Solid Gold?" Mutis asked. "They're pretty good."

The Solid Gold team represented a nightclub where female nude dancers hold center stage. The Solid Gold team, however, was not au naturel Sunday. But it was a close call.

Morales took note of sparsely clad male racers representing Le Bare, a Broward County dance club.

Which brings up a point about how the bed race—this was the 15th edition—has evolved. If it were a movie, it might not win a G rating, though it might get a G-string rating. Many participants and spectators dress to get just about as much sun as possible in public.

But for fully dressed John Schulz, 44, the event simply amounted to a welcome break.

"I came with some friends. We came down here from Pinellas County to work on rebuilding. We take our spare time and spread it around. We've gone to Calle Ocho and Metrozoo and Islamorada," said Schulz, who works with windows and screening.

For the sports-minded, the competition's other victors were Budweiser in the Open Division, Hooters in the Women's Division, and People's Telephone in the Fun Division.

The ultimate winner was the Muscular Dystrophy Association, which receives money from Bed Race food, beverage and souvenir concessionaires, said event official Terry Weaver. (p. 3B) Reprinted with permission of The Miami Herald.

COMING TO YOUR SENSES

Roy Sorrels (1986), a correspondent for *Writer's Digest* magazine and a novelist, offers this exercise for "sensuous writing"—that is, writing with your senses. Here's what he suggests:

To make your own writing more sensuous, take a series of blind walks. Ask an understanding friend—another writer maybe—to help.

Close your eyes and let your companion guide you gently through a few environments. Down a city street, perhaps, past the busy school yard, into the park. At first, you will be a bit nervous with your vision cut off, but relax and you'll become more and more aware of all the rich input from your other four senses. Relax into the sounds, notice the surface under your feet—gritty sidewalks, cobblestones, dirt in the park, lush or scraggly grass. Smell the world—can you tell when you pass by the bakery or the fishmonger? With your friend's guidance, touch things in the park—grass, tree trunks, a worn park bench.

Of course, you can do this on your own, just closing your eyes for a few minutes sitting at a sidewalk cafe, or on a bus, or lounging under a tree.

ENHANCING WRITING WITH FIGURATIVE LANGUAGE

Many writers who leave lasting images in the minds of their readers know how to use figurative language in an effective manner. Simply put, figurative language is a device that helps readers understand your meaning. Commonly, journalists use concrete words and their modifiers for precision in meaning. Experienced writers also know when to use the two of these forms known as *metaphors* and *similes*. Writers also often use *allusions* and *personifications*. These are not, of course, the exclusive turf of fiction writers such as classic poets or short story writers.

Metaphors and similes create impressions in readers by comparison of things that are usually not associated. "Combine two previously isolated categories and something mysterious happens. Synapses sizzle. New connections appear. Synergy fashions a new form greater than the sum of the parts," explains *The Oregonian*'s Jack Hart (1989, p. 1).

Metaphors describe something in terms of something else. They imply comparisons. Similes are more direct comparisons, commonly identified by use of *like* or *as*. The allusion is simply an indirect reference. This occurs most often by using some sort of reference commonly known by writer and readers. Personifications give objects human characteristics.

The Orlando Sentinel Washington bureau staff writer Sean Holton used an entertaining hog and pork chops metaphor to discuss the "pork-barrel" nature of $45 billion in federal funding awarded for the National Aeronautics and Space Administration. This is how Holton (1992) began the story, which ran on the front page of a Sunday edition of his newspaper:

BEST SOURCES FOR DESCRIPTIVE AND COLOR WRITING

People and their opinions
Direct quotations
Dialogue
Your own observations
Actions
Environments
Your own perceptions
Your own attitudes/emotions
Your personal experiences
Personal experiences of others

WASHINGTON—This story is about NASA and Congress. But first you need to imagine a hog—one of the biggest hogs that ever was—a hog so big that butchering it would make 45 billion pork chops.

Next, spread those pork chops throughout the country. Ship 13 billion of them to California. Send another 5 billion to Florida. Go through all 50 states, and don't stop until you've dropped off the last 550,000 pork chops in the outback of North Dakota.

Then consider how grateful the recipients of those prime cuts of pork would be. Think how eagerly they would fight to keep their pork and work to make you happy in the hopes of getting even more.

Now shift the context back to Washington. Think of the hog as NASA's budget, the pork chops as the $45 billion the agency has spent on prime space-program business and research contracts since 1987, and the grateful diners as NASA boosters on key committees in Congress.

This is NASA's coast-to-coast political pork network. It's a money-and-jobs pig roast that welcomes every state in the union (and, of course, the District of Columbia), and it reserves places of honor for several guests whose plates are piled with hundreds of millions of dollars a year. (p. A-1)

Tools such as metaphors enhance written communication. Without the pork metaphor, the story about NASA funding might have been just another boring budget analysis read only by the hardest core government watchdog. But this touch by the writer makes the story more interesting and a little more appealing to an average reader. As Hart explains, you are not only serving readers when you use figurative language, you are serving yourself. For most writers, such writing is a welcome diversion from the routine, and this might help you remain interested in the art and craft of writing.

PROFESSIONAL'S POINT OF VIEW

Madeleine Blais
University of Massachusetts at Amherst

Detail and color in a piece of journalism should work ideally in the same way they function in poetry or in fiction. They should function metaphorically or they should help create a mood. They should contribute to a sense of momentum, not clutter.

In the kind of journalism that is only interested in record keeping, details and color are often used to telegraph the fact that the reporter was an actual witness. In this approach, quotations are also used to prove the presence of the reporter. Thus, quotations are often included that contain little or no information and contribute not a whit to the overall design. Such pieces peter out rather than build and that is why cutting from the bottom makes sense.

Journalism that attempts to be literary narrows the gap between writing that only entertains and writing that only informs. How can you train yourself to know what details to include?

First, keep up with your reading of literature. Second, when you are out on a story, use all your senses, not just your ears. I remember once interviewing a woman who wanted more than anything else to rid herself of a bad situation. She kept saying as much, over and over, as she stood in her kitchen, but nothing she said spoke to her pain as insistently and clearly as the way in which she kept sponging and sponging an already immaculate kitchen counter.

I once wrote a story about a schizophrenic woman. It is one thing to say that she lives in a disordered world, another to say: "Two years after Trish's mother died, she wrote her a letter, asking for cigarettes."

Once I wrote a short piece entitled "Monica's Barrel" about a woman who had immigrated from Jamaica and who periodically sent home barrels, big cardboard cylinders with tops made of tin, to the people she had left behind. At first I was going to write that if she had stayed home she would be poor. On prodding from my editor I wrote: "In Jamaica Monica's brightest prospect would be a job at the bra and underwear factory making $50 a week in an economy where $5 buys a pound of rice."

Another time I wanted to convey the sense of a beach resort as the epitome of safe haven: "We spend all winter telling the children never to say hello to strangers, yet here the stranger is likely to be a woman with gray hair wearing a belt with whales who happens to be circulating a petition to save St. Joseph's parsonage from being sold to developers."

When in doubt, turn to Strunk and White's *The Elements of Style* before embarking on an important piece: read it, reread it, memorize and then proceed (Blais, personal communication, 1988).

Madeleine Blais is a free-lance writer and associate professor of journalism at the University of Massachusetts at Amherst. Blais spent 8 years as a staff writer for Tropic, the Sunday magazine of *The Miami Herald*. She is the winner of the 1980 Pulitzer Prize for feature writing. She has also worked for *The Boston Globe* and *The Trenton Times*. She has been a Nieman Fellow at Harvard University, and she was featured on the Public Broadcasting System series, "Writer's Writing."

6

The Human Interest Article

A man leaves his child on the roof of his car, drives off to the interstate highway nearby, speeds up to 50 m.p.h., and the baby flies off the car and onto the roadway. A terrible tragedy? No, the baby was not hurt. It's one of those *unbelievable* people stories. It's a happy-ending story. It's a "boy, was that a stupid thing to do" story. However, it was a story that begged to be told. Chris Reidy, a reporter for *The Boston Globe*, got such an assignment. All the elements were there: a man, his baby, drama, a crazy mistake. And, oh yes, it was Mother's Day and the husband had to tell his wife about the little problem with their baby. Human interest such as this can be big news, the major story of the day, in fact. Reidy (1992) told of the Murrays' miraculous good fortune in the day's front-page lead story for *The Globe*, with a jump-page sidebar on how people misuse car seats for children, written by another reporter. Here is Reidy's story:

MILLBURY—After his 3-month-old son sailed off the roof of his car at 50 m.p.h. and landed unhurt in the middle of an interstate highway in Worcester on Sunday, Michael Murray decided to break the news to his wife gently.

It was, after all, Mother's Day, and Murray, a 27-year-old factory worker, said yesterday he did not want to say right out that he had "messed up" by absent-mindedly driving off while his son was strapped into a car seat that he had left on the sunroof of his bronze 1987 Hyundai.

As her husband sheepishly held Mathew, who was sleeping serenely in white pajamas and sunbonnet, Deanna Murray, 28, recounted the phone call she received from her husband.

"'Come to the emergency room,' he told me."

A surgical nurse, Deanna Murray was on duty at the Medical Center of Central Massachusetts in Worcester when her husband's call came in. The emergency room is down the hall from her work station.

"'Just come down here,' that's all he told me," Deanna Murray said, describing the phone call. "'Mathew has fallen,' he finally said. I ran all the way down the hall."

After learning the full story, Deanna Murray said, "I was in shock. The nurses had to sit me down and hold me. It's a miracle. It really is."

"It's a good thing he didn't tell me on the phone," she said, adding, "Every time I hear the story I could burst into tears."

Deanna Murray heard the story a lot yesterday as the media descended on the Millbury farmhouse where she lives with her husband and two children.

The Murrays obligingly went through the details over and over again, but Deanna Murray balked when a photographer requested that Michael reenact the sequence of events with Mathew posed in his car seat on the top of the car.

"You're not going to put him on the roof again, are you?" Deanna Murray said, the only time she expressed a hint of displeasure with her husband.

As Michael Murray recounted it, things began innocently enough around noon Sunday when he decided to drive Mathew and his 20-month-old sister to the hospital, where Deanna was working the day shift. He wanted to drop off her Mother's Day gifts—a gold necklace bearing the legend "Number One Mom" and a single rose.

After presenting these gifts, Michael Murray carried his two children back to the indoor garage where he parked the car. Murray put his daughter into her car seat but then got into the car with Mathew still on the sunroof.

"The garage was dark," Murray said when asked how he could have forgotten about his son.

Murray then proceeded to drive through the streets of Worcester. Traffic was heavy, he said, but no one beeped at him to indicate that anything was amiss.

As he accelerated onto Interstate 290, the highway that cuts through Worcester, Murray heard a scraping sound on the roof of his car.

"You could hear it slide," Murray said of his son and the car seat. "I looked to where he should have been. Then in the rear view mirror, I saw him sliding down the highway."

Fortunately, the driver following Murray does not believe in tailgating.

"I was coming over Route 290 South about noon," said James Boothby, 67, a retired antiques dealer from Worcester. "I saw something in the air. I thought it was garbage, something somebody had tossed out. Then I thought it was a doll. Then I saw the doll open its mouth. I couldn't believe it. It was a little baby."

At this point, I-290 is three lanes in each direction, and Mathew landed on "the driver's side of the middle lane," Boothby said.

If Boothby had swerved, the Murrays believe their story would have had an unhappy ending. Instead, he came to a stop in the middle lane, halting the flow of traffic. Boothby said he was driving the speed limit—about 50 m.p.h.—when he caught sight of Mathew and his car seat.

"It just landed on the road," Boothby said of the car seat. "It bounced a couple times, but it never tipped . . . . It just sat right down."

Murray, who estimated that Mathew was on the roof for a total of about 1 mile, said he stopped his car about "25 to 50 yards" past the point where his son had become airborne.

With his car blocking traffic, Boothby got out to investigate. What he found was a baby uninjured and a car seat undamaged.

"I picked the little fellow up, and he looked all around," Boothby said. "When he started crying, I knew everything was all right . . . . He looked at me as if to say, 'Who are you?' He knew I wasn't daddy or mama. That's when he started to cry."

"Thank God for him," Deanna Murray said of Boothby. "I can't thank him enough."

Commenting on the heavy traffic that had come to a sudden halt behind them, Boothby said, "It's amazing there weren't any fender-benders."

When Michael Murray reached Boothby, he snatched up his son, telling him, "When the police show up, tell them I went to the hospital."

At the hospital, Mathew was deemed to be uninjured, though he was kept overnight for observation. While doctors scanned the son, the father was cited for driving to endanger.

State Trooper Mario Tovar, who issued the citation, said, "I have never seen or heard of anything like this. It was kind of shocking, the whole thing."

"He was a very happy kid, all smiles," Tovar said of Mathew at the hospital. "The doctor gave him a good bill of health. He's a miracle baby. What a Mother's Day gift! The result was one in a million."

Michael Murray noted that "the doctors said that with the shape of the car seat, it actually flew like an airplane."

Murray's car is a hatchback, and its shape may have helped put Mathew into a glide path.

"We're definitely writing to the car seat company," said Deanna Murray.

The seat was identified as a Gerry Guard with Glide, manufactured by Gerry Baby Products of Denver.

When not used as a car seat, it can be converted into a mini rocking chair, hence the word "glide" in the chair's name, said company spokeswoman Stephanie Aragon.

The seat is designed for infants weighing less than 20 pounds, she said.

Said a grateful Deanna Murray: "The Gerry Glider—it certainly lived up to its name." (pp. 1, 18) Reprinted with permission of *The Boston Globe*.

Just about everyone likes to read, or listen to, a good story such as the Mother's Day episode involving Michael and Deanna Murray and their baby Mathew. Human interest articles should always be based on *good stories*. It is that simple. These articles are the sort of stories you can curl up with on the sofa and enjoy for a few minutes. Readers react by feeling sad for those involved in tragedy. Readers feel happy because someone has beaten the odds and won a battle against a bigger foe, as young Mathew did. Sometimes, readers smile because they remember a similar experience they have once been through. A human interest article is often a success because the story that is told is *true* and involves people in your own town or someone who is just like you, but from a faraway place. Readers find these human interest articles a change of pace from the normal flow of spot news. Furthermore, as *McCall's* managing editor Don McKinney (1986) says, these stories serve readers in another way: They offer inspiration and hope for readers who might be experiencing the same troubles or frustrations.

Just what is a human interest article? This type of article has several labels. Some publications, like *McCall's*, just call it a *human interest narrative*. Some label it a *true-life drama*. McKinney says that regardless of what they are called, these articles are stories told by writers about people who have been involved in real dramas and these emotional stories are usually told in narrative form. These articles are quite popular with readers, research shows, and some publications try to balance their editorial content with these sorts of stories appearing regularly.

Atlanta Journal and Constitution staff writer Actor Cordell, who writes for the newspaper's North Fulton County People section, wrote a compelling human interest feature about a young physically challenged woman who would soon be entering college with hopes of attending law school some day. Cordell interviewed the young woman, the mother who adopted her over a decade earlier, and one of her high school teachers who supported and helped her for this typical daily newspaper human interest feature. Cordell also took the color photograph that accompanied the article. Here is what Cordell (1993) wrote about Lisa Olson:

Lisa Manyata Olson plans to enter Lee College in Cleveland, Tenn., in the fall to begin studies toward a degree in law.

"My teachers have told me I like to talk so much, I should make a great lawyer!" the Roswell High School senior said, and she laughed.

Lisa's left arm measures a few inches. Her left leg ends at the knee, and on her right side, there is no arm or leg at all.

Born in 1974 in India, Lisa is a victim of "a condition known as Total Amelia born without limbs," said her adoptive mother, Marie Olson, 64.

"Usually the cause has been blamed on drugs, such as thalidomide. We do know that thalidomide was being taken by women in India around the time of Lisa's birth to a poor couple who already had seven children."

Going off to college may seem a formidable challenge for Lisa.

But people such as Roswell High math teacher Eddie Echols are certain the grit that's gotten her over other hurdles will see her through.

Mr. Echols nominated her for a "Beats The Odds" award in the program begun in 1990 by Fulton County to honor graduating seniors who've achieved academic excellence and shown leadership qualities despite adversity.

She and the six other winners of $1,000 scholarships will be honored at a dinner tonight at the High Museum of Art.

"They're going to pick me up in a limousine to go to the banquet," she said last week after zipping down the hall at Roswell High in her electric wheelchair, sounding a high-pitched horn as she turned corners.

With a prosthetic left arm, Lisa can eat unassisted, use a typewriter, paint, use the telephone to call her pals and even swim.

Marie Olson, now 64, a native of Staten Island, N.Y., was director of Hope Town, a residential school for the handicapped in Carmel, N.Y., in 1979 when she was contacted by a Christian girls' home for the handicapped near Bombay, asking if she could take Lisa.

The U.S. Immigration Service was not enthusiastic about the proposal and later informed Ms. Olson medical visas from India had been stopped; to get Lisa to the United States, she would have to adopt her.

"She was 5½ years old and weighed only 17 pounds," Miss Olson recalled of their meeting in India. "I'd try to feed her and she'd turn her head away. I knew no Maharani, her native language, but she was quick to learn English. I held up a mirror and said, 'Hi, funny kid'. She looked into the mirror and said, 'Hi, pretty kid.'"

"I don't have any memories of India," said Lisa. "I don't think they were very good ones, and I probably just blocked them out."

In Carmel, after three years at Hope Town, she progressed enough to enter public school. After Miss Olson's retirement in 1991, the two moved to Roswell, having become acquainted with the area through Miss Olson's sister, Doris Martin of Sandy Springs.

Lisa plays the omnichord, a keyboard instrument "that I run my arm down and it sounds like a harp." She hates math, likes English and Spanish, and has watched "L.A. Law" from the beginning.

A former poster child for Variety, an organization in New York state that assists disabled children, she has performed in its fund-raising telethons. For several summers, she has served as program director for 4- to 6-year-old inner-city children at New York's Camp Joy.

At tonight's banquet, her guests will include school chum Suzy Keegan; Roswell High Principal Tom Zachary; her staff aide at the school, Sandy Clarke; two officials from the Variety headquarters; and a former aide from Hope Town.

This summer, she will be a law office aide in downtown Atlanta.

At age 8, she was featured in a "March Of Dimes" film, "The Same Inside." (p. H1) Reprinted with permission of the *Atlanta Journal and Constitution*.

As in this story, the key to telling these stories is the *human element*. This is a people story. There must be plenty of emotion experienced by the primary characters/subjects in the article, as well as emotion experienced by the reader: horror, amusement, excitement, joy, depression, sympathy, sadness, anger.

Your assignment as a human interest article writer is to make your readers a vicarious participant in the drama. You react. You want Lisa Olson to succeed in school. You root for her. Your readers' personal involvement in the news draws them further into what you have written and into the publication generally. These articles are most often the odd and unusual stories about people.

Newspapers occasionally run human interest articles in sidebar format to accompany other articles on the same subject. Magazines like these articles to contrast with other types of articles, such as travel articles, interview articles, hard-hitting investigations, and regular departments and columns. You will find the time element is of secondary importance in many human interest articles. It mattered more in the story about Mathew Murray than it did in the story about Lisa Olson. In fact, some human interest subjects are really timeless and could be published just about any time. Articles such as those sprinkled throughout this chapter are as interesting to read now as they were when they were originally published. Often, the material that forms the story takes years, or even a lifetime, to evolve into the story. Only when the series of events culminates does the writer enter and begin to chronicle it for readers.

Fort Lauderdale Sun-Sentinel staff writer T.M. Shine (1993) wrote an interesting anniversary story about the little girl at the beach who was the model for the well-known Coppertone tanning products advertisements over the past four decades. This story is not affected by time and the events unfolded in the story occurred over a period of 40 years. This is his full story:

"I'm 68 years old," Wanda Villani says. "How much longer am I going to be around?"

Long enough to put the word out about her Coppertone baby one more time.

This gets her going every few years or so. This time it was an article about the 40th anniversary of Little Miss Coppertone and how Schering-Plough HealthCare Products has a big publicity campaign going to find a new

Coppertone girl and how so and so's daughter was the original Little Miss and
. . . .

"It's got to stop," says Villani, who lives in Lighthouse Point. "I get so mad. That's
my daughter up there, and Coppertone just keeps refusing to acknowledge it.
They like the controversy. It just gives them more publicity."

"To me the disputes about who was the original Little Miss just add to the aura
of the story," says Doug Petkus, Schering-Plough spokesman.

Back in '53, when the ad first appeared, Villani says her ex-husband, Peter Porter,
did the art work. "They didn't want the bathing-beauty image, so all that was
left was children and animals, " Villani says.

Porter always worked from live models and snapshots to do his drawings. He
looked at a few snapshots but ended up using his own daughter Robyn as the
model. Villani has one of the photos taken the day Robyn posed. "Her sisters
were laughing at her when she got her pants pulled down. She was so upset."

You look at the photo and say, "That's the Coppertone girl."

That's because it is, Villani says.

But, while Villani—and a few other families—have claimed to provide the model
over the years, Schering-Plough is sticking to its story. Company officials say
Joyce Ballantyne, a New York artist, was hired by a Miami ad agency to create
the logo and used her own 3-year-old daughter.

The only problem is, Ballantyne wasn't on the scene till the late '50s after the
original art work had been destroyed in a fire, Porter insists. "She made some
slight changes in the original—the hands and the pigtails—and may have very
well used her own daughter as a model. But this is all about the original, the one
that made the company famous in the early '50s. And the original is our daughter,
Robyn."

Porter says the situation has gotten so convoluted over the years that all he can
do now is laugh. "But my ex-wife wants some kind of vindication for our
daughter, and I can understand that."

It's not about money or compensation, Villani says. Over the years, she has told
all her family and friends about Robyn—now 42 and living in North Carolina—
being the Coppertone girl. And then one of these stories comes out in the paper
and makes her look like a liar.

"People I haven't heard from in years call up and say, 'Hey, I thought you said
your daughter is the Coppertone girl.'

"Well, she is." (pp. 1E, 6E) Reprinted with permission from the *Sun-Sentinel*, Fort
Lauderdale, Florida.

Writing human interest articles requires a unique touch on the part of the
writer. Not only do you have to have the right frame of mind to find the story,
you need the right strategy to handle it. Approach the usual story in a certain

way and it is still only a routine news item. If you take that same story and tell it with a *human angle*, it comes alive and becomes a better overall story, a human interest story.

Natural disasters and medical problems are common sources of some of the best human interest articles. Disasters such as tornadoes that strike in the Midwest, earthquakes, and floods are only a few examples of events that nature brings to test human resilience. Medical problems can touch the heart like nothing else, especially those involving suffering children. The stories of children who need transplants of organs, those who are handicapped, and those who have terminal diseases are always widely read and usually evoke a strong outpouring of support and offers to assist the families.

WHY WRITE ABOUT PEOPLE?

Names make news—still. This is the primary explanation if you wonder, "Why write about people?" People want to read about their neighbors and neighborhood businesses, especially when unusual events occur involving them. Articles about people, not institutions or other organizations, fill publications such as weekly newspapers and newsletters in small communities. Articles about people are being used more often in larger newspapers, too, to maintain readership. Local magazines can apply the same principle, but, of course, this becomes more difficult for national and general interest magazines. However, magazines that focus on personalities and human interest, such as *People* or *Parade*, are quite successful in the marketplace.

A newspaper, magazine, or newsletter that is writing about people only in a personalities-celebrities page or even in the entertainment section just is not doing its job in the mid-1990s. Readers seek more people-oriented writing in their newspapers, magazines, and newsletters—in all sections and departments. And, it follows, these people should be local people, not just always the meaningless names of people who live a thousand miles away.

So what makes people so interesting? Human interest feature writing is sometimes a catch-all phrase used in newsrooms and magazine offices to describe a story about people. Whatever the subject, these stories are interesting and popular with readers because they focus on people in unusual and odd situations. Just as all features tend to emphasize the unusual and odd, these articles do so in the most human fashion. People simply want to read about other people. Readers like to see how they "measure up" to others in similar situations. They enjoy seeing how others live, especially the celebrities, personalities, and leaders of our society. And as a human interest writer, you can bring the lives of these people to your readers.

Human situations and problems are the most popular subject of writers. Everyday occurrences translate into articles and even books partly because you, as a writer, also have that common experience. Your approaches and ideas often come from that base of experience you have had as a child and an adult, and these experiences, combined with your own values, make you a writer about people. You will see that, for example, someone's personal mannerisms or other behaviors might spark a story idea. As you begin to write human interest articles, you might have to depend on suggestions from others, but as you become more experienced as a writer, you will see these stories will be easier to identify and write.

There may be no more compelling human problem story within a strongly religious community than when one of its leaders falls from grace. Deeply religious Mexican-Americans in New Mexico felt the pain of such troubles when a revered and respected church leader was accused of sexual misconduct. *Boston Globe* staff writer James L. Franklin (1993) described the problems of the widely supported first Hispanic archbishop of Santa Fe, New Mexico:

ALBUQUERQUE, N.M.—Emilia Santillanes remembers the bells ringing all day in the church of San Felipe de Neri, the center of the 18th-century adobe settlement from which this modern city grew.

Not since J Day, the day that marked the Allied victory over Japan in World War II, had they tolled as they did that day in 1974.

The occasion: The pastor of San Felipe, Rev. Robert Fortune Sanchez, was named archbishop of Santa Fe, the first Hispanic archbishop in the United States.

He was a native son, the chancellor under Archbishop James Davis, and he was the top-ranked nominee of the three recommended by a committee of clergy and lay people named by the archbishop.

"We cried for joy. We were so proud to have an archbishop born in New Mexico and of Hispanic descent," said Santillanes, who cried again as she read the column she had written for the *Albuquerque Journal* on the fall this year of Archbishop Robert Sanchez.

Even in 1974, some knew that the popular priest had not always stayed within the lines. Catherine Stewart-Roache, who served on the committee, said in an interview that panel members knew Sanchez had been involved with a woman in Albuquerque.

"But in the context of the 1970s, with so many clergy opting for laicization—in my parish we had seven priests in five years who left to get married—Sanchez seemed to have indicated . . . that he wasn't going to get married," said Stewart-Roache, who is a hospital chaplain. "I said, with others, that he would make the best candidate."

Sanchez, 59, offered to resign on March 19 after acknowledging to associates that he had had sexual relations with at least five young women from well-known New Mexico families in the 1970s and 1980s. He was less explicit in two letters to the people of the archdiocese.

The result was great anger and even denial. Some in the Hispanic community blamed the archbishop's accusers, particularly because the charges were first made in a television program, a CBS 60 Minutes broadcast in March. Others, from a variety of backgrounds, are still urging him to return.

Church officials complain about news coverage. Reporters have asked about the archbishop and the handling of sexual abuse charges against 14 Santa Fe priests and residents of the Paraclete House in Jemez Springs, a retreat for clergy with alcoholism and other problems.

Bruce Pasternack, a lawyer who says he represents the three women who took part in the 60 Minutes broadcast, sees a connection between Sanchez's personal life and the problem of sexual abuse by priests in the archdiocese.

"The tragedy is the requirement of celibacy. Robert Sanchez for his whole life wanted to help people, and to help people he made a vow that nobody could keep . . . . When priests and families told him Father So-and-So had molested children, Robert Sanchez was paralyzed by hypocrisy. His whole sexual activity crippled him."

Santa Fe is a rural diocese, with 90 parishes and 300,000 Catholics in 75,000 square miles.

Relatively few of the Hispanic and Native American Catholics who make up a large part of the local population have become priests, so many clergy come to New Mexico from elsewhere.

In this setting, Sanchez was a reconciler. He changed the name of a chapel in his cathedral in Santa Fe from La Conquistadora, celebrating the Spanish conquest of the heathen Americas, to Our Lady Queen of Peace, and he was careful to visit native peoples on the feast day of their patron saints.

Although Hispanics predominate in the state and in the Santa Fe church, they, too, had felt at odds with its leadership, which is often drawn from outsiders.

Some priests and bishops "have no concept of our culture and make no allowances for tradition, which has caused a lot of pain," Santillanes said. "Being one of our own, Archbishop Sanchez was able to pull us all together, and everyone was accepted without judgment." (p. 5B) Reprinted with permission of *The Boston Globe*.

THE ASSOCIATION-IDENTIFICATION ELEMENT

The successes of regional and city magazines and community sections of major metropolitan newspapers in recent years have been due, in part, to the fact that these publications are writing and editing their editorial products for *local* markets. The appeal to readers is broad, but one strong reason for the local appeal is the ability of readers to identify with the people, places, and things that they read about. About two decades ago, leading daily newspapers such as the *Philadelphia Inquirer, Orlando Sentinel, Milwaukee Journal,* and *Chicago Tribune* began to publish specially edited neighborhood sections that are "zoned" or distributed on a regional level within the larger market that the newspaper serves. These newspapers hoped they would be better able to write stories about people in the smaller neighborhoods and communities—the cities within the cities. The space for these stories became available because smaller advertisers could now afford to purchase less costly advertising space for their shops and stores. And editors, guided by their own intuition as well as current market research, decided the best way to fill the sections was with a large amount of human interest feature material about the neighborhoods' people, churches, and schools. Most editors and experts feel the approach is working.

The same applies to the magazine industry, but in a slightly different way. Regional and city magazines in major metropolitan areas have developed to reflect a lifestyle of young adults in dozens of metropolitan areas such as New York, Los Angeles, Chicago, Atlanta, Miami, Cincinnati, Indianapolis, Orlando, and Sacramento over the past three decades. Yet these magazines filled another void in the metropolitan market also, providing still other outlets for human interest articles as well as other forms of reporting about urban and suburban life.

Other types of magazines also depend on human interest articles to draw readers. General interest personality magazines such as *People* focus on celebrity human interest writing. *McCall's* and other women's magazines draw heavily on this category of features. *Reader's Digest* has always used these types of features. Columns such as "Life in These United States" are just one example. Small town daily and weekly newspapers have traditionally depended on a large number of human interest articles in their editions.

Writer Hank Stuever of *The Albuquerque Tribune* found a superb human interest story in what might have seemed like a routine wedding. Stuever wrote a remarkably detailed account of the wedding of a local couple. His newspaper produced an entire special section for the package of Stuever's article, numerous color photographs, and a chart detailing the costs of the event. The couple, from families of modest means, got married and celebrated at a reception attended by 800 persons at the Albuquerque Convention Center at a cost of about $25,000 to their families, themselves, and their friends. The special 8-page Lifetimes section told the story of how the young man and woman met, dated, and became engaged. The story then re-created the tension of arranging and carrying out the wedding and the party afterward. Stuever told readers about the bachelor and bachelorette parties, too. To do all this, he allowed the participants to describe their feelings and thoughts through numerous direct quotations. Stuever also provided rich description throughout the story. Early into the story, Stuever (1992) explained to readers what this feature attempted to do:

> This is a story about a wedding, one of those runaway trains in life where you set the date months ahead of time and figure it will never get here, only to marvel at the speed with which everything collides. Absolute limits are overspent

anyway. Someone could get too drunk and say the wrong thing at the wrong time.

It's a North Valley drama as simple as this: A pretty secretary with a spiral perm meets and falls in love with a nice man who drives a pickup truck and coaches Little League. Rings are purchased, a reception is planned and tears, invariably, are shed. Tensions surface in the nightmares of a bride-to-be, images of wet hair and jilted lovers broken suddenly by the blare of the snooze alarm and the soothing voice of daddy.

Good morning, mija . . . .(p. B1)

Stuever not only told readers the story behind this major event in the lives of these two families, but forced readers to wonder whether this sort of event is "too big, too much, too many, too this, too that?" Stuever wrote, "In the North Valley, two families celebrate and endure the traditions, expenses and emotions of a summer wedding" (1992, p. B1). The story, like all love stories should, began when the couple met. This one ended, appropriately, when the newlyweds returned from their Las Vegas honeymoon. "We had fun and that's what counts," Stuever wrote in the final sentence, offering the couple's ultimate justification for it all. Stuever's article was honored as a finalist in 1993 for the Pulitzer Prize in feature writing.

You can make your human interest article easier for the reader to enjoy by providing lots of direct quotations from the people you are writing about. This is what strengthened Stuever's memorable wedding story. You can also improve the story by giving the reader detail and description, as was discussed in the preceding chapter, especially when photographs are not used. Direct quotations capture the way the person speaks and, sometimes, how the person thinks. They enliven the human interest article because quotations allow you to tell the story in the source's own words. Description makes the person come

---

THE ELEMENTS OF A HUMAN INTEREST ARTICLE

McCall's managing editor Don McKinney (1986) identifies three types of human interest stories:

1. *An extraordinary experience.* This type of story involves natural disasters such as floods, earthquakes, blizzards, hurricanes, fires, and the like. Persons who survive these have a story to tell. There is life in jeopardy or even death. There is suffering. There is property loss, often of priceless and precious possessions.

2. *A common problem.* Men and women who experience a relatively common human problem and succeed in battling it have a good story to tell. It may be a singular experience or a family experience. The story focuses on how this person dealt with the tension and stress in a situation that readers can easily identify with while reading the article.

3. *A national issue.* People who suffer because of problems that are on the minds of the citizens of a nation are often heavily in demand and heavily read.

alive in your reader's mind. How is your subject dressed? How is the person's hair styled? What is the person's occupation?

It all comes down to one point—human interest articles must be written and edited so readers can see some of themselves in the article. You need to write in terms of people and not in terms of numbers or widgets. Readers do not "see" themselves in an article directly, of course, but they can imagine themselves as the principals of your article. Readers can see this person could have been themselves or is somehow like themselves. The events are described in a way that readers can see them occurring in their own homes or in their workplaces. A reader should be able to say, "Wow! That could have happened to me!" All of this occurs because of the common purpose, lifestyle, ideas, values, sensations, or characteristics of the human condition between readers and the subject of your article. It is the association and identification element of a human interest article that permits readers to think, feel, and even act as they imagine the experiences of the person about whom you write.

THE EMOTION ELEMENT

Emotion is a powerful element in any writing. Novelists use it in their work. In nonfiction, it is used to create closer ties between the reader and the article. With emotional elements in the right mix, you might produce one of those articles that readers just cannot put down until it is finished—regardless of the length.

Emotion, psychologists tell us, has four general levels: intensity of feeling, level of tension, degree of pleasantness or unpleasantness, and degree of complexity. Emotion is a strong feeling, either general or specific, about a subject. It is manifested in a number of physical and psychological ways. The most common emotions in human experience, of course, are joy, anger, fear, and grief.

There are also emotions that we write about that are associated with various physical experiences such as pain, disgust, and delight. Some other emotions are tied to our own appraisals of ourselves. These include feelings of success and failure, pride and shame, and guilt and remorse. Many times, in reading a good human interest story, you can help readers experience emotions pertaining to other people. These include feelings of love and hate.

Some of the stories written from Bosnia-Herzegovina during the civil war there have been head-shaking, powerful accounts of the human condition. These stories are dominated by emotions such as love and hate. *Palm Beach Post* staff writer Nancy Nusser (1993), who was in the war-torn region on assignment for her newspaper, wrote this lead to a story about a Bosnian woman who was raped by a Serbian soldier and who gave birth to the resulting child. The story is about the hate felt by this woman for the soldier and the "Chetnik" child:

TUZLA, Bosnia-Herzegovina—The pale Bosnian woman sitting in a health clinic said she hates her newborn son and could not bring herself to look at him before nurses took him away.

The baby's father is the Serb soldier who raped her.

"The child is a Chetnik," she said. "I hate the child. My brother was in a concentration camp for 10 months, and I was raped by Chetniks."

What some call hate of the baby, other victims describe as fear, said Amra Mesic of Tuzla, who has counseled rape victims.

"We are afraid that deep inside they might also be Chetniks," she explained.

In Bosnia, Muslim women generally are Westernized in clothing and education. Many look as though they would be comfortable in an American mall. Though not intensely religious, many hold tight to traditional values—opposing sex outside of marriage and convinced that rape is almost like death.

More to the point for those who were raped, the aggressors were Serb soldiers who often also killed or imprisoned the women's families and burned their homes.

Pope John Paul II has urged the raped women of Bosnia to bear the children.

Some, like the 20-year-old Muslim woman, do give birth, but say that keeping the child is beyond the limit for them.

"If I had gotten pregnant and couldn't have an abortion, I would probably have killed myself," said an 18-year-old rape victim, also interviewed in Tuzla.

She and the 30-year-old woman withheld their names . . . .(p. 1A)

As Nusser does here with such strongly felt emotion as the hatred between the Bosnians and Serbs, you should seek a strong emotional theme in a possible human interest article. It might be the unifying element you need to write a good piece. Remember that emotion can be disruptive to your readers. It can be arousing. These reactions will link your article to the reader. Emotion is often the difference in an average feature story and an award-winning feature. For example, Dan Luzadder earned a Pulitzer Prize for the *Fort Wayne News-Sentinel* in 1983 for his description of the dreams destroyed by a devastating Indiana flood in Spring 1982. The impact of his article came from the myriad of emotions conveyed to readers who could identify with his description of homes, cars, businesses, and other important possessions under water.

Stories such as this inextricably link the reader and the story. They do so with honesty and clarity. Writers let the emotions do the job and do not have to overwrite the story to make a point. They remain simple because of the double duty that the emotion element carries in the story. Although 1990s journalists will not write the type of "sob story" that was common early in this century, emotion remains the thread to tie together many human interest stories. They are stories from the heart.

Occasionally, writers will encounter stories that have to be told but, for overwhelming reasons, they cannot help but become involved in the story. This sort of reaction is quite normal, writers being people themselves, so it might become an asset if handled well. Compelling stories such as these will demand that you write first person or write third person with your own perceptions and reactions becoming a part of the article. It is hard, for example, not to react to a child dying of liver disease who needs a transplant.

Writer Madeleine Blais won the 1980 Pulitzer Prize for feature writing for a 1979 article about an old man who was a World War I conscientious objector and who had been given a dishonorable military discharge but who sought to upgrade it to honorable status. Blais, who wrote that article for *The Miami Herald's Tropic* magazine, likes to get very involved with the topics of her articles and the sources themselves:

> Sometimes when I do stories, I can really tell that I've done something that's really worthwhile. I can tell it sort of lives very vividly in my mind while I'm doing it. Even afterwards, I have this level of caring about the people, almost like a kind of friendship forms because of the story. At some point in the research something happens. Either somebody says something or there's an event that moves me in some way, that seems important to me. And then I start feeling this passion about creating through the reader the exact same psychological steps that I went through to get to the point where these people were moving to me . . . to do that for the reader as well. (Blais, 1984)

You need to remember when you do react to such a story, your own journalistic observations can become affected by the experience. If this is not desired, and in some types of feature writing it is not, Rivers (1992) suggests solving this possible problem: "When an event makes a writer react emotionally, his or her impressions are especially vulnerable to distortion. You can often resolve this problem by recording your impressions immediately after the event to capture its details and then later, at a more tranquil time, assessing your first account to find and correct for distortion" (p. 141).

FINDING UNIQUE PEOPLE STORIES

Author Daniel Williamson (1975) has stated that most human interest feature writers are "incurable people lovers." They have to, as he says, "relish the strange, inconsistent antics of the human race and, to a large degree, earn their livelihoods by astutely observing and reporting these antics" (p. 112). Therefore, Williamson observes that if a man bites a dog, it is not news as much as it is a human interest article. You'll soon find, if you have not already, that human interest stories are often about people down on their luck, the people in society who have been dealt a losing hand.

In the early part of the 1990s, one of the most significant social issues involved a person's right to die. Numerous terminally ill patients wanted dignified ways to die, such as those provided by hospices, or the chance to live their last days at home with family and other loved ones. Some wanted to, and did, take their own lives to end their suffering. Regardless of personal feelings about the issue, there were legal issues involved in many states. In Michigan, a doctor assisted many terminally ill individuals and instructed them how to commit suicide. Most Americans became familiar with the cases and patients of controversial Michigan physician Jack Kevorkian. A slowly dying Ohio woman sought to use his services because she suffered from terminal disease, but the state lawmakers of Ohio, like those in the state of Michigan, would not permit it. Her story was told by writer Linda Vaccariello (1993) for *Cincinnati* magazine. Here's how the article ran:

> One Sunday afternoon last May, Jean Frenz was doing the same thing thousands of other Cincinnatians were doing. She was mowing her lawn.
>
> When she finished, she stopped her riding mower, stepped off, and fell flat on her face.
>
> This May she won't be mowing her lawn. If she has her wish, she won't even be around to see it.
>
> Jean Frenz has ALS—amyotropic lateral sclerosis. When she was diagnosed, she learned the real name for Lou Gehrig's Disease. She also learned that the chances of surviving ALS are the same as they were when the Iron Horse of baseball died fifty years ago. None.
>
> But worst of all, Frenz says, was learning what her remaining life would be like. This is not the way she wants to live. Not the way she wants to die, either. She can't change her life. She wants to have a choice about her death.
>
> Frenz is too frail to be a political activist. (That's a role taken by her daughter, Karla Addington-Smith.) But she wants to explain why she believes assisted suicide is her fundamental right, a right that ought not to be denied by Ohio lawmakers. Whether or not one agrees, her experience represents a hard reality that refuses to be reshaped by politics, medicine or religion.
>
> Frenz was diagnosed with ALS last July. Following the May tumble, she had fallen once on the job (she owns her own cleaning company) and felt a persistent weakness. The 56-year-old woman, a lively, independent divorcee, simply didn't feel like herself. She didn't sound like herself, either; her voice had taken on a peculiar quality. Then one day in the grocery store, reaching for change, her hands began to move in slow motion. "I thought, this is something really serious."
>
> What followed was two months of specialists, tests, examinations, and labored phone calls when the results of those tests and examinations were not forthcoming from those specialists. Doctors later explained to Frenz and her family that pinpointing this condition is a process of elimination, there is no definitive test.

But Frenz finds it ironic that a friend calling long-distance heard about her physical problems, listened to her faltering voice, and said, "Sounds like you have ALS." Two months and $20,000 worth of doctors' bills later, she got the same medical opinion.

Frenz felt that she was being passed around during those weeks, then dismissed when her diagnosis was final. "Everybody got a piece of me," she says. "Then they sent me home to die."

Today she is in touch with only two physicians: her family doctor—very compassionate and concerned, she says—and Dr. Jack Kevorkian.

Everyone remembers how *The Pride of the Yankees* ends, with Gary Cooper delivering his farewell to the stadium crowd. But that isn't how Lou Gehrig's life ended. When Frenz began to understand how her life could end, when she fully grasped the consequences of ALS, she contacted Kevorkian, the controversial Michigan physician who has assisted terminally ill patients to commit suicide.

ALS attacks motor neurons in the brain and spinal column which control the movement of voluntary muscles. It is a progressive disease; limbs become weak, reflexes are lost, muscles atrophy. Included in the devastation are muscles that control speech, chewing and swallowing. In the normal course of the disease, death comes two to five years after the onset of symptoms. Most ALS patients are eventually supported on a respirator, tube fed, mute and immobile.

But aware. ALS spares the mind and the senses throughout the course of the disease, encasing them in a fishbowl of a body that cannot respond. "In the later stages, I will only have use of my eyes," she says. "That is devastating."

To her daughter, this disease virtually defines "hopeless." Terminal, progressive, untreatable as well as incurable. Addington-Smith has a mountain of material she collected in the days after her mother's diagnosis, piles of research, notes from calls to major medical centers all over the country. "It was like *Lorenzo's Oil*. When we first learned about it, we were determined to fight this. We were going to be the one-in-a-million."

Reality set in fast. ALS is rare enough that drug research is limited. One of the few possibilities Addington-Smith found was a treatment that was being prepared for clinical trials at UC Medical Center, a treatment that might slow the progressive muscle weakness caused by the disease. But by the time the study began in January, it was virtually pointless for Frenz to participate, her daughter says. She was already profoundly debilitated.

As this story is prepared, Frenz can still speak, but with difficulty. She can swallow small bites of food, but cannot feed herself. She can use the toilet with assistance, but cannot turn herself in bed. As her muscles deteriorate, the pain in her joints gets worse.

Her son, Eric Addington, is now her primary caregiver, assisted by nurses' aides during the week and his sister on weekends. He points out that this situation is neither short-term nor static. It is permanent and progressively worse.

"I tell my children it's like an inchworm," Frenz says. "Every day it inches up on you a little more."

And every day there are hints at what the future will hold. Frenz tells the story of the nurse who came to care for her one afternoon. The woman fixed lunch on a tray, set it down in front of Frenz and her virtually useless hands, and went into another room. "She forgot to feed me," Frenz says with amazement. "I thought, oh Jean, if this happens when you can still talk, what will happen when you have no voice?"

Within a few weeks of receiving her diagnosis, Frenz abandoned the hope of a cure, or even the fantasy of a miracle. "I realized I was going to be getting very bad. And I didn't want to lie here and be in that situation. I would rather die." That's when she told her son that she wanted to call "that doctor."

It was several months before he complied. But eventually he placed the call, gave his mother the phone, and she said, "Dr. Kevorkian, I need your help."

"And she changed," he recalls. Frenz says she felt a tremendous relief. "I felt as though it would soon be over."

Hope is a relative concept. For Frenz and her son and daughter, it was the possibility that the Michigan doctor would assistant in a suicide. They sent the information he requested—a written statement, medical records, the attending physician's name and number—and continued to have regular telephone conversations. When Michigan passed an emergency law barring assisted suicides and Kevorkian was investigated for the circumstances surrounding the death of patient Hugh Gale, the family was no longer able to have direct contact with him.

Now Frenz says she is back where she started. She doesn't want to live the life and die the death that she sees ahead of her, and she doesn't see any alternative. She does not have the ability to take her own life—cannot swallow pills, cannot die by her own hand.

What she can do is talk about how she feels about the legislation pending in Columbus that would make assisted suicide a crime. Recently her daughter has been quite public about the issue, and, Addington-Smith says, "I know people think I am using my mother." (She points out that terminally ill people can't very readily show up in Columbus for public hearings.) Both women are willing to risk the backlash that could come with public exposure.

"I don't want people protesting in my front yard," Frenz allows from the hospital bed that now occupies much of her living room. "And I couldn't go through a court battle," she adds (somewhat needlessly; it would be difficult for her to leave the house). "But I want to get this before the public."

It's a basic right, she says: a terminally ill person of sound mind with no recourse for cure or recovery has the right to chose to end his or her life. "If I could help one person be able to choose to exit without the law trying to control what he can or can't do, it would be worth it. It's not a lawmaker's issue, it's a human issue."

And, in her view, the most personal decision there is. "No one can realize what a nightmare this is . . . how horrible this is unless you live through it.

"I was healthy all my life. Then, all of a sudden, I fall.

"If it can happen to me, it can happen to anyone."

Public controversy during a crisis isn't something most families would court. A friend of Addington-Smith's has argued with her, comparing it to abortion, an analogy which she says is "totally unfair." The family doesn't much like to talk about Kevorkian, because they feel the media have sensationalized and misrepresented a man whom they have found to be highly compassionate and extremely ethical. Addington-Smith's guest column in the *Enquirer* attracted a caller who told her the illness was caused because "Your mother isn't wearing the armor of Christ."

True, tiny Jean Frenz, with her gray curls framing delicate features, does not look like she is wearing anybody's armor. But she is far from defenseless. She has formed a bond with her adult children which is stronger because of her illness. She has the comfort and support of the minister and friends at her church in Kenwood. Her straightforward approach is such that she isn't much bothered by the "armor of Christ" remark.

And while she says she is "as helpless as a baby," she still has emotional strength. She is most sad when she talks about her grandchildren. One is 3, the other was born just nine months ago—the same day she learned she had ALS. They're so young that their memories of her will have to be augmented by family stories. Like all family stories, they will recount the way Jean Frenz lived and died.

"I hope they understand I gave it my best shot." (pp. 84–86) Reprinted with permission of *Cincinnati* magazine.

For human interest articles that are based on human suffering and illness such as the Jean Frenz story, the ones that seem to touch readers most, you have to proceed with caution. Check medical facts and diagnoses. Be clear about the situation. Medical and legal issues need to be explained carefully and in detail. For example, in Vaccariello's article, she is careful and thorough in explaining the medical condition of Jean Frenz, but Vaccariello does not do the same effective job with the legal issues in the Cincinnati case. Had she given the legal issues the same attention, it would not be uncertain about what prevents Kevorkian from talking to an Ohioan (the case would not involve Michigan law). Ohio's current legal environment or what has been proposed is not a major part of the story.

Some sources may attempt to fool you. In cases such as that of Jean Frenz, there was no doubt of her illness after visiting the patient or talking to her physician. Of course, most experiences told to you by a source will be true. However, a story occasionally will be exaggerated or simply untrue. Not long ago, newspapers and magazines in South Florida were contacted by a woman who was having difficulty getting public assistance for her ill child. She painted a picture of bureaucratic delays that might cost the child its life. A newspaper reporter checked the woman's story and found that most of the facts were true. Yet, because she did not reveal all the facts about the illness, there were missing pieces. The reporter found out from a physician whom he had telephoned for background that the illness was serious, but not as immediate a problem as the woman claimed. In fact, the child could expect to live a number of years before the illness turned serious or fatal. The newspaper decided not to publish the written story in light of the new information. Another newspaper, however, *did not* check the facts as closely and did run the story.

Children, as you saw in *The Boston Globe* story at the beginning of the chapter, make good human interest subjects regardless of their plight or the location of the story. Although it has been argued that the local human interest story is preferred, occasionally some stories are so compelling that geography matters little.

To find these sorts of stories, feature writers must keep in touch with the world around them and people in that world. You will find the stories in many places. For starters, try the local courthouse. Criminal and civil courtrooms are filled with this type of human drama that has, for various reasons, reached the need to be resolved before a judge. Usually the court cases that make the best human interest stories have a broader social issue element within them, *McCall's* managing editor Don McKinney (1986) explains.

Certainly good human interest articles come out of hospitals and other health care institutions. Similarly, you can expect to find good stories at schools and churches. Government social services offices can often bring you in contact with good stories, too, if you can build dependable sources there. Each of these is a place where people gather and interact. You can expect to learn a lot if you take the time to talk and listen.

Established writers know these stories find their way to them. If you are new to a community, it might take some time before people seek you out to tell you their stories, but eventually they do. Certainly neighbors and acquaintances often can lead you to stories. Listen to what they have to say. Remember people you meet and where they live and work.

Even other publications can produce good ideas for you if you take time to read the newspapers, magazines, and newsletters in your area carefully. Reading carefully for run-of-the-mill news stories, you might find a missing angle or perhaps the next step that was not taken. Try it and see for yourself.

In searching for that good human interest article, award-winning feature writer Madeleine Blais (1984) recommends not heading into the story right away. Give yourself time to look around even when you have a subject before you zero in on a theme or unifying thread. "My technique . . . was listening, hanging out, absorbing—a kind of inventory. It seemed ridiculous to be standing here stockpiling every little quote or whatever because I really needed more to get impressions than facts," she explained about her strategy on one assignment (Blais, 1984). Blais also suggests looking for the *little* things in your prospective articles. "I love, as a writer," she says, "to take things that are not readily observable as monumental and try to find the monuments in them."

Minnesota free-lance writer Steve Perlstein (personal communication, 1993) adds that human interest article writing often depends on the editor you serve:

> Human interest is dicier [to free-lance] because it is so subjective. What one editor thinks is a great human interest piece, another thinks is just dumb. I wrote a piece for *Modern Maturity* about Garrison Keillor and how he puts together his radio show every week. That magazine thought it was a wonderful idea and commissioned it almost on the spot, but when I tried to sell it to other markets I got nowhere. The second book I'm working on is going to be 300 solid pages of human interest—the chronicle of the first year of the Northern League, an independent minor league, which one principal has called "the second chance league." It will be made up of young hopefuls passed up by the big-league organizations and veterans who've been released and are looking for another go-round. It's dripping with emotional potential. My original agent tried four major publishers who thought this would make a lousy book and who wouldn't spend a cent on it; that agent eventually agreed with those editors. My new agent showed it to editors at five other major houses, and every one is bidding for the book.

INSPIRATIONAL, MOTIVATIONAL HUMAN INTEREST

Inspirational features are a type of how-to motivational essay. The purpose of such articles is to arouse and prompt readers to take action of some form to reach an objective or goal, even to set an objective or goal and strive for it. Or to get involved in a social movement, maybe; to perform on the job better; to stick to a diet; to break a bad habit. Inspirational feature writers often offer their successful experiences, or the experiences of others, in describing events that have changed a life or otherwise made life better for an individual or group, or helped some people improve themselves, sell more, or succeed in what they want to do. These are typically short articles with strong personal and human interest elements.

Inspirational and motivational feature articles are a growing interest area for some magazines. Magazines such as *The American Salesman, Reader's Digest, Home Office Computing, Personal Selling Power,* and *Selling* use them frequently.

One free-lance feature writer who specializes in motivational, or inspirational, human interest articles is Susanna K. Hutcheson (personal communication, 1993). She uses a very simple formula based on personal experiences for these stories. Here's how she says she does it: "They're quite short really. They're an interesting article to write in that they require no interviews. They're basically an essay based on some experience the author has had that will inspire others. They require excellent writing and an ability to inspire with your words."

YOUR BEST SOURCES FOR HUMAN INTEREST STORIES

People: Interviewing and Observing
    Neighbors
    Workplace friends, acquaintances

Institutions: Interviewing and Observing
    Hospitals
    Social services offices
    Schools
    Churches, synagogues
    Funeral homes
    Civil courts
    Criminal courts

Places: Interviewing and Observing
    Parks, playgrounds
    Clubhouses
    Festivals and celebrations
    Senior citizen centers
    Missions, centers for homeless
    Schools
    Churches, synagogues
    Halfway houses, rehabilitation centers
    Courthouses
    Libraries

Hutcheson says she has a formula that results in two approaches to the articles. She follows one or the other in her work:

> Often I write a very brief outline before I write. But more often than not, I simply start to write and then do a rewrite and then a polish. I have found that the more of these I write, the less work they require. Most of them are from 700 to 1,200 words and take little time. I try to paint a picture for the reader. I first lay out the problem. In one that I did on insurance sales, the problem was making more sales. Then I use a few quotes from prominent people on the subject, put in some facts and figures, and back it all up with personal experiences or experiences of others. I always wrap up my articles with a summary of what I have said at the beginning. I leave the reader feeling good and thinking to himself or herself, "I can do that!"

PERSONALITY-CELEBRITY FEATURES

The international fascination with celebrities of all types is not a new one. We commonly read articles about entertainment, sports, political, social, literary, and religious celebrities. Many general interest newspapers and specialized magazines and newsletters have, though, placed a new emphasis on coverage of personalities and newsmakers in film, music, sports, and other entertainment areas, for instance. You do not have to look far to find people-oriented columns and sections in your daily newspapers. Many newspapers devote prominent portions of their news sections, as well as larger amounts of feature sections, to personality-celebrity news. Other publications simply edit their wire or bureau news into personality-celebrity roundup columns featuring a half dozen or so items and pictures about well-known people. And some, of course, exist solely to report about celebrities. However, the point is clear— these items reflect the growing public interest in celebrities and personalities. These features tell us the daily activities of famous people—with whom they are seen, where they are going, their latest work, their personal lives. And, surely, there are emotional stories that can be told about the famous as well. Because these people may be internationally known, or even just known across their communities, others care about them and what happens to them. When a local radio disc jockey falls ill, if a popular nightclub singer gets married, or members of a royal family are having problems, the events become human interest story material. You write about this in the same manner in which you would handle any other human interest story.

The ongoing emphasis on people stories, combined with the growing attention to personality-celebrity news, is a response to the strong demand for personality human interest features in newspapers, magazines, and newsletters.

WRITING HUMAN INTEREST

You have a number of alternatives in writing a human interest article. Much of the time, the material you have collected can dictate the form of the story. Organizationally, you often choose from these approaches:

1. Suspended interest approach.
2. Storyteller's chronological approach.
3. Narrative approach.

The *suspended interest approach* is a pyramid organizational strategy. The lead is only a partial summary of what happened, saving resolution of the human drama for a later point in the article. Most of the time resolution comes at the ending. The article's body, or main section, is a description of the main events in chronological order. Finally, the article winds up with its outcome, or revelation, in the conclusion-climax. This approach has its advantages, primarily that it forces the reader to stay with your story for the big ending or "moral to the story." This plan is not unlike that of the novelist who unveils the murderer on the last page of his mystery.

The second major strategy for organizing human interest articles is to approach writing as you would tell a story: Tell the entire story in *chronological order*. This sort of plan is simple and easy to write once you get your facts straight. The sequence of events does the work for you. This sort of approach does not fit all human interest stories. It works well when events culminate with a major action on the part of a principal source in the article.

Narrative organization is also easy to use and works particularly well for beginning writers. Like the chronological form, this approach is dictated by the information you collect. Your major decision will be how to start a narrative article, because you are not necessarily bound to start with the first event in any sequence. *McCall's* Don McKinney (1986) says a human interest narrative article lead should "lure the reader (and this includes the editor, who will decide whether the reader gets a chance at it or not) into your story and capture that person's interest so that he cannot put it down until he learns how it comes out" (p. 27).

Narrative organization, then, just tells what happened by running from beginning to end. In this case, narrative is different from the suspended interest because the best material is saved for the end, and different from chronological because it does not lead with the first event or end with the last event. You have the most flexibility with narrative writing by not forcing what becomes the beginning, middle, or end through a chosen structure. You can merge elements of the story using narrative organization, pulling from two divergent tracks, or themes, if needed.

Pulitzer Prize-winning feature writer Madeleine Blais, now a college journalism professor, likes to use metaphors to structure her articles whenever possible. Blais (1984) says: "The structure should rise from the material. The way to make it happen is to make yourself an authority, to know so much about your subject that you know almost as much about your subject as your subject knows about himself."

PROFESSIONAL'S POINT OF VIEW

Maryln Schwartz
Dallas Morning News

Sometimes writers find it hard to distinguish between a feature and a news story. This is the best way I can explain it:

We all know the biblical story of Noah and the Ark. Just before it rained for 40 days and 40 nights, Noah built an ark. He took his family and two of every kind of animal that was then living on earth. Every living creature on the ark was saved from the flood.

That is a news story.

If I was writing about that event, I'd want to talk to Mrs. Noah, who was probably having to clean up after all those animals for 40 days and 40 nights.

That's a feature story.

When I'm writing my newspaper column, I look for the small details that give the readers a clear view of the big picture.

For instance, when Prince Charles visited New Mexico, I wanted to give an example of what it means to be royalty. I didn't want to just write that people were bowing, because we already know that people bow to royalty. So I just watched for a little while.

Then I noticed that Prince Charles was the only person at the party who wasn't wearing a name tag. And this wasn't a "B" party. Cary Grant was there and he wore a name tag.

This is the kind of touch that separates real royalty from mere legend. I did the same thing recently when I was watching the Miss America contestants give their predictable prepageant TV interviews. They were all insisting they weren't beauty queens, they had a message to give the world. They didn't want to discuss sex appeal. They wanted to talk about nuclear disarmament.

Then I would flip channels to interviews of the presidential candidates. The political analysts kept trying to talk about Michael Dukakis' charisma or George Bush's sex appeal.

I knew I had my column when I began to realize that politics and beauty pageants have somehow become confused with each other: "Would someone please tell me what's going on? Why is it that Miss Montana can't wait to discuss Manuel Noriega and George Bush only seems to want to discuss his grandchildren?"

To write a good feature story requires as much observing as it does writing. You can have a beautifully crafted story, but no one will really care unless you have something to say. Information is the most important aspect. There will always be an editor who can help you turn a better phrase. But all the editing in the world isn't going to help if your information isn't interesting.

You don't have to have been at a major news event to find a good feature story. And you just have to train yourself to see details that other people overlook.

Actress Farrah Fawcett was the most interviewed actress in the country when she was starring in the "Charlie's Angels" TV show. My editor asked me to do a story and to be sure to mention that the actress had been named one of the "10 Most Beautiful" on campus when she attended the University of Texas.

The story had been done again and again. I didn't think anyone would even want to read it. Instead, I decided to find out what had happened to the other nine most beautiful. The story went on the wire and was used in about 40 newspapers.

I got my information by phone. It took only 2 days (Schwartz, personal communication, 1988).

Maryln Schwartz is an award-winning feature writer and columnist for the *Dallas Morning News*.

7

Profiles and Personality Sketches

In a recent issue of *The New Yorker* magazine, writer Susan Orlean (1993) profiled an unlikely subject: an inner-city New York City high school student. This teenager was an athlete, and Orlean's article told readers how Felipe Lopez was handling his upcoming chance at big-time college and professional basketball. Her article spotlighted the young man's future, and this is how she used a touch of contrast to set the profile's focus and context in the opening:

> White men in suits follow Felipe Lopez everywhere he goes. Felipe lives in Mott Haven, in the South Bronx. He is a junior at Rice High School, which is on the corner of 124th Street and Lenox Avenue, in Harlem, and he plays guard for the Rice Raiders. The white men are ubiquitous. They rarely miss one of Felipe's games or tournaments. They have absolute recall of his best minutes of play. They are authorities on his physical condition. They admire his feet, which are big and pontoon-shaped, and his wrists, which have a loose, silky motion. Not long ago, I sat with the white men at a game between Rice and All Hallows High School. My halftime entertainment was listening to a debate between two of them—a college scout and a Westchester contractor who is a high school basketball fan—about whether Felipe had grown a half inch over Christmas break. "I know this kid," the scout said as the second half started. "A half inch is not something I would miss." The white men believe that Felipe is the best high school basketball player in the country . . . . (p. 74)

Some profile writers will tell you that profiles are short, vivid biographies. Orlean's substantial profile of Felipe Lopez is much like that. We learn a great deal about Lopez in her profile, even in just her lead. Profiles such as these are similar to the efforts of portrait painters or sculptors. An artist paints a life-like portrait of a person with oils or watercolors. A sculptor might use clay or marble to create a bust. As a writer, you can also create a portrait of a person using your command of some very different communication tools—words and language.

Still, personality sketches and profiles are a bit different from biographies and different from other portrait art forms. Obviously, a profile for a newspaper, magazine, or newsletter will not be as long as a book-sized biography. Some newspaper, magazine, and newsletter profiles do run thousands of words and some are even occasionally published in installments. And some are excerpts from book-length studies of an individual—biographies. Most, however, are much shorter—in the 750-word to 1,500-word range—and more concentrated and focused. Writer and former magazine editor Art Spikol (1979) says article profiles require a different treatment because of their length, but also because article profiles have different focus: "A biography deals with the entire life of the subject, whereas in the profile . . . the focus is current. The question, 'Why are we interested in this person?' is always answered, 'Because he is such and such *today*'" (p. 8).

Daniel Williamson (1975) calls profiles in-depth stories about an individual designed to capture "the essence of his personality" (p. 151). Profiles have been a part of the nonfiction writer's portfolio for generations. In the early part of this century, magazines in New York, particularly *The New Yorker*, began to publish personality-based stories labeled *profiles*. *The New Yorker* readers thumb through new issues, looking for profiles to see who's who. Personality sketches and profiles are important feature articles in the overall content mix of newspapers, magazines, and newsletters of the mid-1990s. Newspapers and wire services use them to introduce new newsmakers to readers on an almost daily basis. Someone receiving a high government appointment at the national level is almost guaranteed to be profiled by the major news organizations. This also occurs at the local level, of course. New government officials, especially appointed individuals, are profiled on page one. Star athletes having a good year or who have just completed a record effort are highlighted in sports. Award-winning singers and musicians are subjects for the entertainment section. Some magazines regularly present profiles of industry or profession leaders and newsmakers to their readers in sections devoted to highlighting individuals. Continental Airlines has named its in-flight magazine *Profiles* and each issue highlights several prominent or otherwise interesting persons. *The New Yorker* has used its profiles regularly for decades, and newer magazines have recognized the value of regular profiles.

The usual newsmaker profile focuses on a new appointment or other newsworthy achievement by an individual thrust into the limelight. This is the "news peg" or "nut graf" for the profile. Something recent usually has happened to the individual to justify the attention. In addition to spot news stories about the decision and announcement, these profiles serve as sidebars. Editors use them because they believe their readers want to know more about the individual in the news. For instance, when President Bill Clinton made some changes in the White House staff early in his administration, he named David Gergen, former *U.S. News & World Report* editor and, at the time, a columnist and at-large editor, to a new post. He became a counselor to assist the president in political matters involving communication with the public. It was an unusual appointment because presidents seldom name members of the opposing political party to important policy posts. Some Americans knew the Gergen record, but many did not. As an example of a newsmaker profile in sidebar form, this is how Associated Press reporter Christopher Connell (1993), in Washington, began AP's profile on Gergen:

WASHINGTON (AP)—Pundit, writer and policy wonk David Gergen spent eight years inside the White House helping three Republican presidents polish conservative messages. Now he's back, trying to help Democrat Bill Clinton pull off an early political correction.

"When a president asks for help, there is only one good answer: How soon should I start?" the middle-of-the-road Republican said on the Rose Garden steps Saturday. "Patriotism must come before partisanship."

Gergen, 51, is giving up a lucrative career as a columnist and editor at large for *U.S. News & World Report*, commentator on the "MacNeil-Lehrer Newshour" and speechmaker to become a White House counselor with oversight of Clinton's troubled communications shop.

He knows the precinct well.

He helped sell Reaganomics to the country in 1981 as Ronald Reagan's communications director. At age 30, he was a top speech writer for Richard Nixon and later, special assistant to Gerald Ford.

Now, his mission is to focus Clinton's message and bring him back to the policies he espoused as a founder of the centrist Democratic Leadership Council before winning the White House.

Gergen bemoaned in the May 10 issue of *U.S. News* that the Clinton administration was "lurching to the left too often, emphasizing tax increases over spending cuts."

"Instead of sticking to the economy and jobs, he began dealing with a bewildering array of issues," Gergen wrote a week earlier. But he cautioned against writing Clinton off too soon: "He could well bounce back, proving himself a big-league president, even a hall of famer."

Gergen said on CNN Saturday that he expects to disagree with some of Clinton's decisions, but "I worked in a Reagan White House where I didn't agree with some of the decisions either" . . . . (Connell, 1993)

Although most profiles focus on people, these days profiles do not have to be about people. You will find profiles of cities, companies, sports teams, management teams, musical groups, acting or dance companies, committees, and other subjects. These organizational and institutional profiles are popular in certain sections of newspapers such as business, sports, and entertainment, and in similar departments of magazines as well. The ability to produce a profile and personality sketch is a necessary skill for the versatile nonfiction writer. This story form should be a part of your standard writing repertoire. You will get a look at the basics of the profile and personality sketch, and the different approaches to writing these stories, in this chapter. Your first stop is with the basic elements of writing profiles.

BASIC PROFILE CONTENT AND STRUCTURE

Profiles have common content and generally follow a standard organizational format. You will find variations, of course, but most profiles include certain basic information. The result is a structure that has evolved over the years. When profiling an individual, whether it be for a newspaper, magazine, or newsletter, you should include biographical material offered in a mostly chronological order, an environment or surroundings description, anecdotes or stories by and about the subject, personal information, and family information. It does not have to be presented in that order, of course. A combination of these elements should produce a full, insightful picture of the individual or subject.

Writing the article will be easiest to do for beginners if you follow the general format for profiles. After you have done a profile or two, you will probably begin to experiment with other organizational approaches as well as other means of focusing on the individual.

A standard profile can have several purposes and forms. A *full profile* will be a narrative article of considerable length depending on whether the profile is for a newspaper, magazine, or newsletter. Many publications are publishing profiles in capsule form, called *thumbnails* or *sketches* by some editors. These are abstracted profiles with only the basic facts presented in a summary or listing format. For a beginner, a traditional profile formula has four major parts:

1. Lead paragraphs.
2. "News peg" or "nut graf" outlining spot developments of significance.
3. Subject's current successes/accomplishments.
4. Biographical chronology.
5. Ending or conclusion.

The lead can be built by using several parts or only one component. Like other articles, it is two or three paragraphs that are interest-arousing for the reader. These can be stirring quotations, a dramatic scene description, or a telling anecdote. The lead should melt into the current accomplishments portion through an effective transition. That is the article's news peg. This is where you tell your reader: This is why you should read about this person. This is the point of the story where you describe the subject's achievements and responsibilities. Associated Press arts writer Dana Kennedy (1993) achieves this in the descriptive beginning of an A-wire—the main AP news wire—advance for Sunday editions that profiled singer and recording artist Cyndi Lauper. Kennedy went to Lauper's white-collar Manhattan apartment for the interview and used a description—complete with a bit of blue-collar Queens dialect—of the visit as the basis of the story's lead. Lauper had just released a new album and was attempting a comeback a decade after her sudden burst onto the pop scene:

NEW YORK (AP)—Cyndi Lauper walks into her living room looking like a musician. Very grunge. No makeup, dark roots peeking out of peroxided hair, a black T-shirt and baggy gangsta jeans. Barefoot.

But her voice takes care of the visual cliché.

"Jeez, how are ya?" Lauper says, leaning against the black Baby Grand piano and picking her toenail. "Can I get you some CAWFEE or something?"

Lauper has just moved into the Apthorp, a grand Upper West Side building known as the poor-man's Dakota. But if you close your eyes, you'd swear you were sitting in a two-family in Queens.

Ten years after she became famous with her first album, "She's So Unusual," and more than 20 years after leaving her unhappy home in Queens, Lauper makes no effort to hide her working-class origins.

But her distinctive accent and kooky image have all but vanished from the pop-star radar screen in recent years.

As the cab driver on the way over to Lauper's apartment put it: "Oh yeah, the one with the squeaky voice. Whatever happened to her?"

Lauper hopes her comeback album, "Hat Full of Stars," will answer that question. "It was a long path to get to here," she says. "But this album is all mine. Every song is about me and what I wanted to say."

It turns out that the girl who made "Girls Just Want to Have Fun" into something approaching a national anthem found it hard to practice what she preached.

After the disappointing sales of her third album, "A Night to Remember" in 1989, and a flop film, "Vibes," with Jeff Goldblum, Lauper took a break. She came back determined "not to be anyone's puppet anymore."

"I was fighting everybody," says Lauper of her last album. "They were telling me what to do, what to wear. I was writing songs and they were handing me tapes of other people's work.

"It got to the point where I felt like saying, 'How old you have to be to do your own . . . record the way you want it?' I'd started to repress myself. I need to work with kindred spirits."

Lauper co-produced "Hat Full of Stars," due in stores next month, and co-wrote all the songs, most of them at her new house in Connecticut. She directed the album's first video, "Who Let in the Rain?"

She also has a new movie coming out with Michael J. Fox called "Life With Mikey." She even has a new husband, actor David Thornton, and calls herself a "newlywed."

"It's a full circle to me," says Lauper, settling down cross-legged in a hassock. "I've come home to myself" . . . .

Following the lead, a profile establishes the news value of the story. What is the person doing? Why is this individual in the news? These portions are italicized in Kennedy's lead excerpt. This also serves as a form of transition from the lead to the middle of the story. With a good transition from the lead, you move to that portion of the article where the personal background on the individual is presented. How did the individual get to where he or she is? This is a biographical section, told most of the time in chronological order from childhood (or beginning of professional career, perhaps) to present. This will usually demand the variety of sources necessary in a profile to give a complete picture. But beware: This section can be dull unless it is spiced up with anecdotes and direct quotations, even some storytelling by the subject or others close to the subject.

The ending is linked to the rest of the article in several ways. The most common method is to bring the reader back to the present in the chronology, connecting with the points made in the "news peg" section. Another method is to link up with an anecdote offered in the lead or some other observation made by you, the subject, or another source, near the beginning of the article.

Using the Q & A Format for Profiles

Some publications prefer to publish profiles in a question and answer format. The Q & A has certain advantages. One is brevity. A second is the sense of realism, the feel of listening to the conversation that readers often get from the presentation style. They sense they were there during the interview. A key to success, however, is organization of questions and other information prior to the interview. These interviews do not have to be verbatim, of course, because it would then become a transcription. You have to edit and select material to be used as much as you would in the more traditional format. Because there is a strict Q & A format, the ordering of questions and answers must be as logical as any other sort of writing. There will also be need for some sort of editor's note to introduce the interview. You can write it, of course, for the editor, but this brief introduction needs to explain the who, what, when, where, why, and how of the Q & A.

This format also has its share of disadvantages. One is a lack of writing creativity. Of course, your editing creativity may substitute for it. There is often need for precision in question asking and in recording responses. There is temptation to leave extraneous material in such articles, also, to keep them more realistic. But this is a reason to edit carefully and thoroughly. Make certain the answers stick to the questions and do not drift.

Gulfshore Life magazine, which serves readers near Naples and Fort Myers in Southwest Florida, uses a large number of lifestyle features in its monthly issues. A recent article by writer Tom Whitaker (1993) illustrates how profiles can be done well in Q & A format, focusing his skills on longtime professional golfer Chi Chi Rodriguez, who stays in Naples when he is not playing on the Senior Professional Golfers Association Tour. Whitaker kept questions short and allowed Rodriguez's answers to be lengthy and insightful for golf fans.

CHECKLIST OF BASIC PROFILE INFORMATION

Biographical material
    Birthdate, birthplace
    Schooling
    First job, other positions held
    Family (parents, brothers and sisters)
    Childhood friends

News peg information
    Promotions, appointments, advancements
    Awards, honors, citations
    Present situation

Environment/surroundings
    Home, workplace description, decor
    Former living and working environments (for contrast)

Physical characteristics
    Physical appearance of person
    Mannerisms
    Clothing style
    Hair style

Anecdotes/stories
    Embarrassing moments
    Greatest accomplishment
    Memorable first times

Family
    Spouse, marriage information
    Previous marriages, commitments, or other relationships
    Children, ages and names
    In-laws
    Pets

Personal
    General lifestyle, philosophies of living
    Plans for the future
    Dreams and fantasies
    Hobbies, special interests
    Favorite foods and music
    Recreational activities
    Religion
    Military service
    Volunteer work or other civic/community service
    Club memberships
    Major traumas and problems (current or past)

newsletter published by the Poynter Institute in St. Petersburg, Florida, the institute's Don Fry profiled the new interim dean of faculty for the internationally known media center. The format worked well with a brief editor's note setting the context of the interview followed by brief questions and longer responses for the 1-page "People" page feature (Fry, 1993).

Industry and trade publications also use the Q & A format for profiles of prominent individuals in the business, often because of its efficiency in presenting information and its simplicity in organization. A recent issue of *American Bookseller* featured a Q & A format interview with Waldenbooks president and chief executive officer Charlie Cumello by the magazine's editor, Dan Cullen (1993). The article, written for a magazine read primarily by members of the American Booksellers Association—the people who manage bookstores, publish books, or distribute them—focused on industry trends such as growth of "super" bookstores, consumer habits, retailers, and the future of Waldenbooks.

Playboy magazine's longtime series of interviews by Larry Grobel also effectively uses Q & A format to profile newsmaking individuals, partly because of the lengthy introductions often given to the Q & A interviews, but also because of the actual depth of the interviews and the answers to Grobel's questions as well.

A Difference in Purpose

Art Spikol, former editor of *Philadelphia* magazine, says there is a clear distinction between the interview story and the profile. "Even if the terms are occasionally used interchangeably by beginning writers, the fact is that the two types of writing bear little resemblance to one another" (1979, p. 7). Spikol says an interview is just that, a conversation with someone. He adds:

A profile is something else: It is an article whose main subject is a particular person, and it is rarely based exclusively on an interview or on interviews with that person. In fact, profiles are probably at their least expository—and writers at their laziest— when written with information supplied by their subjects. After all, no subject—particularly one with some sophistication dealing with the press—will supply information that might be damaging or embarrassing; the only anecdotes the writer will get will be those the subject wishes to share. (1979, p. 7)

Your Profile's Tone and Writing Approach

Do you have to love your subject? Trash them? Profiles should not be entirely positive or laudatory. Most are neutral or balanced in presentation. In fact, some profiles will be written about a person who has been responsible for criminal activity or other socially unacceptable behavior. Your readers are likely interested in these persons as well.

Some profiles will seem to write themselves, up to a point. Usually you can tell your readers the news and the past about the person. It is possible, as Spikol says, you might wind up without a good ending. "Profiles are like that. You have swooped down on a subject and caught him at a certain point in time; naturally, you'll have to swoop away and leave him to act out the rest of the script. About all you can do is speculate a little about the subject's future" (1979, p. 10).

THE SUBJECT AS *THE* SOURCE

How do you choose the right person or subject for a profile? People and organizations are chosen for profiles because they are newsworthy. Because of what has happened to them lately, these persons are thrust voluntarily or involuntarily into the public eye and readers want to learn more about them. Judgments about the newsworthiness of a profile of an individual by editors are usually based on recent developments in the person's personal or professional life.

As noted earlier, people are not the only subjects of profiles. Cities, for instance, can be profiled. Or institutions. Or organizations. Such an article uses the same basic formula described for profiles of people—multiple sources, observations, a chronological summary of the city's recent history, and factual support for generalizations (a university study, among other sources).

In choosing a subject, you should consider that a person will be a good candidate to be profiled if the individual is well known. Individuals may be popular because of their professional activities. Or the person may be controversial because of a position on an issue that may divide a profession, community, or even a family.

Another reason to profile people is because they have reached a new level in their career or personal life. This means there has been a promotion, a new accomplishment, career change or shift, or other step recently taken. You also want to select an individual based on a third reason—leadership. The sort of person to profile is an industry or business leader who serves as a role model.

You should try to select individuals for their talkative nature and fluency of speech. A profile often is, in part, based on the thoughts of the person being highlighted. Someone who is not so glib or garrulous, for example, might not provide you with strong material for your story. Furthermore, it is also helpful to a successful profile for the subject to have a large circle of professional and personal acquaintances who are willing and able to discuss the subject of the article.

But you do not always have to profile someone because of fame or recent accomplishments. Sometimes, especially for feature treatment, a profile can focus on someone who is not a celebrity. These "common" people, the rank-and-file, often also make good human interest stories that are appealing to readers. For example, *The New Yorker* magazine publishes a newsletter as part of its education program. The publication goes to teachers and others who use the magazine as a teaching tool. In one recent issue, the newsletter, named *Talk of the Classroom*, profiled a university teacher who uses the magazine in her classes. The detailed article for the "Classroom Close-up" department of the newsletter utilized a full page of the 12-page publication. The article told other teachers about the educational successes enjoyed by Professor Owene Weber, including, of course, how she uses *The New Yorker* as a "textbook" in her English composition and literature courses. Although the profile is purely descriptive, without direct quotations, it discusses this teacher's style, manner, and her research focusing on a *New Yorker* writer. The article contains advice of strong practical value for the newsletter's readers (*The New Yorker* staff, 1993).

The idea of profiles that focus on "ordinary people," of course, is to emphasize what makes this individual, who might otherwise be like your readers, a bit unique or successful. The profile of Professor Weber achieves that goal. Spikol (1979) says profiles should be chosen depending on the answers to five questions:

1. Is the subject everything he seems to be?
2. How did the subject get that way?
3. How does the world react to, and perceive, the subject?
4. How does the subject perceive himself?
5. What can we learn about the subject by analyzing his environment—the people, places, and things with which he surrounds himself?

After deciding the person is right for your attention and effort, you need several things to fall in place. For starters, to do the profile you need cooperation from the subject. A profile will rarely succeed without a subject agreeing to be interviewed. Ideally, the person to be profiled will agree to the idea and allow one or more interviews. This is not always an easy matter because the type of person you will often profile is usually quite busy and in demand by many other people at work, home, and in the news media. Some people, such as those who feel they have been treated poorly by reporters, may resist you. But most people like to be profiled and will agree to it.

You need a significant block of time with your subject to get to know the person. If possible, request interviews in several different environments. You need to talk with subjects in their creative or work environment, but it adds a dimension to talk to subjects at their home in a more relaxed setting. Being at both the work environment and home environment allows you the chance to see the subject in distinctly different (most of the time, at least) environments. If possible, find a neutral location as well, such as a park where your subject likes to jog or a quiet coffee shop, for conversations, too. The more variety of atmospheres you can use, the more you will learn about the individual.

Subjects who do not want to be profiled or do not have time to talk to you can still be profiled. The job is just harder, requiring you to do more work in your research and in interviewing others who know your subject well. For example, Gay Talese's (1963) widely read and reprinted profile of Frank Sinatra, which first appeared in *Esquire*, characterized the entertainer without the author directly interviewing him. Instead, Talese carefully and tediously observed Sinatra and talked to Sinatra's friends and acquaintances to gather his information for the article, "Frank Sinatra Has a Cold." He watched Sinatra during the filming of an NBC television program and he watched him with his friends in a Beverly Hills bar. Talese wrote down conversations he heard for passages of dialogue in his article. He noticed what the singer ate and drank. He watched Sinatra's mood changes. Talese (1966) incorporated all this research into his profile of a man who was, in Talese's words, "the champ." Here's how his article began, setting a scene and atmosphere displaying Sinatra's unusual mood:

> Frank Sinatra, holding a glass of bourbon in one hand and a cigarette in the other, stood in a dark corner of the bar between two attractive but fading blondes who sat waiting for him to say something. But he said nothing; he had been silent for much of the evening, except now in this private club in Beverly Hills he seemed even more distant, staring out through the smoke and semidarkness into a large room beyond the bar where dozens of young couples sat huddled around small tables or twisted in the center of the floor to the clamorous clang of folk-rock music blaring from the stereo. The two blondes knew, as did Sinatra's four male friends who stood nearby, that it was a bad idea to force conversation upon him when he was in this mood of sullen silence, a mood that had hardly been uncommon during this first week of November, a month before his fiftieth birthday . . . . (p. 89)

OTHER SOURCES THAT MAKE A DIFFERENCE

As with other types of feature articles, one source is not enough to give a full picture of what you are writing for your readers. Even if that source is the subject of the story, you should not stop with just this source. You can be fooled by a good interview or series of interviews with your source into thinking you have everything you need to write.

You don't.

Good profiles are balanced in their use of sources. You should attempt to give the positive and negative elements of the individual and you usually have to go beyond the subject for that. Writer Lou Ann Walker, who has completed numerous profiles for magazines, including a profile of Candice Bergen for *New York Woman*, strongly recommends this approach. "Become friendly with the people who work with the person you're interviewing," Walker (1992, p. 323) suggests. "Charming a secretary who is snooty can lead to important revelations. One such secretary confided in me that the actress I was interviewing was just breaking up with a man and dating someone new. I would have never have found that out if I hadn't done a little buttering up."

So, how many interviews are enough? Seldom do you need to interview as many as 50 people. Some writers will do this, but usually that kind of depth is necessary only for a book. Generally, you can get a good sense of the person by talking with half dozen to a dozen sources. This is no magic range. The real trick is variation in the type of source you use. Too many similar sources will not tell you anything new. You need to try to find a balance of friendly and unfriendly sources, and family and professional sources, for example. There are seven categories of human interview sources you can most often use. Here's a list:

1. Family members such as brothers and sisters, parents, spouses, and children. Former family members such as ex-spouses should be included.
2. Neighbors and former neighbors.
3. Business associates where the subject works.
4. Business associates through professional organizations.
5. Competitors and rivals in the workplace.
6. Personal friends.
7. People who work where the subject shops and places where the subject goes for entertainment.

You will want to incorporate as many anecdotes as possible into your article to help generate "insight" into the subject's personality. During your interviews, encourage the subject and your other sources to tell these stories. These should be informative, amusing, and profound.

There are two other types of research to use in a profile beyond interviews. You should also check clippings of other articles written about the person (this is particularly true of newspaper writers who have access to such libraries). Although magazine writers might not have such resources as easily available, because many newspapers have computerized their libraries and now sell access to the public, research for free-lancers and magazine writers without office libraries is not as serious a problem as it was a decade ago.

Another form of research to complete in preparing your profile is public records. You may find interesting details about a person by reviewing civil and criminal court files, police records, property records, and other public documents of similar nature. This is especially applicable to profiles of individuals in public service, such as appointed and elected government officials. It will also be an effective strategy to learn more about business executives, entertainers, athletes, and others widely known in your community or region whose activities are on the public record.

OBSERVING YOUR PROFILE SUBJECT

In the last section, it was suggested that profile writers take the time to watch profile subjects do what they do best. Why are you writing about this person? Is the individual a top dress designer in a market? Then try to watch this person designing, or at least, introducing some work at a show. If you are profiling a politician, watch the person interacting with constituents, on the floor of the legislature, and in a political party meeting. Each experience will tell you more about the person and help you write a more complete profile of the individual. This will help you create a better, more complete picture of this person in your mind, and, consequently, in the minds of your readers. Note the subject's mannerisms. How does your subject deal with other people? Is this person's work behavior with others different from behavior with superiors? With family? Friends? If so, why?

You can approach this in two ways. Depending on the individuals and their activities, you can observe them without the subjects' knowledge you are doing so. This can be in public places, of course, when the individual is performing, speaking, or whatever. You can also, under circumstances where you might not be able to remain anonymous, watch as a known observer to the subject. This might be necessary when you watch in a small-group situation for demonstrations or less public forms of work.

Some of the best profiles are built on research through firsthand *observation*. For profiles of public people who lead very public lives, this is not difficult. Go out and watch them do their thing. If you have an assignment to profile an entertainer, go to some live performances. If the subject is a politician, go to public meetings and attend some speeches. If the subject is a social leader, try to get invitations or tickets to some of the parties or charitable events this individual supports and attends. But *watch* them work.

The descriptions of the individual will add an entirely different dimension to your work. The information you obtain from an interview or two with the subject is critical, no doubt, but these observations give you richness in detail that you cannot always find in interviews. You *see* and, perhaps, *hear* how the person works. You see subjects interact with others in their most comfortable milieu.

Lou Ann Walker, who specializes in writing profiles of entertainers and other celebrities, believes this is one of her most useful tactics in creating a profile:

> One of the best tactics is to stay with the person all day, particularly on a movie set. Academy Award-winning actress Marlee Matlin allowed me to tag along on a free day, and we had a most illuminating time. I let her drive me all over Los Angeles. (Frankly it was a death-defying stunt. She's so excitable that when she uses her hands to sign, she often takes both of them off the steering wheel.) She took me to visit her elderly grandmother in a nursing home, and I could see the family affection. We went to a Beverly Hills restaurant where she used her TTY . . . to have a conversation with her boyfriend, an actor on location in Canada. It was these small moments that made our interview memorable. (1992, p. 323)

These moments can also be obtained secondhand, of course, by interviewing others. There is no real substitute for the real thing and being there yourself. Of course, this creates access issues. To be able to spend time with a busy actress such as Matlin requires arrangements well in advance. Access to celebrities, major business executives, political leaders, and other busy individuals in the news and public spotlight is not often easy to obtain. If access is granted, the additional depth to the story is superior to most other observation.

This does not prevent you from spending time watching the individual in public. For some persons, this will not occur often. Reclusive individuals are most difficult. But for some profile subjects, public appearances are part of their lives and therefore easier to observe and to profile.

Miami Herald staff feature writer Rene Rodriguez, who writes for the newspaper's lifestyles section called Living, wrote a telling profile of model Beiron Andersson. Rodriguez talked to Andersson while he was in Miami Beach working on an assignment.

The profile describes the subject of the article at two distinct levels. There are *physical descriptions*, such as how people react to seeing Andersson on the street ("'Oh my God, he's so . . . beautiful'," or "the model smiles and complies politely"), and there are *attitudinal or philosophical descriptions* ("Andersson knows that when it comes to money, none of the hoopla matters much," or "Andersson is trying to remain levelheaded about what's coming next"), which tell readers how Andersson is handling all of this success. Both are forms of observation. One comes from looking and seeing and the other comes from listening carefully. Rodriguez's story was written to establish Andersson's potential to become a major supermodel and the story establishes early that Andersson is one of the first men to achieve such status in the world of high-fashion advertising, calendars, and magazine covers. The story incorporates considerable observation of Andersson during his working session at the beach, including re-creation of dialogue and detailed description. Rodriguez's observations are firsthand and add much to the article, including the entire scene used for the lead to the story. This is Rodriguez's (1993) profile of the upcoming male model, integrating his observations with an ample supply of direct quotations from Andersson:

> It is Friday afternoon, and the sidewalk cafes along trendy Ocean Drive in South Beach are packed. Eternally cool actor Dennis Hopper strides by, but few heads turn. This, after all, is a jaded crowd.
>
> But they notice Beiron Andersson. The 27-year-old Swedish model, in Miami to shoot photographs for a 1995 calendar, is drawing lots of curious glances, and some downright gawking, as he poses for a photo on Ocean Drive.
>
> "I think I've seen him on TV," one woman says.
>
> "Is he an actor?" another asks.
>
> "Oh my God, he's so . . . beautiful," a third sighs.
>
> Through it all, the model smiles and complies politely. He has become used to the attention since he began appearing in magazine ads for Guess? jeans last October.
>
> "In my case, it's nothing like a big actor, where people go crazy," he says. "People ask you to sign a magazine or take a picture or whatever. It's low-scale."
>
> Andersson may soon be looking back at these days of "low-scale" attention with nostalgia: He is poised to break through the printed page and into the public consciousness as a male supermodel.

A male supermodel? Unheard of. Attaining super status is a feat only women—the Cindy Crawfords, the Claudia Schiffers, the Naomi Campbells—have achieved.

Granted, some male models are popular (Marcus Schenkenberg was profiled last year on Entertainment Tonight and in national magazines after his sexy ads for Calvin Klein raised eyebrows). And, granted, an ever-growing list of magazines is devoting space to men's fashions (*GQ*, of course, but also *Details*, *In Fashion*, *Interview*, *Men's Journal* and others). But no male model has ever become a household name.

"If you ask the average person who are the top supermodels, three or four names will come to mind right away—and they're all women," says Mala Ransamooj, director of Working Models Agency in New York. "If you asked who are the top male models, I will bet you 10 out of 10 people on the street will not know."

If initial reaction is any gauge, however, Andersson might change that.

"I think Beiron is a supermodel," says Patricia Sklar, president and owner of Landmark Calendars, which will publish his calendar in June 1994.

"He has a kind of appeal that's ageless. I was looking through a magazine and I saw Beiron in the Guess? jeans ad and I was stopped in my tracks. I thought, 'What a gorgeous man.' He has great-looking eyes. I felt that he would appeal to a vast majority of women."

Apparently he does. "Guess? is now making notebooks, postcards, posters, everything," Andersson says. "They've gotten a great response. I get letters from teachers who say their girls' books are covered. I've gotten letters asking me out on dates, asking me to the prom."

Hollywood has also come calling. "I've had calls from all the big agencies—CAA, William Morris—offers for movies, television. I just haven't been ready. I just got going with the modeling, so I don't want to stop that, because I'm making a good living at it."

Still, Andersson knows that when it comes to money, none of the hoopla matters much.

"If a male was in Cindy (Crawford)'s place, the one that people would think would make the most money, he would be beat by a girl that's maybe in 30th place in the women's ranks," he says. "She would make the double of what the top guy made."

But he understands why the inequity exists: "Obviously, you have more money to make on women. Women look at fashion more, and they also buy more."

It only follows that the real supermodels—the ones people who never pick up a fashion magazine can still recognize—are women.

"In all honesty, the modeling industry is a beauty business," says Michaela, an agent for the L'Agence modeling agency in Miami. "It's one of the few industries where the women make more money than the men. Not that men aren't beautiful; it's just predominantly a woman's industry. But the men's market is getting bigger."

"There are a couple of things attached to the phrase ‹supermodel›: high price tag, crowd appeal and celebrity status," says Ransamooj. "They can compare to any of the Hollywood actresses in terms of mass appeal.

"Back in the 1970s, famous models like Cheryl Tiegs were known for different reasons. There wasn't that movie-star image attached to them. They didn't make seven to ten thousand dollars a day."

The men's fashion industry didn't really begin until a few years ago. "It came into its own and became a viable industry in the late '70s to early '80s," says Brian O'Hara, booking agent for Miami's Irene Marie Agency. "A definite market has developed for the men, other than being accessories in the women's pictures, which is basically what they were used for."

Andersson began modeling as a fluke. The Stockholm native first came to the United States as a high school exchange student in Chico, Calif., then decided to stay after serving a one-year stint with the Swedish army.

Two years ago, he decided to open a gym in Chico. On a visit to Los Angeles to get ideas from the larger gyms there, he began to get invitations from agents, suggesting he try modeling.

Though he had received offers before, Andersson had never seriously considered them. "Then I thought if I was going to be working as a fitness instructor or whatever within the gym, I might as well model a few hours on the side for a little extra money."

"I had walked in with a few snapshots I took in the park the day before, and that was all I needed."

He started small, appearing in national and local department store ads and catalogs. Then he caught the eye of Paul Marciano, president and director of advertising for Guess?.

They met for dinner last August. "After one hour, he just told me, 'You will be everywhere. I'm going to push you like you won't believe.' That was my first meeting with him. I was booked for the (Guess?) job right here in Miami."

So far, Andersson has appeared in two Guess? ad campaigns. The first, featuring a tropical beach setting, was shot on South Beach two days before Hurricane Andrew hit and appeared last year. The second, currently running in such magazines as *Entertainment Weekly*, *Details* and *Premiere*, pairs Andersson with model Anna Nicole Smith in a series of black-and-white ads inspired by Raging Bull.

Despite all the attention, Andersson is trying to remain levelheaded about what's coming next. "I'm never going to be a real actor. I'm going to get the roles where my look is right. I know why these offers are coming. I've had offers to become a new rock star. I can't sing. They told me 'We don't care! We'll take care of that. You've got the right look.' That's not me."

Andersson married his high school sweetheart Tina seven years ago. They have a 3-year-old daughter, Alexandra.

Tina's "very special," Andersson says. "I think there's very few women that would accept what I do. Before I started modeling, we went through everything, we talked. I told her if things started going good, I'm going to be gone a lot and working with beautiful women. If you're going to have a problem with it, I'm not going to pursue it. And she said 'Go for it.'"

His family helps keep Andersson grounded. "I think it's a good thing in this business to have something solid behind you, because it's not a normal lifestyle. You're always staying in these great hotels, clients pay for your dinner, you go out to bars for free, you hang out with a very selective group of people looks-wise, and so on.

"People think we can only stand and look pretty in front of a camera. It would be nice to be able to inform people that that's not the way it is. All the models that do really well have to have a head on their shoulders, because it's use or be used. And if you're not smart about it, you're going to be used and thrown out very quick." (p. 1E) Reprinted with permission of *The Miami Herald*.

SPECIAL PROBLEMS INVOLVING CELEBRITIES

As noted, there are numerous barriers to gaining access to celebrities such as Marlee Matlin or a supermodel-in-waiting such as Beiron Andersson. These people are always in demand by writers for stories of all types. These barriers include secretaries and receptionists for business executives; bodyguards, publicists, and press agents for entertainers; public information officers and media relations liaisons for individuals in high levels of public service. Their jobs include "protecting" their employers from people who might want to interrupt or disrupt.

There is a strategy to get to your source for the interviews you need for your article. Your first step is to fully identify yourself and directly ask the celebrity's assistants for their help, explaining what work you are doing and why. Because your work is *legitimate* and *serious*, you might get to your subject to request the interview. You might also be asked to wait while your request is taken to your subject for a response. If you work for a publication, your reputation and your publication's reputation can be an asset. Do not be afraid to use it to help you.

If you are still denied access, then try to work your way around the barriers. One way is to find the subject leaving the workplace, or where the subject shops on weekends, or at some other *public* location where you can introduce yourself and state your purpose. This direct approach will often work, even though it requires extra effort. There are occasions when writers, stopped by a subject's staff, get an interview because they went to the extra effort to ask directly. It is possible, and often is the case, that the subject never got the original request submitted to an intermediary.

Still another strategy for the hard-to-get interview is offered by Chicago columnist Bob Greene. He writes letters to tough-to-reach subjects. This is the way he managed to obtain his well-known interviews with Richard Nixon, Patricia Hearst, and multiple murderer Richard Speck. These accomplishments early in his career helped him toward becoming a syndicated writer (Schumaker, 1983).

You can also use published or broadcast quotations from other sources that you locate in your research. Of course, this means you must attribute the information to its source in your article. You can take these from speeches, press conferences, and similar public events. And it does not harm your article to tell readers that you made attempts to reach the person but were refused for whatever reasons.

If you are fortunate enough to get an interview with your subject, then you must, like any other interviewer, get yourself prepared. Larry Grobel (1978), who has interviewed celebrities for *Playboy* magazine, says it helps to have certain expectations for the "star" interview. "Know what you are getting into. Find out in advance if there is a time limit . . . . Good interviews are ones in which the subject is as interested as you are. That's difficult with celebrities, who have to hear the same questions over and over, but that's not impossible" (p. 20).

You may have restrictions other than time. You might be asked to conduct your interview with another writer in a small-group setting. You may have a language barrier and need translation, so you actually interview the translator. You may be told that you have to conduct the interview with this busy celebrity in an unusual environment—in a car, backstage, or even at home with the kids screaming and dogs barking.

Prepare your major questions in advance and write them down. You might wind up not needing them, but these serve as a crutch when awkward slow moments occur. And tape your interview for accuracy. For very important interviews, use two tape recorders to guard against mechanical failures. This also lets you participate more in the conversation because you don't have to spend so much effort taking detailed notes. Grobel also recommends that you should work to keep control of the interview. This means you should be in charge of the direction of the conversation. Change topics if you must do so when a pause or interruption occurs.

THE NEED FOR FOCUS

You now know that a good profile has *focus*. When you are beginning to work on a profile, you need to think about what focus it will have about the subject. Most subjects that are worthy of profiles have multiple elements of their personalities and accomplishments that will force you to choose a particular direction for the profile. When you are restricted on length, particularly for traditional newspaper or newsletter profiles of 750 to 1,500 words (3 or 4 pages), you cannot afford to drift aimlessly in your description of the individual. You can probably get deeper into an individual in magazine profiles if the luxury of a longer manuscript (5,000 to 10,000 words, or 20 to 40 pages, for example) comes with the assignment. This would permit you the chance to probe several directions. But most profiles do not permit such depth and require more writing discipline through limited focus. Some profile writers also call this focus a *theme* for the article. Whatever it is called, the point is the same—give your article some direction. The direction might become apparent in your research before you begin interviewing or writing. Even if it is not after you have completed most of your research, you can still look for the focus during your interviews with the subject and others.

University of Florida professor Edward Yates (1985) suggests that, in searching for that theme, you remain flexible. "If he or she (the writer) has selected a theme from pre-interview research and a more interesting one develops during the questioning, he or she must be ready to switch directions" (p. 210). Yates says themes will often concern a subject's range or type of experience, personality or character traits, aspirations in life, personal achievements, or philosophy of life.

WRITING PERSONALITY SKETCHES

A personality sketch is not as involved with the subject as a profile must be. Although some personality sketches are as long as some newspaper or magazine profiles, sketches generally are short and to the point. The article is designed to give us a quick look at an individual and to tell us why the subject is important. These articles usually lack the depth of profiles and must not waste words with the reader.

William Rivers (1992) says a personality sketch is a tough assignment, forcing you to "become a keen observer and recorder of significant details" (p. 254). These articles, Rivers notes, contain imagery created by details that you find in profiles. However, there is just not as much in these shorter pieces. You must show; don't tell. You have to do this in your own sketches. Rivers (1992) also suggests that sketches are strengthened by use of anecdotes. These have tremendous value to you as a writer and offer much strength to your sketch. "Anecdotes, by their nature, are not great world-shaping events. They are human looks at something. They have small cores, but radiate ramifications" (p. 260).

WRITING CAPSULE AND THUMBNAIL PROFILES

Brief or capsule profiles, often called thumbnail profiles also, are growing in popularity with newspaper and magazine editors. These profiles are quite short, just a few hundred words, and usually follow a standard format developed by the editors of the publication or news service. These formats may even vary within the publication, with different sections or departments offering their own profiles depending on the nature of the subject being profiled.

There is also a trend toward writing profiles of nonhuman subjects such as institutions, corporations, sports teams, network programs, films, and similar

---

BEST SOURCES FOR WRITING PROFILES

People
- Subject
- Family
- Neighbors
- Workplace associates, rivals, and competitors
- Businesses where subject shops

Observations
- Subject at work
- Subject at home with family, friends
- Subject enjoying personal activities

Library research
- Resume, press kits
- Public records
- Writings by subject, if any
- Previous newspaper, magazine article clippings
- Film and videotape, if available

---

subjects. These articles follow a certain content outline, usually set by the individual publication based on a dozen or more categories of information, and are regularly offered. A new company, a successful business, or a new investment category might be profiled by a business magazine, specialized company or industry newsletter, or business section of a newspaper. At the beginning of a new sports season, standardized profiles of teams or leagues might be part of a special section or part of the regular coverage of a top game of the day or week. In the news section during election campaign periods, personality sketches or capsule profiles of all serious candidates are standard fare. In entertainment, profiles of new movies, books, records, and other art forms are commonplace. Each of these serves a purpose for the reader: The capsulized profile is an information digest for a quick read. These capsule profiles can be placed within larger articles on broader subjects as a sidebar or placed beside articles of equal importance.

Some publications ask subjects to profile themselves by answering a short standard list of questions. This form is an abstracted version of what you might write in a full profile, but without the elaboration. These short profiles are the bare bones. There are no wasted words, and they are direct to the point.

AVOIDING PROFILE PROBLEMS

Can you err in writing profiles? Yes. You can permit yourself to be *overly positive*, or *impressed* with the "star" quality of the person you are profiling, or be *intimidated*, or *superficial*. These are four major pitfalls of many beginners, especially students. And you can talk too much during the interview, for example. Some interviewers get involved in the interview to the level of talking too much and getting less from the source as a result. Or you can waste valuable time with terrible questions. To avoid mistakes, exert self-control and discipline. Be careful not to depend on only your subject. Perhaps worst of all, you can be "steered" by your subject to a certain agenda and focus of the subject's choosing.

One way to avoid some of these problems is to use numerous sources representing a variety of perspectives. Do your homework, of course. Research for background will provide a strong foundation for the story and your interviews.

As for writing the story, there are some tips for that part of the profile assignment also.

- Don't write in chronology only. Select a strong focus for your article.
- Don't drift.
- Don't jumble your facts together.
- Use good transitions to connect the pieces.
- Above all, do not forget your "nut graph" (the news peg to the story).

With these things in mind, you are probably ready to try your first profile.

PROFESSIONAL'S POINT OF VIEW

John A. Limpert
The Washingtonian magazine

Profiles are a big part of magazines like *The Washingtonian*. Here are mistakes we see profile writers make:

Thinking it's an easy payday. When writers tell me they like to write profiles, it sets off warning bells. Often they mean an easy personality piece from a quickie interview. Best-selling author Judith Viorst was one of our best profile writers. She would first read about the subject, then call the subject and say: "I'd like to do a story on you. I've read a lot about you. Before we talk, can you give me the names of people who know you well, both friends and enemies?" Famed trial lawyer Edward Bennett Williams said he never asked a question in court he didn't know the answer to; writers should know most of the answers before they start asking the questions of the profile subject.

Loving the subject too much. In a variation of the Stockholm Syndrome, in which hostages begin to identify with their captors, some profile writers develop too much empathy with their subjects. When it comes time to write the profile, the writer worries more about the profile subject than the reader. The writer has to make a shift in mindset after the research: When you sit down to write, your loyalty is to the reader. You owe the reader a clear-eyed, professional look at the subject, and you can't worry about pleasing or displeasing the subject.

Hating the subject too much. Again, you owe the reader a clear-eyed look even if the subject has been difficult to deal with or runs into one of your biases.

Trying to be too clever. Some writers try to cover up weak research or a dull subject with very clever writing. It's harder to fool readers than many writers think. A good editor has a sensitive BS detector and won't let you get away with it. A corollary: Write about sophisticated ideas in simple language, not the other way around.

Giving up when the subject won't cooperate. Some of our best profiles were done on people who wouldn't talk to us. It takes a lot of smart reporting to do this kind of piece, and, again, don't let the subject's feelings toward you poison your attitude, but the lack of cooperation allows you more freedom to make judgments and draw conclusions. And we've often found that uncooperative subjects become cooperative when they realize we're going to do a good reporting piece on them whether they talk or not.

Not thinking enough about how you're going to get the reader into the subject. Leads—usually a good scene or anecdote—are important, but also think about what kind of headline, art, captions, and pull quotations the story needs. Editors appreciate suggestions (but not demands). If you were the reader, what in the story would interest you the most? Suggest that these points be highlighted. Many readers graze through publications, looking for a picture or caption or headline or pull quote that interests them. Then they may read your story.

Not protecting your reputation. Some writers try to build a fast name for themselves by doing what we call "hit" pieces. It's the journalistic equivalent of an assassination. I've seen it work for some writers for brief periods of time, but media subjects are getting more sophisticated. Before they talk to you, the subjects will do some checking: How fair are you? How accurate are you? Is your main goal to leave a lot of blood on the floor? Conversely, some tough profile subjects will talk to you if you send them copies of stories you've done along with a letter explaining what a fair, thorough, knowledgeable writer you are. (Limpert, personal communication, 1993)

John A. Limpert is editor of *The Washingtonian* magazine. Limpert has worked for United Press International and has served as editor of newspapers in Warren, MI; San Jose, CA; and Washington, DC. He worked in the office of Vice President Hubert H. Humphrey and was a Congressional Fellow. He joined *The Washingtonian* staff at the end of the fellowship in 1969. He is a winner of the American Political Science Association award for distinguished reporting in public affairs. *The Washingtonian* has won five National Magazine Awards since 1982.

8

Seasonal Feature Articles

When you think of *seasons*, perhaps you think of the weather. Or sports. Maybe food. Perhaps special clothing. Or the holidays. Or vacations. Family gatherings. There are many different types of seasons, and people associate as many or even more different activities and traditions with them. We often associate vacation camp with summer, for example. In the spring each year, typically, many newspapers and magazines devote attention to summer camps. As part of this annual activity, parents and children spend countless winter hours talking about camps and deciding what they will do that upcoming summer. Same camp as last year? Something new? As a seasonal feature, articles help such discussions with new information and descriptions. *USA Today*'s Life section feature writers usually assemble a seasonal feature advancing summer camp season. Staff writer Tamara Henry recently wrote one such package of advance articles, focusing on specialty summer camps that offer more than just the usual summer vacation for kids. These camps, she wrote, provide advanced educational opportunities, as well as a beautiful setting in the countryside. Henry's (1993) story began this way:

> Summer camps are as American as apple pie, and just about as diverse as America itself, with choices ranging from foreign languages to cave explorations, circus arts and weight loss.
>
> Camp programs have become so popular that parents often scramble to enroll students long before the snow melts and thoughts turn longingly to summer.
>
> "Camps are here to stay and they are growing," says Karen Rosenbaum of the American Camping Association (ACA). "The big thing is that people's stereotype of camp still exists and is flourishing".... (p. 4D)

As part of her total *package*, Henry cited some of the more popular camp specialties and included a short sidebar listing the most successful camps featuring space study, computers, creative writing, horses, canoeing, tennis, and cave exploring. A second sidebar listed questions to ask when checking out a camp for a child. In her main story, Henry took a consumer approach to her story, listing features and prices for these camps. She also gave some national statistics on participation and the number of summer camps in business.

Journalists often write feature articles about the seasons and seasonal activities such as summer camp. Seasonal articles celebrate the regularity of life—the cycles and rhythms of nature and human life that govern our lives. Summer camp is one of those great American traditions that is part of growing up in many families—something many adults remember from childhood and something children usually look forward to each summer. Traditional seasonal stories such as the *USA Today* package call readers' attention to the beginnings and ends of important segments of our lives—such as the shift from winter to spring and summer—to special dates and events that demand our recognition and memory.

Seasons, as a force of nature, transcend all human life. The seasons dictate the parameters of human life: Seasons affect plant life, animal life, the world climate, Earth's natural and seemingly unnatural events, migration, hibernation, and the Earth itself. British author Anthony Smith (1970) said quite succinctly that "the complex rhythm of our planet Earth, rotating upon its axis in its orbit around the sun, encircled all the while by its neighbour the moon, provides the basis for the ceaseless rhythm of life itself" (p. 16). The growing concern with man and our life rhythms emphasizes the regularity of life. The cycles of life have evolved over thousands of generations to what we now know of it.

In this century, modern writers have provided seasonal articles for their readers to help them prepare for changing natural seasons, for the end-of-year religious holidays such as Christmas and Chanukah, for the beginning of vacation, for the start of a new school year, for graduation, for ethnic celebrations, for national and regional birthdays and anniversaries, for special days for mothers and fathers, and even for the loves of our lives. Few publications overlook marking these events in some fashion each year. For some publications, entire issues may be built upon the season or holiday. For others, a brief article may be sufficient. But for most, something in between is preferred.

Unusual perspectives are often what it takes to get a reader's attention to a routine seasonal event. In a recent St. Patrick's Day issue, the *Palm Beach Post* highlighted its March 17 Accent section, which contains lifestyles and other features, with a lead story about wearing green. *Palm Beach Post* fashion editor Loretta Grantham (1993) wrote the cover article that gave readers suggestions for dressing in green for the parties and other events of this special Irish day, and for other days as well. Green was making a comeback, she wrote in this lead:

It's *got* to be on your mind today.

Green-spangled St. Patrick's Day soirees. Green beer. (Green complexions come morning.) Green garb, or get grabbed. You get the idea.

But pause for a moment. Pop in a New Age CD. Think about green apart from today's festivities. Tell your boss it's a Mother Earth thing.

Green is no nouveau hue. Nature aside, it's probably been around since the first caveboy kindergartner glopped blue and yellow tempera paint on the same rock.

But lately, the color's gained a new respect.

"When I was selling in stores a few years ago, green was called a markdown color because nobody would buy it at regular price," said Carole Jacobson, vice president of the Fashion Footware Association of New York.

"But in the past two years, green has become most important." (p. 1D)

For a beginning feature writer, perhaps one of the more basic articles to master is a seasonal feature article, no matter what section or what time of the year. These articles are necessary throughout the year and appear in just about every part of every newspaper, magazine, and newsletter, and there are ample opportunities to write them.

"Seasonal articles are not particularly hard to write—in fact, I think they are easier than general articles" (p. 44) says veteran seasonal article writer Clinton Parker (1975). "They do require a certain depth of research, however, and absolute historical accuracy. That's why it is best to specialize in a particular event or field. Once you have done the basic reading for the specialty, the articles are much easier to write" (p. 44).

Whether you specialize in seasonal articles or not, you will find that much of your feature article writing will be controlled by the calendar. Newspapers, magazines, and newsletters will run features to highlight special events on the calendar each year. Readers expect it. Seasonal features are not much different from other types of features. In fact, you will probably mix some of the different elements and types of feature articles when writing a seasonal article. There may be *humorous* seasonal stories. Or highly *personalized* stories. Or stories with great *human interest* elements. Or a *review* of traditional holiday season music, food, or dance. The focus in this chapter, however, is on the *context* of the article regardless of the approach taken.

One significant point, however, is that seasonal features should reflect the tone and the theme of the season. This is largely dictated by local customs and traditions. A seasonal feature can be ruined with the wrong approach. It would obviously be in poor taste to write an irreverent feature about the military for Memorial Day or Veteran's Day. Then again, a newspaper reporter or magazine writer who does not try to be especially creative and tricky on April Fool's Day or Halloween is completely missing the point of those special days.

It is not unusual for newspapers to run several seasonal articles at the beginning of and throughout a major holiday season. The *Atlanta Journal and Constitution* devoted a recent food section cover story to the lost art of traditional formal ladies' luncheons on holidays such as Mother's Day. Columnist Celestine Sibley's (1993) lead article focused on a 1940s and 1950s white-gloved tradition that was lost on more recent generations of modern Atlanta-area women. Sibley's feature was supported by several additional articles by dining critic Elliott Mackle, who told what current tearooms and other restaurants offered such services to contemporary Atlantans for Mother's Day. Their articles appeared on the Thursday before Mother's Day.

Compare that idea with how the *Los Angeles Times* handled the same Mother's Day. It was a little different in approach and purpose. In View, the *Times'* lifestyles and trends features section, staff writer Bettijane Levine wrote a tribute to mothers by confessing to her readers that mother *does* know best. Levine's article focused on that advice in the newspaper's celebration of Mother's Day. The *Times* had earlier in the spring asked readers to submit the best advice their mothers ever gave their children. She quoted from the best submissions, of course, in her article. She talked with a few experts about parenting, too, and to other experts about the soundness of the advice ("'Learn to type, so you'll have something to fall back on' isn't as obsolete as it might seem," Levine writes). In addition to a boxed sidebar highlighting the 16 best entries (the first one, "Life is like a bank account; you get out of it what you put in," was submitted by a reader living in Los Angeles), the main article generalized about relationships between mothers and their children and how children often ignore what their mothers tell them. But in the end, of course, Levine admits "mother knows best." Levine's (1993) salute to mom's wisdom began this way:

> If she told you once, she told you a thousand times: "Elbows off the table. Stand up straight. Go before you leave the house. Two wrongs don't make a right. If Johnny jumped off a cliff, would you jump, too?"

> But did you listen?

> Nope. In one ear and out the other.

> Mom was undaunted, however. She knew her job: To verbally pummel you until wisdom was indelibly etched in your brain; to repeat and repeat until you mouthed her maxims before they even left her tongue.

> "Oh, so the egg is teaching the chicken?" she'd ask. "Well, this hurts me more than it hurts you. But when you have your own children, you'll understand."

> And, apparently, you did. Because when the Los Angeles Times asked readers to submit the best advice their mothers ever gave them (in 50 words or less), hundreds of men, women and some children sent classic lines . . . .(p. E1)

Although it is more common to publish a major article or feature *package* of several articles, as *Times* editors did with Levine's Mother's Day stories, some newspapers produce entire special sections in recognition of local festivals or holiday periods. Similarly, it is not unusual to find a monthly specialized magazine devote a cover and a majority of its top articles in the issue to a seasonal theme. Food and entertaining magazines often prepare special holiday issues featuring new recipes, party and gift ideas, holiday getaways, and, of course, their versions of the ultimate Easter, Thanksgiving, or Christmas feast.

Author Daniel Williamson (1975) says a seasonal feature is "an account of an annual event or an aspect of that annual event which captures its spirit" (p. 170). Think about all the Christmas, Thanksgiving, and other holiday stories you have ever seen. Hundreds, no doubt. To make the special season come to life, you have to capture the sights, sounds, smells, tastes, and even feel of the season. These stories lean heavily on your descriptive abilities when you write about events and activities surrounding these special moments in our lives.

WHY WRITE SEASONAL FEATURE ARTICLES?

There are numerous reasons for writing seasonal articles. First, there's professional opportunity. Although editors generally have enough copy for the routine issues of their newspapers, magazines, and newsletters, there always seems to be a shortage of good seasonal material. This editorial need means seasonal features are an effective way to crack the free-lance market and to get an editor to notice your work above and beyond others'. Even experienced writers often overlook seasonal article opportunities. These articles, geared to a special time of the year, can also open the door to you for other nonseasonal opportunities, writer Clinton Parker (1975) says.

The importance of seasonal features extends beyond the need to entertain readers by describing the occurrence of holidays, annual events, major anniversaries, or even the changing natural weather and growing seasons. Wire service and newspaper articles focusing on weather often look at the seasonal nature of weather. Some features highlight it. In the Northeast and Midwest, the cooling fall means the season to go into the countryside to see nature's colors. In the South, along the Gulf of Mexico, summer means the rainy season or, as some call it, hurricane season. The following are two wire service weather news feature leads, written by staff members from the respective Miami bureaus, beginning with the United Press International story lead, about the traditional beginning of a new season:

> MIAMI (UPI)—As the Atlantic-Caribbean hurricane season officially began Tuesday, the year's first tropical depression edged away from Florida and over the Bahamas and the northern Caribbean islands.
>
> The scattered spiral of thunderstorms dumped more than 8 inches of rain over parts of south Florida on Memorial Day, but was not expected to strengthen into a tropical storm.
>
> "It'll continue going out over the waters of the Atlantic and it will probably lose its tropical characteristics in the next 48 hours or so," said National Weather Service meteorologist Bob Ebaugh. (United Press International staff, 1993b)

And the Associated Press version:

MIAMI (AP)—The first tropical depression of the Atlantic hurricane season arrived a little early and dumped as much as 10 inches of rain on Cuba, Florida and the Bahamas.

The storm formed on Monday in the Caribbean and prematurely kicked off the 1993 hurricane season, which officially begins today and ends Nov. 30.

Forecasters expected the storm to fizzle today after some morning showers.

A tropical depression before the start of the hurricane season is rare but not unheard of, meteorologist Robert Molleda said.

"This isn't an indication of a strong hurricane season," he said. (Associated Press staff, 1993)

In addition to the spot nature of these two seasonal wire feature stories, seasonal feature articles are also used by newspaper, magazine, and newsletter readers well in advance of the seasons or holidays to help prepare for the celebrations, the changing weather, and any special activities associated with seasonal events. There is a certain functional value to seasonal stories that extends past their pure entertainment value. A well-written seasonal story will educate readers about a religious holiday or about a national hero. It will teach our children the value of remembering an important family day such as Mother's Day or even a routine civic activity such as voting. These stories will help readers prepare for potential weather disasters such as winter blizzards, spring tornadoes, flooding, or subtropical hurricanes. The articles can teach your readers how to make, prepare for, and understand the meaning of a special meal such as a Passover Seder.

DEVELOPING SEASONAL IDEAS

To begin generating seasonal article ideas, take a look at any calendar. For starters, there is a list of major annual holidays and seasonal occasions later in this chapter. But you can go well beyond this list, because these are only the major national dates you should know. There are, of course, various other national holidays (such as those in Mexico) that are celebrated in the United States. There are also unique regional holidays and state holidays that are peculiar to the regions and states. You can probably think of one of two in your own state that are not on the list included with this chapter.

Many of the *local* holidays and seasons will not appear in nationally sold calendars and appointment books, so don't depend on these sources for complete lists. Instead, check with local libraries, school systems (for their own calendars), local newspaper files, and even local museums, ethnic groups, and civic–business groups. This will help you especially if you are a newcomer to an area or, for example, you want to write for a publication in another region of the country that you might not live in or be familiar with the customs and history of.

However, a serious feature writer—regardless of whether at a newspaper, a magazine, or free-lancing—will get organized about writing seasonal articles. There are many ways to keep up, but the most obvious method is to keep your own calendar for the current year, and also for the next 2 years. This helps you work ahead and in the present. You might be working a day or two or a week or two in advance on seasonal articles for a newspaper, or several months ahead for magazines, and you need to be tuned into needs far ahead, not today. You will see more about this in the next section.

Another good place to check for seasonal ideas is an almanac. Most general annual reference books such as *The World Almanac* and *Information Please Almanac* are quite thorough in listing public and religious dates of significance throughout the year. These books are annually updated and will often run special events date listings for many years beyond the current year.

Another good source category is theme appointment books. These books come ready-made for persons who wish to specialize in certain subjects, such as quilting or computers. They are easy to find on sale in most bookstores. Inside these books, in addition to the regular listings, will be special dates such as anniversaries unique to that theme or subject (e.g., when the first personal computer was placed on the market, or Microsoft founder and chairman Bill Gates' birthday). You might have to look a little to find these, but you can usually find them in specialty shops or advertised in specialty publications such as organizational newsletters.

The key to getting the right idea for a seasonal article is *anticipating*, being able to successfully guess what is going to be on your readers' minds when the season nears. You must be thinking about what people will want to know about a holiday or special event *long before* that event is on the general public's mind. You are trying to anticipate interests: What activities will be interesting? What foods will be tasty? What ceremonies are essential? You must be able to think about seasons that have not yet arrived. Also, you must be able to find a fresh approach to a story that has been told dozens of times before.

Successful seasonal article ideas must be *timely*. You cannot write stories about Thanksgiving meals that require a week's preparation if they are written or published 2 days before Thanksgiving. You cannot jump the gun too much either, because even good ideas are forgotten if they come along too far ahead of the big day. A strong idea will draw readers into your story by making them think to themselves as they read your lead: "Yes! This would be fun to do. I want to find out more about this."

Laurie Goering's *Chicago Tribune* feature story about the allergy season arriving in the Chicago area was timely when a recent spring brought the usual sniffing, sneezing, and other allergic reactions to newly growing plants. Goering, a *Tribune* suburban affairs writer, could not delay publication of her story because it was a seasonal feature with a strong spot element within it. People were reacting to the allergies *at that time*, not a month or two later. An

184 8. SEASONAL FEATURE ARTICLES

annual health problem, such as spring allergies or winter flus and colds, could be anticipated also, and articles could be prepared in advance in some areas as more of a preventative medicine story, of course. As you read Goering's complete story that follows, notice how she mixes description of the reactions to the change in seasons, the allergic reactions, and the comments and explanations of allergy and plant experts. The rich direct quotations, combined with her descriptions, provide for a complete story. This is what Goering (1993) wrote:

This is Allergy Awareness Month. Odds are you're already aware.

Odds are you or someone around you is sneezing, wheezing, cursing empty tissue boxes and making fruitless late-night raids of the medicine cabinet.

That's because for the 40 million allergy sufferers in the United States, May is not the start of summer fun. It's the start of that unremitting annual plunge into histamine hell: hay fever season.

"The allergy season has come in like gangbusters," said Dr. James A. Thompson, a Flossmoor allergist who began tending to the walking wounded last week. "And we're just getting under way."

At first, it appeared things might be better this year. Winter hung late, delaying the pollination of trees and keeping hay fever sufferers safely indoors, suffering delusions that this year would be different.

Then a week ago, spring hit like a tidal wave. Temperatures went from 30 degrees to 80 degrees overnight, tempting everyone outdoors. And then the long-delayed trees, as if lying in wait, joined with early grasses to release a tornado of pollen that has wafted on the breezes ever since.

That double whammy, from plants that usually sprout weeks apart, has produced what Floyd Swink, a plant taxonomist at the Morton Arboretum, called "a pretty rough sneeze season."

"I know somebody who's never had symptoms and this year his eyes are watering so bad he had to go home and take eye drops. There's something to it," Swink said.

Weather has everything to do with hay fever. In years when cool and dry days prevail, plants bloom less, mold doesn't grow and everyone breathes easy. Hot, humid weather, on the other hand, is what keeps pharmacies in business.

But it's not entirely that simple. Hot and dry weather, like that during the drought of 1988, considered the best allergy season in years, can kill mold and slow plant growth. And cool, rainy weather slows mold growth and washes pollen out of the air.

Last week's cool weather, however, didn't include much rain. And the pollen grains still wafting in the air from the week before were sticking to test slides like flies to an empty soda cup.

At the Des Plaines rooftop testing site of the Board Certified Allergists of Greater Chicago, tree pollen was measured at more than 500 grains per cubic meter of air. Anything over 200 grains prompts an allergy alert.

Mold was worse, with readings of up to 4,788. A reading of more than 1,000 spores prompts an alert.

But those readings aren't the whole reason so many more people seem stuffed up and fed up these days, said Dr. James A. Thompson, an allergist with South Suburban Hospital in Hazel Crest.

First, we just plain know more about allergies these days than we did years ago. That makes us less likely to write off a stuffed-up nose as just one of life's trials.

Second, many more of us now live in the suburbs, having traded in the city's concrete for close proximity to cornfields, trees, bluegrass lawns and thousands of other potential allergens.

"There's a reason you find the bulk of allergy offices in the suburbs," Thompson noted.

Finally, researchers believe an increase in other kinds of pollutants in the air— auto exhaust, ozone, dander from more indoor pets—is irritating airways and setting up mild allergy sufferers for a bigger reaction when the pollen lands.

All of that, combined with the recent rapid changes in weather, which leave the body struggling to adapt, means "many people who may not have considered themselves allergic have complaints now," Thompson said.

That's a big problem, and not just for the suffering hordes rubbing their itchy eyes and feeling miserable. Allergies are the second-most common reason people lose days from work or school, according to Dr. Cheryl Lynn Walker of Northwestern Memorial Hospital. The first is the common cold.

That means allergies are "a very important thing to treat," she said. "Some people say, 'It's just allergies,' and don't seek help. But getting help can make your life better."

Treatment varies, depending on the severity of symptoms. A mild sufferer may get relief by taking an over-the-counter antihistamine and keeping the windows closed, especially at night when the pollen counts are highest.

The truly miserable need to do more. Prescription antihistamines and decongestants that don't cause drowsiness are now available and should be taken before symptoms occur for best effect, doctors urge.

Sufferers venturing outside to do yard work also may want to try wearing a pollen mask, or at least tying a linen handkerchief around the face, regardless of the smirks from family and neighbors. And the hardest-hit may just want to stay inside as much as possible, venturing out only after rainstorms wash the air clean.

And, of course, there are shots. Allergists suggest that the severely allergic roll up their sleeves, grit their teeth and remember: Shots, taken first weekly, then monthly over five years, desensitize the overenthusiastic immune systems of allergy sufferers and help 80 percent of them feel better and reduce their use of drugs.

With hordes of the sneezing and wheezing spending $4 billion a year on allergy medication in the United States, that could mean big savings.

But shots aren't effective immediately, doctors warn, and the time to get ready for 1994 is now.

"People say, ‹I'll wait a little› and then their symptoms subside and they never go," said Dr. Donald Schwartz, president of the Board Certified Allergists of Greater Chicago. "They forget that we're going to have grass and trees next year too. If we don't, we're in real trouble."

And don't forget to mark your calendar: Ragweed season starts Aug. 15. (pp. 1–2) © 1993 Chicago Tribune Company, all rights reserved, used with permission.

Good seasonal features also have strong *visual potential.* Try to select topics that will lend themselves to strong photographs or other forms of illustration to help tell the total story. *Chicago Tribune* editors enhanced Goering's story by running two full-color photographs with her article on the top front of the Chicagoland section. The photographs showed metropolitan area residents doing typical outdoor spring activities, such as sketching a landscape and smelling flowers in a garden. Try to suggest to your editors that they use photographs with your story. Suggest potential photographic content, also. How about proposing a schematic diagram that shows how to make an object? How something happens? Perhaps a boxed set of instructions that includes a recipe? For newspapers, magazines, and newsletters, packaging is important with seasonal features and, if you want maximum attention given the article you write, plan to propose strong graphics in addition to your well-written and reported article.

Free-lance writer Clinton Parker (1975) recommends developing a specialization as a seasonal feature writer. Become an expert on a certain season. Parker's specialization? He has been a pastor in Plymouth, Massachusetts, so he focuses on the Pilgrims and Thanksgiving. "Much of the trick to selling seasonal material is to stick to a certain holiday or event, mining it for neglected angles," he says (p. 30). For feature writers, this means you should simply think about the regional activities that are occurring around you, and perhaps one or more of these will develop into a specialization for you that can be sold. He suggests looking not only at the regional calendar but thinking about annual local festivals and fairs for your prospects.

WRITING IN ADVANCE OF THE SEASON

There is no doubt that much seasonal feature article writing is produced in advance. This is particularly true for monthly and less frequently published magazines, but it is also true for newspapers. The major difference is that the lead time varies. For a newspaper, work on a seasonal piece for a Sunday supplement magazine would be not much different from the deadlines you will face for a weekly to monthly magazine or newsletter. Newspaper feature editors like to work as much ahead as possible while keeping their articles as timely as possible. This assists in production of graphics such as large color illustrations, posed photographs, and so on. Even for the spot seasonal feature, done a day ahead, the advantage goes to the writer who finishes early in the day to permit time for revision and collection of new information as deadline nears.

For a magazine or newsletter published monthly or even less frequently, you have to be particularly conscious of "lead time" in preparing stories with content sensitive to seasonal changes. Some monthly magazine and newsletter editors work 4 to 6 months ahead of the current calendar. So, if you are reading this in December or January, you should be thinking now about summer vacation, Father's Day, Fourth of July, or graduation stories. Admittedly, this is hard to do when there is snow outside and temperatures do not easily suggest going to the beach or picnics.

The reason for this? Preparation time. Lead time is that period of time between the decision of a writer to write the article or the decision by an editor to buy it, and the appearance of the article in the publication. Preparation time includes securing rights, assigning photographers and illustrations, editing, fact verification, typesetting, paste-up, proofreading, printing, and even distribution. With all that to be done, it is no wonder that you have to finish writing your Thanksgiving cooking article in May or June to get it into the hands of readers in early November so they can begin thinking of your ideas for their own tables at the end of November.

Jacqueline Shannon (1984), a seasonal feature writer and former magazine editor, says the mastery of timing is critical to your success. Four months, she says, is a dependable industry average for magazines that use color. But she warns:

> If you're submitting on spec[ulation], your lead time is obviously not the same as the publication's lead time. To give your article time to be considered, you must add "reporting time" to lead time. Therefore, if the reporting time for your targeted publication is one month, you must submit a seasonal story five months in advance. But don't stop counting yet. There's the possibility that your story will be rejected. So you must also figure in a couple of months to market it elsewhere. That brings us up to a free-lancer's lead time of six or seven months. In other words, start circulating "Christmas Ornaments from Pine Cones" in May or June. (p. 34)

Shannon says the same rule applies for queries on seasonal articles. In fact, she observes, many publications will provide minimum lead time for you in listings of market information. Also, she advises, there is such a thing as too much lead time. Up to 1 year, she recommends, is acceptable, but only for important events such as an Olympics, an election, or a major public anniversary. So, she says for the usual material, do not submit over 7 months in advance. This leaves a golden window of advance work from 4 to 7 months for magazines and some newsletters. You become a calendar juggler, but to be an effective seasonal writer, this is part of the job. Some writers such as Shannon keep a seasonal picture wall calendar, turned 6 months ahead of the present date, on their desks. All this requires a seemingly simple decision: to plan ahead when writing a seasonal article. This means developing an "editorial body clock," as Shannon calls it.

It also requires writing alertness and discipline. All the while you are working in August preparing an article for February readers, you have to keep references to "this year" and "last year" straight in your mind—or readers will be confused for sure. Shannon also recommends saving a good article idea when the timing is off. As long as the subject is *timeless*, she says, it can be held a few months in the interest of timeliness when it is submitted to an editor.

Author William L. Rivers (1992) suggests seasonal feature writers should try thinking like department store managers and advertise their Christmas specials in July. Editors, like store managers, often need additional "stock" to use. "Editors also need stories that are not time-bound, stories that could be published at any time of year without losing their newsworthy qualities," he says (p. 97).

FRESH ANGLES FOR ANNUAL ARTICLES

One thing all newspaper and magazine feature editors want to avoid is the same old seasonal story each year, so it is necessary for writers to work with their editors to come up with a creative, fresh angle for an annual seasonal article. When it is a certainty that you will need to write that St. Valentine's Day romance article, and the idea of another local couple's 60th or 70th wedding anniversary story bores you (and probably your regular readers, too), it is time to work on a new approach. Ask yourself, "What's new this coming Valentine's Day?" Check with retailers such as card shops, candy stores, and florists. Check with small companies that offer special services such as breakfast in bed or singing telegrams to find out what unique ideas they will be offering for the coming special day. You will find that these businesses will at times come to you with their ideas in hopes of some advance publicity to foster business. Thus, you will find a cooperative source anxious to help you with your article. The strategy is to not limit yourself to the traditional story. Why stop short on a seasonal feature when you can give your readers a better story? Why do the same old story if something stimulating is just waiting to be written?

Clinton Parker (1975) says the formula is simple for the new angle: Fresh material plus solid background equals a successful story. Like generating any good story idea, as you remember from the chapter on developing story ideas, a good seasonal feature must be the product of thorough looking around, extensive talking to lots of people, and careful listening. It also takes thinking and an ability to put things together. This approach will result in some solid article idea leads that could develop into that story you wanted for this year.

Of course, there are times when a very old idea will work for a seasonal article. There are times when an idea or theme has not been used for years, or at least, it has not been used as the basis of an article. Two decades ago, in a classic seasonal "what-if" feature story idea, reporters for the *Florida Times-Union* in Jacksonville were sitting in their newsroom at Christmas time, a traditionally slow news period, trying to come up with a good Christmas Day page one feature for their readers. Reporter Jerry Teer (1973) wondered if it might not be fun to see if the true Christmas spirit still existed in Jacksonville. "Do people really believe all this Christmas stuff?" he asked. "And if they do, how deeply do they believe it?" To find this out, he asked the managing editor: "What if I wrote a story about what happens when myself and a pregnant woman, apparently my wife, visit inns around the city on Christmas Eve in search of a room?" (p. 24). With his editor's okay, he asked a young female friend to join him as the two went from motel to motel looking for a place to stay for the night. They looked a bit ragged, wearing old clothes and carrying their belongings in a duffel bag. They told innkeepers they had no money and, with the help of a pillow, Teer's friend was dressed to appear pregnant. This modern-day version of the Biblical story of Joseph and Mary on Christmas Eve was a widely read feature in the newspaper the next day. Although he hoped to find one Good Samaritan, Teer and his friend found no free rooms among the 15 "inns" they visited. This angle, far more interesting than a story about leftover Christmas trees, demonstrates what is meant by a fresh angle on an annual season or holiday assignment.

In another highly creative Christmas holiday feature, Denver-area feature writer Robin Chotzinoff (1990) decided to turn an ordinary holiday story about store Santas into something more. She used her storytelling and research skills to produce a witty, fun-to-read seasonal feature. She consumer-tested Santa Clauses. A writer for the weekly publication *Westword* for nearly a decade, Chotzinoff wrote a feature highlighting the holiday season by "testing" Santa Clauses at Denver-area shopping areas such as malls. The test was conducted in early December, and the story ran during the following week—in plenty of time for shoppers to take advantage of her discoveries. She used her 7-year-old nephew as the "official tester" and proceeded to rate Santas at 10 different locations over a 3-day period on several levels (e.g., setting, handout "loot," additional fun nearby, and the appearance and general quality, or realism, of the Santa). Working with her nephew, she recounted the conversations Santa had with the boy and other important details that contributed to a holiday atmosphere. When the article was published, it included ratings of the Santas and concluded that the best Santa of that season was one who told the boy about the meaning of Christmas and about loving and caring for people, and that he was the most sincere and honest Santa of all those visited. Chotzinoff told judges of the J.C. Penney–Missouri Journalism Awards, which awarded her a Certificate of Merit in consumer features in the 1991 competition:

> Both Nick and I were surprised at how exhausting such a lighthearted story turned out to be—we drove almost three hundred miles, were accosted by countless mall survey takers and ate way too much junk. Also, I realized that the breathless Christmas feeling I experienced as a child—an entirely nonreligious feeling, I might add—was entirely foreign to Nick and others of his generation. This made me sad. On the other hand, watching a seven-year-old begin to understand the breathless feeling of writing made me very happy . . . . All in all, the Santa survey made no lasting impression on mankind, or did I expect it to. It did impress upon me, however, the importance of presenting a child's point of view as no more or less valid than that of any other source. (Chotzinoff, 1991)

Holiday and seasonal features are a lot of work. To find out what is new for the summer vacation season or what is different for Easter this spring, you have to be willing to do some digging. It takes time to find the right travel agents, hotels, or tourist commissions to get that vacation story that comes out in late May or early June, the start of vacation time for many families, in the middle of winter. It might seem early, but this is when the decisions are, or already have been, made. The same goes for the religious holidays such as Easter. You should not only contact stores for the commercial side of the story—new candies, stuffed toys, and the like—but also should contact churches of the many denominations in your community for the celebrations that are scheduled. Depending on your deadline, you must work ahead and often press individuals for information to make your story more timely when it appears in the newspaper, magazine, or newsletter.

USING LOCAL SOURCES FOR SEASONAL FEATURES

The best-read seasonal material is localized. It is interesting to know what people are doing for a holiday a thousand miles away, but readers really care most about what's interesting in their own neighborhoods and communities. The neighborhood parade for Flag Day might be just the story your newspaper needs. Or a city or regional magazine might want to begin the summer vacation season with an article on nearby vacation destinations. You cannot ignore the activities in your own areas for the highest percentage of sales to newspapers and, if the market permits, magazines.

Local angles are defined in different ways, of course. A magazine looks at localization differently than does a newspaper. Most national magazine editors would consider too much localization a potentially serious flaw in an article. Then again, a local or regional magazine might just be looking for that localized article on coping with winter storms. Newspapers are much the opposite. Most newspapers are edited for their specific communities—a market usually defined by the name of the newspaper. Some major metropolitan newspapers serve multicounty and even statewide markets. A few others, of course, are nationally circulated. In short, know the market and write for it in an appropriate fashion for seasonal articles just as you would any other feature article you write. In the following example written by *Fort Lauderdale Sun-Sentinel* staff writer Lee Eric Smith, this type of approach is taken to a Memorial Day seasonal feature for the front page of the newspaper's Metro section. This story, not an advance on the holiday but a day-after story summarizing all the activities that occurred on the holiday for the next morning, uses local sources and local events only. Rainy weather—with how the rain affected the traditional outdoor activities, such as picnics and memorial services—was the focal point of Smith's story. Smith captures the mood, though, by telling readers in the *round-up format* story that people who ventured outdoors on the rainy holiday mainly did so to go somewhere else indoors such as a movie or mall. Smith (1993), whose reporting was supplemented by Lane Kelley, depends much on direct quotations gathered from interviews with Fort Lauderdale metropolitan area residents and dignitaries in various locations throughout the day. This is the full story:

Memorial Day was more drizzle and frizzle than sun and fun, and to many that meant malls and movies instead of parades and picnics.

For the most part, beaches and parks were rained out, and people turned to indoor activities for the holiday.

But not everybody gave in to the rain—about 200 people participated in a parade in Pompano Beach.

The parade began at 10 a.m. and lasted only 10 minutes. Veterans marched, followed by the Coral Springs High School Marching Band.

After the parade, there was a short service. State Rep. John Rayson, D-Pompano Beach, linked the rain to famous events in World War II.

"Did it rain in Corregidor? Did it rain in Bataan? That never stopped American soldiers from fighting, and it should not stop us from honoring them," he said.

Parade organizers in Davie bypassed their annual parade altogether, instead gathering at the Davie Rodeo Arena for a Memorial Day program, where Mayor James Bush spoke. Several veteran groups were also on hand, Town Administrator Irv Rosenbaum said.

The program, sponsored by the Town of Davie and several area Boy Scout troops, featured a Civil War re-enactment as well as the Fort Lauderdale Drum and Bugle Corps performing in Revolutionary War uniforms.

"The rain didn't slow us down," Rosenbaum said.

But other people were not as lucky.

Ever since Tom Meek moved to Fort Lauderdale in 1979, he has spent Memorial Day at the beach, then returned home to barbecue. Yesterday, he found himself sitting in The Galleria Mall. And his barbecue?

"I poured some Liquid Smoke on some ribs, and I've got them in the oven, not on the grill," said Meek, 39. "We'll be eating inside, but this is not what I planned."

Between the weather and the opening of several blockbuster films, The Movies at Lauderhill had a busy weekend, general manager Robert Boswell said.

About 8,500 tickets were sold from Friday through Sunday night, and 2,200 tickets had been sold on Monday before the evening shows, he said.

"That's normally what we do in a week, and way more than we usually do on Memorial Day," Boswell said. "People usually go out for picnics, so it's usually not that big of a holiday for us."

But Dave Barnabei and his friends were determined to have fun. They went to the beach and played a little 3-on-3 football. Despite the rain, they had been out most of the day, skateboarding, swimming, and having fun. "We started rollerblading, but it was too wet," said Barnabei, 21, of Fort Lauderdale.

After the football game, the plan was to go inside, eat some barbecue, drink some beer, then hit the beach again.

"We like it like this," said Sean Boroughs, 23. "We wanted it to rain. This way we get to keep the beach all to ourselves."

Staff writer Lane Kelley contributed to this report. (p. 1B) Reprinted with permission from the *Sun-Sentinel*, Fort Lauderdale, Florida.

SEASONAL COLOR ARTICLES

Although you may have already given thought to writing color feature articles, it is important to point out that many successful seasonal articles mix in the elements of strong color and descriptive writing. Writers will use seasonal article assignments as a chance to exercise their imagination along with their descriptive writing skills.

Marco R. della Cava, writing the Life section cover story for a *USA Today* weekend edition, tried to capture the unusual nature of Bike Week, the annual early March gathering of about 250,000 persons at Daytona Beach, Florida. This seasonal event commands a descriptive colorful approach to the story and della Cava's story delivers the necessary images to readers to accompany the color photographs on the page. In the story, his writing conjures up images of lots of chrome, Harley-Davidsons, black leather jackets, loud engines, and the tattoo-covered "Born to Be Wild" bikers. Photographs of bikers parading down the street and dressed to the max in black leather strengthen the stereotype. But perhaps you didn't think of all the ordinary working folks, many of them professionals, who now constitute the majority of the persons attending Bike Week's activities. This is the story that della Cava (1993) wrote about the closing weekend:

DAYTONA BEACH, Fla.—Main Street is every cow's nightmare this week.

Acres of black leather jackets, pants, vests and bikinis parade down this teeming drag, worn by 250,000 fans here for the final weekend of Bike Week.

But there is a levity to all this darkness as the swap meets, races, shopping and contests brew up a camaraderie common to most cookouts.

Despite the menacing images of "bikers" sketched by Hollywood, the face of motorcycling is changing.

No longer is biker a synonym for Hell's Angel. Only 1% of riders are "hard-core"—replacing them are baby boomers—dubbed RUBs, rich urban bikers—intent on capturing their easy riding youth.

For all its menacing look, Bike Week is a giant costume party starring grandmothers, kids and Christians, a place where you bump into a mean-looking guy only to find he's a nice dentist from Toledo.

Or an undertaker from Lilburn, Ga.

Bill and Carole Head have been coming here for eight years. Their massive Honda Aspencade—bought from a motorcycle cop friend—provides transport that's as psychological as it is physical.

"We see so much sorrow at work, so we live like there's no tomorrow," says Carole, who shocked her son recently by marking her 50th birthday with a "butterfly tattoo to my fanny!"

Adds Bill, a silver skull capping off his black outfit: "This bike here is my golf, my tennis, my fishing and my hunting. I love the freedom."

That feeling has stung Peter Guldan's friends. The 36-year-old engineer from Memphis owns six bikes and a few cars, and he's here—brazenly mainstream in shorts and a white T-shirt—for the party.

"This is a two-wheel Mardi Gras. The ladder-climbing yuppies I work with are into it," he says. "The traditional scene is being swallowed up by white middle-class males who want to get away from their PC's and cellular phones."

That world is nowhere in sight on Main Street.

First to strike is the noise, a demonic growl that sounds like a thunderstorm that won't quit.

Next come the exhaust fumes, swirling up from gleaming tailpipes in such abundance that they become a familiar elixir.

Providing both are riders from around the globe, including Ralph and Katherine Wenig, who flew in, bikes and all, from Munich so they could cap a Daytona marriage ceremony with a tandem cruise on Main.

Sidewalks swell with spectacle: The tattooed man with a macaw, a goggled dog in a sidecar, horned hats that could make a steer envious.

And then, as always, there are Bike Week's women, a saucy mix of no-nonsense bike owners and scantily-clad passengers who occasionally indulge the crowd's call to bare untanned flesh.

But this may not be the scene at Bike Week in 2003. A conservative bent may calm future gatherings, much as it has already fueled the rebirth of one American legend.

Ten years ago, Harley-Davidson held only 23% of the "big-bike" market, a lone U.S. stalwart battered by Japanese imports. This year it claims 65%.

The Milwaukee-based company—which turns 90 this year—now sells every bike it makes. The average buyer? Married, 32, college-educated and earning $39,200 a year, according to the Motorcycle Industry Council.

Good thing, too. Harleys aren't cheap, ranging from $5,000 to $15,000, not even counting a glossy 130-page catalog of accessories that can nearly double a bike's final price tag.

They dominate the scene here, due to a resurgence in quality as well as Stateside patriotism. The company knows a fiscally good thing when it sees it, and soon will launch a major leather-plus clothing line.

"I think people enjoy playing a role, especially one that's so dressed down and natural," says Karen Davidson, designer and the co-founder's great-grand-daughter.

Without a touch of irony she says her $400 black jackets—toddlers can get suited up for $150—and other Harley fare are a hot trend in Japan: "They love what is classically American."

And for that, look no further than the chromed steed, says Buzz Kanter, publisher of *American Iron* magazine, Norwalk, Conn., a thriving equipment mag that stands out in a sea of women-draped-on-bikes fare.

"There's a bit of *Easy Rider* and *The Wild One* in all this, but a lot is just being able to get away. It's a real stress-breaker," he says. "I like one Harley T-shirt. It says, 'If I have to explain, you'll never understand.'"

Kanter has no trouble explaining why circulation has jumped 400% in two years, to 85,000.

"We got so many letters saying the same thing, 'I have young kids and don't want to have to explain to them why my magazines have nude women in them.' We keep it clean, and people seem to want that."

Though bikers are a communal lot, they treasure the individualism riding seems to nurture.

"In a society where people can get lost in a crowd, biking gives you a sense of identity," says Los Angeles attorney Russ Brown, whose magazine ads bill him as a 33-year riding veteran and founder of Bikers Against Manslaughter, "a AAA for bikers."

"But," he adds, that identity "is an illusion more than a reality."

An illusion that finds a willing subject in Kevin Jones.

"I love the sound of those engines, I love the prestige," he says, the envy of Main Streeters for pulling off the ultimate American double: squiring his vintage Harley with a gleaming red Corvette.

"I haven't missed this in 23 years," says Jones, 37, who "does amazingly well" as a bellman at nearby Disney World. "I've met doctors, lawyers, some normal looking, some with ponytails, and all the nicest people you'd ever want to meet."

Those types no doubt bring a smile to the face of Bill Donahue, owner of D & L House of Leather. He takes a break from a quick $1,000 sale ("Couple of jackets, some vests, a shirt") to remark on the changes he's seen over the past few years.

"It's so upscale now, it's amazing. These shops used to be dens (for bikers). They used to be dark. Now it's light, the streets are clean. Now this whole thing is socially acceptable." He pauses.

"I tell ya, there's no recession here. Why? Because everybody is tired of being squeezed. Everyone has to have some fun sometime."

Bingo. Hang out here long enough and you're engulfed in something no survey can quantify: passion. Whether it be for escaping reality or embracing fellowship.

No one need remind motorcycle fans that they ride in the land of the automobile. They lobby against laws they feel restrict them (helmets are an issue), and pray to avoid cars that (as compared with European thoroughfares) largely ignore them.

Enter Bike Week.

If it can deliver nothing else, what it bestows on aficionados from all walks— whether ex-con from Kansas or dentist from Toledo—is the promise that for one sunny Floridian week each year, it's a biker's world after all. (pp. 1D, 2D) © 1993 USA TODAY. Reprinted with permission.

Description, such as that in della Cava's story, is important to some seasonal features. The event's unique atmosphere is present because of it. Readers sense it. However, use this descriptive and color-laden approach with caution and deliberate skill. Author William Rivers (1992) says "the worst flaw in seasonal stories is that the writer tries too hard to be overpoweringly descriptive. Instead, the writer should be content with touches of description: a few visual verbs, an unpredictable adjective or two, an adverb that is allowed to do its

MAJOR HOLIDAY AND SEASONAL ARTICLES CALENDAR

January
> New Year's Day (1st)
> Martin Luther King's birthday (15th, officially, it varies)

February
> National Freedom Day (1st)
> Groundhog Day (2nd)
> Constitution Day (Mexico, 5th)
> Abraham Lincoln's birthday (12th)
> St. Valentine's Day (14th)
> Susan B. Anthony's birthday, also Women's Liberation Day (15th)
> George Washington's birthday (3rd Monday)
> Ash Wednesday (varies)
> Mardi Gras (varies)

March
> Baseball training season opens (varies)
> St. Patrick's Day (17th)
> First day of Spring (21st)
> Mardi Gras (varies)
> Palm Sunday (varies)
> Good Friday (varies)
> Easter (varies)

April
> April Fool's Day (1st)
> Daylight Savings Time begins (varies)
> Palm Sunday (varies)
> Good Friday (varies)
> First day of Passover (varies)
> Pan American Day (14th)
> National Secretary Week (3rd week)
> Easter Sunday (varies)
> Easter Monday (Canada, varies)
> Arbor Day, Bird Day (last Friday)

May
> May Day, also Labor Day (Mexico, 1st)
> Loyalty Day (1st)
> Mother's Day (2nd Sunday)
> Victoria Day (Canada, varies)
> End of school year (varies)
> College, high school graduation (varies)
> Armed Forces Day (3rd Saturday)
> National Maritime Day (22nd)
> Memorial Day (last Monday)
> Traditional Memorial Day (30th)

June
> End of school year (varies)
> Summer vacation season begins

College, high school graduation (varies)
National Smile Week (varies)
Flag Day (14th)
Father's Day (3rd Sunday)
First day of Summer (21st)

July.

Canada Day (1st)
U.S. Independence Day (4th)

August

Civic holiday (Canada, varies)
Ecology Day (varies)
National Aviation Day (19th)

September.

Labor Day (U.S., Canada, 1st Monday)
Summer vacation season ends
Start of school year (varies)
Football season opens (varies)
Grandparents Day (11th)
Independence days (Mexico, 15th–16th)
Citizenship Day (17th)
Rosh Hashanah (varies)
Yom Kippur (varies)
First day of Autumn (22nd or 23rd)
American Indian Day (4th Friday)

October.

Child Health Day (1st Monday)
Columbus Day, Discoverer's Day, Pioneer's Day (2nd Monday)
Columbus Day (Mexico, 12th)
World Poetry Day (15th)
Thanksgiving Day (Canada, varies)
United Nations Day (24th)
Daylight Saving Time ends (varies)
Halloween (31st)

November.

Election Day (1st Tuesday after 1st Monday)
Veterans' Day (11th)
Remembrance Day (Canada, 11th)
Sadie Hawkins Day (1st Saturday after 11th)
Elizabeth Cady Stanton birthday (women's rights, 12th)
Thanksgiving Day (4th Thursday)

December.

First Day of Chanukah (varies)
Basketball season begins (varies)
Bill of Rights Day (15th)
Forefather's Day (21st)
First Day of Winter (21st)
Christmas (25th)
Boxing Day (Canada, 26th)

BEST SOURCES FOR SEASONAL ARTICLES

- Published specialized or theme wall calendars.
- Topical or theme appointment books.
- General almanacs such as the *World Almanac* or *Information Please Almanac*.
- State travel department calendars.
- City and regional chambers of commerce.
- Holiday festival committees and organizations.
- Historians and history museum curators/directors.
- Encyclopedias and annotated bibliographies.
- Newspaper, magazine, or newsletter files from a year before the annual event.
- Retail store sales managers and clerks.
- Product manufacturers' regional sales representatives.
- Subject experts.

---

work because it's in a crisp sentence rather than in a sentence burdened with other adverbs" (p. 251). Does the Bike Week feature accomplish this more subtle approach? Probably. Like other color articles, many times a good seasonal story with a strong dose of color will use anecdotes to open the article. This form of storytelling draws the reader into the article easily, Rivers says.

PROFESSIONAL'S POINT OF VIEW

Doug Jimerson
Better Homes and Gardens

Obviously timing is essential when you're free-lancing seasonal material. Every publication, whether it be a newspaper or magazine, has its own lead time that you must take into consideration if you want to successfully market your story ideas. At *Better Homes and Gardens*, for example, we plan our editorial calendar 1 year in advance of publication. This doesn't mean that we wouldn't accept a better story idea closer to deadline, but it does indicate how vital it is to be aware of your target magazine's schedule and plan accordingly.

More importantly, you should know the editorial content or philosophy of any publication you solicit for free-lance work. Nothing is more frustrating to editors than to receive unsolicited manuscripts about topics that aren't even remotely related to their publication. For example, our magazine never publishes poetry, songs, book reviews, celebrity interviews, or first person humor stories like "How I Raised Bumper Crops of Broccoli In My Bathtub." Yet, every week we're inundated with submissions like this from misguided writers across the country, usually with a tag line on the bottom of the page asking us to send payment as soon as possible!

I realize that this all might sound a pretty basic, but I can't emphasize enough the importance of research. Always take time to read and critique a few issues from the magazine or newspaper before you charge ahead with your own story ideas. It's also smart to check an up-to-date masthead and read the bylines of all stories. You need to know the names (correct spellings, please) of the appropriate editors you'll contact later. And remember, don't take notes from mastheads that are over 1 year old. Editors retire, die, get promoted, and move on to other publications. One of my pet peeves is that I'll often receive unsolicited manuscripts that are addressed to the garden editor who was with the magazine in the 1950s. That shows me that the writer hasn't done homework about the direction or scope of our magazine.

In conclusion, I'd also like to suggest that you think about specializing in one or more subject areas. There's nothing wrong with being a good generalist, but if you strive to become an expert in a particular field, such as money management, electronics, parenting, architecture, food, environment, sports, or even horticulture, you'll have a leg up on the competition when a publication is looking for someone to write that "special" feature. It's also a smart marketing strategy. If you can sell yourself as a proficient writer with a strong background in a particular subject area you'll stand out from the rest of the thundering herd. (Jimerson, personal communication, 1988)

Doug Jimerson is Garden Outdoor Living editor for *Better Homes and Gardens* magazine, Des Moines, Iowa.

9

Reviews, Criticism, and Entertainment Features

Writing about entertainment is changing with the times. Not just "previews and reviews," editors for consumer magazines and daily newspapers have taken new looks at how reviews, criticism, and entertainment features are extending beyond the routine. New sections have been created for newspapers. New departments in magazines are parts of redesigns. These publications have broadened how they cover the arts and they have added more depth. Entertainment journalism is growing to full maturity alongside the more established opinion-based reviews and critiques (Bednarski, 1993; Bunn, 1993; Hellyer, 1993; Vawter, 1993).

Many aspiring nonfiction writers associate writing artistic reviews and criticism with a glamorous career filled with opportunities to mix with both the famous and infamous artists of our time. The work is attractive to beginners in the news media because reviewers and critics are often working at the cutting edge of such creativity as filmmaking, book writing, television program production, music and dance performance, and theater production. Perhaps the lives of those who do reviewing and critical writing are often filled with glitter, bright lights, and black ties for the successful few who are nationally known full-time reviewers or critics of the arts. For most people who do reviewing or criticism, it is a part-time specialization and seldom offers the lifestyles of the rich and famous. Reviewing and critical writing are still two of the most popular forms of feature writing among young writers. With the strong appeal of the performing arts to young adults in particular, it only makes sense that many beginning writers seek to develop talents as reviewers and, ultimately, as critics.

However, it remains difficult for a nonfiction writer to build a career in reviewing and critical journalism. Most newspapers, magazines, and newsletters, when they use a regular schedule of reviews or critical analyses of the arts, use feature syndication services and part-time or even volunteer writers—such as experts—for their articles. Only the largest of metropolitan- area daily newspapers, newspaper wire services, and features syndicates retain full-time reviewers and critics in the arts. It is not uncommon to find as many as a half dozen to a dozen persons on a large daily newspaper's arts or lifestyles section staff. However, small and medium daily newspapers cannot often afford full-time critics or reviewers on staff. They turn to full-time staff members who specialize in other types of reporting and writing or editing to do reviewing as additional work. Many use regular part-time writers to extend their staff coverage. Or, of course, these newspapers also turn to free-lance writers.

Magazines and newsletters that publish reviews and criticism of the arts will most often use regular part-time, free-lance, or volunteer sources. Like newspapers of all sizes, some magazines will depend on news services and features syndicates to provide their reviews and criticism. Few magazines or newsletters have full-time critics on staff unless they are highly specialized publications devoted to one or more of these arts.

Reviewing and critical writing are quite different from other forms of professional feature writing. Generally, professional feature writers will not often cross the line from fair and objective writing into subjective writing and personal opinion, but reviewers and critics must take this bold step for their work to contain value to readers. That's why reviewers and critics are so widely read and valuable to consumers.

It is difficult to discuss reviewing and criticism without discussing entertainment reporting also. For many arts writers, the job involves regularly writing both reviews or critiques and news from their beats. A good reviewer or critic will be a major asset for a publication by covering the arts as important news-based feature material. For example, film reviewers or critics are often called upon to write the local story when a film crew goes to a community to shoot on location. Regular book reviewers or critics are assigned to profile a local author who has written a successful new book.

There are numerous roles the reviewer and critic play in serving their readers and the region's arts community. Rutgers University communication professor Todd Hunt (1972) points to eight functions of reviewers and entertainment writers in covering the arts:

1. *First, and foremost, the reviewer informs readers about the arts.* Readers learn about the existence of new works from their favorite publications.

2. *Reviewing and criticism help to raise the cultural level of the community, the region, and the nation.* By setting standards for performance, the cultural community is, in the long run, improved.

3. *Reviewers and critics impart personality to the community.* By writing lively copy, expressing well-supported opinions, and by being a little bit different, the reviewer and critic provide a unique personal dimension to their feature writing.

4. *Reviewers and critics advise readers how to best use their resources.* Reviewers and critics help readers decide what films to see, books to read, restaurants to visit, and theaters to attend. With limited entertainment budgets, many readers depend on their local reviewers and critics to guide them in making these decisions.

5. *Reviewers and critics help artists and performers to fine-tune their works.* As an educated consumer, a qualified reviewer or critic can make suggestions that will help artists and performers to improve their efforts in later performances.

6. *Reviewers and critics identify the new.* Whenever new works are offered to the public, and, at times, before these new works are presented for the first time, reviewers and critics are able to identify, interpret, and explain trends and new developments in the arts to their readers.

7. *Reviewers and critics record history.* One of the best sources of performing arts history is the review. As many nonfiction news writers do, reviewers and critics write arts history on a daily basis.

8. *Reviews and critical writing are also entertaining.* As reviewers and critics impart personality, they also entertain with timely and interesting writing.

Many consumers think of critics as arts snobs who influence the public, writer William Ruehlmann (1979) says. But, he adds, this is far from reality. The reviewer and critic *do not* influence readers. Reviewers and critics have an important role in the relationship of the arts and their communities. Reviewers and critics are, in many ways, in the middle of the arts on one hand and the public on the other hand.

So, who cares about the opinions expressed? Reviewers and critics actually have several constituencies. Consumers are in the front row. Artists and performers are also part of the group that seriously considers the work of the reviewer and critic.

What does it take to get a job as a reviewer? Much depends on the publication. Some small newspapers and magazines without big budgets cannot afford to pay well and will offer opportunities to beginners for little or no financial rewards. Some even use volunteers who write for the "clips"— that is, to get the experience and published articles known as "clips"—but not for remuneration. Editors of these publications allow their reviewers to "learn" on the job. Most publications are more discriminating and require greater preparation of reviewers and critics. Although your *writing skills* are probably most important in determining your success as a reviewer, the more *educated* you are, the more *knowledge* you possess about the art form, and the more *experience* you have as a reviewer, the better chance you have in finding a job. *Motivation* is also a key to be a reviewer or critic. Professor Todd Hunt maintains that you must have a profound concern for perpetuation and improvement of the art form. He also says you need the roots of a newsman, that is, a sense for news, on which you build your interests in the arts.

REVIEWER OR CRITIC? WHICH IS WHICH?

There is a significant difference in a review and critical writing, although some arts writers feel the distinction is an artificial one and not really necessary. But such matters are substantial and worth noting. Reviews are generally written by less authoritative writers and often take the perspective of the consumer of a particular work. Some critics feel the content of most reviews is less substantial, more like high school or college book reports. These articles tend to summarize the work and its major features, but are not so evaluative. The review describes the work and its genre. It can also discuss the skill of the artist or author, and even the quality.

The major distinction between reviewing and criticism is *expression of opinion*. When writers begin to include personal opinion in the form of evaluation, they leave the realm of objectivity for subjectivity and their assessments of artistic performance are offered. The line into criticism is crossed. This is also a more sophisticated, perhaps worldly, view of the art form.

Critical writing at this level usually requires specialization and higher education. One of the most important differences between reviewers and critics is educational background. Most successful critics are college- or graduate-level educated in the art form they criticize. To be a critic, you must have some form of specialized education, and perhaps even amateur or professional experience as a performing artist yourself. After all, what better credentials to criticize performance or an art form than to have been there yourself? Certainly individuals educated with majors in drama or film are going to be better informed critics about the correct or preferred techniques in theater or movie production than someone who is not. An English major or author will likely be a better book critic than someone who is not. A person who majored in food and nutrition or has been a professional chef would be better qualified to be a restaurant critic than someone who simply likes food and wants to dine out on an expense account.

The point is rather simple: To be a critic, you must know what standards to apply in assessing professional or amateur performance. You must be able to write what you think about the effort in a *skilled* manner. You must know what levels represent truly excellent work and what ones do not. In fact, some experts on reviewing and criticism feel that because there are many unqualified reviewers and critics it might be better for news organizations to utilize artists as reviewers and critics.

It is becoming easier for beginning writers to specialize in the arts when in school. In addition to reviewing and criticism, these writers also will be covering the arts as news. Furthermore, because most newspapers, magazines, and newsletters cannot hire individuals solely for coverage of the arts, general feature writing or news writing and reporting skills are necessary. Universities and colleges with programs in mass communication and the arts are the best locations for academic preparation for careers as reviewers and critics. Schools that offer journalism majors in newspapers and magazines and also provide students with a chance to double major in an art such as music, drama, or creative writing permit maximum development of talents necessary to be a professional reviewer and critic in the next decades.

WRITING ENTERTAINMENT FEATURES

Most reviewers and critics also write entertainment news and features. It is a natural extension of the specialization to be able to write both news and features, in addition to opinion about the arts. At many publications, it is part of the beat responsibilities to cover breaking news, to write Sunday features, and to review or criticize. The work is therefore a mix of objective and subjective forms of feature writing.

However, writing entertainment features is as difficult as any other type of feature writing. It requires the same reporting and writing skills. It may demand even more patience and resourcefulness because of the unique nature of the artistic community. There are many responsibilities covering entertainment and few people to cover entertainment beats at most publications. Like other forms of reporting, perhaps the most important ability is source cultivation. Developing sources of information about the entertainment world is your bread and butter. After all, reporters are reporters.

Entertainment feature writing is often more nationally focused than other types of feature writing. Many entertainment stories, especially in metropolitan areas, have national interest and appeal. For television beat writers, for instance, there is a mix of national and local stories, but many of the programs are national in origin because they air on broadcast or cable networks and must have national focus. National stories, even if they are about television programs, have a local impact at the stations that air them and in the homes where they are watched. At the same time, local television stories must have a priority because they involve persons and companies in the areas served by local publications.

Entertainment writers also seem to have more autonomy in their work than most other reporters at mainstream newspapers and magazines. As beat reporters, they are specialists. They are expected to know more about what is happening in their areas of expertise than others in the newsroom. Although entertainment reporters are specialists, it is possible to be even more specialized with beats within entertainment, such as television-radio-cable, dance, restaurants, music, and so forth. Thus, it is up to the writer to generate story ideas and complete them. On occasion, editors will propose or assign stories, but, for the most part, entertainment writers are expected to develop a high degree of enterprise in their work. Some individuals, particularly beginners who cover entertainment, like the independence, but others prefer direction because they feel they just cannot come up with good material day in and day out.

Along with that, many entertainment writers—as well as reviewers and critics—work from locations other than the newspaper newsroom or magazine office. Many work from offices in their homes. Part of the reason is the nature of their work—it is not in the office and at unusual hours. For example, Fort Lauderdale *Sun-Sentinel* popular music writer Deborah Wilker, who has covered entertainment beats and has written reviews and criticism for more than 10 years, does much of her work from an office at home. But she still must be a *reporter*, she says. Wilker begins most of her workdays on the telephone. She spends about 3 hours each morning talking to artists, agents, promoters, and other sources. "I am on the phone all day long," she explains, "relentlessly pursuing any source I can regarding what concerts are occurring and what albums will be coming out and when. If I get a release date on an album, I want to make sure I have that album in my hand a week before the release date. At night, I usually write, all night long . . . or if there is a concert, I'll go to the concert" (Wilker, 1993).

Wilker's colleague, Tom Jicha, who covers the television and radio industries, as well as regularly writing reviews and criticism about television and radio for the Fort Lauderdale *Sun-Sentinel*, uses similar techniques and depends on the telephone a great deal. "We [entertainment reporters] are a lot like cops; all reporters are. Without sources, we'd be dead. The way you get those sources is that you cultivate them on the phone. A lot of the time, I'll call people up just to chat, to maintain the lines of communication" (Jicha, 1993). That, it seems, is the nature of entertainment feature writing: people, chatting, interviewing, information gathering, and story writing.

Local newspaper, magazine, and newsletter entertainment feature writers have an advantage over their broadcast and cable counterparts because they can get advance material much more easily. Telephone interviews can build stronger advances for big shows in a community, for example. It is difficult, if not impossible, for local market television entertainment reporters to do this.

Entertainment reporters must develop publicists as sources for their feature stories. Some entertainment feature writers are generalists—covering all types of entertainment and the arts—but others are highly specialized. The generalists must cover all aspects of the art world and must be comfortable with a wide range of arts and recreational activities. Specialists are focused on film, television-radio, popular music, and so forth. Some are highly specialized. They don't just write about music, but focus on pop music, classical music, or jazz. And it is more difficult for generalists writing entertainment features to have a depth of sources to call on for stories, but they do have a greater breadth of sources.

Just because the subject matter may be lighter and less complex than most other news beats, it cannot be less accurate or timely. The effort is seemingly endless for some entertainment reporters. Even covering the glamour events such as the Academy Awards program, the Grammy Awards show, a multimillion dollar concert tour, or other national mega-events can be exhausting. Getting to a location early, waiting, and then being ready at an instant's notice can be stressful and physically demanding. Often covering events such as the Academy Awards means standing in crowded rooms, screaming questions at sources who ignore them, being subjected to herd-like instructions of publicists, and other less appealing situations. In fact, most entertainment reporters at a major awards event never get into the auditorium. They wind up covering the event from an auxiliary room (or adjacent building) set up with a television monitor. When postevent interviewing occurs, it takes place in a press conference forum with a chance for only one question, at best, if the reporter gets called on. There is rarely any exclusive interviewing that takes place at such events.

Most entertainment reporting at the local level does not involve such spotlight events. Those assignments might be the reward for a year of covering more routine entertainment news at the local level. These stories focus on shows at the local auditorium or arena, touring artists and performers who come into the area, an occasional interview with a celebrity who visits the area or who lives in the area, and a lot of features about amateur productions and artistic effort at neighborhood theaters, local colleges, and perhaps even high schools. The types of stories are often classified as nothing more than previews and reviews, some editors like to say. There is much truth to that, but enterprising entertainment reporters go much further with profiles, human interest stories, seasonal stories, and a wide array of approaches to their beats. It is up to you and your skills to make the most of being an entertainment reporter.

USING THE ESSAY STRUCTURE

Although entertainment features use a variety of organizational approaches, most reviews and critical articles find their way into an *essay* structure. This is a simple approach that permits the maximum development of writing. A good lead (or introduction) opens the essay with a statement of what you want to do. The body of the essay is a synthesis of generalizations about the work that are supported by evidence and illustrations that are taken from the work. The conclusion summarizes your points. And all this is done in just a few hundred to a few thousand words. Writer William Ruehlmann (1979) recommends 10 points about the basics of what he calls judgmental features. To reach success as a critic, he says:

1. *Make yourself an expert.* The more you know about writing books such as novels, the more authoritative you will be and the better you can handle your assignment.
2. *Don't flaunt your expertise.* Do not write over the heads of your readers. Teach, but do not assume too much about what readers know.
3. *Do not talk down.* Assume your reader is intelligent and can understand what you write.
4. *Avoid overdependence on plot summary.* Do not tell your reader everything that happened. Tell the reader how and why something happened, but not what.
5. *Explain the work in context of our lives.* In other words, he asks, is the work good entertainment? Does it help us understand ourselves or the world around us better? If so, it is art.

6. *Find a strong lead and ending.* Be specific and arresting in your lead. End with a snap.

7. *Cite specific examples to support your views.* If you say something good or bad about the work, show readers. This gives insight by providing your own reasoning behind the assessment.

8. *Write well and write cleverly.* Apply the same standards for good style and structure that you expect in the work you are reviewing to your own writing.

9. *Take your stand with conviction.* Do not be timid. Write with confidence and assurance.

10. *Have a little charity.* Remember this in particular when you are writing about amateur artists instead of professionals. But even in dealing with seasoned professionals, take into consideration all factors when you decide you love or hate something.

Ruehlmann says that the structure of a review can be as varied as any other type of feature article. He says you must remain flexible to permit the review to take the form necessary to make your points understandable. He also emphasizes the need for readable reviews. This is done, he adds, by use of specific examples to support opinion and to enliven the critical writing.

Good writing is what sells your work, regardless of whether you are a staff writer or free-lancer. Writing must keep readers interested. Andy Rathbone (personal communication, 1993), San Diego-based editor of the nation's largest regional computer weekly publication, *ComputorEdge*, and a former editor at Harcourt, Brace, Jovanovich, writes both product reviews and restaurant reviews. He believes opinion writing should be *stimulating* for readers. "You have to hold the reader's interest by going close to the edge, but not over. Nobody wants to read a boring opinion. However, if you go too far in one direction, you'll be branded as a radical, and lose the reader's respect and, more important, the reader's long-term interest. Walking that edge—being radical enough to be interesting, yet still have that truthful edge that makes people nod their heads—is the key."

Although straight entertainment feature writing is normally in third person, there are two schools of thought about perspective in personal opinion-based writing. One side argues for first person writing. The other advocates third person. There is more to it than just use of personal pronouns, however. Consider what you are saying to a reader by writing in first person. You are saying, "I am important enough to be a major part of this review." It is, of course, convention in professional journalism to write most nonfiction, such as general feature stories, in third person. The rules change in the case of personal opinion, especially reviewing and criticism. Use of first person is more acceptable. Still, many reviewers and critics prefer to write in third person. It is really a matter of each publication's own style of writing or, perhaps, that of the individual writer.

In review writing, the philosophical approaches of reviewers and critics fall into two schools: authoritative and impressionistic. Todd Hunt (1972) defines the impressionistic approach as one that "generates an expression of the critic's . . . reaction to the work, exclusive of standards or precedents" (p. 26). Authoritarian writing perspective tends to be third person and is highly comparative, Hunt argues. "The particular work is evaluated in reference to historic models which have been previously judged worthy. The authoritarian critic must have considerable background preparation and exposure to the art form, and he necessarily accepts a set of fixed standards of rules" (p. 26). Most contemporary reviewers and critics are somewhere in the middle of the two approaches, Hunt says. Most attempt to take the best of both schools rather than fit into one or the other. "[M]ost feel free to switch into the more comfortable personal essay style, often leading to an 'I-like-it-because' conclusion"(p. 29), Hunt says.

As in all other forms of features, selection of the lead is a big decision. How do you begin? This part of your review will set the tone of the entire article and should be carefully considered before you begin. Perhaps you can open with something startling about the artist. You have decided the work is pretty bad and you want to warn readers at the beginning, so you choose an inverted pyramid approach by getting the "news" about your evaluation at the top.

Whatever you choose to say in the lead, your first several paragraphs need to establish the *context* of the review or critique. What work is being reviewed or criticized? Who is involved? When and where? As you move into the body of your essay, you begin to tell your readers how and why. Some beginning reviewers are so anxious to get into the opinion, they forget to present the basic facts near the beginning of their essay. You should also avoid clichés associated with reviewing and criticism of a particular art form, especially in a lead. These worn-out statements or phrases only drag down the quality of your own writing and bore the reader. Find new and interesting ways to make your points.

Pressing deadlines may change the approach you take when writing reviews. It is one thing to dwell on a work for several days before committing your ideas to paper. For a debuting new play, film, television program, or touring musician, you might get just one shot and only a few hours to complete your work.

For newspaper and weekly magazine reviewers and critics, this is generally the case on all new work. For monthly magazine or newsletter writers, deadlines present a different set of problems—remaining timely when you must produce your feature or review weeks, or even months, before a movie or book debuts. The problem is so severe for some magazines that they simply do not try to review certain types of material unless they can get considerable lead time through previews and advance copies. For some magazines and newsletters, for example, book publishers may provide paperbound "galley proofs" or "special advance reading editions" for reviewer or feature writer use before the book has been hardbound and distributed to bookstores for sale to the public.

A thorough review will offer readers comparison and contrast. Readers want to know how a new book compares with the earlier works of a favorite author or how a new album will stand against the earlier efforts of a group. What is similar and what is different? Why? Is it relevant? Similarly, many essay reviews will compare and contrast the works of different artists on the same subject or same level in a single review. It is not unusual, for example, to find a set of summer movie reviews packaged together or one review that discusses all the new summer releases at the same time. The technique is also popular with book reviewers who might look at new books on one subject— such as the 1992 presidential election campaign or a trio of new competing books about the British royal family—in a single review.

It is also important to provide readers with a highlight or information summary with a review or critique. These information summaries are often "boxed" typographically by editors to run within or beside the review. However, it is your responsibility, as the reviewer and critic, to provide the information used in these boxes. As you read about the major forms of reviews and criticism in the following sections, you will learn what specifically is commonly needed in the information box for each art form. These inserts in your reviews and critiques focus on the basics, but each publication has its own variation of how it should be done. These are general guidelines, however, and it is essential that you present the facts in a consistent style that your publication uses.

WHO HAS THE RIGHT TO SAY WHAT?

Do readers really care about what you say in your reviews? Do they care about your expressed opinions? Some do and some don't. Some will accept what a writer recommends because the writer recommended it. Some will ignore the comments or even laugh at your carefully weighed assessments. A few will get very upset if you criticize their favorites. And, it seems, some readers just do not get involved one way or the other. As reviewers or as qualified critics, writers have been given the right to comment on the arts of their town by the editors or publishers of their publication. It is a significant role in the arts community that must be kept in perspective at all times. It is a form of public trust not unlike that of the city hall or statehouse reporters who cover—and assess—government for the public. It must be done responsibly.

What are the limits of writers producing reviews and criticism? Do you, as a reviewer or critic, limit your work to art only? Or do you include the larger arena of entertainment? Certainly the umbrella that covers reviewing and criticism in the mid-1990s has enlarged itself. As you will see from the subjects covered in the last half of this chapter, reviewing and criticism have extended beyond pure art to entertainment.

Another important consideration is the legal limitations of criticism under the First Amendment and the various state constitutions. How far can a reviewer or critic go in expressing opinion before it is unacceptable? In terms of law, a reviewer and critic must be concerned with libel because of the potential for defamation of character of an artist. Because libel law varies from state to state, the limits of criticism will also vary according to state libel law. What a critic says might not be considered damaging by a jury in a major city as easily as it would be in a small town in the more conservative regions of the country.

Generally, though, reviewers and critics are permitted to express their opinions, even if defamatory, on topics that are interesting to the public. This is the conditional privilege of *fair comment*, a defense that has existed since the beginning of this century. Mass media law professor Don Pember (1993) explains: "The basis for the defense of fair comment is the notion that both our democratic system of government and our culture are enhanced by the free exchange of ideas and opinions" (p. 187). He adds, "Statements of opinion are often immune to a successful libel action. The courts have said that the rhetorical hyperbole—broad, exaggerated comments about someone or something—are obviously not assertions of fact, and cannot stand as the basis for a successful libel suit" (p. 189).

Mass media law professors Dwight Teeter and Don Le Duc (1992) add that common law and state statutes extend to "even scathing criticism of the public work of persons and institutions who offer their work for public judgment: public officials and figures; those whose performance public taste in such realms as music, art, literature, theater, and sports; and institutions whose activities affect the public interest . . ." (p. 227).

However, Pember (1993) says the fair comment defense against libel in a review must be based on certain requirements: (a) the comment must be an *opinion*; (b) it should reflect on the *public aspects*, not the private, of the person's life; and (c) the comment should have a *legitimate public interest*. Still, Pember cautions, the difference between fact and opinion is not that clear. The courts, he says, still wrestle with the distinction. This makes life difficult for aggressive critics and reviewers. Perhaps the best legal advice is that you should be able to back up what you say in the public interest with evidence, and that you should be concerned with the context of the statement and the words themselves. This way, Pember says, the public has the ability to develop its own opinion about the performer or the work itself.

FILM REVIEWS/CRITICISM

The names of the best-known film reviewers and critics over the past 30 years are household words among moviegoers—Pauline Kael, David Denby, Rex Reed, Gene Siskel, Roger Ebert, Judith Christ, Andrew Sarris. You can, no doubt, add names of outstanding local and regional film critics. The art of writing film reviews and criticism is perhaps the most visible of any type. Film reviews are usually written when a motion picture makes its commercial debut. When they do write an evaluation, reviewers and critics employ a number of strategies to evaluate a new film. The most common concerns are:

1. Quality of story line (plot), social relevance of the story line, or the original source material.
2. Performance of leading actors and actresses.
3. Performance of the director.
4. Consistency and quality of work of the technical support staff (such as special effects, cinematography, or film editing).
5. Use of conventions such as symbols or color.
6. Audience reaction and the film itself as a social event.

Dwight Macdonald, who criticized film for more than 40 years and influenced many of today's critics and reviewers, says reviewers and critics need to judge film on different standards, but two rules of thumb include "did it change the way you look at things?" and "Did you find more (or less) in it the second, third, nth time? (Also how did it stand up over the years, after one or more 'periods' of cinematic history?)" (1969, p. xi). To those main points in his book, *Dwight Macdonald on Movies* (1969), he adds five other standards by which he judged movies:

1. Are the characters consistent, and in fact are there characters at all?
2. Is it true to life?
3. Is the photography cliché, or is it adapted to the particular film and therefore original?
4. Do the parts go together; do they add up to something; is there a rhythm established so that there is form, shape, climax, building up tension and exploding it?
5. Is there a mind behind it; is there a feeling that a single intelligence has imposed his own view on the material? (p. ix).

It is also common for film reviewers to provide adequate background on key individuals involved in the film. Film scholars who focus on the director as the author of the film subscribe to the *auteur theory* (Kael, 1979; Sarris, 1979). Professor Todd Hunt (1972) says, however, a majority of film audience members are just not that interested in the author as a focus of a review. Most, he says, look at importance or relevance of the film. Bill Cosford (1993), late film critic for *The Miami Herald*, felt the film industry may be witnessing the end of auteurism. "We no longer know for sure . . . whether the movie we have just seen is the movie the director intended, or whether it will be the same one that, in just a few years or months from now, is the movie our friends will be seeing, and the movie we'll see is the movie we were *supposed* to have seen," Cosford said. "The reason for this, irony of ironies, is the burgeoning of the vaunted 'director's cut'" (p. 1G).

Film reviewers and critics watch a lot of films. An average week for a full-time reviewer or critic for a major publication includes enough time to view 5 to 10 full-length films. Some are shown in theaters, requiring even more time to travel back and forth, but others, such as classics or new versions of existing films, are available on videotape. Devoted film scholars who review or criticize films will see some films much more than just a single time. In fact, dozens of viewings of a single film are not unusual for the very best ones, or for personal favorites of veteran reviewers and critics over a long period of time. There is also the time spent each year at film festivals, industry meetings and conventions, and other special events. Just routine viewings, at 2 hours per film, are quite a time investment for a single work week. Much of this time is spent in preview screenings. These special private screenings are an important means of getting to see a film before the public does. But they are not always final cuts, either. Smart reviewers or critics will not leave a film early, no matter how badly it may begin.

Viewing advance screenings is essential to the success of the film reviewer and critic, however. To gain access to previews, reviewers and critics work with studio publicists and promotion specialists, as well as their own local theater managers and distributors. These individuals will contact reviewers who are associated with publications, but beginning free-lancers must find these individuals until they become known to the industry. Often, these showings will be after hours when theaters are available (some after midnight). Showings are usually early in the same week a film is scheduled to open (such as a Monday or Tuesday for a typical Friday opening). At other times, reviewers and critics will travel to Los Angeles or New York to see special screenings set up by the studio.

Getting started in film reviewing may involve taking a backup role to a more established writer. This means you have to have a willingness to review the less important films that might not even rate preview showings. Other opportunities exist at less mainstream publications such as college newspapers, alternative and entertainment-oriented weeklies, and small regional arts magazines.

Miami's Bill Cosford was a workhorse film critic, like many writers who cover industry news, write an occasional column, and criticize several hundred films a year. A longtime student of the motion picture, he often taught film criticism to university students. Duties for a metropolitan daily include writing several film criticisms a week, a column on occasion, and breaking industry news (such as covering the Oscars or writing an obituary of a prominent film star or director) as it becomes necessary. Cosford's newspaper reviews were seldom magazine-length but usually ran from 750 to 1,000 words.

Film reviews and criticism typically are accompanied by synopses of information about the film. This "information box" commonly used by newspapers and magazines usually contains some, or all, of the following information:

1. Name of film, local theaters screening it, their addresses, opening date.
2. Director and producer, production company.
3. Leading actors and actresses in the cast.
4. Screenwriters, cinematographers, and music scorers.
5. Running time.

6. Motion Picture Association of America audience rating.
7. Quality rating by reviewer/critic.

RADIO AND TELEVISION REVIEWS AND CRITICISM

One of the newest types of reviewing and criticism to evolve is broadcast and cable program reviewing. Newspapers and, to a limited extent, magazines are now covering the broadcast and cable industries and reviewing or criticizing programming at levels like never before. Beginning in the late 1950s and early 1960s, programming coverage was sporadic. Through the 1970s and 1980s, this new type of reviewer and critic emerged. In the 1990s, these individuals focus on reviewing and criticizing new regular programs, major sportscasts, special programs, and other unusual activities of interest to local audiences. Many full-time reviewers believe they have the responsibility to reinforce experiences in common with viewers and listeners. They also feel it is their duty to alert viewers and listeners to worthwhile events, to comment about excellence in programming, and to inform readers on developments at local stations.

Central Michigan University broadcasting professor Peter Orlik (1988) says television and radio writing generally finds its way into one of these five formats: the personality or gossip feature, the audience reaction column, previews, program reviews, and opinion essays. Although the focus in this chapter is on program reviews, it is important to note the context in which program reviews occur. Program reviews, Orlik notes, deal with several types of television and radio programs. First, reviews are written about series programs. Second, they are written about special programs such as "sweeps week" miniseries shows. Third, there are one-time programs that are often reviewed.

Opinion essays are also important contributions of television and radio reviewers. These are not limited to single programs or series, but can become more philosophical about trends, questions, and issues involving the indus-

---

USEFUL ENTERTAINMENT/ARTS-ORIENTED NEWSLETTERS

Academy of Family Films and Family Television—Newsletter
Celebrity Bulletin
Circus Report
Entertainment Research Report
Marquee
PCAN: Popular Culture Association Newsletter
Street Artists' News
Under the Big Top
What's Happening

Note: Many other entertainment-oriented and entertainment industry newsletters are published by fan clubs and other organizations about particular artists and performers.

tries and their audiences. Orlik notes this "contemplative approach" is often taken by magazines because it fits a magazine's production schedule more easily and appeals to more specialized audiences attracted by magazines. They are also different in that they tend to be longer and more thoughtful. "Such think pieces and the issues they raise are seen as mooring masts to which can be anchored the shorter and more transitory personality and audience reaction columns—previews and reviews" (1988, p. 44), Orlik argues.

As film reviewers depend on advance showings for much of their work, so do broadcast reviewers. These showings are usually available on videotape or at the local stations in the community where the reviewers work. Much advance viewing is done with special videotape copies of programs sent to reviewers and critics a few days or a week before the scheduled broadcast. Of course, special opportunities are provided to preview shows in New York and Los Angeles, where many television, radio, and cable networks are headquartered, during tours and special promotional events during the year.

Like other commentary writers, television and radio reviewers and critics must do their homework. It means watching and listening to a large number of programs each week. For Fort Lauderdale *Sun-Sentinel* television critic Tom Jicha, a veteran journalist of nearly 30 years, it means receiving and viewing as many as 10 to 20 videotapes a day. He explains how he does his job:

> I'll never review a show without watching the whole thing. But I won't watch a lot of shows at all. I just have to make a decision based on whether I have any interest, or if it is a new program or a miniseries. There a lot of people who are going to be looking to me—and I know it sounds a little pretentious—for guidance: "Is this worthy of my investment in time?" You have to tell them. But some of the programs that show up on the Discovery Channel, the Learning Channel, or Arts & Entertainment, some of that is the best programming on television, but some of it isn't. You make a judgment at some point that people aren't going to tune in to watch certain programs. So why bother? So I don't watch a lot of the tapes I get. But the ones I do watch, I watch from beginning to end. (Jicha, 1993)

Daily newspapers are the dominant outlets for broadcast and cable reviewing because of the timing of publication deadlines. For the same reason, most magazines do not get involved in broadcast and cable reviewing. Some weekly magazines, such as the news magazines or *TV Guide*, are able to do so in advance because of lead time given them by sources seeking maximum promotional value for a special program or series in a big circulation publication. Similarly, these weekly magazines will review or cover the broadcast of programs after the fact if a program has strong impact or if ratings show an unusually large audience.

A review or critique of a television or radio program can actually serve a dual purpose. It may also serve as an advance story, alerting viewers of the coming program. Thus, with a dual purpose, writers have to be careful not to reveal too much that would spoil viewing.

Many of the nation's major television industry beat writers, reviewers, and critics collect information on a 3-week press tour of Southern California each summer. The tour is grinding, with writers beginning their days at 8 or 9 each morning and going nonstop through midnight. The days are filled with previews of new fall programs and interviews with the new programs' stars, producers, directors, and other individuals involved in the industry. It is often difficult to find time to write while on the road with such a tight schedule. "It's 19 straight days of screenings like that," says the *Sun-Sentinel's* Jicha (1993), who has been taking the tours for more than a decade. "And people think we are having fun. We work hard during those trips."

Jeff Jarvis writes television criticism for *TV Guide* in a regular feature named "The Couch Critic." Part of his work is viewing new programs (e.g., Fox's "Tribeca") and revisiting existing ones (e.g., "Evening Shade") or network services (e.g., QVC network programming). He also comments on the value of these programs for the millions of viewers who read the magazine each week. Jarvis used a review of the Fox series "Tribeca" as an opportunity to discuss a general philosophy behind the series, which uses an anthology approach instead of the more conventional series approach. This is Jarvis' (1993) review of "Tribeca":

I like the idea of an anthology, a series with different writers, stars, and stories each week—a series about surprises. It's not easy to keep an anthology going, to keep the quality up, and the audience coming back. But it's worth it if an anthology can bring variety to prime time.

So here comes Tribeca from Robert DeNiro's own company, an anthology set in a cool New York City nabe (which is so nice and neighborly it looks like Mayberry). Philip Bosco as a coffeehouse owner and Joe Morton as a cop are the only regulars who traipse through each tale: a drama this week, a comedy next. The structure is fine and the shows are well-produced. But the series is inconsistent. It's on the right track . . . just in the wrong train.

The premiere was promising: Larry Fishburne and Carl Lumbly played brothers, a cop and banker searching for success in New York. Then one was murdered. The show resisted clichés: there is revenge, but there is no justice. It was well-acted and beautifully photographed. It was a good beginning.

Next I saw a trifle written by, directed by, and starring Melanie Mayron, as a single woman who's still thirtysomething and still whining. Her boyfriend, Richard Lewis, wants to move in because his therapist says it's time. But they break up. Then her grandmother moves in and tells her, "It's a rotten life ahead of you." The show has nice touches of whimsy, like a roaming executive on roller skates. Too bad it doesn't have more of a story to glue its fun scenes together.

Then I saw a show about a homeless man (Stephen Lang) who lives in a park, taking care of war memorials, until Morton the cop kicks him out. In this show, angry poetry about New York is shouted at the camera. The homeless man invades a coffeehouse to deliver a soliloquy on kisses. Then Morton and his artist-wife have the homeless man over for brunch. It's pretty heavy-handed. It's a thud.

Tribeca tries to be so arty. It is obvious that DeNiro and company want us to watch and shout: "But you can't do that on television!" Oh, but you can do anything on television—witness Roseanne, Picket Fences, Larry Sanders, The Simpsons, "Barbarians at the Gate," David Letterman. Too often, movie people who make TV shows don't watch enough TV to know that TV got better without them.

In the toughest time slot in prime time—on Fox's new night, replacing Key West (yeah!) and competing against Roseanne—Tribeca tries to be a new kind of series and a magnet for fresh talent. That makes it a noble experiment. Sadly, the experiment is not a success. (p. 7) Reprinted with permission from *TV Guide®* Magazine, Copyright © 1993 by News America Publications Inc.

When stories are written from press tours or other more local sources, information boxes are common in many publications, especially newspapers. The information box (if brief enough, information sometimes runs in a trailer—a paragraph at the end) for a television, radio, or cable program advance and/or review usually contains some or all of the following information:

1. Name of program, network (if appropriate), local station(s) broadcasting it.
2. Scheduled air time(s), program length(s), and date(s).
3. Major actors and actresses.
4. Content category (drama, comedy, and so on).
5. Capsule summary of content.

LIVE MUSIC AND CONCERT REVIEWS

For many younger arts writers, there is no more exciting assignment than to cover a live concert by a well-known band or solo artist. In fact, many reviewers and critics start out reviewing concerts or albums of recorded music. Newspapers, magazines, and newsletters approach live music and concert reviews differently, mainly because of timing and deadlines. For newspapers, there are two types of situations that concern reviewers and create different writing strategies. First, there are musicians who are on tour and may make only one appearance on one date in an area. Second, there are extended concert appearances and dates by musicians in a community. You cannot handle each situation the same way.

For the one-night performance, a review might not be as helpful to readers from a consumer point of view. After all, they cannot use your review to decide to go after the fact. A way around this is to review an earlier performance by the same musicians in a nearby community if possible. Nevertheless, reviews of one-night concerts are still part of the coverage of the arts of a community.

Certainly, persons who attended want to know how others assessed the show. It is important to note that those who did not go are interested in what happened from a critical perspective.

For concerts that are scheduled for more than one day in a community, you have more latitude in what you can do. A regular review will serve readers in major ways, such as helping them decide whether to attend. Naturally, it is best to publish the review as quickly as possible after the first performance. Daily newspapers usually publish the next day, or at worst for a very late evening show, on the second day.

Most daily newspaper concert reviews stick to the basics because of their deadline constraints. These reviews, as in other print media, focus on staging; sound quality; length of performance; audience size, reaction, and involvement; names of songs performed; special performers present; unusual deviations in the performed music (such as live versions dramatically different from recorded versions of well-known songs); and the effort of the warm-up act.

Veteran Fort Lauderdale *Sun-Sentinel* popular music reviewer Deborah Wilker (1993) says she must work very hard to produce a good concert review. It is not always a fun night out on the town with the sole purpose of finding out gossip about the performers. "When I am assigned to go to a concert, I am assigned to write a thoughtful, provocative review of what the singer did, what instruments were played, what songs were performed, and more. I'm not there to report on who was in the audience and gossipy things like that," she explains.

Magazines and newsletters, on the other hand, must take a different look at reviewing live music because of their less frequent publication schedules. Some magazines and newsletters simply do not attempt it because it is not part of what they want to offer to readers. Others do not review music because of their infrequent publication schedule and the months of lead time they require for production. Weekly magazines do so in a manner somewhat different from newspapers. Most weekly magazines, such as the major news magazines, that attempt to write about live music focus only on major artists and do so by writing a round-up style review of a tour. This type of review is generally more descriptive than critical and incorporates information from several stops on a national or international tour, adds nonperformance highlights, and any other aspects of the events that surround a tour by a world- or national-caliber musician or group. These articles are part review and part color (or atmosphere) feature, and perhaps even a little human interest feature as well.

Your best single sources for information about a tour are an artist's public relations representative or the tour's road manager. Often, the management of the concert facility can provide helpful local information also. Press kits and other background information are provided most often by these sources if you make yourself or your publication known to them.

Miami Herald pop music critic Leonard Pitts (1993) recently reviewed a live concert by veteran performer Neil Diamond. In his review, he summarized the songs performed, the quality of the effort, the sound of the show, and the energy of the performer. Not liking what he saw and heard, Pitts took Diamond to task for a very lackluster effort. The detailed review provides strong reasons for why the effort was not appreciated, as you will see from the reprinted article that follows. But critics who strongly criticize artists have to be prepared for the reaction to those comments. Diamond's highly loyal fans reacted with a deluge of calls and letters to the newspaper complaining about the point of view offered by this award-winning critic, even after Pitts had written a very long and generally positive advance leading up to the two sold-out shows. This is his full review:

Here's some consolation for you if you were one of those people who was unable to get tickets for Neil Diamond's sold-out two-night stand at the Miami Arena: You would have been better entertained sitting at home listening to your hissing and popping old copy of Sweet Caroline. Fact is, you'd have been better entertained sitting at home organizing your sock drawer.

At least, that was the case for lo-o-o-ong stretches of Diamond's Sunday night show (the second performance is tonight at the Arena). As for the other stretches, well, we'll get to those in a minute.

Suffice it to say that most of the show was nothing to write home about unless it was to say, "Don't go. Stay home. Save your money." Diamond, who is reputed to be one of the most electrifying performers in pop, acted as if the plug had been pulled Sunday night—walking through much of his set. He wasn't the only one to blame.

The sound mix was flat and without presence, losing Diamond's voice for crucial parts of the show. And that voice was definitely—you should pardon the atrocious pun—a diamond in the rough . . . a harsh, gritty sound with much of the nuance obliterated.

And the audience wasn't much help either. At some points during the set, you would have thought you had wandered into a Bible study class to judge from the level of crowd enthusiasm. It's a phenomenon that's been witnessed in enough different venues and with enough different crowds (from Public Enemy to Bruce Springsteen to Bryan Adams) that you can no longer ascribe it to coincidence.

Something in the air, something about the mugginess of the subtropics, something about the size of the skeeters, something makes people sit on their hands down here when they should be up and urging their heroes on.

Performers feed on that response—it's the thing that challenges them. Diamond didn't get it except, curiously, when the lights came up, at which point the audience would suddenly cheer and become one big party animal. It's a shame. He could have used their support.

Without them, he walked through a cavalcade of oldies without much inspiration or invention. Cherry Cherry, Sweet Caroline, Brooklyn Road—they all went down pretty much unremarked by the crowd. You'd have thought Diamond actually was a Solitary Man to judge from the lethargic applause that greeted that chestnut.

And then came America and suddenly, they were alive. Alive! Up and pumping their fists and going nuts. Given the fact that that song is more of an adrenaline-charged anthem than most of the rest of Diamond's repertoire, the difference in audience response was stunning.

Diamond rode that into Song Sung Blue, a gentle sing-along accented by thoughtful staging—blue spotlights circling the crowd. He even breathed life and drama into the vapid duet You Don't Bring Me Flowers Anymore.

It was, you might reasonably argue, too little too late. But it was at least something. A pulse. Coming as it did from a performer who had failed to challenge his crowd and a crowd that had failed to push their performer, it was a welcome moment.

Because, on both sides of the equation, much of the rest of the night was about an audience and a performer who seemed to be pacing themselves. Conserving energy when they should've been blowing the lid off.

A person sitting next to me opined that it was like visiting your dad. You love him and all and you kind of enjoy yourself, but there's no surprise because you always know what's coming next.

I can't put it any better than that. (p. 1C) Reprinted with permission of *The Miami Herald.*

The information box for a concert advance or opening night review in either a newspaper or a magazine for a series of performances (not a one-time show) usually contains some or all of the following information:

1. Name of main group or artist.
2. Name of warm-up group or artist.
3. Date(s) and location.
4. Ticket sale dates and times, price scales, locations of ticket sales points, additional remote-site ticket service fees.
5. Reviewer/critic rating of the performance.

Generally, information boxes do not run with concert reviews that are written on performances that are one-time shows in a particular area.

RECORDED MUSIC REVIEWS AND CRITICISM

Just about all adults and most children listen to recorded music in one form (compact disc, tape, or record) or style (classical, rock, jazz, rap, country, easy listening, and so on). Because recorded music is so popular with the public, demand for qualified reviewers and critics in the mass media is high. Also, the need for information about records has been growing since the mid-1960s (evidenced most prominently by one-time alternative newspaper *Rolling Stone* magazine's upcoming 30th birthday in 1997), more popular mass media devote considerable attention and space to recorded music than ever before, a turf once reserved only by specialized publications.

Reviews are more popular than ever before. Because record reviews appear regularly in many newspapers and general interest and news magazines, they are written a little differently than when they were found only in specialized newspapers, magazines, and newsletters. There was a time when only the most devoted music listener could interpret the special language of these reviews. But because of the mass interest in records (let's use this term for convenience), reviewers have to write to be understood by more people. The review, taking on this added educational function, has helped bring up the public's level of knowledge of records and musical styles.

Preview copies help record, tape, and compact disc reviewers do their jobs in a timely fashion. Just as film and broadcast/cable reviewers preview their art, so do record reviewers. The record companies will ship preview copies to reviewers once they get on the company's promotion department mailing lists or to generic addresses, such as "Music Reviewer, Arts Department," at a publication. And there are different levels of lists. Some are more important—that is, perceived by the publicists to be more influential—than others. To get on a promotional mailing list, contact the record companies with a legitimate request to be included. You will have to furnish the name of the publication you work for and its address, and you may be asked to submit some clips of previous work.

In fact, preview copies are one reason many music reviewers work at home. They can listen to the newest compact discs without distraction on their home systems. For reviewers and critics for daily newspapers or music and entertainment magazines and newsletters, it is not unusual to receive as many as four or five dozen new recordings a week. That makes a lot of music to consider. Reviewers cannot listen to it all. There is simply not enough time in the day. The Fort Lauderdale *Sun-Sentinel*'s Wilker (1993) sets a limit of 10 CDs a day. After that, she says, it all seems to run together and "you are not doing anyone a service. I wish I could give these people more attention."

There are numerous approaches to writing a record review. Some writers prefer to read the *liner notes*—the words on the back of an album cover or tape or CD container—as they listen to the album. Some listen to the album first without taking any notes, just to get a "feel" for the album. Then they will listen a second time for technical purposes and for details to cite in their review. And some reviewers like to turn their stereo system high for full effect, whereas others prefer a headset. You might try a variety of approaches until you find a way that works for you.

Regardless of your approach, your basic purpose is to provide a description of the content of the album. After that, you should evaluate the work and provide as much background on the album content and the artist as space permits. At best, you want to be clear and practical for your readers. At worst, you will write solely for other record reviewers in a language only the members of the "club" will understand. Of course, you want to avoid that because you are serving no one but yourself.

Classical music and opera provide exceptional opportunities for recorded music reviewing. Much of what has been said in this section relates to popular contemporary music. Todd Hunt (1972) properly suggests that education is a most important function of reviews of classical music and opera. "Because many readers are unfamiliar with all but the best-known works of the major composers, the critic must turn teacher when evaluating performances of music by lesser-known persons," he says (p. 136). Hunt also emphasizes the need to analyze the technique of the artist when considering classical music and opera. This is, of course, applicable to performance of established works. A particular challenge, he says, is new works. Changes in styles, techniques, and even instrumentation are worthy of your attention.

The information box for a record review usually contains some or all of the following information:

1. Name of album and artist or group.
2. Record, tape, or disc label and catalog number.
3. List price of record, tape, disc.
4. Release date (if appropriate).
5. Reviewer/critic rating of the recording.

BOOK REVIEWS AND CRITICISM

If you enjoy reading, writing book reviews may be an easy extension of that pleasure. There are a large number of daily newspapers and weekly or monthly magazines and newsletters that regularly publish book reviews. These books are often mass market or trade books found in most bookstores. There is wide interest in them. On the other hand, there is also a growing market for specialists who write for more specialized magazines, newsletters, journals, literary reviews, bulletins, quarterlies, and other publications with readers interested in the latest book news and reviews.

USA Today, for example, regularly publishes book reviews by free-lance contributors, such as authors and editors, about general interest books, such as novels by known authors, and nonfiction, such as travel books, public affairs books, celebrity biographies and autobiographies, and so forth. Its reviewers are often free-lance contributors such as magazine editors, book authors, and other writers. Bruce Allen (1993), a Maine writer, began a recent free-lance USA Today review about Robert Boswell's new novel, Mystery Ride, leaving no doubt how he felt about the book. Then he proceeded to describe what the book does and doesn't do:

Robert Boswell's third and best novel powerfully confirms his place among the best writers who emerged during the 1980s. It's an intricately constructed story of unstable familial love, and of "mysteries" implicit in human relationships, here both ingeniously dramatized and passionately, directly expressed.

Protagonist Angela Landis (later, Vorda) and her first husband, Stephen, find their marriage unraveling in rural Iowa when city-bred Stephen decides he can make himself into a farmer, and Angela realizes she and their young daughter Dulcie must leave him. The novel's action is divided between 1971, their crucial Iowa year, and 1987 when Angela, remarried and living in L.A., briefly leaves her adulterous husband to shepherd rebellious teen-ager Dulcie to Stephen's farm for the summer.

Though it lacks a linear plot, the novel is generously crammed with vivid incident and boldly drawn conflict . . . .(p. 4D)

There are numerous local outlets for book reviews. The leading ones are Sunday newspaper book sections and magazine book departments. Specialized publications such as business magazines often devote considerable space to reviews of books relating to the industry, so don't ignore this potential market.

Poet, novelist, playwright, and essayist John Updike knows something about writing and, of course, book reviewers and critics. Updike once gave the art of book reviewing some thought in one of his essays, the foreword to *Picked-Up Pieces* (Updike, 1976). His five rules of book criticism included:

1. Try to understand what the author wished to do, and do not blame him for not achieving what he did not attempt.
2. Give enough direct quotation—at least one extended passage—of the book's prose so that the review's reader can form his own impression, can get his own taste.
3. Confirm your description of the book with quotation from the book, if only phrase-long, rather than proceeding by fuzzy *precis*.
4. Go easy on the plot summary, and do not give away the ending.
5. If the book is judged deficient, cite a successful example along the same lines, from the author's *oeuvre* or elsewhere. Try to understand the failure. Sure it's his and not yours? (pp. xvi–xvii).

Updike also recommends not accepting review assignments you might be predisposed to like or to dislike. There are many reasons for either stance. Furthermore, it is important to note that some newspapers, magazines, and newsletters will not solicit or accept reviews of second or subsequent editions of books. These may seem new to the author and the publisher, but most publication editors prefer to use reviews of completely new books. Exceptions are possible, of course, when a major change occurs in the new edition. For the most part, individuals new to book reviewing are best advised to work on first editions unless an editor specifically assigns a later edition. You may discover a similar attitude often accompanies sequels to books. These are more likely to be reviewed than second editions, but they will be less sought after than reviews of the first book in a series.

Book reviewers and critics, like other reviewers and critics, must keep up with new developments in their field. Following the book industry is relatively easy if you look in the right places. Book publishing industry organizations, such as the American Booksellers Association, or writers' groups, such as the Authors Guild, will keep members informed of developments. Their publications are helpful to monitor also. The ABA publishes *American Bookseller* magazine, and the Authors' Guild has an extensive newsletter issued regularly to members. Other publications are *Publishers Weekly, The New York Review of Books,* and the *New York Times Book Review,* commonly available to the public by subscription or at newsstands. There are many others, of course, both designed for industry insiders and for the book-buying public.

Most of the time, general interest publication book reviews are written by individuals who have a specialization in the subject that the book is about, not people who specialize in writing book reviews. Editors look for staff and free-lance specialists in specific subjects because of the levels of expertise necessary to evaluate a new work. Individuals who write book reviews need to know something about books, the authors, and book publishing. Reviewers for the top-of-the-line national publications are often themselves editors or authors. These individuals are rarely staff members and write their commentaries as free-lance reviewers. Their depth of knowledge comes from writing itself, working in the industry, and sophisticated study such as college and graduate-level majors in literature or other specializations.

If you are looking for prospective books to review, Boston free-lance book reviewer Mark Leccese (personal communication, 1993) recommends doing your homework. Leccese, a former full-time reporter and editor in the Boston area for 13 years, writes four to six book reviews and book articles a month. He decides what to review based on his publishing industry research:

> Get the publishers' seasonal catalogs or *Publishers Weekly's* seasonal preview, pick a few books you would like (and feel qualified) to review, and query book review editors proposing to review a specific book. Free-lancers don't get to do the 'big' books, so look for high-quality niche books. When you query, make it brief and clear, and always send clips. Choose areas of specialty for yourself (fiction, political books, etc.), and tell the editors you're querying. Never miss a deadline, always write to length and, at least when you're starting out, don't argue about money.

Some beginners even volunteer as reviewers to establish themselves and get clips.

The best literary critics strive to achieve the level of excellence attained by the late Irving Howe, who wrote for many years for *Dissent,* which he founded, but also for the *New York Times Magazine* and other publications. Howe was known as the book critic's critic. Although he wrote his own award-winning

A BOOK REVIEWER'S TIPS FOR WRITING

Free-lance book reviewer and Boston University adjunct professor Mark Leccese regularly writes about books for the *Boston Business Journal* and the *Boston Phoenix Literary Supplement*. He says his book review structure is flexible, depending on who will be reading the review:

The form, shape, and content of my book reviews depend on the publication's audience, the space I have, and the book itself. A piece about writing about books (or music, or film, or art) falls somewhere, I think, on a continuum: On one end are "reviews," ("It's good/It's fair/It's poor; here's what it's about") and on the other end is "criticism" (which tries to place the work in a larger context: of literature, of works in the field, and so forth). Where I aim on that continuum depends on what the editor (and that means the audience) wants.

I have no formula for a review. The book itself, and what I have to say, will determine the shape and tone of the piece. I do have a few touchstones, though:

1. *Take careful notes as you read.* I use the (blank) first page inside the cover to note thoughts and comments I have, page numbers of important parts of the book, notes that outline the structure of the book. I underline, I dog-ear pages, I scribble in the margins. As a reviewer, you have to have something to say.

2. *Write clearly, simply, and directly.* There's no excuse for pompous, turgid writing, and too many writers think that's how you're *supposed* to write about books. It ain't—not if you want readers.

3. *Understand the point of the book, not just the plot.* What is the writer (novelist or nonfiction writer) trying to say? Why, in other words, did the author write the book? When you understand, tell your reader.

4. *Quote from the book.* Don't just tell the reader about how the author writes and what the author writes about—*show* the reader. When you make a point, *prove* it.

5. *If you can, read previous work(s) of the author.* This helps put the current work in context. (personal communication, 1993)

books, he was widely known for his thoughtful essays and criticism. He was an independent thinker who avoided trends and trendy writing throughout his five decades of work. Individuals as successful as Howe, for instance, improve with experience and depth of study. Howe taught university-level English literature. He knew his material.

Some analysts feel book reviewing is changing. Bill Marx, a book and theater critic in the Boston area, believes book reviewers are too soft and are often too positive. Marx feels 1990s reviewers are not as critical and are far too consumer oriented. "More critiques are crammed into less space; demographics rather than individual taste, frequently dictate what gets selected [for a review]. More ominously, there's a growing perception that reviewers should be the place for gossip or opinion, not complex thought," Marx argues (1993, p. 36). He also feels that too many reviewers are too quick to praise new works and that there are problems with authors criticizing other authors, resulting in conflicts of interest and what he calls questionable ethics. Marx says book reviewers should be encouraged to produce "critical writing whose independence, intelligence and passion excites readers" (p. 36). There is a danger, if these trends continue, of reviews being seen, but no longer holding any credibility with readers, Marx says.

Even beginners these days must know their material. This is an important step in getting started. To get the review process underway, get to know the book contents, its genre, and the author well. Look through it and then read it. Read the title page; note the publisher; and read the acknowledgments, introduction, and foreword. This is where you find out what authors say they are trying to do with the book. Skim the table of contents to get an idea of the scope of the book. Then turn to page one and *read the book* from front to back. Perhaps it may be surprising, but there are reviewers who do not read an entire book, or even parts of it, and try to write a review or even simply interview the author. A review can be written without reading the book, but the quality of the review invariably suffers and, thus, so does the service provided to the author, publisher, and the book-buying public. There are countless stories, and even comedy routines, based on talk show hosts, journalists, and others who did not prepare their work properly.

Some research about the author(s) is also important to understanding the book you are reviewing. At times, the publisher will provide some of this information for you on the flyleaf or on an author page at the end of the book. Some publishers, when sending out review copies to publications in advance of an announced publication release date, will provide a press release-biography of the author. "Advance reader copies" are available as much as 6 months before official publication, but often these are uncorrected proof editions with minor flaws and are usually only available in paperbound form. These are extraordinarily helpful in getting an advance look at a book, providing time for you to read the book before actually writing anything about it. There may also be summaries of the plot on the flyleaf or back cover that can be helpful to you in deciding if you want to review it at all.

In reading a review, readers want to know something about the authors. Who are they? How did they come to write this book? A good review will integrate such information about the author and tell readers something about the author's previous work. It also makes sense to read as much of the previous work of an author as you can before you take on the current effort. This gives your review perspective and gives you the chance to compare and contrast within the author's own writing. Certainly, it also helps your readers if you, in your review, compare and contrast the book to others like it that have previously been published. Like record reviews, a thorough book review will summarize content without giving away plots, in addition to educating readers about the author. An information box accompanying a book review usually contains some or all of the following information:

1. Author and title of book.
2. Publisher and location, edition number (if applicable).
3. Book availability in hard or softcover, prices.
4. Publisher's official release date (if appropriate, this is the date it is usually available in bookstores).
5. Length of book in pages.
6. Special distinguishing features.

DRAMA AND DANCE REVIEWS

Along with film, books, and television, drama is one of the traditional major subjects of reviewing and criticism in the United States. Interest in dance, such as ballet, is growing and becoming an important specialization in the arts for those writing features for the mass media. Although the "national theater" remains centered in New York, most people who write about drama and theater *are not* in New York. These are the people in the hinterlands and other metropolitan areas writing about regional and local theater productions at the professional and amateur levels. Theater has spread across the country like wildfire in the past 30 years, resulting in a rather sophisticated system of regional and community theaters and drama companies that are no longer solely focused in Manhattan. There are audience-supported theaters in just about every metropolitan area that offer drama and dance.

As a drama critic, you have the duty to look at all the drama performances in your area, good or bad. Todd Hunt (1972) says:

> [T]he critic, who must attend *all* the plays, sees a theater that includes occasional ineptness and a great number of not-too-near misses. He knows that it is easiest to write a rave notice . . . . But more often he will have to struggle to explain a play's apparent purpose, where it failed its goal, and what rewards remain to be found . . . . What makes it worthwhile, of course, is the occasional evening in the theater when the mind is engaged, the imagination is stretched, the intellect is rewarded (p. 83).

Like reviewing and criticizing other art forms, you must be well prepared to write a drama or dance review. Some reviewers read plays before seeing them performed—easy to do with established works but not so easy with debut material. Others do not read plays, regardless of whether they are available. What you can do, if possible, is read other material by the same playwright.

It is also important to learn as much as you can about the cast prior to the performance. Learn their names and roles, just as a sportswriter learns the numbers of key players in a game before it begins. Also note the producer, director, and the other behind-the-scenes personnel who contribute to the production. You can get some of this background from the playbill or program, but you can also obtain it from the promotion department of the theater a few days before the performance.

As in book reviewing, be careful not to reveal too much of the story line when reviewing a dramatic performance. Telling too much spoils the experience for others. The critical elements in a drama review must address the play's plot and its relevance, the performance of major actors singly and as a group, the direction they received, staging and sets, costuming, sound, lighting, audience reaction, and overall assessment of the night's entertainment. Any unusual developments, such as technical problems, should also be addressed if they affected the experience. Of course, reviewers often compare and contrast a current production with earlier versions of the same work by different companies or, in some cases, the same one.

The information box for a theater advance or opening night review for a series of performances (not a one-time show) usually contains some or all of the following information:

1. Name of play, author or choreographer.
2. Major actors and name of the touring company (if any).
3. Date(s) and location.
4. Ticket price scale, locations of ticket sales points.
5. Reviewer/critic rating of the overall performance.

Generally, these information boxes do not run with theater reviews that are written about performances that are one-time shows in a particular area.

Dance, although not nearly as popular in most areas as dramatic theater, still provides creative opportunities for reviewers and critics. Modern dance companies, many with uncertain support levels, certainly deserve the critical attention of the local media. More traditional dance groups, such as ballet companies, are perhaps more stable and generally receive critical review when new performances are staged. Like classical music reviews, dance reviews must educate the public. Few readers of dance reviews thoroughly understand what they have seen enough to not want assistance in interpreting what the performance achieved or did not achieve.

What do you concern yourself with in a dance review? The focus must be on two levels: the effort of the dance group as a whole or an entity and the effort of the troupe's star dancers or directors. Because many dance groups are dominated by a single performer or director, this is an important point of view. Hunt (1972) suggests re-reviewing dance companies to measure the degree of growth and change in the company over a season. Because performances are not always the same, this is a helpful strategy if time and space permit it.

New York Times drama and dance reviews most often are published in the national edition on Mondays. Dance reviewer Jack Anderson (1993) recently wrote a three-section review of a dance program celebrating choreographer George Balanchine at New York's Lincoln Center. He focused on the three distinct works on the night's program and organized his review in that manner. Each section of his review was separated by a "bullet" and focused on a different performance. This is how he opened the review, focusing on the most important performance on the night's program:

> Watching "Movements for Piano and Orchestra" is like watching bolts of lightning. But because this lightning is choreographed by George Balanchine, everything is always under control, and the electrical storm is awesome without also being threatening.
>
> Gestures are jagged and patterns are restless throughout the work, which was offered by the New York City Ballet on Thursday night at the New York State Theater at Lincoln Center as part of the Balanchine Celebration. Balanchine obviously listened closely to the Stravinsky score that serves as the ballet's title. What he heard inspired him in several ways. The choreography's nervous energy is obviously a response to that of the music. Yet the score never grows hysterical; Stravinsky created an ultimately orderly wildness. So did Balanchine .... (p. 16)

An information box for a dance performance advance or opening night review for a series of dance troupe performances usually contains some or all of the following information:

1. Name of dance troupe and the title of performance or program.
2. Names of the company director or choreographer, lead performer, and other artists, such as musicians, if appropriate.
3. Date(s) and location.
4. Ticket price scales, locations of ticket sales points.
5. Reviewer/critic rating of the performance.

Generally, information boxes do not run with dance reviews that are written on performances that are one-time shows in a particular area.

FOOD AND RESTAURANT REVIEWS AND CRITICISM

Life as a restaurant reviewer or critic is a life of diversity, and, of course, calories. Amid the menus and wine lists are certain ways of handling the job, certain liabilities, and certain deadlines. Most food and restaurant critics are occasionally told how fortunate they are to have their jobs. *Milwaukee* magazine restaurant reviewer William Romantini (1987) says, "Everyone tells me how lucky I am to have the job . . . . But, though eating for free can at times be a lot of fun, it involves some major liabilities" (p. 49). First, he jokes, his friends won't have him over for dinner. More realistically, he says he must endure several bad meals for every good one.

Most restaurant critics want to dine anonymously. If they are known to the employees of a restaurant, it is possible for a restaurant to give unusual and extraordinary attention to preparing the reviewer's meal. Some restaurants, sensitive to a reviewer's power and influence in affecting public opinion, keep pictures of reviewers on the walls of the kitchen for waiters to study. Most restaurants prefer reservations, and reviewers should make them. To remain unknown, use a dining partner's name, however. Of course, the experience of making reservations becomes part of your assessment of the service you receive at the restaurant.

Andy Rathbone, a free-lance restaurant reviewer in the San Diego area, occasionally contributes his restaurant reviews to a suburban newspaper. "My wife and I wrote restaurant reviews for a local paper, the *La Jolla Light*. We wrote under a pen name, so the wait staff wouldn't let our names influence our service. I'd take notes surreptitiously during the meal, and my wife and I would discuss the meal on the drive home," explained Rathbone (personal communication, 1993), a San Diego Press Club and Society of Professional Journalists award-winning writer.

Many restaurant reviewers take a consumer approach to their work. They review the food, not as food authorities, but as consumers. What did you get for your money? Was it worth it? Why? Rathbone argues this is the most important part of a restaurant review:

> The most significant element of a food review is the price of the food. Is a gratuity added on to the final bill? Do the "dinner specials" include a drink? After price, the next most important quality is a restaurant's overall experience. For instance, fine food can be marred by poor service. Fine service, an exceptional view, or live entertainment can occasionally make up for mediocre food (as long as that's made clearly understood in the review). Least important? Perhaps the restaurant's location. Most people are willing to drive out of their way for an extraordinary dining experience. (Rathbone, personal communication, 1993)

Robert Hosmon, a nationally syndicated wine and restaurant critic based in Miami, has been commenting on restaurants for 15 years. Currently the house restaurant critic for *South Florida* magazine after writing for several years about restaurants, food, and wine for *The Miami Herald*, Hosmon (personal communication, 1993) says he considers five important factors for his monthly essays:

1. *Food ingredients and preparation.* Is the food properly prepared as it is listed on the menu? Are the ingredients fresh? Is the presentation of the food satisfactory? One clue to judging a restaurant's capability is to select those dishes that are identified as specials, often carrying the chef's or the restaurant's name on the menu.

2. *Service.* Is service efficient and courteous? Does the serving staff hover, creating an awkward situation for diners, or does it disappear, leaving diners to fend for themselves, waiting for more water, waiting for the check?

3. *Decor.* Is the restaurant, visually, a pleasant place to be? Does it live up to its intentions and diners' expectations?

4. *Ambiance.* Does the combination of decor, service attitude, size of the dining room, music, lighting, and patronage in the restaurant add up to a pleasant dining experience?

5. *Price.* Is a visit to the restaurant worth the expense? Are any food items overpriced? Is the wine list prepared with reasonable mark-ups? Is the entire experience worth the price?

Milwaukee magazine's Romantini (1987) adds three other areas of concern of the restaurant reviewer. Those are:

1. The *entrance* to the restaurant and the first impressions you get as you enter.
2. The *attention* you receive as you are seated and the appearance of your table (settings, its preparedness, and so on).
3. Not the least important, the *taste* of food served, its *temperature*, and *timing* of service.

In evaluating food, be concerned with the main dishes, but do not forget the significance of soups, salads, other appetizers, breads, and desserts. Writing the review should be easy if care is taken to note details during the dining experience. It is difficult to write a review from memory, without some sort of notes. Try to obtain a menu. Some restaurants will permit it if you ask. Others will sell you a menu. If you cannot take a menu with you, ask for an itemized check. And, of course, take some descriptive notes while you are at your dinner table. This might give you away, but it does not have to do so. Many business people write notes during a meal. With some practice, you can become inconspicuous in your note taking for your review.

Many reviewers write about their dining experience in chronological order. Romantini (1987) says writing should always be done with concern for the effect of what you say. "[K]eep in mind the effect your opinion will have. Can you look yourself in the eye and honestly write what you feel no matter what the consequences? Remember, it's easy to say nice things about someone, but an abundance of tact is needed if you've got to criticize" (p. 52).

Some publications, because of monthly deadlines, or even less frequent deadlines, choose to review several restaurants in a single article. For these roundup-style reviews, try to find unifying themes for the selected restaurants. This could be done using a style of food (e.g., Mexican), a neighborhood (e.g., the city's East Side), a category of service (e.g., guaranteed fast business lunches), and so forth. For a national magazine, it could be a city's top restaurants. This is how reviewer John Mariani (1993) approached his assign-

---

ADVICE FROM A RESTAURANT AND WINE CRITIC

Dr. Robert Hosmon's wine column appears in 240 newspapers and other publications each week through the Knight-Ridder Tribune News Service. Hosmon has written about food, restaurants, and wines sold in the United States for nearly two decades. Currently his wine column is based at the Fort Lauderdale *Sun-Sentinel* and he writes monthly restaurant reviews for *South Florida* magazine. He also regularly contributes to *Wine & Spirits* and *The Wine News*. It's a lucrative free-lance lifestyle that a lot of writers both admire and envy. Hosmon offers these comments about restaurant reviewing:

Unlike other critics, restaurant reviewers have a unique responsibility to the subjects they review. A negative architectural commentary isn't going to cause the razing of a building. A bad movie review won't drive a theater to bankruptcy. The critic who finds fault with a dance company or symphonic orchestra's performance isn't going to provoke the demise of the company. But a negative review of a restaurant can, and often does, put that restaurant out of business forever. Therefore while restaurant critics serve the public, they must also remember the responsibility they have to the men and women whose future livelihood depends on their opinions.

Standards for a good restaurant critic should include extensive knowledge of food ingredients and preparation, esthetic judgment, and an understanding of how restaurants function as a business. Each of those qualities requires experience, experience that can be developed through study and personal investigation. Conscientious restaurant critics dine out often and in many places. In the process, restaurant critics develop a professional approach to the evaluation process.

The professional restaurant critic will, in the final analysis, consider the intent of a restaurant when making a value judgment. A family-oriented, budget restaurant is not trying to provide the same experience as a gourmet French emporium. But either restaurant can be judged as excellent—or poor—according to how well they succeed in doing what they set out to do.

A good restaurant critic is never a casual consumer; he or she is a consummate observer, analyzing every food and every operation within the restaurant. Dining out for a restaurant critic is not a social occasion; *it's a job*. (Hosmon, personal communication, 1993)

---

ment when *Travel & Leisure* asked him to write reviews of several restaurants in New Orleans. Mariani could not write about all the outstanding places in that city, so he was careful to begin his review by discussing the differences in Creole and Cajun cooking. Then he choose five establishments of growing and already established reputation to highlight, with a series of mini-reviews of several hundred words each. This is how he creatively began his feature for the "eating around" department of the magazine:

In some towns, steamy tales of impropriety involve sex, politics or grand larceny. But in New Orleans, they usually have more to do with overeating and drinking. A century ago Mark Twain explained the local colloquialism *lagniappe* by writing, "When you are invited to drink—and this does occur now and then in New Orleans—you say, 'What, again?—no, I've had enough,' the other party says, 'But just this one time more—this is for lagniappe.'"

A wise traveler soon realizes that this voracious city is first and foremost a Creole town. Cajun food is regarded as, at best, a heavy "country cookery" and at worst, an aberration that has nothing to do with the refinements of Creole "city cuisine." Mention jambalaya and a Creole will sniff, "Oh, that's Cajun food." Then he or she will try to persuade you to try some delicacy like shrimp ravigote, perhaps followed by chicken Clemenceau and finished off with bread pudding and cafe brulot—*Creole* dishes . . . .(p. 68)

The information box for a restaurant review usually contains some or all of the following information:

1. Name of restaurant, address or location, reservations telephone number.
2. Hours of operation.
3. Type and price range of food served per person.
4. Dress code, if enforced.
5. Reviewer/critic rating of the meal (often categorized by quality of food, price/value, service, and decor).

WRITING PRODUCT REVIEWS

A relatively new subject for reviewing and criticism is the area of consumer products. Although a few specialty publications, such as *Consumer Reports*, have been doing such reviews and evaluations for a long time, other newspapers, magazines, and newsletters have recently begun devoting more space to experts who write product reviews. These individuals know the industry and how the products should be performing. They acquire advance copies of the products through loaner programs or testing services and try them out for a period of time.

The range of products literally covers the marketplace. Automobile writers often review and write about new models of automobiles or other vehicles. Outdoor writers do the same with new boats, motors, or other fishing gear. Computer specialists write about new hardware and software based on their experiences *using* the products before they go on to the market.

For example, *Condé Nast Traveler* regularly offers "gear in review" to readers. This department of the magazine features new products of interest to travelers. One recent article by contributing editor Bill Marsano (1993) discussed picnic baskets, Thermos-type containers, and other totable food and beverage containers for people on the go. The review described the best new products by their trade name, suggested retail prices, model numbers, manufacturers, sizes, and most important features of each item. Needless to say, selection of items for this department fits nicely with the general focus on upscale international travel stressed by the magazine.

Free-lance writers who want to produce product reviews must begin by seeking the market. What is your expertise? Children's toys? Computers? Bicycles? A musical instrument? What publications regularly publish these product reviews? Some market research will determine these answers.

Andy Rathbone, the free-lance writer you met earlier in this chapter as a restaurant reviewer, also writes computer product reviews for numerous computer periodicals. Here is how he says he handles a computer product review:

> First, I find the market for the product review. Second, I call the product manufacturer's public relations person and arrange for an editorial loan of product. Then I play with the product for a while, and write what I think about it. Other times, the publication sends me the product, and I review it.
>
> The last product I reviewed was the Manes/Andrews book on William Gates. Cathy Conroy sent me the book, and asked me to review it for CompuServe's online magazine, *Online Today*. I spent a month or so reading it, and taking notes in the margins. I liked the depth of the book, didn't like some of the overstatements, and wrote a review recommending the book. I also review computer software and hardware for a local computer magazine.
>
> The most important element is price. That single issue affects everybody. After that, the review should discuss the product's quality: How it handles the job it purports to accomplish. Then the review should compare how the product stands up against other products making similar claims. The review should also compare the product against other, similarly targeted products, even those from different price ranges. (Rathbone, personal communication, 1993)

OTHER SUBJECTS OF REVIEWS AND CRITICISM

There is a wide variety of other reviewing and critical writing specializations that have evolved in recent years or have existed for longer periods in specialty publications. Among them are:

1. Live entertainment (ice revues, comedy shows, circuses, and so on)
2. Architecture
3. Painting
4. Sculpture
5. Photography

Live entertainment reviewing and criticism have many of the same concerns as dramatic reviews and concert reviews. As Todd Hunt (1972) says, it is hard to say anything negative about such all-American institutions as ice

BEST SOURCES FOR BACKGROUND INFORMATION IN THE ARTS

Films and Movies
Local theater managers
Regional or local film company publicists
National film company publicists
Distribution company publicists
Actors and actresses
Specialized industry-trade publications such as *American Cinematographer* or scholarly publications such as *Film Comment*
Producers and directors
Film credits

Broadcast-Cable Television and Radio
Television and radio network publicists
Local affiliate publicists and promotion departments
Radio station publicists
Syndicated program distributor publicists
Specialized industry publications such as *Broadcasting, Electronic Media,* or *Radio & Records*
Program credits

Live Music and Concerts
Recording companies of touring musicians (see below)
Road managers
Tour publicists
Musicians
Specialized industry publications such as *Billboard* or *Daily Variety*
Specialized consumer publications such as *Rolling Stone, Spin,* or *Ray Gun*
Concert site facility management

Recorded Music
Recording companies promotion departments
Regional or local record company publicists
Musicians
Specialized industry publications such as *Billboard, Record World,* or *Radio & Records*
Specialized consumer publications such as *Rolling Stone, Spin,* or *Ray Gun*
Jacket information of albums/tapes/compact discs

Theater and Dance
Theater playbill night of performance
Theater managers
Actors and actresses, dancers
Specialized industry publications such as *Daily Variety* or *Back Stage Shoot*
Directors and choreographers

Books
> Book jacket or flyleaf
> Introduction, foreword, and acknowledgments of book itself
> Publishers' promotion departments
> Regional or local publishers' publicists and sales representatives
> Specialized industry publications such as *Book Week, Publishers Weekly,* and *American Bookseller*
> Authors

Food and Restaurants
> Menus
> Restaurant managers, chefs
> Public relations representatives of company
> Local health inspector
> Specialized industry publications such as *Restaurants and Institutions* and specialized consumer publications such as *Bon Appetit*
> Local and state restaurant associations

Architecture
> Gallery, museum, or show curator
> Architects
> Contractors, builders
> Specialized industry publications such as *Architecture, Progressive Architecture, Architectural Record,* and *Historic Preservation*
> Financing sources
> Local building inspector
> Local and state architects' groups

Painting and Sculpture
> Artist or sculptor
> Specialized industry publications such as *Art in America, Arts, Artforum International,* and *Art News*
> Published major exhibition catalogs/books
> Gallery, museum, or show curator

Photography
> Photographers
> Published major exhibition catalogs/books
> Specialized industry publications such as *Popular Photography* and *Aperture*
> Gallery, museum, or show curator

Popular Live Entertainment
> Specialized industry publications such as *Daily Variety* and *Back Stage Shoot*
> Theater program on the night of the performance
> Theater managers
> Performers
> Performers' public relations representatives

revues and circuses. These articles tend to be more review and less criticism. But, as he observes, there is a limit to how much you can hold back. Judgment based on local standards may be your best guide here.

Architecture reviewing has become increasingly important since a Pulitzer Prize for criticism was awarded *New York Times* critic Ada Louise Huxtable. Architecture critics such as Paul Gapp of *The Chicago Tribune* are well known in their cities and in the industry. The role of major structures in creating the personality, or face, of a community has been illustrated by the construction boom in the Sun Belt in the past two decades, and it continues. The new cities of this century have been characterized by their architecture, and the role of the critic is becoming more significant. A handful of newspapers and magazines use architecture critics as their cities continue to change. Because there is no second chance in terms of buildings, these critics should be on the inside of what is happening in terms of planning in the community before it happens.

Other arts such as painting, sculpture, and photography are most often presented in galleries and museums in special exhibitions and in standing or permanent exhibitions. These exhibitions often say much about the cultural state of the community that displays them, placing a degree of importance on criticism of these exhibitions. Most written evaluations of these exhibitions are descriptive, as they should be, for persons who might want to see the exhibits.

Often, Hunt (1972) notes, painting, sculpture, and photography exhibits are housed in a facility together and a single reviewer or critic will be called upon to discuss each in a single or perhaps separate reviews at different times. In these reviews, attention is seldom given to a single item unless it is so dominant that it commands the attention. Showings are also often presented by artist or by group of similar style artists.

ETHICS: WHO PAYS FOR THESE 'FUN' ASSIGNMENTS?

In 1992, *New York Times* food critic Brian Miller spent about $100,000 on restaurant meals and other expenses (Hosmon, personal communication, 1993). That's $274 a day, every day of the year! Although Miller's expenses are quite extraordinary, more organizations are paying for what used to be provided free by restaurants, theaters, or record companies. The slick full-size travel magazine owned by American Express, *Travel & Leisure*, publishes its policy on the table of contents page of each issue. The policy includes such concerns as restaurant and entertainment review expenses. "We always pay for airfare, hotels, meals and other trip expenses for all editors, writers and photographers on assignment for this magazine. We do not accept press trips or any other free travel that might influence our coverage," the policy states (*Travel & Leisure* staff, 1993, p. 9).

Who should pay for the entertainment you review? Should you pay for the free tickets? Records? Books? Dinner? Like *Travel & Leisure*, many publications are no longer accepting "freebies" for reporting about the arts, food, or travel.

Most newspapers, magazines, and newsletters have two sets of rules for this important feature writing issue. For full-time staff members, most major newspapers, magazines, and newsletters will reject free entertainment items unless the free ticket or book is used by a legitimate reviewer or critic in the completion of an assignment. Other books, records, and similar items are usually donated to local charities when received from a source. For part-time writers or free-lancers, these rules may or may not apply. At some publications, part-timers or free-lancers are left to their own decisions about who pays.

Why? Usually there are expectations associated with the gift of free tickets, records, and books. The expectation can range from simple recognition of the new work in print (news space publicity for little or no cost) to positive reviews. There has been a changing mood and a new set of expectations from such sources in recent years, however, as ethical standards have tightened. They expect less.

Clearly there are certain advantages to the special considerations such as good seat locations, receiving books or records in advance of release dates, and so on. It helps you do your job. But there is a chance of abuse of these special considerations if you are not careful. The price is high, too, in terms of your credibility as a reviewer. Once you are "bought" you can never achieve the same level of integrity in the business. It is a tough concession to make. There is the problem of dealing with sources. At times, reviewers and critics have the opportunity to become too close to their sources. The result? The temptation to write unwarranted favorable, or too favorable, reviews. This also diminishes your credibility. The two things reviewers or critics have from the beginning of their career are *integrity* and *credibility*. They are worth keeping, regardless of the cost.

PROFESSIONAL'S POINT OF VIEW

Michael Larkin
The Boston Globe

Most people, readers and other journalists included, view critics and reviewers with bemused envy, seeing only that someone could get paid for watching movies or attending rock concerts, eating dinners or reading some hot new novel. It's hardly work, right?

Consider, though, sitting through a screening of "Rambo XI: Thin Blood" and trying to think of something informed and entertaining to write about Sylvester Stallone's peculiar, enduring artistry. Or how about hunkering down in front of the tube for a night of the new fall season: What to say about "Hocus Focus," a new hour-long drama about magician crime solvers? Perhaps Anne Tyler's new book is out. But, then, you've already been assigned five books for the week and the book editor has given that one to someone else . . . well, maybe you'll get to it on your vacation (if you've the slightest desire to read anything more involved than the back of a Cheerios box).

It is, I think, the most difficult, underestimated, long-term assignment in journalism: Do for a living what other normal people do for relaxation and fun. Not only that, do it on deadlines only crazed sportswriters live with and do it with the understanding that everything you write will prompt a disagreement with someone—readers who know more (or often less) than you do, even probably your editors who have seen the same performance and are hideously callous in venting their opinions. Consider, too, the artists' responses. A sample: "Bigger jerks than me review books, Nathan," writes Philip Roth in *Zuckerman Unbound*. And above all, don't make a factual error; you're the expert and your performance is as public as any play or TV program.

So how does anyone do it? The critics I know love their work; almost all of them—despite crushing schedules—are trying to figure out how to cover one more thing or are panting about some upcoming event. Constantly learning about their specialty, they devote their lives to studying it: reading, seeing even performances they'll never write about, speculating about an entree's ingredients at a dinner party. They thrill when someone achieves excellence or expands the definition of the form; they are mortified yet enthralled (though they may not write it that way) when they witness an all-too-public flop. Mostly, though, they deeply care about the attempts at creation. It is a caring that stems from a lifelong affection for the art; it is the key element in doing this job.

No one gets to be a respected critic simply because someone gives them the job. Usually, critics gave themselves the assignment when they were young, and have spent most of their lives and education trying to figure out why some books are more moving, some films more exciting, some rock stars rockier. It is this fascination that endures. The best have it as a constant and are able to communicate it. It gives them an understanding of the past, an appreciation for the present, and enthusiasm for the future, all essential elements in the confidence necessary to make judgments about the ambitious efforts of others, to review and to criticize with personal vision and voice.

Without all this, a critic might as well be going to the theater for fun. (Larkin, personal communication, 1993)

Michael Larkin is Sunday Editor of *The Boston Globe*, overseeing all advance sections of the newspaper. In 20 years with *The Globe*, he has been a news copy editor, assistant sports editor, assistant business editor, editor of *The Boston Globe Magazine*, and senior assistant Metro editor for zoned news sections. For 5 years, he was living/arts editor, supervising *The Globe*'s feature writing, reviewing and criticism, and contributing occasional book reviews. For fun, he says, he likes to think about what to do next.

10

Aftermath, Follow-Up, and Depth Series Articles

In a horrifying instant late on a spring evening, a group of 27 children and their chaperones met their deaths in a preventable disaster of unparalleled proportions. Forty other persons survived, but some of them were seriously injured. They were the victims of the worst drunk-driving accident in U.S. history. A church group had been riding in a school bus on Interstate Highway 71 in northern Kentucky. The group had just finished a day of fun and frolic at an amusement park in southern Ohio. At 10:55 that night, a 34-year-old man driving a pickup truck, legally drunk it was later determined, was headed up the same side of I-71 in the wrong direction. Despite warnings from truck drivers flashing their lights, the truck hit the bus, punctured the gas tank, ignited the gasoline, and set the bus on fire.

It was a difficult 5 years after the 1988 accident. The survivors and family members first endured a long investigation by authorities and then the trial. Even 5 years later, they continued to suffer from lingering physical and psychological problems. What had happened to the hundreds of people involved in the disaster was a story waiting to be told. When the fifth anniversary of the accident approached, *Lexington Herald-Leader* editors assigned reporter and feature writer Mike Estep to tell the story of what had happened since the accident. Estep's stories appeared in a Sunday edition of the newspaper, just a few days before the actual fifth anniversary of the event. His lead story, which began on the front page of the Sunday edition, focused on how the survivors had been living with their grief. It told about what happened to some of those individuals willing to talk about the past 5 years. He also wrote a single story that discussed the changes in bus safety and drunken driving laws that the state legislature passed after the accident. The main story looked at the numerous victims willing to discuss their experiences since the accident. Family members described their feelings about the losses they suffered. Estep also wrote in detail about the pickup truck driver and what happened to him (he was serving a lengthy prison sentence for manslaughter). The story, a follow-up feature, was loaded with rich direct quotations from victims and their families that permit the people closest to the event to describe their feelings and emotions. The driver who caused the accident, however, was contacted in prison and refused to discuss the incident from his perspective. Estep's main story was nearly a full newspaper page in length. It was illustrated with 5-years-later photographs of survivors or family members of victims. Here's how Estep's (1993) lengthy story began:

Two symbols of the nation's worst drunken driving wreck are gone.

Last week, salvage-yard employees destroyed the charred hulk of the church bus in which 27 people died in a fire in 1988. They cut it in half, crushed it into a chunk of metal 10 inches high and took it to Louisville to be ground into shavings—carrying out a court order to make the bus unrecognizable.

Then they crushed the Toyota pickup Larry Mahoney was driving when he hit the bus at 10:55 p.m., drunk and going the wrong way on Interstate 71 near Carrollton.

But as the fifth anniversary of the May 14 crash approaches, the people whose lives were shattered don't need reminders. The memories are never far from the minds of the 40 survivors and the families of those killed.

Rick Uhey remembers every detail of the late-night call that made his heart race; getting pulled over for speeding; his frantic search at hospitals in Louisville for daughters Pam, who lived, and Crystal, 13, who died.

"I can tell you everything just as vivid as if it was yesterday, and I'll be able to do that in 10 years," Uhey said.

The crash happened as members of the Radcliff First Assembly of God church and guests returned from a trip to Kings Island amusement park in Kings Mill, Ohio. The crash punctured the bus fuel tank and ignited the gasoline, cutting off exit from the front door.

As flames raced through the bus and toxic fumes from burning seat material choked the air, panicked passengers became tangled in the narrow aisle and fell atop each other, clogging the rear door.

Three adults and 24 children and teens died.

Their families and the survivors, some badly burned, became "the bus people," bound together by a numbing tragedy that made headlines around the world.

They search for ways to describe the enormity of the tragedy, but say words can't do the job . . . .(pp. A1, A14)

When major news stories such as the Kentucky accident break and they are in the public's eye for several days, weeks, or even months, eventually a variety of types of articles are written. New developments call for second or third looks at the story. Anniversaries, recurrences of the dates when these benchmark events of our lives occur, also signal a time to revisit an event. Feature articles are often the manner in which we write about these special dates and events.

These feature articles have evolved into three basic types of articles that are becoming more important to depth coverage. Those approaches are *aftermath* articles, *follow-up* articles, and *depth series* articles. What are they, exactly?

Aftermath feature articles are written in the immediate wake of a major news story, typically an unpleasant or tragic event. These stories are assigned and written in the few days after a big story breaks, giving new insights into what happened and the effects of those events.

Follow-up feature articles are written after a period of time has passed, such as a few months, a year, or even several years. Follow-up stories often offer new information to shed new light on known events or revisit events to reinterpret them. These stories have a more evaluative, analytical, or interpretive purpose through use of experts, witnesses, and others involved in the story in some manner.

Depth series feature articles are a collection of articles that take a subject into greater depth and scope than a single story could achieve for a publication. In addition to being published in parts, as the nature of a series would require, the depth series is more highly organized and offers broader perspective through use of human and written sources of information. Depth feature articles in a series incorporate many of the characteristics of aftermath and follow-up stories, of course.

These three types of feature articles, each a little different from the other, offer explanation and perspective that were not available when the story first developed. The articles use large amounts of description, extensive direct quotation from interviewing, and narration to tell readers more about the events that are the cause for the story to be written.

Accidents, fires, bad weather, natural disasters, famine, rioting, war, and other events that cause high levels of human suffering usually demand additional coverage in the form of aftermath, follow-up, or depth series feature articles. On the other hand, positive events or significant changes that bring happiness and joy to a community are also an occasion for these features.

By showing the human angle, the story becomes less facts and figures and more "people-ized." It should also have a *local* perspective. Typically, aftermath articles appear on the second, third, or fourth days after an event. Follow-up features begin to be written in the weeks, months, or annual anniversaries after the event. It is also not unusual to use such follow-up stories even years afterward. Some editors use these articles a year, 2 years, or more after an event as *anniversary* articles.

In the early summer of 1993, for example, 25 years after the assassination of Senator Robert Kennedy in Los Angeles, most news organizations wrote follow-up stories looking at what happened in the time since Kennedy died, supposing what might have happened if he had continued his run for president and perhaps been elected, and looking back at a generation of "what ifs" by interviewing many of those persons close to Robert Kennedy, who knew him, worked for him, and carry on the spirit of his plans and his political ideals. Writing for the national wire out of Washington, Associated Press reporter Jill

Lawrence (1993) wrote her follow-up feature story, distributed on a Saturday afternoon for Sunday morning, the anniversary date. Taking a broad, sweeping view of things over such a long period of time, she speculates through her sources and talks to family members, individuals close to the Kennedy family and to the 1968 Robert Kennedy presidential campaign. Here's how her story began:

> WASHINGTON (AP)—The nation has traveled far in the quarter-century since Robert F. Kennedy was murdered. Yet his contributions have endured through the turbulent 1970s, the complacent 1980s and into the current era of Democrats who label themselves new and different.
>
> "The fact that 25 years after Robert Kennedy's death at the age of 42, he is still such a vital figure in the imagination of many people, including young people who were born after his death, shows he struck a deep chord," said Arthur Schlesinger, a historian and author of "Robert Kennedy and His Times."
>
> At the heart of Kennedy's legacy—a mix of compassion and pragmatism—lie several principles: Society has an obligation to help and protect the vulnerable; individuals have an obligation to try to make a difference; and those tiny individual ripples can form a current "that can sweep down the mightiest walls of oppression and resistance," as he put it in 1966 in Cape Town, South Africa.
>
> Kennedy's causes echo in President Carter's foreign policy, which elevated human rights to a top priority; in President Clinton's talk of personal responsibility, racial reconciliation and the dignity of work; and in a memorial organization dedicated to exposing injustice and aiding the needy.
>
> "He appealed to the best in all of us. He gave people a vision of what America could be," said Kerry Kennedy Cuomo, a Kennedy daughter who runs the memorial's Center for Human Rights.
>
> As a senator from New York and later as a presidential candidate, Kennedy visited Indian reservations and Appalachian hollows, migrant workers in their fields, poverty-ridden families in Brooklyn, N.Y. and the Mississippi Delta. (Lawrence, 1993)

These articles are commonly found in daily newspapers and sometimes used in weekly newspapers, but they also appear in magazines. News magazines, for example, use aftermath and follow-up articles often as a device to deal with their once-a-week publishing schedules, especially on an anniversary of an event, but also as an approach to coverage of a major event in the first issue to appear after the event. Although this happens each week, you might recall such recurring coverage in news magazines for events such as the terrorists' bombing of New York's World Trade Center or the long standoff and then the fiery conclusion of the siege at the Branch Davidian religious group's compound outside Waco, Texas in 1993.

When something *good* happens to a community, such as a national sports championship or a major economic development like the decision to build a new automobile assembly plant nearby, these stories also become highly read items. Whereas readers are naturally curious about disasters and other public traumas such as the Waco standoff and eventual deaths of many of the religious group's members, people truly savor the more positive success stories from our communities. Major successes also command thorough coverage, and part of this includes aftermath, follow-up, and series articles.

The return of strike-ridden daily newspapers to a metropolitan area is one type of positive development, of course. This occurred in Pittsburgh, where both of the city's newspapers were shut down by a strike by delivery truck drivers and other circulation personnel. When the strike ended, only one of the two major newspapers had survived. Newspaper readers were still happy to have their *Pittsburgh Post-Gazette* in hand, even though it had bought out the larger *Pittsburgh Press* and closed it down during the strike. Associated Press reporter Claudia Coates (1993) wrote an aftermath feature about the effect of the strike and the significant changes in reading habits and sales patterns in that city's newspaper market after the newspaper returned. Her story, taking a strong business-oriented approach by looking at competitors such as smaller newspapers and marketing strategies, told readers interested in the industry what had happened in the Pittsburgh area newspaper business in the aftermath of that strike. This is how her story began:

PITTSBURGH (AP)—Every day, Cora Scott picked up a copy of the *Pittsburgh Post-Gazette*—until last year, when a strike stopped the presses.

Then the paper resumed publishing in January, and she started buying it again. But not every day; perhaps half as often as before. She remains angry, she said, because of all the obituaries she missed over eight months.

"We were deprived because a lot of people would pass on and we wouldn't know," she said, handing a vendor 35 cents.

The Post-Gazette didn't earn her wrath—or that of other readers—but is stuck dealing with it, more than a year after the strike began.

It was *The Pittsburgh Press*, the afternoon paper and the larger of the city's two dailies, that prompted the strike by trying to force 605 delivery drivers into a new distribution system cutting 75 percent of their jobs.

The strike against the Press Co.—which printed and distributed both the *Press* and the smaller, separately owned *Post-Gazette*— began May 17, 1992, and lasted through the summer, fall and into the winter.

It ended with a surprise: David swallowed Goliath. Blade Communications Inc., the owner of the *Post-Gazette*, bought the *Press* from E.W. Scripps Co. and shut down the paper.

Tom Herrmann, *Post-Gazette* circulation director, said the paper has no reliable way to tell how many people, like Ms. Scott, have fallen out of the habit of reading a paper every day.

But sales figures show readership is down. Before the strike, the Sunday circulation for the *Press* was about 554,000. The *Post-Gazette* is printing about 530,000 copies, although it hasn't determined yet how many newspapers are actually sold. The weekday run totals 290,000, far short of the papers' combined circulation of 365,000 before the strike.

The strike couldn't have come at a worse time . . . . (Coates, 1993)

A CLOSER LOOK

Often an event is big enough that it cannot be handled as a single event or single story. Rather it becomes a series of events and dozens or even hundreds of stories over several weeks, months, or even a year. Recent local events of national and international interest in Florida, Louisiana, and California and illustrate this. The events surrounding the power and fury of Hurricane Andrew in 1992, the nation's worst natural disaster to date in terms of damage, and the scope and emotion of the devastation of the urban rioting that occurred in Los Angeles after the 1992 criminal court decision acquitting police officers in the videotaped beating of motorist Rodney King, called for enormous packages of aftermath features, as well as a lengthy series of follow-up stories in dozens of newspapers in the regions affected by these events. A closer look at the types of stories helps further define and explain the roles of aftermath and follow-up feature articles.

Florida and Louisiana Publications React to Hurricane Andrew

There were literally thousands of aftermath and follow-up articles published by Florida and Louisiana newspapers in the wake of Hurricane Andrew in late summer and fall 1992, but also throughout most of 1993. For individuals living in those areas, the story never seemed to go away. There was always something else to write. After the initial aftermath coverage in the weeks immediately after the storm struck, the follow-up feature stories came in several waves.

Many of the first set of aftermath stories were written as spot, or breaking, news stories. An equally large number of them were written as people-oriented features. These aftermath articles were published in the first week immediately after the storm struck in August 1992. These spot news articles focused on the scope of the damage brought by the storm, as officials began to measure it. The feature aftermath stories focused more on how people were devastated by the disaster. The stories told affected residents how to get medical help, where they could find emergency water, the effects of curfews, how to find food, what to do about temporary housing, how to find telephones, ways to hook up temporary electricity with generators, how to prevent looting, ways to cope with traffic and transportation problems and dangers, and what the different levels of government and volunteers from the private sector were doing to assist the many thousands of victims. Many of these aftermath stories were told at a very personal level so readers could easily identify with the people in the feature stories.

Typical of the dozens of such aftermath articles in the first week after the hurricane was a story by *Miami Herald* reporter Jacquee Petchel (1992) from the center of the storm-damaged area at the southern tip of the Florida peninsula, Florida City, on the third day after the storm struck. She wrote this story without the usual facilities of a reporter for a major daily—working telephones, bureau computers nearby, and easy transportation. Because of blocked roads and other traffic problems, just getting into and out of the area was a major challenge for most reporters to overcome. She managed to file her aftermath story about the suffering of hundreds of migrant farm workers living in the heart of the area. This is how she began her very descriptive and moving story for the Thursday editions of the newspaper after the Monday storm:

FLORIDA CITY—In the heart of South Dade's farm fields, on Hurricane Andrew's growing map of misery, Florida's migrant workers feel forgotten.

Jesus Muniz, farm worker and lemon picker, has seen relief and rescue planes flying over his rubble-strewn labor camp, but he wonders: "Why does it seem like they can't see me?"

"We have no family to go to, no money, no clothes, no nothing," said Muniz, the father of three small children. "It is like no one can see us, or they don't care about us because we are just farm workers."

Muniz and his family were among hundreds of migrant workers, mostly Mexicans, left homeless and all but broke Monday when Hurricane Andrew leveled their shanty-like trailer camp. Not one of 400 rental trailers is standing.

Dozens of families, with nowhere to go, were left to camp among the splintered remains, sleeping on cement slabs, under trucks and in their cars, and on mattresses unearthed from the soggy ruins.

Nineteen-year-old Norma Vega and two other families—17 total—spent Tuesday sleeping on a mattress under a farm truck. Raw sewage is seeping up from the ground nearby.

"We don't know what to do, but we try to stay together and help each other," she said. "We don't have anyone else. We cannot believe what has happened to us."

In the wreck of a nearby trailer, Alicia Mendez slept between slabs of wood with her five-month-old baby. She said she wept most of the night.

"I do not cry for me, but for my baby," she said Wednesday. "I have two other children, too. We have no clothes, no nothing."

They dug holes in the ground to cook, took their water from two fire hydrants, and scrounged through heaps of wood and fiberglass for unscathed boxes and cans of food.

There was little. In fact, almost none.

"Everybody is hungry here. My baby needs milk," said Generosa de Valle. "They just forgot about us and we need new lives."

Residents of the Everglades camp at 19400 SW 376th St. didn't see anyone from outside the camp until Wednesday afternoon, when a search and rescue crew arrived to look for casualties. None was found as of Wednesday afternoon.

No one has brought food or clothing, although rescue crews were trying Wednesday to persuade residents to leave and be bused out to nearby shelters . . . . (p. 22A) Reprinted with permission of *The Miami Herald*.

After the most immediate emergencies, such as the dangers the migrant residents were found to be experiencing, had passed, a first wave of follow-up stories evolved. These focused on less critical, but still pressing problems. Readers were told how to repair their homes and businesses, how to select the more reputable contractors, or how to find the right tools and supplies. Stories also advised victims on how to deal with insurance companies, adjusters, and banks. Readers learned about potential problems dealing with the overworked building and zoning offices of the county government. And readers were given follow-up stories about the dangers of using unlicensed contractors and inadequate materials to repair their homes and businesses. These articles related experiences of victims. Readers were able to learn from the experiences of others.

A second wave of follow-up articles, 6 to 12 months after the storm, focused on assessing how well or how poorly the recovery effort was going. Many of these stories had more of an evaluative tone, focusing on special programs set up by governments and their successes and failures at a broader level. Other stories took a much more personalized approach by looking at individual families and how each was battling its own problems. These stories outlined the painstaking efforts to rebuild homes and neighborhoods, as well as efforts to keep families—which had been split up by changing schools, jobs, long-distance commuting, temporary residences, and other factors—together. Several newspapers used graduation time in the spring of 1993 to write follow-up features about Homestead, Florida, high school students at their senior prom and how they had endured a most unusual and traumatic senior year. And 9 months after the storm struck, a handful of enterprising feature writers even did lighthearted human interest follow-up stories about the sudden jump in the area's birth rates. This sort of follow-up reporting continued for most of the first full year after the storm struck. Because the story affected so many people in so vast an area, and did so much property damage, the follow-up feature approach seemed to fit the coverage well. This sort of reporting and feature writing was characteristic of most South Florida and Louisiana newspapers in the year following the storm.

Southern California Reacts to Urban Rioting

Los Angeles and Southern California also experienced a major regional trauma in 1992 when the area reacted to the state criminal court decision acquitting police officers of charges in the beating of Rodney King. Several days of rioting occurred in South Central Los Angeles, as well as other neighborhoods, burning large areas of the city and resulting in deaths and injuries to residents.

Southern California newspapers reacted in a manner similar to the way journalists reacted to the Andrew disaster, but they had only hours to respond at the beginning. In the days and weeks following the disturbances, major daily newspapers in Los Angeles, Long Beach, Orange County, and other nearby urban areas in Southern California first wrote aftermath feature articles about the tremendous human and property losses suffered by the community as a whole, but also the tremendous losses of businesses, jobs, and homes suffered at individual levels. There were memorable stories of heroism in rescues, but also stories about the fear, disgust, and frustration. Much aftermath coverage focused on the neighborhood that was destroyed and the people who lived there.

Later, follow-up stories were developed about what occurred during the trial itself, the opinions of the jurors, the police officers on trial, and other court officials involved. The entire Los Angeles Police Department and city government were given in-depth follow-up attention as additional investigations proceeded. Still other stories followed up by focusing on residents' confusion about the legal system and how it worked. Some stories looked at Rodney King himself. In the end, hundreds of aftermath and follow-up feature and news stories were published in the year following that spring week, describing how people were refusing to give up and describing what was happening in South Central Los Angeles in the wake of the civil problems.

Work of this magnitude is seldom at an individual level. In these cases, it involved the newsroom staffs of two very large daily newspapers. Each individual working on a story contributed to the total effort. Teams of editors, graphic artists, photographers, and reporters were needed at newspapers such as *The Miami Herald*, the Fort Lauderdale *Sun-Sentinel*, *Palm Beach Post*, and *New Orleans Times-Picayune* to cover the wake of Hurricane Andrew as the storm cut across Florida, the Gulf of Mexico, and then Louisiana. In California, literally hundreds of journalists were required to cover the events in the aftermath of the Rodney King criminal court decision. The *Los Angeles Times*, the *Los Angeles Daily News*, the *Los Angeles Herald Examiner*, *Orange County Register*, and *Long Beach Press-Telegram* each committed the maximum of their resources to cover this major local story that had very high national and international interest.

The staffs of *The Miami Herald* and the *Los Angeles Times*, in fact, were awarded 1993 Pulitzer Prizes for their work. *The Herald* won for meritorious public service for its aftermath and follow-up coverage of the natural disaster, and the *Times* won in spot news for its responsive second-day spot and aftermath coverage of the manmade problems in Los Angeles in spring 1992.

PURPOSE OF AFTERMATH ARTICLES

Aftermath and *follow-up* are terms that are often used interchangeably. However, there is a difference that you may have noticed from the discussion and examples so far. Aftermath articles occur most often in the days immediately after a major event or series of events take place. Follow-up articles return to significant events in a community's life also, but more time has passed and new information comes to the story through that passage of time. These revisit the major stories from time to time and, as a result, are a form of aftermath articles. The follow-up article is written with a stronger news approach and is often based on new or updated information, the facts and additional details that were not available in earlier coverage of the story by a newspaper, magazine, or newsletter. Many publications still try to "featurize" such reporting when it is published. New developments in a story often lead to these articles in newspapers, magazines, and newsletters.

There were dozens of aftermath and follow-up articles in the wake of the Branch Davidian religious cult tragedy in central Texas in 1993, stories focusing on cult leader David Koresh, his relationships with his followers, the treatment of children living at the compound, the survivors, and countless other aspects. Each follow-up story shed, in some way, new light into the workings of this mysterious group that caught the world's attention. How did these stories do that? They relied on investigations, interviews with relatives or the few survivors, release of information collected by local, state, and federal government agencies involved in the case, and other reporting. Slowly, readers interested in the group learned more about how it formed, existed on a daily basis, and, ultimately, died in a firestorm on that spring day.

The aftermath is the *result* of an event, often an unpleasant result, in fact. Newspapers, magazines, and newsletters continue to tell their readers about a major event in the first days immediately afterward by assigning writers to write aftermath articles. These magnify the focus on a story and remind readers of the importance of the story. Feature writer Daniel Williamson (1975) says aftermath articles are features that give new perspective "to a disaster, tragedy or profound news event that captures the impact and dimensions of the event by humanizing its effect" (p. 179).

Aftermath articles tend to contain more of a people approach than the traditional news follow-up. And although these articles often focus on disasters and tragedies, they also focus on other actions, decisions, and developments in the community. When a river overflows in an unusual spring flood, how does it affect those involved? Readers want to know the basic facts, such as deaths, injuries, daring rescues, and damage amounts, but they also want to know the human element—the reaction to all this. How do people endure?

What are their feelings? Thoughts? Emotions manifest themselves in many ways. An effective writer will try to capture those displays of emotion to truly tell the story in the article. This is what happened during the Hurricane Andrew disaster and again when a severe flood tore through Fort Wayne, Indiana. The description in writer Dan Luzadder's (1982) column, written on daily deadline for the *Fort Wayne News-Sentinel*, gave his personal reaction to the disaster. He told readers in a compelling way how this event changed the lives of residents of his community on that day and, probably, forever. Because it was a column, it had many personal observations and feelings from the writer instead of the usual variety of nonpersonal sources. Luzadder went to the neighborhoods where the flood hit hardest and talked to many Fort Wayne victims. Still, his generalizations about the community's reactions captured the mood and portrayed the plight of the victims. There was no one named, no heroes—except the community itself—and no one directly quoted. Although it was a highly personal approach, it still achieved what an aftermath story seeks to do—and Luzadder's column earned him the Pulitzer Prize a year later for local general spot news reporting.

Writer Daniel Williamson (1975) says the aftermath articles about such events as floods and building collapses use one or more of four different approaches:

1. *The epitome of the victim or the victims.* This strategy focuses on the one person or group of people who have endured the disaster, such as a plane crash or a hotel fire. There may be only one real victim for the focus of the article, such as a child who becomes trapped in a well and must be rescued before death. You try to focus on these individuals by finding the survivors, who become your key sources. If none are accessible, then friends or relatives may assist in telling the story to readers. Jacquee Petchel's story discussed earlier in this chapter demonstrates this approach.

2. *The mood piece.* These articles employ many of the techniques of color articles and are dependent on description by those on the scene. These articles are often rich in detail and help those who were not present to gain insight into the atmosphere of the site, using witnesses, survivors, photographs, and other means of re-creating what happened. Dan Luzadder's award-winning column described earlier is an example of a mood approach.

3. *The hero.* In some assignments of this type, the best way to tell the story is to focus on the individual who saved the day. There will be times when this person is accessible and quotable. It creates a much-desired angle for the article because most people love to read about a hero and this form of the great American success story. Numerous hero stories were written in the aftermath of the Los Angeles rioting, notably the rescue by several black residents of white truck driver Reginald Denny from his beating in an intersection by several black youths.

4. *The goat.* Occasionally, someone, or some organization, unfortunately causes a tragedy, such as the drunken driver of the pickup truck who caused

the Kentucky bus accident. The story becomes a strong angle if you can tell the story from that person or institution's point of view. Because most people or organizations are understandably reluctant to talk to a reporter if they have caused a death or large amounts of property loss, this is a difficult angle to pursue. Regardless, if it can be told this way, it is a compelling story because it is a *human* story, one of accidental or intentional human error.

You might not have a choice about which angle to chose in handling your assignment. Much of the time, the course of events will determine how you handle the story. But on some stories, you may have the choice of one or two or three approaches.

WRITING AFTERMATH ARTICLES

You have a number of writing decisions to make when you are working on an aftermath article. You must develop your lead, decide the article's structure, locate sources, select a writing style, and decide the article's mood. Let's look at these in a bit more depth:

1. *Aftermath lead.* The lead of the article is most important. Here you set the stage for the entire piece, and your decisions about how you plan to tell the story to readers are revealed. Aftermath leads can be anecdotal, focusing on an individual or an example of the major point of the article. This approach makes specific points to illustrate the larger problem—the suffering of one victim can show what an entire group of survivors has experienced and how they feel. Claudia Coates' lead to the Pittsburgh newspaper strike story for the Associated Press is an example of this sort of lead. Take another look at that lead on pages 243 and 244. Rereading it, you can see how Coates focuses on a typical frustrated newspaper customer to exemplify the readership and sales problems facing the newspaper.

2. *Structural plan.* Think through what you are trying to achieve with the aftermath article before you begin to write. How will you organize it? What are the major sections? What are the major points? In what order?

3. *Sources.* At the same time you think through the organizational plan, consider what sources are necessary for information to make your major points. Will it be victims? Their families? Official sources such as police and firefighters? Other people? Reports? Observations?

4. *Writing style and mood.* Your chosen style and mood for the particular article should reflect the type of event you are covering. In other words, for an article that describes the joy of a small town several days after it has won a state high school basketball championship, an informal, casual, and upbeat style might be appropriate. But for a natural disaster, such as a tornado striking that same small town, the style should be more serious and respectful.

Williamson (1975) offers four more considerations for writing aftermath articles. Your approach, he says, should stir the imagination of readers by going beyond the basic facts of the event that are found elsewhere, such as other articles in the same issue or earlier issues. Here's what he suggests to strengthen your writing:

1. *Play heavily on human emotion.* Use descriptions of sorrow, fear, happiness, and other emotions to enhance your article. This comes through direct quotations and observation of what happened and its effects on people and places. Can you accurately convey what people experienced? Exercise your vocabulary for this— accurate word choice will make all the difference.

2. *Try to help the reader identify with the victims.* Will readers think that it might have happened to them? If so, you have probably succeeded in helping them identify with the victims. Writing with detail will permit this to happen in most articles. Be alert, and observe to recapture the situation.

3. *Write tersely and briefly.* A tightly written article will still get to the point and will permit more perspective to get to the reader in the same amount of space your editor has assigned to the article.

4. *Concentrate on a fast-moving, strong lead.* Good leads set the tone for the article. For aftermath articles, you must write a lead that gets the reader involved and still explains the purpose of the article.

It is important in writing aftermath stories to bring in the local angle as much as possible. This is easy enough for local events. It might not be so obvious for events that occurred hundreds or thousands of miles away.

WRITING FOLLOW-UP FEATURE ARTICLES

The follow-up feature approach is often an appropriate alternative for stories of this type because, after a time, readers need background information as well as the new information to remind them of events surrounding the original story. Whereas it is traditional in newspapers and the wire services, the second-day, or follow-up, approach is also used by some magazines and other specialized publications to cover a major story. Using the follow-up approach is routine for news magazines such as *Newsweek, Time,* and *U.S. News & World Report.* With their once-a-week publication schedule, editors and writers at the major news magazines are forced to find new angles in writing featurized follow-up articles that also serve as round-ups on the event.

Most newspapers believe in the importance of follow-up stories. In fact, in 1992, *The Orlando Sentinel's* editors invited readers to call them with suggestions for follow-up stories they would like to see in the newspaper. Hundreds of readers responded, suggesting various subjects and events about which they wanted to learn more. Highest on the list was the tragic story of an 11-year-old Orlando-area boy who was injured at a convenience store on

Christmas Day 1984, nearly 8 years earlier. The boy's injuries—the booby-trap gift-wrapped bomb had cost him his right leg—had healed the best they could. The boy and his family—they were too poor to buy any Christmas presents then—had been flooded with gifts, $135,000 in donations, free hospital care, and a new mobile home. But what happened to him? The newspaper responded to readers by assigning reporter Jim Leusner to find the boy and follow up on what had happened to the youth. Leusner discovered, to the shock of readers, that things were not much better for the young man. This is how Leusner (1992) began his lengthy follow-up:

> On Christmas afternoon 7½ years ago, his 11th birthday, Paul Jewell's life was shattered by a gift-wrapped bomb.
>
> People opened their hearts and pocketbooks to the mangled, badly burned victim of the booby trap that had been set outside an Orange County convenience store.
>
> The boy eventually lost his right leg, but $135,000 in donations, a new mobile home, and free hospital care seemed to insure a bright new start for the fourth grader, whose family was too poor to buy him Christmas presents.
>
> But such stories often end happily only in the movies.
>
> Today, Paul Jewell is 18 and living in a small town in eastern Ohio. He is jobless, trying to recover from yet another of two dozen operations, and he sleeps in his car.
>
> Sometimes, he says, he mentions suicide to his mother.
>
> "I'm trying," Jewell said in a recent interview with *The Orlando Sentinel*. "This stuff gets you down. Sometimes you just think about giving up.
>
> "I've been going through a rough time, since my accident. It was a real crummy deal," he said.
>
> Jewell says he quit school in the ninth grade in Ohio because he tired of students making fun of his burn scars and artificial leg. He also says he doesn't understand why he can't have easier access to $123,000 remaining in the trust account that was filled by thousands of Central Florida donations.
>
> The person responsible for his injuries—in what apparently was a random bombing—has not been brought to justice. And Jewell has no hopes of suing anyone to recover money for his anguish.
>
> Former teachers and acquaintances, however, contend that Jewell was an unmotivated child of the welfare system who has not taken advantage of the extraordinary help provided him by generous Orlando-area residents....(pp. A-1, A-10)

A few days after a teenage boy was discovered to have made a daring life-threatening stowaway flight in the unprotected wheel well of a jet freighter flying from Colombia to Miami, new information came to light about the boy. The story was still fresh in the minds of residents of South Florida, where the

---

BEST SOURCES FOR AFTERMATH AND FOLLOW-UP ARTICLES

Participants, victims
Friends and relatives of participants, victims
Neighbors
Witnesses
First persons to arrive on the scene afterward
Spokespersons from investigating federal, state, and local agencies
Public records and reports as they become available
Private sources of information released to the public

---

story originally broke. A typical second-day spot news approach might start like this United Press International (1993a) staff-written story, distributed about 24 hours after the youth was discovered at the Miami airport. This story, written with standard wire story brevity, focuses solely on the new information about the already existing story:

> MIAMI (UPI)—A woman in Colombia says she is the aunt of a teenage boy who said he stowed away in the wheel well of an airplane and made what medical experts called an impossible journey to the United States.
>
> Lucely Cardona told Radio Cadena Nacional in Colombia Saturday that the youngster identifying himself as Guillermo Rosales is really Juan Carlos Guzman, and that he is 16 years old, not 13.
>
> She said her nephew is unstable and that he travels the country looking for adventure.
>
> "I saw him on television. It's him. There's no doubt. I was shocked. I even felt like crying," Cardona said.
>
> Cardona said the teenager is the son of Yolanda Betancur and Oscar Guzman, who are dead. She said he does not have an aunt in Miami as he had claimed, but he does have distant cousins.
>
> The claim had little impact on Rosales' celebrity status. He has been taken into the home of Jairo Lozano, a brother of Miami police officer William Lozano, who was acquitted last month of manslaughter in the deaths of two black motorcyclists four years ago. The Lozano family is from Colombia.

The follow-up feature approach taken by Alina Matas and Gail Epstein (1993), two *Miami Herald* reporters, was more human interest and community reaction oriented. Despite that approach in the lead, their story still contains the new revelation about the youth's identity and age, and the development that the U.S. Immigration and Naturalization Service (INS) was investigating the boy's story. Their follow-up story had a more personal approach, starting with the lead's emphasis on the boy's first trip into the city after he was released from INS custody to a Colombian family living in Miami. The story answers reader questions such as "What is he doing?" "What is new with this story?" "How is he?" and "Who is caring for him?" Compare *The Herald* story's beginning with that of the UPI national wire story:

> On his first outing in Miami, Colombian teen Guillermo Rosales went out for a Big Mac and a milkshake, but also got a shower of effusive greetings at a Coral Way McDonald's from customers in awe of his stowaway story.
>
> Tipped by the television cameras, men and women came up to the boy and hailed his courage. A little girl walked from across the opposite end of the fast-food restaurant to give him a key chain from Colombia.
>
> A woman ran to his table and tightly hugged him, wiping tears from her eyes.
>
> "I just wanted to hold him in my arms," said Gloria Bejarano, who left Cali 14 years ago and heard the news about Guillermo, who says he is also from Cali. "He comes from my homeland. It's as if I know him."
>
> Meanwhile, back in his homeland, a woman claiming to be his aunt told Radio Cadena Nacional that Guillermo's real name is Juan Carlos Guzman and that he's 16, not 13. Lucely Cardona said her nephew is unstable and that he travels the country looking for adventure.
>
> "I saw him on TV," she said . . . .(p. 1A)

The UPI story was necessarily shorter and more to the point—true to wire service style—and focused on the new information about the youth. However, *The Herald* story, with more length and depth, let readers get to know the youth. The story also delves into the feelings of the Miami family responsible for the boy, reviews known background on the boy's journey in the unpressurized, below-zero-temperatures landing gear area aboard a cargo plane full of fresh flowers, and provides some reaction comments from around the United States, including those from a man and woman who called from Washington state to say they wanted to adopt the boy. The story then describes INS efforts to find relatives and check out the story the boy told the INS when he was discovered a little more than a day earlier at the Miami airport cargo area. The story also provides comments from aviation experts who questioned the boy's original story, saying that the boy could not have possibly survived the trip in the wheel well and that he was likely smuggled aboard the plane somehow. The story also says that INS would investigate, because if the boy had been smuggled into the United States, the airline would be responsible. The story closes with a description of the boy's activities on his first day of supervised "freedom" in Florida and with available background information on the boy's family—the boy said his parents had died in an accident. The follow-up ends with a revealing direct quotation from the boy: "I hope they let me stay here," he told the reporters (p. 1A).

Follow-up articles such as the Colombian stowaway story have wide application in all types of publications. In addition to news coverage, such as the stowaway example, follow-up articles are often used in sports coverage as second- or third-day stories, meaning they give new information such as players', coaches', or fans' reaction to the conclusion of a major sports event. They are common in entertainment sections after events such as the Academy Awards, a major concert or special performance, or other similar events of note. They give readers the inside story about entertainers' reactions, emotions, and explanations for why they succeeded or did not.

These types of feature stories, with their new information combined with the already-known information, help readers. Earl Maucker (1993), managing editor of the Fort Lauderdale *Sun-Sentinel*, says that his newspaper's research shows readers want relevance and ability to understand the events of the day from their newspaper's follow-up on major stories. "They want to understand their world," he says. "They want follow-ups on stories. They want those follow-ups to be balanced and fair, to list information, to explain and describe trends, to provide analysis, and to show them, not tell them." Follow-up feature stories can help readers to understand why something has occurred and to share the reactions other people have to the event if they are written well. They are, as Maucker explains, essential supplements to coverage of events by newspapers, magazines, and newsletters.

WRITING DEPTH SERIES FEATURES

There are times when routine feature coverage, whether it be aftermath, follow-up, or other types of feature articles, just cannot do the job in a single article. Even longer magazine articles might not be adequate for certain subjects. Major topics, such as a presidential election campaign or a public health issue dealing with AIDS, often demand more than a single article can accomplish. Usually this occurs because of one or more of these characteristics:

1. *Magnitude of the issue.* An issue will often affect many individuals and communities. Public policy issues, such as taxation or care for the elderly, affect many individuals and often demand depth coverage. Coverage telling how many people are impacted must also tell the human side of the story by illustrating it through the eyes of the people involved.

2. *Seriousness of the problem.* Certain matters are necessary to cover in depth because of the serious nature of the subject. For example, discovery of contamination of a major source of public water requires thorough attention. Aside from the straight news approach, feature approaches will examine the personal effects such a problem brings to a community by looking at individuals and at the group.

3. *Immediacy of the event or issue.* Because certain subjects are current now, they cannot wait. Public concern about an issue, such as the potential risks of AIDS or the potential dangers of nuclear power, requires attention in such a way that articles serve the community's thirst for information right away. Fear of the unknown often creates problems that compound existing troubles, so educational-instructional articles are a public service. These articles illustrate

the situation by humanizing the problem so readers can identify with the subject at their own level. Answering questions such as "How does this affect me?" makes a depth series successful.

4. *Broad scope of the story.* A depth feature series usually evolves when a subject is broad in scope, encompassing a number of subtopics that must be covered in adequate depth to make sense to readers. Often, a trend is significant enough to justify thorough analysis and illustration through a series of features. The effects of the growth of Vietnamese and other Southeast Asian refugee communities on the West Coast over the past decade, for example, have been covered by a depth feature approach by various publications.

Author William Rivers (1992) says that some inexperienced writers feel writing short articles is easier than writing long ones. Actually, it becomes easier to handle longer material because you have more opportunity to use the information you have collected. It is also easier because of the additional dimension of organization that serialization permits.

The feature series should be a highly organized study of a subject that is neatly and cleanly divided into parts of equal significance. The pieces within each series need to be linked together with transitions. The pieces of the series should be presented in logical fashion with linkages as well. Series are often accompanied by editor's notes, sidebar boxes, or other short editorial devices to explain to readers what the purpose of the overall series might be, as well as the role of the individual story that they are reading in an issue.

Each part should be written to stand alone: The individual story should be strong enough and self-explanatory enough to be useful to readers who did not see earlier, or will not see later, parts. The series approach is common in newspapers, magazines, and newsletters, but perhaps it is more frequent in daily or biweekly newspapers and weekly or biweekly newsletters because their publication frequency is conducive to publishing pieces over a short period of time. However, magazines also run depth feature series when a subject justifies the treatment over several issues in succession.

Writing a Feature Series for Newspapers

Organization is a key to newspaper series articles. Distinct divisions of the subjects within the overall topic are necessary to determine what goes into what story. A writer or editor planning such a series should outline the project first, then refine each story idea as it develops. There should be minimal overlap of the subjects and there should be an editor's note at the beginning or end of the article to inform readers that the article is part of a series and that other articles have been published and will be published on the topic. Subjects are, of course, varied, but must be broad enough to permit subdivision.

The Philadelphia Inquirer frequently publishes in-depth news and features in series form. The regularity of use of this approach is one of the reasons the award-winning daily newspaper has developed a reputation for investigative and depth reporting over the past two decades. The high quality of the writing and reporting, of course, is the single most important reason. A recent example of this was a 5-part series written by Donald C. Drake and Marian Uhlman (1992) entitled "Making Medicine, Making Money." The articles focused on why U.S. medicine prices are so high compared to those in other countries. The reporters began the series on a microlevel, presenting the problems of four typical patients who must purchase expensive prescription medicine to treat medical problems. Then the story discussed the problem in general and how the pharmaceuticals industry operates. The series was organized in this fashion:

Part 1: Why prices for medicine are soaring out of the reach of most Americans.
Part 2: How drugs are marketed to physicians.
Part 3: How drug companies must clear certain government barriers to make their way to the profits that come from selling prescription drugs.
Part 4: Research and development efforts by drug manufacturers and how they minimize risks in developing new drugs.
Part 5: How other countries such as Germany, Japan, and France hold down drug prices.

These segments were not limited to one story per installment. Drake and Uhlman wrote several sidebar features (such as one that focused on the move by some drug companies from mainland U.S. locations to Puerto Rico to keep their costs low), and the stories were supplemented by numerous informational graphics and photographs. A depth feature story approach kept the stories interesting and personalized, presented at a level understandable to average readers. Just as a sample of how the extraordinarily long series began, this is Drake and Uhlman's lead to the first story in the series:

Eva Smalls Rozier has diabetes, a stomach ailment and high blood pressure. To keep these problems in check, she takes prescription drugs costing $150 a month—more than she spends for food or her mortgage.

Transplant patient Joseph Pearlstein takes pills to keep his new heart from being rejected. The cost: $50 a day.

When John Forrest Jr. suffered a heart attack, emergency room doctors shut off the heart attack with a drug that dissolved the blood clot causing it. The treatment cost $2,200.

Mary Nathan has a potentially lethal ailment called Gaucher's disease, which weakens bones and causes painful swelling of the spleen. Her drug costs $270,000 a year.

These patients have a variety of medical problems, from the ordinary to the unusual, but they have two things in common:

They all owe their lives to drugs.

They are all captives of the $55 billion-a-year pharmaceutical industry.

It is the most profitable business in America.

It doesn't matter if the economy is flourishing or stagnating, if the jobless ranks have swelled or shrunk, if the inflation rate is high or low, or even if America is at war or peace. The pharmaceutical industry rakes in the cash. No other legal business consistently makes as large a profit . . . . (p. A1)

Writing a Feature Series for Magazines

It may seem unusual for a magazine to run a series, right? With all the space a magazine can give to a major article, why would it need to serialize? It is more common than you might think. Monthly magazines, especially the specialized ones, will occasionally run a feature series of two or three or more parts. Usually, this is done not because of a space crunch, but because an editor wants to develop an ongoing readership habit. This is common for new magazines and for those that have a high proportion of newsstand sales instead of subscription sales.

One recent example of a depth feature series in a magazine comes from an unlikely source, a pet magazine. *Cat Fancy* magazine is published monthly by Fancy Publications in Irvine, California, with the focus on cat care by responsible owners. The company also publishes *Dog Fancy*. *Cat Fancy*, established in 1965, has a circulation of 330,000 copies a month. It is a leading magazine in the pet and animal category. A contributing editor for *Cat Fancy* magazine and a managing editor for Fancy Publications, David Blum recently wrote a two-part series of "special report" articles (1993a, 1993b) focusing on how cats communicate with their owners. His articles were based on a survey of about 2,300 of the magazine's readers who wrote to the publication to describe how their cats meowed, yowled, purred, and otherwise used nonverbal movements to say something. For people who truly believe they can talk to their pet cats, this was an entertaining set of feature articles.

The first part of the set focused on how cats tell their owners they are hungry, if they are contented and happy, when they want to play, how they have their own "vocabularies," and so forth. The article used a large amount of anecdotal information and direct quotations from survey respondents. Blum frequently described firsthand communication experiences of cat owners through their own words.

The second article looked at how cats tell owners they are not happy, how passage of time affects how cats and owners can communicate, how cats express sorrow, and how cats communicate with other cats. To conclude the series, he discussed a few other hard-to-believe communication stories that he collected from the responses to the survey. Typical of the article is this middle portion of the first installment of Blum's series (1993a), which focused on the vocabulary of some cats:

There may be no such thing as a plain old "meow," CAT FANCY readers report. Surveys mention everything from "hello" meows to "what's that?" meows to "hurry up" meows and more.

Victoria Ritter of Florida offers this translation guide for her Turkish Angora, Fluffy:

Long, high-pitched meow = "Play with me."

Short, high-pitched meow = "Help me."

Long, loud meow = "Cat outside."

"Jrrrrrrr." = "Bird outside."

Meow/purr = "Breakfast time."

"Meowwww?" = "Where are you?"

Anna Seals of California reports that her black shorthair, Phantom, "chirps when he's chasing bugs, lets out a lighthearted cry for attention and cries terribly when he wants into our room."

Pam Dunnam of California writes that her tabby, Lynx, has a separate, distinct meow for his owner's name. She also insists Lynx says "wa-wa" for water. "Honest!" she writes.

Other owners report growls, chirps, squeaks, "yohrs," "rowrs" and "prrrrps." Carol Hagemeyer, who lives with Sidney, a 9-year-old domestic shorthair, writes, "I am aware of 10 different meows" . . .(pp. 18–19)

Series presentations in magazines are not as common as they once were. Historically, it has been common for magazines to serialize. Years ago, magazines would serialize fiction, especially for readers who could not afford to buy books. With books more available in less expensive paperback editions in the last three decades, magazines that serialize books today tend to use parts of new nonfiction and fiction books as they are being written or soon after the manuscript is finished. A publisher might permit early publication of portions with the hope that it will tease readers enough to encourage them to buy the entire book.

Newspapers also run serialized or excerpted books on some occasions. This can occur when the author is a staff member of the newspaper. Typically, it occurs when major daily newspapers or larger magazines buy rights to new blockbuster books as publishers prepare to release the book. Book publishers like to serialize parts of books to encourage sales of the entire book. It is a marketing "tease" tool. Some newspaper and magazine editors like to run these advance peeks if they feel excitement about an anticipated book is substantial enough to justify it in terms of enhancing readership of their own publications. *The Wall Street Journal*, for example, recently ran exerpts of David Brock's best-selling controversial book, *The Real Anita Hill*, on its editorial page. The book, published by Macmillan's Free Press division, was a study of the Oklahoma law professor who was the key witness in the 1991 U.S. Senate Judiciary Committee confirmation hearings for the U.S. Supreme Court appointment of Justice Clarence Thomas.

The serial approach is also particularly useful for specialized business/industry periodicals, such as magazines and newsletters that must cover issues of a highly technical nature for readers with specialized knowledge. The approach works well for those magazines and newsletters with sophisticated levels of knowledge, but also works for new or not widely known subjects of common interest of readers of a specialized publication.

PROFESSIONAL'S POINT OF VIEW

Mike Foley
St. Petersburg Times

An aftermath story? A follow-up piece? You mean, write a feature story after the news is over?

Is that journalism?

You bet. The feature story done after the big disaster, the crucial vote, the key game, or that triple axe murder is not only real journalism, but it's your time to shine.

You'll have the time, space and, probably, a lot of freedom to decide how best to handle the story. How often do you get an opportunity like that in this business?

But it's also a real challenge. Your usual excuses—or, rather, "reasons"—for a less-than-stirring account won't work. The deadline is farther off than a few hours, or minutes. You can talk to more people. You can get the details. You will be able to sort out the confusion. Then, you can sit down and—can you believe it?—write.

So, you've got challenge, you've got opportunity. Can the possibility of massive, career-ending failure be far behind? Of course not. So, before you blow it, you might consider a few suggestions:

• *Relax.* Take a few deep breaths, a blank piece of paper, a pen or pencil and figure out what you need to do. This preparation should include reading stuff already written on the topic, and planning other research, including public records, historical documents, books and outside experts. (You'll find later that background information is almost as important as the new reporting you'll do.)

• *Talk to your editor.* Your editor has either assigned this story, or, at least, has permitted you to pursue it. Only an expert (or fool, or maybe the publisher's kid) would ever work on a story without talking it over first with the boss. This also will allow you to find out how much time and space you'll have. You also should, at this point and throughout the gathering and writing stages, think of other material that will enhance the story—photos, maps, charts, illustrations. Your editor will thank you for any suggestions. (Editors like to look good, too, you know.)

- *Think about what you want to do.* Sound redundant? Maybe it is. But many writers, especially young and beginning ones, forget to set goals. They're after a "story," without thinking about what the story might be. Sure, the story will change many times as you gather information. But it helps to start with some idea of where you could be going.

- *Don't forget the little things.* The follow-up stories are the detail stories. What's the dog's name? What did the family eat for dinner? What was the dead guy wearing? Take a look at reporter Edna Buchanan's book, *The Corpse Had a Familiar Face*, if you want some examples of how to do this well.

- *Feel it.* Attention, all you aloof, neutral observers: It's time to get real. If you want to write a good story (even gather enough material to fashion a good story), you have to let loose, be a human. Don't take sides or get involved, but use your own emotions to try better to understand what the human in your story might have felt.

- *Tell me a story.* Sure it's journalism, but let's not forget what a "story" is. It's a narrative, with a beginning, a middle and an end. Reread your research, study your notes, shut your notebook (and maybe your eyes for a minute), and tell me a story. Step back and tell it whole.

If you have done your job, I'll even read your story, maybe all the way to the end. And that's my ultimate compliment. (Foley, personal communication, 1993)

Mike Foley is vice president of communications and community relations for the *St. Petersburg Times*. Prior to that, he spent 23 years on the news side, the last 9 years as executive editor and managing editor. He was a reporter and assistant city editor for the now-defunct *St. Petersburg Independent* before becoming assistant metropolitan editor of the *Times* in 1974. He was also metropolitan editor and assistant managing editor of the *Times*. He has also served as a Pulitzer Prizes juror. In his spare time, he is a bass guitarist in a country band, Stalled on the Tracks, and a drummer in a rock and roll band, The Fabulous Nose-caps.

11

Travel Writing

Travelers spend a *lot* of money in the United States. The figure was reported to be $85 billion to $90 billion in 1992. And a *lot* of people travel, also. That figure was reported to be as high as 150 million U.S. travelers in the same year (Clarke, 1993). No wonder it is big business. And no wonder there are a lot of newspapers, magazines, and newsletters devoted exclusively, or in part, to travel.

The American public is traveling more in the mid-1990s than ever before, creating a growing market for travel writing. Books, magazines, newspapers, newsletters, and other printed materials are used for guidance in making travel decisions and for getting the most out of travel budgets. For most writers, travel stories are fun assignments. Perhaps one of the most glamorous feature writing assignments is to write about an exotic, faraway land.

People are enriching their lives by travel, not escaping, recent surveys of travelers tell travel editors. And those who travel do so frequently. They are interested in cultural and historical locations and places of natural beauty instead of night life, luxury, or shopping. A recent national survey found important factors in planning a vacation or other leisure trip included a location with natural beauty (96% said this was important), a place where the traveler has never been (89%), freedom to decide what to do during the trip (89%), and experiencing local culture and history (83%). Less important factors in travel were recreation such as golf (24%), luxury resort areas (39%), night life (51%), and shopping (59%). People who consider themselves seasoned travelers take several trips a year, including destinations overseas. Leisure travelers are not young people and they may have more time on their hands. Market studies show the average leisure travelers to be individuals in their late 40s, female, and living on a household income of about $46,000 (Clarke, 1993).

Much travel writing designed to help both leisure and business travelers make decisions about their trips is done by free-lance and part-time writers. Most daily newspapers have at least one staff writer or editor assigned to travel, and many larger dailies have a Sunday section filled with color photographs, stories, and information about interesting places. Even the largest daily newspapers have few—one to three full-time persons—who work exclusively as travel editors and writers. Small dailies usually offer a special page or pages once a week, and the person handling travel news and features may divide these duties with other features or news duties. Most weekly newspapers devote little or no regular space to travel features unless the publication is in a resort area or has a special tie to the travel industry.

Magazine editors depend on articles with travel-oriented features by either staff or free-lance writers. Many national and regional lifestyle consumer magazines offer readers travel stories that appear in every issue or with some other regularity. And, of course, there are numerous travel-oriented periodicals, such as *Condé Nast Traveler*, *National Geographic*, *National Geographic Traveler*, *Travel/ Holiday*, and *Travel & Leisure* on the consumer magazine market, dedicated to a person's urge to wander. State and regional publications, such as *Arizona Highways* and *Texas Highways*, also focus on travel in their respective states and regions.

Leading monthly consumer travel magazines such as *Travel & Leisure* and *Condé Nast Traveler*—their circulations were each at 1 million a month in late 1992—publish issues of about 200 pages in a large-page full-color format each month. These magazines generally have five or six main feature articles, including the cover article, plus regular monthly departments, such as those devoted to letters from readers, food, shopping, personal care, wine, the world weather outlook, books, business travel concerns, upcoming current events in major cities around the world, new travel products, and opinion articles such as columns and editorials. Naturally, this list is just a sprinkling of the possibilities for major travel publications to focus on. Pick up copies of these publications at a nearby newsstand or at the library and see for yourself what they are doing.

There are also growing magazine and newsletter markets for travel-related manuscripts in industry and trade travel-oriented publications. These include periodicals of travel agents, hotels, convention and tourism organizations, convention planning organizations, tour operators, bus companies, attraction operators, rail lines, cruise lines, airlines, recreational vehicle businesses, and similar travel-related markets. These publications are geared to individuals who work for businesses associated with the travel industry. Examples of these publications include California's *RV Business*, published for the recreational vehicle industry, and Illinois' *Bus Tours Magazine*, published for charter operators.

These days, consumers turn to the news media for help in making travel planning decisions. A major purchase, such as a vacation package, requires the traveler to gain the expertise to make the proper decisions. Airline deregulation has made a quagmire of airline routes, service, and ticket prices. Ground travel is no different. Automobile travelers are constantly affected by unpredictable weather and often wildly fluctuating gasoline prices, for example. Thus, a good travel feature can make a difference as readers turn to their favorite newspapers, magazines, and newsletters for assistance. Travel writing, then, can include an element of consumer reporting. One distinction University of Miami journalism professor and former *Miami Herald* travel editor Alan Prince (personal communication, 1993) recently noted is that you must be honest with readers:

The reader who is stimulated by a travel writer's destination piece doesn't return home with a computer or a television set. Instead, he or she's got an airline ticket stub, photographs, and souvenirs, and, most of all, memories. That's not a lot considering today's cost of travel.

The reader should understand that he is paying money for an experience, not for an appliance.

Henry David Thoreau wrote, "It is not worthwhile to go around the world to count the cats in Zanzibar." Both the travel writer and the traveler must understand that.

For some 5,000 years of recorded history, the only way humankind could travel faster than on a horse was to fall out of a tree. And most people stayed close to home.

Today, people travel to distant areas in a matter of a few hours—and that means the travel writer faces a credibility standard. The standard is set by the thousands who have visited a place before the travel writer gets there.

The travel writer must realize that in his or her mass audience there are many readers who know more about the place than the travel writer can learn in a brief visit. There's no way the writer can pull the wool over these readers' eyes. He can't fake it and keep his credibility. It's that simple.

The other share of your audience—those who haven't been there—might someday go. And if they find the destination to be quite different from what the travel writer has pictured, they will never again believe—or will always be skeptical of—anything that travel writer ever writes.

It's a matter of trust.

Travel writers, especially those who are on newspaper staffs, don't have the luxury of spending weeks in a destination. Two to four days are more likely, and that's hardly enough time to get to know the place—especially when you're supposed yo be an expert when you leave.

There's no question in my mind that the most important element in competent travel writing is "knowing the place" before you get there. You can accomplish this by reading anything and everything you can get your hands on.

A reporter doesn't begin an interview with a celebrity by asking how the celebrity spells his or her name. The reporter already knows that and, one hopes, a lot more about the celebrity. The same principle applies to doing a destination piece. Otherwise, the destination piece is going to be awfully "thin," and that just isn't good travel writing.

At the 1987 annual convention of the Society of American Travel Writers in Melbourne, Australia, *San Diego Tribune* editor Neil Morgan (*Editor & Publisher* staff, 1987) said travel writing is getting to be more credible with the public. Travel writing has gained this new level of respect from readers because of the "courageous and consistent" efforts of newspapers, magazines, and newsletters to upgrade quality. Skepticism about travel writing brought about by flattering writing and free trips that existed in the 1970s has been overcome by increased reader trust, Morgan said. "Newspapers and magazines should be able to tell readers about travel as reliably and convincingly as about abortion and AIDS," Morgan, an experienced travel writer himself, said (1987, p. 13).

Even the short-distance or regional traveler needs information to best use his or her time and resources. Travel writing serves this purpose when done well. Business travelers need guidance on all aspects of their travel (including airlines, ground transportation, hotels/motels/inns, restaurants, and entertainment), and an entire industry catering to business travelers has evolved in this century. Included in that movement is a subdivision of the travel publication industry that produces magazines and newsletters aimed at veteran travelers.

Simply writing about your recent vacation won't get the job done. Most travel-oriented publications provide a standard fare of information for the traveler, or the person thinking of traveling, or the person simply daydreaming about traveling some day. "Travel writing is an overcrowded field and much of it is poorly written," says Southern California-based free-lance travel writer Kit Snedaker (personal communication, 1993). Snedaker, whose work is syndicated by Copley News Service and who is a member of the Society of American Travel Writers, believes good travel writing means hard work; it is *no* vacation: "Too many travelers believe they are travel writers after managing a postcard and the rest are in it for the free trips. They write payback stuff. But the best make stories out of it. The biggest fault is what I call the 'Summer Vacation' story. 'We climbed on board and then we went to . . . and then . . . and then . . . .' It's a diary and about as interesting as watching a fly climb up the draperies."

Readers of the travel pages, as well as readers of the business pages of contemporary publications, are generally erudite. These people are those in the higher income brackets with the money and time to spend going places. Thus, many of them are likely to be well-traveled and informed readers of your stories. And, as some travel editors will tell you, the writing must simultaneously serve two distinct audiences: people who have not been to the place you write about and people who have already been there.

Christopher Baker, an award-winning full-time travel writer and photographer who specializes in adventure travel articles, has published work in most of the nation's major travel magazines. He describes what makes a travel manuscript a winner: "A successful travel article does more than conjure up unforgettable images and lead readers by the hand. It entertains, provides reliable and useful information, and tells the truth," Baker explains (1989, p. 22). "But if you fail to place your reader vicariously on that mountaintop or on that beach you've described, you will not sell your article in this highly competitive market."

How can you succeed? What do you write about? You write about places to visit. You tell readers about historical places, annual festivals, national

OBSERVATIONS OF A VETERAN TRAVEL FEATURE WRITER

Kit Snedaker
Copley News Service feature writer

According to surveys, everyone travels for three reasons: shopping, eating, and sightseeing. But there's another reason: We travel for the excitement of another reality and, for writers, the chance to tell everyone about it. Alas, anyone who has written a postcard believes he could be a travel writer, little knowing it is a tough gig. Editors can spot a beginner at once. He starts at the beginning of his trip, uses the first person, and trudges through to the end. The reader has bailed out long since. Editors call this travel story "How I Spent My Summer Vacation."

Pros frequently use the first person, too, but only when it's appropriate and then only to give the journey immediacy. In fact, some newspapers and magazines prefer third person and refuse to accept first-person stories. It also helps to have some writing experience behind you, to know about the active voice, positive language, and to have a decent grasp of grammar. It is also important to have a point of view, not entirely enthusiastic, and not to be afraid to present it. Was the meal dull? Were the beds lumpy? The reader is as interested in this as he is in the great view and the shopping bargains. More interested. Now he knows what to expect and what to avoid.

This reader looks for pieces about places he's been or places he plans to visit. For that reason, the United Kingdom is always a prime story destination. So are Paris, Italy, and most of Europe. The Far East has its admirers, but Borneo, Sarawak, and such odd corners of the world are not frequently published for good reason. There are not a lot of people who have been there or want to go there. They sound like an editor's dream, "never before written about!" But they are an editor's nightmare.

I once went to Togo on a dreadful trip, came back and devoted about 2,000 words to this nightmare, both the good and bad. My editor called me in and said warmly, "Who the hell gives a damn about Togo, wherever it is? And look at the space you've wasted on this needle in the armpit of Africa!"

This aspect of travel writing really belongs under marketing, but then for a free-lancer, half the battle is selling stories. Consider not only newspaper travel sections, which seem to be drying up, but also travel magazines and inflight magazines of both domestic and foreign airlines. Look at newsletters, some of which are upscale and well edited. Indeed, look at anything that will pay and provide a tearsheet. Current tearsheets are often the key that opens the door to a new market.

Travel writing is an overcrowded field. Writers from other areas gravitate to it, looking for free trips and, with experience, they have the edge. However, more and more newspapers and magazines do not accept articles based on sponsored or free trips. At least they say they don't. Many give this lip service and then never really ask. Still, this is something to consider. (Snedaker, personal communication, 1993) parks, cities, resorts, and inns. You tell them about places to stay, restaurants with views, and the easiest and cheapest ways to get there. You convey the richness, the color, the excitement, the fun, the moods, and the atmosphere. You give important information such as admission prices and times for an attraction. But you also relate personal experiences, such as the best place to park in a busy neighborhood—New Orleans' French Quarter or Boston's North End, for example—to make your story complete.

Thus you find the unusual, the unique, the odd, and the entertaining. Writing professor Shirley Biagi (1981) says: "Visiting Waikiki may have been fascinating for you, but asking a travel editor to buy 6,000 words about 'gorgeous white sand beaches' is an insult. The successful travel writer chooses the offbeat, photographs the unusual, visits the out-of-the-way" (p. 24). Christopher Baker (1989) says the unusual is essential, but writers must also "breathe *possibility* into your readers' own travel plans—and make your destinations come alive" (p. 22).

Curtis Casewit (1988), author of a dozen books on travel, recreation, and photography, believes travel writing requires *enthusiasm* to succeed. He is right: This is something you have to want to do to do it well. Some people travel because they must; others do it because they love it. "You cannot enjoy being on the road without a genuine enthusiasm. For some of us, travel is almost a physical necessity. It springs from a chronic curiosity and desire to uproot ourselves," Casewit says (p. 6). Casewit also observes that the most successful travel writers have finely developed skills and traits involving observation, accuracy, humor, flexibility, patience, curiosity, and ability to overcome adversity.

Have you ever taken a major trip? Have you ever gone that one step further by writing about it? What would you tell your friends about the trip? This can be the foundation of a good feature. Travel writing requires good reporting, though, because it is much more than going from point A to point B by jet. Most successful writers are experts, too, and know the details of a successful journey from planning to budgeting to itineraries and more.

With a good market, you need to consider what works for those already in the business. Start out by reading the weekend travel section or page of your local newspaper. Also study it. What kinds of stories are published? Photographs? Where do they come from? Does the section contain more than basic "destination pieces?" If so, what else? In the stories, what sources do the writers use? What is the writing style? Is it narrative? First person? What supplementary material comes with the stories? Photographs? Locator maps? In this chapter, we consider all the elements of travel writing.

Who do you contact and with whom do you work? Travel editors, of course. The individuals who review your work have various responsibilities and titles. Most are called travel editors, but some are features editors or Sunday editors at daily newspapers. At many magazines, they are called travel department or features editors, depending on the level of specialization of the publication. These are highly educated, well-traveled individuals. They are also experienced journalists who have earned the coveted position they hold. And they often really love their work.

FIVE MAJOR TYPES OF TRAVEL WRITING

Regardless of whether the articles are written for newspapers, magazines, or newsletters, there are five common types of travel writing:

1. *Destination article.* Destination stories simply tell readers the basics about places they might go on a trip. What's there? What is there to do? What sort of accommodations are available?

2. *Attraction article.* Attraction stories are more specific than destination articles. These tell readers about a particular place, such as a park or historical site.

3. *Service article.* The service story explains how to travel better by letting the reader understand the mechanics of traveling. This includes articles about buying airline or cruise line tickets or negotiating customs and other legal hurdles in a country known for its tight import/export and immigration rules.

4. *Personal experience article.* Personal experience stories may do the same as any of the three previous approaches, but they interject a personal experience perspective, including such things as emotional responses to the experiences. As personal features, these stories have high levels of anecdotal content.

5. *Roundup article.* These stories give readers a summary view of a subject by theme. Two examples might be the "5 best-kept secrets of Maui" or "10 bargain deals for this winter's Caribbean cruise season," in which the writer assembles information from different places and summarizes them in listed or other organized formats.

WRITING STYLES: FINDING THE BEST APPROACH

The experienced traveler-turned-writer is the travel writer of the mid-1990s. Your job as travel writer is to take the reader there on destination stories, to give your reader the facts for service stories, and to provide opinion about current travel and tourism industry issues. Most travel writing is narrative. It remains descriptive, however, as writers use their command of the language to paint a mental picture for the reader. Remember, not all travel stories are illustrated with color photographs or graphics, so you must use your vocabulary to convey impressions of the subject through precise adverbs and adjectives.

Travel writers often utilize a more personalized style of writing. Whereas most features in a newspaper, magazine, or newsletter are written in an objective, third-person style, travel writing allows several different writing style approaches, including a growing emphasis on a first-person, personal experience approach. The personal approach puts the author into the story as a principal source of information. It is firsthand experience writing. It is friendly and casual. Use of the first-person pronoun "I" is characteristic of this style. It is storytelling just as if you were telling it to your friends. Your own observations and reactions are important in this approach. Re-creation of dialogue using direct quotations of brief conversation is common in this style also. Although first person is not as common in other sections or departments, it is a trend in today's travel writing that makes the story more appealing to readers. Full-time free-lance travel writer Arthur Harris, Jr. (1992) says that you must study a newspaper or magazine first to determine what writing styles it prefers for what types of travel articles. "If uncertain what approach a travel section takes, I pop several dollars in an envelope and mail it to the paper's circulation department requesting a recent Sunday paper" (p. 21).

A simple, but successful, formula for travel articles begins with a dramatic or, at the least, interest-arousing lead. You have to sell the story to the reader. There are plenty of travel articles out there. The story must convince readers this one is worth their time. Some writers do this with an anecdotal lead, some use a dramatic moment, some use heavily descriptive openings to create impressive images in the reader's mind, and others try a summary approach that simply creates an atmosphere or mood of the place.

After deciding what works best for your story for the lead, set the rest of the story up by providing some sort of thesis or "nut graf" for the readers. Tell them why they should read on. What is the point of the story? Why should they care about the dogwoods blooming in east Tennessee in April? Or the side trip you took in Hawaii to that remote waterfall? This portion of the story has to tell the readers why they should read the article and what is going to follow. Let them know what you are going to do with their time, in other words, even if it is only 5 minutes for a shorter piece, and especially so if it is 15 minutes for a much longer magazine-length article.

The remainder of the article must carry out the promises made. Put people and places into this story. Travel writing is about people and places. Share that. Let readers travel with you. Christopher Baker (1989) strongly recommends that travel writing show, not tell, to be effective. "The ability to share travel experiences with others relies on your skill in painting strong and sensual pictures with words," he says (p. 24). One way to accomplish this, he says, is to rely heavily on similes and metaphors in your writing. Another effective means is to use of dialogue to re-create conversations of those at the scene.

Writer Kevin Paul DuPont took the personalized, yet descriptive approach to his article about travel in winter. DuPont, an experienced winter traveler after more than a decade of news and feature reporting about the National Hockey League, shared some of his firsthand knowledge in his article for the travel section of *The Boston Globe*. His personalized writing is not limited to his own observations; he also peppers the article with re-creation of dialogue to make the story more lively and interesting as it dispenses valuable advice. But in the end, readers gain from this lighthearted approach to the problems of getting anywhere in the northern U.S. and Canada during the winter months, especially if it involves airline arrangements. Here's DuPont's (1993) article:

> BRRRRR, North America—It's the dateline that fits almost all my stops across our continent. After more than 15 years of reporting on the National Hockey League, I know cold. I know snow. I know sleet and hail.
>
> Turn me upside down, and $1.38 in Canadian currency, frosty to the touch, tumbles from my pocket—just ahead of 3 inches of packed powder from Banff, Alberta, the place of hot springs, superb skiing and a dry, biting cold that will challenge even a Diehard battery.
>
> With apologies to Paul Simon, I have holes in the soles of my shoes—and I think they're all from the salted sidewalks of Winnipeg or Calgary or maybe Bloomington, Minn.
>
> So now it's your turn to join the jet-set world of gloves, hat and galoshes? Fine. Good luck and welcome to the not-so-wonderful wonderland of winter travel.
>
> Above all, pack your patience first. Nothing you can jam into a carry-on bag will serve you better, especially if your point of departure is some place snowy.
>
> While the rest of the world dreams of poolside piña coladas in the Caribbean, the bone-chilled traveler to and from wintry places fantasizes of flights that run on time (hah!), wings that don't need de-icing and airport lounges with deep, cushiony seats, mountains of free popcorn and waiters who don't suggest self-immolation when you order your fifth soft drink.
>
> Booze mixes with fatigue, aggravation, long delays and air travel—if ever your flight does take off—into a concoction that delivers the mother of all migraines once in the oxygen-thin air of the flight cabin. So push the fluids, but perish the alcohol. Instead, save your nightcap for the warm hotel bar that's keeping a light on for you, somewhere, even if only in your dreams.
>
> Every man and woman who works behind the counter at an airport gate—those friendly faces who make that final check of your seat assignment before boarding—is a liar. "Why is the plane not here?" you ask.
>
> "Uh, fog in Bangor," says the man behind the desk. "Yeah, can't get off the ground."
>
> It just so happens the plane you're waiting for is coming from Cleveland.
>
> "If it's stopped snowing, and we're already two hours past departure, why can't we leave now?"
>
> "Well, you see, there's a problem with the windshield wiper, and . . ."
>
> Lo and behold, only 10 minutes later, 33 additional passengers come shuffling to the gate. It wasn't the windshield wiper after all, just some creative storytelling to camouflage a connecting flight. Five minutes later, everyone boards.

Really, what does it matter what they're saying? When the plane leaves, it leaves. Until it does, read your book, do your crossword, make your phone calls, listen to your tapes, fill out your expense account, savor your snack.

Never, however, stray too far from the gate once the waiting game has begun. They may be saying no one is going anywhere for an hour, but it's amazing how time flies (and the plane does, too) when those 33 connecting passengers arrive. Don't trust gate people, and don't let them out of your sight.

Baggage is another bugaboo. I once arrived at LaGuardia Airport in Flushing, N.Y., two hours ahead of an early-evening flight to Nova Scotia. With bag checked, boarding pass in hand ("Aren't you early?"), I loaded up on newspapers and paperbacks and went for dinner.

An hour later, thick fog covered the airport. Two hours more, my flight was postponed until 9 the next morning. ("Postponed" is airlinespeak. They should just say, "Fly in this weather? Are you crazy?")

Meanwhile, my bag, impossible as it seemed, was already on its way to the Maritimes. I had been so early that Air Canada popped my suitcase on an earlier flight to Nova Scotia (gee, if only they had asked me to go, too). Back I went to Manhattan to spend the night, while my clean shirt, underwear and socks were being delivered to Nova Scotia.

Business travel with a bag lost is one thing, but vacation travel is another. If you're going somewhere special—and I do hope it's a sunny, phone-free zone—then absolutely, positively do not check anything that, if lost, would keep you from enjoying your arrival in paradise.

If you're overloaded, though, don't forget that many of the "gotta haves" will fit in your pockets. I've begun packing for more than one trip by putting on my bathing suit before I put a single thing in a suitcase.

Funny, but you don't get many chances to swim in Winnipeg. (p. 6F) Reprinted with permission of the *Boston Globe*.

WRITING THE TRAVEL ARTICLE

The single most important step in writing a good travel story is preparation. Although taking the trip and writing the story may seem important, these steps cannot be as successful without laying groundwork before leaving home. The biggest reporting assets writers have in travel journalism are the telephone and the fax machine. Use them often. They can offer the basis for a good story and save you a lot of time and trouble in the long run. Don't forget the mail as well. When and where you need information but are not in a big hurry for it, send postcards or letters for background information, such as press kits. Get on mailing lists of public relations firms that represent the travel industry. You will soon have more information than you know what to do with.

If you plan to get into travel writing, either for a magazine or newspaper, start a set of reference files. Organize them as you see fit, but try to put information you collect in some system so it can be found quickly when needed. One easy approach is to begin an alphabetical system based on destinations and attractions. You could also begin a set of files on service-related topics that is organized by subject. Keep a telephone number file, too.

To get you thinking about what goes into reporting and writing a travel story, here are some suggestions for a good start:

1. *Call sources ahead of time.* When you decide you will do a story, call or write sources at the locations several weeks (if domestic) or several months (if foreign) in advance to gather the advance information mentioned previously. Call tourism offices that are usually government-operated and government-sponsored. The best possible help on foreign sources comes from the domestic offices of government travel bureaus. Many are located in major metropolitan areas and ports of entry such as New York, Chicago, Los Angeles, Miami, and Washington, D.C.

2. *Contact local business organizations.* These include chambers of commerce and convention bureaus. These organizations can provide economic reports to give you a better feel for the area. They can also give you the best information about hotels, motels, restaurants, and transportation. Often they also have information about historical sites, popular places to visit, and more.

3. *Use visitors' bureaus.* Popular vacation and resort locations will have sophisticated visitors' offices and will be anxious to help you before your trip. These persons can also arrange tours once you arrive.

4. *Use sources at your hotel.* Don't forget the hotel or motel where you plan to stay. Many times the management of these places will offer help in advance if you request it.

5. *Go to the library.* Check out books about the areas you will visit. Review articles from periodicals that have been recently published so you can get a better idea of what might be a "new" angle for your story.

6. *Build your own travel library.* As you go to a new place, add a book about it. Eugene Fodor's series of country and city guides, published in paperback annually by David McKay, is a good example. Arthur Frommer's guides offer a similar perspective. Don't think these two examples are the only ones; they are not. Simply visit the travel section of a good local bookstore and you will see a wide range of travel guides—most written by experienced travel guides and travel editors. There are also a growing number of travel-oriented newsletters available by subscription. These vary a great deal in their approach, focus, and price, but can be the most up-to-date sources of information available to you as a travel writer. Examples? *Consumer Reports Travel Letter*, *ASTA Notes*, and *Entree*.

7. *Contact specific site sources.* Once you know where you are going and when, start to ask specific questions when you write or call. Contact the individual sites and begin to request information to provide the needed

background for your story. But always remember the wide range of possible sources you have at your disposal. A good travel writer, like any reporter, has multiple types of sources.

8. *Use a wide variety of sources.* Many good sources serve the travel industry. These sources are individuals working for hotels, airlines, cruise lines, automobile clubs, and the specific attractions. Many are in public service, such as city and county tourism commissions, state tourism offices and departments, and regional agencies. Many are in private service, representing businesses such as local and state chambers of commerce, tourism cooperatives, and promotional organizations. But you must exercise care in dealing with industry sources. These sources have a particular point of view and a positive perspective to represent and may try to influence you toward their way of thinking.

9. *Call to confirm appointments and visit dates.* Your time is valuable, but so is the time of the person who might be your tour guide or source. To help your work, be reliable and keep appointments.

Free-lance travel writer Barbara Claire Kasselmann (1992) talks to local residents for color and other details when she visits a destination for a travel article. "I always talk to the people in a region to get the flavor of their accents, their interests, and their styles that make that part of the country or the world special," she says (p. 23). "If you make these people come alive in your writing, it will pique the prospective traveler's interest in the destination about which you will be writing." She says these sources also provide local lore and provide tips on the best places to eat or tour that might be off the beaten path.

Many offices are set up to deal with drop-in visitors such as journalists. But others are not, so consider the source and determine if the people you need to see will be able to see you at a moment's notice, or if these people need a call ahead of time. It never hurts to call ahead. Use the telephone and fax machine to your advantage.

USING YOUR OBSERVATIONAL SKILLS

After your research stage is complete, after all the appointments are made, and after you arrive, your on-site reporting work begins. Remember your own senses will be serving as the senses for your readers when the time comes to write the story. Good observational skills are critical here and these are developed through discipline and practice. A good travel writer always has an eye or ear open for new possibilities. There are stories you do not expect that will develop, forcing you to abandon part or all of the original plan. You cannot be so rigid as not to consider the chance this will occur. If you are fortunate, you could encounter a new angle on a story that you planned to write. This will not only be exciting for you, but it will also excite the readers of your story. You must constantly look at the story with the idea there is something new to this approach.

A good observer will use the senses to the fullest and convey this to the reader. Consider colors, sounds, and smells. Notice textures and tastes. All of these, if written with the right adjectives and adverbs in your story, will take the reader to that special place that you write about each time.

Another word about writing: Avoid clichés in travel articles. Most editors detest them and they can be the "kiss of death" for an otherwise sound manuscript. There is special temptation to use them to convey impressions. Don't use them, because clichés often turn off readers. Work a bit harder to find the words you need to describe what you saw, heard, or felt. It will pay off.

A similar warning can be issued about perpetuating stereotypes. This is a problem especially when you are writing about foreign countries and their cultures and peoples. Strive to find fresh and innovative ways to describe the areas you visit and the anecdotes you include in your articles. It is quite possible to write about national or regional customs, beliefs, and other traditions without feeding on stereotypes. It might require some work below the surface, but it will pay off in the form of more appealing travel features.

The following are checklist charts of major sources for newspaper, magazine, and newsletter travel writers. Some of these sources are important to you because of the organizations they represent. Others are going to be important to you because of the positions they hold within an important travel-oriented organization. The best advice for you is to use them often because they will be there to help you before, during, and after your trip (when you are writing about it).

WRITING DESTINATION ARTICLES

One of the oldest, and still one of the most common, forms of travel writing is the destination piece. These stories are designed to focus on a place the reader might want to visit or has already visited. It is generally a descriptive story. The story is designed to tell the reader about the place, whether it be an exotic location, such as Honolulu or Singapore, or a more traditional vacation destination, such as Niagara Falls or the Smoky Mountains.

These stories focus on cities or specific attractions. They must be crammed with facts. The reader will be seeking the best information about these locations as possible destinations for a meeting, vacation, or other purpose. Tell readers what they should see. Tell what should be avoided and why. Tell your readers about the major parks and other public facilities. List historic sites. Give details of hours of service, costs, and other necessary information. Where do readers write for additional information? You should know this and should tell the readers.

Destination articles should be rich in detail and offer direct quotations from *local* authorities to back up generalizations about places you have written about. Quote residents and experts. Talk to historians and visit historic sites.

Talk to food critics about the best restaurants. Ask other travelers to comment about the same things you experience. Then summarize the most important facts in a special abstracted form known as the *facts box*. This will help your readers by providing a fast reference list when they are is in the car or plane.

DESTINATION ARTICLE FACT BOXES

A popular approach to writing destination features is to include a *facts* or *if you go* typographic box with the story. This information goes beyond what is contained in the main article but also supplements the article with an abstract of key information for readers who skim the section or who are interested in clipping only the most basic information about this destination.

What do you include? Here is a list of the 10 most common categories of information for the box:

1. *Directions.* How do you get there? What is the address? How do local visitors get there by car, train, boat, bus, or air?
2. *Parking.* Where do you park? What is the cost? When does the lot open and close?
3. *Days and hours of operation.* When are the attraction and accompanying facilities open?
4. *General information.* Whom does a visitor contact for general information, such as advance tickets or brochures?
5. *Contact.* What is the contact telephone number and address?
6. *Lodging.* Where can readers stay? What are the price ranges?
7. *Food and other facilities.* Can you buy food? Are there restaurants? What are the price ranges? What other facilities (or the unusual lack of them) are worth mentioning to your reader?
8. *Souvenirs.* Can you buy anything? Is taking anything (e.g., at a national or state park) illegal?
9. *Tours.* Are there organized, regular tours? How do you sign up or reserve space?
10. *Special upcoming events.* What's in store for the current or next season?

WRITING SERVICE FEATURE ARTICLES

One of the most practical types of travel features is the service article. These pieces provide useful and important information to help readers make decisions about an upcoming trip or what to do with their time while on the trip. Service stories also provide another important function because these stories, short or long, offer tips and ideas for simplifying the trip and the means for making the trip.

276 11. TRAVEL WRITING

For example, a travel service story will help your readers negotiate a major international airport—such as Atlanta's Hartsfield, Chicago's O'Hare, or New York's Kennedy—by offering descriptions of the terminal, concourses, parking, fees, luggage storage, and security policies. These are stories that will tell your readers when and how to book reservations on cruises or at a popular area resort by providing information such as names and addresses, deposit amounts, and deadlines. Service stories also give tips on getting good camera angles when photographing sites such as national parks or historic neighborhoods or buildings.

Every traveler seems to have an opinion about airline food. It is a natural service article topic, especially when major changes are occurring in the industry. *Newsday's* Tom Incantalupo (1993) wrote a Sunday travel section feature, distributed throughout the United States, that focused on redesigned menus and other modifications of in-flight food service offered by airlines. He used information from industry authorities and the airlines to tell travel section readers what to expect the next time they took a flight. This is his article:

One of the top 10 ways to annoy an airline flight attendant, David Letterman once claimed, is to ask whether the Salisbury steak can be used as a flotation device.

Airline meals get dumped on almost as much as New Jersey, by comedians and passengers—sometimes unfairly and sometimes for good reason. But the airlines are trying to change that.

One by one over the past two years, most airlines have redesigned their menus, trying to improve what they serve aloft and also, not incidentally, to reduce the cost of it, which totals about $1 billion a year industrywide.

In some cases, that means no meal when you expected one or a cold one instead of a hot one, which costs more to prepare and store. To save money, some carriers are eliminating meals on shorter flights, usually those under two hours that are airborne between normal meal times.

Some are reducing the variety of entrees available and making seemingly inconsequential labor-saving changes that can add up to big money—like serving melon in crescent-shaped slices rather than in cubes or curls.

On some routes, eliminating meals not only saves the cost of raw food and its preparation, but also might allow the airline to reduce the number of attendants on a flight, says Andrew Nocella of Avmark Inc., an aviation consulting firm in Virginia. "If you're going to serve food to 150 passengers," he says, "you need more flight attendants than are required (by the Federal Aviation Administration) for safety."

To make their food more appealing to an increasingly health-conscious public, the airlines are making meals lighter and more nutritious, eliminating things like breaded meats and sauces and other cholesterol-laden fare.

The latest effort, by American Airlines, took to the skies earlier this month, when the nation's largest carrier introduced an all-new menu—representing, it says, the most complete overhaul in its history. It was done, American says, under the guidance of a panel of chefs from top-drawer restaurants.

No. 2 United overhauled its domestic program last June and its international menu last November. The new overseas menu, says United, features more grains, vegetables, legumes and pastas. "Lighter sauces and glazes that enhance flavors instead of masking them will also be emphasized," its announcement said.

Not all of the menu changes are aimed at promoting healthier eating, but they are all designed to win friends.

American's new menu substitutes chateaubriand for filet mignon on first-class dinner flights. Passengers on some flights will be offered deep-dish pizza made at a well-known pizzeria in Chicago. And United offers a boxed McDonald's cheeseburger on certain flights if passengers reserve them in advance.

American, which says it serves 180,000 meals and snacks and 156,000 soft drinks in the air each day, says it is not removing food from any flights. But United says

---

PUBLIC AND PRIVATE TRAVEL INFORMATION SOURCES

Public Sources	*Private Sources*
Neighborhood tourism offices	Specific attractions
City and county tourism offices	Hotel, motel offices
Multiple area tourism boards	Development boards
State tourism departments	Airline travel desks
Parks and recreation offices	Airline public relations offices
Public relations firms under con- tract to local governments	Tourism boards
National tourism offices	Chambers of commerce
	Hotel, motel associations
	Business associations
	Restaurant associations
	Local corporations

LEADING TRAVEL INDUSTRY SOURCES

Human Sources	*Written Sources*
Local editors, reporters	Tour books (annuals)
Tourism directors, staffs	Local authors' books
Hotel staff where you stay	Local newspaper files
Public information officers	National and regional travel maga- zines
Managers of attractions	
Residents of area you visit	Auto association guide books
Tour guides	Attraction press kits
Shop merchants	Telephone directories (usually a local information section)
Local authors	
Local historians	World atlas
Local museum directors	History section at a local bookstore
Cab, bus drivers	U.S. atlas
	Hotel, motel room guest books
	Airline in-flight magazines

it has eliminated meals from some flights of under 800 miles that don't coincide with normal meal times. TWA announced last June that it would eliminate meals on flights of less than 549 miles.

Behind the effort to cut costs are staggering losses at most major carriers—the result of the recession and of fare wars. The industry lost an estimated $7.5 billion in the past three years.

Like leg room and the interior decor of planes and airport waiting lounges, food has been a marketing tool for the airlines for decades. Lee Howard, an expert with the consulting firm Airline Economics Inc., in Washington, D.C., says the culinary wars began in earnest during the 1960s as airlines scrambled to fill an increased number of seats that came with the introduction of jet aircraft.

"We're constantly looking for some differentiation because, essentially, we're all flying the same planes and leaving at the same times," says TWA spokesman Jerry Cosley.

For all the talk—and jokes—about it, experts say food ranks quite low in importance among passengers. Stan Plog, whose Reseda, Calif., company, Plog Research, does customer survey work for airlines, says business travelers rank seating comfort as most important, followed by a convenient schedule, on-time performance, the existence of a frequent-flier program and, finally, amenities like food.

For leisure travelers, Plog says, ticket price is most important and food is hardly a factor at all in the choice of an airline. "Almost never does the question of food come up," he says. Most people, he thinks, have low expectations about airline food.

But, Plog says, the media, especially travel writers, pay a lot of attention to an airline's food and bad publicity about it can hurt.

A prime example: the saga of United Airlines and the macadamia nuts served to first-class passengers. Whether fliers cared is questionable, says Plog, but the decision by United's bean counters (no pun intended) in the 1970s to substitute less-expensive peanuts triggered wide and, for everyone but United, funny news media attention. (p. 11F) Reprinted with permission of *New York Newsday* and *The Los Angeles Times Syndicate.*

To tell someone about changes in airline food service, for example, you have to know the in-flight food service standards and you have to talk to the experts. For an article explaining how to negotiate a foreign city's complicated public transportation system, you have to know that destination and its underground rail system inside and out. These stories are strongest when they draw on the experience of the travel writer who has been there. This means you must get out on the road as often as possible to write these types of articles.

It is not impossible, however, for you to write good service articles from where you work. Many times a story, such as the example about reservations for a busy vacation spot, can be done by telephoning to the right source. Or, if you are writing for a market outside of the region where you live, a local

POPULAR TRAVEL BOOKS AND PERIODICALS

Books	Consumer and Industry Periodicals
Hotel & Travel Index	*National Geographic*
Official Hotel and Travel Guide	*Signature*
AAA tour books	*Frequent Flyer*
Arthur Frommer's guides	*National Geographic Traveler*
Fodor's guides	*Condé Nast Traveler*
Travel Research Bibliography	*Official Airline Guide*
Steve Birnbaum's guides	*Travel & Leisure*
Air Traveler's Handbook	*Endless Vacation*
Goode's World Atlas	*New Departures*
The Travel Writer's Handbook	*Family Motor Coaching*
Curtis Casewit's *How to Make*	*Travel-Holiday*
Money from Travel Writing	*World Traveling*
	Travel Smart
	Odyssey Hotel & Travel Index
	ASTA Agency Management
	The Travel Agent
	Travel Smart for Business
	Southern Living
	Sunset
	AAA magazines, such as *Home & Away*

story might be appropriate for that market and the story would not necessarily require you to leave the office to do it well.

The service article requires good timing to be valuable to your reader. If you want to write the type of story readers will clip and save—sometimes these are called "refrigerator stories" because people clip them to their refrigerators or put them on office bulletin boards—you have to produce the story with sufficient advance timing to get it to the reader when it is needed. Usually this requires months for magazines and weeks for newspapers.

Service articles do not always follow this more conventional approach. A successful service article in a newspaper or magazine does not even have to be in traditional story form. The mid-1990s travel sections and departments will continue to provide important travel information in tables, charts, and boxes that stand alone (without a story). These are called *informational graphics* and they are a specialization in the news media. However, it is still the responsibility of the travel writer to gather the information for the graphic artists who compile it with their mastery of art and the computer.

For an effective service article, you must know your traveling readers' information needs. This takes research and a thorough knowledge of the traveler and the reader of your particular market. Writers who do not know the market won't have their stories read if they are published, and a free-lance travel writer won't get the stories published very often.

Service articles most frequently take the form of one-shot feature articles. These stories are designed to stand alone. But there are other forms. Some travel editors and writers produce columns that are functional with service-type information to help consumers make those big decisions about vacations and business trips. And there is the opportunity on certain service subjects to develop a series. Ideas? How about highway safety and auto maintenance in preparing the family car before a long trip?

SPECIAL NEEDS OF MAGAZINES

In the past decade, there has been a surge in the number of travel magazines in the United States. There has been a boom in the national and regional travel magazine market. *Traveler* was founded by Condé Nast Publications, its first such publication, in 1987. Other existing travel magazines retooled. Take a look at any free-lance writing market book (such as *Writer's Digest*'s annual volume entitled *Writer's Market* or *The Writer*'s annual *The Writer's Handbook*) and you will get a good idea of what magazines want from free-lance travel writers. Most magazines maintain very small in-house staffs of full-time writers. These publications require the services of free-lance writers to fill their space.

What do they want from free-lance writers? New Jersey's *Vista/USA* magazine is published for the Exxon Motor Club. The magazine has a circulation of about 800,000 copies four times a year and approximately 90% of the articles it publishes are from free-lance writers. Because it is a quarterly, the editors want material well in advance, as outlined in a recent edition of *Writer's Market* (Kissling, 1992). This is the sort of material *Vista/USA* editors seek:

> We are looking for readable pieces with good writing that will interest armchair travelers as much as readers who may want to visit the areas you write about. Queries about well-known destinations should have something new or different to say about them, a specific focus or angle. Articles should have definite themes and should give our readers an insight into the character and flavor of an area or topic. Stories about personal experiences must impart a sense of drama and excitement or have a strong human-interest angle. Stories about areas should communicate a strong sense of what it feels like to be there. Good use of anecdotes and quotes should be included. Study the articles in the magazine . . . .(p. 689)

Travel & Leisure, one of the leading travel magazines produced by American Express Company, depends on regular free-lancers for material on travel and vacation places, food, wine, shopping, and recreational sports. Nearly all of the articles for this magazine, however, are assigned to experienced and proven writers.

Travel-oriented newsletters, because they are so specialized, are perhaps more demanding on writers than magazines. *Travel Smart*, a monthly travel newsletter published in Dobbs Ferry, New York, seeks articles about "good-value" traveling. In *Writer's Market* (Kissling, 1992), the newsletter's editors say they are:

> [i]nterested primarily in bargains or little-known deals on transportation, lodging, food, unusual destinations that won't break the bank. Also information on trends in [the] industry. No destination stories on major Caribbean islands, London, New York, no travelogs, "my vacation," poetry, fillers. No photos or illustrations. Just hard facts . . . . When you travel, check out small hotels offering good prices, little known restaurants, and send us [a] brief rundown (with prices, phone numbers, addresses). Information must be current . . . .(p. 688)

With the additional space often afforded major features by consumer travel magazines, writers can be more eloquent in their writing about the destinations or services that their articles focus on. These articles often have a storytelling quality to them or are much more descriptive and detailed. Writer David Michaelis wrote enthralling words when he described the Great Lakes region of the Midwest, America's Mediterranean, for a recent issue of *Condé Nast Traveler*. Michaelis sought to focus specifically on the Great Lakes region around northern Michigan for readers, zeroing in on Mackinac Island and the Upper Peninsula lakes region. This is how Michaelis (1993) descriptively began his first-person lead article for the magazine, trying to establish the feel as well as the scope of America's Great Lakes region:

> The sound went right through me, like a gunshot. Even up here, 440 feet above the shoreline, at the edge of the highest sand dune outside of the Sahara, I could hear the waves—the crack of the breakers down on the beach. I felt it in my ribs. It was my second day on the Lake, high up in Michigan, and I was still absorbing the fact that this was not the sea.
>
> In the far distance, more than halfway up the sky, the visible horizon edged across to nowhere. A gull, swooping down nearby, slapped the water. Farther offshore lay shipwrecks, powerful currents, turtlebacked islands. Swells, rolling through hundreds of miles, brought ashore the cadences of vast watery plains, tidal restlessness, seething turf, foaming water.
>
> This wasn't lakeshore. Lakes are places where water stays put, idling under the dock. This was coastline, a ten-thousand-mile coastline passing through eight degrees of latitude, seventeen degrees of longitude, and spreading through eight soft-shored states and one rocky Canadian province. The water on this coast spills eastward across seventeen hundred miles, from the head of Lake Superior . . . . (p. 86)

Another example of a specific travel market to target is airline in-flight consumer magazines. Instead of being subscriber-based, these periodicals are provided to passengers on the airplanes and in waiting areas free of charge. Most are produced for an airline by a contracting publishing company and these companies often need free-lance contributions from serious writers.

Airline in-flight magazines are a solid market for travel writers. Often over-looked, especially at the international level, these publications need destination and service articles for their readers. Most airline magazines are monthlies, but some of the smaller airlines have bimonthly or quarterly editions. These publications usually run major features in front, regular departments in the back, perhaps some columns mixed in, and some listings of events, in-flight programming, safety matters, or other useful en route information.

For travel writers, airline magazines are an opportunity to present major features and shorter pieces for the regular departments. *Major feature articles* need to be tuned to cities and people served by the airlines, of course, and the major activities within those areas. Articles typically highlight upcoming events in destination cities, the best restaurants, sight-seeing, recreation and entertainment of other forms, profiles, lifestyle concerns of travelers such as business executives, new technology, and vacation ideas. *Specialized columns* can cover a wide range of topics but are often written by regularly contributing experts on such subjects as finance and money, business and management, personal health and fitness, and living or lifestyles. *Regular departments* focus on information about the airline itself, safety features onboard the airplanes, movies and music available on the flight, games or quizzes and puzzles, and other diversions.

To write for travel magazines and newsletters, you must know the market. Study these travel magazines before you begin to write for them. Each one is a little different in what it likes to publish. Know the particular style of writing and presentation. Know the approaches. Magazines and newsletters are tough markets, but if you can meet the orders of your editors, you will have a widely read article.

TRAVEL COLUMNS AS FEATURES

Travel columns are permanent fixtures in most newspapers and many travel-oriented magazines. These columns are given a wide variety of titles, such as Jane Lasky's "Business Travel Report" (distributed by the San Francisco Chronicle Features Syndicate), *Los Angeles Times* travel editor Jerry Hulse's "Travel Tips" (Los Angeles Times–Washington Post Syndicate, Peter Greenberg's "The Savvy Traveler" (Los Angeles Times Syndicate), and Laura Bergheim's "Weird, Wonderful America" (King Features Syndicate). The question-and-answer format is also popular in newspaper travel sections and magazine travel departments. These columns typically answer questions posed by readers and are either answered by experts or by staff writers. One example is *The New York Times'* Sunday "Q and A" column. This column is compiled and written by members of the travel section staff. Columns and features such as these come in wide varieties of presentation formats, such as single-author, multiple-author, or just staff credit. Some publications run edited travel columns that list no credited author. Some are weekly and some are monthly. Most run from 600 to 800 words, but some are longer, 1,000 to 1,500 words per article.

Smaller publications often depend on syndicated material and wire services for their travel columns or material that makes up an edited travel column. Magazines usually will depend on free-lance writers to provide material on a regular basis and editors pay by the item. Syndicated travel columnists cover a variety of subjects. Popular 1990s topics for specialized travel columns include camping and other outdoor recreation, cruising, international travel, business travel, bargain and money-saving travel, and solo or senior citizen travel.

Travel columns can be used as a collecting point for shorter items that come to your attention but might not make a publishable story on their own merit. Calendar information, such as upcoming events, hours of operation, and free information by mail, fits neatly into a column. Put together, rewritten into tight form with minimal promotion to the source (such as a commercial enterprise), the information can be practical and go well with the longer features in the section or department.

The column is also a feature in its own right, with the author taking advantage of the regular space and appearance date (weekly or monthly, for example). In this format, writers such as editors of sections will present their personal perspectives on subjects. Travel editor Mike Shoup of the *Philadelphia Inquirer* handles his column this way.

Many columnists choose this personal approach because of their extensive backgrounds. Whereas this sort of commentary might be inappropriate in other sections or other articles in the travel section, you can express opinions, reactions, interpretations, and generally comment on current travel industry developments. Donald Pevsner (1993) writes occasional free-lance travel industry features that are presented as guest columns and his work demonstrates what a travel writer with expertise in another subject—law—can accomplish. A consumer advocate and former regular newspaper travel columnist, he writes about current issues and events in the travel industry. He is an attorney who often takes cases involving airlines and other parts of the travel industry. Pevsner, also an occasional world tour operator, will write about such topics as bargain fares, legal rulings affecting travelers, and how to take advantage of ticket pricing policies. One recent feature focused on involuntary "bumping" practices of airlines, in which some ticketed passengers are not permitted to board oversold full flights. In that column, he discussed what the current federal policies and court rulings stated about the rights of passengers and how those relate to the policies of many major airlines. He also writes about other travel law issues, such as the matter of automobile rental car insurance. However, the legal approach in his articles is sprinkled with his strong opinions to guide consumers through the maze of travel decisions that must be made in planning an out-of-town business trip or a vacation.

WRITING OTHER FEATURES WHILE TRAVELING

Not every article that you plan to write from a trip out of town has to be based on the trip itself. You must remember that you can generate other sorts of feature articles while traveling to unusual or faraway destinations. Mix the types of articles you plan to write if necessary to generate the maximum benefits from the trip. If you are a free-lance writer, this may be essential to paying your expenses and turning a profit from expensive travel.

Phil Philcox, a New York free-lance writer and author of numerous books and articles, recommends writing mini-profiles of businesses while traveling to foreign countries, for example. Philcox (1989) reminds free-lancers that there are several thousand trade and business periodicals in the United States that would consider queries or manuscripts about businesses and business practices in foreign nations. "What these [magazine] readers have in common is that they're in business, and all businesspeople want to know how other businesspeople operate," he says (p. 27). "Would a florist in Cleveland, for example, be interested in how a florist in Munich buys and maintains an inventory? . . . Almost certainly."

Similarly, other assignments can be generated about people, especially individuals from your region or community who have relocated elsewhere and become successful or otherwise done something newsworthy. For example, a former public schools superintendent in your community may have moved to another state to accept a bigger and better position. How is he or she doing? This story prospect is clearly not a travel feature but might be the ideal assignment to free-lance, along with other more travel-oriented plans you have.

Simply remember that you are not limited to writing for the travel section of the Sunday newspaper or the travel department of your favorite magazine. You can write about sports on a travel-oriented assignment. Or recreation. Or business. Or fashion. Or health and medicine. Remember these stories can be marketed as well, but just not as travel features. And it is likely that the fact that you went after the story, sometimes a long distance, can't hurt. This effort should make the story at least a little more appealing and, at the least, compel an editor to give it a closer look during the query process.

CONTEMPORARY TRAVEL WRITING ISSUES

Travel and recreation have emerged in recent years to become major subjects for coverage by magazines and newspapers. Sections and departments have enlarged beyond simple articles on destinations. There are numerous issues facing travel writers and editors in this decade, not the least being ethics and objectivity.

Ethics Involving Subsidized Travel

The primary travel writing ethics issue of the mid-1990s relates to what is called *subsidized* travel. This means finding sources other than the newspaper or writer to pay for the sometimes high expense of domestic and international travel. Often, travel writers accept free hotel space, complimentary airfare, and free meals while touring an area. But the expenses are paid by interests represented by those areas, such as the resorts, tourism commissions, Chambers of Commerce, national or regional airlines, restaurants, and other groups with a financial interest in the area that seek news and feature articles providing instant credibility and positive publicity in place of advertising.

Whereas larger newspapers and magazines can afford to pay for their staff writers to travel, many smaller publications and most free-lance writers cannot do this and also expect to earn a living. The travel writing field, both editors and their free-lancers and staff writers, is divided over the issue and no simple solution seems readily available, but an increasing number of publications seem to lean toward disclosure; that is, revealing to readers who paid for trips that are the focus of articles.

Use of Subjectivity

Although the issue of subsidies is a major topic, so is whether travel writers should take an objective or more subjective approach to their work. Both schools of thought have their supporters. Some editors feel travel writing should be as objectively presented as any other news or features in the newspaper or magazine. Others, however, prefer a more personalized and subjective approach to the presentation with the hope that it will be more appealing to readers.

Public Policy Issues in Travel and Recreation

There are other concerns based on public issues related to travel and recreation. Serious news and feature articles discussing public and private travel and recreation issues and controversies, many focusing on public spending, the environment, development matters, and quality of life concerns, are found in addition to the more traditional destination or service piece in the travel section of the Sunday newspaper or the travel department of your favorite magazine.

American society seems to be moving in two distinct directions. First, there are individuals who are working more and more hours per week. The percentage of persons working long hours has risen. But secondly, and even more important, the percentage of unemployed and underemployed has also increased. Researcher Thomas Kando (1980) has written: "The point is that those persons who have increasing free time on their hands are involuntarily retired, poor, unskilled, chronically unemployed. Thus, there is a growing category of people condemned to leisure, as well as a growing minority of persons who, of their own volition, work increasingly hard" (p. 13).

Other research tells us people do certain things with their leisure time, including travel, and these studies raise certain issues travel writers might investigate for their readers. Here are six general trends relating to travel and leisure time issues that you should consider in your writing:

1. *The idea*. What is the general idea of leisure? What constitute travel and vacationing patterns in your region?

2. *Types of leisure*. What are the prevailing community types of leisure activities? Vacations? What seem to be the different philosophies about leisure time usage in your area?

3. *Priorities*. How do your readers spend their personal funds on travel and leisure? How do they spend their time? Is it local? On the road? Simply, what do people think, feel, and do about their nonwork time?

4. *Development of attitudes*. You will not only want to know the characteristics of leisure, but you might benefit from understanding how these priorities have developed. What are the conditions leading to decisions? What does government policy toward travel and recreation/leisure have to do with it? What are the influences of the private sector?

5. *Social problems*. A reporter using this approach can ask: "What are the leisure/travel needs of different sectors of the community/market I serve?"

6. *Promotion*. What are the best ways a community can promote its travel and tourism? What are the roles of government and the private sector?

Economics alone cannot explain leisure and travel activities. It is difficult, if not impossible, to split the economic from the social, political, and technical factors, according to sociologist Max Kaplan (1975).

PROFESSIONAL'S POINT OF VIEW

Mike Shoup
Philadelphia Inquirer

Travel writing by its very nature tends to be positive, but that doesn't mean it has to be puffery, and it certainly doesn't mean that normal standards of fairness and accuracy can be ignored or compromised. There is simply no substitute for good, old-fashioned reporting with pen and notebook. If the facts aren't there, or they are wrong (and my finding is that this is often the case), the story will simply never get off the ground.

My wall is practically papered with the humorous errors of would-be-writers, including no less than 37 wrong spellings of my last name—Shupe, Shamp, Shout, Sharp, Shroup, Short, Schub, Shoop, and Soup, to mention but a few. And my reasoning is this: If the writer can't get the editor's name right, what guarantee is there that any place or name spellings in a story are correct?

Travel writing is not simple. I receive from 50 to 100 manuscripts a week in my job and reject 99% of them. Some are inaccurate, some are sophomoric, but most are just plain boring, dull, and lifeless. It doesn't have to be that way.

Those who are not brilliant writers (and most of us aren't) should look for the details and nuances that make one part of the globe different from another. It is these same details that breathe life into a narrative and make each story different from the next. Writers should employ concrete examples rather than hyperbole, and be sparing with the use of adjectives.

Most travel stories written for newspapers seem to occur in a vacuum that excludes humanity—there are no people in them. It doesn't hurt any to inject characters into a story, when and if they fit.

The best stories, in my opinion, accurately reflect the whole travel experience, whether good or bad. They also reflect preparation and research, and often have a historical or societal perspective. It is difficult, for example, to write a travel story about Mexico City without at least mentioning the air pollution, or the street beggars. This does not mean it is necessary to dwell on such subjects, but mentioning them in passing gives the reader the idea that he is, after all, in the real world and not in some make-believe La-La Land invented by a travel writer whose trip is paid for by the Mexican government.

My final word would be my first: There is no substitute for basic reporting and writing skills. Those intent on travel writing—or any form of writing— will find a year or two of newspaper reporting invaluable.

Meanwhile, yes, it is Soup. But with an "H," please. (Shoup, personal communication, 1988)

Mike Shoup is travel editor of the *Philadelphia Inquirer*, a position he has held for 14 years. He has also served as managing editor of *Inquirer Magazine* during his 23 years at the newspaper. He enjoys biking, hiking, running, gardening, and, yes, traveling.

12

Service Articles

Service publications are catching on with readers. More and more readers are discovering publications that serve them by providing practical information. Yes, entire publications are devoted to *service journalism*. Many of them are aimed at women, but some recent efforts have been aimed at men as well. And some women's magazines are going through major changes. Readers like the practical value of service articles. You know the titles of many national magazines that have strong service components: *Family Circle, Woman's Day, Ladies' Home Journal, Good Housekeeping,* and *Better Homes and Gardens* to name a few. Although those are geared to women, some men's publications are service oriented also: *Popular Mechanics* and *Popular Science* are sound examples. And many city and regional magazines have strong service content each month.

Service features should help people live their lives better. "Any subject can become service journalism," writes University of Missouri magazine writing professor Don Ranly (1992). "It's simply a different approach to writing. The one word that best characterizes a service article is the word 'useful'" (p. 18). The articles and other content help readers to make better decisions as consumers, to take better care of themselves, to improve relationships, to make things, and cope with "realities of everyday life, and not matters of cataclysmic importance," says Pamela Fiori (1992, p. 78), executive vice president and editorial director for American Express Publishing Corp., which produces *Travel & Leisure* among other products. "Service magazines . . . are more apt to be micro than macro; local as opposed to global; practical and directional, a bit flat-footed at the minimum and bordering on gimmicky when they try too hard. But at their best, they can have tremendous impact: They can change the way readers think or act, alter the way they spend time or money, influence style, eating habits, and travel plans, improve relationships, diminish biases" (p. 78).

Many feature articles are written to provide this type of service to readers. Fred Tasker, feature writer and columnist for *The Miami Herald,* combined two of the major forms of service journalism when he wrote his award-winning consumer package entitled "The Cost of College" (Tasker, 1992). Published in the Living Today section, the articles provided an overview of the high costs of college for parents who were just beginning families at the time his article was published. Eighteen years later, Tasker told readers, a baby born in 1992 might cost $260,000 for 4 years at Yale or $121,000 at a state university in Florida. After shocking readers with that revelation, Tasker proceeded to discuss the many creative ways of financing a college education. He suggested in the *how-to* portion of his package what could be done to begin saving now. He *listed* long-term investment options for parents, summarizing the pros and cons of each option. He offered strategy tips, also, presenting lists of ways readers could time their investments to maximize them. Using experts on taxation, he listed suggestions to save money through various tax strategies. Tasker reviewed college loan programs, scholarships, prepaid tuition programs, such as those offered in Florida for state universities and colleges, military tuition aid, and where to find information. A well-designed chart took readers through, in step-by-step form, computing how much a person would have to pay to put a student through college in the years ahead, depending on the age of the child. A sidebar gave readers explanations of financial aid procedures and packages and where to find information.

Perhaps what made Tasker's effort particularly effective was the consistent use of examples throughout his articles and listings. Using two typical families, which he named the "Bluecollars" and "Whitecollars," Tasker was able to show various scenarios in real-world conditions. The Bluecollars were an average middle-income ($30,000) family. The Whitecollars earned more ($80,000). All examples of funding and financial aid computations were based on these families and their financial status, which Tasker outlined in detail.

In addition to the articles, charts coached readers through computations of tuition costs and investment needs. One chart required only five easy steps of computations to determine how much the reader's family would pay for their son or daughter to attend college in any given year. Another one created an investment worksheet in nine steps, using certain information provided in companion tables. This is how Tasker's (1992) lead article laid out the presentation package, which won the best consumer article category in the 1993 JCPenney-University of Missouri newspaper feature writing awards:

So you went to Yale, and you want your bouncing, red-faced little Gladys—just born today, bless her—to follow in your footsteps when she's 18, in the year 2010.

Well, boola boola for you.

But four years at Yale, by then, will cost $261,605. If you start saving today, in an investment that earns a generous 10 percent per year before taxes, you'll have to put away $384 a month.

What? You say you'll compromise on the University of Florida? Even better. By 2010 it will cost only $121,178. You have to save only $178 per month.

Scary, huh?

Inflation's beast has sunk its teeth into college even deeper than into other aspects of our lives. Costs rise by 7 to 9 percent every year. Tuition at Florida's nine state universities leapt 15 percent just last year.

It's the old double-whammy: Booming college enrollments require costly new building programs just as Reagan-era federal budgets and tax-starved state governments reduced college funding. And the academic programs growing fastest—business and engineering—employ professors who demand the highest salaries to resist the siren call of private firms.

It doesn't mean your kid can't go to college. There's an astonishingly generous array of financial resources out there: Pell Grants and ROTC scholarships, subsidized loans to Buddhists, work-study programs and outright gifts to descendants of Confederate soldiers. Some are based on need, some on grades, some on the fact that your daddy was in the Brotherly and Protective Order of Elks.

There are also dozens of ways to start your own fund for Junior or Sissy's education, letting the white knight of compound interest cross lances with the dragon of college inflation.

Problem is, it almost takes a college education to understand all the resources.

But despair not. On Pages 4E and 5E is a compendium of tips on both college aid and college savings.

Don't just file it away for future reading. Act today. Saving works best if you start with the first inkling that you someday might have to finance a college education for your progeny.

As Rita Wax, college-finance expert for Dade schools, puts it:

"Don't wait until they're born. Start the morning after they're conceived."

A guide to ways to raise money for your child's education, Page 4E.

How to figure out how much college aid you can get, Page 5E. (p. 1E) Reprinted with permission of *The Miami Herald.*

Newspaper, magazine, and newsletter service journalism, such as this consumer-oriented package by Tasker, has been around for a long time. The earliest efforts were published in the traditional women's publications such as *Ladies' Home Journal* and *Good Housekeeping*, first developed over a century ago. Much of their content was service-oriented information about the home. These articles are not necessarily "spot news" in the sense that we usually talk about news. Service feature articles are an important part of any newspaper, magazine, and newsletter, and readers depend on these articles as part of their total newspaper or magazine package. These articles help readers do something better; they help make life easier. These articles are usually found in four forms: *how-to-do-it, listings, art of living articles,* and *chronological case histories.*

1. The *how-to article* explains how something is made, built, cooked, protected, purchased, or otherwise accomplished by an expert on the subject. These articles are often found in home and garden sections, food/cooking sections, and increasingly so in consumer-based sections of newspapers and in the similarly named departments of magazines or newsletters. How-to articles are the most frequently published form of service article. It is certainly a popular story form with editors, says Professor Louis Alexander (1975). "[I]n a pragmatic nation, Americans look more and more to magazines to advise them and show them how to do the things that are important in their lives," he writes (p. 213).

2. *Listings* have become more interesting in recent years in newspapers, magazines, and newsletters. Sports sections of newspapers and sports-oriented magazines offer lists of records and interesting trivia as regular features for readers. Business and finance-oriented publications frequently run lists of top businesses, top salaries of executives, real estate transactions, and so on. Feature sections of newspapers and city and regional magazines have, for many years, listed in calendar form the major events of an upcoming weekend or month and have listed top restaurants and theaters in their circulation areas.

3. *Art-of-living articles* teach us how to get more out of life. These often are inspirational articles, with readers feeling uplifted after reading about someone else's skill at making their life better. Sometimes these articles (and books) are called self-help articles and are simply narratives or essays that affect readers in one way or another and give them ideas about how to improve their own lives or the lives of family members or friends. These articles include subjects such as retirement, love and family relationships, and making tough decisions.

4. *Chronological case histories* teach us about something by looking at a particular example in depth. Readers are served by the lesson learned from the case history. These can include descriptions of purchasing a house, curing a medical problem, or resolving a conflict between neighbors.

The four approaches to these articles are not limited to single articles. There are entire magazines that specialize in how-to journalism, for example. Books, too, have been written on hundreds of subjects to help readers in the same way—everything from career choices, resume writing, and job hunting, to personal finance, automobile repair, and relationships with the opposite sex.

BASIC APPROACHES TO WRITING SERVICE ARTICLES

American Express' Fiori says service magazines and articles "help the reader to cope—with aging parents or one's aging self, an alcoholic co-worker, a serious illness, unemployment, change of address or change of life. They might even inspire the reader to contribute to society—by volunteering his or her services, by writing to Congress, by joining a local environmental group. Or, closer to home, by spending more time with the kids" (1992, p. 79).

How do these articles achieve these seemingly lofty goals? Although the service article seems self-explanatory, there is more to it than the topic description indicates. The best service articles provide information that results in action or behavior change on the part of readers. Often the information gleaned from the article is the sole reason for a reader's use of the article. By providing information, you are offering readers the best advice you can find on the subject. This is done in a readable fashion, but at the same time in the clearest way possible because you are explaining how something works or how something is done. Service feature articles take one or more of these three fundamental reporting and writing approaches:

1. *Writer-as-expert perspective.* Many how-to articles are written by individuals who are experts on the subject. As writers, they are able to communicate their expertise to persons who want to know about the subject. Merrill Lynch, the financial services firm, has published numerous editions of its 30-page booklet, *How to Read a Financial Report*, since it was first published in 1973. The firm's expertise adds credibility and authority to the effort.

You can often write as an expert from your own personal experiences, thus combining the best elements of a personal experience feature with a service how-to feature. Eugenie McGuire, a free-lance writer specializing in horses and other agricultural animals, produces a large amount of how-to feature material based on her own expertise and experience. "I personally find that if I haven't done it, I cannot write effectively about it," McGuire (personal communication, 1993) explains. "For me the practice of actions is a requirement to get the words on paper correctly. My articles start out as blow-by-blow descriptions of the action, almost as if I was looking at a movie of the thing and describing it to someone who was blind. The articles get refined from that point but still retain the first-person feel." For the publications that she has written for, such as *Southern California Riding Magazine* and *The Hoofprint*, she believes this works well. But she cautions, "I'm not sure this would be suitable for more mainstream features."

2. *Someone-else-as-expert perspective.* This is the more common approach to how-to service articles. This approach requires you as the writer to find one or more experts on a topic and relate in detail to readers how they do the activity. Finding these experts is relatively easy—there are hundreds of them in your own community at colleges and universities, government offices, and in private business. In this story, your task is equal to that of the reporter-as-expert approach by which you must take the approach of the expert and tell readers how the expert does it. Many times, these articles are primarily for enjoyment and not necessarily to be used by readers to improve their lifestyle.

3. *Writer as source or generator of informational graphics devices*: As the primary organizer for a service article, the writer has the responsibility to gather information for creation of lists, boxes, short sidebars, informational graphics

such as "exploded diagrams," calendars, recipes, step-by-step instructions, and so forth. Writers rarely put these in final form for publication, but editors depend on them to produce the raw information for these elements either on the writer's authority or on the authority of expert sources found by the writer.

CHOOSING THE BEST SERVICE ARTICLE SUBJECTS

Possibly because there are so many subjects and sources available for how-to, lists, and other service articles, some experts feel how-to articles are one of the easiest ways to break into print. Feature writers Clay Schoenfeld and Karen Diegmueller (1982) make that point in discussing service features. Subjects that readers want to learn about tend to make the best service articles. These are day-to-day "how-to-live better" subjects of a rather routine and practical nature. These include subjects on personal health care, fashion, car and home repair/care, home and office decoration, gardening, food preparation, money and finance, shopping, and a variety of arts and crafts subjects. Readers often depend on their hometown newspapers and regularly read magazines and newsletters for advice on living better. American Express magazine executive Pamela Fiori (1992) says "readers want intelligent choices and solid judgments delivered in a compelling way" (p. 80).

Minneapolis feature writer Steve Perlstein (personal communication, 1993) believes how-to articles are important forms of service features that should be mastered by all feature writers:

> There are few better ways to sell a piece to a magazine than to offer a title and topic like "10 Ways to Get Your Kids to Eat Their Veggies" or "How to Make a Killing on Health Care Stocks." Editors love this stuff. These ideas can come from virtually any slice of life you run across. The ideas I get for *Parenting*—things like microwaving baby food and how to know what to believe in newspaper nutrition stories—come from real questions my wife and I have asked ourselves. This way, I can find out the answer and make a lot of money at the same time. I'm writing a how-to book that guides parents through work-family options like family leave, job sharing, telecommuting, compressed workweeks, and part-time scheduling. The project stemmed from when I took family leave when our son was born. We wanted to learn more about how to go about taking such a leave, but nobody had written anything; that's where I came in. The old adage goes, "write what you know." With how-to stories that can be adapted to go, "write what you want to know," because somebody else is probably wondering the same thing.

Service article writers should also be concerned about their own attention span in dealing with a subject. For service articles, pick subjects you really care about and have interest in. This makes your effort much less difficult when you have to spend a large amount of time learning about the subject.

What are hot service topics? If you are a good researcher, use your skills to compile unusual idea lists. How-to articles can include a variety of topics beyond home and garden usuals such as how to hang wallpaper or how to grow a bonsai exhibit. Include timely and socially or financially important topics, such as how to survive sex in the era of the Acquired Immune Deficiency Syndrome (AIDS), how to survive the extreme ups and downs of the stock market, or finding full-time employment during the seemingly wild fluctuations of the job market.

If you are not an expert in such complex stories as AIDS and securities, then you must locate authorities on the subjects to help you do the story. A problem with these stories is simple enough: Some experts make a living from their expert advice and they might be reluctant to share it with a newspaper or magazine writer. A counterargument is publicity. Some reluctant sources may respond if you remind them that publicity can help them build their businesses. You may need to go to several local or national authorities on the same subject to put together your story.

Writer's Digest contributing editor Art Spikol (1984) says his best advice for how-to writers is to pick the right subject. "The secret of success is to identify a need that isn't being sufficiently filled, and to fill it. In other words, take on a job that nobody else wants" (p. 15). This is the case for service articles, he says. "If you weigh the time you must put into them against the money you earn from them, you have to strain to reach the poverty level. That's the bad news. It's also the good news, because that's one of the reasons that nobody else wants to do them" (p. 15).

Spikol says service articles should do legwork for readers. You become the reader's helper. If you can select subjects that do this, you will have a successful service article. He points out their importance today: "[T]hey sell magazines. They're staples, often staff-written, at many publications. Especially today, when special-interest publications abound" (p. 15). To get assignments from your ideas, Spikol recommends querying editors with a few ideas *before* investing time and money. This way, if an editor likes an idea but wants a slightly different focus or different sources, you can make the changes early into your work.

WRITING AUTHORITATIVELY AND SHARING EXPERTISE

Novelist and short story writer William Browning Spencer (1992) says that all writers, fiction and nonfiction, need to use the voice of *authority*. Using authority results in "the impression the author gives that he is in control of his material" (p. 28). This, Spencer says, can be achieved in several ways, but getting the facts right, of course, is most basic of all.

When you have firsthand expertise in a subject, it is easy to speak with authority. Because you experienced it, you know it. For example, a journalism graduate student at the University of Miami combined her interest in magazine writing with a specialty in South Florida wildlife (she had an undergraduate major in zoology). Some students double major in college and can use their second major with their journalism major to create a specialization. Regardless of how you obtain it, your expertise should dominate the service article. Without conscious effort, it might become difficult for you to write for readers who do not know the subject as well as you do.

When you know the ins and outs of a subject, you know the detail and precision needed for such service writing. But when you do not, and you are a feature writer with no particular specialty or if you are just starting out, then you must be able to give your articles the sense of authoritativeness when you go to other sources for your expert information.

Gary Stern (1993) and Leonard McGill (1984), both authors of how-to books, say you can accomplish the same type of firsthand authoritativeness in your writing even if you go to other sources for your how-to article. Stern argues that for free-lance writers, "the art of instant expertise is a must" (p. 35). McGill says, "Two traits are essential: Curiosity. A willingness to use your inquisitive pick and shovel to unearth information that makes you sound authoritative. I've recently sold articles on how to order clothing from Hong Kong, how to combine various sports in an exercise program, and how to cut the cost of shaving. Before researching these subjects, I knew about as much about them as I do about building submarines. Nothing" (p. 26). McGill also recommends that you seek four types of information when doing research: (a) specific descriptions, (b) "subject-bound" terminology, (c) concrete examples, and (d) expert facts.

As Stern and McGill say, experts talk shop by using specifics. They just do not generalize. If you are writing about bicycles, for example, you just do not talk bicycles. There are racing bicycles, sport/touring bicycles, all-terrain bicycles, women's bicycles, and children's bicycles. Then you can begin talking about frames, gearing, brake systems, rims, tires, and hubs. Take this specific type of description, combined with correct technical language used by the bicycle industry (terms such as freewheel, derailleur, crankset, or head tube angle), and you can write with the authority of a veteran. Current examples make these terms come to life—discussing whether or not to get a particular brand's front or rear derailleur on a sport/touring bicycle begins to make sense to readers when applications are made (e.g., a specific brand of bicycle). Facts, such as the number of new products on the market or prices, make the story practical and useful.

Stern's secret to instant authoritativeness is logical and simple: "There are always experts who can answer your questions, and lead you to new sources" (1993, p. 36). The trick is finding the experts, right? Stern recommends this list of one dozen ways to become an instant expert:

1. Brainstorm for sources.
2. Find an "angel" or mentor to help you find other sources.
3. One expert source will lead you to another.
4. Be wary of self-serving experts.
5. Use clip files.

6. Ask your editor for suggestions.
7. Use trade and professional publications.
8. Find a dissenting view.
9. Use think tanks and their experts who are paid to study subjects such as the one about which you are writing.
10. Use reference experts at the local library.
11. Consult public relations directors and public affairs coordinators of companies and organizations.
12. Keep a list of experts for future reference, but be wary of "rounding up the usual experts."

As Stern suggests in his list, multiple sources make a difference in service journalism. When you are writing authoritatively about something you actually know little about, you must consult as many different sources as possible. The wide variety and diversity will give you insurance against conflicting information and advice. McGill (1984) warns of two additional concerns:

1. Make certain you are not presenting opinion instead of facts. Multiple sources will help filter out opinion.
2. Present the facts and instruction as yours, not someone else's. A number of interviews with different sources will lead you to certain conclusions of your own and make this easier to do. You can become authoritative on your own in this way.

McGill (1984) advises against overuse of the pronoun *you* in how-to articles. Most editors complain about this, he says. Do not rely on it and use it in a limited fashion.

Dr. Carin Smith is a veterinarian who loves to write. Some observers may say she is a writer who loves veterinarian medicine. But she is an *expert* who uses her high levels of specialized knowledge as a basis for her award-winning book and feature writing. "I'm a veterinarian/writer who has been fairly successful selling my how-to articles on a free-lance basis," she says. "I write business articles for veterinarians and pet health articles for pet and horse owners." Smith, author of three books and numerous magazine articles about animal health care, and a contributing editor to *Horse Illustrated* and *Cat Lovers* magazine, explains her approach to how-to writing:

My best-selling articles are those that answer the questions that I hear everyday. These are the "average" questions, the ones that appear simple on the surface. For instance, an article on flea control will sell much better than one on fancy new methods of brain surgery in dogs. You don't have to pick an obscure or complicated or highly technical subject. To any potential writer, I'd say: Think of what you know the most about—whether it be plumbing or gardening or computing. Then consider the typical conversations you have with friends or co-workers. What questions are you asked most often? About what kinds of things do people ask you for your advice or turn to you for answers? Why are you the one they ask? If you aren't the one, then what do you need to do to increase your knowledge in that area so that you know more than just about anyone you talk to? Once you are in that position, you know enough to write an excellent how-to article.

Assume your readers are very intelligent, but that they know absolutely nothing about your field. That way you avoid talking down to the reader, but you still don't go over their heads with words they don't understand. Explain every technical word, but learn to do so without making a big deal out of it, so the reader isn't offended if he or she already happens to know what the word means. (Smith, personal communication, 1993)

WRITING HOW-TO ARTICLES

Perhaps the major type of service article focuses on how to do something: How to cook a particular dish, how to make a piece of furniture, how to repair a broken appliance, how to set up a computer, how to buy a car. These are the bread-and-butter articles of service feature writing and a form that all feature writers should master early in their careers. Some free-lance experts say the how-to article is free-lance writing's biggest single market.

How-to articles accommodate a lot of approaches and related forms of approaches. If you can write how-to articles, then you should also be able to write "what is," "where is," "when is," and "why is" features. They each have a common element of authority and expertise that makes the articles appealing to readers needing information about a subject.

These articles are not usually the exciting, award-winning forms of journalism you might have aspired to produce when you first became interested in writing nonfiction. However, these are the practical types of articles that help free-lancers to make a living and staff writers to keep their editors happy. "[F]ew literary reputations have been built upon, and no Pulitzer awarded for, how-to tomes," writes Colorado full-time free-lance writer David Petersen (1992, p. 38). "I write how-to because free-lancing helps pay my bills, and how-tos probably comprise the largest single slice of today's free-lance market. Instructional nonfiction is where the assignments are, and where the money is."

Petersen, who has written several hundred how-to features over nearly two decades, uses a basic formula. Like most articles any feature writer would outline, his how-to articles have three major parts: the beginning, middle, and end. Each has an important role, though, as he explains: "An old journalistic truism—you've no doubt heard it—holds that every article should have a beginning, a middle, and an end. Well, in how-to writing, it's more than a truism, it's a mandate. And none of those three distinct parts is more important than the opening hook" (p. 38).

1. *Lead.* The "hook" as Petersen labels it, is the first few paragraphs with which you get readers interested and entertain them at the same time. This is the portion of the article where the stage is set. The introduction tells what the story will accomplish. It contains a paragraph that is a statement of purpose. It helps the readers so they do not have to struggle with your article to figure out what will be gained from reading it. Writer Leonard McGill (1984) recommends "letting readers know you will teach them something valuable" (p. 28). State the benefits of your advice, he says. Tell readers you are going to help them solve a problem, if that is the point of your article. At the end of the beginning there should be a transition to the middle of the article.

2. *Middle.* Petersen recommends outlining the middle of how-to articles during the writing process to keep them highly organized. Start with decisions about the main points and purpose of the article. What are you trying to do? And how do you accomplish that? Generally, the step-by-step portion of your article follows. Take readers through the process to get to their goal. This is detailed and should leave no guessing. You must be careful to explain all steps with the assumption that your reader does not know certain basic points about the process. McGill says readers expect information in how-to articles in a "cadence" approach. This means writing the body of the article in a cookbook style in the instructional portions. For example, you might write in four quick and short sentences: Collect tools: drill, bits, ruler, pencil, dry wall mount. Measure location of picture. Drill hole. Screw mount into wall. "Readers expect to receive how-to information in such a cadence," he says (p. 28).

3. *Closing or ending.* This portion of the article "weaves it all together," Petersen explains (p. 40). You have previewed, explained, and now you are recapping. Some repetition is important here, especially on the most significant points. The conclusion can also offer a bit of final advice for your readers. These tips might hint at troubleshooting, set-up, or maintenance, for example.

TEN TIPS ON SERVICE FEATURE BOXES

Pamela Fiori (1992) is executive vice president and editorial director of American Express Publishing Corp., and she developed this checklist of 10 tips for preparing service items such as lists and boxes:

1. *Keep it simple.* Give great information, not great literature.
2. *Make it lively.* Material should be inviting.
3. *Be kind to the reader.* Graphics should be legible.
4. *Display the material prominently.* Don't diminish material by burying it.
5. *Be accurate.* Fact check because it is essential. You can't risk losing trust of readers.
6. *Avoid giving the reader too much.* Be selective. You can do too much.
7. *Stick to one style.* Develop and use a standard format for presentation.
8. *Coordinate with the art department.* They produce the artwork.
9. *Exercise restraint.* Too much irritates and confuses readers.
10. *Don't fake it.* There should be a legitimate reason for the box or list.

Writer Art Spikol (1984) urges that you also create a chart to help keep organized when producing service articles. "List everything you want to know about whatever it is you are investigating," he says (p. 16). "In constructing such a chart, you might begin by listing the names, addresses, and phone numbers" (p. 16) of your primary sources, along with other essential information about the sources. In short, a key to success is being organized when gathering facts. This should also benefit you when you begin to write the article itself. Your urge to keep the article brief might have to be quelled in the interest of clarity in service features. Additional words, used in the right places, might make the difference in a positive direction in this type of feature writing.

A good way to double-check your approach is to write a rough draft and then ask someone who knows absolutely nothing about the subject to read it to see if the article makes sense. This way you will likely spot unclear passages before it goes to your editor. You want to be certain to eliminate ambiguous or vague content that would lead to guessing on the part of readers. Because you are so familiar with the material, it is easy to lose sight of a detail that someone else unfamiliar with the process will easily spot. On the other hand, if you are unfamiliar with the material, you might have the same problem spotting problems with details. Even after you have checked your article, your newspaper or magazine will also give it a thorough once-over. For example, many major newspapers, magazines, and newsletters test new food recipes and review other how-to food articles in their own kitchens or in the kitchens of experts before publication. Editors of how-to publications such as *Popular Mechanics* check potential how-to articles by building the furniture or equipment or by testing repair hints in labs or workshops before an article is published.

There are thousands of how-to articles published each year. Some publications exist for the sole purpose of publishing how-to service articles. Students can write them for other students. These are good "training ground" features, in fact. Some examples:

- A major university's student employment office newsletter recently published a helpful article that focused on controlling stress. Written and edited by undergraduates, the newsletter often uses articles of this type to help student employees cope with life on campus a little more easily. A recent article discussed stress caused by exams, term papers, campus jobs, and other conflicts. The article gave "helpful hints" from experts about coping at the end of a semester.
- *Pennsylvania Angler* magazine recently published a major article entitled "12 Tips to Becoming a Better Angler," simply presenting a dozen ideas that experts believe help the average outdoors-oriented person to be more successful when fishing.
- *Home & Condo* magazine, published for winter visitors as well as year-round residents in Florida's southwest coast region, recently ran a helpful how-to feature that told readers ways to finance the purchase of their first Florida home.

- *Mustang Monthly* magazine, a national publication geared to lovers of the Ford Mustang automobile, recently carried a special full-color 32-page pull-out section entitled "How To: Restore Your Mustang." The issue featured articles about planning the restoration, budgeting for costs, safety in the repair shop, research and detective work in finding authentic parts, interior evaluation, organizing and disassembly of the car, finding parts (a four-page listing of parts suppliers as well as an article), parts cleaning and sheet metal work, working on the engine, the undercarriage, the body, and even the "ten most common mistakes" during restoration of the car.

- *The Miami Herald*, with its readers still reeling in 1993 from the damage of 1992's Hurricane Andrew, published a 40-page how-to tabloid section focusing on two main themes: preparing for future hurricanes and restoring homes and businesses damaged by Andrew. The section contained dozens of articles and informational graphics by staff writers and free-lance experts instructing readers on such topics as storm tracking, insurance, equipment, tools, storm shutters, banking, roofing, and government assistance.

Sarasota magazine, a regional monthly on Florida's west coast, provided its readers with a very practical how-to article in a summer issue aimed at weekend vacation trips to the nearby Orlando area. Writer Janis R. Frawley (1992) took Sarasota readers on a personalized tour of Orlando-area theme parks. Her lead connected the idea to Sarasota area residents and seasonal visitors. Then she executed her article's plan by offering general how-to tips about theme park touring. The final two-thirds of her article took readers through the nine major attractions in the area, with each receiving mini-reviews of approximately 500 to 1,000 words. The result was a major package filling five advertising-free pages in the magazine. As you read the beginning portion of her article that follows, notice how Frawley wrote in a highly appealing personal manner, but also how she combined her experiences with solid advice and a logical organizational plan.

> Okay, I'll confess. I'm a theme park junkie. There's no better way to take an ordinary day and fill it with adventure and thrills. Especially when the theme park capital of the world, Orlando, is only two hours away!
>
> I know what you're thinking—the throngs of people! The lines! But with a little inside information, you can escape the maddening crowds and have the time of your life.
>
> First of all, **schedule your jaunts during the least crowded times of the year**. For example, Disney's Florida Resident Salute offers discounted passes and hotel rates to encourage Floridians to take advantage of park lulls. Suggested times: May 1–June 7; Aug. 16–Sept. 30; Nov. 29–Dec. 20; and Jan. 1–Feb. 9. Believe me, that's when you can make the most of everything.
>
> **Steer clear of ticket booth lines** at the entrances by buying admission tickets at local outlets such as Sears, Ticketmaster and (for members) AAA, which offers a

20 percent discount throughout the year to non-Disney parks. Disney tickets are discounted only during special promotions. But addicts can buy annual passes that offer unlimited entry.

Arrive when parks open, as reservations to most restaurants and special shows fill up early. Later in the morning, head for the opposite end from the park entrance for crowd-free cruising. Evening is an excellent time to tour the parks; crowds thin out and there are often spectacular closing ceremonies.

LET'S DO DISNEY
Highlights from Disney attractions

THE MAGIC KINGDOM
It doesn't get any more magical than this.

Nobody does it quite like Disney. It takes days to experience everything within Disney World. But the original Magic Kingdom remains my favorite . . . . (pp. 19–20)

Frawley's article is typical of travel- and recreation-oriented how-to articles that serve readers with a roundup unified around a theme. Writer Jim Bennett (1993) took a somewhat similar approach with his how-to feature for the American Automobile Association's *AAA World,* a national magazine produced in editions for specific states by AAA. Bennett wrote an article that told readers of this organizational membership magazine how to make sure a used car was technically sound before deciding to purchase it.

Bennett's article incorporated a checklist approach in its presentation, telling readers that experts recommend certain tests, which he described, be conducted on any used car. For readers who depend on their cars and who might be in the market for a used car, this was undoubtedly must reading.

The U.S. Department of Transportation reports that the average lifespan of a car is currently 12 years or 128,500 miles. Although today's new cars last longer than ever before, they still depreciate very quickly—25 percent or more in the first year alone. This means there are plenty of used-car bargains available. Of course, most cars on the used market need some maintenance or repair. To spot potentially "big ticket" problems, you need to take the car for a thorough inspection by a qualified technician.

A good inspection usually costs between $40 and $120—more if additional tests are performed or if the car is rare or exotic. "You must be willing to pay to have a good job done," warns Steve Larchuk, president of Auto Critic Services, Inc., a mobile used-car inspection service. "Most people don't appreciate the time it takes to do a good job."

You need to balance the cost of the inspection against the cost of the car. The higher the purchase price of the used car, the more worthwhile the up-front investment for an inspection. Spending $50 to $100 for a technician's inspection makes more sense on a newer, low-mileage car than on an older, high-mileage one that costs a few hundred dollars.

Before you pay for a technician's test, however, prequalify the car you're interested in. Do the small stuff yourself. Check the tires for uneven wear. Make sure all lights and power accessories work. Inspect the body for signs of extensive body work, damage, or rust. Take the car for a 20- to 30-minute test drive. (See "15 Signs of a Good Used Car," *AAA World*, May/June 1990.) Take notes to give to your technician.

It may not be easy finding an owner willing to part with the car long enough for a mechanic's inspection. "Many dealers will do it," says Larchuk, "but private sellers don't want to lose control of the vehicle." Often, private sellers cite insurance concerns . . . .(p. 10)

The remaining portions of Bennett's article focused on how the reader can qualify the technician who will inspect the car and the seven tests that should be performed on a used car, such as electronic diagnostics, air conditioning inspection, and so forth. He concluded the feature with advice that the technician be asked which repairs, of those deemed necessary, need to be made immediately.

USING ILLUSTRATIONS WITH YOUR ARTICLE

One way to strengthen your service article by making it clearer to readers is to use *analogies*. This helps you look more authoritative and readers understand the material far better. If you have the chance and space to use them, *illustrations*, such as photographs, drawings, or charts, will make things even clearer. Many how-to articles are presented with illustrations to help describe the process, a critical step, or even the final product. Artwork includes such tools as statistical tables, charts, maps, diagrams, graphs, "exploded" diagrams in which things are taken apart slightly, labeled photographs, "staged" photo illustrations, and tables.

Charts and tables can provide such information as summaries of steps necessary in a process, such as cooking, outlined one at a time. Another example for an article might be a rundown of costs for a repair or renovation project or the different options available in a major purchase. Graphs, maps, and diagrams can show how steps or stages in a procedure tie together. As an expert on the subject, you should work closely with artists to make certain such graphs are correct to every detail.

Much of the time, photographs known as *photo illustrations* do the trick. Photographers will pose the subject matter as an illustration and it is presented with your article. You should attempt to tie these in with references to such illustrations in the text of your article. An alternative is to label parts of the photograph through the cutlines or legends under the photographs or to identify parts of the subject of the photograph with identifications using lines or arrows. Collaborating with copy editors, graphic artists, informational graphics editors, photographers, and page designers makes the total package work better. The tasks of writing and preparing artwork for how-to or other service features should be team efforts if possible. Most editors and artists appreciate, but often simply require, the advice and assistance.

POPULARITY OF SERVICE ARTICLES AND BOOKS

There are countless how-to books on the market, many of which have grown out of original newspaper or magazine articles. A quick look at the *Writer's Market* shows a large number and wide variety of publishers involved in producing these specialty books. The 1993 edition presents nearly a full page (p. 287) of listings of both major and minor publishers who consider manuscripts on this subject.

Specifically, another popular magazine category in recent years has been *self-help* or *self-improvement*. The *1993 Writer's Market* also contains a section listing five publications, including *Changes Magazine* and *Celebrate Life*, that seek manuscripts on psychology and self-improvement. The section describes the demand for these types of articles: "These publications focus on psychological topics, how and why readers can improve their own outlooks, and how to understand people in general. Many general interest publications also publish articles in these areas" (p. 528).

How-to audiotapes and videotapes are also popular, with these evolving from articles and books on personal development subjects (exercise and stress management), sports subjects (golf and tennis), and personal finance (real estate and stock market investments).

LISTS AS SERVICE FEATURES

It is not unusual to find stand-alone lists in contemporary newspapers, magazines, and newsletters. However, you can enhance your service feature by combining the best of the narrative article and a listing. The listing thus becomes a sidebar or remains a major portion or purpose for the article. These approaches are often given titles such as "Ten Richest Women in the State" or "Five Steps to Losing Weight Overnight." Newspapers such as *USA Today* have capitalized on the curiosity such lists arouse in readers. Combining the *USA Today* staff talent for inviting graphics, these lists are often provided as a visual feature for readers.

To be successful at listings, you have to have a creative energy for research. Compiling lists often requires multiple sources in different locations. At other times, information may be found in one place. Listings must also be current and timely. Readers must be given the most recent and current information available from the most authoritative sources. Therefore, your list is also the most accurate.

Newspapers, magazines, and newsletters that publish listings are often considered authoritative sources on their own and find their published lists cited and reproduced elsewhere. *The Chicago Tribune*, for example, has recently placed more emphasis on child-oriented feature content in the newspaper. Editors are aiming at the "tween" ages of 9 through 14 in particular. Each Monday, the newspaper devotes a portion of every major section of the newspaper to children's news. As part of this coverage, child-oriented articles explain current events, offer advice, provide lists of information, and provide a number of other services not found elsewhere in the newspaper. Among the lists commonly used are those that give readers, both young and adult, ideas for things to do during the week.

List information is used in many different ways. Readers like to keep them, turning them into "refrigerator features" that are clipped and stuck on the refrigerator door with a magnet or piece of tape. Some lists can become publicity sources for the publication, too. For example, many morning drive-time radio program announcers like to pick unusual listed feature information out of their local newspaper or news magazine to read to their audiences (e.g., David Letterman lists, best- or worst-dressed lists, and top-attended movies of the past weekend).

Most stand-alone lists are short and to the point. These are usually a top 10 or top dozen. Too much information is usually not retained nor read in listed form. Thus, a brief list of the top 10 busiest airports might be appealing, but a top 100 becomes useless and overly thorough unless it is part of a major project or a complete list of all the elements in a group and the detail is necessary. Most published lists are presented in tabular form. Tables are quick and easy to read. Paragraphed information of the same kind is just not as easily skimmed and understood.

ART-OF-LIVING ARTICLES

Articles such as self-help or self-improvement pieces are part of a broader category of service articles called art-of-living articles. These have been made popular by their regularity in widely read publications such as *Reader's Digest*. Art-of-living articles can be an easy market for beginning feature writers, says *Reader's Digest* senior staff editor Philip Barry Osborne (1987). These articles include features that are inspirational narratives and essays, inspirational essays on faith and religion, and self-help articles. Inspirational and motivational features are also a type of human interest feature and were discussed at some length in chapter 6.

As you may recall, inspirational narratives and essays tell stories with a message to readers. The main difference is in approach. Narratives are chronological, whereas essays are in essence dealing with philosophy and "feel."

A RECIPE FOR SUCCESS IN HOW-TO FOOD WRITING

Nanette Blanchard
Free-Lance Writer

Root vegetables, recipe software, the history of corn, low-fat ice cream and vegetarian cookbooks are some of the subjects I've written about as a free-lance food writer. Getting paid to test chocolate recipes or try out new restaurants may not seem like writing, but it is. Food writing is one of the most enjoyable and versatile types of free-lance writing.

You can get ideas for food articles anywhere and everywhere. Start paying more attention to what people are eating. Listen when friends start talking about a new restaurant. Read cooking magazines and the food section of your newspaper.

Even television can help you with ideas for food articles. Check your local television listing for daily food and cooking shows. CNN's weekly show "On The Menu" is a particularly helpful program for food writers with information on food trends and news in the world of cooking. For instance, one recent show discussed how apple sauce and prune butter can be easily substituted for the oil or butter to lower the fat content of cookie, cake or muffin recipes.

Seasonal topics are always in demand by food editors. Because many magazines work 6 months in advance, keep a calendar near your desk when sending food article queries to editors. I keep a spiral notebook and write in pertinent information for each month of the year. That way, I can quickly glance through my notebook and find out that blueberries are in season in July or that March is National Peanut Month.

Don't limit your article topics to national holidays that are traditionally associated with food like Christmas or Thanksgiving. *Cooking Light* ran an article on President's Day with recipes inspired by U.S. presidents such as Brown Rice Pilaf with Peanuts (in honor of Jimmy Carter) and Jelly Bean Cookies (in honor of Ronald Reagan). Many magazines run low-calorie and spa food recipes in their January issue for all the after-the-holidays dieters.

I usually come up with some recipe ideas before I query the publication and offer a sample recipe list. I then look through cookbooks and my extensive recipe files for some preparation ideas and ingredient suggestions. I try to use simple, descriptive recipe titles. I often include some type of short introduction with each recipe such as, "This recipe is a family favorite and I adapted it using brown instead of white rice." If your recipe can be prepared in a different manner or prepared ahead, this information should be included in the recipe's preface.

The style of the recipe varies. Many food magazines send recipe guidelines to free-lance writers at the time an article is assigned and some of these recipe guidelines are quite complex. Check each magazine you're writing for and follow the recipe style exactly. Some magazines spell out Tablespoon, some just use T. or Tbsp. Always list all ingredients in the order used in the recipe.

I find that including an ingredient's weight as well as number is often helpful. A recipe that includes two potatoes in its list of ingredients is less scientific than one that states two potatoes, about ½ pound each. Also, include information on how to test for doneness in addition to cooking or baking times. Rather than just stating "Bake about 20 minutes or until done," write "Bake about 20 minutes or until toothpick inserted in center comes out clean."

When testing a recipe for an article, always make it twice. This can help you discover any problems or be certain that the ingredient amounts were correct as written. Save your grocery receipts as the magazines may pay your recipe-testing expenses. The directions of a recipe can be copyrighted although the ingredients cannot. If your recipe closely resembles another published recipe, with only a few minor changes, it is always smart to mention the original author and the inspiration for the recipe.

Almost every magazine published today can be queried with a food-related article idea. Don't limit yourself to food magazines. Travel magazines, women's magazines, men's magazines, children's magazines, health magazines, airline magazines, and even romance and confessions magazines all publish food articles.

You can write about the history of wheat for *Smithsonian* magazine, famous food scenes in movies for *Premiere*, 15 ways to disguise broccoli for your kids in *Parents* or that wonderful farmer's market in Provence for *Travel & Leisure*. Study several back issues of each magazine you wish to query and you can narrow down a food or cooking topic for every one.

Food writing is an always fascinating field of writing and you don't have to be a Cordon Bleu chef to get published. With a little study of the food markets and a lot of enthusiasm, anyone with a love of leeks or a yen for yams can be a successful food writer. (Blanchard, personal communication, 1993) Reprinted with permission of the author.

These are "good" stories about people that make readers feel better after finishing them. Inspirational essays on faith and religion are not always sermons; these are, instead, articles on worship, personal revelation, prayer and meditation, and love. As Osborne points out, these can vary greatly in length as much as in topic.

Osborne offers five tips for art-of-living articles:

1. *Guard against overwriting.* Do not get too ornamental or exquisite in your writing. "[T]hink more in terms of creating a small, delicate watercolor, rather than a giant oil painting," he advises (p. 22).

2. *Steep yourself in what you're writing about.* Simple themes, he says, require much more than simple or superficial research.

3. *Pinpoint your lesson or message.* This is a fundamental requirement, so give the article what *Reader's Digest* editors call a "takeaway"—some theme that readers can take with them after finishing the article.

SELF-HELP NONFICTION THAT SELLS

San Francisco Bay area writer and psychotherapist Eric Maisel (1993) recommends an 11-step self-help program to writing self-help articles and books. These are his suggestions:

Getting Ready

1. Identify a workable and compelling issue.
2. Frame appropriate questions to give focus to the project.
3. Serve the reader as a mapmaker, not an expert.
4. Reframe problems as challenges for motivational purposes.

Building the Book or Article

5. Decide on the structure of the project in terms of general information, individual stories, and self-help strategies.

Write the Book or Article

6. Provide examples, vignettes, and illustrations.
7. Use available research.
8. Create classification schemes to help convey concepts.
9. Offer workable strategies to readers.
10. Describe available resources and support services.
11. Look to the future to tell readers where they can go from here.

---

4. Sharpen your eye for the telling anecdote. These articles are about people, so use anecdotes. In fact, anecdotes can become the entire basis for an article.

5. Don't be afraid of ghosting. Writing under someone else's name is acceptable at *Reader's Digest* because art-of-living stories are best told in first person. Thus, write for experts who cannot do it themselves, he says.

CHRONOLOGICAL CASE HISTORIES

You can often learn easiest from example. This is where *chronological case histories*—some writers also call them *case summaries*—enter the category of service feature writing. Just as how-to articles, listings, and art-of-living articles teach readers, so do chronological case histories. A good case history can hit home for your readers. A patient who has had heart trouble and has made it through major surgery to repair the problem has a story to tell. Other patients and their friends and families will benefit from the story.

A chronological case history will outline the case of the patient for readers in a moment-by-moment, day-by-day approach. Many times, in fact, these articles are organized by date and time. In telling the story of the heart patient, no detail should be spared. And in concluding it, resolution must be achieved. Tell readers whether the efforts of doctors and nurses paid off—did the

---

BEST SOURCES FOR SERVICE ARTICLES

There are a number of individuals who will be your best sources for service articles. Here is a list of major categories:

How-to Articles

Craftspersons	Chefs/culinary experts
Builders/contractors	Authors of books
Mechanics	Consumer advocates
Carpenters/electricians	Inventors
Artists	Scientists
Gardeners/horticulturists	Investors
Technicians	Decorators

Lists and Listings

Historians	Museum curators
Statisticians	Government studies
Reference librarians	Census data

Art-of-Living Articles

Ministers	Psychologists/counselors
Physicians	Psychiatrists
Lawyers	Financial advisors

Chronological Case Histories

Social workers	Teachers
Physicians	Police
Psychologists	Sociologists
Psychiatrists	Historians

---

problem get solved? Did the patient live? Are there breakthroughs in health care to result from this?

USE CAUTION IN WRITING SERVICE FEATURES

It is quite possible to get so enthusiastic about service articles, especially how-to articles, that you can forget potential dangers related to these articles. As a writer, you must emphasize safety at all times. Especially dangerous, or potentially dangerous, subjects, such as those involving poisons (in gardening) or electricity (installations), might need an extra dimension of safety written into them. As a writer, you do not want to de-emphasize the possibility of risk in the stories you write—if it exists. On the other hand, non-health-threatening stories that involve other kinds of risk, such as investments, should be written just as carefully and thoughtfully for readers. You cannot write enough cautions and safety reminders into these types of articles.

One particular area of concern is the subject matter itself. Although it might have been interesting and entertaining reading, quite a controversy arose when *Progressive* magazine published a now-famous article over a decade ago about how to make a hydrogen bomb. On a more practical level, there is still concern about how much you tell readers, even if you personally know or if an expert is willing to discuss it, on certain subjects.

The ethical considerations on stories about crime such as auto theft, for example, are many. Do you write an article about how parking lot car thefts occur? How much do you tell? Is it right to have a former thief as your source—and is it proper for the source to describe, in detail, how to produce tools to break in and steal a car? Or, if your community has a problem with arson in a particular neighborhood, should you write an how-to article about how an arsonist does the job?

One recent newspaper feature highlighted a one-woman crime wave. This woman, the article related, broke into countless homes of wealthy individuals by dressing the part of a well-to-do visitor—including wearing fancy clothing and driving a luxury rental car. Too much information about how this woman managed her 300 to 500 burglaries might suggest the idea to someone else. However, it can also alert persons to a potential thief in their neighborhood. Content of such articles must be governed by a fine line of judgment.

In another case, three Florida teenagers were once arrested for making an incendiary device—napalm—after reading how to do it in a book, *The Anarchist Cookbook*, written nearly 20 years earlier. They were mixing the substance in their kitchen when they were discovered by local authorities. Even the newspaper reports of the arrest described in detail the ingredients the boys were using. Would you write that article for publication?

PROFESSIONAL'S POINT OF VIEW

Joe Oldham
Popular Mechanics

If I had the opportunity to say only one thing to a young writer who was interested in making a living as a feature writer for magazines, newspapers, or any other medium for that matter, it would be this:

Write the way you speak.

Be natural. Write the words as if you were having a conversation with someone. Imagine that you're telling the reader a story or giving the reader some new information. This is especially true of service-oriented and/or how-to articles. Here, it's essential that you get the interest of the reader with the lead, then hold his interest by transmitting information in an easy, accessible style. For most of us, that means, again, writing the way you speak.

Just about everyone can speak to another person and transmit a thought. That's really all nonfiction, feature writing is. There's nothing mysterious, nothing magical about it. It's just transmitting a thought. Then another. And another. Until finally, you've written an article that transmits many thoughts in a logical sequence.

"Talking" to another person on paper should give your article a conversational tone. Unless you're writing a formal paper or treatise, you want that conversational tone in all your feature writing. That means speaking (on paper) clearly, using common language, and just being yourself.

For instance, most of us speak in contractions. We say "You're going," not "You are going." So write that way. Your sentences will flow a lot better.

Most of us speak in the vernacular. It's true that we all have several different vocabularies, and that our writing and speaking vocabularies are not the same. Still, good writers don't differ much in the way they write and the way they speak. An easy, conversational tone is always the end result—and with it, a well-written article.

It always amazes me when someone I know as a regular guy writes something in a pompous, affected style that is totally unlike his natural manner and normal speech pattern. Somehow, when some people sit down at the computer, they feel that they have to become more formal or stodgy or achieve a so-called higher tone than they usually operate in as a person.

Wrong.

Just the opposite is true.

Good writers are who they are all the time. They don't take on a different personality when they sit down to write. Instead, they extend their own personality right into the words and sentences and paragraphs they're writing. They never step out of character.

Good nonfiction writers also write to one person at a time, no matter what the circulation of their publication. Each month, *Popular Mechanics* staffers write for over 9 million readers—one at a time. Especially in nonfiction, service, how-to and the like, you've got to talk to that one person out there reading your stuff. When you reach him, you've reached them all. Use the word *you* a lot. Not the word *I*. You should do this. You shouldn't do that. You should buy this. But don't buy that. Sometimes the *you* is implied. But it should always be there.

Be yourself. Be natural. Relax. Write the way you speak. Then you'll be a good writer. (Oldham, personal communication, 1993)

Joe Oldham is currently editor-in-chief of *Popular Mechanics*, a Hearst Corporation magazine, in New York. He's been an editor at The Hearst Corporation for over 20 years in various assignments. Oldham was assigned to *Popular Mechanics* in 1981 and became editor-in-chief in 1985. Under Oldham's leadership, *Popular Mechanics* has won a prestigious National Magazine Award and been nominated two other times. The magazine has also won two *MagazineWeek* Editorial Excellence Awards and over 100 awards for graphic excellence.

13

Personal Experience Articles

It is a horrible situation no one would ever want to consider, much less have to face. How do you deal with a mother's suicide? This is the question writer Jeanne W. Amend tried to answer in her cover article for *The Weekly*, a small newspaper published in Orlando, Florida. Amend took a first-person approach when she wrote the article 6 months after her mother took her own life. The article captures the essence of *personal experience* feature writing. This is how Amend (1992) began her very telling story about her family's crisis:

Around 3 p.m., on Saturday, April 4, I was dusting my living-room furniture when the phone rang. As soon as I heard my eldest sister's voice tell me to sit down, I knew she had called to tell me our mother had died. It had been exactly a month since Mom had been rushed to the hospital with seizures. For almost a year, she'd been battling lung cancer that had metastasized to her brain.

"What happened?" I asked, anticipating the words "seizure" or "blood clot."

"She shot herself," came the reply.

"WHAT? WHERE?"

"In front of the post office."

"Oh my God."

***

My rational mind had always believed that suicide was the greatest act of cowardice and selfishness, the easy way out of a difficult situation, a permanent solution to a temporary problem. Now that I've seen close-up the journey that leads a person to die violently by her own hand, however, my dim view of suicide has been painfully illuminated.

***

No news could have shocked me more on May 16, 1991, than to be told that my mother had lung cancer. It was a nightmare come true. Since she'd had thyroid cancer 12 years earlier, one of my worst fears was that she would have a recurrence. Now, I literally shook, uncontrollably and for hours, at the thought that she would be taken away from me far sooner than I was willing to let her go.

In a flash, my life and my family's life were turned upside down. The focus of my world shifted from life in New Orleans to the corridors of the southwest Louisiana hospital where my mother's cancerous lung was removed . . . .(p. 1)

Amend's article was a deeply personal one, as you note from the anecdotal approach taken in her lead. The remaining portion of her feature described the events that occurred during the year leading up to her mother's death and the 6 months following it up to the publication of her article. She told readers how she coped with this family tragedy and tried to describe how young adults handle such a difficult-to-understand event in their life. Insightful writing like this is one goal of personal experience feature writing. A personal experience article allows you to do much more than the usual feature article, because you, as a writer, can become highly involved in the storytelling. Most beginning writers have been encouraged to take themselves out of the story—to *de-personalize* the article—as much as possible. However, personal experience feature writing offers something unique in journalism—the chance to become part of a personalized story.

Most nonfiction writers have experienced events in their lives that would make good foundations for personal experience feature articles. Some of these events are much less serious, tragic, or life-changing than Jeanne Amend's award-winning family story. Furthermore, her article for a mid-sized *weekly* shows that such personalized features are not limited to large daily newspapers or 200-plus-pages-a-month consumer magazines that typically have more space and can give writers more time to develop the stories. One enterprising college student writer jumped out of an airplane (with a parachute) to write a feature about skydiving for her biweekly campus newspaper. Without that frightening experience, she might not have had the right mood, the touch of drama and fear, and the right words for her first-person feature article about skydiving.

Corvette Quarterly magazine, a Michigan publication devoted to the popular Chevrolet sports car, has a regular feature entitled "I Drive A Corvette," featuring celebrities and other individuals who own Corvettes. In these articles, the automobile owners describe their particular models, how they acquired them, what they are like, and why they like them so much. One recent issue featured an article, written by Robert Charm (1993), describing the experiences of Corvette owner Gary Wolf, writer of the Oscar-winning film, "Who Framed Roger Rabbit?"

When you become part of your story as do these car owners in *Corvette Quarterly*, your readers become closer to you because they find they can identify with you. You gain detail in your writing from close-up observation. This type of personalized feature article can be as simple as spending a shift at work with someone—getting involved personally. Personal writing is a broad-based approach to your craft. Your own point of view makes a difference in any story, but on these types of assignments, you can let it become part of the story itself.

APPROACHES TO PERSONAL EXPERIENCE ARTICLES

Generally, there are only two approaches to personal experience articles:

1. *Personal experiences of others about which you write.* These articles describe in detail the unusual and appealing experiences of individuals in a highly personal approach, but are not written first person. These are your descriptions as a writer who uses the experiences of another person for the basis of the article.

2. *Personal experiences of your own.* These are commonly called first-person articles. These articles draw on your own experiences for primary material for the article. These articles are often stories of medical problems, trips, crime incidents, life or death accident situations, human relationships, family experiences, and countless other similar events. You are the reporter, storyteller, and the central source—or one of the major sources—in the article. These can be everyday occurrences, but the articles that receive the most attention are unusual, adventurous, frustrating, or dramatic.

San Jose Mercury News feature writer Mike Weiss wrote a riveting story about the personal experience of someone else—a San Jose Police Department officer—for his newspaper's Sunday magazine, *West*. Weiss produced a 9,000-word story of conflict, sexual harassment, fear, danger, internal police politics, and citywide controversy. The story, Weiss stated, was based on "court documents, internal police reports, and interviews with about two dozen people inside or close to the police department" (1992, p. 12). The story was not only a recap of what happened to Officer Deborah Morris after a fellow officer made sexual advances toward her, but it was also a story about what happened in the 5 years after the incidents occurred. After she repelled him and filed a complaint, the rest of the story unfolded. What happened to Morris is both startling and insightful to readers not familiar with the culture of law enforcement. Readers were given a lesson in police department procedures, local politics, policy, internal investigations, and what can happen to a female officer in the tradition-bound and male-dominated field of law enforcement. Weiss' article not only gained the attention of West Coast readers, it also earned a certificate of merit from the JCPenney-University of Missouri newspaper feature writing awards in 1993. This is how Weiss (1992) began his article entitled "The Shield That Failed":

IT WAS A POLICE OFFICER'S nightmare: The suspect was resisting arrest, fighting off the handcuffs Officer Deborah Morris was struggling to clamp on his wrists. Morris couldn't drag him close enough to her patrol vehicle to reach the radio and call for help. It was just after dark, August 1987, in the Evergreen area of Southeast San Jose.

Finally she got one hand around the transmitter, and gasped for a Code 3 fill—emergency in progress, dispatch other cars with lights and sirens.

The rookie dispatcher didn't copy her call sign. Morris had to move away from the transmitter again—she needed both hands to keep hold of her suspect, who was wrestling free.

Then she heard the dispatcher transmit a message that should bail her out: "Can any unit I.D. the female officer requiring the Code 3 fill?"

Radio silence.

So the dispatcher repeated herself. Silence.

The rookie dispatcher didn't know what the silence meant, but Debbie Morris did. Her adrenaline hit her heart with the force of revelation. Nobody was coming. She was being abandoned.

Now the dispatcher was calling Officer Rosa Garcia, the only other woman on Morris' team on this swing shift. "Was that you?" she asked.

No, said Garcia, not me. But Garcia didn't add what she must have known: If it wasn't her, it had to be Debbie Morris.

So Morris subdued the suspect herself.

As soon as the shift was over, she asked Garcia for a 10-87, a window-to-window meeting in their patrol vehicles.

"You knew that was me requesting that Code 3 fill," Morris demanded. "Why didn't you tell the dispatcher?"

Garcia was just as blunt. She said about the worst thing any street cop can imagine hearing from a fellow officer, especially another woman who might be expected to understand what Morris had been through these past four months.

"It's not my responsibility to look out for you," Garcia said, slowly and distinctly. Then she gunned her motor and drove away.

Morris was left alone, exposed. She was not safe.

WHAT HAPPENED TO Debbie Morris began on a warm April afternoon as she assembled a cheap stereo cabinet in the living room of a safe house on Bluegrass Lane. She was excited. Only 23 years old, she was working her first undercover burglary sting, after just 18 months as a cop. These stings were known to be Chief Joseph McNamara's pet projects.

She was posing as "Nicki," the lover of "Mike," who was in fact Reese Gwillim, the sergeant running the sting. Gwillim was a departmental fast-tracker. He had become friendly with Morris about a year earlier and had pushed to bring her into BPU, the Burglary Prevention Unit, for this operation. Soon they were to begin buying stolen property and drugs.

The assignment was dangerous. They would be dealing up close, deceiving crooks and crackheads, and things might suddenly spin out of control.

But this was what Morris had always wanted. She had been only 8 years old when she declared her intention to become a cop. Her family had lived in the

Santa Cruz Mountains near Los Gatos, and her oldest brother was increasingly in scrapes with the law. "I'm going to be a police officer someday," she told him, "and straighten you out."

Eventually she studied criminal justice at Cal State Hayward. She felt she had the bravery it took. At 17, she was held at gunpoint by two robbers; she had remained calm and got good descriptions.

Morris stretched and went into the bedroom of the apartment in search of a hammer. She was about 5 feet 7 inches tall, slim, athletic and wholesome, with long pretty brown hair. The spirit of a serious enthusiasm was within her—she laughed easily, she was in the bloom of youthful good health. Men noticed her, Reese Gwillim among them.

There were rumors circulating in the department, in fact, that the only reason Gwillim wanted Morris up there was to put the make on her. Some more experienced women officers who had also coveted the assignment clearly resented her, but she had spoken to them about it, and to Gwillim as well.

About a year earlier he had told her how much he was attracted to her, even though he was nearly engaged. But now he pretty much laughed it off, saying she was picked because crooks didn't know who she was, she didn't look like a cop, and she was sensible.

It was an assurance she welcomed, because if the two suddenly found themselves in trouble only Gwillim would be at her back. Originally a third officer had been assigned to their team, but Gwillim had said they didn't need the backup man. For nine months he and Morris would pose alone as lovers and criminals.

Gwillim was relaxing on the bed. It was an unseasonably warm afternoon and he had stripped off his shirt. He was naked to the waist, his torso V-shaped and muscular.

"Reese," she said, "Do we have a hammer?"

Gwillim said he wasn't sure, smiling at her. Reese Gwillim had a smile and a way that made him one of the most popular cops in the department. He was a darkly handsome, soft-spoken 11-year veteran who had built up a reputation as an up-and-comer working narcotics. As with Morris, this was his first sting.

Still smiling, Gwillim said, "Why don't you come over and check out the bed? It's really comfortable."

Morris thought: Oh no, it's starting again.

A week before, they had been alone like this in the hot house across town, where they would be doing the buying, when suddenly Gwillim had kissed her, his tongue in her mouth. The kiss had lasted what seemed an eternity, but while a million thoughts spun through her mind she had returned the kiss, frozen in indecision.

Then he had reached into her bra.

"Knock it off, Reese," she had told him. She tried to talk to him, telling him they had a strictly working relationship, reminding him of his girlfriend, Cheryl. As she talked she touched his hair, feeling the need not to bruise his ego. He was the man who would assess her performance on this most crucial assignment to her future.

Almost immediately, he had apologized and said it wouldn't happen again. She accepted his word—what choice did she have?

"C'mon over and check out the bed," Gwillim said again now. "I'm not going to bite you, Deb."

Summoning her courage, she touched the mattress with her hand. Gwillim, who was strong—Morris knew because they had lifted weights together—suddenly grabbed her and pulled her down, rolling on top of her and pinning her arms.

"Let me go," she said.

"Just once, please," Gwillim besought her. "You don't know how many times I thought about having sex with you. Just this one time, Deb."

Debbie Morris repeated, "Let me go. I don't want to have to hurt you."

He laughed at her. "Yeah, like you're really going to hurt me."

She tried to roll free, shaking her head as he forced his lips against hers. She felt his erection rubbing against her through his pants. "Please," he kept saying, "Just this once."

Morris couldn't bring herself to knee him in the groin, she was so confused. Gwillim opened her blouse. She was wearing a front-snap bra, but Gwillim impatiently pushed the cup aside and began to suck her nipple. Somehow she rolled free and got off the bed.

"I'm sorry," he said at once. "I shouldn't have done that." He asked her to come back to the bed.

Without a word she went into the living room and sat motionless on a couch. He stayed in the bedroom for a long time. When he finally came out, Morris asked Gwillim again, this time angrily, if that was the only reason he had brought her up to BPU for the sting—so he could mess around?

He answered no, no it wasn't.

That was April 1987. It has taken almost five years, until this February, to resolve all the disputes and discords that arose from those few minutes on Bluegrass Lane. During that time the San Jose Police Department became bitterly divided into camps. There were the very few who supported Debbie Morris. There were the many who lined up behind Reese Gwillim. And there were those who wanted to speak up but were afraid of the consequences. Many officers and commanders call it the most divisive internal issue of the last decade.

It resulted in a criminal conviction, lawsuits that cost the city $350,000 in settlements alone, and an angry closed-door meeting of the City Council. It forced a new sexual harassment policy and training on the police department. Yet it escaped virtually all public notice.

The Debbie Morris/Reese Gwillim imbroglio caused two departmental chiefs to experience sudden memory blackouts while being questioned about their roles. It caused a respected investigator the department assigned to the case, who defied orders from above, to undermine his own investigation.

It drove Debbie Morris to the brink of suicide.

But most revealing of all, perhaps, was the glimpse it offered through court documents, internal police reports, and interviews with about two dozen people inside or close to the police department, of the intimidating backstage style of ex-Chief Joseph D. McNamara, whose wrath was feared by most of the cops he commanded, and whom one ex-captain calls "a master of deception". . . .(pp. 12–13) Excerpt reprinted with permission of the *San Jose Mercury News*.

Feature writer and teacher Nancy Kelton (1988) says personal experience articles such as the compelling personal story of Officer Debbie Morris by Mike Weiss should look at the world as honestly as possible, "seeing the truths— both the dark and the light—within our experiences so that we can share them with other people who will nod and say, 'Yes, that's how it is. I've been there, too'" (p. 24).

COMPONENTS OF PERSONAL EXPERIENCE FEATURES

A personal experience article must provide readers with an unusual story, an adventure, or a real-life drama. A personal experience article should also attempt to put that story in context. Often, the context will be current trends in the community or society, such as those affecting medical care or employ-ment. Yet it could add the dimension of historical context as well. There are three major components of personal experience articles, according to Kelton (1988), a specialist in personal experience article writing:

1. *A point of view.* What is the unique way in which you can present the situation? How are you or your source involved? What perspective do you offer? An inside view will generally be preferred. Usually, Kelton says, this fares better than filling the article with descriptive details of the actions of others at the expense of personal reactions and opinions. You have to tell how it felt, what it meant, and how you grew as a person during and after the experience. This, she says, is the best way to write a personal experience article.

2. *Arrival at some basic truth.* After you have made your trip, been released from the hospital, survived the criminal assault, or floated to the ground after parachuting from an airplane, you should be able to reach a conclusion about what you have learned. "[S]omething should become clear to you," Kelton

says. "You should reach a new level of understanding that you convey to your readers" (1988, p. 22).

3. *Emotional involvement.* It helps readers to share your experience if you can place them in the middle of your emotional reaction to the situation. You cannot afford to hide your feelings in writing such an article. You have to offer a complete description of what you felt. Write in such a manner that you can put your reader next to you, watching the experience all over again.

Putting these three main components to work is the key to a successful article, Kelton says. Here's how she does it:

1. *Pick an experience you care about deeply.* Some writers, Kelton relates, like to say that subjects pick writers, not vice versa. Although you do not have control over the events that you might use for an article, you can control your selection of those that you feel most strongly about. These are the ones to use for your articles.

2. *Don't make publication your primary goal.* Your primary objective should be to discover how you feel about an experience by writing about it. Afterward, in writing, you also will try to publish the article, and you have an added benefit. "Your initial satisfaction should come from the writing and the discoveries you make in the process," Kelton says (1988, p. 22). Her new experiences with motherhood, which she eventually wrote about, were her reasons for thinking about and trying to understand these new emotions she felt.

3. *Don't write a personal experience article to vent anger, indignation, or other negative emotions.* Sometimes you will experience something that makes you angry. It might be bad service at a garage or an annoying neighbor's lifestyle. Personal experience articles should not be used to vent these feelings. The anger may make it difficult or impossible for you to express your feelings.

4. *Have the courage to reveal yourself honestly.* You must convey feelings by opening yourself to others, perhaps thousands of others. That takes nerve, Kelton says, and is not for everyone. These feelings are not always positive and bright. "You must be courageous enough to reveal yourself honestly," Kelton (p. 22) says.

5. *Don't tell what you went through—show it.* To show it means to dramatize it. Reset the scene and put yourself and the reader there together. Often this means telling the story in chronological fashion. This is a simple step-by-step process that takes readers from beginning to end.

6. *Don't show everything—don't write about the mundane details of the experience.* Much of the time, too many details will drag the story down. The clutter can get in your way. Is the detail relevant to the story? If so, include it. If not, forget it.

IDENTIFYING INTERESTING EXPERIENCES

What have you done that makes interesting reading for others? From some of the examples discussed so far, you are aware of successful personal experience articles. Much of it is simple good or bad luck—depending on the nature of the event. Free-lance writer Howard Scott (1992) believes feature writers often overlook their own experiences. "In the search for subjects, many writers ignore an obvious possibility: their own personal experiences," he says (p. 359). "Although these events do need some drama, tension, and a resolution (or solution), they don't have to be earth-shattering or catastrophic. Most of us have such experiences, and writers can make them come alive on paper."

Writers may find themselves in a place to develop a story by sheer coincidence. Your sound news sense will often be a good guide. The elements that make a good feature will become even stronger if you are personally involved in that topic or event. So, instead of a routine story about the problems people have settling with insurance companies after a break-in, an automobile accident, or natural disaster, the story takes on more meaning if you have had the misfortune to experience such an event yourself and can write about it. Scott (1992), who has written personal experience features for magazines and newspapers, feels you should consider several things when thinking about your own experiences as potential material for features: "Think of a personal experience as a series of events that happened to you, and might be worth sharing with others. . . . What else constitutes a personal experience? Have you ever spent time with a famous person, lived through a medical crisis, lived in or visited an exotic place, taken up any strange hobbies? Have you had a close brush with death—an accident or a sickness, recovered from a disabling addiction, attempted and accomplished a difficult feat?" (p. 359).

Sometimes the routine at home makes good material. Many columnists do this. They are not at all hesitant to discuss topics such as sex education by using their own families as the example for others. Writing in first person, such writers even mention husbands, wives, and children by name in relating stories to readers and making their points in their regular features.

Unusual adventures that most people cannot experience are the focus of many appealing personal experience articles. Writer George Plimpton has made a career of trying unusual sports and other activities and writing magazine articles and books about the experiences. He has been an athlete as well as a jet fighter pilot. In a recent article prepared for *Popular Mechanics*, Plimpton wrote about his experiences flying an $18 million F-18 Hornet at Mach 2 speed above the Atlantic Ocean.

Taking a lighter personal approach, *Florida Today* local section columnist John McAleenan (1993) recalled an experience of his younger days as an introduction to a more contemporary concern regarding the Atlantic Ocean beaches around Melbourne, where his newspaper is located. The amusing story he tells is an example of how a writer can use a personal experience for humor and to get to another point in an article. This is part of his column:

> This is not my official nudist camp story; that's already been written. But I want to borrow from that, just a few lines, so that I can go on and talk about some other nude stuff.

Anyway . . . it was a lovely June morning, circa 1969, and myself and a couple of friends had piled into the old VW van and headed for Cypress Cove, a nudist camp near Kissimmee we had heard about.

I had called ahead, mentioning that we wanted to do a story about all this, but wanted to experience it also. Assured that would be just fine, we left with a wonderful spirit of adventure—and as it turned out—were not disappointed.

We were met at the gate by the proprietor, ushered onto the grounds, all the while peering over his shoulder at a bunch of nude folks gamboling along the lakeside.

"So," says the owner, "you will be nudists for a day, right?" I assured him that was our intention. He was wearing a towel and a baseball hat. We were wearing shoes and socks and underpants and pants and belts and shirts and stuff like that. The conversation stalled.

"Uh . . . what do we do now?" I asked. "Well," he said, "you can start by taking your clothes off. Then we'll go meet some people."

My friends and I took turns at looking at each other. We seemed frozen on the spot.

Finally I asked a question—one that will forever remain the best straight line I've ever spoken. "Well," I said, "where are the dressing rooms?" The owner seemed only slightly taken aback. "Dressing rooms? You'll be naked, right?" And with that, we stood in the dusty parking lot and began to undress. Right in front of each other. It was a heavy moment. But when the deed was done, the owner gathered us into a little platoon, and off we went to meet some people.

It turned out to be one of the best days, one of the funniest days, and perhaps not surprisingly, one of the more liberated days any of us had experienced.

And with that introduction, I must tell you the bureaucrats at the National Park Service, charged with tending our National Seashore Park at Playalinda, seem singularly uptight about all this nudity business. The threat of arrests loom once again.

"There is much more to it than nudity," says park superintendent Wendell Simpson. "They are going into the dunes. They walk in the dunes—and we have a mission to protect this resource . . . . We cannot take a group of fifth graders there. Or a group from Iowa. Or a church group, or whatever. There is sexual activity up there and homosexual activity. We have documentation of that."

That suggests, I would guess, that someone out there is filming all this. Smile everyone. This is nothing less than show biz. (p. B1) Reprinted with permission of *Florida Today*.

Of course, more serious subjects such as public safety and health make good personal experience stories. A first-person approach to modern health issues is illustrated by the case of a student journalist who was once a cocaine addict. Her experiences gave a critical dimension to her story about the impact of drugs on a middle-class coed that she could not achieve as meaningfully from a source in an interview. If the student can bring herself to write about this trying part of her life and others learn from it, then the story has had impact. Her story, which was written for a university newspaper's monthly magazine, chronologically told how her increasing dependency on drugs cost her a promising career, her marriage, and an entire lifestyle. Her article described how she eventually managed to win the battle with drugs and told the high price she paid. From this writer's rare personal situation, we learned that a peek into someone else's life can teach us much about a woman's highs and lows and how she put herself back on the road to a productive life.

Ideally, personal experience stories should relate to broader community concerns, if possible. Although some incidents can be interesting as isolated happenings, an experience takes on more value if it is placed in a more meaningful big picture. The final test is to determine if the experience is "writable": Can you tell this story to someone else? Would someone else want to know about what you experienced? If so, then you might have a good story idea.

FINDING THE BEST STORYTELLERS

In every community there are storytellers. You might have occasion to tell your own personal experience stories from time to time, but much of your grist will be from other sources, people known as the local storytellers. Who are they? They take many roles—minister, Boy or Girl Scout leader, historian, police officer, and social worker. People who are involved with other people on a regular basis often have the best experiences to tell you. If you can find one or more of these persons, you will have rich potential for a story.

Research, as you are often reminded, makes a difference even in personal experience storytelling. You might be aware of events that can be the basis of a good personal experience story. By searching records and newspaper clippings, you can often get the names of persons who were witnesses, victims, or otherwise involved in the event.

These are your storytellers.

TELLING A MEANINGFUL STORY

Some personal experience feature articles can be called factual short stories. This might help you to remember a good approach to writing a meaningful story—write and organize it as you might handle a short story, but just be sure to keep the content factual. Accomplishing this is easier than it seems. It helps a great deal if you use the storytelling techniques of short story writers:

1. *Dialogue.* Use an ample number of direct quotations and reconstructed conversation between key individuals.
2. *Description.* Bring in plenty of rich descriptive words and detail. This includes using active verbs and adverbs and impression-filled adjectives.

3. *Plot.* If your story permits, try to organize it so your story has a plot or story line. Make it suspenseful if appropriate. Give the story a moral. You should introduce the plot/story line early in the article and stick with it throughout.

4. *Facts.* Stick to the facts. Do not embellish or falsify to enhance the story line. Use real names of those involved, real places, actual dates and times, and other factual details. The reality adds a truly valuable dimension to the article that cannot come from any other type of writing device or technique.

There can be problems that come with telling a story. One of the most serious ones is selective or failing memory. On some personal experience story assignments, you might depend on memories of events that occurred months or years ago. Your memory gets hazy. There may be no written record of events, either. Fading memory filters out certain details over time. If this happens to you, it can happen to your sources, too. You must be prepared to go to extra lengths for details that might be forgotten. For example, you may be able to use yearbooks, photo albums, and other records to stimulate detailed recollections.

Many writers, when faced with missing information, are better off admitting to readers that they cannot recall some detail or piece of the puzzle. Don't guess. This openness and honesty are personal touches that make the article even more appealing to readers.

USING YOUR OWN EXPERIENCES

Has anything extraordinary ever occurred to you? Would it make an appealing story? Can others learn from your experiences? There will be unusual events and circumstances that will occur in your life that could generate an article. Newspaper reporters and magazine writers experience the full range of human experiences and you should be prepared to write about the unusual events that you experience. Of course, the ordinary activities in your life might make good feature article material, too. Ana Veciana-Suarez, a Living section features writer and a former suburban section editor for *The Miami Herald*, has often written about her family in her parenting features and columns. As her children have grown, readers have been able to learn from her family's experiences. Sharing the many experiences in her column is not only humorous and entertaining, but also educational for other parents.

Washington Post reporter George Lardner, Jr. may have taken on the most difficult assignment of his career when he decided to write an article about the death of his 21-year-old art student daughter, Kristin. Lardner's article was a description of how the criminal justice system failed in protecting his daughter from a jilted boyfriend who stalked and murdered the woman in Boston in 1992 (Kurtz, 1993; Lardner, 1992). Lardner, a 30-year veteran of the *Post* staff, is normally an investigative reporter. He wrote about the assassination of Robert Kennedy in 1968, the Chappaquiddick incident involving Ted Kennedy, the Watergate cover-up trial, and the Iran-Contra scandal. But he turned to a very different writing style—a much more personalized feature approach—in telling the story of his daughter's death and her murderer's suicide. His article, "The Stalking of Kristin: The Law Made It Easy for My Daughter's Killer," was published in the newspaper's Outlook section. In first-person style, he described what he wanted to achieve with the article: "This was a crime that could have and should have been prevented. I write about it as a sort of cautionary tale, in anger at a system of justice that failed to protect my daughter, a system that is addicted to looking the other way, especially at the evil done to women" (Lardner, 1992, p. C1). Lardner said his work on the story began when he spoke with a Brookline, Massachusetts, police officer. Lardner discovered, after talking with the officer, how little he really knew about what had happened to his daughter. In his efforts to find out the truth about Kristin's case and her death, he collected information that would grow into his article, which won the 1993 Pulitzer Prize for feature writing. This is how Lardner (1992) began his lengthy article:

THE PHONE was ringing insistently, hurrying me back to my desk. My daughter Helen was on the line, sobbing so hard she could barely catch her breath.

"Dad," she shouted. "Come home! Right away!"

I was stunned. I had never heard her like this before. "What's wrong?" I asked. "What happened?"

"It's-it's Kristin. She's been shot . . . and killed."

Kristin? My Kristin? Our Kristin? I'd talked to her the afternoon before. Her last words to me were, "I love you Dad." Suddenly I had trouble breathing myself.

It was 7:30 p.m. on Saturday, May 30. In Boston, where Kristin Lardner was an art student, police were cordoning off an apartment building a couple of blocks from the busy, sunlit sidewalk where she'd been killed 90 minutes earlier. She had been shot in the head and face by an ex-boyfriend who was under court order to stay away from her. When police burst into his apartment, they found him sprawled on his bed, dead from a final act of self-pity.

This was a crime that could and should have been prevented. I write about it as a sort of cautionary tale, in anger at a system of justice that failed to protect my daughter, a system that is addicted to looking the other way, especially at the evil done to women.

But first let me tell you about my daughter.

She was, at 21, the youngest of our five children, born in D.C. and educated in the city's public schools, where not much harm befell her unless you count her taste for rock music, lots of jewelry, and funky clothes from Value Village. She loved books, went trick-or-treating dressed as Greta Garbo, played one of the witches in "Macbeth" and had a grand time in tap-dancing class even in her sneakers. She made life sparkle . . . . (p. C1)

Lardner told the story chronologically after setting it up with this lead. Following the description of his daughter, he traced the history of the relationship—how Kristin met the man who would stalk and kill both her and himself. Lardner gave readers detailed biographical material about Cartier, her murderer. As he did, the story became more third person in voice. Lardner quoted friends of his daughter and persons who knew Cartier, a man with psychological problems. The detail of Lardner's writing included numerous incidents and anecdotes recounted by people who knew the couple. He also used his investigative reporting skills in locating and reviewing public records involving his daughter's murderer. His eye for detail was evident in this paragraph midway through the story:

> Left in her bedroom at her death was a turntable with Stravinsky's "Rites of Spring" on it and a tape player with a punk tune by Suicidal Tendencies. Her books, paperbacks mostly, included Alice Walker's "The Color Purple" and Margaret Atwood's "The Handmaid's Tale," along with favorites by Sinclair Lewis, Dickens and E.B. White and a book about upper- and middle-caste women in Hindu families in Calcutta.

> Her essays for school, lucid and well-written, showed a great deal of thought about art, religion and the relationship between men and women. She saw her art as an expression of parts of her hidden deep inside, waiting to be pulled out, but still to be guarded closely: "Art could be such a selfish thing. Everything she made, she made for herself and not one bit of it could she bear to be parted with. Whether she loved it, despised it or was painfully ashamed of it . . . she couldn't stand the thought of these little parts of her being taken away and put into someone else's possession." (p. C1).

Still another insightful passage utilized another writing technique. Lardner re-created dialogue in this portion:

> What did she see in him? It's a question her parents keep asking themselves. But some things are fairly obvious. He reminded her of Jason, her friend from New Zealand. He could be charming. "People felt a great deal of empathy for him," said Octavia Ossola, director of the child care center at the home where Cartier grew up, "because it was reasonably easy to want things to be better for him." At the Harbor School, said executive director Art DiMauro, "He was quite endearing. The staff felt warmly about Michael."

> So, at first, did Kristin. "She called me up, really excited and happy," said Christian Dupre, a friend since childhood. "She said 'I met this good guy, he's really nice.'"

> Kristin told her oldest sister, Helen, and her youngest brother, Charlie, too. But Helen paused when Kristin told her that Cartier was a bouncer at Bunratty's and had a tattoo.

> "Well, ah, is he nice?" Helen asked.

> "Well, he's nice to me," Kristin said.

Charlie, who had just entered college after a few years of blue-collar jobs, was not impressed. "Get rid of him," he advised his sister. "He's a zero."

Her friends say they got along well at first. He told Kristin he'd been in jail for hitting a girlfriend, but called it a bum rap. She did not know he'd attacked Rose Ryan with a scissors, that he had a rap sheet three pages long.

Kristin, friends say, often made excuses for his behavior. But they soon started to argue. Cartier was irrationally jealous, accusing her of going out with men who stopped by just to talk. During one argument, apparently over her art, Cartier hit her, then did his "usual thing" and started crying. (p. C1)

Lardner finished the article with a continuation of the chronology of his daughter's relationship, their breakup, the stalking, and the final days of her life. In great detail, he reconstructs what happened in her life for the 3 months leading up to the day of the murder. He also reviewed events that occurred following her death: his efforts to trace the weapon used in the murder-suicide and detailed descriptions from public records of his daughter's efforts to stop the stalking and harassment after she had ended the relationship with the man. The final portion of the article was devoted to explaining how the judicial system failed to protect her. This section alone is a startling lesson to readers. He questioned, "How many . . . [people] should have known she was in grave danger?" (p. C1). But his concluding paragraph summarized in an effective manner just how little the judicial system worked: "The system is so mindless that when the dead Cartier failed to show up in Boston Municipal Court as scheduled on June 19, a warrant was issued for his arrest. It is still outstanding" (p. C1).

Writer Nan Robertson (1982) told another amazing personal story for the *New York Times Magazine* that explained to readers her battle against a medical condition known as *toxic shock syndrome*. The article, appealing because of the very personal story it tells, earned her the Pulitzer Prize the following year for feature writing. Robertson wrote in rich, precise detail about her experience with the rare medical problem. Structurally, she takes a chronological approach, beginning just hours before she was stricken. She takes readers through her near-fatal attack, the ride to the hospital, diagnosis, and treatment. Her article uses direct quotations of recalled dialogue during her attack and treatment. She also depended on family members and friends to remember details and quotations, and she used a diary one friend kept for her during her hospitalization. After setting the scene—her trip to the hospital in Illinois— readers are told:

This is the story of how, almost miraculously and with brilliant care, I survived and prevailed over that grisly and still mysterious disease. Almost every major organ of my body, including my heart, lungs and liver, was deeply poisoned . . . . This is also the story of how—with luck and expertise—this life-threatening disease can be avoided, detected, monitored, treated and destroyed before it reaches the acute stage. (p. 30)

Robertson's article, written in first person, is understandable even when she discusses the medical reasons for the disease. Readers are able to share the experience of her personal fears, her suffering and her pain, and her joy in winning the battle. Yet, she also incorporates into her article considerable discussion about the disease by experts from the Centers for Disease Control and other medical research centers. Woven into her own experiences, this makes the article instructional as well as entertaining.

The Veciana-Suarez, Lardner, and Robertson examples illustrate how reporters with a variety of experiences that appeal to readers can use their own lives as the basis for personal experience articles. Veciana-Suarez writes about daily occurrences that can be meaningful to other parents. Clearly, neither Lardner nor Robertson would have wanted to go through their experiences. But they did and eventually turned them into learning experiences for themselves as well as others. Whereas one writer chose to use her own amusing family experiences as material for lifestyles features and a parenting column, the other two turned dangerous, even fatal, situations into valuable stories from which others are able to learn.

ORGANIZING NARRATIVE ARTICLES

Personal experience features require care in organizing the sometimes large amounts of material. Because you, or someone you are working with, have experienced the subject firsthand, writing about the experience can become difficult because you or your source are so close to it. Many features rise or fall because of their organizational structure. A strong personal experience story will depend on organization also. Because many personal experience stories are not written in the traditional inverted pyramid—with the most important facts first—a strong lead will make a difference. This lead is the first step in the organizational effort. It must capture the flavor of the article by hinting at its essence without giving away the outcome or moral. The lead must arouse readers by piquing their curiosity, teasing them, and even raising their eyebrows in reaction to what they have read. *Miami Herald* feature writer Mark Silva's (1983) lead to his feature about the problems he experienced during an airline strike is successful because he uses ample description, personal reaction, and surprise:

> I was weary, worn out by the last strong September sun and an afternoon of bathing in the hot confluence of a boiling spring-fed river and a cold trout-filled stream in Yellowstone National Park, when I learned that the airline that got me there had gone bankrupt.
>
> There is something seductive about imagining, for a moment, that one's vacation will never end . . . .(p. 1B)

Most personal experience articles are organized as essays written in chronological order, simply recounting a series of events that interest readers. Still, an essay requires a basic organizational structure also—a beginning/introduction, body, and ending. Chronological stories must be told in a time-based order of events—often including the times to help the reader understand the sequencing. It is essential that you stick to the topic—that is, remain focused—in your article. Because it is often a personal story you are telling, the temptation can be great to drift away from the real focus.

You must also keep the story moving. Doing this requires pacing and a skilled use of transitions. You can tell each single episode that contributes to the entire experience an item at a time, but you must constantly try to tie each item together with good transitions that remind the reader of the links. For example, using times of the day or days of the week in a chronological piece will aid readers a great deal. Helter-skelter movement around a series of events confuses readers and can lose them.

Staff feature writer Jocelyn R. Coleman (1993) compiled a collection of 11 personal experience stories for the People section of *Florida Today* entitled "Miracles Do Happen: Unexplained Wonders Touch Brevard Lives." Her article is a series of ministories of unusual, "miraculous" experiences of individuals who live in the newspaper's market in central Florida. Coleman does not attempt to find scientific explanations for what happened. Instead, she simply allows the individuals who experienced or witnessed the unusual events to describe them, most often in their own words. The article relates a series of sad, amusing, and simply unbelievable personal experience stories. This is her article:

Early in 1958, Jean Martin of Indian Harbour Beach was driving north of Melbourne on U.S. 1, on a mission to collect pledges to build what now is Holmes Regional Medical Center.

Her then 3-year-old son, Mike, and newborn baby, Cindy, were in the back seat.

Suddenly Mike said, "Mommy, Cindy looks funny."

Then Martin stopped the car, she was terrified to discover Cindy had stopped breathing. This was before CPR was very well-known, so Martin immediately began to pray for a miracle.

As she stared at her daughter's blue face, Martin said she felt a hand push her head down onto her child's face to breathe into her nose and mouth.

Soon a passerby stopped and drove them to a hospital. Cindy was OK in an hour. Martin is convinced that God was the one who urged her to perform mouth-to-mouth resuscitation on Cindy. She thanks him every day for that.

Martin is just one of the many Brevardians who recently shared their recollections of miracles with *Florida Today*. Here are some of the other responses we received:

328 13. PERSONAL EXPERIENCE ARTICLES

STALL OF A LIFETIME

At 5:45 p.m. Dec. 30, 1967, Florence McCall, now of Melbourne, was running late. She was taking her brother and his fiancee from her home in Fairfax County, Va., to National Airport in Washington, D.C.

On the way, they had to cross a railroad crossing that had red flashing lights but no gate. Drivers familiar with the area looked both ways and kept going because the freight train that used the track usually crept along at a slow 35 mph.

As McCall approached the track, she saw the train, but decided to try and beat it and pushed down on the accelerator. But the car went dead. Lucky for her it did. The train coming down the tracks wasn't the slow freight, but a passenger train going about 85 mph. After it whooshed by, McCall's car started back up without a problem.

"Somebody up there turned my motor off," McCall says.

THE TRANSFORMATION

Paul Procko of Indian Harbour Beach and his brother were nearby as their 80-year-old mother lay near death. They were sitting in the kitchen across from her bedroom when her heavy breathing suddenly stopped.

They jumped to their feet and rushed to her side. While Procko tried to revive her, he felt a calm engulf him as if to say relax and just watch.

The woman's wrinkled head swung to the left side. She wasn't breathing. Suddenly, a golden glow surrounded her body until she was in a golden circle of light. The glow turned into a beautiful blue sky with white clouds.

All the wrinkles disappeared from her face. Her straight gray hair changed into the "most beautiful black braided hair I have ever seen," Procko wrote.

By the end of this moving transformation, which went on for a few minutes, Procko was looking at a beautiful 30-year-old woman.

Then, without any warning, the heavenly surroundings disappeared. Her gray hair and wrinkles came back, and her mouth and eyes snapped wide open. All the ugliness of death returned to her face.

But for a moment, "it was the most beautiful vision of loveliness I have ever seen," Procko said.

CAR FLIPS THREE TIMES

Six years ago, Janis Chieca of Palm Bay was driving her friend's Toyota on Long Island, N.Y. Suddenly, the left rear tire blew out and the car started veering to the left and going off the road. Chieca turned the steering wheel in the opposite direction, but over-corrected and started spinning. When the car stopped, she was facing oncoming traffic.

"They are going to kill me," Chieca exclaimed out loud before she looked around the automobile convinced that it was going to be her tomb. That's when she started praying.

"Dear Lord, help me. What can I do?" she asked.

He answered her prayer and came to be with her in the car, Chieca said. He gave her specific instructions to: Push back in the seat as far as possible, close her eyes and hold on to the steering wheel with all her might.

Then he was gone.

Just as Chieca's eyes were beginning to close, she saw the car go straight up in the air before overturning three times.

During the ordeal she felt only a tap on her head. When the car landed right side up on the other side of the road it was totaled, but Chieca was fine.

Chieca's miracle had an earthly assist: She was wearing her seat belt.

A HEALING

Last May, Helen Lynch of Scottsmoor entered Parrish Medical Center in Titusville for gall bladder surgery. It was supposed to be a one-day procedure, but instead of getting better she took a turn for the worse.

The doctor accidentally cut the bile cord, and infection spread through her body. She was put in intensive care and hooked up to a breathing machine. By June, the doctor was saying she wouldn't make it.

That's when friends and relatives began praying night and day. Three days later, she began to improve. She came home shortly thereafter.

"If that isn't a miracle," said her husband, James, "I don't know what it is."

DROWNING VISION

Margarete Miller of Melbourne Beach will never forget the surety she felt two summers ago. Her son John Niland and his family had traveled from Houston to visit family members in Brevard County.

One day, everyone gathered at the Indialantic home of Miller's daughter, a registered nurse. Because the dining room was adjacent to an inground pool separated from the room only by sliding glass doors, the adults told the younger children to play only indoors. They didn't want Anne, Niland's 8-month-old daughter, to crawl outside.

Time passed. Before the adults noticed anything was amiss, one of the grandchildren yelled that the baby was in the pool. She was floating face down when Niland jumped in the water to pull her out. Her face was blue.

Everyone in the house started to panic. Everyone, that is, except for Miller, who simply froze. During that time, Miller says, she experienced a miracle.

A clear image of the baby laughing and clapping her hands appeared before her. It only lasted two seconds, but it was enough to encase Miller in an easing calm and convince her everything would be all right.

"I have tried to rationalize it, but I cannot . . . . I am not particularly religious and did not ask God or any higher power for help. The image appeared to me on its own volition," she said.

Miller proceeded to dial 911 relaxed and with assurance. While her daughter performed CPR on the child, Miller assured the rest of the family that everything was going to be just fine. Miller was the one calm enough to open the front door for the rescue workers.

The baby was rushed to Holmes Regional Medical Center and kept overnight. She was released the next day good as new, just like Miller had predicted.

"I will never forget the utter surety of it," said Miller, who usually doesn't talk about the moving experience.

". . . I have my little vision that I recall from time to time and it makes me smile and feel glad to be alive. Miracles do make you humble, and for that, one's perceptions about things alters for the better."

ANOTHER POOL MIRACLE

Jane Walker's husband of 48 years died unexpectedly in January 1992. About five weeks later, Walker's youngest daughter, Wendy Hankins, and her two children traveled from Chulota to cheer Walker up.

Before they arrived, Walker turned on the pump to their solar-heated pool, which is covered with a plastic bubble. Hours later, Walker and Wendy were reading, when, Wendy said, her father reached down from heaven, touched her on the shoulder and asked, "Where's Mr. Todd?" Mr. Todd is the family nickname for Wendy's 15-month-old son, Todd.

When Wendy called out for the youngster, she received no answer. Walker suddenly realized that she had left the sliding glass door to the pool open. When she pulled back the cover, they found the boy at the bottom of the deep end.

With the help of the 911 operator, Walker and Wendy administered CPR and got one gasp before the ambulance arrived. They were afraid it was Todd's last. But after the rescue workers slit his little arm for a blood oxygen count, out came a faint but blessed cry.

Todd was airlifted to Holmes Regional Medical Center in Melbourne, then taken on to Arnold Palmer Hospital for Children and Women in Orlando. He was kept restrained for two days. When he woke up he looked at the red lights on the instruments in his hospital room and said "Hot." The family sighed in relief, realizing there was no brain damage.

Mr. Todd is now taking swimming lessons.

THE HEALED HEART

Doyle Whipkey of Palm Bay had experienced a heart attack and was scheduled for a heart catheterization the week she went to Sunday worship service at a Dayton, Ohio, church.

In the middle of the sermon, the pastor stopped preaching and stated that someone in the sanctuary needed a prayer for healing.

The minister asked for that person to stand. Whipkey said to herself, "What have I got to lose?" and stood up. As the pastor began to pray, Whipkey felt a warm glow flow from her head, down through her body, clear to her feet.

At the time, Whipkey says she did not know what the sensation meant. It wasn't until the doctor who performed her heart catheterization days later told her there was nothing wrong with her heart. He actually asked her why she was scheduled for the procedure in the first place.

Today she is able to do anything a 69-year-old can do.

A MALL MIRACLE

R.J. Van Vonderen summed up his miracle into one sentence:

"Last fall, my wife and mother-in-law went shopping at Burdines in the Melbourne Square mall . . . neither of them bought a thing."

REAL ESTATE MIRACLE

Helen Pirson of Barefoot Bay and her late husband, Wallace, owned a summer home in Franklin, N.C., 2,400 feet up the side of Gold Mountain.

Then Wallace suffered a severe heart attack that forced them to put the house on the market. Unfortunately, almost nothing in the area was selling at the time, and properties that did sell went for far below the market value.

While praying and meditating, Helen visualized a huge sold banner across the front of the house. Then something moved her to place an ad in Melbourne's *The Little Paper*.

The day after it ran, a Palm Bay woman called for details.

By the end of the telephone call, the deal was basically done.

"I never read the ads in *The Little Paper*, but it was on my desk and I skimmed through it while on hold on the telephone," the woman told Pirson. "I want your property. I'll send you a cashier's check for $1,000 as a binder, and you'll have it by Monday."

Both the Pirsons and their friends were stunned—no one buys property sight unseen.

The next Monday morning, sure enough, a postal truck came up Gold Mountain, but it didn't deliver a check for $1,000. Instead, the Pirsons were handed one for $3,000.

Meanwhile, Wallace Pirson's health was failing fast. The buyer had said she would be up in three weeks, but after hearing of his condition, she came the next weekend.

The deal eventually was closed a mere 12 days after the ad appeared. To her family, Pirson says, this was a miracle.

A TRIO OF MIRACLES

Barbara Kreher of Palm Bay says she has experienced three miracles in her lifetime.

When Kreher's daughter Caroline was a teenager, she developed a pain behind her eye. Because one of Kreher's brothers had died of brain cancer, she immediately took Caroline to a doctor, who took X rays and found a growth.

The young woman, who was in intense pain, was scheduled for a spinal tap in Orlando. Shortly after they checked into the hospital room, a cheerful group of women dressed like the good fairies from Disney's "Sleeping Beauty" entered.

"We're from the Episcopal Church here," they told them. "We read on the card that your family is Episcopalian, so we've come to pray with Caroline. You can both go home. We'll take over now."

The women were so positive that Kreher and her husband had no problems leaving Caroline in their hands.

The next morning, the spinal tap showed nothing of a foreign nature behind Caroline's eye. And the Krehers have the before and after X rays to compare.

Miracle No. 2: Kreher was outside her home in a Connecticut subdivision with her children when her son Jonathan, then a baby, crawled into the usually quiet road. In the distance, a truck was heading straight toward Jonathan, and the driver wasn't paying attention.

Kreher's heart was in her mouth. She was running faster than she ever had run in her life. Jonathan giggled, thinking it was a game, and crawled toward the truck's path even faster.

Suddenly, a man in a car leaned on his horn, causing the truck driver to veer into the grass away from Jonathan.

"What a miracle," the car driver said. "I wasn't supposed to come home for lunch today, but something was pulling me back here."

Miracle No. 3: Kreher's children and her former husband had packed up to travel from Melbourne to Connecticut in the World War II trainer plane he owned.

During the trip, Kreher's husband told her over the intercom: "I'm not going to land at the airport below. I'm going on to the next one."

Right after Kreher settled down for some more riding in the clouds, she heard a "voiceless voice" that clearly stated: "You do not have enough gas."

Sure enough, the plane ran out of gas on the final approach to an airport in South Carolina. They had to glide in and land on a highway. On the way down, they chopped down a tree. The airplane was totaled, but Kreher and her family walked away without a scratch.

Since childhood, Kreher has believed in guardian angels. Today she says she always will believe a gigantic hand reached out and made a glide slope to safely bring the plane down.

SOURCE IDEAS FOR PERSONAL EXPERIENCE ARTICLES

These are some of the most commonly used sources to write about the personal experiences of others and personal experiences of your own:

Researching the Experiences of Others
>Other newspapers, magazines, and newsletters
>Civil and criminal court files
>Radio and television talk shows
>Neighbors and friends
>History books
>Local museums and schools

Your Own Experiences
>Family albums
>School yearbooks
>Observation
>Notebooks, diaries, or logbooks
>Home movies and videotapes
>Conversations with family and friends

"Miracles do make you humble, and for that, one's perceptions about things alter for the better"—Margarete Miller, Melbourne Beach. (p. 1D) Reprinted with permission of *Florida Today*.

USING THE FIRST-PERSON APPROACH

Like travel writing, personal experience features are often written in first person. When you are telling a story that you have experienced yourself, it is often easier to write about it in first person. In assistant managing editor David Hamilton's feature for *Newsday* (1985), he wrote about the changes his own family experienced when it got its first personal computer. Rather than take a detached third-person perspective, he chose to write in first person and discussed how the new machine affected mom, dad, and the children. Using pronouns such as "I," "we," and "our," Hamilton lets the world know how his "family user group," as he called it, became high tech. In addition to describing the individual reactions, Hamilton also provided a list of "useful tricks" for other families that have recently acquired, or might consider acquiring, a PC. Here's how he used personal pronouns and his own experience to describe the decision to get the computer:

> But we are an optimistic group, ever bent on progress, and so we emerged from the decision huddle vowing that the interest and need of each family member would ensure their care and concern. Yes, we cannot always manage to put the cheese away and close the refrigerator door in a single trip to the kitchen, but no we would not neglect the instrument our 3-year-old dubbed, importantly, the "the 'puter." I'm here to testify that we've done about as well as might have been expected. (p. 3)

This story gives us a very real look at a family situation that many readers can easily identify with throughout the article.

The key to deciding whether to tell a personal experience story in first or third person is whether you believe that you, as the writer "I," should be a major component of the story. In David Hamilton's case, and in the case of many of the other examples we have discussed in this chapter, it was critical to the success of the feature story. You should also remember that when writing a personal experience story from someone else's experience, the best writing approach is third person. Taking a first-person approach is only confusing to the reader if your byline is on the article and someone else is really telling the story.

PROFESSIONAL'S POINT OF VIEW

John Mack Carter
Good Housekeeping

To my way of thinking, the personal experience feature is the core of magazine journalism, one of the hallmarks that sets us apart from the news media. In one form or another—the first person article, the case history, anecdotes, nostalgia—I consider personal experience the most important part of the mix of features in *Good Housekeeping*. In *Good Housekeeping*, these articles may take any of 10 different formats:

1.*The exclusive celebrity interview.* Two examples of this type of article that we've run in *GH*: "My 12 Years with Prince Charles" by Stephen Barry and "Diana's Life as a Wife, Princess and Mother."

2. *Crime and suspense.* Two examples:

"Shattered Night," the trial of the wife of a famous heart surgeon who, after suffering years of physical and psychological abuse, shot and killed her husband.

"Who Killed Patricia Gilmore?" This young woman was killed by her former boyfriend after the authorities failed to take his threats seriously.

3. *Weight-loss stories.* We look for new but sound breakthroughs on weight-loss products, techniques, or diets. An example: "I Lost 100 Pounds Through Hypnosis."

4. *A miracle or legal first.* Two examples:

"A New Life for My Joi." This is the story of the first pancreas transplant as a treatment for severe diabetes.

"The 14 Million Dollar Woman." Story of Dorothy Thompson, who initiated and won a landmark antidiscrimination suit against the U.S. government.

5. *A woman's personal courage triumphs over a difficult challenge.* Example:

"Alice Williams' Impossible Dream." Inspiring story of how a sharecropper's daughter, the only one among her siblings to graduate high school, managed to put her own 11 children through college.

6. *A provocative issue.* Examples:

"Doctors and Rape." The trial of a young nurse who accused three doctors of raping her.

"Malpractice." A doctor and expert witness opens his casebook on malpractice suits, some of which have made medical and legal history.

7. *Personal stories of medical oddities.* Examples:

"I Froze to Death—But Lived." A young girl, caught in a Minnesota blizzard, was frozen literally as stiff as a board—but much to her doctor's amazement, she recovered fully.

"My Heart Stopped While My Baby Was Being Born." Doctors thought there was a high probability that neither Laura Spitler nor her baby would survive—but they both beat the odds.

8. *Unique family lifestyle.* Examples:

"A Very Different Kind of Family." A fascinating glimpse into what it was like growing up in a polygamous Mormon household with 47 brothers and sisters.

"His, Mine . . . Ours." What happened when a mother of two married a widower with four—and got his former mother-in-law as well.

9. *The brief, personal, nostalgic essay.* Examples:

"A Spoonful of Love." The precious gifts passed down from mother to daughter.

"Watch Out, Great Grandma is Coming . . ." An anecdotal tale of multigenerational life.

10. *A woman's problem and how she solves it.* Examples:

"My Husband Was a Tightwad."

"I Fell in Love With My Doctor." (personal communication, 1993)

John Mack Carter is editor-in-chief of *Good Housekeeping* magazine, a position he has held with Hearst Magazines in New York since 1975. He was honored in 1990 with the Henry Johnson Fisher Award from the Magazine Publishers of America—the industry's highest honor—for his lifetime achievement. It is the magazine industry's highest honor. In 1990–1991, Carter served as president of the American Society of Magazine Editors. He has also been director of magazine development for Hearst Corporation since 1979. Under his direction, *Country Living* and *Victoria* magazines were created. *Victoria* has been categorized as the most successful launch in the history of Hearst Magazines. In 1989, his magazine won a National Magazine Award in the Special Interest Category. He formerly edited two other major women's magazines—*Ladies' Home Journal* and *McCall's*. He was also editor-in-chief and chairman of *American Home* and *American Home Crafts*, as well as associate editor of *Better Homes & Gardens*. He is the former host of the cable television program, "Good Housekeeping's Better Way." Yet he still finds time to write. He produces a monthly column on the magazine industry for *Adweek*, and has done so for the past 9 years.

14

Writing Humor in Feature Articles

The market for high-quality prose humor is always strong. Truly funny and creative writers can just about fill in the blanks on their own paychecks for full-time work or free-lance assignments. Some publications in the United States specialize in humor, but most simply use it along with other content. Some magazines and newspapers use humor as spot features; others use it as a regular item in columns or departments. Still others will use humor only as fill material. Regardless, if you have an eye and ear for funny stories, and if you have an ability to express things in a humorous way, humor might be a potential specialization for you.

To be successful as a humorist—as Dave Barry, the late Lewis Grizzard, Garrison Keillor, Alice Kahn, Roy Blount, Jr., Art Buchwald, Erma Bombeck, or James Lileks have been—requires a combination of keen wit, hard work, and a little luck. These are some of America's best contemporary humorists:

- *The Miami Herald's* Dave Barry, winner of a Pulitzer Prize for his satirical commentary, is syndicated by Tribune Media Services and Knight-Ridder/Tribune News Service and is the author of numerous best-selling humor books about working, traveling, children, and health. His unusual, distinctive approach to ordinary topics is part of what has made him popular.
- The *Atlanta Constitution's* Lewis Grizzard was the author of numerous books about life in the South and was widely read across the country. He took many of his experiences from growing up in rural Georgia, as well as the people he knew as a child and young man, and turned them into stories that have delighted readers across the region and in other parts of the country.
- Garrison Keillor, perhaps best known for his work on National Public Radio, began as a writer for *New Yorker*. His stories for the "Prairie Home Companion" have entertained both theater audiences and radio audiences for many years. His books and occasional magazine features focus on the life and values of people living in mythical Lake Wobegon in Minnesota.
- The *San Francisco Chronicle's* Alice Kahn writes a humor column that is distributed by the Los Angeles Times Syndicate. She has written several books using her sarcastic view of life on the West Coast (Astor, 1988).

- Roy Blount, Jr. may be best known for his long list of books, including novels, but he is a frequent magazine writer and is a contributing editor at *Spy* magazine. Blount, a jack-of-all-writing-trades, often combines humor with sports and contributes to *Sports Illustrated*. He is also a poet, lecturer, performer, sportswriter, and dramatist.
- Art Buchwald has authored numerous best-selling books and newspaper columns satirizing politics over a long and distinguished career that includes a Pulitzer Prize for commentary. He authors a Los Angeles Times Syndicate column from his home base in Washington, D.C.
- Erma Bombeck has established a wide following for her best-selling books and humor columns that focus on motherhood, family, in-laws, children, money, and home life. Her appeal is particularly strong with women readers, but she has been popular with all readers for many years.
- James Lileks writes his twice-weekly column for the Newhouse News Service and the New York Times News Service. Based in Washington, D.C., he focuses on politics and American culture.

Most writing experts say that humor is among the toughest types of writing to master. Because humor writing has this reputation, few people try it and, of course, even fewer succeed. Such success requires basic hard work. Yes, you have to have something funny to say, but you must also have the wide-ranging experiences and unique perspective to make it work. Hollywood writer Larry Wilde (1976) says humor writers are "hypersensitive, indulgent, indefatigable, disciplined, sentimental, highly intelligent, and well-educated individuals. Their influence on society is immeasurable. They are the word-picture painters, word coiners, phrase makers, colloquial-expression designers of our times" (p. 6).

Among periodical and book publishers, humor can be big business, too. There is intense competition for the truly successful humor writers and editors, and publishers are constantly searching for new voices with talent. Many humor writers start with small publications and work up to major newspapers and magazines and then to book authoring. However, some humor writers begin their careers as stand-up comics and then try their hand at writing. American writing has a rich tradition of writers with an ability to entertain and make readers laugh. "From Artemus Ward and Mark Twain to James Thurber and Peter De Vries, American popular literature has been plentifully supplied with humorists," writes *Publishers Weekly's* Robert A. Carter (1990). "And in publishing there's no doubt that humor is a serious business" (p. 24). Much of the success of both a writer and the publisher depends on luck and timing, many experts say. "More than any other genre, humor is a fragile contraption. Tricked out in cartoons, amusing essays, or cheeky one-liners, what's funny to one person is stupid, offensive or utterly mystifying to another," Robert Dahlin (1992, p. 23) wrote in *Publishers Weekly*. The author, however, not the subject, ultimately sells humor, Dahlin rightly observes.

This chapter cannot teach you everything about humor writing. In fact, entire books are devoted to this subject (for example, see Gene Perret's *How to Write and Sell (Your Sense of) Humor*, Writer's Digest Books). However, this chapter shows you the basic elements of writing funny stories, columns, and other material. Although humor can be both fiction and nonfiction, spoken or written, the chapter's focus is on written nonfiction. This chapter discusses formulas that make writers such as syndicated newspaper and magazine humorist Dave Barry, who won the 1988 Pulitzer Prize for his humorous commentary, so successful. Although you might not become an Erma Bombeck or an Art Buchwald, you will learn about writing briefs and brights as well as the longer humor columns and articles. You will see how proven humorists have built their reputations—one funny word at a time.

WHAT IS HUMOR?

What is funny to you? Or to someone else? Is there a difference? One dictionary says humor is a person's disposition or temperament, sort of a state of mind. *Webster's New World Dictionary* defines humor as whim or fancy. Then it adds, well into the definition, "the quality that makes something seem funny, amusing, or ludicrous; comicality . . . the ability to perceive, appreciate, or express what is funny . . . ."

Scholars have been studying humor since the days of the Greek philosophers. Humor takes many different forms. As a writer, your humor can be jokes, brief fillers, quips, sketches, essays, columns, or even a more traditional feature article. Humor remains an elusive concept and there still is no agreement on how humor should be defined. The bottom line is simple enough—what is humorous is different to each individual. Humor historians Walter Blair and Hamlin Hill (1978) put it this way: "[L]aughter is a highly subjective response. So writers who are foolhardy enough to discuss the humor which does or doesn't produce it are an endangered species" (p. vii).

J. Kevin Wolfe (1990), a producer for radio personality Gary Burbank in Cincinnati, says there are two keys to good humor. He argues that people laugh at two different things: surprises and misfortune of others. "We laugh in *surprise* at the union of two things that don't fit together, such as the Pope skateboarding. Surprise humor leads you in one direction and then takes a sharp turn," he notes (p. 19). "We also laugh at people's *misfortunes*: of the rich and famous, of the poor and ethnic, of living where you do, of being yourself. This type of humor has a butt. Think of jokes you've heard recently. Who did they slam?" Another point Wolfe makes is that humorists often combine surprise and misfortune. Surprise can be a misfortune and misfortune can be a surprise. Many comedy performers, cartoonists, and humor writers employ this strategy, he observes.

DRAWING HUMOROUS IDEAS FROM REAL LIFE

Some of the funniest stories we find to write about are not made up. When we hear or read one, it might seem as if some very creative person just thought it up, but the best is what happens on a daily basis. Just keep yourself on alert for the possibilities.

Political humorist Mark Russell, perhaps best known for his television performances for Public Broadcasting System stations and live performances around the nation, also writes a syndicated humor column and occasional magazine articles. His political humor is based entirely on what is happening in Washington and other power centers of the nation. Although he lives in Buffalo, Russell says he reads the *New York Times*, *Washington Post*, and *Wall Street Journal* to keep up with current events and to find ideas for his material. "It's almost too easy, when you've got Congress, the White House and both political parties writing the material," Russell explains (Belcher, 1988, p. 1F).

Like Mark Russell, syndicated columnist Art Buchwald uses the daily newspaper for most of his ideas. A new Buchwald column, usually about 600 words, begins when he reads the newspaper. Often he will see something he will file away for later use. Then he looks for the news peg for whatever idea he has filed away—in other words a reason for writing about that subject. Then he writes. He repeats this process three times a week, or more than 150 times a year.

Longtime humor columnist Erma Bombeck has built her highly successful writing career on her own experiences. She writes about the common elements of marriage and family. Her readers can easily identify with her topics within that broader range of domestic life subjects. Bombeck, who lives in Arizona, has been writing her column since 1965. She began with an Ohio weekly newspaper, the *Kettering-Oakwood Times*. The formula for her success is writing about husbands who are not perfect, children who are not always a pleasure to be around, and the notion that home owning is often torture. She writes what many people think, and she writes it in an entertaining fashion. Bombeck appeals to women in particular. She frequently describes everyday experiences common to many Americans managing homes and families—such mundane things as laundry and stopped-up plumbing—and makes them entertaining subjects about which to read (Brodeur, 1993).

Humor writer Mary Ognibene (1975) says her humorous articles are based on her own experiences. "The only humor I can write is based on the idea that every dumb thing that happens to me also happens to everybody else. I add a little exaggeration and the formula seems to work," she explains (p. 1).

Some writers feel that finding ideas is the most demanding part of the job of the humor writer. That's how humor columnist Richard Benedetto (1975) sees things. "The hardest part of column writing is coming up with ideas. I pound the pavement and stay awake nights trying to find them. And once one is selected, I begin to worry about the next one. Readers, colleagues and friends often offer suggestions, which are sometimes used," he says (p. 5).

Lewis Grizzard's humor columns and books stem from his own experiences in Georgia. They focus on family members, his dogs, his former family members (such as his three former wives), life in the South, landlords, neighbors, religion, relationships, Northerners, politics, and much more. He tells short anecdotes and long stories. But he bases his material on what he sees and hears.

New Orleans Times-Picayune columnist Angus Lind also uses real stories but has even advertised for humorous stories from readers. His strategy works because his readers call—even long distance—to tell him of their experiences. Lind uses the best material for his column.

Similarly, syndicated humor columnist James Lileks comments about politics. He jokingly says, "I love the opportunity to be one of the more incoherent political voices out there" (Lamb, 1993, p. 35). Lileks grew up in South Dakota and went to school at the University of Minnesota. He began writing for an alternative weekly and then moved to the *St. Paul Pioneer Press.* He characterizes himself as an essayist, and he frequently uses satire to make his point.

David Blum, a contributing editor who writes the Fun City humor column for *New York* magazine, devoted one of his columns to a tongue-in-cheek explanation of where he gets his ideas for his essays. Blum (1990) says he depends on his friends:

> One way I come up with ideas for columns is to bribe my friends. The arrangement I have worked out is this:
>
> If a friend comes up with a fully formed notion for a column that meets with my editor's approval, he (or she) gets a steak lunch at Sparks. The only restriction is that he may not make me feel bad by using witty euphemisms throughout the lunch, like "That was a tasty piece of cow flesh" or "I'm in the mood to do the horizontal hula."
>
> If a friend's idea leads me to a column but isn't an idea in itself, then he does not get the lunch.
>
> If the friend says something funny that I use in a column as my own joke, then I tell him I will buy him lunch, but when the check comes, I tell him that I'd had the same idea myself . . . .(p. 30)

Funny writing often takes advantage of unusual and ordinary experiences coming from a variety of directions. Journalism professor Shirley Biagi (1981) says humor writing depends on a writer's ability to form images and word pictures, along with the surprise or unexpected finish or resolution of the story. The strategy keys on building up to the end by taking a small step at a time to tell the story, allowing momentum to grow. By using a combination of little jokes, she says, you can then break the punch line.

J. Kevin Wolfe (1990) suggests there are four elements in telling humorous stories used by humorists ranging from Mark Twain to Dave Barry. These elements are a funny opening, colorful narration, colorful characters, and a concise plot. Tom Ladwig (1987), writing for the daily *Columbia Missourian*, simply told a funny story and let situations in the story do the job. The story was based on a series of incidents involving a Missouri couple who took a trip filled with strange, but true, incidents and coincidences. As Ladwig tells the story, it becomes increasingly funny from the first step to the conclusion. And it is quite entertaining reading. His eye for a good story and his ability to retell it won Ladwig first place in the 1987 humorous column category of the National Newspaper Association writing contest. This is Ladwig's story:

This story is intended for those among us who think we've had a bad day.

It doesn't seem to have one whit of historical significance, but it is a story that probably will be told and retold.

Adam (not his real name) is a man of the cloth. He and his wife were missionaries for many years, and he now teaches in a bible college in southeast Missouri.

For the first time in many years, they have weekends free. To enjoy them more, Adam purchased a small pickup and had a camper shell installed. They explore the Ozarks and occasionally help a fellow minister when he needs a Sunday off.

They filled in for a colleague one Sunday last summer. They started home early Monday and passed one of those tourist attractions where you see all sorts of wild animals in a pseudo-natural setting.

It was early, and it seemed like fun so they drove in. After buying their tickets they saw all the animals they wanted to see from the safety of their pickup camper.

As they neared the end of the road, they found a huge elephant standing in the middle. Adam, a calm man, edged the truck closer. The elephant didn't budge. Adam edged closer.

Possibly patience and prayer would have worked better, but Adam honked. The elephant did move. It sat down, right on the hood of the truck.

The rear end of the camper went into air and Adam, now in desperation, honked and honked. The proprietors came and sent the elephant keeper who finally convinced his charge to leave.

Of course the management arranged for the damage to be repaired and left Adam their business card with the insurance firm's telephone number. The motor still ran and Adam decided to limp home.

They had driven about 20 miles on the four-lane when they passed a wrecked car. Seeing there were other travelers assisting they drove on.

Four miles down the road, a highway patrol car approached and as it came abeam, wheeled across the median and flagged them down with siren and lights.

The trooper approached and told Adam he was investigating a hit-and-run accident a few miles back and asked Adam how his truck came to be damaged.

Adam said: "Officer, you're not going to believe this. An elephant sat on my hood." The trooper said: "You're right, I don't believe it. Get out."

It took a while for Adam's story to check out, The trooper, a 20-year veteran, still shaking his head in disbelief, told them they were free to go.

By this time Adam's head ached. He asked his wife to drive while he rested in the camper. They made good progress. Adam's wife made a rest stop at a service station. Adam awakened and decided this was a good idea.

When Adam returned he found the camper gone, his wife obviously thinking him still asleep in the camper. He walked to the highway and sat on the curb to plot his next move. While there, the same patrolman drove by. Seeing Adam, he stopped and asked: "What now?"

Adam explained. The trooper said he was going toward Adam's hometown and could drop him off. They took off and somehow arrived before Adam's wife and the pickup camper.

It was still daylight, and Adam, the keys to the house still in the truck, thanked the trooper and said he would just sit and wait.

It wasn't but a few minutes before Mrs. A turned into the drive.

As she approached the house, she caught sight of Adam waving from the porch. She jerked her head violently back toward the camper. And while in the position, her battered pickup slammed through the garage door.

Fortunately, Adam's wife was not injured. And nothing unusual happened to Adam and his wife for the remainder of that day. Or since for that matter. (p. 20) Reprinted with the permission of the *Columbia Missourian*.

MAJOR HUMOR WRITING TECHNIQUES

The market for humor is ready and waiting for copy such as Ladwig's funny story because it is entertaining and an escape for readers from their day-to-day concerns. The pay for humor writing is not so bad, either—some magazines pay $100 to $400 per item for brights and more for longer pieces. Topically, however, most publications do not want off-color or sexist humor. Taking shots at others, such as telling ethnic jokes, is not welcomed much by contemporary mainstream publications, either. So, a smart professional humor writer will stay away from these out-of-favor subjects and approaches.

Humorist Patrick McManus, author of books and articles, offers four major tips for writing short (up to 1,500 words) humor. First, he says the idea should be covered by *a single theme*. Second, *develop the characters* in the story. Third, *list the bits of humor*—the jokes, in other words—you can fit into your prescribed length in words. And fourth, *start writing and rewrite frequently*. Concentrate on the lead, because it is often the hardest part. But McManus says you should make it funny to alert readers that the piece will be funny. He then

then recommends using exaggeration, but it should be appropriate exaggeration (Finley, 1988).

The best humor writers employ 10 standard tools in writing humor. These are satire, parody, exaggeration, contrast, understatement, asides, irony, grammatical and typographic emphasis, puns, and logic-internal consistency. These assist humor writers in achieving their goal of entertaining readers.

Satire

Writers often ridicule a subject's vices, excesses, abuses, follies, or stupidities. This is *satire*. This form of criticism is perhaps one of the most widely used in contemporary humor writing. When someone prominent is caught in the act, perhaps drinking a little too much, using an illegal drug, or otherwise breaking the rules, and the story is reported in a serious way, it does not take long before humorists take the victim's mistakes as fair material for their writing. Satire often becomes the approach used to criticize a gun-toting leading citizen who takes a position for gun control, for example. Portraying the individual as using his weapon to protect himself against overly aggressive children who want their weekly allowances might get the point across.

Even the news magazines will use satire for some of their feature items. Recently *Newsweek* ran a "Newsmakers" department that made fun of a decision made by editors at *Sports Illustrated*. This is how they worded the item (*Newsweek* staff, 1993):

> Even in the summer, Canadian soccer teams don't usually play in the buff—yet there they are, 11 burly members of the semipro Richmond Hill Kick, naked from the ankles up. Of course they're only posing for an Adidas uniforms ad. Scheduled to run in Sports Illustrated's new Canadian edition, the eye-catching photo was iced at the last minute by SI editors in New York. Were these perpetuators of the sexy SI swimsuit issues flinching at a bit of beefcake? "Such a comparison," declared SI spokesman Roger Jackson, "is a matter of apples and oranges. Or, perhaps, bananas and oranges." (p. 49)

Dave Barry often uses satire in his column. One recent example made fun of a mid-1990s literary trend. He pokes fun at novels by lawyers, such as those by John Grisham and Scott Turow, and the amazing popularity such "blockbuster legal thrillers" enjoy. Barry not only satirizes the mystery genre, but he also takes shots at the people who read such books. His article was actually a mininovel satire structured as Grisham might write one of his books. Ultimately, Barry takes all attorneys to task for their inability to communicate effectively in writing. Barry (1993) produced his own "blockbuster legal thriller" for his loyal readers. Here is how it began:

> "Ohhhhhhh," she cried out. "OOOHMIGOD."

> "I'm sorry," I said, "but that's my standard hourly fee."

Like most people, I can always use an extra $7 or $8 million, which is why today I have decided to write a blockbuster legal thriller.

Americans buy legal thrillers by the ton. I was in many airports over the past few months, and I got the impression that aviation authorities were making this announcement over the public-address system: "FEDERAL REGULATIONS PROHIBIT YOU FROM BOARDING A PLANE UNLESS YOU ARE CARRYING *THE CLIENT* BY JOHN GRISHAM." I mean, everybody had this book. ("This is the captain speaking. We'll be landing in Seattle instead of Detroit because I want to finish *The Client*.")

The ironic thing is that best-selling legal thrillers generally are written by lawyers, who are not famous for written communication. I cite as Exhibit A my own attorney, Joseph DiGiacinto, who is constantly providing me with shrewd advice that I cannot understand because Joe has taken the legal precaution of translating it into Martian . . . . (p. 27)

Barry uses also satire in his account of a lunch date with Sophia Loren. Barry got to take his peek at the world of the rich and famous and told his readers about it. He uses satire—he makes fun of himself by writing that he was "working" when he lunched with the movie star (and a lot of other people). He satirizes the lifestyle of the luxury residential complex that the luncheon event and Loren promoted. He pokes fun at the free food and champagne, the high prices of the exclusive apartments, the press kit descriptions, and even the press itself. When it comes time for him to ask her a question, he asks her about cockroaches in her own luxury apartment at the complex. Here's Barry's (1986) entire article:

My original plan was not to have lunch with Sophia Loren. My original plan was to eat a chicken salad sandwich, then go pick up my son at kindergarten. In fact, I had actually purchased the chicken salad sandwich at The Miami Herald cafeteria when a person in the Business Section asked me if I wanted to have lunch with Sophia Loren. "Sure," I said. This kind of thing happens all the time in the news game.

So I called my wife. "Could you pick up Robby?" I asked. "I'm going to go have lunch with Sophia Loren."

"Sure," she said, in a sweet and kind and totally understanding voice. She will get even.

The reason I was invited to lunch with Sophia Loren was that she was promoting something. Somebody is always promoting something in the news business, and it is our job, as communications professionals, to go and find out what it is, even if this means eating a lot of free food. In this case, Sophia Loren was promoting something up in North Dade called "Williams Island," which, according to the press packet, is "a luxury, 80-acre island resort residence community on protected waters just off the Intracoastal Waterway." It's very nice. I would recommend

Williams Island as a potential residence for anybody, whether he had $250 million or just $245 million.

No, seriously, the brochure says they have "residential offerings" there starting at a very affordable $180,000, which I bet you could round up just by walking around and picking up the money that blows off the balconies of the nicer units. One of those units is occupied, when she's in town, by world-famous raving-beauty movie actress Sophia Loren, who also does promotional work for them in exchange for money. (Yes! Even Sophia Loren!)

We had lunch at the restaurant on Williams Island, the Island Club. They have a new kind of Very Trendy food there called "tapas," which also was being promoted. According to Richard Lamondin, director of marketing and sales for Williams Island, "The Tapas Experience is now one of the North American rages."

So we media people all sat down at our assigned tables and had the Tapas Experience, which consists of eating things off little plates. I thought they were great, except this one plate that I swear to God had a small dead octopus on it. Probably it was a prank. Probably back in the kitchen, they said: "Look what Lester found in the protected waters just off the Intracoastal Waterway! Yuck! Let's see if the news media will eat it, because it's free food!"

After the Tapas Experience, they served us lamb chops, during which Sophia Loren herself came over to our table and sat down to chat with us personally. You ladies have heard, of course, that Sophia Loren is very, very beautiful, especially for a woman of 51, but let me tell you something: When she is up close, when you really get a look at her, she is Beyond Perfect. I'm sorry, ladies, but there you have it. Genetics. If it makes you feel any better, there is probably some area in which you are superior to Sophia Loren, such as playing the accordion.

So after we had just looked at her for a minute, we asked her some questions. This is where I would hate to be a famous movie actress, because she got asked, for example: "Is there any message you would want to give to the women of the world?" Think about that. There you are, trying to eat your lamb chop, and you have to come up with a message for the women of the world. I know if it was me, I'd blow it. I'd say something like, "Well, they should floss their teeth." But Sophia Loren, she was very poised. She said she felt the women of the world should be Generous. She came up with that right off the top of her head.

I had given careful thought to what question I would ask her. I wanted it to be the kind of question you, my readers, would want to ask in the astoundingly unlikely event you ever had a personal lunch with Sophia Loren.

"Have you found any large insects in your apartment?" I asked.

"Insects?" she said.

"Cockroaches," I said. "They get huge down here." I held my hands about a foot apart so she'd get the idea.

"Not yet," she said.

So there you have it: an exclusive interview with the lovely Miss Sophia Loren at her South Florida residence, the luxurious and cockroach-free Williams Island. If you want my opinion, you all should head over there as soon as possible and try the tapas and maybe purchase yourself a residence offering. And I don't say this just because they gave me a lot of free food. I say this because they also gave me champagne. (p. 1B) Reprinted with permission of Dave Barry.

Spy magazine often uses satire and other devices for its irreverent and entertaining writing. Here is how *Spy* (1993) magazine introduced a summer movie preview guide for readers:

For as long as there have been summers, for as long as there have been movies, for as long as *hot* has also meant "fab," there have been hot summer movies. But only in the last couple of years has there been a new genre of hot summer movie: the super-hot summer movie that goes instantly stone-cold dead if opening weekend grosses don't top $25 million, a phenomenon that baffles even the studios' top physicists. And only *this* year has there been a completely alien and freshly malevolent addition to the hot-summer-movie experience: the SPY Hot-Summer-Movie Guide.

Unlike hot-summer-movie guides you will be eagerly poring over in *Premiere*, *Entertainment Weekly*, *People*, *Us*, *Time*, *Newsweek*, *The New York Times* and your local shopper, only the SPY Hot-Summer-Movie Guide appears in SPY magazine. Only the SPY guide allows you to directly compare hot summer movies, telling you which films contain precocious imps, shiny helicopters, already-boring morphing, or child-satiating dinosaurs. Only the SPY guide has the pomo decon DramaGram (TM), a consumer-friendly contrivance that outlines plot devices and stock characters in an easy-to-follow, formal logic equation based on Boolean operators. (For God's sake, don't just stare at the word; look it up.) And finally, only the SPY guide was put together with virtually no cooperation from studio publicity departments, guaranteeing you that the information presented herein will be inaccurate in ways other than the producers intended. (pp. 32–34)

Parody

Parody is another one of the trendy humor approaches of the 1990s. Subjects vary widely, but parodies are popular with contemporary readers. Parody is the best approach for some humor. At times, there is an opportunity to imitate the style of an individual, place, object, or institution. This is basic parody. To do parody well, you must study the subject about which you plan to write. Popular subjects in recent years have been preppies, yuppies, entire publications such as magazines, and various ethnic groups. Once you have mastered the characteristic style of the subject, you take a nonsensical approach to the subject. This works best with serious subjects such as political leaders or revered institutions. For example, a local humor columnist might use parody to write about a local public official who has made a bad political decision or squandered public resources. *Spy*, *National Lampoon*, and *Mad* magazines have used parodies for many years with great success.

Writer Larry Tritten (1993) parodied several genres of fiction when he wrote an article for *Writer's Digest*. He discussed "the nuances of personality and behavior that a writer in a particular genre might feel compelled to affect" (p. 80). Here is Tritten's advice to people who wish to become mystery writers:

> Think of your pseudonym as an alias. Watch *America's Most Wanted* to get story ideas. Know what a MacGuffin is and use plenty of them. Refer to your dust jacket photo as a mug shot. Insist on fingerprinting your agent. Wonder what Nancy Drew would have thought of Kinsey Millhone. Make your own Christmas cards using a series of cut and paste letters. Have an aunt who won the Miss Marple Look-Alike Contest. When you autograph books, use a code or cipher for the inscriptions. When you can't find your keys, calm down and consider the situation in the manner of Poirot or Holmes. Hang out with retired safe crackers, ex-cops, hookers and crooked lawyers. Win an Edgar and a Raven, but don't be satisfied until you also have a Gold Dagger. If you write spy novels, mourn the end of the Cold War. If you get low advances for your novels, consider using your ideas to commit real crimes. (p. 80)

Exaggeration

In telling funny stories, a useful technique is *exaggeration*—to enlarge, distort, and overemphasize to make a point. Although the size of the cockroach on your kitchen table might not be quite equal to that of your Irish setter, it makes the point better when you stretch the fact a little. This emphasizes your perspective and conveys to readers that the insect in your kitchen really did scare you into jumping onto a chair and causing you to cry out for help. Remember that when you make a point using a technique like exaggeration, you make a promise with readers to have a reason for it. Exaggeration and overstatement for nothing more than the purpose of overstating often do not work.

Exaggeration can be used on yourself as a subject also. Writer William P. Holton (1993) took himself to task for his bad work habits. He amusingly described in a column for *Writer's Digest* how he made up answers "that stretch the truth" when his wife would call him from her job to ask how his writing at his home office was going (p. 6). Rather than tell her the truth about his writer's block, how he had not managed to finish (or even start) his household chores, and how he had nothing to show for a day's effort, he made his effort seem like more than it was. He uses a "What I say" and "What I'm actually doing" approach. Here's three examples of his technique:

What I say: I'm cleaning up a few odds and ends.

What I'm actually doing: Disassembling my five-box paper-clip chain because I want to try my hand at the tricky, tri-clip braid.

What I say: I'm conducting some research.

What I'm actually doing: Flipping the dial between *Donahue, Oprah,* and *Geraldo.*

What I say: I'm just finishing up a chapter.

What I'm actually doing: I'm three quarters of the way through the latest Stephen King opus . . . .(p. 6).

Columnist Art Buchwald, whose columns appear in several hundred newspapers each week, also uses exaggeration in his humorous commentary on political and other national issues. In the following column, Buchwald (1993) makes a series of exaggerated statements about airline frequent flyer programs and their financial status:

EVERY TIME that you see an aviation executive on television, he's crying poverty. All the airlines are losing money and nobody knows why. I do. Just this morning I received my latest frequent flyer accounting statement. For taking three flights to Newark, I was entitled to five free trips around the world or one business-class seat on the next space shuttle from Cape Canaveral.

Apparently, there's nothing you do today that does not entitle you to a free airline ticket. When I opened the frequent flyer envelope, all sorts of colored coupons fell out informing me how I could build up airline mileage. If I used Purina dog food, it would go into the computer. If I stayed in a hotel, I would get points for just sleeping there. If I used my microwave to heat up a can of chicken soup, I could get a round-trip ticket to visit Aunt Milly in Hawaii.

The airlines seem to be the only industry that gives away the very commodity that it's supposed to be selling.

Jay McKenzie, the marketing director for Southern Freebie Airlines, is very proud of his company's free mileage policy. "Frequent flyer mileage is our way of saying thank you to all the people who take our airline—or are thinking of taking our airline in the future."

I said: "I can understand you rewarding those who fly your airline, but it doesn't make much sense to give away free trips to people who jog in Central Park."

"The airline wants to attract many people who ordinarily don't fly—teenage baby-sitters, green-card holders, people in state prisons," Jay told me. "To do this, we must persuade them that there is something in it for them. If we can provide an Orkin man and his wife with a free trip to Acapulco, we consider that we've done a good merchandising job."

"Don't all these trips cut down on your cash flow?" I asked.

Jay replied, "Admittedly, we could benefit from more profits. But once you go down the frequent flyer glide path, it's hard to turn back. The competition is always breathing down your neck. We heard that TWA is offering 20,000 miles if you watch 14 hours of basketball a week. Obviously we have to top that if we're going to stay in business."

"How do you plan to do it?"

"We're working out a deal with the iceberg-lettuce people. Every time you buy a head of lettuce, we'll credit you with 2,500 miles."

"If you're handing out free mileage for everyone, what are you using for money to keep your planes flying?"

"We're giving our mechanics 25,000 free bonus miles for every plane they fix correctly. They love the incentive and will work late into the night to earn enough to get them to Europe."

"Dare I inquire how the stockholders are doing with all the free rides?"

Jay said: "Not bad. We give them a 4,400-mile bonus for every point that the stock goes down."

"Nobody loses according to your marketing campaign."

"Aviation is something that requires special selling. If a guy knows that he can stay in a bed-and-breakfast hotel and get frequent flyer miles, he's going to sleep better. If he buys a set of golf clubs and gets a ticket to Argentina, he is ahead of the game. The next time he wants to fly somewhere, he'll take Southern Freebie Airlines."

Jay handed me a certificate.

"What is this?"

"We're crediting you with 14,000 miles for wearing a blue shirt." (p. 13A) Reprinted with permission of Art Buchwald and Los Angeles Times Syndicate.

Contrast

Contrast can also be described as incongruity. In using contrast, you establish a lack of harmony with the world; you show unreasonable and unsuitable situations. There are times when something that is expected and routine becomes something completely unexpected and nonroutine. For example, a story about a business trip that was well planned with hotel and rental car reservations, airline bookings, and other details turns into a series of humorous situations when the realities of the trip include an airline strike, a rental car breakdown, hotel reservations denied by a clerk, and just plain bad timing (for example, you finally arrive at the hotel at 11:15 p.m., hungry and tired, but find out that room service closed at 11 p.m.).

Understatement

Just like exaggeration, *understatement* works to create emphasis and reaction on the part of the reader. An intentional, softer comment will draw attention when it is contrasted with the expected. If, for example, you were referring to the real summer heat that the local readers know was 98° with 80% humidity by saying, "It was a little warm outside yesterday," then you have understated the case dramatically and no doubt drawn a reaction from your reader.

Alice Kahn, the sarcastic columnist from San Francisco, says in her columns that she adores her editors. In one column about getting writing published, she discusses the writing and editing process and the need to work with a variety of different editors. Using understatement, Kahn (1990) concludes the column: "But I'd hate to leave you with the impression that I'm down on editors. I have a very good relationship with mine. The section of the paper I write for has one contributor who is a convict in a federal penitentiary. I like to show my editor that I know my place by referring to myself as 'your other prisoner' (p. 39)."

Asides

Many humor writers like to use *asides*—short messages in parentheses or other form—to communicate with readers on a quasi-private level. This is a technique often used in acting that permits the actor to communicate only with the audience. In writing, humorists who use asides are attempting the same technique as if to privately communicate with you (and not the book's editor). Did you notice? The previous sentence contained an aside. You don't have to use parentheses all the time. Some writers prefer dashes (—) or other typographic devices to accomplish the same thing. Some writers will even use footnotes for the same effect. Dave Barry is one contemporary humorist who likes to use asides in his writing.

Irony

Similar to contrast, *irony* is a technique that employs contradictions through writing tone and subject. Irony focuses on the direct opposite of what is usual or expected. The outcome of the story is different from what is expected by readers. The distance between what happened and what should have happened or what is said and what is intended is irony. Writers using irony set up the story they tell by leading the reader to expect one type of finish through a combination of circumstances or steps involving the principals of the story. Then the reader is stunned by the opposite or inappropriate conclusion of the episode. This technique is used often in writing short humorous items known as *brights*.

Grammatical and Typographic Emphasis

Some writers will make points in their humor writing by intentionally over-using and abusing English *grammar* or *typography*. One such technique is overuse of exclamation marks (e.g., multiple exclamation marks after a word in the middle of a sentence or a string of typographic symbols such as "*@!*!#$%&!!@" to represent bad or strong language). Another is capitalizing improper nouns (e.g., a term such as Campaign Trail) used in generic references rather than specific contexts. These tricks draw reader attention to certain words and terms in an extreme fashion and help place focus where the writer wants it. Other humor writers intentionally invent words or new usages of existing words when they cannot find the right word to express their feelings or actions (e.g., the seemingly endless different ways the characters in the film "Wayne's World" referred to what doctors commonly call "regurgitation"). These diversions from the ordinary uses of grammar are functional and help writers as they tell the story.

Humorist Roy Blount, Jr. used a variety of grammatical devices in a *Sports Illustrated* spoof on the obsession some baseball fans have for statistics. Blount decided the sport of baseball did not collect certain key statistics and took the opportunity to *create* ways to compute them with a series of scientific-looking but nonsensical formulas. One example in his article focused on the overgeneralization commonly made that when a player makes an outstanding defensive play, the same player "often" leads off his team's next turn at bat. Blount (1991) amusingly argues that we should be able to calculate this, as we do just about everything else in baseball. Here is a portion of his essay for *Sports Illustrated* that explains the formula for Blount's new statistic:

> Trouble is, no one has figured out how to quantify spectacular stops, incredible throws and circus catches. In this day and age!

> Let's see. If you let g stand for ground covered, adjusted by p (position differential); and s for percentage of snow-cone effect (how much of the ball is still visible outside the glove at the moment the fielder gains control); and d for distance between the fielder's toes and spot at which they left the ground (this applies to either a leap or a dive); and t for distance of throw, if any (again adjusted by p); and a for angle of body to the ground at moment of release (which pretty well covers off-balancedness of throw)—well, I don't see why we couldn't come up with something like this: $gp+s+d+a(tp)=GP$. GP standing for Greatness of Play. (p. 133).

Puns

For many centuries, humor writers have used *puns* for a good laugh from readers. In recent years, it seems, puns have gained a bad reputation. It seems that some writers (and readers, too) feel puns are categorically bad. However, this is not the case; the use of puns may be the problem. Much of the value of the pun is in its use. A pun is a writer's device that uses plays on words to provide double meaning. One common use of puns by some contemporary humorists is in references to sex. No doubt you can think of countless puns you encounter in everyday conversation, reading, and your own writing.

Logic and Consistency

Logic is the science of correct reasoning and valid thought. Logic involves correct reasoning through induction or deduction. Some successful humor is based on its internal logic. Crazy behavior and absurd conduct by people make up much of modern American humor. But after everything else, the humorous story must maintain its internal logic. One way to do this is to begin a story with an absurd premise and keep that premise throughout the story as it is told. Related to that is internal consistency. Changing the focus in the middle of a story will often hurt it more than help it. Writer J. Kevin Wolfe (1990) calls internal logic and consistency two of the major building blocks of humor writing.

Other Humor Writing Techniques

There are other techniques humor writers use. For example, Art Buchwald likes to use dialogue in his columns, creating fictitious conversations that *might* have occurred. Dave Barry also uses conversations frequently. In fact, most humorists find dialogue to be an essential device for their writing and use it often. Stanley Bing (1992) wrote an essay for *Esquire* about the unemployment plight of middle-level corporate management in America. In the middle of his humorous essay about the paranoia over employment security that permeated corporate America at the beginning of the 1990s, Bing uses conversations with invented persons and with himself as a major humor device. At one point in the piece, he created this telephone conversation to show how quickly middle-level company managers seemed to be losing their jobs:

> First I dialed Arnette, president of the High-Speed Metal Shaving Group in Fresno. "Art!" I hollered into the phone, whose connection seemed very strange. There was a kind of whistling, as if a lunar wind were blowing in the bones of the fiber-optic line.
>
> "Mr. Arnette has left the company," said a digital voice absolutely devoid of gender.
>
> "Since this morning?" I screamed.
>
> "Mr. Arnette's business was basically a break-even operation with only moderate potential in the intermediate term," said the voice. "It has been sold to its closest competitor for good value, and Mr. Arnette has chosen to take the generous severance offer made by the company. Who may I say is calling?"
>
> I hung up. Arnette gone. At one time he was in line for a division presidency. Now he was . . . going home. (p. 46)

BRIGHTS, QUIPS, AND OTHER SHORT ITEMS

Much humor published in American newspapers, magazines, and newsletters takes the form of short, brief stories that fit in various places throughout the publication. Some newspapers like to run front-page one-line chuckles or quips and editorial page one-paragraph funny stories. Other publications incorporate such short humorous material into regular news or columns. These are collectively referred to as *brights* or *brites*.

Some publications simply use these funny feature articles as fill material when it is needed to complete a page or fill a specific space. Magazines such as *Reader's Digest* use regular humor features such as "Humor in Uniform" and "Campus Comedy" that are collections of brights about American military and college life. And they're very popular. Research at *Reader's Digest* shows these sections are among the most popular in the entire magazine. They can be lucrative also: *Reader's Digest* pays $400 and more for brights and other published short articles. These brights are typically amusing stories that offer, as writer Daniel Williamson (1975) defines them, "a humorous and unusual quirk" (p. 117). These items can come from reporters on the police beat, the courts, meetings, or from callers.

University of Houston professor Louis Alexander (1975) says the main purpose of a bright is "to change the pace and tone of the newspaper, the magazine, or the broadcast. Being so short, a brite makes a fine filler, fits anywhere to complete a page, round out the makeup of a section or fill out a broadcast. And in this process, brites accomplish their main purpose: they provide variety" (p. 30).

Quips are similar, just shorter. Quips use word play, such as puns, to get attention and reader reaction. Selma Glasser (1990), a free-lance writer and book author who has published many shorter humorous items in national publications such as *Reader's Digest* and *Good Housekeeping*, says quips are an easy way to get published. "I give simple words or phrases new sparkle, variety, energy, and meaning. Timely subjects act as dynamic idea generators, recognizable because of their relevance to topics of the day. Just being alert and observant can pay off" (p. 16). Example? She sold the three-word line "Need anything colorized?" to "Dennis the Menace" cartoonist Hank Ketchum, who produced a cartoon showing the boy with his crayons asking that question of his mother. Quips and brights can be a gold mine for writers, Glasser (1992) believes. "The only qualifications are alertness, perservance, and adaptability. The words are all in the dictionary. It's how we choose to 'doctor them up' that counts. Be alert and ready to jot down inspirations. You can add your own touches, a new title, or interpretations later" (p. 19).

Author and comedy writer Gene Perret (1987) says writing these short humorous anecdotes is easy and takes little time. It is quick and fast writing and it is fun and a challenge, he argues. Brights are particularly popular with the news services, which use them for both the newspaper wires and the broadcast wires. They are then used by editors, radio announcers, or television anchors as counterpoints to the day's usually serious news.

The writing style dictates that these items remain brief, using the most concise writing. People and places cannot be thoroughly described or themes developed in detail. The usual bright is a couple of sentences to a couple of paragraphs in length. Usually, this means fewer than 50 words, but no more than 300 words.

With such short, funny items, structure is important. Brief and to-the-point leads work best for brights. They must be terse. They should be fast-moving and skeleton-like. Many briefs are written in inverted pyramid form, but some stories lend themselves to chronological writing. Structure is dominated by a strong lead and an even stronger ending. The best material goes last. There should be an unexpected outcome, a surprise finish. If readers will expect one sort of resolution, the bright will strike them as funny because it does the opposite.

Brights have a "twist," as some humor writers explain them. This twist is the uncommon point of the story, the writer's statement about human nature. It can be the punch line described in the preceding paragraph. Louis Alexander (1975) describes the main characteristics of brights:

1. They make fun of human nature and human errors.
2. They must have a news peg (be about someone and be recent).
3. The situation should be unusual.
4. They must be cleverly written.
5. The item should end with a punch line.
6. There should be good transition elements.

Some brights will not have a punch line finish. Brights without a punch line must leave readers wondering why something happened, who was involved, or simply what happened. This is usually a finish forced on writers because no resolution is available. For example, did the man ever get his keys out of the car? Did the child get the ink off her face? Did the student pay the overdue book fine?

Finding brights is easy, writer Gene Perret (1984) says. His advice is to review your own personal stories, to trade stories at gatherings, read a great deal and remember what you read, stay aware of what is going on in your community, and be alert of what is happening around you.

Brights, it should be added, should not be written with the solution in the lead. This spoils the effect for readers and destroys the value of the item. A well-thought-out bright will hold its best for last. In addition, Alexander recommends avoiding the inverted pyramid structure in writing briefs. You write a brief much like you tell a joke. Not all brights have to be funny. If brights are not going to bring a laugh, they should draw out sympathy or another emotion. They can draw their reaction from the reader's intellect. Brights are not always time-bound. Some editors compile them for use in columns and other regular features. The entertainment value of brights is more important than the time element, yet a timely bright is even more valuable when it is available.

Perret (1987) recommends another approach—writing the bright backwards. Begin with the ending when you write. Then build toward that ending and be compact. The beginning, he advises, should be "a short explanation of

SUBMITTING BRIGHTS FOR PUBLICATION

Gene Perret (1984), who has written humor for Bob Hope and Carol Burnett, recommends three rules for submitting short humorous anecdotes, quips, and other similar material for publication:

1. *Send your submissions in batches.* No less than five should be in each envelope you send, although you can submit as many as a dozen each time. Giving the editor a few to read through each time helps your percentages.
2. *Send each anecdote on a separate page.* On each sheet, include your name, address, phone number and Social Security number (the last will help speed payment).
3. *Neatly prepare all submissions.* Don't cut corners because it's "only" an anecdote. Be professional. Buyers don't want to read through handwritten or messy submissions. Make sure your printer has a new ribbon and double-space submissions for easier editing. The usual SASE (self-addressed, stamped envelope) is not required because most periodicals don't acknowledge these submissions except when and if they send an acceptance check.

why you're telling this story" (p. 29). The good bright writer is also a good reporter. The funny story, as tempting as it may be, cannot invent facts or even stretch them for the effect the stretching might bring. Stick to the facts: Good reporting helps get the facts right. Now let's look at a bright from a recent issue of *Reader's Digest* to see how it works:

From "All in a Day's Work"

On a very windy day, I was driving to my assignment as a home health-care worker. Suddenly a woman dashed out of a shop, apparently chasing a small, hairy dog. Before I could stop, it ran right under my wheels. Through my tears, I tried to tell the woman how sorry I was.

"Honey, don't cry," she said. "My best wig is still at home."

—Contributed by Carol Danielson (1993, p. 79)

Reader's Digest, founded in 1921 and boasting a circulation of about 28 million copies a month in 17 different languages, seeks several dozen brights like that one in each monthly issue. In *Reader's Digest*, potential contributors are told about sections such as "All in a Day's Work," "Campus Comedy," "Humor in Uniform," and "Life-in-These-United States": "Contributions must be true, unpublished stories from one's own experience, revealing *adult* human nature, and providing appealing or humorous sidelights on the American scene" (*Reader's Digest* staff, 1993, p. 4). Readers are also advised in each issue what editors look for, because many contributors are magazine readers as well as professional feature writers. The maximum length is 300 words, and an accepted item earns $400.

Does the bright about the wig mistaken as a small dog achieve its goals? Structurally, yes. It sets the situation up and then delivers a surprise ending that may bring a smile to a reader's face. It contains description, but not overwritten description. The scene is set in a very few concise, but clear sentences. There is only one direct quotation, but no dialogue.

Here is another example:

From "Campus Comedy"

"While walking through the biology department at Lamar University in Beaumont, Texas, I noticed this sign on the door of the microbiology lab: STAPH ONLY!"

—Contributed by Lauren LaFleur (1993, p. 126)

This bright is very short; it is only an observation. The quoted sign is critical because the two short words, a pun, on the sign are the punch line.

Another example:

From "Life in These United States"

A friend, a Vermont native, inherited 100 acres of farmland, including several ramshackle buildings. He heard that out-of-staters buy old places and rebuild them country style. He put one of the buildings up for sale.

Soon a prospect looked at it and said, "I'm interested. Are you flexible on the price?"

"Ayup," the Vermonter replied. "I could go up."

—Contributed by R. Scott Rehart (p. 100)

This bright contains a brief conversational exchange. Nothing elaborate, only two very short quotations. However, the author's description of the way the Vermonter speaks adds a new dimension of realism to the story. Use of "ayup" instead of "yes" lends authenticity and character to the incident. It is a part of what makes the bright successful.

HUMOR COLUMNS

Art Buchwald's four decades of political satire column and Erma Bombeck's three decades of family-oriented humor are two of the leading examples of success at humor column writing. Buchwald's humor focuses on big government but is not inappropriate for family consumption. The column on frequent flyer programs is just one example of this approach. Buchwald writes a regular column 3 days a week. His ability to regularly produce amusing material is rare. What is funny varies, depending on the reader, so Buchwald says he writes to please himself. He says he likes to laugh at his own material and tries not to think about whether a reader will think it is funny or not.

Bombeck's work, like Buchwald's, has passed the test of more than one generation of readers. She has carved out a subject area that permits countless ideas for columns. Like politics, domestic life generates an endless stream of stories that Bombeck has had a keen eye and ear to record and recreate in her short essays. By writing about human shortcomings, such as hair loss or weight gain, and common complaints involving passport photos, children, houses, neighbors, and backyard-fence gossip subjects, she has become known by most standards as one of America's best-known humor columnists and even as America's first lady of humor (Brodeur, 1993; Carter, 1990). She writes about normal things her readers can see affecting their own lives. "The world's going to hell in a handbasket and people are so depressed and then they get to a part of their lives that I've outlined and then they say, 'There's something still here to laugh about,'" Bombeck explains (Brodeur, 1993, p. 3C).

Although many humorists are syndicated and write from an independent base—such as Buchwald and Bombeck—major newspapers and magazines often have a humor columnist on staff. The most popular "local" humorists, such as Bombeck, Grizzard, and Barry, have become syndicated and their followings have grown from the regional to the national level.

Most columnists will focus on their own experiences, observations, or current events. The usual run of current events involving our leaders provides enough material for most humorists—stories about the presidential campaign style and appearance of billionaire Texas businessman Ross Perot, the controversial testimony about sexual harrassment during the confirmation hearing of U.S. Supreme Court Justice Clarence Thomas, or Gary Hart's presidential campaign and his personal involvement with a model.

For almost 7 years, William Geist wrote real-life humor for *The New York Times*. Before that, he wrote a column for *The Chicago Tribune*. Although he has moved on to write books and to write and produce humorous segments for the "CBS News Sunday Morning" program, he still writes about the people, the environment, the scenery around him, and the most commonplace activities he experiences. He looks for ideas in his own neighborhood. Geist explains he finds material for his regular regimen of writing in this manner: "I always look for a story where there's a conflicting sense of values or ethnic groups, or anything where something doesn't fit, is out of whack, in order to get insights on what people are really like" (Spielmann, 1988, p. 30). An example: He focused on class conflict when he wrote about "driveway dress codes" in suburbia—all brought about by a New Jersey community's ordinance preventing certain vehicles (e.g., service trucks) from being parked in driveways overnight.

THE DIFFICULTIES OF HUMOR WRITING

It is worthwhile to remind you that humor writing is not easy. Most professional humorists agree and are often frustrated to even attempt to describe how they do it or how you should do it. Some say it cannot be taught. Here's how *Writer's Digest* columnist Art Spikol (1986b) sums up writing humor:

> It's hard to write humor. I can teach any half-decent writer to write a salable magazine article, but I can't teach anyone to write funny. That ability really comes from an inner voice, and that inner voice may not necessarily be there when you need it. After a few years of developing the muscle, you'll be able to flex it at will—but you'll never get that far if you're not somebody who thinks funny to begin with. (p. 18)

Spikol is right. You need that certain unusual perspective on life to write quality humor. And you need a mind for it, as well—you must know your market and what makes it tick. If you write for a general audience, as most newspaper writers do, then you have a different humor challenge from those who write for specialized magazines. Those who write humor for specialized magazines know the "inside" issues and concerns that inside jokes can be built on. As Spikol says, humor is not written in a vacuum.

And there's no substitute for grand creativity. A very imaginative individual has an edge in writing humor. *Miami Herald* staff reporter Stephen Doig's (1987) inspired April Fool's Day hoax displays this sort of approach. His story told readers that pigeon and snipe hunters had found a cache of weapons in the Everglades area west of Miami. The story was laced with hints (such as trick names) and deliberate typographic errors (such as FBI spelled FIB) as indications that it was a joke and sharp-eyed readers saw them. This was his lead: "A couple of serious hunters who spotted a light flashing Morse code in the Everglades early this morning stumbled onto a cache of arms worth at least $411,987, according to puzzled authorities" (p. 1B).

The suggestion that pigeons and snipe were involved should have tipped off some readers. Another hint is in the amount of money. Did you note that it is really the date? Topically, the hoax is perfect for South Florida readers because the ruse involved possible drug smuggling, arms, and the mysterious, swampy Everglades. The subject and presentation as a "straight" news story on the front of the local section misdirected readers into thinking the story was genuinely serious news. For those who read the story but did not catch on, the newspaper ran a second story the following day that explained the little April Fool joke (*The Miami Herald* staff, 1987). Doig's genius in creating this article with its numerous tricks and other devices made the article a success. It was amusing, entertaining, and clever. Readers appreciate such efforts and respond.

Although well-known humor writers get the best publication breaks, it is not impossible for you. And you might want to start at a low-pressure level by writing humor when you are inspired to be funny. By writing infrequently and thinking small in the beginning, you will gain confidence one step at a time. Small newspapers, such as your community or neighborhood weeklies, and small magazines or newsletters will be easier markets to crack. Dave Barry and the late Lewis Grizzard did not become successes overnight. Their careers developed slowly and methodically from local levels into their national superstar levels.

And once success as a humor writer is achieved, it must be maintained through hard work. Inspiration, as Dave Barry told *Writer's Digest* writer Marshall Cook, is not enough if you make a living off the writing. "I write seven days a week," Barry says (Cook, 1987, p. 29). "If I don't write, I feel guilty. There's real work out there, and I'm not doing it. The least I can do is write."

PROFESSIONAL'S POINT OF VIEW

Alice Kahn
San Francisco Chronicle

I am often asked: "Alice, how can I join the exciting and glamorous world of article writing and hardly work at all and make tons of money?"

There are several foolproof methods of achieving this goal. The most common are the sleaze dig, the trend invention and the integrity-ectomy. Let me give you an example of each.

Recently a young woman called me and asked if she could interview me for a paper she was writing for her journalism class. It was a profile of John Raeside, editor of the *East Bay Express*, the paper where I got my break.

She asked me many probing and interesting questions about the influence of Raeside on my *oeuvre*. I was only too happy to go on at length about how much my old editor had encouraged me, how lucky I have been to work with supportive editors, the importance of including the writer in the editing process, and so on. Obviously, time had glossed over whatever battles we had had, because I couldn't recall a single fault in my former editor other than his being born with the genetic defect of frugality.

After she asked me about Raeside's particular qualities, we got to the hidden agenda. "How long have you known him?" she asked.

"About six years," I answered.

And, lifting her shovel for the sleaze dig, she said, "And did you have what we might call a *personal* relationship?"

"Are you asking if I slept with him?"

"Just trying to dig something up," she said.

Now, I could understand, if she were interviewing me in person, how she might think a swell-looking babe like me would have no other way of succeeding than by sleeping with editors. But this was a phone interview.

I don't know what they're teaching them in journalism schools these days, but they'd better get one thing straight: "Bay Area Writer Sleeps With Editor" is not going to have the same market potential as "Liz Taylor Found in Pat Robertson's Love Nest."

Within hours of my conversation with the student journalist, I got a call from an experienced writer who is on the staff of a major metropolitan newspaper. She asked me if I could give her some "quotes" for a story she was doing. You see, she was on deadline, so she didn't want to have a discussion. Just gimme some quotes and keep your stinkin' ideas to yourself.

She said she was writing something about yuppie despair. She had a major trend going. That is, she had three yuppies who were willing to be desperate— on the record. Now she needed something from me as an expert on yuppies. I had written three articles on yuppies. I was an expert.

I said three things. Those became three quotes. A trend was born.

When the final call of the day came, I realized I needn't write any more. I could just fill requests. The person wanted to know what I thought of something or other. He was writing an article that consisted of nothing more than calling up other people and asking them what they think of something or other. He didn't even have the integrity to dream up a trend or fantasize someone's weird sex life.

Now, we here at The Alice Kahn Column consider ourselves a full-service agency. We are only too happy to oblige the readers by providing them with further information about the important subjects covered in this column. But I am serving notice on all writers of articles in search of a point that if you want me to pop open your idea, it's gonna cost you.

Henceforth, a 10 percent surcharge will be added to your bill for intellectual corkage. (Kahn, personal communication, 1988)

Alice Kahn is a syndicated columnist for the *San Francisco Chronicle*. She is author of several books, including *Luncheon at the Cafe Ridiculous* (1990), *My Life as a Gal* (1987), and *Multiple Sarcasm* (1985). She resides in Berkeley, CA.

15

Writing Science and Technical Features

Writing about science and other technical subjects, such as medicine and health, can be doubly rewarding. You can provide an educational service to readers who learn about the latest medical or engineering developments. This, in turn, helps readers to live more complete, enjoyable, and fulfilling lives. Increasingly, this is a major role of the science feature writer in our society. Concern about AIDS in recent years, with the mixture of rumor and fact, left the public confused over the truth about this disease. Governments around the world turned to the news media to help to disseminate the known facts about AIDS and to educate the public about how to avoid the fatal epidemic. These public health information campaigns depended in part on science writers and medical writers for their success. Citizens in the mid-1990s are now generally better informed about AIDS but still turn to the news media for the latest developments in the prevention and treatment of the disease. The public's dependence on the news media for such valuable information underlines the significance of science and health feature writing. Through news stories, and through feature articles about discoveries dealing with AIDS and other medical problems, the public is educated and better served.

You are part of a new generation of serious science and high technology. They pervade all aspects of your life. The same applies to magazine, newspaper, and newsletter readers. There are vital issues involving contemporary science that never existed before. Most, in fact, were not even in the minds of our best scientists a generation or two ago. Few people could have anticipated a medical problem such as AIDS, for example. The first mainframe computer was developed a half century ago and desktop personal computers are still less than a generation old. Manned aviation itself is less than a century old. It would have been hard for most scientists in the early 1940s to imagine an energy source that could be as inexpensive or as dangerous as nuclear power. The list of these types of recent major scientific developments is endless.

It is one of the news media's most important duties to provide the latest science and technology information to those who live in our communities. Certainly, reporting about new developments that are lifesaving techniques, or simply just timesaving, can be particularly satisfying for science feature writers.

Staff writer Mike Toner (1992) of the *Atlanta Constitution* wrote a startling six-part "occasional" series about the diminishing effects of pesticides and antibiotics entitled "When Bugs Fight Back." Explaining how insects develop resistance to chemicals in the human effort to eradicate them, Toner was able to teach readers about the science behind such work by making a complicated topic involving chemistry and biology easy to understand. He interviewed dozens of scientists and other experts. Toner illustrated the problem with numerous actual medical cases and examples. He discussed the problem by reviewing its history and development. Toner's efforts earned him the Pulitzer Prize for explanatory journalism in 1993 and the JCPenney-University of Missouri Newspaper Feature Writing Awards certificate of merit for a series. This is the first part, a 3,300-word installment, in Toner's highly enlightening series:

Editor's Note: The bugs are fighting back. And they are getting very good at it. The world's simplest creatures—bacteria, viruses, insects and weeds—are unraveling the chemical security blanket that has nurtured a half-century of progress in both public health and agriculture. First in an occasional series, "When Bugs Fight Back."

The death certificate attributed the 58-year-old heart patient's demise to "complications" following bypass surgery. The real reason made even his doctors cringe. Antibiotics didn't work anymore.

For four months, doctors at the University of Michigan Medical Center had struggled to control a bacterial infection that had invaded the man's chest cavity. The germs, however, were resistant to every available drug.

In the end, the bugs triumphed—and doctors at one of the country's premier medical institutions were as powerless to prevent it as doctors were 50 years ago, in the days before penicillin.

"If he hadn't had such a resistant strain, he would have made it," says Dennis Schaberg, professor of medicine at the University of Michigan medical school in Ann Arbor.

"I hate to sound like Chicken Little, but with certain micro-organisms, we are back to a point in time where we have no options left. It's tough to explain something like that to the family of the patient. Very tough."

A growing number of patients—and their families—are discovering a grim new reality of medicine in the 1990s. Antibiotics, those too-good-to-be-true compounds that have provided mankind with mastery over infectious disease, don't work like they used to.

The bugs are fighting back. And they are getting very good at it.

On city streets, in remote jungle clinics, on the farm and in back yards, the world's simplest creatures—bacteria, viruses, insects and weeds—are unraveling the chemical security blanket that has nurtured a half-century of progress in both public health and agriculture.

Whether we are conscious of it or not, the ability of these mindless creatures to adapt to the chemical warfare we wage on them has become a significant force in our daily lives. Look closely at any infectious disease for which there is a cure and you'll find bugs with a cure for the cure.

Have a child with an ear infection that won't go away? Deep in the recesses of your toddler's middle ear, there is probably a resistant bug to blame.

Having trouble getting rid of Fido's fleas or the cockroaches under your sink? Chances are, they're resistant too.

Did your stomach tie itself in knots after your last trip to a restaurant salad bar? If it was food poisoning, chances are one in three that the bug you took home with you was resistant.

Like the villains in a late-night horror show, resistant strains of mankind's oldest enemies are finding ways to sabotage our most sophisticated technology. And even the malevolent microbes of "The Andromeda Strain" or the angry hordes of "Killer Bees" aren't as scary as the real-life "superbugs" that are now emerging throughout the world.

In U.S. hospitals, where most people go to get well, 2 million people a year get sick after they check in—and the Centers for Disease Control (CDC) estimates that 60 percent of those infections are now resistant to at least one antibiotic. Because drug-resistant germs are twice as likely to be fatal, they contribute to 50,000 hospital deaths a year. And because they take twice as long to cure, they add as much as $30 billion a year to the cost of hospital care.

The toll in hospitals, however, is only the most documented facet of an insidious trend. Resistant strains of some of man's oldest enemies—malaria, tuberculosis, gonorrhea, food poisoning, pneumonia, even leprosy—are undermining public health throughout the world.

Some new strains of tuberculosis, resurgent after 30 years of decline in the United States and Europe, have become resistant to so many drugs that they are virtually as untreatable as they were before the discovery of antibiotics.

Malaria, which claims at least 1 million lives a year in the tropics, is on the comeback trail too, bolstered by the malaria parasite's growing resistance to drugs, and pesticide resistance of the mosquitoes that carry it.

Even that familiar nemesis we call pneumonia, which claims more than 3.5 million lives a year worldwide—up to 50,000 of them in the United States—is becoming steadily more resistant to penicillin, which has controlled it for nearly 50 years.

Almost every human infection—from drug-resistant "superclap," which has become a worldwide problem, to stubborn staph infections that linger in nursing homes for years—is now resistant to at least one major class of antibiotics.

TRACTOR-TOWED BLOWTORCHES

Among the insects, things are no better. On Long Island, where the Colorado potato beetle is now resistant to every major class of pesticides, potato farmers use tractor-towed blowtorches to kill the insects—one of at least 17 "superbugs" that are now resistant to all pesticides.

Weeds are getting tougher too. More than 100 species are now resistant to at least one herbicide, and wheat growers in Australia and the United Kingdom are encountering the first multiply-resistant "mega-weeds," which scientists say could threaten the world's wheat supply.

Farmers' problems, of course, quickly become consumers' problems.

The clouds of pesticide-resistant sweet potato whiteflies that devastated last winter's vegetable crops in California, Texas and Florida triggered supermarket sticker shock that gave us $3.50 cantaloupe and $2-a-pound tomatoes.

There is no great mystery about what is happening. The bugs, whether single-celled microorganisms or the six-legged variety, are doing what comes naturally. They're surviving.

Bacteria have been on the Earth for at least 3 billion years; insects for at last 850 million years. Like all living things, they are constantly mutating, testing new traits that may give them an edge in a hostile environment.

With a new generation of bacteria every 20 minutes, trial and error can be a powerful survival tool. And when one bug finds something that works, it passes it on, sometimes even to other species.

With eons to adapt, bacteria have learned to live in the Earth's most hostile environments—from superheated deep-sea vents to the frozen slopes of Mount Everest. The few thousand antibiotics and pesticides that mankind has thrown at them have been, by comparison, a minor challenge.

The bugs' subversion of man-made chemicals has been unwittingly aided by the industries that market them, by "experts" who overuse them, and by ordinary people who treat them as technological "no-brainers" that promise, for a time, to change the course of evolution.

"The problem is not chemicals; it's the irresponsible way they are used," says University of Illinois entomologist Robert Metcalf. "Our shortsighted and irresponsible use of antibiotics and pesticides is producing strains of monster bugs resistant to nearly everything in our arsenal. The outlook is dismal. And it is getting worse."

The benefits of the 20th century's chemical "miracles" are indisputable. In the decade after the introduction of antibiotics, U.S. death rates from pneumonia, TB and influenza dropped 50 percent. Worldwide, penicillin is thought to have added 10 years to life expectancy. And the heavy chemical use that fueled the Green Revolution has helped feed a burgeoning population.

Resistance is not a new phenomenon. The emergence in the 1940s of penicillin-resistant staph infections in hospitals and DDT-resistant houseflies proved that bugs could fight back.

Until recently, however, human ingenuity always pulled some new solution from technology's seemingly inexhaustible bag of tricks. Now, like an audience that has seen the magician's act before, the bugs are getting harder to fool.

In recent years, resistance has become so pervasive that some experts now fear medicine and agriculture are on the verge of regressing into the technological dark ages that preceded the era of antibiotics and pesticides.

THE ULTIMATE NIGHTMARE

For most people, for most illnesses, antibiotics still work. But in a growing number of cases, like the 58-year-old Michigan heart patient who died of mediastinitis caused by a hard-to-treat strain of enterococcal bacteria, the bugs' ability to accumulate resistance swiftly to several drugs at one time conjures up the ultimate nightmare.

"For some infections, we are very close to the end of the road," says Fred C. Tenover, the head of antimicrobics investigations for the CDC. "The worst-case scenario is almost here. We are very, very close to having bacteria resistant to every significant antibiotic ever developed. Only this time, there are no new drugs coming down the pike."

No aspect of the problem has dramatized the predicament more than the resurgence of tuberculosis—a disease that was once thought to have been vanquished by antibiotics. Although the numbers are relatively low—26,283 cases in the United States last year, 909 in Georgia—the upward trend and the growing prevalence of resistant TB worry many experts. A 50 percent increase in cases in Atlanta last year left the city with the highest TB rate in the country.

"TB is out of control," says Dixie Snider, who heads the CDC's tuberculosis control division. "These outbreaks we have seen in the last year may be just the beginning."

But while tuberculosis gets the headlines, resistant strains of other diseases have been spreading almost unnoticed. Salmonella infections, which cause up to 4 million cases of food poisoning a year in the United States, have been rising steadily for 15 years—and antibiotic-resistant strains now make up one-third of all cases.

Health officials say the spread of resistant food-borne germs, which often acquire resistance genes from exposure to antibiotics used to treat farm animals, will mean larger outbreaks of food poisoning in the future—like a 1985 case of contaminated milk that sickened 180,000 in the Midwest.

New strains of resistant bugs are spreading globally. In Georgia, soaring rates of penicillin- and tetracycline-resistant gonorrhea—once unknown outside of Southeast Asia—have rendered obsolete drugs that controlled the disease for three decades. In five years, drug-resistant gonorrhea has increased tenfold in Georgia, enough to give the state the highest rate in the country.

Several antibiotics are still effective against gonorrhea, but pockets of resistance to these "last resort" drugs are already emerging in other countries.

"There is a global movement of these gonococcal strains, so it is probably only a matter of time before we have them in the United States," says Joan Knapp, an epidemiologist with the CDC's division of sexually transmitted diseases. "We are standing at the edge of a crisis. Every new antibiotic we have thrown at this bug has ended up making it more resistant."

Old enemies aren't the only ones learning new tricks. The AIDS virus is already resistant to the first three drugs approved to treat it.

Development of two other AIDS drugs was curtailed this year after researchers discovered that the virus had developed resistance after only 12 weeks of treatment.

INVASION OF THE WHITEFLIES

Insects are proving every bit as adept at chemical countermeasures as the microscopic "bugs" that cause human disease.

When Rachel Carson warned in 1962—two decades after the introduction of DDT—that repeated pesticide use would create a crisis in which "only the strong and fit remain to defy our efforts to control them," 137 insects were resistant to at least one pesticide.

Today, resistance has been documented in 504 species of insects and mites, 273 weeds, 150 fungi and other plant pathogens, and five kinds of rats—and there are at least 17 insects that are resistant to all major classes of pesticides.

When pesticides fail, the consequences can assume almost biblical proportions— as they did during last year's invasion of sweet potato whiteflies in California, Texas and Florida.

"We had fields that were completely devastated," says Nick Toscano, an entomologist at the University of California at Riverside. "It was like the plagues of locusts and grasshoppers that they have in the Middle East and Africa. At times, the clouds of whiteflies were so thick, it looked like a dust storm. If you drove through one of the clouds, you had to stop and scrape off your blackened windshield so you could see."

The U.S. Department of Agriculture has launched a five-year research program to seek new solutions to the problem.

But "Invasion of the Sweetpotato Whitefly II," the sequel, may be only months away—and experts say the insects, which thrive on cotton and peanuts, could soon become a major headache in Georgia, Mississippi and New Mexico, too.

"Control may not be impossible, but it's going to be very expensive," says Gary Herzog, research entomologist at the University of Georgia's Coastal Plain Experiment Station in Tifton. "I had to tell a farmer the other day to expect a couple of years of serious hardship before we come up with a solution."

The rising tide of resistance is by no means an unbroken trend. The boll weevil, which almost instantly became resistant to DDT, is as susceptible to parathion as the day in 1949 when it was first sprayed on Southern cotton fields. Penicillin is still as effective against syphilis as it was when GIs were treated with it during World War II.

At other times, compounds that took years to develop have sometimes been rendered ineffective within months of their introduction.

Sometimes the bugs leapfrog ahead of technology. Farmers, using a class of chemicals called pyrethroids for the first time, have discovered insects that were already resistant. The same gene the bugs used to beat DDT also works against pyrethroids—and the trait has persisted even though DDT hasn't been used in the United States for 20 years.

Man-made chemicals of all kinds apply the same kind of "selective pressure" that Charles Darwin first described more than a century ago.

But the unrelenting use of antibiotics and pesticides has, in effect, thrown the evolution of resistance into fast forward.

In 50 years, bacteria have evolved more than 100 resistance factors to survive the onslaught of antibiotics. The same 50 years have seen the evolution of at least 1,640 combinations of insect-insecticide resistance.

'RACE BETWEEN MAN AND BUGS'

From the bugs' point of view, the pressure to succeed is enormous.

Americans use 700 million pounds of pesticides and herbicides and 30 million pounds of antibiotics each year to treat everything from acne and gum disease to farmed catfish and feedlot cattle. Worldwide use of antibiotics and pesticides is three to five times that of the United States.

In the long run, the effects of this chemical blitz are not all for the better. Even though U.S. farmers use 33 times more pesticides than they did in the 1940s, pests now destroy 37 percent of the annual harvest, about what they did in medieval Europe, where farmers lost "one of every three grains grown."

The record on antibiotics is no more encouraging. Doctors write 220 million prescriptions for oral antibiotics a year, one for nearly every person in the country. But surveys show that about half are unnecessary or incorrectly prescribed. In addition to wasting billions of dollars a year, the misuse encourages the spread of resistant infections.

"The widespread, often inappropriate use of antibiotics ensures their phased obsolescence as new resistant organisms emerge," says Calvin Kunin, professor of medicine at Ohio State University, who has studied doctors' prescribing practices for more than a decade.

"Too many people think antibiotics are harmless," says Thomas F. O'Brien, a specialist in infectious diseases at Brigham and Women's Hospital in Boston. "We need to start persuading them that resistant bacteria can be just as dangerous as high blood pressure or cholesterol. You don't want it—and the way to avoid it is not to take antibiotics unnecessarily."

Although experts in infectious disease and agriculture seldom discuss their problems with each other, they think remarkably alike on one point. As bugs of all shapes and sizes grow more resistant, urgent efforts are needed to preserve the weapons that still work. That means abandoning the quick-fix mentality that has shaped the use of these chemicals for 50 years, and adding an ingredient that often has been missing—common sense.

Some farmers are discovering that simple biological control—insects eating insects—works better than chemicals. Others believe advanced technology will ride to the rescue. Scientists, for instance, are already engineering insecticidal traits and herbicide resistance into hundreds of crops—a generation of plants that could reduce the need for chemical pesticides.

Some insects, however, have already developed resistance to these biological pesticides, and some experts worry that widespread use of such plants could actually promote resistance.

"History is repeating itself," says Marvin K. Harris, an entomologist at Texas A&M University. "Every time we come up with a new class of chemicals, we think we are finally home free. In every instance we have been wrong. There's no reason to think we won't be wrong again."

Advances in genetic engineering also promise a new generation of anti-infective drugs and vaccines, as well as speedier diagnosis of resistant microbes. But if hope springs eternal, it no longer flows with the optimism that greeted the introduction of penicillin a half-century ago.

"This is a race between man and bugs," says Colin Marchant, associate professor of pediatrics at the Tufts University School of Medicine. "The bugs have been very clever about finding ways to evade the drugs we make. So far we have been very clever about devising new ones, but I don't know how much longer we will be able to." (p. A/1). © 1992 Atlanta Newspapers Inc. Reprinted with permission of Atlanta Newspapers Inc.

Toner also developed a chart focusing on the "do's and don'ts of antibiotic use" for the first installment of the series. His other stories discussed global spread of resistance, "tougher" germs in hospitals, how doctors and drug companies encourage resistance, the growing difficulty in controlling weeds and insects, and the dwindling supply of "magic bullets."

Staff writer Jacqui Banaszynski wrote a series of articles for the *St. Paul Pioneer Press* in 1987. Her subject was AIDS in America's farming heartland, something few people had considered at that time. She focused on the life and eventual death of an AIDS victim in telling the story from a compelling human perspective. She was able to write about a difficult medical subject in human terms. The effort earned Banaszynski the 1988 Pulitzer Prize for feature writing. This is how Banaszynski (1987) set the context of her project in the beginning portion of the first article of her award-winning three-part series:

Death is no stranger to the heartland. It is as natural as the seasons, as inevitable as farm machinery breaking down and farmers' bodies giving out after too many years of too much work.

But when death comes in the guise of AIDS, it is a disturbingly unfamiliar visitor, one better known in the gay districts and drug houses of the big cities, one that shows no respect for the usual order of life in the country.

The visitor has come to rural Glenwood, Minn.

Dick Hanson, a well-known liberal political activist who homesteads his family's century-old farm south of Glenwood, was diagnosed last summer with acquired immune deficiency syndrome. His partner of five years, Bert Henningson, carries the AIDS virus.

In the year that Hanson has been living—and dying—with AIDS, he has hosted some cruel companions: blinding headaches and failing vision, relentless nausea . . . .(p. 1)

The excellence in *Baltimore Evening Sun* feature writer Jon Franklin's two stories about a new brain surgery procedure is built through detailed description of the complex operation on a 57-year-old woman. Franklin uses an approach he calls the *nonfiction short story*. This approach, applied to writing about science and other technical subjects, makes the material more appealing to readers. "The principal difference between the short story of old and the nonfiction short story of today is that in its modern form, the story is true," Franklin wrote (1986, p. 27). The effort won Franklin his first of two Pulitzer Prizes, this one in 1979 for feature writing. Franklin (1978) began the short story-like article about the complicated surgical attempt to untangle and remove a knot of abnormal blood vessels in a woman's skull. He set the up dramatic conflict between the surgeon and what the patient called the "monster" internal growth that was slowly killing her:

In the cold hours of a winter morning Dr. Thomas Barbee Ducker, chief brain surgeon at the University of Maryland Hospital, rises before dawn. His wife serves him waffles but no coffee. Coffee makes his hands shake.

In downtown Baltimore, on the 12th floor of University Hospital, Edna Kelly's husband tells her goodbye. For 57 years, Mrs. Kelly shared her skull with the monster: No more. Today she is frightened but determined.

It is 6:30 a.m.

"I'm not afraid to die," she said as this day approached. "I've lost part of my eyesight. I've gone through all the hemorrhages. A couple of years ago I lost my sense of smell, my taste. I started having seizures. I smell a strange odor and then I start strangling. It started affecting my legs, and I'm partially paralyzed.

"Three years ago a doctor told me all I had to look forward to was blindness, paralysis and a remote chance of death. Now I have aneurysms; this monster is causing that. I'm scared to death . . . but there isn't a day that goes by that I'm not in pain, and I'm tired of it. I can't bear the pain. I wouldn't want to live like this much longer."

As Dr. Ducker leaves for work, Mrs. Ducker hands him a paper bag containing a peanut butter sandwich, a banana and two fig newtons.

Downtown, in Mrs. Kelly's brain, a sedative takes effect.

Mrs. Kelly was born with a tangled knot of abnormal blood vessels . . . . (p. C-1)

Franklin proceeds to tell this dramatic story with a chronological approach. Yet, readers do not find out what happened until the struggle ended 7 hours later on the operating room table. With detailed description, Franklin puts readers in the operating room as observers. He lays out Mrs. Kelly's story as a fiction writer might write a short story. As this real-life drama builds in his story, the condition of the patient is left hanging. At the same time, a very difficult medical procedure becomes understandable and meaningful to readers. It isn't until the last sentence of the article that Franklin reveals what happened to Mrs. Kelly. "The monster won," Franklin simply wrote in that final sentence (p. C-1).

Why did these three writers succeed? Why did each win such high-level recognition? Each one has mastered science feature writing. Although the topics were different and each was approached by the author in a somewhat different manner, each told his or her story in a manner understandable by readers.

This chapter outlines the basics of writing science, technical, medical and health, and other specialized features. Toner, Banaszynski, and Franklin succeeded because of their abilities to take complicated subjects and write them in an accurate manner that could be understood by readers without medical backgrounds. For example, Franklin's article displays the uncertainty and tension surrounding any surgical procedure that risks human life, particularly the drama of a revolutionary technique. The story is even more effective because of the humane approach to the article—readers get to know the patient and the neurosurgeons because Franklin develops their roles in the story beyond just name and identification. This type of science and technical writing is sensitive and dramatic through its narrative description. It's a good read. That's what writing about complicated subjects should do—allow readers to learn from, and enjoy, the subject.

DESCRIBING SCIENCE AND TECHNICAL FEATURES

Science and technical feature topics literally cover the universe. Some of the hot topics in the mid-1990s include personal health and fitness, medicine, computers, astronomy and space travel, psychology and psychiatry, nutrition and diet, sports and exercise science, geography and oceanography, meteorology, and biology. Take any of these topics and each can be broken down into numerous subdivisions that are important topics themselves. In medicine for example, the focus will continue to be on drug abuse, AIDS, cancer, paralysis, burns, heart disease, children and childbirth, sleep, and sex.

Award-winning science writer Karla Harby (personal communication, 1993), who is based in Long Island, New York, notes there is an increase in public interest in science news. "A new survey by the Scientist's Institute for Public Information in New York City finds that the general public is hungry for science reporting, especially medical reporting. These stories are some of the easiest to sell as a free-lancer. I think the future of science journalism is very bright and exciting," she observed.

It seems there are more subjects in science, technical, medical, and health writing than there are sciences. It is up to you as a writer to determine which of those subjects are marketable and appealing to readers. You can be certain that subjects such as those already mentioned will appeal across the board. Increasingly, newspapers and consumer magazines and newsletters are devoting portions of their content to personal health and fitness subjects, for instance. *Working Woman*, devoting its monthly content to feature articles about such diverse topics as motherhood, career advancement, clothing, enterpreneurship, and more, has major content devoted each month to health and fitness topics. In one recent issue, there were major articles about managing job-related stress, stress clinics, and how food and nutrition affect job performance.

What does it take to be science or technical feature writer? First, it takes some interest in a scientific subject such as the environment, medicine, space, or computers. Second, it takes some education in the sciences. It is not necessary to be a science major, but some general science education, especially at college, is very helpful. Third, it makes a difference if you specialize. This focuses your "learning curve" in a particular area.

Bill Steele (personal communication, 1993), a Cornell University graduate working near the school in Ithaca, New York, began college as a physics major but wound up in psychology. He says he was more interested in people than things. Steele, who has written numerous articles as a free-lance writer for national general interest magazines such as *Family Circle, Working Mother, National Wildlife, Popular Electronics*, and *Health*, as well as trade and business publications, specializes in medicine, computers, and more general science writing. He explains how his education has helped him:

> In my work as a science writer I drew mostly on the basic courses I took in the first couple of years. Today, I draw much more heavily on what I've learned since college. For example, when I was an undergraduate, there was no such thing as molecular genetics, yet today that's a subject I write about far more often than physics. I've made a point of becoming informed about it, and probably know more about it now than I know about physics. Or psychology.

> A good scientific education teaches you how to *do* science. To write about it, you need to know the basics, and the vocabulary, so you can understand what a scientist or engineer is telling you. You also need to be up on the state of the art, so you know what's news. After that you use the same interviewing and

storytelling skills you use to report on business, law, sports or anything else: Here's the expert who knows what's going on and you have to find out what that is and ask questions or do research until you can explain it to your audience in terms they can understand. (Steele, personal communication, 1993)

DEFINING SCIENCE AND TECHNICAL WRITING

Pennsylvania State University English Professor Robert Gannon (1991) describes a confusion involving science writing, technical writing, and scientific writing. These are each different types of communication about science, he notes, explaining:

Science writing is often confused with technical writing and scientific writing. It is neither. The difference lies mostly in the audience. The technical writer prepares "technical" material—reports, memos, brochures—for a captive audience that needs data: a client, a colleague, an organization. A scientific writer, preparing scientific papers, writes for readers who want the information—many of whom are in the discipline and must keep abreast of what's happening.

But the science writer (or science journalist) addresses the lay public. This job is much more complicated. The science writer must make complex theories and systems clear to a large, diverse readership, and must do so with the utmost clarity, accuracy, and excitement . . . .(Gannon, 1991, p. v)

Science writers, at least as a group, have worked in a recognized specialty since 1934. That was the year the National Association of Science Writers was founded in New York. There are other groups of writers worldwide who concern themselves with scientific and technical material—groups such as the Council for the Advancement of Science Writing and the American Medical Writers Association. There are courses on the subject at many universities and colleges offered through journalism programs or science departments. It is a growing specialization in feature and news writing.

Many newspapers have reporters assigned to specific science and technology beats. Among the most common beats are health and medicine, the environment, aviation and transportation, and energy. With the growing interest in science and high technology, many major newspapers have science and technology sections or pages on a regular basis.

Typical of much daily newspaper science writing is that based on scientific research findings. Many reporters find these story ideas from reading the major journals. *USA Today* reporter Kim Painter (1993) illustrates this with her aftermath article explaining to readers research focusing on treatment of AIDS with the drug known as AZT. A new study said AZT may not be as effective as originally thought. Painter's story summarized a letter about the findings that was published in the British medical journal, *The Lancet*. She also reported reaction to the controversial announcement by interviewing authoritative members of the AIDS research community and the medical education community about how they are handling the AZT controversy. This is Painter's easy-to-understand story:

> For years, U.S. AIDS experts have told people infected with the AIDS virus that early treatment could give them months or years of healthier life.
>
> That advice hasn't changed with the news of a European study that suggests there are no long-term benefits from early treatment with AZT, the drug now routinely prescribed before symptoms appear.
>
> U.S. experts say AZT is not the only component of early treatment, and the study, even if correct, doesn't show AZT has no role in early treatment.
>
> In the course of the three-year study—described Saturday in a letter in the British medical journal *The Lancet*—researchers saw just as many deaths and full-blown AIDS cases among infected people who got AZT when they had no symptoms as among those who got it only after symptoms appeared or tests showed declining immunity.
>
> Because of the study, "some people are asking, 'Why should I bother taking AZT or even getting tested?'" for HIV, the AIDS virus, says Mark Bowers, a spokesman for Project Inform, San Francisco. "We think that's a big mistake."
>
> Bower's group, which runs a national hot line, tells callers:
>
> • The European study, like U.S. studies before it, shows patients getting early AZT are less likely to develop AIDS in the first year of treatment.
>
> • New research focuses on switching or combining drugs to suppress HIV— meaning long-term AZT treatment isn't the only option.
>
> • There's some good news in the study: In three years, only 18% developed AIDS; only 7% to 8% died, adding to evidence that rapid progression is rare.
>
> • The study shows early AZT treatment does no harm—even at doses much higher that those used in the USA.
>
> At Gay Men's Health Crisis in New York, "We're getting people asking if they should stop taking AZT," says spokesman David Eng.
>
> "We're saying there's no reason to do that and that you should consult with your doctor before you do anything. We're also saying that the study does not show that those who started early are harmed. Once we explain that, a lot of people calm down."
>
> U.S. researchers will meet with the Europeans soon and plan to review treatment guidelines within a few months. But for now, "no physician or patient should change the approach they're using based on this study," says Dr. Daniel Hoth, AIDS research director at the National Institute of Allergy and Infectious Diseases.
>
> "This study has not shown that AZT is a useless drug," he says. "We believe that the most likely outcome, after we've seen all the data and reviewed everything, is that we'll see AZT is a drug that provides benefit, but of limited duration.

"There are lots of drugs we use that are beneficial but of limited duration," he says, using cancer drugs as an example. "You have to keep it in perspective. You don't hold it up as the magic bullet or cure, but you don't throw it away."

These are the current government recommendations:

• Any person who thinks he or she has been exposed to HIV—for example, through unprotected sex or sharing drug needles—should get tested.

• Those who test positive should see a doctor regularly and be monitored for drops in CD4 cells, infection-fighting blood cells killed by HIV.

• AZT treatment should begin when CD4 counts drop below 500 per cubic millimeter. Normal levels are 800 to 1,200.

When the levels drop still lower, doctors prescribe drugs to prevent AIDS-related pneumonia, a killer becoming less common because of early treatment. (p. 6D) © 1993 USA TODAY. Reprinted with permission.

Some consumer magazines, with their well-defined markets, specialize in scientific content. Some are generally about science. They include publications such as *Discover, Omni, Scientific American, Popular Science, Science Digest,* and *Science,* the official publication of the American Association for the Advancement of Science. Whereas these consumer magazines are devoted to general science, there are other major consumer magazines devoted to health, personal care, and medicine. These include four of the top 100 magazines in the country: *Prevention, Health, Weight Watchers Magazine,* and *American Health—Fitness of Body and Mind.* Many other magazines have departments devoted to medicine and health, space, engineering, the environment, technology, and the like.

Thus, you have probably deduced by now, science and technical writing is subdivided into numerous specializations. Some writers are able to handle the general science assignment as it comes up, but most try to develop their own specialties within the science because of the difficulty of the subject matter.

The basic feature writing and reporting skills are no different in science and technical writing from other forms of feature writing. However, the growth in information and in interest in science requires it be treated as a specialization of newspaper and magazine feature writing. Beyond the basics in writing and reporting, there is one critical difference. You must be able to gather this usually complex scientific information, digest and understand it, and then translate it into understandable information for the general public. This requires a feature writer willing to accept this challenge and able to overcome it. You must often cope with a technical language unique to a specific science. You must be able to write along a fine line that keeps well-educated readers interested without losing the less sophisticated ones. It is always a difficult assignment.

You must also be able to define and explain. It is critical to maintain accuracy in use of unique scientific and technical terminology. Such words must be explained in your article; you must take the time and effort to define terms and then use them in precise fashion in your article. What does the story mean to the average person? How will the information in the article affect the reader's life? Or the lives of succeeding generations? This determination of meaning often is the most difficult challenge of all science and technical writing.

Although you are faced with the challenge of writing about new scientific and technical developments that affect our lives, there is still another challenge. You must also be able to write about subjects that readers already know about in a manner that is appealing and new. This may be more difficult for a writer than a story dealing with new developments. Making the old and familiar seem new is a tough assignment.

The work of most science and technical writers is difficult to generalize about. Newspaper writers who specialize in science and technical writing many times have other duties. Although science writers for small daily newspapers might focus on the medical beat, they might also have assignments to cover schools or city hall. Many science and technical writers for smaller consumer magazines work free-lance and must be able to generate assignments on their own initiative and enterprise. This effort requires paying attention to developments by reading and talking to the leading information sources in the area.

Darrel Raynor, an independent computer consultant who writes free-lance technical articles about computer hardware and software, lives in suburban Dallas. He offers a cookbook approach to writing technical feature articles:

> First, I identify a hot topic I think will be of interest to specific readers. Then I spend about a half hour finding out if there is enough interesting research material. Then I hone a three-sentence description I can pitch to editors-publishers as I talk to them. If approved in writing, unless I have a long relationship with the editor-publisher, I start gathering research material immediately and keep at it! My averages are 1 hour pure research time per 500 words, if I already know a lot about the topic, and about 1 hour research per 250 words if I am less familiar with the topic . . . . Then I outline the piece to find out if fill-in research, quotes, or interviews are required. I start actual writing 1 day ahead of deadline for every 100 words in the piece (this is my rule of thumb to avoid deadline fever and 3 a.m. mistakes). I then get an unsuspecting friend to edit. I pay attention to what they say and finish in time to let [the manuscript] rest at least 2 days for final edit and review. I send in at least 2 days before deadline. (Raynor, personal communication, 1993)

Despite such organized approaches, science and technical writing have their problems. Free-lance science writer and former managing editor of the *Journal of Nuclear Medicine* Karla Harby says changing reading habits are not helping, but she is not overly pessimistic:

> The overall decline in newspapers affects science writing by forcing those stories to compete more strongly with the rest of the paper. Illiteracy and competing uses for leisure time also hurt us. As the baby boom generation ages, it will

become even more interested in health information than it already is. Those persons now in their late teens and 20s show a keen interest in environmental stories. When I was a student, no one cared about that subject; now there are a dozen magazines to address it, and newspaper coverage seems to have grown, too. (Harby, personal communication, 1993)

Research about science and technical writing has determined that there are four factors that affect reader interest in science and technical subjects, according to Michael Shapiro, a science writing researcher at Cornell University. Two concepts do influence a person's interest in science articles, but two others seem less likely to, Shapiro says (1988). The two that certainly affect interest are:

1. *Relevance of the subject.* You must, as a writer, find a way to help readers see how the subject is important to them. If you do, this enhances readership.
2. *Entertainment value of the article.* The article must be prepared in such a manner that it satisfies the readers' need for stimulation if you want a widely read article.

The two concepts that have traditionally been associated with readership now seem less likely to influence interest, the study reports:

1. *Ease or difficulty of the subject material.* Even though it seems that difficult subjects would be less inviting to readers, there is little evidence that interest in science articles is related to subject difficulty.
2. *Topic familiarity.* Although many writers have believed that people turn to material that they already know, this is true only for actively sought material. For casually encountered articles in newspapers, magazines, and newsletters, familiarity has little affect on interest.

WRITING FOR THE RIGHT AUDIENCE

You have an assignment. You must write about unhealthy levels of asbestos found in local public elementary school classrooms. How much does your publication's average reader know about the complicated subject? How much do you have to explain and define as you write this article? You must make these types of decisions before you write one word. Your science and technical writing approaches will vary considerably—depending on whether you write for a general audience or a specialized audience.

The General Audience

Much of the science and technical writing you will do in consumer publications will be oriented to the general public. The wide range of educational levels will put a special demand on you to write in an interesting fashion for the reader with a professional degree as well as the reader who did not finish high school. But you must know as much as you can about this general audience because it might have special interests. For the general audience, it is best to err on the side of stating the obvious and too much explanation. Remember, part of your work is educational, too.

Writing for the general audience is not automatic. Translating complicated information into understandable form requires effort on the part of the writer. Free-lance writer and editor Wendy Grossman who specializes in computers and paranormal science from her flat near London, says writers who deal in complicated subjects benefit from talking to everyday people. "Stay in touch with real people. This is a problem you see often among computer journalists—they know too much and the result is they don't understand what's difficult for anyone else," she says. "The other thing is to maintain some detachment from your subject—in my case, I'm a writer who happens to be writing about computers and science. If you're the other way round—a computer junkie who happens to be writing about them (instead of selling them or making them), it will be much harder for you to write for a general audience" (personal communication, 1993).

The Specialized Audience

Some science and technical writing you may do will be designed for a specialized audience of high sophistication. Feature writers for business and industry periodicals, for example, will prepare articles for those with high interest levels in a subject and, it is likely, high knowledge levels as well. Most specialized audience readers will have some experience with the subject themselves, either through their work or their education. This expertise on the part of readers requires that you have an even greater awareness of audience when you write. You do not want to make the mistake of assuming too little, and thus bore the reader. Nor do you want to assume the audience knows too much and turn it off by leaving too many vague explanations or unanswered questions. Some preliminary research about your readers may help solve this problem.

Most newspaper and magazine editors have a particular audience and subject range in mind for each article they accept. For example, *Writer's Market* (Kissling, 1992) reports the editors of *Popular Science* seek applied science feature writing for their unique market:

> *Popular Science* is devoted to exploring (and explaining) to a nontechnical but knowledgeable readership the technical world around us. We cover all of the sciences, engineering and technology, and above all, products. We are largely a ‹thing›-oriented publication: things that fly or travel down a turnpike, or go on or under the sea, or cut wood, or reproduce music, or build buildings, or make pictures, or mow lawns. We are especially focused on the new, the ingenious and the useful. We are consumer-oriented and are interested in any product that adds

to the enjoyment of the home, yard, car, boat, workshop, outdoor recreation . . .
. Freelancers should study the magazine to see what we want and avoid irrelevant submissions. (p. 618)

"A good science article is an easy read; it carries the readers along effort-
lessly, with fascination," says Penn State's Gannon (1991, p. vi). "And when
readers are finished, they are often surprised (if they think about it) at just how
much highly technical material they have picked up along the way."

KEY SOURCES FOR ARTICLES

In science and technical article writing there is a vast, rich lode of sources to
mine. These include organizations such as professional and trade associations,
professional and trade groups' conventions and exhibitions, regular local and
national professional meetings, articles in professional journals and busi-
ness/industry publications, researchers at local and state universities and
colleges, area research and technical institutes and centers, research groups
and foundations, scientists on staffs of museums, and commercial research
organizations—just to mention a few possibilities.

Specialized publications can be a good starting point. Familiarize yourself
with those in the subject areas that interest you. There are numerous special
handbooks, guidebooks, and directories available for reference. Many are
written specifically for reporters and writers by specialists in a field. Some are
produced by journalists for other journalists. For example, Edward Edelson
(1985), science editor of the *New York Daily News*, wrote *The Journalist's Guide
to Nuclear Energy* for the Atomic Industrial Forum, a collective of organizations
involved in peaceful use of nuclear energy. This book and ones like it contain
explanations, definitions, diagrams, and other helpful resources for writers.

Veteran free-lance feature writer Bill Steele uses research to find the human
sources he needs. He says he goes wherever the needed information can be found.
He uses both experts and principals involved in events about which he is writing:

Sometimes on small jobs, it's just the library. Mostly I prefer going to live people
who are the principals in the event or the experts in the subject. Library research
will give you clues as to who and where these people are, as well as telling you
what's already been covered. But writing entirely from what's already been
covered isn't journalism; it's more like writing a paper for school. You sometimes
have to go through PR people to get to the primary sources, and they can send
you literature, but they're not worth much as sources themselves; again, what
they tell you is what's already been covered, by them. In writing about science I
always follow up references to technical journals, but don't find them very useful
except for getting precise numbers and names of things right. They usually cover
one narrow research event, and seldom put it in context. (Steele, personal
communication, 1993)

Another free-lance science and technical feature writer, Wendy Grossman, uses computer databases and networks of people for her reporting. She explains:

> I use the magazine databases on CompuServe a fair bit. When I'm reviewing products, I also like to look in the vendor forums and see what people are complaining about. For the paranormal stuff, I use the network of skeptics; for computers, a lot of what I do is ask PR people to come up with appropriate contacts. I rarely read computer magazines, except, once in a while, *Byte*. *Science News* was recommended to me as a good source of science coverage, but in fact I'm finding *BusinessWeek* more useful, and I now have a subscription—it covers technology companies very well. One unfortunate thing is that most editors here won't let me quote from other magazines, which I think is unfair if the magazines have uncovered really useful material. A lot of journalists complain about PR people, but to a free-lancer they can be enormously helpful: Arranging loan and review equipment, supplying information about their clients, finding someone for you to talk to and making sure that person actually follows through with the interview, and so on. We're pampered far more here than journalists are in the U.S., partly because most of the magazines are so underfinanced. You have to watch it, of course, because obviously PR people are paid to put the best face on the company they can, but nonetheless they can save you a lot of time chasing people. (Grossman, personal communication, 1993)

Many American organizations and events are buffered by the public relations specialists or other media liaisons whose job it is to provide writers with access to scientists and technicians who have the expertise needed for your article. With this in mind, let's look at these major categories of science and technical sources in more detail:

Scientific Journals and Other Publications

The literature of a particular discipline or field is the best place to seek out story ideas. Most science and technical writers who specialize in a subject (medicine or environment, for example) read the major publications. When possible, it is advisable to subscribe to these publications. In medicine, two of the leading publications are the *Journal of the American Medical Association* and *The New England Journal of Medicine*. Yet, there are dozens of more highly specialized medical journals, magazines, and newsletters. General science and official organizational technical publications, such as *Science*, are also good for story prospects.

Professional and Technical Organizations

In science and technical subjects, professional organizations exist for exchange of new knowledge and for continuing education. Most leading researchers participate in these organizations in one way or another. Examples include the American Psychological Association, the American Chemical Society, and the

---

BEST SCIENCE ARTICLE SOURCES CHECK LIST

Organizations such as professional and trade associations
Resource books prepared for the news media
Professional associations and trade group conventions and exhibitions
Professional meetings
Professional journals and newsletters
Bibliographic indexes and abstracts
Online access bibliographic database services
Business/industry publications
Universities and colleges
Research and technical institutes and centers
Research groups and foundations
Museums and libraries
Commercial research organizations
Information hotlines

American Institute of Architects. These groups hold regional, national, and international gatherings on an annual basis and they provide a perfect forum for story ideas. Most scientific organizations also produce newsletters for members, or produce their own journals and magazines. These publications can be excellent sources.

Conventions and Meetings

In addition to regular organizational meetings, industry- and profession-wide conventions or symposia are regularly scheduled—generally once a year—to permit leading experts to gather and discuss the latest developments. Often, the latest research findings are discussed at these meetings and the leading authorities on topics gather to discuss trends, plan research, and share findings. These meetings transcend individual and institutional interests and provide even better opportunities for writers to develop story prospects and sources. Many groups that hold national and international annual sessions have subdivisions by specialization and interests (for example, cardiologists within the American Medical Association) and regional subgroups (for instance, by state or county).

Universities and Colleges

You probably have one nearby. Major universities and colleges that have research missions (usually the larger state and private 4-year schools) will provide a ready, and usually willing, series of sources for new information on just about any subject. This is particularly true about universities with medical and other professional schools and centers. A look at a current catalog will let you know what programs exist at the university and, from that, what types of research are being conducted. For more specific information, contact individual departments or the institution's public relations offices. In addition to these sources, some universities and colleges have begun to offer science and technical writing programs. One such program, at Lehigh University in Pennsylvania, allows students to specialize in science writing.

Institutes, Centers, and Research Groups

Perhaps the best-known organization that supports science and technical development is the National Science Foundation. This is not only a national funding source for research, but it is also a source of information about the research it is funding. Other sources exist at independent institutes, centers, and groups that can provide the latest information on topics of current concern. For example, one major source for changing weather patterns is the Climate Research Group at the Scripps Institute of Oceanography at LaJolla, California. Scientists there can be available to discuss their most recent work in meteorology and other related subjects.

SCIENCE AND TECHNICAL WRITING TROUBLE SPOTS

Writing about science and technology, even with the best sources available, can have its trying moments. As a feature writer involved in writing about complicated information, you must be able to discern fact from opinion. One way this can be done is by using multiple expert sources. Diversity of authoritative sources is often necessary when writing about scientific research and similar work at the cutting edge of a subject, where the lines between scientific opinion and fact are frequently blurred. Scientists frequently disagree about matters, especially new developments and theories.

Science writers also have the occasional opportunity to write about what some authorities call "maverick" science. This involves writing about very unorthodox or unusual scientific theories such as those that would predict

---

NEED SOURCES? TRY THE SCIENCE INFORMATION HOTLINE

It's a science writer's 911 number. The Media Resource Service hotline that is operated by the Scientists' Institute for Public Information receives numerous calls each week. Established in 1980, the hotline helps when science-based stories break in the United States and elsewhere. Such major stories as new AIDS developments and natural disasters create a need for fast, authoritative information.

Feature writers can call the service toll free by dialing *1-800-223-1730*. The service will refer writers to experts who can help them. Callers will be given names and telephone numbers of potential sources. The line is monitored for fast response even during nonbusiness hours such as evenings, weekends, and holidays.

earthquakes or propose miracle cures or treatments for major diseases. The least-preferred—but perhaps most tempting—approach to this, conventional journalistic practices dictate, is to tell readers what to think about these maverick theories. Traditions of objectivity and fairness do not support this approach, however. Most science writers feel they should be more critical of these maverick explanations and the individuals who advocate them than they would be of more conventional sources with more credible explanations. Research at Michigan State University suggests that because science writers already depend on authority figures for the content of stories about scientific controversies involving maverick theories, they should also depend on these expert sources for *interpretation* of the context of the controversy (Dearing & Kazmierczak, 1992).

The late University of Texas professor Warren Burkett (1986), author of *News Reporting: Science, Medicine, and High Technology*, advised all science feature writers to remember:

1. To plainly tell readers when a discovery or medical procedure is experimental, and thus not available as accepted medical practice. Or, put negatively, "raise no false hopes."

2. There is no drug without side effects, even when the public relations people tell you so; share this with readers.

3. Advise readers that just because something works in a lab experiment or on a few patients, there is no guide to whether or not it will work in a production process or become accepted medical practice. It usually takes about 10 to 15 years for a new science discovery to reach application and acceptance.

4. Be careful in using the word *breakthrough*. Scientists, doctors, and experienced science writers object to use of this word, because it is usually misleading.

Science and technical feature writing runs the risk of being incomplete as well. At times, sources may be unwilling to discuss all aspects of their work. Incomplete reporting causes confusion and uncertainty, and this results in lack of clarity. At times, sources are unprepared to talk with reporters, or they cannot adequately explain their work to you. If this occurs, how can you expect to make sense of things for your readers? Nevertheless, scientists can be skeptical about you and your effort to communicate their work to the world. You must make a concerted effort to gain their confidence and trust.

Science and technical writers can get involuntarily involved in the politics of the scientific community as well—especially when hard-to-get funding is at stake from public and private sources. Writers must be able to cut through the competitive nature and hype of some scientists and technicians to get at the heart of a matter.

Cures and solutions to difficult scientific problems must be viewed with skepticism on your part, too. At times, announcements of study results can be premature and create unjustified optimism in readers. Writers must be careful not to overdramatize the importance of results of studies they report.

THREE MAJOR PROBLEMS IN SCIENCE JOURNALISM

Robert Logan
Director, Science Journalism Center
University of Missouri, Columbia

The significant problems in science, environmental, and medical reporting today seem to revolve around innumeracy and the need for reporters to independently evaluate the empirical information supplied to them by government, public interest groups, universities, independent institutions, foundations, and corporations. Critics of the news media's reporting of medicine, science, and the environment usually point out inaccuracies and a lack of context to help the public understand issues.

At the foundation of accuracy and contextual problems is a common journalistic inability to independently evaluate scientific data and little understanding of relative risk. Although some key writers in the National Association of Science Writers, American Medical Writers Association, and Society of Environmental Journalists are notable exceptions, the vast majority of reporters, editors, and producers in most U.S. print and broadcast newsrooms are unable to independently judge whether a scientific environmental report is professional or unprofessional.

A journalist who has provided leadership to encourage his peers to become more independent of sources in adjudicating scientific data is Victor Cohn of the *Washington Post*, who is the "dean" of medical writers in the United States. Cohn and other critics explain that reporters and the public are too often at the mercy of an organization that can best put on a press conference featuring the quasi-scientific with celebrities to generate interest in news coverage.

In 1989, when the National Resource Defense Council (NRDC) wanted to criticize the EPA and FDA's handling of Alar, a chemical preservative for apples, its officials prepared some scientific data, a legislative and legal chronology, and asked actress Meryl Streep to appear at a news conference decrying the safety of apples. To make sure every news organization attended, they leaked the story to "60 Minutes" for broadcast the night before. The NRDC followed exactly the same formula in Great Britain where it presented the same "evidence" and used a well-known British actress, who cried (as did Streep) about how her children's health was jeopardized by a multinational conglomerate and indifferent governmental bureaucracies.

Reporters naturally trusted the NRDC. It had won the Nobel Prize. The environmental record of multinational conglomerates and the U.S. and British governments had merited widespread criticism and skepticism for the past 30 years. But there were almost zero challenges from journalists about the data the NRDC offered—and it was internationally reported as

What would have happened if most of the reporters and their editors were trained in epidemiology and risk assessment in the same way many journalists care about grammar, sentence structure, and graphics placement? For one thing, most would have discovered weak statistical associations, methodological flaws, and poor sampling techniques that would not pass peer review in serious scientific publications. The research presented simply did not merit the conclusions the NRDC reached, which the press faithfully reported. Although the NRDC's data were too flawed to be published, millions of persons worldwide were told by the news media that apples and apple products contained dangerous carcinogens and unsuspecting children were particularly at risk. Sales plummeted, jobs were lost in apple growing areas, and public confidence in the food supply was jolted without solid evidence—as most reporters later discovered.

All journalists need basic training in statistics. As the Alar example demonstrates, journalists should cover epidemiological data regarding environmental issues with a solid, working knowledge of what a "p value" is and how scientists make statistical estimates. It is interesting that news organizations, which will avoid sending someone to cover a baseball game if they cannot explain an earned run average, think little about sending in reporters with little basic technical knowledge to cover some of society's most highly personal and vital health policy issues.

The bottom line to understand scientific, biomedical, and environmental issues is to review the evidence independently—this enables a reporter to evaluate the honesty and reliability of a scientific source. If journalists cannot do this—particularly when public health or epidemiological questions are raised—then it is not surprising that serious mistakes are made in newspapers, magazines, and on television every day.

A second key issue is the lack of comparative perspectives about relative risks and the reluctance of reporters to point out inconsistencies between what persons take for granted and what frightens them. Perhaps these issues are best pointed out by biochemist Bruce Ames at the University of California-Berkeley. Ames has asked why natural carcinogens in natural fruits and vegetables are seen as benign, whereas far lower traces of man-made pesticides in foods are seen as a significant risk to public health (that demands public policy action).Why don't reporters, as part of their basic training, point out relative risks in news stories?

A third emerging problem is the intervention of public relations firms that seek to heighten publicity for a client engaged in litigation against large corporations for negligence usually linked to an expensive illness or disease. In personal injury litigation, it is to an attorney's advantage to obtain favorable publicity about the pain and suffering of clients who are alleged to have contracted cancer because of a toxic waste site near their property. Although there is rarely a question that the client is seriously ill, the epidemiology that links cancers to many environmental factors is less direct that most persons realize. The fact a cluster of persons become ill does not mean there is an environmental cause and it reflects a profound, but common, misunderstanding of statistics and reality to assert otherwise. Under some circumstances, reporters may be deliberately manipulated to obtain publicity leading to a more favorable verdict for a client. In most other judicial activities, journalists would not intervene on a side—so why is this behavior accepted in reporting about cancer clusters and alleged environmental malpractice?

Paradoxically, a major barrier to remedying these problems is the inconsistency among many press critics about whether the news media should evaluate information and confer legitimacy on one scientist or another. For example, most food chemists want journalists to independently assess the epidemiology of a pesticide. But many food chemists do not want a journalist to assess global warming evidence; the food chemists would rather see the charges and counter charges with little press intervention—make up their own minds. The example is not an isolated one.

In the scientific or biomedical arena, experts are consistently urging journalists to become more literate, better informed, and make distinctions about who are legitimate sources, who has the best evidence—and they ask reporters to actively discredit, or ignore persons with less evidence to advance scientific claims. But as soon as experts move outside their discipline, their message to the news media is the reverse: Just publish what you find and let us make up our mind.

In science and environmental coverage, the scientific community is sending a flawed, mixed message to journalists. Although the press is asked to decipher and elucidate evidence part of the time, most people can't make up their minds whether reporters are the first line guardians/gatekeepers of scientific credibility. For the news media to make progress, it is important for the scientific and biomedical community and the public to decide what role they want journalists to serve. The most desirable scenario would be for the public to insist that reporters learn statistical and epidemiological risk assessment and that reporters use their own judgment to ascertain if claims are based on evidence. It is really this issue and innumeracy—more than even a fundamental understanding of science and medicine—that is the current barrier to progress in reporting about medical, science, and environmental issues. (Logan, personal communication, 1993)

Still another caution about science sources involves the illegitimate source. You will occasionally encounter sources who attempt to provide evidence about new discoveries that is faked or artificially enhanced. There are still other individuals who try to gain attention through tricks and hoaxes played on the news media. To avoid being duped by a hoax, it is important not to depend too much on the information provided by a single source. Science writers should go beyond press releases and research reports in collecting information. These sources are only starting points, really, and should be supplemented by interviews and other written sources where possible.

Public relations staffers for companies involved in research and development of new products can be helpful to you, but they can also be an obstacle.

These individuals can stop you in your tracks from getting important information that they see as negative for their clients. They will often have different ideas about how to use new information. It is up to you to get around these barriers by talking to the scientists and managers directly whenever possible.

On occasion, it might be appropriate for you to double-check your story's first draft, or parts of it, with your primary sources. This is done solely in the interest of *accuracy*. Although this is not normal procedure in most feature writing, it is sometimes necessary when writing on highly scientific and technical subjects.

It is also important to discuss sensationalism in science and technical writing. Despite your impressions about the value of the story and the enthusiasm of your sources, be careful about "hyping" the story. Because science writing is not often glamorous and does not often command page one or cover-story levels, there is a temptation to overwrite an article and exaggerate its importance to gain an editor's attention. For example. Jim Sibbison (1988), a U.S. correspondent for *The Lancet*, a British medical journal, says too many reporters are drawn into the magic of "breakthrough" medical reporting. Sibbison says, "Medical scientists often criticize the news media for proclaiming major breakthroughs on the strength of what are, in fact, no more than tentative findings . . . . But the scientists can't rightfully unload all the blame on the media. Some of them can, on occasion, be found egging on the press with exaggerations of their own" (p. 36). He adds an observation that seems to be central to the whole problem: Good medical articles that are properly qualified tend to be of low news value. "Stories that say a salve performs miracles are more attractive than ones that say there may be flies in this particular ointment," he writes (p. 39). He says there is a simple test that can be a solution to this problem. He advises: "If [your] story includes words or phrases such as 'for the first time,' 'cancer-causing peanut butter sandwiches,' 'dawn of a new age,' 'milestone,' or 'breakthrough,' a second scientist's opinion may be in order" (p. 39).

HOW TO READ A SCIENTIFIC JOURNAL

Most scientific journals that report the findings of new studies in a discipline follow the same general model for publication of articles. Some sections are more important than others for nonexpert readers. Here is a list of those main sections and their value to science and technical feature article writers:

1. *Introduction and literature review.* This section can be skimmed but usually has minimal value to you. In it, you will find out about the problem being studied, what has previously been done by other researchers on the subject, and justification for the present study.

SCIENCE AND TECHNICAL WRITING REFERENCES

Alley, Michael, *The Craft of Scientific Writing*, Englewood Cliffs, NJ: Prentice-Hall, 1987.

American Psychological Association, *Publication Manual*, third edition, Washington, DC: APA, 1983.

Bly, Robert W. and Gary Blake, *Technical Writing: Structure, Standards, and Style*, New York: McGraw-Hill, 1982.

Booth, Vernon, *Communicating in Science: Writing and Speaking*, second edition, New York: Cambridge University Press, 1992.

Burkett, Warren, *News Reporting: Science, Medicine, and High Technology*, Ames: Iowa State University Press, 1986.

Burger, Jr., Edward J., *Health Risks: The Challenge of Informing the Public*, Washington, DC: The Media Institute, 1984.

Cohn, Victor, *Reporting on Risk: Getting it Right in the Age of Risk*, Washington, DC: The Media Institute, 1990.

Eisenberg, Anne, *Effective Technical Communication*, New York: McGraw-Hill, 1982.

Farr, A.D., *Science Writing for Beginners*, Boston: Blackwell Scientific, 1985.

Gannon, Robert, *Best Science Writing: Readings and Insights*. Phoenix, AZ: Oryx Press, 1991.

Hirschhorn, Howard H., *Writing for Science, Industry, and Technology*, New York: Van Nostrand, 1980.

Houp, Kenneth W. and Thomas E. Pearsall, *Reporting Technical Information*, fifth edition, New York: Macmillan, 1984.

Katz, Michael J., *Elements of the Scientific Paper*, New Haven, CT: Yale University Press, 1985.

Leedy, Paul D., *How to Read Research and Understand It*, New York: Macmillan, 1981.

Logan, Robert A., with Wendy Gibbons and Stacy Kingsbury, *Environmental Issues for the '90s: A Handbook for Journalists*, Washington, DC: The Media Institute, 1992.

Olsen, Leslie A. and Thomas N. Huckin, *Principles of Communication for Science and Technology*, New York: McGraw-Hill, 1983.

Singer, Eleanor and Phyllis M. Endreny, *Reporting on Risk*, New York: Russell Sage Foundation, 1993.

Sherman, Theodore A. and Simon S. Johnson, *Modern Technical Writing*, fourth edition, Englewood Cliffs, NJ: Prentice-Hall, 1983.

Turner, Maxine T., *Technical Writing: A Practical Approach*, Reston, VA: Reston, 1984.

Warren, Thomas L., *Technical Writing: Purpose, Process, and Form*, Belmont, CA: Wadsworth, 1985.

2. *Statement of hypotheses or research questions.* This part is more important because it tells you the particular focus of the study. What does the researcher want to find and, in the case of hypotheses, expect to find?

3. *Method.* Almost all research reports should have a section devoted to study procedures. What materials and methods were used in the study? What type of study (survey, experiment, and so on) was it? This section is valuable

to reporters only if the procedures used are controversial, revolutionary, or otherwise noteworthy.

4. *Findings.* The findings are far more valuable than the previously noted sections. Usually these are reported as text, but findings may also be placed in tables for quantitative studies. What did the study determine? The article should tell you in this section. What do you think of the findings?

5. *Discussion.* Interpretation and conclusions may be as important to you as the findings. Much of their value depends on the quality of this section, but this is the place where the researcher tries to make sense of the findings. The key point here is for the researcher to describe the meaning of the findings and simply not retell them.

Other common parts of research journal articles include the abstract, the author's identification and acknowledgments, data tables and graphics, and, of course, appendices.

COPING WITH QUANTITATIVE INFORMATION

One reason some writers shy away from science and technical writing is their aversion to anything involving numbers. This is especially true if the numbers are so small or so large most people cannot comprehend them. Readers often have the same aversion to statistics. Science and technical articles with many numbers or articles burdened with statistics simply turn off certain readers. It is up to you to judge the right amount of quantitative information in your articles.

Jack Hart, writing coach for *The Oregonian* in Portland, says we must be prepared to deal with numbers because there is no way of avoiding them. "The march of science and the computerization of government means that counting things becomes more and more fundamental to the process of daily life," Hart says (1991c, p. 1). Hart says just because journalists are not always good with numbers, they cannot avoid them. We must not only get numbers right, we must keep stories that contain them interesting and meaningful. Hart proposes that writers do the arithmetic for readers. Check how a number was computed and its accuracy before the story is published. He says it helps to visualize what the numbers represent. He also advises writers to use comparable forms of numbers (e.g., percentages or fractions) when using more than one statistic in a sentence or paragraph and to make the numbers meaningful by putting them in terms average readers understand.

It is also beneficial to use only the numbers you need and eliminate others. Minimize numerical density and avoid excessive detail, Hart says, by not packing too many numbers into a single paragraph. Often, making numbers in science and technical articles reader-friendly means finding ways to sugarcoat the statistical medicine for readers. The information may be critical to the article and you must use it. Being creative helps retain readership. Here are some additional tips to beat the technical game:

1. Use informational graphics, a subject discussed in more detail later.
2. Rounding off or shortening the detail of certain numbers. Although you cannot do this on all statistics, it can be done on very large or small numbers.
3. Put numbers in a meaningful context for readers with examples. If you have statistics for an entire state or country, reduce them to a level that makes more sense.
4. Interpret unusual statistics. Tell readers what they mean. Is a statistic good or bad? High or low?

A BASIC STRUCTURE FOR WRITING

When you sit down to write a science or technology article, the usual rules for writing and organization apply. Because of the unusual nature of the material involved, a little extra effort will make a difference. Regardless of the organizational plan you choose, if you accomplish these four goals in the article, you will probably succeed:

1. *Get the reader's attention.* Using whatever lead you choose, draw the readers into the article. Make them want to read it. Create drama. Use tension. No matter what you do, do not lose your potential readers with a slow, unimaginative start.

2. *Get the reader personally involved.* After you have the readers' attention, show readers how this subject affects them. What does it mean to them? Can you help them identify with the subject? Have you written it in a personal way so that it appeals on an individual level? How can your reader benefit from the article's content?

3. *Illustrate your points.* If you achieve this goal, you are showing readers what you are writing about. Give examples and case studies. But try to provide situations that can be understood at the level of your reader—whether the general public or the sophisticated specialist.

4. *Explain the meaning.* Tell readers what this development means. Do not leave your readers with the feeling, "So what?" when they put down your article. This is the major point of your article, so be certain you have made this assessment at some point. Many writers recommend the "so what?" be placed near the end as part of the conclusion.

TECHNICAL AND TRADE PUBLICATIONS

Although technical and trade publications might be an excellent source for some of your feature writing ideas, have you ever considered these publications as possible markets for your features? If you have an interest in science and technology writing, then you should consider these publications as outlets for your work, especially if you want to be a free-lance writer. If you want full-time employment as a science and technical feature writer, then these publications might be your new home.

These publications are highly specialized and require that you have extensive knowledge of the subject as well. Alert students should consider a second major in addition to journalism that might create that specialization. For example, if you have an interest in transportation, an engineering second major would be useful.

For writers getting into the profession after their college experience, think about your undergraduate major as a possible specialization. It is not uncommon to have a "previous life" before an interest in journalism, and this experience can often be the ticket to a specialization in these highly defined publications.

There are many business and industry, or trade, publications in the United States. Thousands of such trade periodicals mean thousands of opportunities for a writer. *Writer's Digest* columnist Art Spikol (1987b) sums up your opportunities with these publications: "[I]t's hard for me to think of any field of human endeavor for which a trade publication doesn't exist. And since many of you do something else with your time when you are not writing—like holding down full-time jobs—chances are you already know enough about something to come up with some articles you can sell to the trades themselves" (p. 18).

Some trade magazines and newsletters are in-house publications. That is, they represent and are published by institutions, organizations, corporations and other businesses—each with special interests. The nature of these publications reflects the sponsor or source, of course. In many cases, however, these publications are produced for the technical community of the organization and are often no different in subject matter approach from consumer, publications that frequently use scientific and technical articles.

Spikol (1986a) says there are some differences, however, that you must remember if you consider writing for such a publication. "Of course, corporate publications are *supposed* to be different from consumer publications. What makes them different, are, among other things, the selling of advertising, the advocacy position (the corporate publication is supposed to enhance the corporation), the captive audience, the clearances required, the free distribution" (p. 16).

ILLUSTRATIONS HELP TELL THE COMPLEX STORY

Visual communication techniques, such as informational graphics, help tell the science and technology story that contains complicated statistics, numbers, or other quantitative information. However, that is only one important use of graphics and illustrations in science and technical writing. Newspapers, magazines, and newsletters have found new artistic and computational means to create visual tools such as *infographics* to help explain complex issues. These illustrations combine factual information with visual techniques such as graphs, charts, maps, or "exploded" diagrams to tell a story. *USA Today* pioneered much of this and remains an innovator in the field.

The Fort Lauderdale *Sun-Sentinel* regularly presents major science stories to readers using full-color, full-page informational graphics. Recently this newspaper has used *open pages*, that is pages without advertising, once a week to show and explain science features. Examples include pages on space science featuring the NASA shuttle Endeavour, an environmental presentation focusing on Florida's coastal mangrove areas, a study of the so-called "big bang" theory of creation of the universe, and a profile of marine beasts called manatees, the "gentle giants" of the waters off the southeastern U.S. These packages mix the science writing of staffers with the artistic skills of informational graphics reporters. Typically the page will be highlighted with a major graphic, but there will also be as many as a half dozen smaller inset graphics and text from the article merged into a single explanatory presentation.

With more and more publications using color, the value of these visual packages in explaining complicated science, medicine, or technical subjects is growing. Because computers, informational graphics software, and photocopies are aiding in the rapid preparation of these images as well, they can be prepared more easily on shorter notice by art departments.

At times, photographs can be the answer. At other times, posed photographs used as illustrations will make the point. Art, such as drawings, maps, and graphs, can show the interrelationships of parts, procedures, and plans to clearly explain it. In many cases, it is appropriate and necessary for you as the writer to take the lead in suggesting visual applications for an article. These techniques are particularly helpful for science and technical writers. For example, in explaining how the space shuttle disaster occurred, many publications used color graphics to supplement features that were written weeks and months after the accident.

The principle is no different from certain types of service articles such as the how-to article. To make information more understandable—something as routine as bypass surgery or as unusual as a nuclear reactor fire and explosion—illustrations such as informational graphics are necessary to tell the story.

PROFESSIONAL'S POINT OF VIEW

Patrice Adcroft
Omni magazine

Nobody but nobody wants to read technical writing. It does nothing that good writing ought to do: inform, entertain, and move the reader in some way. Expose an idea to the air, convert a nonbeliever. Instill a sense of wonderment. Let the reader in on a universal truth.

What science writing should be is really up to you, the writer. Every piece should carry with it some kind of agenda; a determination to arrive at something greater than just a set of facts. I can tell you what good science writing—good journalism—should not do: It should never intimidate, pontificate, or confuse. Even the most complex scientific breakthrough can be described in ordinary terms. Writers who rely on jargon are either (a) befuddled or (b) snobs. I wouldn't want my readers to have to put up with either of these.

Telling a good story is fundamental to good writing. Don't forget to leave a trail that guides the reader from lead to end. Just be sure that the trail consists of something more substantive than breadcrumbs. The trail should be clearly marked, with a few resting places along the way where a reader can stop and catch his breath and reflect on what's been said.

I really care about the way an article sounds. If one of my editors is having trouble with an article, I'll tell him to read the piece aloud. Then he gets an idea of how it will sound in the reader's head. If a sentence just clunks along, or you can't get its meaning from one reading, there's a problem.

Science writers should know how to interview professionals. That means getting them to talk on the average person's level. If you don't understand a concept or formula, neither will the reader. I have something I call the amazing dumb animal question. When there's something terribly complex to grasp, the theory of chaos, for example, or automata, I preface my questions with: "OK. This may sound like a dumb animal question, but . . . ." I've asked bioengineers to compare artificial organs to washing machines, neurologists to compare the central nervous system to the New York subway lines. (The article was going in a publication geared for New Yorkers.) Always ask your source to compare whatever he's talking about to an everyday item. Seek out an image the reader can hang on to. This will make the item, concept, equation, live.

A few words about the best science/technology stories I've published: All contained some human element (a maverick scientist's struggle with a staid institution, for example); all were clear, but not simple-minded; all took the reader on a journey that left him more aware of himself and the world around him. Many were cleverly packaged—an article on the future of films appeared as movie treatments, actually written by famous directors who were told to pretend that they had the most futuristic technology at their fingertips. Good science writing doesn't just report on a breakthrough and leave it at that; it investigates the consequences of the discovery or breakthrough. (Adcroft, personal communication, 1988)

Patrice Adcroft is the editor of *Omni* magazine, Omni Publications International, New York. She had been a senior editor before becoming the first woman in the editor's position of a national consumer science magazine. Before joining Omni in 1983, she was senior editor of *Family Weekly* at CBS. She has also been managing editor for Family Media's *Alive and Well* and a staff writer for *Good Housekeeping*.

III

The Collegiate
and Professional Writer

16

Writing Feature Articles On Campus

Senior Amy Grewe was an assistant news editor for *The Murray State News* when she took on the assignment of writing three major feature articles about college students and money. It was an important project for the Pacemaker Award-winning weekly campus newspaper at Murray State University in Murray, Kentucky. Grewe's full-page spring semester project, an assignment for her public affairs reporting class, focused on the financial future for graduating seniors. She wrote about how students about to enter the job market can begin to save money for their future, how loans can help create needed cash flow, and how important the companies behind the policies can be when seniors consider purchasing their own automobile, apartment, and health insurance policies for the first time. "I had intended the stories for graduating seniors leaving school," Grewe (personal communication, 1993) says. "Most freshmen, sophomores, and juniors don't ever think about those things. I know I didn't. Most students depend on their parents for financial support and management."

Grewe's stories were supplemented with graphics about cash flow, managing credit cards, and how to buy insurance. She interviewed insurance agents, bankers, financial planners, and other money experts in western Kentucky where her school is located.

The stories were published on the newspaper's Focus page, a regular feature that gives readers "in-depth writing in a variety of ways each week," says *Murray State News* faculty advisor Dr. Ann Landini (personal communication, 1993). "We try to concentrate on subjects of high interest to our students." In addition to writing and reporting the features, Landini said, Grewe also laid out the page as part of her "capstone" senior project. The lead story was one of her strongest efforts as a student, her teacher believes. "I thought that story was the best work she did at Murray State," Landini said. "She enjoyed business writing and I told her she should try it. She did, and this page was the result" (personal communication, 1993).

Grewe, who went to work for the weekly *McLean County News* in Calhoun, Kentucky, as a reporter and photographer after graduating, said she taught herself about money management when she began the class assignment. "First, I had to get an idea of the different plans available. I had to educate myself," she said. Her lead article discussed methods area experts recommended to save money for the long term. In a small town, she explained, finding authoritative local sources for such a set of stories was not easy. "Finding sources was the hardest thing about that story," Grewe (personal communication, 1993) stated. "Once I found people to talk to, it was easy to do. It was tough to decide what to leave out once I did the interviews. There was so much. But that is a nice problem to have." When she had assembled all of her information, Grewe wrote this lead story, "Grads Need Savings Plan":

> The last thing that young adults want to worry about is saving money for the future. However, by establishing a savings plan early they can save themselves a big headache later in life.
>
> Dave Hornback, executive vice president of the Bank of Murray, said that students should begin saving money as soon as they graduate.
>
> "When you're 21 or 22 years old, 45 seems so far away, but before you know it you're there and you haven't paved the way," he said.
>
> Betty Boston, certified financial planner and investment broker for Hilliard Lyons, said people should try to put 10 percent of each paycheck into some type of savings, beginning with an emergency fund.
>
> "Things do come along and if you have four to six months living expenses in a savings account or money market account, you're not in a desperate financial situation," she said.
>
> Hornback said if given the opportunity a person should also participate in a 401K plan.
>
> "It is a plan whereby you can set aside a certain percentage of your salary and a certain percentage would be set aside by your employer and they are placed in an interest-bearing savings account," he said. "For example, you could put in 6 percent of your salary and your employer could match that up to 3 percent, so you've got 9 percent of your savings every month going to a savings account. If you're able to start early it could mass into thousands of dollars."
>
> Hornback said most people rationalize why they cannot save.
>
> "Number one we have bills to pay and number two we want to spend our money as soon as we get it," he said. "Often times we want to spend more than we make."
>
> Hornback said even a small amount put into savings each month would help.
>
> "I would say if you were starting out with something like $50 a month, the best way to start would be with a regular savings account," he said. "It may not earn a lot of interest, but, really at that point, the most important thing is just getting into a habit of saving money.
>
> "It's just a matter of forcing yourself to start saving money because you never know when you're going to be out of a job," he said. "These days the economy is so weak and having that money to fall back on is almost a must."

Hornback also said people must live within their budget.

"I would caution people not to think they have to have a brand new automobile and live in the fanciest apartment in town," he said. "If you get into that habit, it's one that becomes a lifestyle and you never save anything."

"You can't get frustrated and compare yourself to everyone else," he said. "You have to look at your own situation and be in control."

Hornback said if a person's intent was to save and he did not want easy access to it, a savings account would be better than a money market account.

"A regular savings account is non-transactional. There are no checks on it and you have to come to the bank to withdraw the money," he said. "A money market account is an interest bearing checking account and it is transactional. Generally it will earn less interest than a savings account," he said.

Boston said once a person has an emergency fund established he can begin investing in such things as stocks, bonds, and certificates of deposit (CD's).

STOCKS

A stock represents ownership in a business and can be bought for about $800 to $1,000. The value of the stock in the future depends on the profitability of the business. They offer the highest earning potential; however, they are also the riskiest because the short-term future is uncertain.

Both Boston and Hornback advise graduates not to invest in stocks when they first get out of college.

Serious investors own several stocks to reduce the risk, but it costs a great deal of money which most young adults do not have, they said.

BONDS

Bonds are similar to lending a company money. Instead of owning a share in a company, a person is guaranteed he will receive, after a certain amount of time, the initial investment along with interest. If cashed too soon, however, a person can receive a penalty.

MUTUAL FUNDS

Mutual funds are a pooling of many investors' money. Instead of using a large amount of money to buy one stock, it is a portfolio of various kinds of stocks and bonds.

They can be started with as little as $250, expanded and can be cashed any time without penalty.

CD's

Instead of loaning money to a company, a person lends money to a bank for a fixed amount of time at a fixed interest rate. They can be purchased for as little as $500. If the money is withdrawn before the fixed time, the investor will receive a penalty.

"One thing I tell people is to put money in a savings account and when it gets up to $600 buy a CD," Hornback said. (Grewe, 1993, p. 5) Reprinted with permission of *The Murray State News*.

If you are a journalism or other type of college writing student, your first experience may not involve a story as complicated as the one written by Murray State's Amy Grewe, but that memorable first feature assignment may be for a writing class or for one of the student publications on your campus. You get the assignment and get started. It is a very good opportunity to get your first story into print.

Student publications serve a noble purpose for their campuses— the primary mass communication means at many schools—and the feature content of those publications is an important part of these newspapers, magazines, and newsletters. Not only do these publications provide a forum for development of student journalistic skills, they also inform students, faculty, and staff members of current events and trends on their campuses. Campus publications are important student voices where there may not be voices otherwise. Similarly, student newspapers, magazines, and newsletters can help protect student rights in the face of some administrators who, if unchecked, would abuse them.

Feature articles are also a significant part of student publications because many student publications are produced on nondaily deadlines. The infrequency of publication often dictates a more feature-oriented approach to writing breaking news that usually would be treated as a news story rather than a feature. Student newspapers that publish once or twice a week have even larger percentages of feature content because of their infrequency of publication. It is one of the ways these publications try to keep stories fresh and appealing. Similarly, campus magazines and newsletters, which publish only 1 to 10 times a year, have large proportions of major and minor feature articles in their content mix.

This means there are numerous feature writing opportunities for a beginning college-level writer. In fact, these opportunities are the best places for you to build confidence in your work and to show others that you can master feature writing. Large colleges and universities may have a dozen or more university-sponsored, student-funded, and independent student-oriented publications. In addition to the more conventional campus newspapers, you may find campus laboratory newspapers produced occasionally by news-editorial or journalism programs or by specific journalism or English classes. There may be other special newspapers produced from time to time by organizations such as student affairs, the athletic department, various academic units, administrative offices such as admissions and enrollments, and the alumni associations. There are similar opportunities with campus magazines. Most major universities and colleges have one or more regularly published magazines. Some are only once- or twice-a-year specialized magazines, such as literary or greek organization publications, but others are issued on a much more frequent basis.

Student journalists should not overlook newsletters as a place for their work. Most student organizations have a need to communicate with their members or potential members and newsletters are frequently used. There are opportunities for beginners looking for a chance for their first byline in all of these publications right on your campus.

Feature stories are probably among the easiest types of articles for beginners to develop on a campus. You will be writing about a place that is familiar to you and using sources that are reasonably easy to contact and develop. There are also the conveniences of geographic proximity and easy-to-get background information that help beginners as well. These experiences will not only build confidence, they will also give novices their first experiences in working with editors. You will have a chance to try out the techniques and approaches you have read about and discussed in class.

These may be the least difficult markets for beginners to crack. Sometimes, beginning college-level writers will be able to sell their work to local newspapers or magazines, but this is rare. It may not take long for a strong and unusually talented writer to develop the skills necessary to make the jump from college publications to more professional ones, but the place for most students to start, clearly, is on campus.

WHAT MAKES CAMPUS WRITING DIFFERENT?

The opportunities you have to write feature articles while you are a student at a college or university will be important ones in your development as a professional feature writer. This experience will be very valuable to you and one that you need to maximize.

This is your opportunity to learn. It is a chance to test the writing and reporting methods that are proven by experience to work. It is also a chance to experiment with new writing and reporting approaches and styles. In an educational environment, there is more room for making mistakes from which you can grow. There is the chance to work closely with professors, publications advisors, and other more experienced writing coaches who may not be as readily available to you once you leave school.

Working with student editors is also a chance for student writers to learn the interpersonal skills needed to function as a professional. The give and take between an editor and writer is not that different on a college campus than it will be once you make the transition as a professional. The concerns and basics of the relationships are the same.

Probably the major reason campus feature writing is different is the fact that it is a learning experience. Although you do not want to make mistakes, you can. Although you don't want to leave problems with editors or sources unsolved, you might. Although you don't want to use bad judgment, you might. In essence, opportunities with student publications are the time to learn by doing. Try the classroom and textbook theory. Put it into practice. We learn from experiences, and the journalistic opportunities you have on campus will enhance your writing. This is the time to experiment with your writing—try things you might not have the chance to try once your career begins. It is the time to stretch yourself and see what your real potential might be.

FEATURE OPPORTUNITIES ON CAMPUS

There are a surprisingly large number of diverse feature writing opportunities on most college and university campuses. Just look around. As a student, you are eligible to write for student newspapers, magazines, yearbooks, newsletters, and other special publications. There are also more professional publications published on campuses as well. Most colleges and universities produce publications for students, faculty, staff, and alumni. Although these are written and edited by professional staffs, students often are given opportunities to take assignments as part of classes, for part-time employment, and for other purposes.

How do you get started? At most student publications, it is as simple as walking into the office and asking to meet with an editor. Introduce yourself and tell the editor that you want to write. An application might be completed along the way, but the big step is asking for, and accepting, that first assignment. Some publications will give you a specific story to begin. Others will be willing to take your own suggestions for stories. Because you may be asked to propose something, be prepared to suggest a strong feature story idea.

Campus Newspapers

As in the commercial world, college newspapers come in all shapes and sizes. Some are broadsheet (or traditional full size); others, tabloids (half-size pages). Some campus newspapers publish as seldom as two or three times a month, others as often as 6 or 7 days a week when school is in session. Some have summer editions whereas others do not. In terms of management, some campus newspapers are independent of the school's central administration, but many are not. Regardless of the type of newspaper on your campus, it is likely your school has some sort of newspaper and perhaps even more than one. This translates into an opportunity for you to learn about feature writing.

Campus newspapers regularly publish feature material. Depending on the school and its size, opportunities to write features for campus newspapers will vary. Some campus newspapers, even the highest quality publications, can never seem to recruit enough news and feature writers. Others, most likely ones published at major state universities and other big schools, have much more competitive situations and any staff writing positions are difficult to secure.

Two of the most popular feature-oriented sections are typically entertainment and sports. A third section embraces student lifestyles and extracurricular activities. These are subjects in which college students often seem to feel most comfortable and would be great places to start. However, remember that there are other sections needing help, too. Opinion section editors are always looking for insightful and interesting columnists with a fresh look at current events or with something to say about the issues. Student activities, both on and off campus, never cease to be potential feature material.

The Vermilion, the Pacemaker Award-winning weekly student newspaper at the University of Southwestern Louisiana in Lafayette, is like many other campus newspapers in devoting considerable space to features about campus entertainment and the arts. Whereas many other campus newspapers offer the standard "previews" and "reviews" features about music and film, some, such as *The Vermilion*, go further on a regular basis by offering articles about what students themselves do. Staff writer Jennifer Brown's feature in the "Tout Le Reste" section of the newspaper focused on a popular dance in Louisiana's Cajun Country known as the *fais do-do*. She talked to a campus dance class instructor and to students who enjoy dancing the fais do-do and listening to the distinctive Cajun band music. This is Brown's (1993) informative article:

> It's more than mastering the motion: two steps forwards, two steps back. It's more than moving to the beat of the music. It's more than a dance.

> It's a zest for life. And a flair for the dramatic.

> It's the rhythm of life down here at the "Fais do-do" and dancing to the melody of a chank-a-chank Cajun band that has always held special magic for everyone in Southwestern Louisiana.

> Fais do-do literally means "go to sleep" and, according to Frank Randol of Randol's Restaurant, it was a phrase Cajun mothers would tell their children at social gatherings. Once the children were sleeping and tucked under the table, the parents could begin dancing.

> Cajun dancing has been a part of life since the Cajuns came from Acadia in French Canada more than 200 years ago.

> Cajun dancing has made its way to USL through the instruction of T.J. Ledet in the Continuing Education Department.

> Elaine Foreman, coordinator of Personnel Development at the Continuing Education Center, said the course is popular and fills up quickly.

> At the present, Ledet is teaching a course for singles and another for doubles.

> "I don't teach for the money," he said. " I do it for the fun."

> For a $30 registration fee, Ledet teaches the waltz, the two step, and the Cajun swing. "I don't like to be called a teacher. I like to share what I know," Ledet added.

> The class isn't just dancing and fun. The students have homework, too. The first week, students are asked to go listen to a live Cajun band. The first thing Ledet asks his students when they come for the next class is, "Did you go practice?"

> "If you take this class once a week and you don't go practice, then you've wasted your money," said Ledet. "There is no reason not to go practice because there's many places in town that offer live music nightly."

Ledet added that at the end of the class, the students throw a party and practice what they have learned.

Not all the students learn how to dance in the classroom.

"In the beginning, I just watched and that helped me learn," said Anne-Scott Bahlinger, a senior in education. "Dana, my sorority sister, actually taught me how to dance."

Bahlinger, a native of Baton Rouge, said she never had seen Cajun dancing before she moved to Lafayette. "It looked like fun and I wanted to learn," she said.

Kim Oliver and Jake Perez, both students at USL, said they find themselves dancing on the average of two to three nights a week.

"It's something I can enjoy doing with my state's culture. And it's a great way to meet people," Oliver said. "It's free fun for all ages. Once you get into it, you can also use your imagination."

She added that the fun and exercise is the best part.

Ryan Still, a junior in advertising, said he learned in clubs when he would go out. "I'd done a little jitterbugging, and I wanted to learn to two-step. It goes with the Cajun lifestyle: You eat good food, you drink a little and you dance.

"I like it because you have a chance to interact with a older crowd. That's what's so great about two-stepping and that type of dancing, you have a chance to learn from each other," he added.

One of the hot spots for Cajun dancing is at Randol's, which proudly boasts about its "two-steppin', toe-tappin', taste tempting" way of life. Native Cajuns from all over Southwest Louisiana congregate at Randol's every evening to twirl to the traditional rhythms of accordions and fiddles.

According to Randol, "This is the place where the young and the old let the good times roll." Randol's also has taken Cajun dancing on the road, traveling to 17 cities across the United States in 1989, and regularly spreading the word of the "Laissez Les Bons Temps Rouler" atmosphere.

"One of the reasons that I find it's so popular," said Ledet, "is that anyone can do it. The steps are simple and when Cajuns picked up the dance, they kept their stuff simple."

"Our culture here is guarded and it's real neat to be able to share that with people," said Ledet.

Still added, "I think it's neat when you go outside this area, where people don't dance like that, and people watch us when we dance. They really like it." (p. 21) Reprinted with permission of *The Vermilion*.

Lifestyles and campus changes that affect student lifestyles are also reasons to write news features for campus publications. *The Daily Orange* at Syracuse University often uses such features. Staff writer Lori Glickman was assigned to write a reaction feature story about how members of a Syracuse social sorority felt about construction nearing completion for their new house. She interviewed members and captured their excitement of looking forward to the move later in the year. Her story was published as a package with a second story she wrote about renovations of other Greek organization houses on campus. Her stories appeared on a special *The Daily Orange* page devoted to "Greek Life." This section is published every 2 weeks in the news section. This is the lead article by Glickman (1993):

> The construction of the new Alpha Omicron Pi House will be a great opportunity for the future of the sorority, said Jen Klebanoff, a junior in the School of Education and an AOPi sister.
>
> "We'll have a house that's just for AOPi," she said.
>
> The sorority has not had a permanent home for several years, said Marie Brown, president of the Chi Corporation, the corporation that funds the sorority.
>
> "This is our seventh move since we recolonized in 1985 when we renewed our charter," Brown said.
>
> "The year 1989-90 we were down on Euclid," said Toni Citera, a junior in the College of Arts and Sciences and current housing director for AOPi.
>
> "It will be the first time we're actually getting our own house," she said. "We're really excited about it."
>
> "The fact that we'll have our own permanent residence means so much to everybody," Brown said.
>
> The AOPi house is now located at 1105 Harrison St. and is rented from the Theta Tau fraternity, Brown said.
>
> "From what I understand, Theta Tau wasn't able to fill the house (in the past)," she said.
>
> AOPi has been living in the house for the past three years, Citera said, and Theta Tau will be returning in the fall.
>
> **A house for the fall**
>
> The location of the new house will be at 106 Walnut St. next to the Alibrandi Catholic Center, and will be completed by next fall, Citera said.
>
> The ground-breaking ceremony will be at 11 a.m. Saturday. Brown said the original vice president, Jan Slagowski, will be in attendance.
>
> The Chi Corporation will fund the project along with contributions from the national chapter and loans from the banks, Citera said.
>
> Brown said there was a fund drive last year and there are plans for another.
>
> Sisters in AOPi have also had to pay building and furnishing fees, Citera said.

Lauri Ricciardi, a sophomore in the College of Arts and Sciences, is a recently initiated sister who will be living in the new house next year.

"I'm living in the house to get closer to the sisters," she said.

Ricciardi said her pledge period lasted only eight weeks and she did not get as much time to know all the sisters as she would have liked.

Ricciardi currently lives in a residence hall and said she is looking forward to more living space next year.

"It's not just going to be living in one room, but a whole house," she said. "I'm definitely looking forward to it," Ricciardi said. "It's kind of like living at home, but with friends." (p. 3) Reprinted with permission of *The Daily Orange*, Syracuse University.

The University of South Florida's Pacemaker Award-winning student newspaper, the daily *USF Oracle*, also often highlights the extracurricular activities of students in its "Features" section. On one recent page, two students were the focus of feature stories describing their interests outside the classroom. One story, written by photo editor Tom Wagner, focused on an "A" student who posed for *Playboy* magazine as "Playmate of the Month." The other student, a philosophy major, was performing in a theater production in Tampa, near where the school is located. *USF Oracle* features editor Andrea Tracy highlighted her stage work by interviewing the actress about her latest effort. The first of the two stories below is written by Wagner (1993):

She may have been in one of your classes or walked past you in the hall. You may have even spoken with her between classes.

What you may not have known is that when the June issue of *Playboy* hit the stands two weeks ago, she was the centerfold.

Alesha Oreskovich might catch your eye sitting in class or walking across campus, but who would guess that this straight 'A' USF student would be Playmate of the Month?

Talk with her and you feel like you have been friends for years; ask her about last night's homework and you will receive an intelligent reply.

Last June, when the Playmate of the Year was announced on television, Alesha was watching.

"It made me think, 'How could I make that happen to me?'" she said.

She picked up the phone and called Michael Moffitt, a photographer friend of hers. She had not spoken with him for a while and when she told him of her interest, his response was too good to be true.

"He told me that since we had spoken last he started working for *Playboy* as a Playmate scout," she said.

So she made some tests shot with Moffitt which he then sent to *Playboy*.

Two days after the photos were mailed she was asked to come to Chicago for a day-long photo shoot.

Soon after, Alesha flew to Chicago for a hectic day of work. She arrived in the morning, posed in the studio all day as the photographer shot almost 30 rolls of film, and traveled home that night to wait for more news.

"You could hear from them, you may not," she said. "I told myself I was going to try and forget about it and go on with my life as usual."

The next morning *Playboy* called and asked her to do a centerfold shoot.

Alesha spent the next week in Chicago, where five days were dedicated to getting one photo.

Once *Playboy* decides which shot to use, it is printed up just like the centerfold. Then the mock-up is sent to Hugh Hefner for approval. No centerfold gets published without his endorsement.

"He either says yes, no, or reshoot it," said Alesha. "If he says yes, he signs it and sends it back. At that point you know if you're getting published or not."

Hefner signed her centerfold and Alesha was notified while she was attending class at USF during the Fall semester of 1992. She made it clear she could not finish the layout until after classes ended in December.

"My education is very important to me," she said. "I couldn't just pick up and leave in the middle of classes."

In January the rest of the photos for the layout were shot on location in Miami and Chicago.

With all the work, Alesha found it impossible to stay in Tampa long enough to attend classes at USF. Her only avenue for continued education was with the University of Florida, which offers correspondence courses.

"Right now I'm taking nine credits and I'll take another six for the summer," she said. "They transfer perfectly to USF, so I won't lose any time while working for *Playboy*."

Her responsibilities as a Playmate sometimes take Alesha away from her boyfriend of two years, Greg Garlik.

"So far it hasn't been too bad," he said, "but I know it's going to get worse before it gets better."

Garlik does not have negative feelings about Alesha posing nude.

"The way I look at it, I'm sharing her beauty with the world, and that is only an image. I'm not sharing Alesha herself—that isn't in the magazine," he said.

So far, Alesha's family has supported her through everything.

"We're behind her 100 percent, we always have been," Marcia [sic] said.

With her family's backing and her own sense of self-determination, Alesha is optimistic about her plans for the future.

"These are opportunities of a lifetime and while they are available I am going to take them," she said. "I've done the modeling thing. I have pounded the streets looking for work and that's not for me. While the jobs come to me and they continue to be exciting possibilities, I'll take them." (pp. 8–9) Reprinted with permission of the *USF Oracle*.

This is Andrea Tracy's (1993) story:

For most college students, juggling a full load of classes and a work schedule is more than enough to test the limits of patience and endurance. But for USF student Heather Cagle, juggling one more activity just adds to the rigorous challenge called college.

Raised in Lakeland, Florida, Cagle moved to the Tampa Bay area last November. In the few months since then she has become very involved in the theater. Cagle was seen on stage several times last year, including performances at The Loft Theater and shows here at USF.

Currently, Cagle is performing in Pig's Eye Productions' "Every Little Breeze Seems to Whisper Louise."

Cagle plays the part of Louise, a young girl with a passion for hopeless causes.

During the course of the play she befriends a young homeless man who feels the same nostalgia Louise displayed for the restaurant, where she works, particularly since it has become his home.

Even though theater is her first love, Cagle is attending classes at USF to earn a degree in philosophy.

"It's just something that I want to know," Cagle said.

During the past school year, Cagle was attending classes, working part-time at a local restaurant and performing in back-to-back shows.

"I have to keep everything really organized," Cagle said. "But I love it, I've never been happier." (p. 8) Reprinted with permission of the *USF Oracle*.

News sections also use features to balance the routine spot coverage of the day. These features often offer unique perspectives and sometimes can set a seasonal tone for readers. This was the case for one writer for the University of Florida's daily student newspaper. Keith Herrel, who was a student feature writer for *The Independent Alligator* in Gainesville, wrote an entertaining Thanksgiving season feature. In the story headlined, "The Lord Provides It, and We Cook It," he tells a warm personal story about a rural family that lives near the university and how it prepares its highly unusual holiday feast in true communal style. Note how the story is enriched by Herrel's use of strong and revealing direct quotations. He allows his sources to tell their story. This is Herrel's (1989) story:

It's easy to find Thelma Markham at Thanksgiving. Just pull up next to the Grove Park store on Highway 20 east of Gainesville, roll down the window and ask for "T.J." One of the many locals who gather around the picnic table will point east and say, "Just follow your nose."

The brief directions are explicit indeed. If Thelma is home and the wind is blowing the right way, the delectable scent of roasting wild meat will mingle with the aroma of fresh vegetables and attract hungry visitors from all over town.

Down the pitted dirt road that leads to Thelma's place, the modern world temporarily ceases to exist. On both sides of the road, amid the trees draped with Spanish moss, stand multi-colored houses arranged helter-skelter like handfuls of tin-roofed dice thrown down by some impetuous gambler.

It's easy to distinguish Thelma's house from the rest. The laughter there is louder, the crowd larger and the welcome heartier.

"Pick up a plate and sit down," is a favorite greeting of Cheristine, Thelma's sister. She will tell you in a friendly bluffness to go into the dining room and fill up your dish.

The food will be in a horseshoe-shaped arrangement in the rustic dining room. But filling your plate may not be an easy task; at any time there might be 40 or more of Thelma's friends and relatives vying for the steaming foods in the compact room. If this is the case, then it is a perfect time to visit the cook.

Thelma, 26, will be in her small kitchen, adjacent to the dining room. She will greet you with a smile and talk to you as she skillfully prepares some of her specialties, ranging from cooter to 'coon and gator to gravy. Some opossums will be in the pot and turkeys in the oven as she wipes her hands with a towel and carries a casserole dish heaped with swamp cabbage into the awaiting holiday throng.

Thelma, who is single and has no children of her own, is the uncontested culinary master of her family. She has been for years.

But exactly how long ago she took command of the kitchen is uncertain.

"She was about 8 years old when she started," Thelma's uncle Johnny Mack, 40, said. Sitting on one of the two living room couches, wearing a gray Fedora and sipping a cold Old Milwaukee, Johnny reminisced about Thelma's earliest meals.

"I started cooking at least 18 years ago," Thelma said.

"She was 11. And the first thing she cooked was a red velvet cake," said Zennie Sheffield, Thelma's 80-year-old great-grandmother.

Although her family disagrees about when Thelma began her cooking, everyone agrees that her food is excellent.

"They better tell me my food is good. 'Cause if they don't, they won't be eating here anymore," Thelma said with determination.

For Thelma's family, having her in the kitchen means having a cornucopia on the table. But exactly how big is Thelma's family?

"I got so many grand, great-grand and greater-grandchildren that if they were all hogs, I'd be rich," Mrs. Sheffield said. "I came down here from Georgia about 45 years ago with my father and my five children. Now I have close to 100 relatives living around here."

Mrs. Sheffield lives in the house next to Thelma's. The two houses, along with the yard that separates and surrounds them, have a personality all their own. The yard is frequented and fertilized by an array of animals, domestic and wild.

Red and yellow hens and roosters, pecking and cock-a-doodling at whim, strut around the amber grass and green shrubs. Armadillo and wild turkeys sometimes venture on the grounds and usually find themselves on Thelma's table. Bunky the cat scampers around, evading the eight or nine dogs that wait not so patiently for a generous handout from Thelma. A black pig named Arnold rounds out the cast.

The cacophony created by those animals sometimes competes with other noises made by various children screaming and groups of men shooting their shotguns in preparation for the day's hunt.

"You should have been here this past Super Bowl," Johnny Mack said. "I brought home a 10-point deer." He spread his arms wide to show the breadth of the animal's antlers with the 10 horns. "It fed about 15 people."

Thelma opened up one of her family's five full-length freezers. It was as full as a supermarket's meat case. She started pulling out the frozen bundles to try and tell what each one contained. After scraping ice off of the basketball-sized chunks of meat, she began to tell what was in each plastic-wrapped package.

"This is some of that wild boar. This is rabbit. This is probably 'coon. I think this is some of that wild turkey. Hmmmmmm. I don't know what this is."

"All of our freezers are like that," Cheristine said as she sat at the table eating some of Thelma's fried opossum and sweet potatoes, garnished with red peppers. "We're prepared for anything—hurricanes, tornadoes, water flows, fire, you name it."

The hundreds of pounds of meat and vegetables tucked away in Thelma's freezers probably could feed the whole family every day for one month before the supply ran out. But the freezers are unlikely to become barren, because everybody constantly adds either animals or vegetables to the stockpile.

"My cousin, he's the one who gets me the swamp cabbage," Thelma said. "He goes down by the trestle where the fishing water is, and there are these pell-mell plants.

"He gets a machete and cuts away at the bark to the middle. Then he brings it to me. You have to cook it longer than regular cabbage though, just like you're cooking a pot of greens.

"Now my granddaddy, he has a garden with red peppers, greens, iced potatoes— just about all the vegetables we eat come from his garden. He's about 68 or 69 years old, and brother, he could sure get around. He's also cheaper on your pockets. All you have to do is go down there and bring him a six-pack, and he'll give you whatever you want."

With bartering like this, Thelma's table is seldom lacking in food, and this fact is never more obvious than at Thanksgiving.

The heat from the wood-burning stove banished the autumn cold and gave the house an old-world scent as Thelma sat at the dining-room table and told how she prepares her holiday banquets.

"In the evening, I start cooking. I'll cook until about five o'clock in the morning, and then I'll go take a nap.

"When I get up, I'll start putting out the food. It will be spread over that dresser, that dresser and this table." She made a sweeping motion with her hand around the room, showing the extent of the banquet area.

"Everybody starts at one end and works their way around. If they don't get enough the first time, they just have to go through the line again. Most people will come with their Tupperware dishes and take the food to go because there wouldn't be enough room for everybody if they stayed here."

The more than 40 guests who Thelma fed last Thanksgiving, however, found ample dining area in the yard and an overabundance of food on the table.

"I had ham, two turkeys, deer, opossum, 'coon. Let's see. Oh, yeah, I had a duck too. My nephew got it. My granddaddy gave us mustard and collard greens, string beans, potatoes, peas in the shell and okra. And we had swamp cabbage, too."

As if trying to establish the logic of it all, she said, "You see, you just can't have one or two meats at Thanksgiving or Christmas."

Her words came almost as an echo of her great-grandmother.

"If the children eat all that's there, there wasn't enough," Mrs. Sheffield said. "I brought them up that way."

To feed squadrons of hungry guests in the hearty manner that Thelma does, one would expect to pay dearly at the neighborhood supermarket.

"I gave my mother $50 to get some eggs, salt, pepper, milk and macaroni from the store," Thelma said. "Altogether I paid less than $40 for the Thanksgiving meal that lasted two days. The rest of the food was all natural. It came from out there." She pointed toward the dense woodland that sprawled behind her backyard.

Thelma's natural, robust personality is mirrored in the way she cooks her food. She abides by a no-frills code when preparing her meals. She has no need for exotic spices or arcane herbs. And she finds no need for a pencil and paper.

"A lot of people come along with a recipe book, and still their food don't taste good," Thelma said.

She went into the kitchen and came out with a one-quarter teaspoon silver measuring spoon. Then she dipped it into an imaginary canister, showing her spicing technique.

"I take a little spoon like this and I estimate. I judge a little bit. At times, I'll use parsley, bay leave, paprika, seasoned salt, celery or oregano. I put whatever I want to put in."

She put down the spoon and picked up a three-inch bone from a plate.

"Could you tell this was once a opossum?" she asked smiling. "Let me tell you about opossum. First, you can't go reachin' in the trap and grab one out or you'll get bit. Then you'll have to make sure they aren't foamin' at the mouth or you'll get sick. Then you swivel them over an open flame to get the hair off of them. After that you wash them down with washing powder and let them sit in salted water for a while to get the burnt taste out."

Thelma has a similar technique for wild turkey. She also has tricks on how to take the wild out of wild rabbit and ways to tenderize even the most sinewy meats. Yet there remain some secrets she won't reveal.

"I don't go giving away all my recipes," she said.

Even if some of her recipes are sacrosanct, most of the pleasure is in the palate, not in the preparation. Except maybe for Thelma.

"Cooking is a wonderful experience," Thelma said with an air of satisfaction. "I enjoy cooking and knowing that everybody knows where they are going to eat. It's just like the Waltons. They say grace, hold hands, and especially the bless the cook." She halted, and with arms akimbo, said, "If they don't they'll get sick!"

Enthusiastically, Thelma went on to tell about her aspirations for a special kind of restaurant.

"I'm gonna have some of everything. I'll be open for breakfast, lunch and dinner and have two bodyguards because of the crime and stuff. And I'm gonna call it, 'The Soul Food and Wildlife Restaurant.'"

If only a fraction of Thelma's friends and family dine at her prospective restaurant, it will become a bonanza. But until then, her intimate clientele will continue its feasting and festivities at her home, realizing how good life can be.

"We do it good in the woods," Cheristine said as she enjoyed a piece of Thelma's wild rabbit. "The Lord provides it, and we cook it." (p. 8) Reprinted with the permission of the *Independent Alligator*, University of Florida, Gainesville.

Magazines

Campus magazines come in several forms. Some magazines are affiliated with campus newspapers and distributed as part of the newspaper, but many are independent publications not tied to the newspaper in any manner. Newspaper-published magazines are campus versions of Sunday magazine sections found in metropolitan newspapers. These publications can be weekly, monthly, or perhaps once-a-semester periodicals. They can be routinely organized, or "formatted," to offer longer features, listings, columns, and other content. Or they can be publications devoted to special topics such as spring break, job hunting and careers, a season preview of a varsity sport, or a special annual event on campus, such as homecoming. Some magazines are special reports in tabloid format published as part of the student newspaper or independently by classes. Some of these magazines and special reports are published as infrequently as once a year.

Campus magazines that are not associated with campus newspapers are often specialized publications. Some are published by magazine programs for distribution on campus and others are published for sale in the neighboring community or region. Still other student-written and student-edited magazines represent the interests of student organizations, academic departments, or other units of the institution. Commonly found in English departments, for instance, are student literary magazines containing a mixture of fiction and nonfiction articles. These magazines will often use nonfiction feature articles and essays in addition to short stories, poetry, and other creative writing.

One example of a successful campus magazine is *Etc Magazine*, published semiannually by students at the University of North Carolina at Charlotte. The magazine prefers general interest articles about student lifestyles. It has regular departments for student-written features about the university and its relationship with the city of Charlotte, ways of dealing with college life and its stresses, the diverse ethnic and racial groups in the college community, and travel ideas for students. Occasional special issues are devoted to a topic such as graduation (Kissling, 1992).

Yearbooks

Many universities and colleges have yearbooks. After a generation of absence or downsizing on some campuses and experimentation with video formats, traditional yearbooks are making a comeback. Although these publications are annually issued, they afford opportunities for student feature writers interested in specialized forms of writing that are not time bound and are more people oriented. Yearbooks are usually dominated by their photographic content, but most yearbook editors seek some sort of balance with a collection of student-written articles that focus on all aspects of student life.

Usually a yearbook has a single editor in charge of the whole book; this editor delegates responsibilities for specific assignments to section editors. Students will find articles about organizations, major unusual events on campus, new facilities, student leaders, annual major activities, outstanding administrators, and the best faculty members on campus. Some yearbooks run extended feature articles much like a magazine would use text and photographs. The main distinction is the perspective the articles take—keeping in mind that yearbook features are frequently explanatory (why or how) or retrospective features. The focus is on people (who) and activities (what) from the past year. Many yearbooks also run short, but informative, features discussing the purposes and accomplishments of active individuals and organizations during the past year.

Yearbooks are dominated by photographs, artwork, and other graphics, so articles usually will not run as long as those found in magazines or newspapers. Because yearbooks are often published each spring or summer, the articles have to take an overview or general approach to the subject. Feature articles include profiles of student leaders and administrators and stories about athletic teams and academic departments. Also common are feature articles about benchmark events on campus such as graduation day, the day one of the athletic teams won a big championship, homecoming, or a visit by a dignitary such as a politician, internationally popular entertainer, or renowned scholar. Other features may be aftermath or follow-up articles that combine a series of related campus events into a single story.

Student writers interested in contributing to the yearbook should study the most recent two or three editions, but each one will be a bit different. These are usually kept in the main library and the yearbook office. It is also a good idea to look at "exchange" yearbooks, ones that your school's yearbook staff receives from other schools in trade.

Organizational Newsletters

There are thousands of small student organizations on campuses across the country. There may be dozens on your own campus. With low-cost computer-assisted publishing technology and fast, inexpensive printing and photocopying available near campuses, it is no longer financially difficult for these usually impoverished organizations to produce newsletters. Thus, many newsletters have started up and are being published on campuses across the United States each year. It seems impossible to count them. Many are published locally on college and university campuses by student, faculty, staff, and alumni organizations and are known to few people outside the members of the organizations they serve. Some, however, are produced on a national or regional level for college-level readers, and command wide attention.

These newsletters may be as small as two pages of typewritten text or as professional-appearing as a slick, full-color magazine in size and printing quality. These newsletters are also excellent places to get experience in feature writing. Why? First, chances are good that you know something about the organization and the special interests it represents. Second, the organization is small and probably needs assistance in producing its newsletter, so access will be easy. Third, you can probably select the assignments yourself—if not in the beginning, not long after you prove yourself. You probably will not get paid for working on a campus newsletter, but you will get your writing published. For a beginner, this is important.

Other College and University Publications

Who is interested in reading about a college or university? Faculty, staff, students, parents of students, alumni, supporters, and even campus neighbors. Magazines are a common medium colleges and universities use to communicate with their varied constituencies. Some universities also produce newspaper-type publications, but the most common formats are slick, four-color monthly or quarterly magazines or regularly published newsletters. Tabloid-format newspapers are sometimes used as less expensive alternatives.

Editors of these publications often seek part-time student writing assistance. This is for several practical reasons. First, these publications want to provide the opportunities for students to learn. Second, they want less expensive help than established professionals would cost. An editor in this situation is willing to trade off some "one-on-one" teaching to get the needed staff assistance when the publication's budget is strained. Advanced reporting courses, practicum classes, internships, college work-study programs, and other opportunities are available for beginning feature writers to help create regular part-time or temporary clerical or writing positions at these publications. Most of the time, assignments are given by professional editors or teachers, but feature writers with initiative—displaying enterprise with strong story ideas—will also make their own breaks.

One example of this type of publication is the *Tennessee Alumnus*, published quarterly by the University of Tennessee National Alumni Association in Knoxville. The magazine is distributed to supporters of the university and alumni at all four of the school's campuses across the state. The magazine typically offers a dozen or more articles in each issue, in addition to occasional feature items in the magazine's regular departments. Features highlight the activities of faculty, alumni, the administration, and students. Articles often focus on travel, but are always strongly focused on university people. Issues in education are also addressed, such as a recent article that looked at mathematics and women. Articles also highlight recent developments in the physical and social sciences, especially the research of faculty in such diverse subjects as aviation, psychology and human behavior, local history engineering, and medicine. President Clinton's science advisor, a former University of Tennessee energy and environment expert, was the subject of a profile. Publications such as these are often major endeavors. The *Tennessee Alumnus*, printed in full color, has a circulation of nearly 50,000 copies.

Similar campus magazines aimed at alumni, donors, and others connected to universities and colleges include *Fordham Magazine, Carnegie Mellon Magazine, Mississippi State Alumnus, Notre Dame Magazine, Rutgers Magazine, Shipmate* (U.S. Naval Academy) and *Ripon College Magazine*. These publications, according to the *Writer's Market*, use from 10% to 75% free-lance material (Kissling, 1992).

Many colleges and universities produce professional-quality newsletters for general and/or specialized consumption. Some of these are distributed

---

LEADING CAMPUS NEWS SOURCES

With thousands of persons on a college or university campus, there are many choices for reliable sources for feature assignments. Here is a list of some of the most used sources on campuses:

Administration
    President's office and support staff
    Provosts and chancellors and support staff
    Vice president of student affairs and support staff
    Deans and department chairs and support staff
    University counsel and other attorneys on staff
    University relations and public relations office staff

Faculty
    Research grant holders
    Faculty authors
    Distinguished faculty chair holders
    Long-term faculty veterans
    Outstanding teacher award winners
    Academic advisors

Students
    Independent, Greek, and other social organizations leaders
    Student government officers
    Academic organization leaders
    Professional society leaders
    Graduate students involved in research or teaching
    Varsity athletics/sports information office

Support staff
    Residence hall advisors
    Health center director and staff
    Employment and placement director and staff
    Dining service director and staff
    Recreation and intramurals director and staff
    Campus public security and parking officers
    Physical plant director and maintenance staff

---

free, but others are subscription-based or tied to membership in organizations that are hosted by the university or college. There are literally thousands of such publications that have highly specialized orientations. These are often disciplinary in nature, focusing on a particular academic interest.

The Center for Peace and Conflict Studies at Wayne State University in Detroit produces a small newsletter, for example. Wellesley College's Center for Research on Women publishes a small semiannual newsletter. On the other hand, the College of Engineering at the University of Florida produces a much larger bimonthly newsletter, *Florida Spotlight on Technology*, which circulates over 8,000 copies per issue. The Agricultural Experiment Station at the University of Arkansas in Fayetteville publishes the bimonthly *Arkansas Farm Research* with a circulation of 10,000 per edition. This newsletter, established over 40 years ago, averages 12 pages per edition and is distributed free. Often student writing assistance is sought for newsletters such as these because these newsletters are produced on shoestring budgets.

WORKING WITH STUDENT EDITORS

At student publications, most of the editors you will work with are also students. Although some may be graduate students, the vast majority will be undergraduates. This means that most student editors have limited experience and are learning as they work. Although the editors might have more experience as a staff feature writer or news reporter than you, they do not have that much more experience. This means there has to be a lot of flexibility in the relationship between student writers and editors. Mistakes will be made on both ends. Questionable decisions will be made. Tempers may get out of control. But you, as a feature writer, need to take as much as you can from the relationship by gaining additional experience and learning from your editor.

Student editors, as individuals also learning their jobs, might not be as well organized as they should be. You may find the direction of your assignment changes in midstream. Some editors might not be specific on the focus needed for an assignment. They might forget details you need or they might not be able to suggest sources as effectively as a more seasoned professional. These individuals have earned their positions by paying some dues and usually have learned something from that experience. You can benefit from it, too. In fact, some students argue that they learn more from their student editors and their experiences writing for these peer "bosses" than they do in writing and other journalism classes because there is no pressure of grades. The practical value of the experience is not to be doubted.

Perhaps the most important part of the student editor–feature writer relationship is for you as the writer to earn *trust* in your work. This is done through meticulous attention to detail. The story must be complete, but it must also be accurate. Student editors are exactly like their professional counterparts in this regard, of course. If you go into a publication office with a hastily prepared, poorly written article with no direct quotations, you will be in trouble right away. An error-prone feature article will not impress any editor, so don't expect to get a second chance. There are few student editors working in newsrooms around the country who can't describe getting copy like that on a regular basis. On the other hand, if that feature story is thoughtfully done with clever writing, sound organization, attention-getting description and personality-filled direct quotations, your story will not only be published, but you will probably be asked to take on more assignments for upcoming issues.

In other words, be prepared. Make a strong first impression even if it is for a student publication. Put time into the effort. It will pay you back in countless ways, but the most significant one will be in the number of opportunities you develop for yourself.

LIFE AS A CAMPUS FEATURE STAFF WRITER

The rigor of working for a campus newspaper, magazine, or newsletter will help you determine how committed you are to feature writing. These is a never-ending demand for effort by staff members on most student publications. The work never seems finished. For campus newspapers, the hours are often long and late. Most campus newspapers are morning publications, and the hours leading to publication of an issue are frequently worked in the middle of the night and on weekends. This often means sacrificing social activities and other extracurricular interests to get an assignment completed.

Student magazines, newsletters, and yearbooks have more laid-back staff workstyles because there are less frequent publication schedules and deadlines to meet. For students writing features for these publications, the hours can also be long and frequently late. Staffs for these publications are often much smaller than those of campus newspapers and the degree of interaction among staff members and editors is also high. The commitment to work on these publications is equally serious and costly, too, in terms of other extracurricular activities.

OTHER CAMPUS WRITING OPPORTUNITIES

There is a wide range of other options for campus feature writing for students. Within academic units and extracurricular programs, numerous publications are produced. Departmental, college, and university publications are among them. One example of a department or school publication is at the University of Nebraska at Lincoln. The College of Journalism produces an annual magazine-type depth report by journalism students that focuses on events and trends around the state. Publications such as this provide additional opportunities for student feature writers. Students in 1992 focused on the small western Nebraska town of Gothenburg. The 48-page tabloid publication was produced by eight student reporters and six student copy editors and funded by grants to the school. Stories focused on a wide range of the aspects of life in that small Nebraska community. The cover story focused on survival in the economically stressed farming area and how people banded together to help one another, its "secret" to survival. Other articles focused on the specifics of the community's economic problems, health care, children and teens who work to improve their neighborhoods, farming, drug abuse, a country veterinarian, and snake hunting. Another set of articles were profiles of a half dozen or so interesting people in the area.

Numerous colleges and universities offer feature writing opportunities like that one. Students in the School of Communication at the University of Miami regularly write special feature article projects for the daily *Key West Citizen*. Students in recent years have produced projects consisting of one to two dozen articles each about the fragile marine-oriented environment of the Florida Keys, tourism in the Lower Keys, the high cost of living on a resort island, and the first year's aftermath of Hurricane Andrew.

Alumni publications, such as magazines and newsletters, offer still more campus opportunities for students. Although many of these publications are university-wide, others are designed to serve specific units, such as a college, school, or department. Sometimes positions on these publications can be obtained through part-time employment or through more formal internship programs.

Athletic department publications offer still other options. At National Collegiate Athletic Association Division I-A colleges and universities—which operate the major athletic programs in the nation—numerous publications are issued for the news media, alumni, students, and for season-ticket holders and supporter clubs and associations. For example, *Scorecard* is a weekly sports tabloid publication aimed at fans of the University of Louisville athletic program. *Hurricane Signals* is published at the University of Miami for its sports fans.

MARKETING CAMPUS STORIES OFF CAMPUS

As mentioned in the preceding section, you may have a chance on some occasions to write a feature story that has interest far beyond your campus publications. The story may originate as an idea of your own or as an assignment from a campus publication editor. Originally, you might complete the assignment for your school's newspaper or magazine. As you began to research the story, conduct interviews, and write it, you may discover that the real potential for the story goes beyond your campus. For example, your story about migraine headache research at your university's medical school could interest many people, not just those who read the school newspaper.

Therefore, you need to look at the feature assignments you complete for campus publications to determine their prospects to be sold elsewhere as well. Most student publications will encourage it. There's nothing wrong with selling two or more articles from the same research. Campus publications, especially, have limited circulation and do not directly compete with commercial publications. In some cases, this might be a conflict, but for the most part, it is not a problem. If you consider this option, as a courtesy, you should discuss with the editor of the publication the possibility of taking your story elsewhere to make certain there are no legal reasons, such as copyright, that would prevent you from doing so.

There is a strong chance you will have to modify or rewrite substantial portions of the original story. It may have to be rewritten in a major way, changing the focus of the topic and the range of sources used. A fresher lead may be necessary, also. But with a minimal amount of work, you might be able to take a story originally written for a campus publication and turn it into a strong story for a local weekly or regional daily newspaper or a regional magazine.

Off-Campus Newspapers, Magazines, and Newsletters

Students should never overlook writing opportunities *off campus* even while they are *on campus*. Local and regional newspapers, magazines, and newsletters are routinely seeking part-time assistance and free-lance contributions. As a student, you should investigate these opportunities as your writing skills mature. If you are not sure if you are ready, ask one of your professors for advice. The number and quality of these off-campus opportunities are often a function of the size of the community in which you live. Larger cities often offer more chances, but there could also be more people, some with better qualifications than yours, competing for those assignments. Weekly newspapers and newsletters are particularly good places to investigate because their staffs are ordinarily quite small and they often welcome help. Specialized magazines, such as trade publications, may also need help but could require some advanced knowledge of the subject.

Stringing, a form of free-lance writing involving a regular relationship with a publication, is another option. The local newspapers and major regional newspaper in the area your school serves might be an option for feature writing opportunities. Similarly, there may be magazines and newsletters in your community that need student staff assistance. These assignments can come on a single-story basis, on a more ongoing basis as a regular part-timer or stringer, or as an intern. To look into these opportunities, check with your journalism or writing professors or contact the publications directly. Stringing for newspapers in other cities and states is a possibility for college students. Some students interested in sports cover their school's varsity teams for out-of-town newspapers. There may be opportunities to write features about successful students for their hometown newspapers. Another category of feature story prospects will be significant faculty research being conducted on campus. Inquiries by telephone or letter may be all that is needed to set up an ongoing relationship with a newspaper or other publication. One thing is certain: These opportunities rarely seek you. You must find them.

News Services Oriented to Campuses

In the mid-1990s, there are several news services at the national level that cater to the interests of student publications. Perhaps the best-known is the College Press Service (CPS). National and regional organizations like CPS gather articles from members of the service and distribute them to other members.

Publications Oriented to Students and Campus Life

There is a growing number of national publications geared to supplement and serve college markets. Among them is *U*, a magazine that focuses on the college and university market. Numerous publishers have oriented their magazines and newsletters to national, regional, or statewide campus markets. Another nationally oriented college publication is *College Monthly*. This lifestyle- and entertainment-oriented magazine likes to publish long student-oriented profiles, travel, personal experience, and humor articles. Departments, which require shorter articles, include fashion, sports, politics, and lifestyle.

Some publications are aimed at particular segments of that market, in fact. One example is *The Black Collegian*, which serves African-American college students and recent graduates seeking career and job information. *First Opportunity*, another such publication, is aimed at African-American and Hispanic students. *Equal Opportunity*, issued three times a year, publishes articles on a wide range of topics ranging from careers to travel to profiles of role models.

Florida Leader, published six times a year and distributed on campuses at private and state universities and colleges in Florida, is another example. This publication encourages student writers to submit feature articles about events, interests, and issues related to campus life.

PROFESSIONAL POINT OF VIEW

Nancy Beth Jackson
American University at Cairo

Students at the University of Missouri, the nation's first school of journalism, find it easy enough to master the basics of the reporter's trade: inverted pyramids, feature leads, interviewing techniques, sourcing, stylebook rules, libel, infographics. What's tough to add to the toolbox is *credibility*.

"You have to go out of your way to be factual. You have a special obligation. At student papers reporters have even less credibility" comes the charge, and not just from J-school profs. Attribute that quotation directly to University of Missouri Chancellor Charles A. Kiesler, who has been burned more than once by writers who didn't get their facts straight or bother putting a story into perspective with enough (or any) research.

Sure, all reporters must strive for facts, but accuracy and sensitivity are even more essential for feature writers, who literally walk into the lives and living rooms of strangers and walk out with stories that will be read by hundreds or thousands of people. A cityside reporter covering a council meeting or press conference can always rely on a more experienced journalist to ask just the right questions. A feature writer does a one-on-one with the subject. Failing to establish rapport, the reporter will have to sweat to pull off the tale.

If you are working for a major daily like the *New York Times*, you can tap into the credibility of the institution. For starters, people return your calls. But in Columbia, Missouri, students at both the *Maneater* campus weekly and the *Missourian* city daily produced by the J-school suffer the sins of their predecessors. The joke goes that in this overly reported town with two dailies, three college newspapers and high school publications, every man, woman and child over the age of three has been interviewed at least once. Many refuse a second or third go-around because they feel the first reporter was unprofessional.

The problem is not unique to the University of Missouri.

"Student newspapers have a problem with continuity. If a source gets burned one semester, it reflects on the next reporter who calls," says Debra Myers, features editor for the San Jose State University *Spartan Daily*.

San Jose State's president had helped solve the problem by routinely briefing student reporters and editors. At the *Missourian*, which has a new reporting staff of about 75 students every semester, staffers must pass on beat reports listing sources and tips.

But even such efforts can't compensate for the ever-changing staffs of student papers. Kathleen Steinauer, editorial page editor of the *Daily Nebraskan*, has found people won't return reporters' calls because staff turnovers mean a different person is calling each time. No name recognition.

Because reporters don't have time to build up byline or personal reputations with readers, students must strive for instant credibility. How? The answer is both institutional and personal.

Establish a publication policy for checking quotations with sources before a story is printed. Both *Maneater* and *Missourian* reporters are required to call back to verify all direct quotations even if it means missing a deadline.

"You have to have a strong policy. If you don't do an accuracy check, quotes don't go in," says Lisen J. Tammeus, who has worked for both papers.

The two newspapers also require multiple sources on all stories, including features, and put a share of the credibility burden on the copy desk, pointing out that errors in grammar, spelling, and details like street addresses can also turn off readers.

On the personal side, student journalists must—like actors—be costumed for their roles. Sweats and sneakers may get the story for you when interviewing contemporaries, but university administrators, city officials, and other nonstudent sources may see sloppy dress as a reflection of a sloppy mind. At the University of Minnesota, where students cover not only the campus but also the state legislature in nearby St. Paul, *The Minnesota Daily* has established a good reputation and is rewarded by being taken seriously by politicians. Sarah Coomber-Greseth recalls how she learned the importance of dress the hard way when she had to race off to the med school in sweatshirt, comfy old slacks, and Birkenstocks.

"It was the most humiliary experience, but I'll never go casual to work again," she promises.

T-shirts, ripped jeans, hair out to there, and nose rings might be the current campus fashion, but they generally are inappropriate for the job. Jacinthia Jones of the Memphis State University *Daily Helmsman*, tells the story of one good writer going off to interview a campus administrator—like two other staff members, she sported a nose ring. The administrator was unimpressed by fashion and telephoned the editor to ask, "What kind of people do you have reporting for you?" All three journalists now remove nose rings when on assignment.

Appearance is only part of a professional demeanor. Prepare for the interview—even more than an established professional. One University of Missouri journalism major heard in News 105 about checking the clips before heading out on a story, but the next semester as a *Missourian* reporter, she raced out to do a feature on a harmonica player. Only after she arrived did she find he had been written about in the *Missourian* 2 weeks before. Neither she nor the editor assigning the story had checked the clips—or read the newspaper!

Whether your subject is a novice at being interviewed or someone swamped by the media, you increase your credibility by letting them know you have done your homework. Pete Bland, a *Missourian* sportswriter who stalked baseball-playing Cardinals and man-eating football Tigers as a part of his undergrad studies, warns never to ask a dumb question of a coach or athlete. You'll be pitched out of the locker room on your ear. "You have to know your stuff, know specifics. A good question is not the obvious question," Pete says.

But your own youth and inexperience can work for you with many subjects. Make them like you. Then they'll talk.

Dora Keeven, a *Missourian* feature writer, has learned a couple of things about building trust with sources:

- Be friendly.
- Try to work in their schedule.
- Make sure you understand what the person is saying.
- Make clear the interview is on the record.
- Smile a lot. (personal communication, 1993).

Dr. Nancy Beth Jackson is an associate professor at the American University in Cairo. She taught for the previous 5 years in the School of Journalism at the University of Missouri in Columbia. She also directed the annual JCPenney-University of Missouri Journalism Awards for newspaper feature writing. She is a former feature writer for *The Miami Herald* and she has written features for the *New York Times* and *International Herald Tribune*.

17

Free-Lance Writing and Marketing

Are you ready to write free-lance feature articles for pay? If so, this chapter and the concluding one discuss how you can get started as a free-lance writer. Many beginning magazine and newspaper free-lance feature writers work part time while they also do something else. Some writers become successful enough that they build lucrative full-time careers as free-lance feature writers. To be realistic, it is not a safe bet that you will find your full-time career in free-lance feature writing—at least, not in the beginning. If you follow the path of most feature writers, especially those writing for magazines, you will become a part-time writer who has a full-time career in another, perhaps related, field. This is frequently the case for magazines, which usually maintain small writing staffs. More and more newspapers are using free-lance writers for material as well. This is not only true for features desks, but also for features for the traditional spot news desks such as the city desk and sports.

Your work as a free-lance feature writer will be tough and demanding. You are your own boss. This puts you in charge of marketing, preparing, and submitting your work. No one will do any of this for you. Some people find this working environment—best of all, the freedom and flexibility—to be to their liking. Others cannot handle it well and prefer staff work. You will have to decide what is better for you.

Some writers feel there is no better time than now to be a free-lance feature writer. There are more magazines, therefore more markets, than ever before. There is greater specialization than the magazine industry has ever known. Although there may be fewer newspapers, there are more editions of the major dailies caused by zoning, or segmentation, of neighborhood coverage.

Yet, other writers say full-time free-lance writing has never been so tough. Pay rates are consumed by inflation, some larger fee magazines have closed, and larger numbers of writers make the work more competitive. Are you ready for that? Free-lancing is not an easy endeavor for beginners, especially younger writers who may lack savvy business skills. That's the point of view of one veteran writer, free-lancer Karla Harby. An award-winning science writer, Harby says individuals interested in free-lance writing need to think of the business side of their work. It is not all writing. "In my experience, most young people are better equipped as journalists than they are as business people," she says. "Mediocre writers can make it as free-lance writers if they develop solid business skills, but only the rare writer with poor business acumen can remain self-employed for long. (And even those guys usually have a trust fund.) But most students discount the business side of things, thinking that their talent and hard work alone will keep them afloat; this is why they don't survive as free-lancers and have to take staff jobs" (Harby, personal communication, 1993).

Whether free-lance writing becomes a good or bad experience, a full-time or part-time career, or a short-term or long-term commitment is completely up to you. Now that you know the basics of writing features, this chapter tells you how to get into print. This is where you turn the corner to a professional writing life. You will learn the basics of *selling*—to be your own agent. You will learn about marketing your work. You will learn about query letters and proposals for articles, preparation of manuscripts, cover letters, photographs and other artwork, and developing multiple articles from a single research effort.

FINDING THE RIGHT MARKET

In recent years, a number of free-lance writing market directories and listings have been published to assist writers in finding the best markets for their work. But you, and only you, still must be very resourceful to find the right market. Take a look at one or more of these directories. At the top of the list is *Writer's Market* (Kissling, 1992), the number one source for nonfiction free-lance writers. This 1,000-plus-page volume is published each fall and lists more than 4,000 publications for articles and publishers for books. *The Writer's Handbook* (Burack, 1992), published by The Writer, Inc., notes over 2,700 markets for manuscripts in its 750 pages. Another popular directory is R.R. Bowker's *MIMP: Magazine Industry Market Place*. Listings of magazines and newspapers also are published annually by *Folio:* and *Editor & Publisher*. Special issues of these two publications, and others such as *Writer's Digest*, *ByLine*, and *The Writer*, list syndicates, new markets, and other reference books.

A relative newcomer to the directory shelf is Gale's *Newsletters in Print*. Reflecting the North American growth in newsletter publication, this directory lists over 11,000 subscription, membership, and free newsletters, bulletins, digests, and other smaller publications in the U.S. and Canada. It describes newsletters in a variety of formats published in business, industry, family and lifestyles, communications-information, agriculture, life sciences, community affairs, world affairs, science and technology, and liberal arts. It also includes newsletter indexes. Similarly, *The Oxbridge Directory of Newsletters* lists in its 1,300-page volume more than 21,000 newsletters on subjects similar to those in the Gale directory. Both directories are comprehensive.

A beginning writer in or near a metropolitan area really needs to go no further than the "publishers" section of the local telephone directory yellow pages for a starting point. This listing will tell you which newspapers, magazines, and newsletters maintain offices in your area. Even if you do not have such telephone directories, you can go to a nearby library that should have the directories or microfiche available to use.

However, you cannot depend just on directories to find markets. You must set up a network by developing your own contacts in the profession. The more people—especially editors—you know, the better. Attend professional meetings, for example, to make such contacts.

You must be patient, also. You must be organized enough to market several ideas and work on several assignments at once. Sometimes you will develop an idea and be unable to find the right market at the beginning of the project. Put the topic on hold for a while, if you can. While you are working on other writing projects that have more easily found markets, your solution to the tough one might come along.

"Don't be afraid to start at the bottom by writing for free. And don't ever say, 'I'd love to be a writer, but I just don't have time.' Writers make time. They don't spend time playing with friends on weekends. They neglect their families more than they should. They don't have time for anything else but writing," says successful free-lance writer Andy Rathbone (personal communication, 1993). "Writers must be able to keep writing, even when the spark's not there. You've got to get some clay on the table; you can always go back and shape it later. Finally, I'll spit out the old cliché: People don't choose writing as a career; writing chooses them."

University of Nevada-Reno professor Myrick Land (1993) also advises that you diversify in your marketing strategy. Try different types of articles. "[Y]ou have a wide range of choices as a free-lancer. Although you may decide later that you prefer to devote most of your time to medical articles or pieces about television personalities, during your early years it would be good to explore a variety of possibilities," Land says (p. 130).

If all else fails, try to locate people who work or are interested in the subject you have chosen for an article. Ask them what they read. Find out their favorite publications. Their answers could give you an idea for new markets. This boils down to persistence. If you keep trying, eventually the effort might be rewarded with an acceptance letter and, later, a tearsheet and check.

Beginning with Newspaper Markets

Many free-lance writers start out building a relationship with newspapers in their communities. Some start with weeklies and small dailies. Others break right in with the major daily newspapers in nearby metropolitan markets. In the mid-1990s, finding full-time positions with newspapers is more difficult than it was a decade ago. Certainly, free-lance opportunities are out there at newspapers for beginning writers, even if less full-time work can be found. *Stringers*, as editors like to call free-lance writers, are a long-standing newspaper tradition. Almost all newspapers need and use them. "Smaller suburban dailies are likely to be receptive to new writers, but the larger dailies usually

BEST SOURCES FOR FREE-LANCE WRITING MARKETS

Books

Gale Directory of Publications, Gale Research, Detroit
Guide to Literary Agents & Art/Photo Reps, Writer's Digest Books, Cincinnati
Hudson's Subscription Newsletter Directory, Newsletter Clearinghouse, Rhinebeck, NY
Literary Agents of North America, Author Aid, Research Associates International, New York
Literary Market Place (agents), R.R. Bowker, New York
Literary Market Place with Names and Numbers, R.R. Bowker, New York
Local telephone book yellow pages (under "publishers")
MIMP: Magazine Industry Market Place, R.R. Bowker, New York
Newsletters in Print, Gale Research, Detroit
Newsletter Publishers Association Directory of Members and Industry Suppliers, Newsletter Publishers Association, Arlington, VA
O'Dwyer's Directory of Public Relations Executives, J.R. O'Dwyer, New York
Oxbridge Directory of Newsletters, Oxbridge Communications, New York
Periodical Directories and Bibliographies, Gale Research, Detroit
Publisher's Directory, Gale Research, Detroit
Working Press of the Nation (volumes I, II), Farrell, New York
Writer's Market, Writer's Digest Books, Cincinnati
Writer's Handbook, The Writer, Inc., Boston

Periodicals

Business Periodicals Index, H.W. Wilson Co., New York
Humanities Index, H.W. Wilson Co., New York
Popular Periodicals Index, Rutgers University Library, Camden, NJ
Reader's Guide to Periodical Literature, H.W. Wilson Co., New York
Standard Rate and Data Survey, Standard Rate & Data Service, Wilmette, IL
The Writer, The Writer, Inc., Boston
Writer's Digest, Writer's Digest Books, Cincinnati
Social Sciences Index, H.W. Wilson Co., New York

Newsletters

American Society of Journalists and Authors—Newsletter
Book Newsletter
Business Publisher
Communication News
EFA Newsletter (Editorial Freelancers Association)
Magazine Week
Newsletter on Newsletters (Newsletter Clearing House)
On Second Thought
Writers Connection—Newsletter
Writers Guild of America (East)—Newsletter
Writers Guild of America (West)—Newsletter

demand journalism experience," says free-lance feature writer Johanna S. Billings (1992, p. 24). "The best way to sell your work to newspapers is to sell yourself first. Once you have chosen a newspaper, find out who the editor is, and then send a cover letter, including a resumé highlighting your writing credits and 'clips' if you have any."

Most newspaper editors would like to establish a regular relationship with their free-lancers. They want to be able to find a writer for fast response on assignments they initiate. They do not want to wait for stories to come to them in many cases, although they most always consider unsolicited submissions. "Because most editors are not looking to buy just one article, they seldom want query letters. Instead, they want to cultivate a working relationship with stringers to whom they can give assignments regularly," Billings (1992, p. 24) wrote. "As a stringer, you will be doing both 'hard news' . . . and 'features.'"

Mastering Magazine and Newsletter Markets

The number of magazines and newsletters being published in the mid- 1990s sometimes may seem overwhelming. It is quite an effort to keep track of the many opportunities that exist for free-lance feature writers. With thousands of magazines in the United States and Canada and thousands more outside North America, there are many different magazine markets for free-lance writers.

First, there are the most commonly seen consumer magazines. There are also thousands of trade, technical, and professional publications. Free-lance writers should always consider the opportunities available outside the mainstream publications. Although many free-lancers may dream of writing for the big fees paid by *The New Yorker, Esquire, National Geographic, TV Guide*, or *Reader's Digest*, it is not realistic for most beginners to shoot so high. Instead, it is wise to look at less competitive markets. Many free-lance writers begin their magazine and newsletter writing careers by publishing in smaller magazines or newsletters or those with specializations with which they are familiar. The fees are much lower, generally, and there is great variation in how much they pay. You don't have to be a specialist, but if you have some expertise, use it. This is especially beneficial to beginners looking for that first break.

Free-lance writer Henry Pratt believes that the thousands of trade publications are a strong option that is "often overlooked" by feature writers (1992, p. 10). There seem to be trade periodicals for just about any imaginable subject. Trade publications—those technical periodicals serving business and industry with articles about news, trends, people, new technology, and research in a particular field—often open up to new writers more easily than consumer publications, he says. "Writing articles for trade journals is fun and profitable, if you take the time to know your customer—the publication, its audience, and the industry," Pratt wrote (p. 10). "[T]rade journals offer writers greater security. Such trades tend to be more stable, and they're not bought or sold as often as some consumer publications. You'll find trade journals are hungry for articles, practical columns, charts, graphs, and photos. Since most have small staffs, the editors depend heavily on freelancers for much of their prose and visuals." Pratt suggests trade features should focus on manufacturing processes, histories and chronologies, and successful elements of businesses such as sales, production, finance, and the future.

Other small magazines offer good publishing opportunities also. There are a growing number of magazines of limited regional or local circulation that remain options for beginning writers, argues free-lance writer Eric Mathews (1991). "In terms of eccentricities, anomalies, and just generally strange publishing practices, these publications, often 'seat-of-the-pants' operations, can be the ultimate test of a writer's patience and professionalism," he says (p. 23). Finding these magazines may be a challenge, but they are often listed in magazine market directories and writers' magazines such as *Writer's Digest* and *The Writer*. With very small staffs, some only one-person operations, these publications also need contributors.

A growing magazine market in the mid-1990s has been regional parenting magazines and newsletters. Writer Mark Haverstock (1993) notes that there may be as many as 140 of these in North America and Australia. "This is a wide-open market for writers, because most of these parenting publications rely heavily on freelance submissions," Haverstock says (p. 6). These publications seek practical feature articles about local activities, places to get help, and advice about child care. *Atlanta Parent*, *Chicago Parent*, and *Seattle's Child* are just three examples.

Regardless of the size or type of the publication, study it and learn as much about it and the market as you can before approaching it. "Target your material to the proper market; know the magazine you want to write for. Magazines are much like people. Each is different, with a distinctive personality and special needs. It's folly to dash off a piece and then frenetically search for a suitable market for it," says free-lancer John Bohannon (1993, p. 22). "One of the most common complaints editors have about free-lancers—and it is a justifiable one—is that they're unfamiliar with the market," agrees full-time free-lancer Charlotte Anne Smith (1993, p. 16).

International Markets

A final piece of advice on free-lance opportunities should focus on international markets. Clearly, Canadian publications are among the most logical places to begin. Not only are the language and culture similar, some of the American media with which you are already familiar are part of the market. Although Canadian cultural content laws try to keep Canada *Canadian*, writers can still sell material across the border if the articles are what the publications need.

British publications and other English-language countries offer additional free-lance markets, especially in the areas of travel, entertainment, sports, and science and health, for example. London-based free-lance writer Wendy Grossman describes opportunities in the British market for her specialties, computers and science writing:

The U.K. market is much, much smaller than the U.S. one, and so is the pool of talent. I think it makes it easier to break in—anyone who's good and professional stands a reasonable chance of making some kind of living. Probably science and technology writers have an easier time than some others—the explosion of computer magazines means there's a fair market for that sort of stuff, and there are an awful lot of journalists in London who are too terrified of technology to write about it even for magazines in other fields.

In non-English-language nations, opportunities also exist. Many publications, if they are interested in the proposed article, will translate it into the native language. There is clearly interest in what is happening in the United States. Some personality-oriented publications in Europe and Latin America, for instance, are a steady market for Hollywood-based writers who focus on the motion picture industry. Some U.S. free-lance travel writers, for example, regularly sell articles to publishers of in-flight magazines for foreign airlines that have routes touching the United States. Although it may take considerable effort to get yourself established in such a market, it is worthwhile.

USING SUBMISSION GUIDELINES

When you have identified a publication that might be right for your work, contact the editor, acquisitions editor, or articles editor to obtain a set of submission guidelines. Whereas newspapers rarely develop printed guidelines, many magazines will send these detailed instructions by mail or facsimile machine to free-lancers on request. One of the most popular outdoors magazines in Pennsylvania, *Pennsylvania Angler*, uses guidelines. As a sample, these are included in Appendix A. *Pennsylvania Angler* Editor Art Michaels explains the importance of reviewing such guidelines in advance of submitting a manuscript:

> Our contributor guidelines are a capsulated view of how to do business with us. They introduce contributors to our magazine. Still, breaking into our market can best be accomplished by studying a few back issues in addition to following the contributor guidelines. Yes, contributors do follow the guidelines closely. I revise them from time to time, but for the most part, the contributor guidelines are current. Most reasons why I reject material can be traced to a contributor's unfamiliarity with the magazine or not following the guidelines. (personal communication, 1993)

WRITING QUERY LETTERS AND ARTICLE PROPOSALS

One of the most important aspects of selling articles to publications is how you conduct yourself as a professional writer. Free-lancer Charlotte Anne Smith strongly recommends a "professional" attitude in how you work with editors. This involves knowing the standards of the profession for preparing and submitting free-lance work. Following general market and specific publication research, it is time to make contact with the publication. Being "professional" is an attitude, but it is also performing at a high level necessary when this first contact is made. "In order to sell, you have to be aware of certain basic facts of magazine publishing," Smith says (1993, p. 15).

Free-lance writer Jay Stuller (1991) believes that an effective inquiry to a magazine, regardless of the form it takes, must be built upon diligent research. "The most critical factor in a magazine article proposal isn't your list of credentials. It isn't even the topic itself," Stuller says (p. 26). "It's how well the idea will appeal to a magazine's audience." Stuller feels writers should find out as much about readers' common interests, age and income ranges, and concerns by checking market research information available through the magazine's advertising department. "Once a writer grows attuned to thinking about audience, the intuition that leads to salable ideas kicks into gear," Stuller says (p. 29).

The right attitude about rejection is also important in free-lance writing. Writers must learn to live with rejection. It happens to every writer. A publication's decision not to use a submitted manuscript or idea proposal does not always mean it is a bad one. It could mean that there were other reasons for not using it. However, many inexperienced writers do not contemplate the reason offered for a rejection, if it is specific, and will give up on the idea. Free-lance feature writer Richard Matthews (1991), like many other successful and persistent writers, believes the next step is not giving up, but revising, refocusing, and resubmitting to "another publication that might be receptive to the same general idea tailored to its editorial content. Restructuring an idea with a different set of readers in mind often meets with success the second time around," he says (p. 22). A distinction between an amateur free-lancer and a real professional, Matthews believes, is how you handle the rejection pile. The worst thing to do, he feels, is to let an idea sit around.

Kevin Robinson (1993), a veteran free-lance writer, agrees that rejection is part of the business, but it *should be* taken personally. He explains, "To be a good writer, you must be human; you must see and feel what those around you see and feel. More importantly, you must see and feel what *you* see and feel," he says (p. 27). If you do that as a writer, he maintains, you react personally to rejection. And, he says, that's perfectly okay. His own rejection rate is about 80%, he says. "I decided long ago that there's nothing particularly noble about suffering in silence or pretending that being rejected isn't painful. But I don't get mad either." His solution, like that of so many other professionals, is persistence. The lesson: Don't give up on an idea until all options are exhausted.

There are numerous reasons editors reject or substantially revise accepted ideas and manuscripts. Veteran free-lance writer John M. Wilson (1990) has identified at least nine reasons for failure. Manuscripts with flaws, he feels, are just unfinished works in progress. Rejected writers simply need to work more to solve the problems. He has created a presubmission checklist that can be helpful in preventing such errors the first time around:

- Angle and focus of the article.
- Appropriate viewpoint and voice.
- Vivid description.
- Logical organization.
- Style in writing.
- Lead that attracts and a distinct, impressive ending.
- Appealing direct quotations.
- Manuscript must reflect what editor assigned.
- Edit and proofread thoroughly.

As a writer seeking a publisher, you must go further than just "discovering" a subject for an article. A subject is simply not enough in the highly competitive mid-1990s writing world. As the American Society of Journalists and Authors, Inc., defines it, the idea is one step toward the finished product (Bloom, Bedell, Olds, Moldafsky, & Schultz, 1992). An idea is a subject combined with an approach, ASJA says. This is your property, even if you do not have the article written yet. Once you get a good article idea, you have to decide when and where it is best to market it.

Writers should not try to query a publication with a subject by telephone. Most professionals prepare a *query letter* or an *article idea proposal*. Some free-lance writers combine a letter and proposal into a single document but, for your purposes as a novice, you should consider them separate steps. A query letter will be briefer, less detailed, and an abstract of a fuller proposal. If you have refined the idea, then develop a separate proposal running 500 to 750 words that will summarize what you plan to do. Your basic strategy is to develop the idea—to describe to an editor what you will do, or have done—without writing or sending the entire article. This is a more detailed outline of the article you plan to write. Editors find these helpful in determining whether your work would fit their plans for an upcoming issue.

Steve Perlstein sold his first free-lance article to the *New York Times*. Now he writes for a variety of newspapers and magazines. He recommends human interest features as a type of article that may increase your chances for success. "When pitching human interest pieces, writers have to tailor their queries to particular markets; editors scan through query letters very quickly, and unless a human interest piece pegs their niche exactly they'll drop a preprinted rejection slip in the SASE [self-addressed, stamped envelope] and be done with it," he says. "When I'm on a hot streak I get maybe one hit in 20 or 30 queries, many of them human interest pieces" (personal communication, 1993).

Free-lancer Andy Rathbone pitches his ideas to editors this way:

First, get the publication's proper name, address, and writer's guidelines. Usually the weary receptionist will recite these over the phone. Next, grab as many back issues as you can find at local thrift shops or a condominium's magazine-swap pile. Your story must fit into a magazine's specific area, or the editor won't take it. Next, write a query letter with a grabbing first graph, followed by a short description of the story, as well as the reason why *you* are the best person to write it. Rules? Make sure it all fits on one page. If you can't sum it up in one page, you haven't found a decent angle for the story. If they haven't followed up in a month, send a follow-up letter. After 45 days, I'll give them a phone call. Don'ts? Don't call the publication unless it's to get their address and current editor's name. Editors don't like being bugged over the phone. And for crying out loud, don't spell anything wrong, either! Editors don't want to work and if they see any misspellings, they know they're in for some serious revisions on the manuscript. (personal communication, 1993)

Another veteran free-lance feature writer, Bill Steele, writes about medicine, computers, chemicals, and drugs. He advocates being prepared when entering the query process. This is especially true of "cold" queries:

My basic rule in querying is to do a lot of homework beforehand. When an editor who knows you calls up and gives you an assignment, it's usually just an idea the editor had: How are lawn-care pesticides affecting the squirrels, or whatever. And you can approach an editor with whom you work regularly with something like that. But when you're querying *cold*, you have to have the work about half finished; do enough research so that you can show the editor there really is a story there and you know more about it than any other writer they might hire to cover it. "According to a study published in the *New England Journal of Veterinary Medicine*, squirrels in the northeast have experienced severe depression after eating nuts sprayed with weed killer, and have been known to carry off small children. I plan to travel to Wallingford, Connecticut and interview Mrs. Ida Klumph, the distraught mother who, after innocently killing a few weeds . . . ." The last paragraph of a query letter is always a brief resumé listing publications in which I've been published. At the beginning I made up stuff, or at least exaggerated its importance. (personal communication, 1993)

Although most articles need proposals or queries to precede them, some articles do not. Publication editors work in different ways. You just have to know the market. This is how British free-lancer Wendy Grossman describes the process in the United Kingdom:

I don't query publications, except very rarely. The first article I ever got paid for writing was a query, to the Women's Page editor of *The Guardian* newspaper. It was a piece about the 20th anniversary of the Irish Family Planning Association, an organization which had been illegal for the first 10 years of its existence, and which was celebrating its 20th birthday by being prosecuted for selling condoms at a Dublin record store. She asked to see clippings, so I sent her a piece from an American humanist magazine on a related subject (church and state in Ireland), and told her I would write the piece on spec[ulation]. I did, and she bought it. Because she answers letters, the once or twice since I've had ideas to suggest, I've written to her.

But editors in London really work on the telephone, so mostly I phone them. I try to avoid days when I know specific editors are trying to put their pages to bed. Everything in London is personal contacts, anyway, and now that I've been around for a few years sometimes people call me and offer me work through recommendations.

Also, in the computer world, all the editors and free-lancers use the same conferencing system, a London-based thing called "cix"; many of the magazines have conferences on there, too. So the other route I use a lot is e-mail. But I'm actually also fortunate in that there are at least two magazines I write for every month, and then it's a question of what I'm going to write, not whether.

But I can't count on this continuing forever, so I do try to think about other markets. It's important to remember that whatever your ideals may be, you're running a business. It's very easy here, for example, to spend all your time going to press conferences or whatever; if you want to make it as a free-lancer, you have to have respect for what your time is worth, and decide how you spend it accordingly. (personal communication, 1993)

This is particularly the case for short articles because editors will want to see the completed work. For editorials, humorous anecdotes/briefs, and most other articles under 1,000 words, a query is not as useful as the finished piece, literary agent Linda Collier Cool (1985a) says. Cool also stresses that query letters must be convincing. "[B]efore you begin writing your query letter, think your article idea through carefully. Imagine you are describing the article to a friend. Could you get the point across in just a few words?" she asks (p. 24). Cool says queries must meet certain physical standards for serious attention to be given to them:

1. Use high-quality computer printer copies (laser printers are best; letter-quality or near-letter-quality printing is preferred over dot matrix) or high contrast photocopies of originals are acceptable.
2. Type letters on personal stationery printed on business-size (8½ x 11 in) paper.
3. Single-space the query letter. Double-space proposals.
4. Submit each idea separately. Do not submit ideas together.
5. Enclose a self-addressed, stamped envelope (SASE) if you want material returned.
6. If you expect calls and are away from the telephone often, use an answering machine.
7. Enclose a self-addressed, stamped manuscript arrival confirmation postcard.
8. Be patient. Wait up to 6 weeks before follow-up.

Some editors prefer only query letters on first contact. If their initial response to your letter is positive, you might be asked to produce a proposal. The problem with many query letters, veteran free-lancer Lorene Hanley

Duquin (1987) says, is that the letter writers do not know what they are really proposing. If so, how can you expect an editor to know?

Some editors like to see clippings of a writer's previously published articles on related subjects. In other words, highlight your qualifications. Previous experience as a writer means a lot to an editor. This is an effective way to establish your credibility as a serious free-lance writer. If you have some copies of articles that you have already had published, you may want to include two or three as examples of what you are capable of achieving. In fact, this has happened to numerous writers: Some editors wind up offering to buy the articles in the photocopied clippings instead of the article you have proposed. As long as you have the rights to the article, you might make an unexpected sale.

Ideally, a query letter will also include the proposal. Or, if you prefer to be more highly organized, send a proposal with a covering query letter that introduces yourself to the editor by describing your qualifications and recent articles you have written. This more personal approach establishes your credibility as a serious professional writer. Duquin says a proposal is the result of a 4-step system:

1. *Capture the idea.* When an idea strikes you, write it down to save it. When the time comes, it will be there for you to take to the next step.

2. *Develop the idea.* Get more information. Think about the idea. Some preliminary research will help. Get the basic facts. Conduct some interviews.

3. *Tailor the idea.* Shape the proposal to the audience that you will try to reach. Decide who would be interested, and devise a writing and reporting strategy that will take you to that goal.

4. *Test the idea.* Ask yourself these questions: Do you really want to do this article now? Are you capable? What is the cost (in time and money)? Can you find other uses for the material?

Read and study the publication you plan to query *before* you prepare the proposal. Call the magazine to get the name (and right spelling) of the proper editor (they do change from time to time and you cannot completely depend on annual directories to be up-to-date). Duquin (1987) says well-prepared and researched proposals get the best attention:

If you've done your homework, you should have all the elements of a good query. Most editors recognize the time and preparation I put into my proposals and they respond personally. . . . More often than not . . . the editor will like the idea, but sees potential trouble spots. Since my proposal is well-developed, the editor can point to those spots and give me the guidance I need to research and write an article that will fit perfectly into the magazine's format. (p. 40)

Southern magazine editor James Morgan (1986) says salesmanship in free-lance writing is most important for success. He points to the timing of being in the right place at the right time with the right product in the right presentation. You control the last "right" but cannot always control the first three, he says. In saying this, he advises writers to avoid gimmicks, sloppy presentations, and dry formality.

Cover letters and accompanying proposals must provide certain basics, regardless of how you organize the information. Here's a list of information to include in a query letter:

1. How to contact you (address *and* telephone).
2. Your background as a writer, free-lancer. (Do not reveal that you are a student or novice. Act professionally and you will be treated as a professional.)
3. Your unique qualifications to write about this subject/idea.
4. Your availability and prospects for completion of the assignment if you get it.
5. A request for a response.

Most query letters are written in traditional business letter format. An appealing, curiosity-arousing opening will get an editor to read more. Letters with dull starts are often not completely read. If you are writing a separate query/cover letter with a proposal, then the letter should be short and to the point.

Article proposals should also have at least seven common elements:

1. Summary of the idea and the approximate word length.
2. Examples or cases to illustrate your focus.
3. Primary expert sources you plan to interview.
4. Facts/statistics from authoritative sources.
5. Time factors affecting freshness of material.
6. Outline of article and tentative title (if possible).
7. Availability of photographs and other graphics.

A proposal should be prepared much like a manuscript. This means it should be typed, double spaced, and free of errors. The depth of your proposal depends on the publication. In essence, then, you have several options in querying. Some proposals will be contained in detailed query letters. Some will take the form of two- to four-page essays. Others may be detailed outlines with other supplemental materials, such as letters and descriptive essays. University of Texas professor Thomas Fensch (1984) advises, "The query letter demands as much practice and attention as does the feature article" (p. 79).

There is some risk of losing story ideas when querying and proposing. Karla Harby, a free-lance science writer, feels this is a minor problem. "Probably some of this goes on, but since you can't stop it there's no sense worrying about it. Just go on to the next proposal. It's always smart to write such a wonderful query that no editor would dream of having anyone but you write the story," she believes (personal communication, 1993).

DEFINITE *DON'TS* IN THE SUBMISSION GAME

Ellen Seidman (1992), an editorial assistant for a major women's magazine, makes her living by looking at letters, queries, and proposals that writers send to her editors. As she says, "I know what makes a query impressive— and which qualities earn it an immediate rejection" (p. 24). This is her list of definite "don'ts" when it comes to submitting manuscripts:

- *Don't* send irrelevant photographs.
- *Don't* mention payments or rights.
- *Don't* send complete manuscripts unless you are writing humor or fiction.
- *Don't* write a long letter, no more than one page.
- *Don't* use a fancy letterhead. Keep stationery simple and professional.
- *Don't* telephone an article idea.

Veteran free-lance writer Gary C. King recalls his first sale was made quickly once he decided to become a free-lance writer:

My first story took me 6 weeks to write, and it sold immediately. But remember that you can't make any money if it takes you 6 weeks to write every story. Now, after nearly 13 years in the business, I can write a 5,000- to 6,000-word story (25 to 30 pages, double-spaced) in about 10 hours. Similarly, I can write a 100,000-word crime book in 3 to 6 months and, again in retrospect, I only wish I had started writing books much sooner. My advice to beginners and college students is to break in with the magazines, but don't wait 10 years to go for the book market. The book market's tougher, to be sure, but if you spend 2 or 3 years carving yourself a niche in the magazine markets, the book markets suddenly begin to open up. (personal communication, 1993)

King also feels querying and proposing ideas require sophistication and the attitude of an experienced free-lancer, even if you are not yet one:

Never admit to being a novice. Write your query letters with an authoritative ring, and convince the editors that you know what you're doing and can do the job. They'll spot the fact that you're a novice when they read your work; so there's no sense in pointing it out to them up front, unless you're looking to make a large file of rejections. And stay away from creative writing classes; you'll only get hurt (journalism classes are okay, even encouraged; but creative writing classes, if I may borrow a phrase from Spiro Agnew, bring out the "effete impudent snobs" who don't know good writing when it reaches out and bites them). (personal communication, 1993)

WRITING A QUERY LETTER: A LOOK AT EXAMPLES

There are many approaches to writing an eye-catching query letter. To show you how it can be done, here is a successful magazine query letter written by

Kit Snedaker, a free-lance feature writer, which she used to sell a food article. She used this form letter in her computer's word processor and filled in the name and address of the editor she sought to contact:

KIT SNEDAKER
ADDRESS WOULD GO HERE
TELEPHONE NUMBER WOULD GO HERE

DATE
EDITOR
PUBLICATION
ADDRESS

Dear Editor:

France's oldest and most prestigious vineyards grow in the chalky, ungrateful soil of Le Medoc north of Bordeaux. Vines thrive with "a sea view and their feet in gravel" as the French say. Wine lovers come from all over the world to visit Chateau Mouton-Rothschild and sample its famous, long-lived vintages.

In "A White Wine Snob Tastes Bordeaux," I compare wine tasting in this, "the largest fine-wine region in the world," according to some authorities, to wine tasting in Northern California. Remember that in a blind tasting in Paris a few years ago, the French were astonished to discover they had rated California wines ahead of their own. A sidebar of nuts and bolts and color slides come with the story.

As food/travel editor of the *Los Angeles Herald Examiner*, I wrote and edited food/wine stories for 10 years. Now I write a weekly column, The Healthy Gourmet, syndicated by Copley News Service, a regular column on Hawaiian cuisine for *Hawaii Magazine*, and free-lance food and travel stories. My pieces have appeared in *Harper's Bazaar, Bon Appetit, Food and Wine, New Zealand's Cuisine* and *Australian Gourmet* and *Traveler* as well as such newspapers as the *Los Angeles Times, Christian Science Monitor, Newsday, Cleveland Plain Dealer*, and *Baltimore Sun*. Clips and a resumé are enclosed.

Also enclosed is a postcard for your decision. If I haven't heard from you in six weeks, I shall call.

Sincerely,

Kit Snedaker

Snedaker, as she notes in her query letter, prefers to use self-addressed and stamped postcards for the convenience of editors in responding to the queries. "Usually, I send a postcard with everything," she explains. "Editors just tic off the proper box or write a note and that's the contact" (personal communication, 1993). She also said that some editors like to exchange short and quickly transmitted notes by facsimile machine.

Free-lance writer Susanna K. Hutcheson sold an article to *Entrepreneur* magazine with a brief, but to the point, query letter to the editor. *Entrepreneur*, a monthly of 325,000 circulation, depends on free-lancers for about 40% of its content, or about 60 to 70 purchased manuscripts a year (Kissling, 1992). Hutcheson wastes no words in the single-page letter. She describes the purpose of the article and its focus. She gives a little flavor of the individual and the woman's company that is the subject of the article. The magazine publishes a lot of "how-to" articles for those interested in running their own businesses, so Hutcheson focused her article on those elements of the Tennessee bakery:

> This short query brought me an assignment in *Entrepreneur*. The idea for it came from a short article in the *Wall Street Journal*. As soon as I read it, I wrote this query and got it off. When the editor called me with the assignment, I phoned the *Journal* and asked where I might contact Ms. Smith. I then had two phone interviews with her . . . . The assignment was for a short article, so I had to really get to the meat in a few words. Note how I get right to the subject in the query. I want to catch the editor just like I would my readers—instantly. I wrote the letter like a terse news story. Then, at the end, I told the editor who I am and why I should get the assignment. (Hutcheson, personal communication, 1993).

Hutcheson's query is also effective because she describes to the editor how her article will benefit the readers of the magazine. "You, the writer, are selling something," she explains. "As a salesperson, you have to sell benefits. The editor, like the buyer, wants to know what this article will do for readers." (personal communication, 1993). Here's her letter to *Entrepreneur*:

SUSANNA K. HUTCHESON
ADDRESS WOULD GO HERE
TELEPHONE NUMBER WOULD GO HERE

DATE
Rieva Lesonsky, editor
Entrepreneur Magazine
2392 Morse Avenue
Box 19787
Irvine, CA 92713-6234

Dear Ms. Lesonsky:

Dot Smith owns a tiny bakery in Tennessee called The Pepper Patch, Inc. Three years ago she took on the state's powerful liquor wholesalers and won the right to buy Jack Daniel's whiskey directly from the distiller rather than retailers. She challenged a state law governing liquor purchases and, by doing so, saved her company tens of thousands of dollars a year.

Now, she is again taking on a giant, this time larger. She is showing that a small businessperson can fight for rights just like anyone else. In fact, she thinks they should.

Lawyers for Campbell Soup Co. sent Smith a letter demanding that she stop packaging her whiskey-laced Tennessee Truffles in a small gold box that they said resembled the containers used by Campbell's Godiva Chocolatier Inc. unit.

Some people would be scared off by a letter from a huge and powerful company's attorney. But not Smith. She sued Campbell before they could sue her, enabling her to fight in her own state. The battle has lasted three years so far. Pepper Patch still packages Tennessee Truffles in little gold boxes.

Your readers may have occasion to fight a giant business. I propose an article profiling Ms. Smith and her business, one that will give encouragement and empowerment to others.

I'm a professional writer but have no major national credits. I do, however, have an article coming out in *Home Office Computing*, a national magazine. I'm enclosing a couple of clips. I could furnish you with a photo of Smith and her business. The article would run about 1,000 to 1,500 words. Interested? Your readers will be.

Sincerely,

Susanna K. Hutcheson

Here is Susanna Hutcheson's final draft of her article as it was submitted to *Entrepreneur*:

When is a gold box just a gold box and when does it belong to Campbell Soup Company? That's the question that's gotten a small Tennessee gourmet food company and its tenacious owner in an onerous legal battle. It isn't, however, the first giant corporation she has successfully fought on behalf of her tiny company.

Dot Smith, 54, started Pepper Patch, Inc. 17 years ago in Nashville. Smith wanted her own identity, credit in her own name, and she didn't want to be bored like so many of her friends.

"This is what has been the driving force behind this business," she says of her need to eliminate boredom from her life.

Success, however, has not come easily for her. She and her tennis partner each put up $1,000 to start the company. Then they needed to borrow another $1,000 to buy a stove. Since they had only been in business one week and had no credit it was no simple matter. But they did get the money after convincing the banker they were a good risk. Smith has now gone from doing business in the branch bank to the corporate lending department in the main bank. She also went from making her products in a cow barn to manufacturing them in three locations. She eventually bought out her partner and is now sole owner.

The Pepper Patch makes 38 products that include pepper jelly and Smith's famous Tennessee Tipsy Cakes.

It was the Tipsy Cakes that pitted Smith against her first giant obstacle, the powerful Tennessee liquor wholesalers. Three years ago Smith challenged a state law governing liquor purchases and was awarded the right to buy Jack Daniel's whiskey directly from the distiller rather than from retailers. The spirits are used in the Tipsy Cakes and other specialties. Her efforts saved Pepper Patch tens of thousands of dollars a year.

Then, another giant stood in her way and again Smith challenged the big guys. She got a letter in May 1989 from Campbell Soup Co. demanding that Pepper Patch stop packaging its whiskey-laced Tennessee Truffles in a small gold box that looked like the containers that Campbell's Godiva Chocolatier Inc. unit use.

Rather than let them sue her in another state, Smith sued them in Tennessee, saving her the cost of fighting the battle elsewhere. While neither side can claim victory yet, Pepper Patch still uses the gold boxes.

Pepper Patch employs 25 people and has gone from a first year gross income of $29,000 to $1.2 million last year. Although besieged by battles, Dot Smith loves being in business for herself. "If you're enthusiastic about what you're doing it makes all the difference in the world," she says. That just may be why she is making a difference in her world. (Reprinted with the permission of Susanna K. Hutcheson.)

DRAFTING A PROPOSAL FOR AN ARTICLE: AN EXAMPLE

Free-lancer Kit Snedaker sells articles about a wide range of travel and food subjects to many different markets. Some article proposals can be mini-articles themselves, ranging up to four or five double-spaced pages to give the full flavor of the proposed article, possible sources, and so forth. "My proposals are always accompanied by a covering letter telling what this is about, describing the enclosed clips and resumé," Snedaker (personal communication, 1993) explains. She says she believes in keeping the proposal short for editors who have a lot to review in the mail each day. The following article proposal is one Snedaker wrote about traditional Christmas in Germany and foods from the Old World holiday season:

KIT SNEDAKER
ADDRESS WOULD GO HERE
TELEPHONE NUMBER WOULD GO HERE

NAME
ADDRESS
PHONE
FAX
DATE

Nobody celebrates Christmas as enthusiastically as Germans. Christmas trees started there, so did Yule logs, Christmas stockings, Advent calendars, Christmas gingerbread, and "Silent Night."

Best of all, though, are the outdoor Christmas markets which open on November 30 and close December 24. Besides toys (many handmade), tree ornaments and gifts, the markets are dotted with food stalls selling Christmas marzipan, gingerbread, Dresden Stollen and Baumkuchen or tree cake.

Originally, it was baked on a spit, batter applied in layers. As each one browned, another was added. When the cake was cut, the edges of the brown layers looked like growth rings of a tree. A version of this, called Spettekka, is found in a small area of southern Sweden. Lithuanians also make a "tree cake" and the Basques in northern Spain bake a cake on a spit, too. Whatever it's called, this cake-baked-in-front-of-the-open-fire predates ovens and has to be the oldest, most interesting pastry in the world.

Doing a roundup of German Kriskindlemarkts and German Christmas food recently, I watched baumkuchen being made on electrified spits and learned how to do this crown jewel of German baking in a springform pan in my kitchen.

Along the way, I visited Berlin's 150-year-old market on the Kurfurstendamm, small, but festive. I saw the biggest Christmas market in Nuremberg, the oldest in Munich (creches are a tradition there), and the most sophisticated in Frankfurt.

Not only markets, but entire towns, street cars, subways, airports, everything is covered with Christmas decorations. It looks as though the holiday was invented there and, in many ways, it was.

If you would like to see a story about: A German Christmas or German Christmas food, Christmas markets in Germany, or Baumkuchen, a story with a Christmas spirit that's older than Scrooge and Tiny Tim, check off the enclosed postcard.

Kit Snedaker

PREPARING A SUBMISSION

Once the article has been queried or proposed, *assigned*, and written, you prepare it in final form for submission to the editor. There is an art to preparing your manuscript in a professional manner. Because you have already been invited to submit the finished manuscript for full review, you have good reason to do this job well. How well you prepare the manuscript and package it is a strong indicator of the professional or unprofessional caliber of your work. If you are sending the finished manuscript on speculation, that is, without any prior correspondence with the publication, you have an even better reason to attend to the details of mailing your manuscript with professional care.

A cover letter is an important part of the final package you mail to the publication. It should be business-like and stick to the point. It can sell the manuscript that you send on speculation. It should make life easier for the editor handling your correspondence. This means you must remember to help editors. You should be as detailed as possible with descriptions or summaries of earlier correspondence (include correspondence dates). "How you handle these [speculation and sale] and similar situations in a cover letter can help build the impression in the editor's mind that you are a professional who understands at least some of the ins and outs of publishing and the author–

editor relationship," editors George Scithers and Sanford Meschkow say (1985a, 1985b, p. 43).

What exactly do you send? Here's a list:

1. *Cover letter.* This should describe what is enclosed and why. Remember that not many editors will remember the details of your project. Help them. This letter should also serve as a memorandum that explains any particulars of the work you have submitted.

2. *Manuscript.* This should be clean (error-free), typed, double or triple spaced. Final copies should always be printed on plain white paper, 8½ x 11 in, and most editors prefer the manuscript be printed by laser, letter-quality, or near-letter-quality printers if you use a computer and word processor.

3. *Artwork.* This includes any visual elements of your story, such as photographs (or negatives), tables, charts, illustrations/drawings, maps, and diagrams. No marking should be included on any visual materials that may be reproduced with your article. It is also best not to write on the back of any artwork. Clip explanatory notes if needed, but do not damage the art.

4. *Protective covering.* If you submit fragile materials such as original photographs or drawings, protect them with cardboard or padding. Specially made shipping containers can be purchased at most office supply stores.

5. *Return envelope and postage.* Especially if you are submitting material on speculation, you should include a self-addressed, stamped envelope for return of materials. Some editors will not return your manuscript and artwork if you do not include the envelope with sufficient postage. An SASE is not needed when the article has already been accepted for publication. Use a large enough envelope to mail the set of materials so they will not be damaged. This means a minimum size 9 x 12 in manila envelope, but if you have a large amount of material, an 11 x 14 in envelope works better.

TRACKING YOUR SUBMISSIONS

Most writers have a system for keeping track of their submissions. As you get more and more into your free-lance writing, you will have a growing list of pending submissions in the marketplace at one time. You need to become organized to track these through the lengthy process of receipt, review, decision, publication scheduling, payment, and even receipt of tearsheets or copies of the articles.

A simple chart will permit such an effort. You can easily keep your records in a word processor file or on a hard copy chart made with a typewriter and ruler. Kit Snedaker (personal communication, 1993), a veteran journalist and free-lance writer, charts the following items on a sheet for every single article—up to 14 article submissions on one page—she submits:

1. The market (note overlapping readerships)

2. Name of the editor
3. Date the query was sent
4. The reply given to the query
5. The submission date
6. Acceptance or rejection decision
7. Photographs or other graphics submitted
8. Publication date
9. Payment received (date and amount)
10. Tearsheet or clipping received
11. Photos returned

Another way to organize such information is to keep separate file folders for correspondence and other documents generated with a submission. The master guide can be an index of the folders, of course, and make finding information easier if needed at a moment's notice (such as an unexpected telephone call from an editor).

WORKING ON ASSIGNMENTS WITH EDITORS

All writers, whether they are staff writers or free-lancers, must work with an editor at some point in the writing and publishing process. The relationship will be very close at some publications. At others, it will seem nonexistent. Most editors are extremely helpful and can even teach their writers new tricks in the process of working with them. They are often willing to spend some time with you and give more precise direction on an assignment. They can communicate what they want and do it in an organized manner. On the other hand, some editors are impossible to work with. These misguided souls are capable of losing manuscripts, failing to issue contracts, forgetting to pay writers, denying payment for legitimate expenses, reneging on promises, and even introducing errors into articles during the editing process. Some have less personal integrity, too. This means some editors will steal ideas, change their minds about accepting and using a manuscript, and even accept a manuscript, pay for it, and then never publish it.

Science writer Karla Harby, who travels the nation on assignment for magazines and newspapers, says the key to working with editors is to listen carefully. "Take good notes and do what the editor tells you to do," she advises. "Keep conversations brief because most editors are chronically overworked. Take deadlines seriously, but don't turn in shoddy work just to meet a deadline. If the article is fantastic, nobody will remember that it came in a day late" (personal communication, 1993).

British free-lance writer and editor Wendy Grossman agrees with Harby and advocates respect for the responsibilities of editors and a professional attitude. "I think the main thing with editors is to remember that they're busy people, and that they and you are, or should be, professionals," she recommends. "Be honest: Don't say you can do things if you can't, because it will only lead to more problems later. Make your deadlines; don't take their comments personally; don't expect them to do stuff to bolster your confidence—you'll have to do that yourself" (personal communication, 1993).

Grossman also suggests that you learn early when to give up your "hold" on a manuscript. It is a mistake to try to work it through the editorial system unless you are specifically asked to assist. "My personal rule is that when the copy leaves my hands I'm finished with it unless the editor asks for a rewrite," she says. "I don't get involved with what the copy editors change, or the headlines, or the choice of pictures. I may request things. I often am asked to supply pictures, either my own or other people's—but once I've handed the stuff over, my job is finished, and it's important to me not to try to do other people's (or I'll have temper tantrums)" (personal communication, 1993).

Relations with editors can become strained, but you cannot let it get to you, Grossman tells beginners. "However badly an editor treats you—and, as one friend of mine said, 'Sooner or later you will come across an editor who doesn't care about you'—it's better not to pick fights with him/her. If there is a disagreement, handle it in a business-like manner; decide what's important to you and ask for it, firmly, but politely. That junior prick who just shafted you is nonetheless in a position to badmouth you all over the profession. Most editors want to behave decently, in any case" (personal communication, 1993).

New York free-lance writer Bill Steele, who worked as editor of a small newspaper before turning full-time to writing, describes the writer–editor relationship from his perspective. "As an editor on a small newspaper (very different from being an editor at a magazine), I was most pleased when people brought me stuff I could use without a lot of rewriting. I was least pleased when people came into the office or called on the phone and took up my time explaining why I should run their stories," Steele (personal communication, 1993) recalls. "So as a writer, I seldom phone editors unless I have something that they need to decide on right away. I will phone, however, if I don't get a reply to a mailed query in a reasonable time. Sometimes that makes them feel guilty and they give me the assignment." Steele has a formula for treating his editors with a fine hand. He explains:

> I think one of the reasons editors come back to me with assignments after I've sold them something is that I give them copy they can use—neat, correct grammar, rhetoric and spelling, and maybe even a little style. My impression is that there are a lot of working writers who don't do that, but who can get the information, so the editors buy their work and clean it up; but they'd prefer not to have to.

> After they've bought your work and start "editing" though, it's important that a writer accept the editor's role and respect his or her expertise. Sometimes you meet editors whose idea of editing is to rewrite the article the way they would have written it, but most are just making adjustments to fit the style of the magazine, space needs, etc. I try to understand this and accept what the editor

does as part of my job. After all, they're paying your salary, and you don't argue too much with the boss. (personal communication, 1993)

Indiana University Journalism Professor Peter Jacobi (1991) recommends a helpful, easy-to-remember checklist of one dozen writing characteristics, all beginning with the letter C, that should gain greater success with editors during the submission process. He recommends being correct, clear, concise, cohesive, complete, constructive, consistent, concrete, credible, conversational, comfortable, and captivating. A writer who can accomplish all of these goals will certainly make friends with editors and readers.

PROVIDING PHOTOGRAPHS AND OTHER GRAPHICS

Although you might fancy yourself as a writer, you will find yourself in a position to be a photographer or graphic artist, or to work in some other form of visual communication. This happens frequently when a magazine or newspaper does not, or cannot, provide a photographer. To strengthen your position to make a sale, you should consider the complete package of your assignment and whether photographs or other artwork will make a difference. If you can take your own professional-quality photographs, it will help a great deal. If you cannot, it is best not to submit below-par photographs with strong writing.

What you can often do to assist an editor is *suggest* visual elements of the total package. You know the material best and will be able to propose photograph subjects, graphs or tables, charts, maps, and diagrams that a professional artist can prepare. You should not have to pay for this service, but you should suggest it to an editor at the time of the query. It strengthens your position if you can propose visual approaches to telling the story. A free-lance travel story will not be as enticing without photographs of the palm-lined beach or snow-capped mountain range. A how-to article or science article is far more understandable with diagrams.

You may be interested in doing your own photographic or informational graphics work. It takes skill development, just like writing. Free-lance science writer Karla Harby is also a photographer. "Being able to take photographs is finally beginning to pay off for me, but it took 8 years of on-and-off effort to make this happen," she explains. "With today's cameras, even a novice can get very good results technically. But to train your eye and learn what is possible with a camera, you should take as many photography courses as you can. You should also study the photos you like in magazines; try to figure what makes them work for you. Anyone who edits a publication with art will greatly appreciate your efforts to illustrate your stories. Good art alone often will clinch a sale. Be alert to the visual possibilities of your writing" (personal communication, 1993).

Another solution is to team with a free-lance photographer and graphic artist. As you begin to increase the frequency of your free-lance work, you may get acquainted with free-lance photographers and artists in your area. Teaming up with these individuals can create a strong offering to an editor that might lead to more good opportunities for everyone involved.

Do not forget that you may be expected to write the first drafts of the cutlines, or captions, of the artwork you submit. These can be short, simple left to right identifications of people in the photographs, or they can be more thorough explanations of procedures and other subjects of the artwork. Your newspaper or magazine's style will dictate how you handle the cutlines—short or long, tight or descriptive, general or detailed—so be sure to familiarize yourself with the way the editor handles these important elements. Always be sure to provide sources of photographs and other graphics for appropriate publication credit if you did not produce them yourself.

MULTIPLE ARTICLES FROM THE SAME RESEARCH

A wise and efficient free-lance feature writer will be able to develop more than one distinct manuscript from research and interviews on a subject. If you can, you will get more income from your investment in time and resources. This is the result of organization and planning. If you are going to make a 500-mile trip for one manuscript—and spend $500 to $1,000—shouldn't you develop a second article prospect for the same trip? Often it is no additional expense to add a second or even a third project; all you give up is additional time. "Full-time writers have to get maximum mileage from each article they produce," says author and free-lance writer Dennis Hensley (1993, p. 32). "That means selling each piece as many times as possible. I do this by marketing from the smallest local publications to the largest circulation periodicals . . . . Most editors don't mind buying a feature that you've already sold elsewhere . . . ." Hensley says multiple sales are acceptable if the previous appearance does not overlap readership, if different artwork can be provided, if the article is rewritten in the style of the second publication, and if new items, such as examples or cases, relevant to readers of the second publication are inserted into the article.

It is smart to consider different markets. There are several ways to focus on a subject, as you know from earlier discussions. Each may represent an article prospect. Focus on both general markets and specialized markets. A general market approach for an article on personal finance will vary a great deal from the specific market approach that a banking magazine would take. Furthermore, consider proposing longer articles in parts. In this way, you are selling two separate, perhaps shorter, articles instead of one longer one. You might earn more for such a sale, but this depends on the rate structure of a publication.

You need the right topic to do this, however. Free-lance writer Tana Reiff (1987a) tells of one such example:

I have a friend who is a lawyer by vocation and a race-car driver by avocation. To promote his racing career, he writes articles for racing magazines. In the course of researching an article recently, he stumbled on a sports psychologist. What a great topic for multiple angles! He's starting with an article on mentally preparing for a race. After that, he'll apply mental preparation to virtually any sport he knows. (p. 24)

PROFESSIONAL'S POINT OF VIEW

Steve Perlstein
Minneapolis Free-Lance Writer

Over the past year and a half—since I left 8 years of newspaper staff reporting for a free-lance career—my efforts to make a living could be summed up in one word: *hustle*.

It doesn't have all that much to do with talent. If I do away with all modesty I can say I'm as good a writer and reporter as anybody who gets $10,000 a pop writing overly long features for *Esquire*. But my optimistic side tells me that I'll be there someday as well, for four simple reasons: I make my deadlines, I write to length, I give editors what they ask for, and I sell myself.

If I sat around waiting for the work to come in, or if I shot off a few queries every once in a while, I might make a little money. But I'm in the unusual situation of supporting my wife, two kids, and a mortgage on my free-lance income. That presents special challenges (like it's nearly impossible), but it also is an impressive incentive to get me downstairs to my office every morning, working hard.

I started small in the winter of 1991—I took a lot of low-paying local work, I wrote for a dizzying array of trade magazines and I scratched up national assignments where I could find them. Usually I couldn't find them. My credo was, "Never turn down an assignment." I still try to hold to that as much as possible, and that is what has kept food on the table and has enabled me to keep my promise to myself that I would not resort to public relations work to earn a living.

Since then, my level of work has remained steady. But instead of averaging around $200 per assignment, as I did when I started, I'm now somewhere around $400. I've done that through a combination of local free-lancing of increasing visibility—including wrestling monthly retainers from two of the Twin Cities' best (and best-paying) free-lance markets—and through dogged pursuit of national markets until I wedged my foot in the door somewhere.

I sent query after query after query—hundreds in all—before *Entrepreneur* magazine called last summer to commission a 400-word piece on a local businesswoman. At 50 cents a word, I only made $200 (and though the piece is long since finished and paid for, it is warehoused and hasn't run yet), but that one assignment opened the floodgates. I was able to put in my query letters, "I have written for *Entrepreneur* magazine, and more than a dozen others." It worked. Shortly after that I had a long feature assignment from *Entrepreneur*, as well as assignments from *Parenting*; *Sky*, the Delta Airlines inflight magazine; *Events USA*; and the nation's largest magazine, *Modern Maturity*.

Still, I constantly have to pitch myself and my ideas to editors. Nobody calls me up begging for my services. There are far too many free-lancers around for that to happen. So everywhere I go, everything I do, and everyone I meet is a potential story. I got my *Modern Maturity* piece about Garrison Keillor's American Radio Company after I attended one of his shows and found it to be charming. I searched until I found a magazine that agreed with me. My wife and I wondered about how safe it was to microwave baby food; that wound up in *Parenting*, with my byline. There is virtually nothing on this earth that can't be crafted to the proper angle and sold to an editor. The key is always to be thinking of what your next story is going to be. It could be something innocuous like the merger of several natural foods cooperatives or it could be something exciting like a travelogue of one of the Clinton/Gore campaign bus trips (both stories I have done).

I can't imagine a free-lancer—unless he or she is a renowned expert on a given topic or named Roger Angell and writing about baseball—who can specialize and make a living. I enjoy how-to and human interest stories, and I write many of them, but I also write a lot about business, politics, health care, parenting, sports, and even banner fabrics, if you can believe it. Free-lancers with a large inheritance or a wealthy spouse can pick a topic and write only that; those of us who have to hustle for a living need to diversify. (Perlstein, personal communication, 1993).

Minneapolis resident Steve Perlstein has been a free-lance writer since 1991, when he left his full-time job as a newspaper reporter. He had developed a successful career at *The Charlotte Observer*, *The Providence Journal-Bulletin*, *The Waterbury (CT) Republican-American*, *The Bristol (CT) Press* and United Press International. After he began his free-lance career, he moved back to Minneapolis, where he had been a student at the University of Minnesota and worked for *The Minnesota Daily*.

18

Surviving in the Free-Lance Business

Kit Snedaker is a veteran free-lance writer who specializes in food, wine, luxury travel, and folk art. Based in Santa Monica, California, she has traveled all over the world. Snedaker is a former daily newspaper staff writer who made the move to full-time free-lance writing a few years ago. She has contributed articles to major publications in the United States and in international markets. Snedaker regularly writes "The Healthy Gourmet" for Copley News Service, and her other feature articles are often syndicated for distribution. She has written several books about cooking, outstanding Southern California restaurants, and the city of Los Angeles. Snedaker has had her travel and food articles published by *Bon Appetit, Food and Wine, Cuisine, Harper's Bazaar, Los Angeles* magazine, numerous metropolitan daily newspapers, and a long list of travel publications. She works in a home office that includes a PC and modem, a fax machine, and other tools of the free-lance writer's trade. She holds memberships in several professional groups, including the Society of American Travel Writers. Snedaker has won awards for her feature writing from several groups and has served as a guest editor for *Mademoiselle*. She grew up in the Midwest and graduated from Duke University. She has lived in Europe, Japan, and on the West Coast.

By all standards, Snedaker is a successful free-lance writer. However, if you haven't detected how she did it quite yet, she has done well because of hard work, discipline, organization, and attention for detail. Her reasons and techniques for success are outlined more fully throughout this chapter. While looking at her work and the efforts of other successful free-lance feature writers like Snedaker, this chapter continues the discussion originated in the preceding chapter.

Free-lance writers work on two levels. The first level is full-time free-lance writing. The second level is "moonlighting"—part-time free-lance writing. This chapter focuses on many important professional concerns of both types of free-lance writing. The chapter discussion begins with the basics of getting paid for assignments. The legal and ethical concerns of free-lance writers are outlined, too. You will learn about professional writers' organizations, continuing educational opportunities beyond college, and contests and awards for quality work.

GETTING PAID FOR YOUR WORK

You earn money as a free-lance writer by being paid for your effort. As you start writing for pay, you will notice variations in how you are paid and how fast you are paid. Checks are the standard, of course, although a few free-lance writers may trade for their services. Checks are issued to free-lancers at various times in the publishing process, but most often after the article is completed, submitted, and accepted for publication. Some publications pay only after the article is printed. On major projects that involve long periods of time, writers should seek an advance or a partial payment in the middle of the project. You have to ask for this, though, because most editors will not usually offer such a convenience.

Most professional free-lancers will include an invoice with their final manuscripts when they are submitted. You need to keep track of such matters, because you will likely have several projects going simultaneously and may lose track of who has paid for what after a period of time has passed. Setting up a ledger, spreadsheet, or a card file system will help you to do this. Sending written reminders for payment are not out of line after a grace period. You should be patient for at least 30 days. After that, send a reminder by mailing a copy of the original invoice to your editor. Editors get busy and occasionally forget to submit payment requests to the publication's business department.

Writer Tana Reiff (1987a, 1987b) says free-lance writing businesses are no different from any other one-person businesses. You should operate with this philosophy. Be your own accountant and practice the basics of good accounting. It will save you money in the long run.

Setting Rates for Your Work

Many beginning free-lance writers are paid whatever their editors decide the going rate will be. They never question nor negotiate fees. This works well enough if you are primarily interested in obtaining clips and, especially, if you have an alternative means of support. There comes a time when most free-lancers begin to take fees as serious business. "[W]hen the rent is due or you want to work at a higher level of professionalism, you need a more assertive approach," says Houston free-lance writer Connie Steitz Fox (1993, p. 6).

Free-lancers must be willing to negotiate for their time and creativity. Editors of most publications set fees for a lot of reasons. They have budgets for free-lancers and can spend only so much. Or they pay depending upon a writer's level of experience. They may have still other reasons.

Fox (1993) says there are several factors to remember when setting free-lance fees. "Consider these factors: What is the market value of your product or service? What is your cost of doing business? What would constitute a fair profit? How much training do you have? How many years of experience? How much natural ability? Do you have expertise in related fields? Can you help to further your client's business goals, including *their* goal of increased profits?" (p. 6).

Gregg Levoy (1991), a veteran free-lance magazine writer, says you need to constantly review what you get paid for your work and ask for more as you gain more experience. Negotiating is essential to getting paid what you are worth, he argues. "When breaking into a magazine . . . writers *should* take whatever terms are offered," Levoy writes (p. 26). "Continuing this practice after breaking in, however, is like turning down raises." In his years as a free-lancer, Levoy has learned three important lessons about negotiating fees: (a) it is surprising what you can get if you ask, (b) the worst an editor can do is say no, and (c) *everything* is negotiable, even editing. However, Levoy says, a free-lance writer's position in negotiating is affected by your performance record, your quality of first impression and presentation, your level of professionalism, the degree of polish you bring to the effort, and the degree of personal contact you have with the individuals on the editorial side of the publication.

There are four ways of being paid for free-lance work. Each one is different and, if you have a choice in the matter, requires that you consider which works best in your own situation. Here are your choices:

First, you can agree to a *flat fee* for completion of a particular writing project. This is perhaps the most common way to handle free-lance assignments. For instance, you write an article of certain agreed-upon specifications and you get paid $75, $150, or whatever amount is established. This does not always take into consideration how much time it takes you to complete the assignment. You will be paid the same amount regardless of the amount of time you need to finish the work. You do, however, have the option of renegotiating the fee if you and your editor discover the assignment will take more time and effort than originally anticipated.

Second, you can work *by the hour* on the assignment. This may be the preferred method from the writer's point of view because it may not always be known how much time is needed to finish an assignment. This is the smart strategy for large projects, because it is seldom possible to anticipate how much effort is required. This approach also requires you to decide how much your time is worth per hour or per day on the open market. This can range from minimum wage to the hundreds of dollars a day that high-powered consultants command. Typical rates for beginning free-lancers are most likely in the $5-per-hour to $10-per-hour range. Veteran free-lancers receive more, ranging from $25 per hour to $50 per hour, depending on the cost of living in a particular region of the country, the size of the publication, and the experience of the writer. Some specialists may be paid even more. Free-lance technical writers, for instance, earn $30 per hour to $60 per hour, according to some published reports. This rate may be the hardest to determine unless you have been in the market. It may be easier after you have completed a few assignments and understand how much you were paid and how much time you used to finish the assignment. On the first few assignments, an "hours worked" log would be very useful for that purpose.

Third, you can be paid *by the word* or by *the column inch*. Some publications stick to the old-fashioned newspaper stringer method of paying by the published length of an article. This can run from 1 cent to $1 or more per word. This does not mean that you are encouraged to write long. Instead, the amount per word is set in negotiation with the editor, and the maximum length of the article is also set by agreement.

Fourth, you can be kept on a *retainer* to write for a publication. This is similar to how some attorneys or consultants work for preferred clients. This involves being paid a set minimal amount per week or per month, regardless of the work assigned and completed. The maximum amount will often be determined by agreement, either by the hour or by the project. This method is not used as often as the others and is used when a writer has become a regular contributor for a publication.

You may also want to charge for special conditions of assignments. Dangerous situations, holiday work, overtime hours, rush work, "no-compete" or "exclusivity" clauses that prevent you from writing on the same subject for other publications, and such extraordinary circumstances may call for higher fees or bonuses beyond the going rates.

Also keep in mind that, no matter which of the four options are used to pay you for your work, your expenses are a separate issue. However, many editors build in ordinary expenses, such as long- distance telephone calls or automobile transportation, into the flat fee paid for the assignment. Additional expenses or extraordinary costs, such as airfare or equipment rentals, must be negotiated to be paid separately. Expenses are discussed in more detail in a later section of this chapter.

How Long Should You Wait Before Getting Paid?

You are entitled to the money you have earned: It is that simple. Payment should occur within a reasonable period of time. Yet, some careless editors and publishers do not quite see it that way. They delay or simply do not pay writers in a professional manner.

Thus, a first step in establishing a payment arrangement is to determine the normal period for the publication. You can ask about this when an agreement to publish your article has been reached. Then you wait.

It is also important to establish a guarantee or a *kill fee* before the work is submitted or even written. If editors change their mind about your article for whatever reasons, you should be compensated for the work you were *assigned* to put into it. If a completed assignment is not acceptable due to no fault of yours as the writer, some professional organizations such as the American Society of Journalists and Authors feel you should be paid a guarantee up to the full amount reflecting the effort put into the article before the decision to "kill" it was made (Bloom et al., 1992). Most professionals agree, also, that you should be paid within a month of delivery. This will vary from publication to publication and the cycle within which the publication's accounting department or business office works. Some process checks only on a monthly basis.

ASJA also recommends in its code of ethics and fair practices that "no article payment, or portion thereof, should ever be subject to publication" (Bloom et al., 1992, p. 51). If a publisher does not pay and you feel you are entitled to your fee, writer Dean R. Lambe (1986) suggests several potential actions to take:

1. Write a politely worded inquiry letter to the editor.
2. Next, write the publisher (if different from the editor).
3. See a lawyer and he will write an inquiry letter.
4. Take legal action through your lawyer.
5. If a bankruptcy has occurred, file a claim so you can get a share when assets are sold.
6. Share your grief with other writers through professional groups.

KEEPING TRACK OF YOUR OPERATING EXPENSES

Free-lance writers are paid for two types of expenses. One is the time spent writing and researching the manuscript. The other type involves the cost of getting the story. Besides your time, you will encounter certain operating expenses when working on an article. As a free-lancer, you must arrange to get these costs paid by the publication that accepts your article or else the cost will come from your agreed fee.

If you have proposed an article, you should estimate expenses and include the estimate in your total fee, especially if the cost will be excessive. At worst, expenses can consume your "profits" from the assignment. At best, expenses should be reimbursed by your employer. Typical writer's expenses include automobile mileage, plane travel, parking, lodging, food, admissions, express mail and overnight delivery services, long-distance telephone tolls, film, photo processing, and photocopying. You should expect your publication to pay reasonable expenses, but you should check these details when an assignment is made or when your proposal is accepted. Normal business expenses such as printer ribbons, printer paper, routine postage, or computer disks are rarely paid as expenses. Overhead costs such as electricity, office space rental, and local phone costs are rarely covered as specific expenses.

Professional writers always keep expense logs and receipts, even for costs that are not directly billable to employers. There are two basic reasons for this: First, you must have a record if you expect someone else to pay for your expenses; second, if you do not get them reimbursed, you can still claim certain business expenses as deductions on your federal and state income taxes—if they are documented. Because tax laws change on a somewhat regular basis, it is best to check with a tax expert on these matters.

Like Snedaker, who must keep her free-lance business organized to enable her to make her living, free-lance writer Karla Harby explains her rather easy-to-use system that will work well for beginners: "I use a cash accounting system, which simply means I keep a book recording income and expenses. You also need a separate checking account for your income and expenses," she explains. For the more advanced, she advises: "All freelance writers need an accountant—preferably a certified public accountant—so have him or her show you what to do" (personal communication, 1993).

Always discuss payment of expenses with your editor in advance, especially if a major expense such as out-of-town travel is involved. You may be given a ceiling for expenses for an assignment by the editor and you will be expected to keep within the limit. For example, if you need to make a large number of lengthy long-distance telephone calls, an editor may budget $100 for that particular expense. Yet, if you foresee going over the limit, ask about it first. Otherwise, you may find the expenses chipping away your income when the editor refuses, after the fact, to pay them.

SOME IMPORTANT LEGAL CONSIDERATIONS

You cannot exist in a legal vacuum as a free-lance writer. In addition to the general concerns all journalists must have about libel, privacy, copyright, open records, and open meetings, you must also consider other legal issues related to free-lance writing. This means knowing the details of obtaining permissions, payment for work particulars, reprint and other second sales rights, contracts, general letters of agreement, and author copyright.

As a writer and reporter, you must be concerned with the laws in your state involving libel, privacy, fraud, copyright, and access to information. There are numerous high-caliber discussions of these subjects in other books and they are not discussed in depth in this chapter. *Mass Communication Law: Cases and Comment*, by Donald Gillmor, Jerome Barron, Todd Simon, and Herbert Terry (1990), for example, is one of several general treatises of concerns affecting all types of feature writers and reporters.

The recent legal problems of one free-lance feature writer may be an illustration of the need to know both state and federal laws dealing with this line of work. A Southern California man recently pleaded guilty to selling phony celebrity stories to supermarket tabloids and was sentenced to federal prison and then home confinement. He admitted to 21 counts of mail fraud and tax evasion for using fictitious sources to sell story ideas and stories to those publications. The judge in the case felt the writer was encouraged to do the work by the publications, but the publications encouraged him, the federal judge said, to protect themselves from libel and other civil action against them. The writer, a former daily newspaper reporter in Los Angeles, agreed in court to assist in investigations into the professional ethics of the publications (*Editor & Publisher* staff, 1993).

Obtaining Permissions

There are times in preparing an article that you will wish to use a substantial passage from another published and copyrighted work. This occurs when quoting other authors, composers, and artists. You must get permission from the source, or rights holder, when you want to do this. Generally, there are four steps to getting permission: find the copyright owner, write a permission request letter to the owner, act on the reply to your request letter (for example, pay a fee or provide a copy of the article), and credit the copyright holder in your article. For short passages, usually up to 250 words or a paragraph, you do not need formal permission. But writers will certainly be asking for trouble if they fail to get permission for use of longer quotations.

OBTAINING AND KEEPING AUTHOR COPYRIGHT

Copyright law in the United States is designed to protect creative works by authors. Such law is almost as old as the nation itself, dating back to 1790. Recent modifications in the law—and it has been changed many times over the past two-plus centuries—focus protection on the author.

As a free-lance writer, you need to know who will own your manuscript once it is published. This should be stipulated in letters of agreement or contracts. Most such arrangements leave ownership—that is, the copyright—with the author. Thus, unless you give up those rights in writing, ownership of the work remains with you as author, according to the 1990 U.S. Copyright Law.

For staff writers producing feature articles in their regular employment role, the work they create belongs to their employers. There can be exceptions to this, but they are rare. Some staff writers, such as extremely popular columnists, negotiate rights to their works when they have become established because they want to publish them elsewhere (e.g., volumes of their collected works). For free-lancers, or for full-time staffers doing articles outside of normal work, the work belongs to the author. If there is doubt, discuss it before you get too deeply into your assignment. Whatever is decided about rights should be placed in writing, also.

Under the revised copyright law, authors are protected when the work reaches final form in any tangible medium. This includes not only computer versions of manuscripts, but also photographs, informational graphics, and other works of free-lance authors. The law protects authors against unauthorized sale and distribution of their work. Although authors do not have to register their work with the U.S. Copyright Office within the Library of Congress (Washington, D.C. 20559; 202-707-3000), it is recommended because any legal action that may occur cannot begin until registration is completed. The process is simple and inexpensive ($20). Authors are also advised to use a copyright notice symbol (©), the word "Copyright," or the abbreviation

"Copr." with the name of the holder and date on all works, although this is not required for protection. Doing so may reduce what is called innocent infringement (Gillmor, Barron, Simon & Terry, 1990).

Reprint and Other Sales Rights

Traditionally, free-lance writers have sold only the one-time publication rights of their work. Reprint fees should be yours as author, ASJA (Bloom et al., 1992) suggests to its members. The publication that prints your article should refer inquiries to you, as well, unless you waive these rights. You hold the copyright unless you grant it in writing to the publication. Any other rights are yours, ASJA says, and it strongly urges writers not to sign any documents that transfer those rights to a publisher.

GET THE DEAL IN WRITING? MAYBE!

Some free-lance writers work regularly with none of the terms of their assignments in writing. Any agreements are informal, casually set in telephone conversations. Although this is admirable, it is also potentially troublesome. It is not smart business practice these days. Perhaps the only occasion when this arrangement between a writer and an editor makes sense is when the relationship is an established one and the terms and details are commonly known by both parties from repeated experience. In all other cases, it is wisest to get a memorandum, letter, or even a formal contract from the editor responsible for the newspaper, magazine, or newsletter that made the assignment. In some situations, such as lengthy or complicated assignments involving international travel or dangerous situations, even more formalized contracts may be required to cover all contingencies.

However, award-winning science writer Karla Harby, who is a member of the National Association of Science Writers, does not often get her assignments in writing. "Most of my journalism assignments are not in writing. It is always wise to send a letter confirming the assignment after you get it, but I'm quite lax about doing this. I've never been stung by an editor—either for a consumer or a trade publication—but I can't recommend my approach! I do always insist on a contract when working for new corporate clients and often for established ones as well. And certainly if you have any doubts about it, get the agreement in writing," she advises (personal communication, 1993).

Harby's situation is probably typical, especially for those free-lancers writing for weekly and small daily newspapers. Magazines and newsletters may be more formalized in their arrangements with writers, but much depends on the size of the periodical. Newspaper editors and small magazine and newsletter editors would probably prefer to work with all free-lance agreements in writing, but their hectic schedules and workloads just do not permit time for it.

Working with a Publisher's Contract

Contracts can be beneficial to writers and editors. If done properly, a contract sets down terms of an agreement between the writer and the editor. Most of the time, the contract will be some kind of standard fill-in-the-blank legal form used for all free-lance employment. If you have been offered a contract with a publication, *read it* thoroughly before you sign it and return it. Contracts will specify certain arrangements between the author and publisher. You may find terms in the document that do not apply to your situation and these should be deleted. Similarly, there may be peculiar aspects of your situation not covered in the document that must be appended. This can be done without significant delays in most cases.

As a writer, you need to look for certain elements of a contract regardless of whether it involves a nonfiction article or something as complex as an entire book. The major concerns about these kinds of contracts, says literary agent Lisa Collier Cool (1985b), include your publication fee, the kill fee (a guarantee if the article is not used), the assigned manuscript length (usually in words), payment of expenses (or limitations), payment schedule, manuscript deadlines, payment of advances, author bylines or credits in the publication, serial rights, book publication rights (usually for collected sets of articles by popular and experienced feature writers), dramatic rights, commercial rights, online database retrieval rights, translations (from English to another language), and frequency of use by the publication (some editors will republish an article from time to time).

Glenda Tennant Neff (1992), assistant managing editor at Writer's Digest Books, advises writers looking at a contractual arrangement to consider their own writing goals:

> As you evaluate a document, consider what you want from your writing. Did you have another sale in mind that selling all rights the first time will negate? Does the agreement here provide the publisher with a number of add-ons (advertising rights, reprint rights, etc.) for which they won't have to pay you again? Contracts are rarely take-it-or-leave-it propositions. Sometimes they are, and the editor will let you know. At that point you will have to decide how important the assignment is to you. But most editors are open to negotiation, and you should learn to compromise on points that don't matter to you while maintaining your stand on things that do. (p. 47)

Using Letters of Agreement

Often it is a good idea to work with a letter of agreement instead of a contract. As the writer, you can originate the letter of agreement if the editor does not offer one. This is a suitable compromise to no written agreement at all and the other extreme of a detailed contract. A letter of agreement, like a contract, should state the terms of the relationship between the writer and the publication. Like the contract, it should list fees to be paid and when, who is responsible for expenses, the topic of the assignment, the length of the manuscript, the deadline, who is responsible for artwork, and other pertinent details.

A sample letter of agreement provided by an author, especially when the publication does not issue any written confirmation of the assignment, is included in Appendix B. This form letter has been drafted by the American Society of Journalists and Authors, Inc., for use when contracts are not appropriate or when the author and publisher prefer not to work with formal contracts.

Some editors like to work with letters of agreement instead of contracts. These letters function as contracts because they have certain details prescribed in them. *National Geographic Traveler* issues its assignments in writing after discussing the terms of the assignment with the free-lancer on the telephone. Senior Articles Editor Carol Lutyk works that way. Her letters of agreement represent the magazine and the publisher, the National Geographic Society in Washington, DC. Her letters outline the topic, length, due date, fees to be paid if used or if killed, and any rights that the magazine retains. Some publications, such as *National Geographic Traveler*, even specify that similar work cannot be done for certain competing publications. Lutyk also asks writers on assignment to agree to certain ethical standards, such as acceptance of discounts or free goods and services. The agreements often also stipulate that writers cannot give the work to someone else to do on their behalf. A copy of Lutyk's *National Geographic Traveler* generic letter used for travel feature article assignments is included in Appendix C.

LAWSUITS AND OTHER LEGAL MATTERS

Lawsuits can arise from just about anything in a written work. The main causes will be claims for libel, defamation, or invasion of privacy, especially in articles that break new ground or are about controversial subjects. You must be concerned with the possibility, whether the cases are legitimate or not.

If your work is *accurate*, then you will have little to worry about. Truth, of course, is the best defense against libel actions. Writer and University of Southern California journalism professor Bruce Henderson (1984) recommends nine ways to "bulletproof" a manuscript:

1. *The idea.* Check whether the story idea is a new one. Be certain you are not copying or plagiarizing a work. Check your own motivations for doing the article. If your work involves revenge or venting anger, forget it.

2. *The assignment contract.* Honor the commitments you make in writing and otherwise. Know what you are liable for, such as legal fees, according to the contract terms.

3. *Research.* Use written sources if possible to guard against legal claims. Keep accurate records about where you find the factual information you use.

4. *Interviews.* Select qualified sources. Be sure sources have no grudges against your subject. Get second sources to verify. Identify sources, whenever possible, in the article. Conduct important interviews in person and tape record them.

5. *Note taking.* Be thorough in taking notes. Organize the notes after an interview or a records search. When you can, note negative results—that you could not find something.

6. *Writing.* Tell only what you know. Do not guess or make up information to fill in holes. If you are not certain of a fact, then avoid using it.

7. *Editing and fact checking.* Do not change information in a story, even if an editor asks you to do so, unless the change is true and accurate. Be ready for a fact checker from the publication to verify information in your story. This may mean calling your sources, too.

8. *Final checks.* Have a lawyer read your final manuscript if you think it might be troublesome. Seeking legal advice before publication is smart and safe.

9. *Lawsuit.* If you ever find yourself served with a suit, contact the publication immediately. The publisher will be directly involved also. Plan to work together.

ETHICS AND FREE-LANCE WRITING

Another important topic for free-lance writers to consider is ethics. Ethics is the set of principles of professional conduct. Even though certain practices in journalism are legal, they may not be ethical. The practices may not be accepted behavior among most professional writers. For instance, there is much concern in the 1990s about invasion of individual privacy.

There are numerous codes of professional standards in journalism. Among them are the codes of the Society of Professional Journalists and the American Society of Journalists and Authors, Inc. These codes are included in Appendices D and E. There are other codes, of course, but they have a similar purpose: to set forward an acceptable way to work as a professional journalist. The SPJ code sets general standards for all journalists and is a good overall model to study. ASJA's code focuses on ethical and economic issues that are the fundamental concerns of writers.

What professional standards should we be concerned about? Ethics codes list more than two dozen different issues pertaining to the relation of writers to sources, editors, readers, and even other writers. Most general codes, such as the SPJ code, focus on responsibilities to the public, need for accuracy, need for freedom of the press, need for fairness, elimination of conflicts of interest and acceptance of gifts in exchange for favors, and the desire to achieve honesty and objectivity. Specific writers' codes, such as the one endorsed by ASJA, are more detailed and propose fair practices in the relationship of writers and editors. ASJA's code, for example, addresses nearly two dozen separate situations ranging from subjects similar to those in the SPJ code, such as accuracy and conflicts of interest, to specific details of writers' publication and payment rights and their expenses.

One mark of professionals is the level of their ethical conduct. Familiarity with the accepted performance standards in your profession will only help in the long run. Because these are evolving standards, they are constantly changing. It is up to you to keep up with them as your professional career expands.

MOVING TOWARD FULL-TIME FREE-LANCE WRITING

Most beginning free-lance writers are moonlighting. Their primary means of support comes from another form of employment. There will come a time for writers who are successful at moonlighting to consider quitting their primary job to open up more time for writing. Two of the hardest decisions a part-time free-lance writer will face are (a) whether to switch to full-time and, if the decision to switch is made, (b) when is the right time to make the change. Besides giving up an existing career, it is a decision that may mean giving up a regular, steady income. It is one that should be made only after thoughtful deliberation and discussion with family and colleagues.

The main *real* difference between a moonlighting free-lance writer and a full-time one is the number of hours per week devoted to writing, says author Robert Bly (1992, p. 24). Once they begin to work, moonlighters and full-timers operate the same way, he says.

Karla Harby, who writes science articles for major magazines and newspapers, says free-lancing requires a major career commitment:

> Don't think that if nothing else works out that you can always free-lance. Deciding to free-lance requires much the same kind of commitment as deciding to earn a degree. Similarly, not everybody will succeed at it. Work at staff jobs for a few years, get to know some free-lance writers and editors, and have some other source of income ready for the first year—a nest egg, a working spouse, inherited money—before taking the plunge full-time. I was never able to free-lance and hold a staff job simultaneously, because I put so much into my job. But many people do make the transition to self-employment this way. (Harby, personal communication, 1993)

Michael A. Banks (1985), an author who quit a factory job to become a full-time free-lance writer, describes advantages and disadvantages to making the big switch:

Advantages. First, there is more time to plan and write. You can take on larger projects, such as booklets and even books. You work as much as you want because you control your time. There is no need for the physical and psychological transition time to go from job one to job two. Also, Banks says, the full-time writing effort gives you a boost in self-esteem by putting you in control of your own career and business.

Disadvantages. You may be the primary wage earner for you and your family. Some economic losses from giving up a steady income are severe and must be reckoned with. You must be able to manage money that comes in uneven surges. You must also endure the operating expenses of being a writer on your own. This means the costs of travel, telephone, equipment, and even ordinary office supplies. You may have to pressure yourself to be productive. Failure can take on a greater significance. There is no supervisory pressure in most cases and you must be self-disciplined. Furthermore, do not forget that you lose all nonpaycheck benefits that come along with a full-time salaried job (e.g., health insurance, pensions and retirement, social security contributions made by your employer [now you must make them], paid vacations, bonuses, sick days, and overtime).

The decision to go full-time must be an economic one. Can you afford it? What is your current part-time income? What would it be full-time if you project it to the amount of time you gain by quitting the full-time job? Is that realistic? Can you find that much free-lance work? What are your basic normal living expenses? Will you cover them? Can you make sacrifices of other things for a while?

Free-lance writer Gary C. King specializes in "true crime" and mystery writing. He has written three books about serial killers and other crime in addition to his numerous articles for publications such as *True Detective* and *Official Detective.* He says he found writing to be addictive. He could not get enough of it as a part-timer. Here's how he says he decided to make the shift:

> When I first broke into crime writing, I was naturally thrilled that anyone would buy my work and in fact wanted more. That was in December 1980. Almost immediately I asked my editor, Art Crockett, if I should give up my job and go full time. His response: "Forget free-lancing on a full-time basis unless you marry a rich widow . . . or until you become a best-selling author and have editors clamoring for your work." I took his advice, but only for a while. By 1984 I was free-lancing full time and putting my family through hell. In retrospect, free-lancing is not something I would recommend to anyone who wants to keep the bills paid on time and food on the table. It's very difficult. Appealing as the prospect of being on your own can be, there's still nothing like a steady paycheck. (King, personal communication, 1993)

Free-lancer Tana Reiff (1987a) recommends diversification of your writing. The more you can write about different specialties, the more you will bring in fees, she believes. She also recommends diversity in the types of projects. Taking on both short and long assignments can keep a steadier supply of income in the mail, she says.

Prepare for the switch by planning ahead. Put aside extra money for the expected slow period at the beginning. Also, save some good writing ideas for

---

WHEN DO YOU QUIT YOUR DAY JOB? A QUIZ

Free-lance writer and editor Dana Cassell (1991) made the switch from moonlighting to full-time writing almost two decades ago. An experienced author of over 1,200 articles in 150 publications, she recommends considering answers to ten key questions before making the leap. A "no" answer to any of these questions may suggest a need to wait, she says. The questions:

1. Do you have sufficient savings to live for 6 months to 1 year?
2. Are you self-disciplined and motivated? Do you start what you finish?
3. Do you have a base to help with expenses, such as an at-home business, to get started?
4. Do you have a business plan? Do you know what markets you want to approach and how to approach them?
5. Have you estimated how much money you average per hour in your writing now? Have you calculated how much income you will need (including taxes)?
6. Do you have good work habits? Do you stick to a writing schedule?
7. Does your move to full-time writing have the support of family?
8. Do you have professional friends and advisors for criticism and support?
9. Do you have private space, equipment, and supplies for an office where you can work undisturbed for the entire day?
10. Can you provide funds for benefits such as insurance and retirement funds for yourself and your family?

---

slow idea periods, Banks recommends. These will help you through tough times. He advises to not "burn your bridges" at your primary job. Try to leave yourself an option to return if things do not work out. Test your career change first by taking a 3- to 6-month leave, if this is available. Sometimes, accumulated vacation time can be taken in one big block for a trial run at full-time free-lance writing.

Brett Harvey is Eastern Regional Grievance Officer of the National Writers Union (NWU) based in the New York City area. She regularly deals with problems between writers who are members of the NWU and their employers and has compiled a list of guidelines that should be particularly helpful for beginning free-lance writers. Her guidelines are reprinted in Appendix F. Harvey (personal communication, 1993) says: "These are especially hard times for free-lancers, in case you hadn't noticed. Magazines are going belly-up nearly every month, and the ones that are left are cutting every possible corner—which means fewer pieces assigned, lower fees, more and lower kill fees, slower payment, and more all-rights contracts." As she advises, guidelines such as hers will not guarantee solution or elimination of problems, but they should minimize the chance for problems to occur.

WRITERS' ORGANIZATIONS, CONFERENCES, AND SEMINARS

After your formal education is concluded, the best way to continue developing yourself as a free-lance writer is to become involved in professional organizations, attend workshops and conferences about writing, and interact often with other professional writers. Writing groups and special events have numerous benefits that far outweigh any disadvantages, such as expenditure of money or time.

Professional Organizations

Professional organizations exist at the national, regional, state, and local levels. It should be easy to find one of more of these to meet your needs. Professional organizations offer writers the chance to meet other writers, as well as editors and publishers. These groups, such as the Society of Professional Journalists (SPJ), may offer special professional development programs that provide continuing professional education. SPJ's membership includes both staff and free-lance journalists, as well as rank-and-file journalists and management.

Other groups focus more on the economic and legal needs of independent writers, not staff writers or editors. Concerns include such matters as fair levels of compensation, health and other insurance benefits, taxation, freedom of expression, uniform standards in contracts, and protection of copyright. Among the best known writers' organizations are the National Writers Union, the American Society of Journalists and Authors, the Authors Guild, the Authors League of America, and the Writers Guild of America. Membership in these groups often requires meeting certain qualifications. Ordinarily, this means you have to be established as a writer. The National Writers Union, for example, requires publication of a book, a play, three articles, or other works.

There are also numerous specialized writers' groups at the national level, each reflecting particular interests. Some specialized groups are divisions of larger organizations. Others are more specific in their interests but independent also. Groups that may interest free-lance feature writers include the American Medical Writers Association, the Aviation and Space Writers Association, the Computer Press Association, the Editorial Freelancers Association, the Jazz Journalists Association, the National Association of Science Writers, the Outdoor Writers Association of America, and the Society of American Travel Writers.

Membership in a professional group might not seem important to you now, particularly if you are still in school, but it will become increasingly important as time passes beyond graduation. However, these national organizations do offer guidance through regular contact with members, officers, and staff experts. This comes through publications and local and national meetings. Many beginning writers, especially free-lancers, find the contacts made at these organizational meetings helpful for story ideas and opportunities to meet editors and other writers. Local press clubs in major cities such as New

York or Washington are also gathering and meeting places for professional writers.

Most professional memberships are not overly expensive, but may seem so to beginning writers. Most require national dues of less than $100 a year—the average seems to be between $50 and $100 annually—and some require additional minimal local chapter dues as well. These business expenses are tax deductible, of course, and are sometimes paid by employers. Regional and local professional organizations are usually less expensive and offer greater interaction among members. Most of the national professional organizations, in fact, offer regional gatherings and local chapters for more frequent interaction among members.

Less formalized writers' clubs and associations are another alternative. These often organize in a community with the goal to further members' careers. These groups can be useful for a free-lance writer if the groups offer speakers, writing critique sessions, readings of works, field trips, and professional contact opportunities. Some offer service to the community, such as helping local schools, as well. Many are organized by towns or neighborhoods. Some have grown as large as statewide groups and have subdivided.

Writers in Florida, Texas, and Georgia each benefit from free-lance writers organizations. For example, the Florida Freelance Writers Association organized to be "the link between Florida writers and editors, public relations directors and other buyers of the written word" (Florida Freelance Writers Association, 1985, p. 1). This particular group maintains a central office, hosts

---

SETTING UP A "WRITING ZONE" AT HOME

Writers need a comfortable and familiar space in which to work. Some may be able to write anywhere at any time, but just like at home, there is a psychological advantage to being in a particularly creative place, or zone, reserved just for writing. Free-lancer Norman Schreiber, writing in *Writer's Digest*, suggests careful decisions be made about creating a personal workspace, because they help change a hobby into a business. These are Schreiber's (1991) recommended components of any home office:

1. A clearly defined workspace (an extra bedroom, basement, or heated garage) and a large work surface devoted just to writing.
2. A comfortable and healthy chair. Remember, you will spend a lot of time in it.
3. Something to write with, preferably a personal computer and printer.
4. Lighting of some kind, preferably task-specific lighting rather than general overhead lighting.
5. Paper storage space such as file folders and cabinet systems.
6. Shelving and drawer storage for writer's tools.
7. Telephone, preferably a separate line for business use, if needed.
8. Office machines such as a fax/photocopier system.
9. Extras such as bulletin boards, wall calendars, and other personal decorations.

an annual statewide conference with speakers, operates a referral system for writer members, furnishes updated state market information, publishes a member directory, and a monthly newsletter, offers a toll-free 800 information hotline, provides a manuscript critique service, helps set up meetings with editors and agents at its annual conference, operates an annual writing contest, has book sales at the annual conference, and offers continuing education programs throughout the year. Similar groups across the country offer similar support and services for a minimal cost each year. Membership in the active Florida group cost $90 in 1993, but the parallel Georgia group membership cost $72 and the Texas group cost $75 (Florida Freelance Writers Association, 1993).

Southern California writers are served by the Independent Writers of Southern California, based in Los Angeles. This group provides numerous benefits for self-employed writers, such as group insurance, a credit union, membership program meetings, a monthly newsletter, a grievance committee for disputes, and subgroups that represent specific counties in the region. Similar local groups to those described above exist in Tampa, Indianapolis, Portland (Oregon), Dallas, and Washington, D.C.

Author Dennis Hensley (1986) recommends that you be selective about these clubs so you can find one that will emphasize writing development over social activities. "Manuscript evaluating is one of the great services a writers club or critique group can provide—if it is done correctly. Too often members offer routine praise to each other and shy away from seriously analyzing one another's manuscripts," Hensley warns (p. 38).

Other Professional Development Opportunities

Some writers prefer not to join organizations. Some journalists are just not "joiners." Others work in rural areas where local membership is not possible or not very convenient. Nevertheless, there are other options for continuing professional education. These come in the form of writers' classes, conferences, seminars, and workshops. *Writer's Digest* annually compiles and lists the major gatherings of writers. In 1993 for example, *Writer's Digest* Senior Editor Thomas Clark and Associate Editor Angela Terez (1993) found more than 400 such events scheduled in the United States.

Such events offer hands-on writing practice and learning; lectures; opportunities to learn from, and to meet, established writers; and the chance to learn new techniques. Most events such as these last only a few days and are often sponsored by schools or writers' groups. The chance to interact with other writers during these events may be the best experience—it gives you a chance to exchange ideas, offer critiques, and help one another in social and working sessions.

Writers should try at least one such conference to see if the experience is beneficial. A little preparation before attending (e.g., reading about speakers, reading the works of speakers, or reviewing the program to choose what you will do) will make the experience more fruitful. Such events afford excellent opportunities to talk to other writers, both beginners and veterans, about their work and about your work. Sessions with speakers are learning situations also, so note taking and tape recording are recommended. Usually there is a chance to ask speakers questions during a session or afterward and it is wise to take advantage of this opportunity. Many speakers at these conferences, especially smaller ones, may be willing to talk with participants afterward. There is also a chance to make contacts for assignments or collaborative efforts, so be prepared to discuss such options.

PUBLICATIONS AIMED AT FREE-LANCE WRITERS

Membership in a free-lance writing or other professional organization normally includes subscriptions to one or more publications. Most common are small magazines or newsletters issued on a monthly or less frequent basis. The Florida Freelance Writers Association, Georgia Freelance Writers Association, and Texas Freelance Writers Association, for example, join forces to publish the *Freelance Writers Report*, a national monthly newsletter about markets, news, tips, perspectives from editors, and activities of members and local groups. There are numerous other similar publications available nationally through memberships.

In recent years, several new newsletters aimed at experienced free-lance writers have begun publication also. These new publications are not associated with organizations and require paid subscriptions. Two examples of these new publications are *Freelance Success* and *Writing for Money*. They also offer readers advice about free-lance writing and free-lance markets. These publications circulate at the national level on a monthly or more frequent basis and are edited and published by veteran free-lance writers.

Although they may not be entirely devoted to free-lance work, many of the monthly writing-oriented magazines also have regular departments or sections devoted to free-lance writing. Leading publications such as *Writer's Digest, The Writer*, and *ByLine* offer regular doses of professional advice and the latest information about new writing markets.

BENEFITS OF CONTESTS AND AWARDS

Some writers love to enter contests and apply for awards; other writers detest such things. The idea of competition and the thought of recognition for excellence often appeal to writers who want to receive systematic professional feedback on their work beyond the fact that they made a sale or not. Winning some contests can be financially rewarding, but other contests simply offer recognition for quality work. Most contests are offered on an annual basis and are specialized by subject. The 1993 *Writer's Market* lists about 100 contests for nonfiction writers (Kissling, 1992) and *Editor & Publisher* annually lists even more for newspapers and magazines.

Contests can provide opportunities for beginning writers. Winning recognition in a contest means greater professional visibility. It means new opportunities. It is a way to be discovered within your specialization. However, winning an award is not the solution to all your professional problems. It is only a sign that you may have taken the step to the next highest level of excellence in your writing. The key to entering contests is to know about these competitions well in advance of deadlines. By doing your homework ahead of time, you have the chance to prepare an appropriate entry with your best professional presentation. Meeting the deadline with a clean entry that follows entry rules carefully is a must for contest participants. Many organizations sponsoring contests and award programs publish the entry specifications and will provide them at no charge if you request them in advance of the deadline. You must always take the time to check your eligibility as well. This should be outlined in the contest rules, but if you are not sure, contact the sponsors.

PROFESSIONAL'S POINT OF VIEW

Art Spikol
Writer's Digest

So you want to be a free-lance writer. Well, I've done it for a while, and I've learned a few things. Here they are—hang 'em over your computer:

• *Don't talk your stories.* If you let it come out of your mouth, chances are it won't come out of your fingertips.

• *Develop a sales approach.* Not a canned pitch, but an effective demeanor for dealing with editors. That demeanor may end up in a query letter or a phone call or a personal visit, but never lose sight of the goal: to sound responsible and competent. If you want success, you can't be just a writer. The biggest cause of failure among would-be-writers is not wanting to deal with the business issues. For instance, a businessperson doesn't write something first and worry about where to sell it afterward.

To be businesslike, ask yourself what kind of magazine you want to sell to. Then what kind of articles that magazine uses. And then make sure that the publication hasn't recently printed an article like yours. And then convince an editor that you're the person to write it. Time is money; don't squander yours.

You'll have to sound not just like somebody who can write a good article, but somebody an editor wouldn't mind putting on a witness stand someday.

Because of litigious times, it may come to that.

If you don't make the sale, don't blame the editor. Editors know what to buy, and they know what their readers want. If you don't sell the article, it (or you) wasn't right for the publication.

• *Do your job like a pro.* If you were a race car driver, neurosurgeon, or astronaut, a mistake could be disastrous. The same applies to writing: Misspell a word, punctuate incorrectly, fail to meet a deadline, and your credibility goes up in smoke. Ultimately, your career will follow it.

• *Take charge of your business.* If, for instance, you wait 10 weeks to get a yes or no from a publication, it's your fault, not the publication's. Take the idea elsewhere—maybe to two or three other markets. If you were trying to sell your car, would you offer it to one person at a time?

• *Don't quit your job.* Sure, you want to be a free-lancer, but don't give up what you have. It will create too much financial pressure to enable you to succeed. Instead, first see if you have the discipline to spend 1 hour a day writing. If you can do that on a sustained basis, stretch it to 2 hours. See what happens—are you selling? Making contacts? Nothing magical happens when you quit your job—except that your income disappears.

• *Don't use best-case scenarios as a guide.* You can earn about $25,000 to $35,000 a year if you write for magazines and hit the best of them every month at their highest rates. Or you can earn $8,000 a year, which is far more likely. Prepare for the worst.

• *Diversify.* If you want to make a lot more than the previous figures, take your writing talent down some more financially rewarding paths. Write newsletters, brochures, annual reports. Write advertising, film scripts, books. They all pay better—for less work—than magazine articles.

• *Finally, love writing.* Practically everybody I meet would like to be a writer, but not many actually want to write. The hard work is sitting down and putting the words on paper.

Now, close this book and do it. May your fingers have wings. (Spikol, personal communication, 1993)

Art Spikol is a Philadelphia-based contributing editor and columnist for *Writer's Digest*, Cincinnati. His column, "Nonfiction," is a monthly feature in the magazine. He is president of an editorial consulting firm that produces business-to-business publications and advertising. He is also a free-lance writer and the former editor of *Philadelphia* magazine. He has written hundreds of magazine articles and columns. His first novel, *The Physalia Incident*, was published by Viking Press in 1988.

APPENDIX A

Guidelines for Contributors:
Pennsylvania Angler Magazine

Art Michaels, Editor
Pennsylvania Angler
P.O. Box 67000
Harrisburg, PA 17106-7000
(717) 657-4518 (8 a.m. to 4 p.m.)
FAX: (717) 657-4549
CompuServe 76247,624

Pennsylvania Angler, published monthly, is the official fishing magazine of the Pennsylvania Fish and Boat Commission, and in turn, the voice of the Commonwealth in matters relating to fishing and to protecting, conserving and enhancing the state's water resources. *Pennsylvania Angler* is a 32-page, four-color, self-cover with no advertising. About 80 percent of the magazine is freelance-written. Every year we buy 100 to 120 full-length article/photo packages and dozens of color slides and some black-and-white prints. The magazine's circulation is about 40,000.

Subjects

The best way to determine our needs is to read and study several recent issues. If you send us a 9x12 envelope affixed with postage for four ounces, we'll send you a sample copy.

Here is a partial list of our needs:

• Where-to articles that include details on how to fish specific Pennsylvania waterways (or a roundup of several waterways), times of day best for action, and technically accurate how-to information. These kinds of articles should include hand-drawn maps showing accesses, main roads, landmarks, parking and hotspots.

• Detailed how-to articles on fishing in Pennsylvania, using specific tackle and strategies in the state's waterways. We do not publish product information or puffery.

• "New" subjects. We like to publish articles that inform readers on the latest fishing methods and trends. We occasionally consider general articles, but "Pennsylvania-ized" subjects get special attention. We do not publish pieces about using a specific product.

• Shorts. We use articles of 600 to 800 words with one to three photos for one-pagers. Subjects include fresh, sharply focused ideas.

• Boating articles. We gear boating features to boating anglers. We favor technically accurate how-to articles on all kinds of fishing boats, equipment, techniques, navigation, piloting and safety. These stories must be slanted toward Pennsylvania waterways.

• Fish and Boat Commission activities across the state. Even though Commission staffers write most of these articles, we gladly consider this kind of material from freelancers.

• Nostalgia and humor pieces are welcome, but they must be strongly slanted to Pennsylvania. We also publish historical articles, and we consider quality Pennsylvania-based fiction and first-person accounts.

• We rarely publish fish cookery articles, but we occasionally consider these features if they have a strong Pennsylvania slant.

• We do not solicit product reviews and roundups, cartoons, poetry, games or puzzles.

• We consider previously published articles and photographs from non-competing markets.

Writing Style

Articles are occasionally aimed at novice anglers, and some material is directed toward the most skilled fishermen. Most articles in *Pennsylvania Angler* cater to fishermen and boaters between these extremes.

Most material we publish is 500 to 3,000 words. With the hard copy we like contributors to send a floppy disk (either size) with their manuscripts captured in MS-DOS ASCII or in WordPerfect.

Pennsylvania Angler is accessible on CompuServe's Outdoors Forum Section 12 and through E-Mail (76247,624). Short copy can be sent via CompuServe's E-Mail. Longer manuscripts can be encrypted and uploaded to the Outdoors Forum Library 0.

Photographs

We use photographs submitted with and without manuscripts. For black-and-white pictures we prefer 8 x 10 glossies with borders, but 5 x 7s are acceptable. For covers we prefer mounted slides (35 mm and larger) shot with Kodachrome 25 or 64, or the Agfa and Fuji equivalents. We require all slide submissions to be originals. Complete captions are required for all slides and photos.

We prefer (but do not require) that photos of boats show current Pennsylvania registrations and all aboard small boats should be wearing PFDs. We prefer photos taken in Pennsylvania, but we accept photos taken elsewhere.

We cannot use obviously non-Pennsylvania backgrounds—snow-capped peaks, saltwater and desert settings, palm trees, and so forth.

Deadlines

Submit seasonal material eight months in advance. For instance, an article on ice fishing in January must be received in May, and an April trout fishing piece must be in our hands in August.

We prefer queries to completed manuscripts, but completed manuscripts are also welcomed, especially for material of 1,000 words or less. Query at least eight months ahead of an anticipated issue date.

Written queries are welcome, as are queries sent by way of CompuServe. Please query on CompuServe with a private message in the Outdoors Forum Section 12 or by way of CompuServe E-Mail.

Payment and Rights

Rights purchased vary. For most material we prefer to buy first rights. If the material you're submitting has appeared elsewhere, tell us when you submit it. Payment for articles and photo packages varies from $50 to $250. This payment is based on quality of the material, research required to complete the piece, length of the copy, and how badly we want the story. Payment for articles submitted without photo support is less than payment for articles submitted with top-quality, usable photos.

When photographs are submitted with an article, the price for the article includes payment for the pictures. The front cover pays as much as $200, depending on rights purchased. The back cover, $150. Wraparound covers pay up to $250. Inside color and black-and-white pictures purchased separately pay $30 to $100 per slide or print. This payment is based on the published size of the photograph.

Be sure to include your social security number with your manuscript or photo submission.

Pennsylvania Angler does not accept simultaneous submissions.

Correspondence

All material—queries, manuscripts, and artwork—are reviewed on speculation. We report on queries within two weeks, and on manuscripts in four to six weeks.

Pennsylvania Angler is not responsible for unsolicited materials.

One final word. Because you're reading these guidelines, you're one step closer to selling material to us than are many others. We are eager to hear from you by way of a tantalizing query, a top-notch completed manuscript, or a color slide that we can't resist putting on a cover.

Send submissions to Art Michaels, Editor, *Pennsylvania Angler*, P.O. Box 67000, Harrisburg, PA 17106-7000. The phone number is (717) 657-4518. FAX: (717) 657-4549. The CompuServe address is 76247,624.

APPENDIX B

American Society of Journalists and Authors, Inc. Suggested Letter of Agreement

Originating with the writer to be used when publication does not issue written confirmation of assignment.

DATE
EDITOR'S NAME AND TITLE
PUBLICATION
ADDRESS

Dear EDITOR'S NAME:

This will confirm our agreement that I will research and write an article of approximately NUMBER words on the subject of BRIEF DESCRIPTION, in accord with our discussion of DATE.

The deadline for delivery of this article to you is DATE.

It is understood that my fee for this article shall be $ AMOUNT, with one-third payable in advance and the remainder upon acceptance (1). I will be responsible for up to two revisions.

PUBLICATION will be entitled to first North American rights in the article (2).

It is further understood that you shall reimburse me for routine expenses incurred in the researching and writing of the article, including long-distance telephone calls, and that extraordinary expenses, should any such be antici-pated, will be discussed with you before they are incurred (3).

It is also agreed that you will submit proofs of the article for my examina-tion, sufficiently in advance of publication to permit correction of errors.

This letter is intended to cover the main points of our agreement. Should any disagreement arise on these or other matters, we agree to rely upon the guidelines set forth in the Code of Ethics and Fair Practices of the American Society of Journalists and Authors. Should any controversy persist, such controversy shall be submitted to arbitration before the American Arbitration Association in accordance with its rules, and judgment confirming the arbitrator's award may be entered in any court of competent jurisdiction.

Please confirm our mutual understanding by signing the copy of this agreement and returning it to me.

Sincerely,
(SIGNED) _____
WRITER'S NAME

PUBLICATION
by _____
NAME AND TITLE
Date

(1) If the publication absolutely refuses to pay the advance, you may want to substitute the following wording: "If this assignment does not work out, a sum of one-third the agreed-upon fee shall be paid to me."

(2) If discussion included sale of other rights, this clause should specify basic fee for first North American rights, additional fees and express rights each covers, and total amount.

(3) Any other conditions agreed upon, such as inclusion of travel expenses or a maximum dollar amount for which the writer will be compensated, should also be specified.

Source: Murray Teigh Bloom, Thomas Bedell, Sally Wendkos Olds, Annie Moldafsky, and Dodi Schultz, eds., *The ASJA Handbook: A Writers' Guide to Ethical and Economic Issues* (2nd ed.), 1992, American Society of Journalists and Authors, Inc., Suite 302, 1501 Broadway, New York, NY 10036 (212) 997-0947.

APPENDIX C

Generic Travel Feature Article Letter of Agreement: *National Geographic Traveler*

Date

Mr. or Ms. So-and-so
Address TK [to come]
City TK, State TK, Zip TK
Dear So-and-so:
We are delighted that you can write a feature story for us on Place TK.

Here are the particulars. (Details about focus, tone, emphasis, and so forth, depending on the nature of the story—national park, museum, city, region, scenic drive, activity).

Here are a few points to keep in mind. Include present-day voices—quotes from interpreters, curators, and/or fellow visitors—as well as voices from the past. Be sure the reader knows where things are, and where you are, as you move through the story; an overall geographical orientation near the beginning would be helpful.

If you encounter any negative aspects that you feel should be passed on to readers, please include them. A realistic assessment of negatives (as opposed to potshots and personal gripes) is a valuable service to readers. Just be sure the overall tone of the piece remains invitational.

Plan on spending TK days in TK PLACE in TK MONTH. You can request an advance on expenses. If, afterward, you think the story should take on a different approach from the above, please give me a ring right away to discuss it.

The story should run about TK words. Our payment will be $TK,000, upon acceptance. The manuscript will be due one month after you complete your fieldwork (no later than Date TK). In the unlikely event that the first draft does not succeed, we will expect you to make revisions if we think they will make the text publishable. If, after that, the story still is not publishable, we will pay you a kill fee of $TK,000.

Our travel office will be glad to arrange for and furnish you with airline tickets, hotel reservations, and car rentals, where required. Please phone them at least 30 days in advance at Phone TK, so they can get the best rates possible. We can arrange a reasonable advance against expenses, to include fees for accommodations. Please heed the word "reasonable," and be conscious of the fact that we do not have unlimited funds for travel expenses; we will be grateful to you for spending only what's necessary to be comfortable and to do your job professionally.

Expenses must be supported by proper vouchers and receipts. Expense-account guidelines are located in the enclosed National Geographic Expense Account booklet and in the Travel and Expense book from the Controller's Office; the Society follows the IRS Travel and Entertainment Regulations. Within two weeks of your return home, upon completion of the assignment, you will be required to file a final report of your expense account and to settle with the Society by returning all unused cash and traveler's checks, according to your records. Final payment for your manuscript will not be made until all travel advances are accounted for and all Society credit cards have been returned.

You are undertaking this assignment as an independent contractor. The Society assumes no responsibility for your health, safety, or property, or that of any person accompanying or assisting you. While on assignment in the field, you will be covered by the Society's accident insurance policy, which provides a payment of $TK,000 to you in the event of total disability or to your beneficiary, specified below, in the event of death, and lesser coverage for other injuries. The policy also provides up to $TK,000 in excess medical coverage, i.e., for costs beyond those covered by your personal accident and health coverages. The above coverage is restricted to you alone.

While working on this assignment, you will carefully avoid doing similar work for publications that *Traveler* would consider to be editorially competitive with it. You will advise *Traveler* promptly of any possible conflict of interest that may develop. You will also take care not to grant any prepublication interviews or assist in any way in the preparation of any prepublication articles or other press coverage in any medium that would reveal the subject matter, editorial content, or the scheduling of an assignment, article, or story for *Traveler*. You will not accept discounts or gratuities of any kind from any person or organization providing information or services to you.

Your manuscript is a specially commissioned work for hire for use in *National Geographic Traveler*, and accordingly all rights (including copyright) in the story shall vest exclusively in the National Geographic Society. You hereby represent and warrant that you have the full right and authority to sell the manuscript and that you have not previously granted, sold, hypothecated, or encumbered these rights. You hereby further represent and warrant the originality of the manuscript, that it will contain nothing of a libelous nature, and that its publication will not infringe any copyright, right of privacy, or other legal right of any other party.

You hereby grant to the Society without additional charge the right to use your name, likeness, biographical material, and any of your textual material for promotional and advertising purposes.

You or your agent will not sell any of your material from this assignment to: *Revista de Geografica Universal* (Mexico), *Revista Geografica Universal* (Brazil), *Airone* (Italy), or *Bunte* (Germany).

Our articles are intensively checked before publication. A condition of assignment is that you turn over all source materials collected during the course of the assignment once the manuscript has been accepted. (Books and pamphlets bought on expense account belong to the Society; those bought with your own funds will be returned at your request.) You are to furnish a marked copy of your manuscript keying facts, quotes, and other information to a separate list of publications, addresses, and phone numbers of people and institutions mentioned in the text, as well as any other sources of information.

This agreement may not be assigned by you. It constitutes the entire agreement between you and the Society and its terms cannot be altered except by an instrument in writing signed by both parties. If its terms are acceptable to you, please sign this letter and return it to me. The copy is for your files.

So-and-so, I'm looking forward to working with you. If you have any questions, please don't hesitate to call me at 202-857-7352. Have a great trip! I'm looking forward to reading about it.

Best wishes,
Carol B. Lutyk
Senior Articles Editor

For the National Geographic Society

Richard Busch

P.S. If you use a computer for word processing, please submit a disk (with a note attached to the disk of the file name containing the manuscript), along with a hard copy of your manuscript and source list. Please indicate below the model of your computer and the name and version of your software.

Model of computer _____

Name and version of software _____

Signature _____

Social Security Number _____

Telephone Numbers _____

Date _____

Insurance Beneficiary _____

Address _____

Please write a brief bio about yourself for publication with this article.

APPENDIX D

Code of Ethics: Society of Professional Journalists
(Adopted by the 1987 national convention, Chicago)

The Society of Professional Journalists believes the duty of journalists is to serve the truth.

We believe the agencies of mass communication are carriers of public discussion and information, acting on their Constitutional mandate and freedom to learn and report the facts.

We believe in public enlightenment as the forerunner of justice, and in our Constitutional role to seek the truth as part of the public's right to know the truth.

We believe those responsibilities carry obligations that require journalists to perform with intelligence, objectivity, accuracy, and fairness.

To these ends, we declare acceptance of the standards of practice here set forth:

•RESPONSIBILITY: The public's right to know of events of public importance and interest is the overriding mission of the mass media. The purpose of distributing news and enlightened opinion is to serve the general welfare. Journalists who use their professional status as representatives of the public for selfish or other unworthy motives violate a high trust.

•FREEDOM OF THE PRESS: Freedom of the press is to be guarded as an inalienable right of people in a free society. It carries with it the freedom and the responsibility to discuss, question, and challenge actions and utterances of our government and our public and private institutions. Journalists uphold the right to speak unpopular opinions and the privilege to agree with the majority.

•ETHICS: Journalists must be free of obligation to any interest other than the public's right to know the truth.

1. Gifts, favors, free travel, special treatment or privileges can compromise the integrity of journalists and their employers. Nothing of value should be accepted.

2. Secondary employment, political involvement, holding public office, and service in community organizations should be avoided if it compromises the integrity of journalists and their employers. Journalists and their employers should conduct their personal lives in a manner which protects them from conflict of interest, real or apparent. Their responsibilities to the public are paramount. That is the nature of their profession.

3. So-called news communications from private sources should not be published or broadcast without substantiation of their claims to news value.

4. Journalists will seek news that serves the public interest, despite the obstacles. They will make constant efforts to assure that the public's business is conducted in public inspection.

5. Journalists acknowledge the newsman's ethic of protecting confidential sources of information.

6. Plagiarism is dishonest and unacceptable.

•ACCURACY AND OBJECTIVITY: Good faith with the public is the foundation of all worthy journalism.

1. Truth is our ultimate goal.

2. Objectivity in reporting the news is another goal, which serves as the mark of an experienced professional. It is a standard of performance toward which we strive. We honor those who achieve it.

3. There is no excuse for inaccuracies or lack of thoroughness.

4. Newspaper headlines should be fully warranted by the contents of the articles they accompany. Photographs and telecasts should give an accurate picture of an event and not highlight a minor incident out of context.

5. Sound practice makes clear distinction between news reports and expressions of opinion. News reports should be free of opinion or bias and represent all sides of an issue.

6. Partisanship in editorial comment which knowingly departs from the truth violates the spirit of American journalism.

7. Journalists recognize their responsibility for offering informed analysis, comment, and editorial opinion on public events and issues. They accept the obligation to present such material by individuals whose competence, experience, and judgment qualify them for it.

8. Special articles or presentations devoted to advocacy or the writer's own conclusions and interpretations should be labeled as such.

•FAIR PLAY: Journalists at all times will show respect for the dignity, privacy, rights, and well-being of people encountered in the course of gathering and presenting the news.

1. The news media should not communicate unofficial charges affecting reputation or moral character without giving the accused a chance to reply.

2. The news media must guard against invading a person's right to privacy.

3. The media should not pander to morbid curiosity about details of vice and crime.

4. It is the duty of news media to make prompt and complete correction of their errors.

5. Journalists should be accountable to the public for their reports and the public should be encouraged to voice its grievances against the media. Open dialogue with our readers, viewers, and listeners should be fostered.

Reprinted with the permission of the Society of Professional Journalists.

APPENDIX E

American Society of Journalists and Authors: Code of Ethics and Fair Practices

Preamble

Over the years, an unwritten code governing editor–writer relationships has arisen. The American Society of Journalists and Authors has compiled the major principles and practices of that code that are generally recognized as fair and equitable.

The ASJA has also established a Committee on Editor–Writer Relations to investigate and mediate disagreements brought before it, either by members or by editors. In its activity this committee shall rely on the following guidelines.

1. Truthfulness, Accuracy, Editing

The writer shall at all times perform professionally and to the best of his or her ability, assuming primary responsibility for truth and accuracy. No writer shall deliberately write into an article a dishonest, distorted, or inaccurate statement.

Editors may correct or delete copy for purposes of style, grammar, conciseness, or arrangement, but may not change the intent or sense without the writer's permission.

2. Sources

A writer shall be prepared to support all statements made in his or her manuscripts, if requested. It is understood, however, that the publisher shall respect any and all promises of confidentiality made by the writer in obtaining information.

3. Ideas and Proposals

An idea shall be defined not as a subject alone but as a subject combined with an approach.

A proposal of an idea ("query") by a professional writer shall receive a personal response within three weeks. If such a communication is in writing, it is properly viewed and treated as business correspondence, with no return postage or other materials required for reply.

A writer shall be considered to have a proprietary right to an idea suggested to an editor.

4. Acceptance of an Assignment

A request from an editor that the writer proceed with an idea, however worded and whether oral or written, shall be considered an assignment. (The word "assignment" here is understood to mean a definite order for an article.) It shall be the obligation of the writer to proceed as rapidly as possible toward the completion of an assignment, to meet a deadline mutually agreed upon, and not to agree to unreasonable deadlines.

5. Conflict of Interest

The writer shall reveal to the editor, before acceptance of an assignment, any actual or potential conflict of interest, including but not limited to any financial interest in any product, firm, or commercial venture relating to the subject of the article.

6. Report on Assignment

If in the course of research or during the writing of the article, the writer concludes that the assignment will not result in a satisfactory article, he or she shall be obliged to so inform the editor.

7. Withdrawal

Should a disagreement arise between the editor and writer as to the merit or handling of an assignment, the editor may remove the writer on payment of mutually satisfactory compensation for the effort already expended, or the writer may withdraw without compensation and, if the idea for the assignment originated with the writer, may take the idea elsewhere without penalty.

8. Agreements

The practice of written confirmation of all agreements between editors and writers is strongly recommended, and such confirmation may originate with the editor, the writer, or an agent. Such a memorandum of confirmation should list all aspects of the assignment including subject, approach, length, special instructions, payments, deadline, and guarantee (if any). Failing prompt contradictory response to such a memorandum, both parties are entitled to assume that the terms set forth therein are binding.

9. Rewriting

No writer's work shall be rewritten without his or her advance consent. If an editor requests a writer to rewrite a manuscript, the writer shall be obliged to do so but shall alternatively be entitled to withdraw the manuscript and offer it elsewhere.

10. Bylines

Lacking any stipulation to the contrary, a byline is the author's unquestioned right. All advertisements of the article should also carry the author's name. If an author's byline is omitted from the published article, no matter what the cause or reason, the publisher shall be liable to compensate the author financially for the omission.

11. Updating
If delay in publication necessitates extensive updating of an article, such updating shall be done by the author, to whom additional compensation shall be paid.

12. Reversion of Rights
A writer is not paid by money alone. Part of the writer's compensation is the intangible value of timely publication. Consequently, reasonable and good-faith efforts should be made to schedule an article within six months and publish it within twelve months. In the event that circumstances prevent such timely publication, the writer should be informed within twelve months as to the publication's continued interest in the article and plans to publish it. If publication is unlikely, the manuscript and all rights therein should revert to the author without penalty or cost to the author.

13. Payment for Assignments
An assignment presumes an obligation upon the publisher to pay for the writer's work upon satisfactory completion of the assignment, according to the agreed terms. Should a manuscript that has been accepted, orally or in writing, by a publisher or any representative or employee of the publisher, later be deemed unacceptable, the publisher shall nevertheless be obliged to pay the writer in full according to the agreed terms.

If an editor withdraws or terminates an assignment, due to no fault of the writer, after work has begun but prior to completion of the manuscript, the writer is entitled to compensation for work already put in; such compensation shall be negotiated between editor and author and shall be commensurate with the amount of work already completed. If a completed assignment is not acceptable, due to no fault of the writer, the writer is nevertheless entitled to payment; such payment, in common practice, has varied from half the agreed-upon price to the full amount of that price.

14. Time of Payments
The writer is entitled to payment for an accepted article within 30 days of delivery. No article payment, or any portion thereof, should ever be subject to publication or to scheduling for publication.

15. Expenses
Unless otherwise stipulated by the editor at the time of an assignment, a writer shall assume that normal, out-of-pocket expenses will be reimbursed by the publisher. Any extraordinary expenses anticipated by the writer shall be discussed with the editor prior to incurring them.

16. Insurance
A magazine that gives a writer an assignment involving any extraordinary hazard shall insure the writer against death or disability during the course of travel or the hazard, or, failing that, shall honor the cost of such temporary insurance as an expense account item.

17. Loss of Personal Belongings

If, as a result of circumstances or events directly connected with a perilous assignment and due to no fault of the writer, a writer suffers loss of personal belongings or professional equipment or incurs bodily injury, the publisher shall compensate the writer in full.

18. Copyright, Additional Rights

It shall be understood, unless otherwise stipulated in writing, that sale of an article manuscript entitles the purchaser to first North American serial rights only, and that all other rights are retained by the author. Under no circumstances shall an independent writer be required to sign a so-called "all rights transferred" or "work made for hire" agreement as a condition of assignment, of payment, or of publication.

19. Reprints

All revenues from reprints shall revert to the author exclusively, and it is incumbent upon a publication to refer all requests for reprint to the author. The author has a right to charge for such reprints and must request that the original publication be credited.

20. Agents

An agent may not represent editors or publishers. In the absence of any agreement to the contrary, a writer shall not be obliged to pay an agent a fee on work negotiated, accomplished and paid for without the assistance of the agent. An agent should not charge a client a separate fee covering "legal" review of a contract for a book or other project.

21. TV and Radio Promotion

The writer is entitled to be paid for personal participation in TV or radio programs promoting periodicals in which the writer's work appears.

22. Indemnity

No writer should be obliged to indemnify any magazine or book publisher against any claim, actions, or proceedings arising from an article or book, except where there are valid claims of plagiarism or copyright violation.

23. Proofs

The editor shall submit edited proofs of the author's work to the author for approval, sufficiently in advance of publication that any errors may be brought to the editor's attention. If for any reason a publication is unable to so deliver or transmit proofs to the author, the author is entitled to review the proofs in the publication's office.

Source: Murray Teigh Bloom, Thomas Bedell, Sally Wendkos Olds, Annie Moldafsky, and Dodi Schultz, eds., *The ASJA Handbook: A Writers' Guide to Ethical and Economic Issues* (2nd ed.), 1992, American Society of Journalists and Authors, Inc., Suite 302, 1501 Broadway, New York, NY 10036 (212) 997-0947.

APPENDIX F

Protecting Yourself in the Magazine Recession (or Any Other Time!)

Brett Harvey
Eastern Regional Grievance Officer
National Writers Union

These are especially hard times for freelancers, in case you hadn't noticed. Magazines are going belly-up nearly every month, and the ones that are left are cutting every possible corner—which means fewer pieces assigned, lower fees, more and lower kill fees, slower payment, and more all-rights contracts. The guidelines that follow come directly from my grievance files. Following them doesn't mean you won't get stiffed; it just means you will have done everything you as a *writer* can do to minimize the possibility.

1. *Get it in writing.* These days, with the advent of the mighty fax machine, there's no longer any excuse for working without a contract. If you're a member of the National Writer's Union, use its Standard Journalism Contract, which will give you the best and fairest possible terms. If you must use the publisher's contract, try to amend it to include payment "on submission" (best) or "on acceptance" (second best), and "First North American print rights only." If the publisher declines to use a contract, think hard about if it's worth it to work for someone who doesn't want to use contracts. If the answer is yes, prepare your own assignment letter spelling out exactly what you and the editor have agreed to, including: (1) how many words; (2) when the piece is due; (3) how much you'll be paid; (4) *when* you'll be paid; (5) the fact that you're selling only first North American print rights; and (6) as much detail as possible about the content of the piece. Verbal contracts are admissible in court, but a paper trail will help a great deal if you have to bring a grievance, and will be invaluable if you have to go to small claims court. Plus, it establishes you as a professional.

2. *Start billing immediately.* Having established when you can expect to be paid ahead of time, include an invoice when you turn in the piece and start pressing for payment immediately. *Don't* let weeks or months (would you believe years?) go by before they hear from you. It's unprofessional and it supports their delusion you don't need the money. And, most important of

all, *they may be out of business by the time you get around to collecting!* My files are full of these cases.

3. *Don't wait to file an action if you haven't been paid.* If you're an NWU member and haven't been paid within a reasonable time from when they promised (I'd say three weeks), write them a letter threatening to bring a grievance and carbon copy your local grievance officer. If that doesn't work, bring a grievance. Promptly. If you are not a Union member, threaten with small claims court action. If you wait until they've folded, you'll never see a penny of your fee.

4. *Don't keep writing for publications that haven't paid you.* If they haven't paid you for one piece, think twice before doing a second. I know this is hard to resist. It's flattering to be asked to write again. But think about it: If they really want you to write for them, shouldn't they be willing to pay for the first piece before you go to work on the second? Chances are very good that by the time you've done the third piece for no pay, you'll find out they're out of business.

5. *Don't sign away all rights unless you absolutely have to.* This should go without saying. However, due to the explosion in electronic publishing, many publications have changed their boiler-plate contract from the standard "first North American rights" to "all rights." If you receive such a contract, cross out "all rights" and write in "first North American print only." Do not be afraid to do this. In many instances, they're just trying to get away with something. They hope the writers are inexperienced enough or scared enough to just sign on the dotted line (and, regrettably, many are!).

This doesn't mean you shouldn't sell the publisher other rights (for example, electronic rights). Just don't *give* them away, which is what you are doing if you sign an "all rights" contract. Make them negotiate those rights separately. *Remember: They will not blackball you if you protest work-for-hire.* The worst they can do is to insist you sign away all rights.

Reprinted with the permission of Brett Harvey (1993).

References

Alexander, L. (1975). *Beyond the facts: A guide to the art of feature writing.* Houston, TX: Gulf.

Allen, B. (1993, May 6). Robert Boswell's dramatic 'Mystery Ride'. *USA Today*, p. 4D.

Amend, J. W. (1992, October 15). Coming to terms: How does one deal with a mother's suicide? *The Weekly*, Orlando, pp. 1–2.

Anderson, J. (1993, May 31). A storm via Stravinsky and etiquette via Japan. *The New York Times* (national ed.), p. 16.

Associated Press staff. (1993). *Tropical weather.* Associated Press A-wire, 9:17 a.m.

Astor, D. (1988, September 10). Writer is a lampooner of baby boomers: Humor columnist Alice Kahn 'fluctuates between disgust and joy' as she comments on the trends and attitudes of a generation. *Editor & Publisher, 121*(37), 48–50.

Atkin, B. J. (1986). Are you a 'magazine' person? In *Magazine publishing career directory 1986.* New York: Career Publishing.

Baker, C. P. (1989, June). How to travel the lucrative road of travel writing. *Writer's Market, 69*(6), 22–26.

Balmaseda, L. (1992, June 4). Neither poverty nor politics can extinguish people's hope. *The Miami Herald*, p. 1A.

Banaszynski, J. (1987, June 21, July 12, August 9). AIDS in the heartland. *St. Paul Pioneer Press Dispatch* (3-part series), p. 1.

Banks, M. (1985, February). Breaking away! *Writer's Digest, 65*(2), 22–26.

Barry, D. (1986, September 12). Dave to Sophia: 'Chow, bella.' *The Miami Herald*, p. 1B.

Barry, D. (1993, June 20). Courtroom confessions. *The Miami Herald*, p. 27.

Barry, J. (1993, May 2). Taking back the neighborhood. *The Miami Herald*, p. 1J.

Bartel, P. (1992, November). Quick and clean interviewing. *Writer's Digest, 72*(11), 36–37.

Barzun, J. (1992, March). *The press and the prose.* Occasional paper No. 10, Freedom Forum Media Studies Center, Columbia University, New York.

Bednarski, P. J. (1993, January/February). Creating a new section in less than two weeks in Chicago. *ASNE Bulletin, 747*, 17.

Belcher, W. (1988, August 30). Poking fun at politics. *Tampa Tribune*, pp. 1F, 6F.

Benedetto, R. (1975, March). The hardest part: Ideas. Editorially speaking. *The Gannetteer, 30*(15), 5.

Bennett, J. (1993, May/June). A technician's test for a good used car. *AAA World* (Florida ed.), *13*(4), 10–11.

Biagi, S. (1981). *How to write and sell magazine articles.* Englewood Cliffs, NJ: Prentice-Hall.

Biagi, S. (1986). *Interviews that work: A practical guide for journalists.* Belmont, CA: Wadsworth.

Billings, J. S. (1992, December). Writing and selling in the newspaper market. *The Writer, 105*(12), 24–25.

Bing, S. (1992, July). Executive summary: Stanley Bing on unemployment. *Esquire, 118*(1), 45–47.

Blair, W., & Hill, H. (1978). *America's humor: From Poor Richard to Doonesbury*. New York: Oxford University Press.

Blais, M. (1984). Writer's writing: Before the first word. Produced by Learning Designs, Inc., and Educational Broadcasting Corp., WNET-TV, New York.

Bleyer, W. G. (1913). *Newspaper writing and editing*. Boston: Houghton Mifflin.

Bloom, M. T., Bedell, T., Olds, S. W., Moldafsky, A., & Schultz, D. (Eds.). (1992). *The ASJA handbook: A writers' guide to ethical and economic issues* (2nd ed.). New York: American Society of Journalists and Authors, Inc.

Blount, R., Jr. (1991, April 15). Staturated. *Sports Illustrated, 74*(14), 133–134.

Blum, D. (1990, August 20). Laugh track. *New York, 23*(32), 30.

Blum, D. (1993a). America's cats speak out, part I. *Cat Fancy, 36*(6), 16–19.

Blum, D. (1993b). America's cats speak out, part II. *Cat Fancy, 36*(7), 24–27.

Bly, R. W. (1992, January). Writing by the light of the moon. *Writer's Digest, 72*(1), 22–25.

Bohannon, J. (1993, February). Successful article writing. *The Writer, 106*(2), 20–22.

Boles, P. D. (1985, April). The elements of your personal writing style. *Writer's Digest, 65*(4), 24–28.

Bottomly, T. (1991, January). Interview strategies. *Second Takes* [*The Oregonian* newsroom newsletter], pp. 3–4.

Bowman, S. J. (1990, November). How to write irresistibly. *Writer's Digest, 70*(11), 38–41.

Breyer, M. (1993, May 15). A mini food court for Texas lawmakers. *Food Service Director, 6*(5), 46.

Brill, D. (1992, September). Setting the right tone. *Writer's Digest, 72*(9), 32–36.

Briskin, J. (1979, February). Research is a snap. *Writer's Digest, 59*(2), 26–28.

Brodeur, N. (1993, May 17). Bombeck pays price for successful career. *The Miami Herald*, p. 3C.

Brown, J. (1993, April 16). The mystique of the fais do-do. *The Vermilion* (University of Southwestern Louisiana), p. 21.

Buchwald, A. (1993, February 22). Flying frequent. *The Miami Herald*, p. 13A.

Bunn, T. D. (1993, January/February). 'hj' turns Syracuse paper into a key youth news source. *ASNE Bulletin, 747*, 20

Burack, S. K. (Ed.). (1992). *The writer's handbook*. Boston: The Writer, Inc.

Burkett, W. (1986). *News reporting: Science, medicine, and high technology*. Ames: Iowa State University Press.

Business Press Educational Foundation staff. (n.d.). *The exciting world of business magazines* (informational brochure). New York: Author.

Campbell, J. (1993, March 15). The interview: Giving to get. *Folio:, 22*(5), 31–32.

Carmody, D. (1990a, March 28). Magazines discover a new audience—men. *The Miami Herald*, p. 1D.

Carmody, D. (1990b, November 11). Magazines face shakeout: Design publications fight for readership share. *The Miami Herald*, p. 19J.

Carmody, D. (1990c, August 12). With sales slipping, Sisters try changes. *The Miami Herald*, p. 1I.

Carmody, D. (1992a, March 12). Bells are ringing for bride guides: More weddings mean more dollars for magazines. *The Miami Herald*, p. 1F.

Carmody, D. (1992b, April 29). New editor wants *Playboy* to 'talk' to men. *The Miami Herald*, p. 1E.

Carpenter, R. P. (1993, May 9). Mining the overlooked jewels. *The Boston Sunday Globe*, pp. B29–B30.

Carter, R. A. (1990, October 12). Tickling the funnybone. *Publishers Weekly, 237*(41), 24–26.

Casewit, C. (1988). *How to make money from travel writing*. Chester, CT: Globe Pequot Press.

Cassell, D. K. (1991, April). When to quit your day job. *Writer's Digest, 71*(4), 22–27.

Charm, R. (1993, Spring). I drive a Corvette: Gary Wolf. *Corvette Quarterly, 6*(1), 34–37.

Chotzinoff, R. (1990, December 5–11). Nick and the fatman: Denver has a lot of Santas, but they're poles apart, *Westword*, pp. 24, 25, 28.

Chotzinoff, R. (1991). *About the story*. Unpublished report to JCPenney-Missouri Awards director.

Clark, T. (1990, December). How to get started as a writer. *Writer's Digest, 70*(12), 24–27.

Clark, T., & Terez, A. (1993, May). The 1993 *Writer's Digest* guide to writers' conferences, seminars & workshops. *Writer's Digest, 73*(5), 36–46.

Clarke, J. (1993, January 17). Travelers' headache No. 1: Answer survey questions. *The Miami Herald*, p. 12F.

Coates, C. (1993, June 7). *Another look—Pittsburgh papers.* Associated Press A-wire, 12 a.m.

Coleman, J. R. (1993, May 30). Miracles do happen: Unexplained wonders touch Brevard lives, *Florida Today*, p. 1D.

Colford, P. D. (1993, May 14). Magazines' baby boom growing. *The Miami Herald*, pp. 1F, 2F.

Conant, C. (1993, June 11). *In search of readers.* Unpublished presentation to Florida Press Association and Florida Society of Newspaper Editors convention, Coral Gables, FL.

Connell, C. (1993, May 29). *Gergen-profile.* Associated Press. A-wire, 3:43 p.m.

Cook, M. (1986, March). Training your muse: Seven steps to harnessing your creativity. *Writer's Digest, 66*(3), 26–30.

Cook, M. (1987, June). Dave Barry claws his way to the top. *Writer's Digest, 67*(6), 28–30.

Cook, M. (1991, March). Ten roads to better article openings. *Writer's Digest, 71*(3), 28–31.

Cool, L. C. (1985a, June). How to write irresistible query letters. *Writer's Digest, 65*(6), 24–27.

Cool, L. C. (1985b, November). Making contract. *Writer's Digest, 65*(11), 39–41.

Coppola, V. (1993, April). The new minorities. *Atlanta, 32*(12), 46–50.

Cordell, A. (1993, May 6). Teen's goals draw near as she 'beats the odds.' *Atlanta Journal and Constitution.* North Fulton People, p. H1.

Cosford, B. (1993a, June 3). 'Director's cuts' make movies a never-ending story. *The Miami Herald*, pp. 1G, 5G.

Cosford, B. (1993b, June 4). Guilty as Sin: Same old story, only duller. *The Miami Herald*, p. 5G.

Couzens, M. (1988, May). Regional magazines: Shakeup and shakeout. *Folio:, 17*(5), 100–103.

Cullen, D. (1993, May). A conversation with Charlie Cumello. *American Bookseller, 16*(9), 72–76.

Dahlin, R. (1992, March 9). Take my book . . . Please! *Publishers Weekly, 239*(13), 23–27.

Danielson, C. (1993, April). All in a day's work. *Reader's Digest, 142*(852), 79.

Davidson, M. (1990). *A guide for newspaper stringers.* Hillsdale, NJ: Lawrence Erlbaum Associates.

Davis, W. S., Byrkett, D. L., Schreiner, P., & Wood, C.A. (1990). *Computing fundamentals: Productivity tools.* Reading, MA: Addison-Wesley.

Dearing, J. W., & Kazmierczak, J. (1992, August). *Newspaper coverage of maverick science: Balancing the unbalanced controversy.* Unpublished paper presented at the annual meeting of the Association for Education in Journalism and Mass Communication, Montreal, Canada.

della Cava, M. R. (1993, March 5). On an upscale cycle: Rich urban riders rev up Bike Week. All chromed up, ready to cruise Main. *USA Today*, pp. 1D, 2D.

DeSilva, B. (1990, September). Secrets of storytelling. *Second Takes* [*The Oregonian* newsroom newsletter], *2*(5), 3–4.

Dickson, F. A. (1980, April). Thinking ahead: 34 article ideas for fall and winter. *Writer's Digest, 60*(4), 33–35.

Doig, S. K. (1987, April 1). Coded message. *The Miami Herald*, p. 1B.

Drake, D. C., & Uhlman, M. (1992, December 13–17). Making medicine, making money. Series reprint published by *The Philadelphia Inquirer*, pp. 1–16.

Dreifus, C. (1993, May 22). ...And I lived. *TV Guide, 41*(21), 8–12.

DuPont, K. P. (1993, March 14). Welcome to winter travel . . . unless there's fog in Bangor. *The Miami Herald*, p. 6F.

Duquin, L. H. (1987, January). Shaping your article ideas to sell. *Writer's Digest, 67*(1), 37–40.

Duscha, J. (1993, June). Consider the alternatives. *Presstime, 15*(6), 64–67.

Eddy, B. (1979, February). Spelling: the curse of the working journalist. *The Quill, 67*(2), 15–17.

Edelson, E. (1985). *The journalist's guide to nuclear energy.* Bethesda, MD: Atomic Industrial Forum.

Editor & Publisher staff. (1987, December 26). Editor says travel writing is getting more credible. *Editor & Publisher, 120*(52), 13.

Editor & Publisher staff. (1993, April 24) Free-lance writer sentenced for selling phony stories. *Editor & Publisher*, 126(17), 72.

Estep, M. (1993, May 9). The Carrollton bus crash: Five years later: "You live with your grief and move on with your grief." *Lexington Herald-Leader*, pp. A1, A14.

Fensch, T. (1984). *The hardest parts: Techniques for effective non-fiction.* Austin, TX: Lander Moore.

Ferdinand, P. (1993, April 8). Medical marijuana pain sufferers who smoke for relief want to end stigma of breaking law. *The Miami Herald*, p. 1J.

Finley, M. (1988, July). Patrick F. McManus and the funny four. *Writer's Digest, 68*(7), 33–34.

Fiori, P. (1992, May). Celebrating service magazines. *Folio:, 21*(5), 78–80.

Fischer, C. (1990). Newsletter journalists find their jobs interesting, rewarding and fast-paced. *Newsletter Career Guide.* Arlington, VA: Newsletter Publishers Association.

Fitzgerald, M. (1993, May 1). Mixed signals: Latest ABC FAS-FAX shows circulations still sensitive to economy. *Editor & Publisher, 126*(18), 10–11.

Flesch, R. (1946). *The art of plain talk.* New York: Harper.

Flesch, R. (1949). *The art of readable writing.* New York: Harper.

Fletcher, R. J., Jr. (1986, March). Trade secrets. *Writer's Digest, 66*(3), 42–44.

Florida Freelance Writers Association. (1985). *FFWA: Florida Freelance Writers Association* (membership brochure). Fort Lauderdale, FL: Author.

Florida Freelance Writers Association. (1993, May 20–23). *Florida State Writer's Conference Report, 11*, 1–24.

Folio: staff. (1992, November). The future of magazines. *Folio:, 21*(12), 140–147.

Folio: staff. (1993). Circulation leaders. *Folio: Special sourcebook issue, 1993, 21*(10), 159–160.

Fox, C. S. (1993, January). How to set your freelance fees. *ByLine, 152*, 6–7.

Franklin, J. (1978, December 12). Tales from the grey frontier. *Baltimore Evening Sun*, p. C-1.

Franklin, J. (1986). *Writing for story: Craft secrets of dramatic nonfiction by a two-time Pulitzer Prize winner.* New York: Mentor.

Franklin, J. L. (1993, May 9). Archbishop's troubles pain N.M.'s Hispanics, *The Miami Herald*, p. 5B.

Frawley, J. R. (1992, June). An insider's guide to Orlando's theme parks. *Sarasota*, 19–23.

Fry, D. (1993, Spring). A conversation with downtown Dean Brown. *Poynter Report*, p. 11.

Fryxell, D. A. (1990, March). Getting organized. *Writer's Digest, 70*(3), 42–44.

Gannon, R. (Ed.). (1991). *Best science writing: Readings and insights.* Phoenix, AZ: Oryx.

Garrison, B. (1990). *Professional news writing.* Hillsdale, NJ: Lawrence Erlbaum Associates.

Gillmor, D. M., Barron, J. A., Simon, T. F., & Terry, H. A. (1990). *Mass communication law: Cases and comment* (5th ed.). St. Paul, MN: West.

Glaberson, W. (1993, May 3). Press: Newspaper publishers consider a heretical new gospel: Just how outdated their products are. *New York Times*, p. D7.

Glasser, S. (1990, October). Read my quips! *The Writer, 103*(10), 16–18.

Glasser, S. (1992, July). Write shorts that sell. *The Writer, 105*(7), 19–20, 45.

Glickman, L. (1993, April 21). AOPi looks forward to new home. *The Daily Orange* (Syracuse University), p. 3.

Goering, L. (1993, May 16). Gesundheit! Allergy sufferers begin paying through the nose. *Chicago Tribune*, Sect. 2, pp. 1–2.

Goss, F. D. (1988). *Success in newsletter publishing: A practical guide* (3rd ed.). Arlington, VA: Newsletter Association.

Grantham, L. (1993, March 17). Green: Whether seafoam, jade or lime, green has stood the test of time. St. Patrick would be proud. *Palm Beach Post*, p. 1D.

Greenberg, H. (Ed.). (1992). *Oxbridge directory of newsletters.* New York: Oxbridge Communications.

Grewe, A. (1993, April 9). Saving for your future: Grads need savings plan. *The Murray State News* (Murray State University), p. 5.

Grobel, L. (1978, January). A star interview is born. *Writer's Digest, 58*(1), 19–23.

Gunning, R. (1968). *The technique of clear writing*. New York: McGraw-Hill.

Hamilton, D. C. (1985, October 27). Sight & sound: The new member of the mid-'80s family. *Newsday*, pp. 3, 21.

Harris, A. S., Jr. (1992, February). Writing the newspaper travel article. *The Writer, 105*(2), 21–23, 44.

Hart, J. (1989, October). Cutting fine figures. *Second Takes* [*The Oregonian* newsroom newsletter], *1*(6), 1, 5.

Hart, J. (1990a, December). Dripping with color. *Second Takes* [*The Oregonian* newsroom newsletter], *2*(8), 3.

Hart, J. (1990b, March). In the reader's shoes. *Second Takes* [*The Oregonian* newsroom newsletter], *1*(11), 1, 3–4.

Hart, J. (1990c, April). Seizing the action. *Second Takes* [*The Oregonian* newsroom newsletter], *1*(12), 1, 3.

Hart, J. (1990d, May). Telling terms. *Second Takes* [*The Oregonian* newsroom newsletter], *2*(1), 1, 8.

Hart, J. (1990e, February). Writing to be read. *Second Takes* [*The Oregonian* newsroom newsletter], *1*(10), 1, 3.

Hart, J. (1991a, October). Building character. *Second Takes* [*The Oregonian* newsroom newsletter], *3*(6), 1, 4–5, 8.

Hart, J. (1991b, November). Building character II. *Second Takes* [*The Oregonian* newsroom newsletter], *3*(7), 1, 4–5.

Hart, J. (1991c, April). News by the numbers. *Second Takes* [*The Oregonian* newsroom newsletter], *2*(12), 1, 3, 5.

Hart, J. (1991d, August). Storytelling. *Second Takes* [*The Oregonian* newsroom newsletter], *3*(4), 1, 3, 5, 7–8.

Hart, J. (1991e, September). The ladder of abstraction. *Second Takes* [*The Oregonian* newsroom newsletter], *3*(5), 1, 4–5.

Hart, J. (1992, March). High tension. *Second Takes* [*The Oregonian* newsroom newsletter], *3*(11), 1, 4–5.

Harvey, B. (1993, May 24). *How to protect yourself as a journalist*. Unpublished manuscript.

Haverstock, M. (1993, March). Writing for regional parenting publications. *ByLine, 154*, 6–7, 21.

Hellyer, K. (1993, January/February). Three ways to satisfy the hunger for useful entertainment news. *ASNE Bulletin, 747*, 16.

Henderson, B. (1984, April). How to 'bulletproof' your manuscripts. *Writer's Digest, 64*(4), 28–32.

Henry, T. (1993, March 29). Giving kids more than an idle vacation. *USA Today*, p. 4D.

Hensley, D. E. (1979, May). Pumping the profs. *Writer's Digest, 59*(5), 34.

Hensley, D. E. (1986, January). Getting the most out of your writers club. *Writer's Digest, 66*(1), 36–38.

Hensley, D. E. (1993, August). 7 simple steps to multiple marketing. *Writer's Digest, 73*(8), 32–33.

Herrel, K. (1989, November 22). 'The Lord provides it, and we cook it.' *The Independent Alligator* (University of Florida), *83*(63), p. 8.

Holton, S. (1992, April 26). Pork flies and NASA does too: NASA contracts spread all around the country ensure Congressional committee support for space program funds. *The Orlando Sentinel*, pp. A-1, A-10.

Holton, W. P. (1993, March). A freelancer's phrase book. *Writer's Digest, 73*(3), 6.

Horowitz, L. (1986). *A writer's guide to research*. Cincinnati, OH: Writer's Digest Books.

Hospital, J. T. (1993, April). Memoir: The site of first dreams. *Victoria, 7*(4), 40–42, 100.

Hunt, T. (1972). *Reviewing for the mass media*. Radnor, PA: Chilton.

Hunter, J. D. (1983, February). Good writing is: Good journalism, good business, an art, good for you, all of the above. *The Bulletin of the American Society of Newspaper Editors, 657*, 5–7.

Incantalupo, T. (1993, January 31). Airline food getting better, scarcer. *The Miami Herald*, p. 11F.

Jacobi, P. (1991, December). 12 ways to win readers (and editors). *Writer's Digest, 71*(12), 34–37.

Jarvis, J. (1993, April 3). The couch critic: Tribeca. *TV Guide, 41*(14), 7.

Jicha, T. (1993, April 8). *Why should we take entertainment reporting seriously?* Society of Professional Journalists program presented at the University of Miami, Coral Gables, FL.

Johnson, O. (Ed.). (1993). *The 1993 information please almanac* (46th ed.). Boston: Houghton Mifflin.

Kael, P. (1979). Circles and squares. In G. Mast & M. Cohen (Eds.), *Film theory and criticism* (2nd ed., pp. 666–679). New York: Oxford University Press.

Kahn, A. (1988, February 24). How to profit from the coming article-writing glut. *San Francisco Chronicle*, p. B4.

Kahn, A. (1990). *Luncheon at the cafe ridiculous*. New York: Poseidon.

Kando, T. (1980). *Leisure and popular culture in transition* (2nd ed.). St. Louis, MO: Mosby.

Kantrowitz, B. (1993, May 10). A fantasy crashes. *Newsweek, 121*(19), 70–71.

Kaplan, D. A. (1993, May 31). The force of an idea is with him. *Newsweek, 121*(22), 45.

Kaplan, M. (1975). *Leisure: Theory and policy*. New York: Wiley.

Kasselmann, B. C. (1992, May). You don't have to go to Spain to write travel articles. *The Writer, 105*(5), 21–24.

Kelton, N. (1988, January). How to write personal experience articles. *Writer's Digest, 68*(1), 22–24.

Kennedy, D. (1993, May 30). *AP Arts: Cyndi Lauper Sunday advance*. Associated Press A-wire, 12:00 a.m.

Kilpatrick, J. J. (1985). *The art and the craft.* The Red Smith lecture in journalism, Department of American Studies, University of Notre Dame, South Bend, IN.

Kissling, M. (Ed.). (1992). *1993 Writer's market: Where & how to sell what you write*. Cincinnati, OH: Writer's Digest Books.

Knight-Ridder, Inc. (1986). *The 1986 Pulitzer Prize winners*. Miami, FL: Author.

Kresch, S. (1986). The changing face of the industry. In *Magazine publishing career directory 1986*. New York: Career Publishing.

Krol, J. (Ed.). (1992). *Newsletters in print, 1993-94* (6th ed.). Detroit: Gale Research Inc.

Kubis, P., & Howland, R. (1985). *The complete guide to writing fiction, nonfiction, and publishing*. Reston, VA: Reston.

Kurtz, H. (1993, April 4). Post wins three Pulitzer Prizes; National reporting, feature writing, book criticism honored. *The Washington Post*, online edition, CompuServe.

Ladwig, T. (1987, October 5). The baddest of bad days gives a couple a good story. *Columbia Missourian*, reprinted in *Publisher's Auxiliary, 123*(20), 12.

LaFleur, L. (1993, April). Campus comedy. *Reader's Digest, 142*(852), 126.

Lamb, C. (1993, June 5). Humorist holds his own in newspapers. *Editor & Publisher, 126*(23), 34–35.

Lambe, D. R. (1986, April). What to do when the publisher won't pay. *Writer's Digest, 66*(4), 36–38.

Land, M. E. (1993). *Writing for magazines* (2nd ed.). Englewood Cliffs, NJ: Prentice-Hall.

Lardner, G. (1992, November 22). The stalking of Kristin: The law made it easy for my daughter's killer. *The Washington Post*, p. C1.

Lawrence, J. (1993, June 5). *RFK's legacy*. Associated Press A-wire, 2:59 p.m.

Leusner, J. (1992, April 26). A bomb shattered a boy's life and the scars are slow to heal. *The Orlando Sentinel*, pp. A-1, A-10.

Levine, B. (1993, May 9). Mama done told me.... *Los Angeles Times*, pp. E1, E4.

Levoy, G. (1991, July). The art of negotiation. *Writer's Digest, 71*(7), 26–29.

Loundy, M. (1992). *Change or die: The inevitable future of information delivery* (Journalism Forum). Columbus, OH: CompuServe Information System.

Luzadder, D. (1982, March 15). A fitful night for those whose dreams lie under the river. *Fort Wayne, Ind., News-Sentinel.*

Macdonald, D. (1969). *Dwight Macdonald on movies*. Englewood Cliffs, NJ: Prentice-Hall.

Maisel, E. (1993, May). The 11-step program for writing self-help nonfiction: Rejection dependent no more! *Writer's Digest, 73*(5), 27–29.

Mariani, J. (1993, May). Eating around: Going over easy. *Travel & Leisure, 23*(5), 68–70.

Markoff, J. (1993, May 7). 17 companies in electronic news venture. *New York Times*, pp. C1, C4.

Marsano, B. (1993, May). Baskets of desire. *Condé Nast Traveler, 28*(5), 194, 196.

Marx, B. (1993, October 25). The decline of book reviewing. *Publisher's Weekly, 240*(43), 36.

Matas, A., & Epstein, G. (1993, June 6). Boy hailed, but INS probes story. *The Miami Herald,* p. 1A.

Mathews, E. (1991, March). Writing for the 'little' magazines. *The Writer, 104*(3), 23–24.

Matthews, R. (1991, January). How to increase your rate of acceptance. *The Writer, 104*(1), 22–23, 47.

Maucker, E. (1993, June 11). *In search of readers.* Unpublished presentation to Florida Press Association and Florida Society of Newspaper Editors convention, Coral Gables, FL.

McAleenan, J. (1993, May 17). One nude story deserves another. *Florida Today,* p. 1B.

McGill, L. (1984, August). Give your how-to articles the voice of authority. *Writer's Digest, 64*(8), 26–28.

McKinney, D. (1986, January). How to write true-life dramas. *Writer's Digest, 66*(1), 24–28.

McManus, K. (1992, November). If you absolutely, positively *have* to talk to real people. . . . *ASNE Bulletin, 745,* 18–19.

Meeks, B. (1991). New databases get behind the scenes. *Link-Up, 8*(2), 9, 12.

Meredith, S. (1987). *Writing to sell* (3rd rev. ed.). New York: Harper & Row.

Merzer, M. (1993a, April 8). L.A. is a city of fear, rumors as beating trial comes to close. *The Miami Herald,* p. 1A.

Merzer, M. (1993b, April 11).The anxious, the bitter, the angry, the hopeful: L.A. speaks its troubled mind. *The Miami Herald,* p. 1A.

Michaelis, D. (1993, May). Far from any sea. *Condé Nast Traveler, 28*(5), 85–88, 154–165.

Morgan, J. (1986, July). The secrets of superlative salesmanship. *Writer's Digest, 66*(7), 30–33.

Neff, G. T. (1992). The business of writing. In M. Kissling (Ed.), *1993 Writer's market: Where & how to sell what you write.* Cincinnati, OH: Writer's Digest Books.

Newsletter Publisher's Foundation staff (1992). *Newsletter career guide.* Arlington, VA: Newsletter Publishers Foundation.

Newspaper Association of America staff. (1993, June). *Facts about newspapers '93.* Reston, VA: Newspaper Association of America.

Newsweek staff. (1993, July 12). Ad hominem. *Newsweek, 122*(2), 49.

Nusser, N. (1993, April 23). Hate begats hate. *Palm Beach Post,* pp. 1A, 9A.

Nuwer, H. (1992, July). You can paraphrase me on that. *Writer's Digest, 72*(7), 28–30.

Ognibene, M. (1975, March). Funniest things are those that really happen. Editorially speaking: *The Gannetteer, 30*(15), 3.

Orlean, S. (1993, March 22). Shoot the moon. *The New Yorker, 69*(5), 74–85.

Orlik, P. B. (1988). *Critiquing radio and television content.* Boston: Allyn & Bacon.

Osborne, P. B. (1987, April). Writing the 'art-of-living' article. *Writer's Digest, 67*(4), 20–25.

Painter, K. (1993, April 5). AIDS study aftermath: Despite questions, experts still back AZT. *USA Today,* p. 6D.

Pankau, E. J. (1993, June). Resources for people research. *Online Access, 8*(3), 40–41.

Parker, C. E. (1975, December). 'Tis the season for seasonal articles. *Writer's Digest, 55*(12), 30–31, 44–45.

Patterson, B. R. (1986). *Write to be read: A practical guide to feature writing.* Ames: Iowa State University Press.

Paul, N. (1993, June 16). Unpublished presentation to Seminar on News Research. The Poynter Institute, St. Petersburg, FL.

Pember, D. R. (1993). *Mass media law* (6th ed.). Dubuque, IA: Brown.

Perret, G. (1984, July). How to build humor, one chuckle at a time. *Writer's Digest, 64*(7), 30–32.

Perret, G. (1987, September). Short investments, sweet returns. *Writer's Digest, 67*(9), 27–29.

Petchel, J. (1992, August 27). Migrants feel new blow—neglect. *The Miami Herald,* p. 22A.

Peters, E. (1992). Where do you get your ideas? In S. K. Burak (Ed.), *The writer's handbook.* Boston: The Writer, Inc.

Petersen, D. (1992, March). How to write the how-to article. *Writer's Digest, 72*(3), 38–40.

Philcox, P. (1989, June). Fare-paying assignments. *Writer's Digest, 69*(6), 27–28.

Pitts, L. (1993, February 22). Neil Diamond: Singer, audience didn't connect during concert. *The Miami Herald*, p. 1C.

Postman, N. (1985). *Amusing ourselves to death: Public discourse in the age of show business*. New York: Viking Penguin.

Pratt, H. J. (1992, November). Writing features for the trades. *ByLine, 150*, 10–11.

Quindlen, A. (1984). *Writer's writing: Before the first word*. Produced by Learning Designs, Inc., and Educational Broadcasting Corp., WNET-TV, New York.

Ranly, D. (1992, June). There's a market for service articles! *The Writer, 105*(6), 18–20.

Reader's Digest staff (1993, April). Wanted: Your laugh lines! *Reader's Digest, 142*(852), 4.

Rehart, R. S. (1993, April). Campus comedy. *Reader's Digest, 142*(852), 100.

Reidy, C. (1992, May 12). A lapse and a 'miracle.' *The Boston Globe*, pp. 1, 18.

Reiff, T. (1987a, September). How to keep the money coming. *Writer's Digest, 67*(9), 22–26.

Reiff, T. (1987b, October). How to keep the money coming, part II. *Writer's Digest, 67*(10), 40–42.

Ritz, D. (1993, March). Inside interviewing. *The Writer, 106*(3), 15–17.

Rivers, W. L. (1975). *Finding facts: Interviewing, observing, using reference sources*. Englewood Cliffs, NJ: Prentice-Hall.

Rivers, W. L. (1992). *Free-lancer and staff writer: Newspaper features and magazine articles* (5th ed.). Belmont, CA: Wadsworth.

Robertson, N. (1982, September 19). Toxic shock. *New York Times Magazine, 132*(45), Section 6, pp. 30–34.

Robinson, K. (1993, June). End piece. *ByLine, 157*, 27.

Rodriguez, R. (1993, April 20). The next supermodel? *The Miami Herald*, p. 1E.

Romantini, W. (1987, May). So you wanna' be a food critic? *Milwaukee, 12*(5), 49–52.

Ruehlmann, W. (1979). *Stalking the feature story*. New York: Vintage Books.

Salant, N. (1993, May 6). *Jury selection completed in New Yorker libel trial*. United Press International west wire, 6:13 p.m.

Sarris, A. (1979). Notes on the auteur theory in 1962. In G. Mast & M. Cohen (Eds.), *Film theory and criticism* (2nd ed., pp. 650–655) New York: Oxford University Press.

Schoenfeld, A. C., & Diegmueller, K. S. (1982). *Effective feature writing*. New York: Holt, Rinehart, Winston.

Schreiber, N. (1991, December). Home is where the office is. *Writer's Digest, 71*(12), 41–45.

Schumacher, M. (1983, January). Johnny deadline to the rescue. *Writer's Digest, 63*(1), 30–33.

Scithers, G., & Meschkow, S. (1985, August). Invisible manuscript. *Writer's Digest, 65*(8), 28–29.

Scithers, G., & Meschkow, S. (1985b, September). Under cover. *Writer's Digest, 65*(9), 42–43.

Scott, H. (1992). Writing the personal experience article. In S. K. Burack (Ed.), *The writer's handbook*. Boston: The Writer.

Seibel, M. (1991, July 22). On reporting: Getting to Fidel. *The Bay View* [*Miami Herald* newsroom weekly newsletter], *29*(91), 1.

Seidman, E. (1992, April). Surviving the magazine slush pile. *Writer's Digest, 72*(4), 24–26.

Shannon, J. (1984, November). Typewriter as time machine: The secrets of selling seasonal material. *Writer's Digest, 64*(11), 33–34.

Shapiro, M. A. (1988, July). *Components of interest in television science stories*. Unpublished paper presented to the Theory and Methodology Division, Association for Education in Journalism and Mass Communication, annual convention, Portland, OR.

Shaw, D. (1993, March 31). Trust in media is on decline. *Los Angeles Times*, pp. A1, A16–18.

Shine, T. M. (1993, April 28). The real Coppertone kid? 'That's my daughter!' *Fort Lauderdale Sun-Sentinel*, pp. 1E, 6E.

Sibbison, J. (1988, July/August). Covering medical 'breakthroughs.' *Columbia Journalism Review, 27*(2), 36–39.

Sibley, C. (1993, May 6). The lost ritual of ladies' lunch. *The Atlanta Journal and The Atlanta Constitution*, pp. W1, W8–W9.

Silva, M. (1983, October 6). Take my plane ticket—please. *The Miami Herald*, p. 1B.

Smith, A. (1970). *The seasons: Life and its rhythms*. New York: Harcourt, Brace Jovanovich.

Smith, C. A. (1993, April). Breaking into magazine article writing. *The Writer, 106*(4), 15–17.

Smith, L. E., & Kelley, L. (1993, June 1). Rain, rain, why this day? *Fort Lauderdale Sun-Sentinel*, p. 1B.

Smith, M. P. (1993, Spring). Redefining news: Knight-Ridder newspapers find new ways to connect with readers. *Knight-Ridder News, 8*(1), 6–9.

Sorrels, R. (1986, March). The sensuous writer. *Writer's Digest, 66*(3), 38–41.

Spencer, W. B. (1992, August). The voice of authority. *Writer's Digest, 72*(8), 28–29.

Spielmann, P. (1988, January). The real-life, stranger-than-fiction humor of William Geist. *Writer's Digest, 68*(1), 28–31.

Spikol, A. (1979, March). Nonfiction: Profiles with punch. *Writer's Digest, 59*(3), 7–10.

Spikol, A. (1984, October). Nonfiction: Service please. *Writer's Digest, 64*(10), 15–16.

Spikol, A. (1986a, September). Nonfiction: Different worlds. *Writer's Digest, 66*(9), 16–18.

Spikol, A. (1986b, January). Nonfiction: Make me laugh. *Writer's Digest, 66*(1), 16–19.

Spikol, A. (1987a, September). Nonfiction: Before the interview. *Writer's Digest, 67*(9), 8–10.

Spikol, A. (1987b, March). Trading in on trade journals. *Writer's Digest, 67*(3), 16, 18.

Spikol, A. (1993, July). Nonfiction: "May I quote you on that?" *Writer's Digest, 73*(7), 54–55.

Spy staff. (1993, June). The hot summer movie thing. *Spy*, pp. 32–42.

Stern, G. (1993, June). Become an instant expert. *Writer's Digest, 73*(6), 35–37.

Stiteler, R. (1993, February). Orlando business: Star search. *Orlando Magazine, 47*(4), 52–57.

Stone, M. D. (1993, April). Word processing: The way you want it. *PC Sources, 4*(4), 264–283.

Strunk, W., & White, E. B. (1979). *The elements of style* (3rd ed.). New York: Macmillan.

Stuever, H. (1992, August 1). Andy & Darleine get married. *The Albuquerque Tribune*, pp. B1–B8.

Stuller, J. (1991, August). The magazine writer's marketing edge. *Writer's Digest, 71*(8), 26–29.

Swanson, M. (1979, May). Covering the campuses. *Writer's Digest, 59*(5), 33, 35.

Sweeney, J. (1993, March). Pay attention to the process of writing. *ASNE Bulletin, 748*, 27.

Swerdlow, J. L. (1993, May). Central Park: Oasis in the city. *National Geographic, 183*(5), 2–37.

Talese, G. (1966, April). Frank Sinatra has a cold. *Esquire, 65*, 89–98, 152.

Tasker, F. (1992, May 29). The cost of college. *The Miami Herald*, pp. 1E, 4E–5E.

Teer, J. (1973, January 20). Florida newsman discovers Samaritans still hard to find. *Editor & Publisher, 106*(3), 24.

Teeter, D. L., & Le Duc, D. R. (1992). *Law of mass communications* (7th ed.). Westbury, NY: Foundation Press.

The Miami Herald staff. (1987, April 2). Every fool has his day; this is yours. *The Miami Herald*, p. 1B.

The New Yorker staff. (1993, Spring). A classroom close-up. *Talk of the Classroom, 5*(2), 6.

Toner, M. (1992, August 23). When bugs fight back. *Atlanta Constitution*, p. A/1.

Tracy, A. (1993, May 20). USF students branch out from academics: Philosophy major shines brightly under stage lights. *USF Oracle* (University of South Florida), p. 8.

Travel & Leisure staff. (1993, May). T & L's editorial travel policy. *Travel & Leisure, 23*(5), p. 9.

Tritten, L. (1993, April). Walk the walk, talk the talk. *Writer's Digest, 73*(4), 65, 80.

United Press International staff. (1993a, June 6). *Colombian woman recognizes stowaway*. National wire, 12:55 p.m.

United Press International staff. (1993b, June 1). *Tropical depression moves over Bahamas*. Southeast U.S. wire, 10:54 a.m.

United Press International staff. (1994, April 21). *Harper's is top magazine award winner*. Southeast wire, 4:05 p.m.

Updike, J. (1976). *Picked-up pieces*. New York: Knopf.

Vaccariello, L. (1993, April). Final exit. *Cincinnati Magazine, 26*(7), 84–86.

Vawter, V. (1993, January/February). Taking 'Detours' to reach new markets in Knoxville, Tenn. *ASNE Bulletin, 747*, 18.

Wagner, T. A. (1993, May 20). USF students branch out from academics: A USF senior is this month's *Playboy* playmate. *USF Oracle* (University of South Florida), pp. 8–9.

Walker, L. A. (1992). How to write a profile. In S. K. Burack (Ed.), *The writer's handbook* (pp. 322–327). Boston: The Writer.

Wallace, R. (1993, May 17). Racy bed race rolls through the Grove, charity wins again. *The Miami Herald*, p. 3B.

Wardlow, E. (Ed.). (1985). *Effective writing and editing: A guidebook for newspapers.* Reston, VA: American Press Institute.

Watson, J. (1993, May/June). Secret gardens: A quintet of gardens to soothe the soul. *Gold Coast, 29*(3), 38–45.

Weiss, M. (1992, March 15). The shield that failed: What happened to Debbie Norris wasn't supposed to happen in Joe McNamara's department. *San Jose Mercury News West* magazine, p. 12.

Whitaker, T. (1993, April). The *Gulfshore Life* interview: Chi Chi Rodriguez. *Gulfshore Life, 23*(4), 45–47, 72.

White, E. (1993, June). Horn of plenty. *Vogue, 183*(6), 182–185.

Wilde, L. (1976). *How the great comedy writers create laughter.* Chicago: Nelson-Hall.

Wilker, D. (1993, April 8). *Why should we take entertainment reporting seriously?* Society of Professional Journalists program presented at the University of Miami, Coral Gables, FL.

Williamson, D. R. (1975). *Feature writing for newspapers.* New York: Hastings House.

Wilson, J. M. (1990, October). How to give an editor nothing to do (except buy your article). *Writer's Digest, 70*(10), 33–35.

Wilson, M. (1992, September 29). Hold on to your top hat, new *New Yorker* is here. *The Miami Herald*, p. 1A.

Winship, F. M. (1993, April 21). HG magazine shot down at 92. United Press International Northeast wire, 1:18 p.m.

Wolfe, J. K. (1990, June). The six basics of writing humorously. *Writer's Digest, 70*(6), 18–22.

Wolfe, T. (1963, November). There goes (varoom! varoom!) that kandy-kolored tangerine-flake streamline baby. *Esquire, 60*(11), 114–118, 155–168.

Wolfe, T. (1966). *The kandy-kolored tangerine-flake streamline baby.* New York: Pocket Books.

Wolk, M. (1991, January 20). Another victim of magazine slump dies. *The Miami Herald*, p. 2G.

Wood, J. (1991, October). A conversation with the *Playboy* interviewer. *Writer's Digest, 71*(10), 28–32.

Wood, T. (1993, March). Getting tough interviews. *Writer's Digest, 73*(3), 28–31.

Wooldridge, J. (1993, May 23). Good morning Vietnam. *The Miami Herald*, p. 1F.

Yates, E .D. (1985). *The writing craft* (2nd ed.). Raleigh, NC: Contemporary.

Zinsser, W. (1980). *On writing well* (2nd ed.). New York: Harper & Row.

Index